Louisiana Women

Louisiana Women

THEIR LIVES AND TIMES

Volume 2

EDITED BY

Mary Farmer-Kaiser and
Shannon Frystak

The University of Georgia Press
Athens

Athens, Georgia 30602
www.ugapress.org

Set in 10/12.5 Minion Pro by Kaelin Chappell Broaddus
Printed and bound by Thompson-Shore, Inc.
The paper in this book meets the guidelines for permanence and durability of the Committee on Production Guidelines for Book Longevity of the Council on Library Resources.

Most University of Georgia Press titles are available from popular e-book vendors.

Printed in the United States of America
16 17 18 19 20 P 5 4 3 2 1

The Library of Congress has cataloged the first volume of this work as follows:

Louisiana women : their lives and times /
edited by Janet Allured and Judith F. Gentry.
p. cm.
Includes bibliographical references and index.
ISBN-13: 978-0-8203-2946-8 (cloth : alk. paper)
ISBN-10: 0-8203-2946-0 (cloth : alk. paper)
ISBN-13: 978-0-8203-2947-5 (pbk. : alk. paper)
ISBN-10: 0-8203-2947-9 (pbk. : alk. paper)
1. Women—Louisiana—Biography. 2. Louisiana—Biography.
I. Allured, Janet. II. Gentry, Judith F., 1942–
CT3262.L6 L68 2009
920.7209763—dc22 2008049614

Vol. 2 ISBN 978-0-8203-4269-6 (cloth : alk. paper)
ISBN 978-0-8203-4270-2 (pbk. : alk. paper)
ISBN 978-0-8203-4903-9 (e-book : alk. paper)

Contents

PART TWO: WOMEN AND WORK

PART THREE: WOMEN AND THE ARTS

Acknowledgments

As editors, we must thank first the eighteen scholars who generously accepted our invitation to be a part of this collection and in doing so joined us on a journey to expand the contours and depths of Louisiana women's history. These writers did a miraculous job managing the edits and varying timelines and deadlines, and they did so with grace and aplomb. It takes much to get an edited collection off the ground, through the rigorous process of numerous reviews and edits and, finally, onto bookshelves. Having the opportunity to work with these eighteen scholars—archivists, folklorists, historians, literary scholars, communications and law professors—has made it all worthwhile. We thank each of them for their scholarly contributions as well as their patience and fortitude in this long process. Most assuredly, they have all been a pleasure to work with.

We also must thank Nancy Grayson, former executive editor at the University of Georgia Press. This second volume of *Louisiana Women* exists because she shared Shannon's conviction that there was much more to say about Louisiana women. We are most grateful that she, too, knew it needed to be said in the Southern Women: Their Lives and Times series. We appreciate also the important guidance and support provided by others at the press, especially Lisa Bayer and Beth Snead. Elizabeth Crowley, Jon Davies, and Chris Dodge also provided invaluable support at critical junctures along the way. The two anonymous readers who reviewed the manuscript for the press offered more thorough reports than we had ever seen, to be sure. We are thankful for their careful readings as well as their requests for more clarity, added scholarly connections, and deeper analysis. Their scholarly service has contributed to the strong collection of essays here. To all of these editorial patrons, we offer our gratitude.

Many Louisiana historians also have provided endless encouragement as we nurtured this collection of essays. Janet Allured, the lead editor of the first volume of *Louisiana Women: Their Lives and Times*, supported our undertaking from the outset and has provided countless moments of much-need perspective along the way. Other scholars associated with the Louisiana Historical Association—far too many to name here—supported this project from its beginning. Over the years, the meetings of the LHA have provided a place for us to gather annually to discuss women's history and to support one another's scholarly undertakings. Beyond this, however, the LHA often provided the place where we, as editors, first met many of the contributors to this collection and they, as authors, first shared the research and tested the arguments offered here. We are grateful for the comradery and scholarly home that the LHA has provided as this collection came to fruition.

We must also thank our friends and family (and one another) for their encouragement and understanding as we collaborated on this second volume of *Louisiana Women*. For Mary, her husband, Douglas, and children, Peter and Irene, came to know the subjects and authors of this labor of love more than they likely thought possible. Her colleagues in the Department of History and the Graduate School at the University of Louisiana at Lafayette too provided much encouragement for this project even as it at times took her away from teaching and administrative duties. She also is especially grateful for the assistance of Stephanie Marker for her invaluable assistance on the index and, indeed, her willingness to take on a task completely new to her (and for her great wisdom to bring Paul Albano into our project). For Shannon, her friends who know her as a writer deserve more words of gratitude than can possibly be provided here. As we worked to finish the volume, she was in Woodstock, New York, and thus wants to thank the Mayapple Woodstock Writers' Group and notably, Judith Kerman, founder of *Earth's Daughters*, the longest continuously published feminist literary periodical in the United States, for inviting her last year to join this amazing group of writers and poets. This was Shannon's second year there, and she could have never imagined how a week spent at a more-than-a-century-old arts colony that more than anything resembles an adult writers' camp would strengthen her writing, both creative and academic. Her colleagues in the Department of History and Geography at East Stroudsburg University of Pennsylvania have been most supportive of her work, and thanks go to Marie Reish in particular. Shannon also thanks her family, most importantly her father, Jerry Frystak. She moved to Bethlehem, Pennsylvania, eight years ago and was immensely fortunate to find a beautiful and rather eclectic cadre of fellow music, craft beer, bourbon, and hiking lovers who have become her family. They include Bobby and Kim, Sharon and Drew, all the Jeffs, Jim, Bill, George, Patrick, Lenny and Jen, and Tom and Michelle. Then there's Joe's gang, her home away from home: Jackie, Justin, Gillian, Bruce, Nicole, J. J., Amber, Matt, Patrick, and Joe. Additionally, there are the friends and family who have been rooting for her for years: Colleen, Ben, Christian, Beth, Fiona, Sean, Shirley, Sarah, Andy, Simon, Charlie, Michelle, Elena, Brad, Preston, Skeet,

Alison, Jude, and Thea. Finally, Sarah Lathrop falls into all of these categories. She has taken care of Shannon's dog Magnolia on numerous academic, writing, and other trips away from home, and Sarah reads everything she writes before anyone else, doesn't hesitate to offer criticism or suggestions, and cheers her on through all the good that surrounds her career. Finally, Shannon's sweet dog Magnolia has sat by her side while she has written for the past thirteen years. Here's hoping there's a few more books in them both.

For all of the above-named individuals (including sweet Magnolia) who have supported this labor of love, we are forever indebted.

Mary Farmer-Kaiser
Shannon Frystak

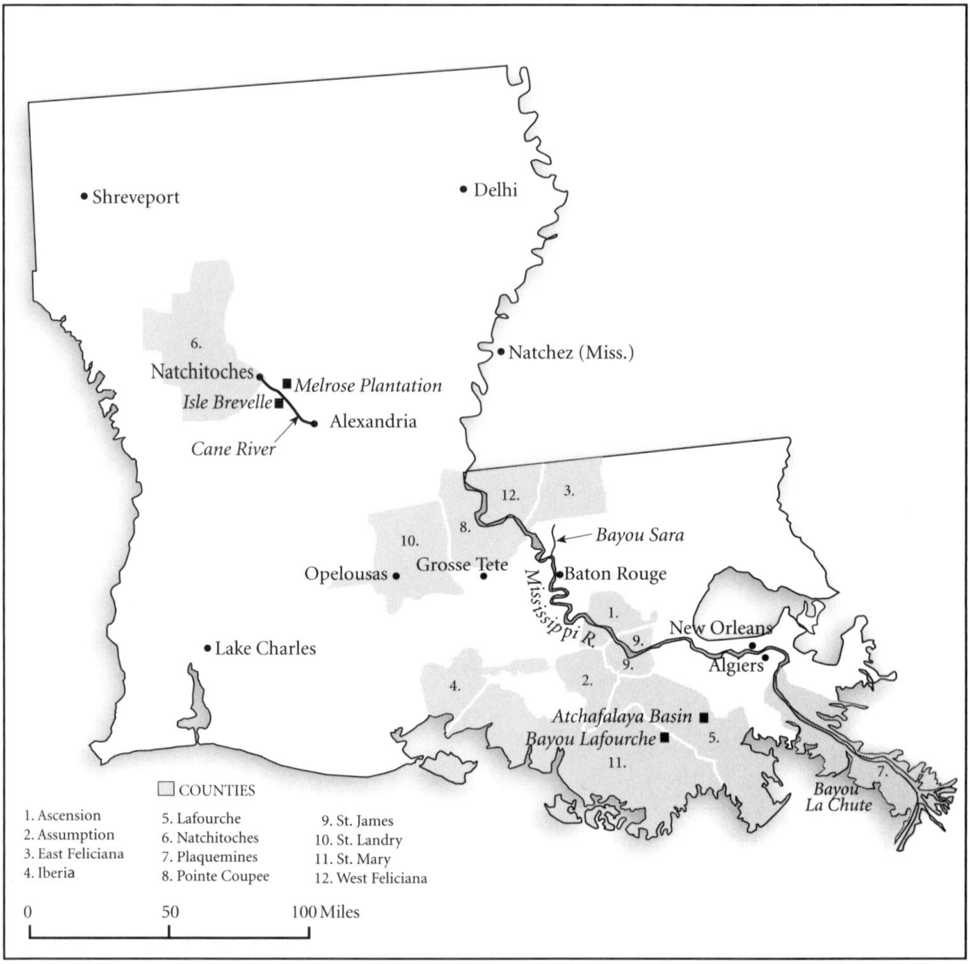
Shreveport
Delhi
Natchez (Miss.)
6.
Natchitoches
Melrose Plantation
Isle Brevelle
Alexandria
Cane River
12.
3.
8.
10.
Bayou Sara
Opelousas
Grosse Tete
Baton Rouge
Mississippi R.
1.
9.
New Orleans
Algiers
Lake Charles
4.
2.
Atchafalaya Basin
Bayou Lafourche
5.
11.
7.
Bayou La Chute
COUNTIES
1. Ascension
2. Assumption
3. East Feliciana
4. Iberia
5. Lafourche
6. Natchitoches
7. Plaquemines
8. Pointe Coupee
9. St. James
10. St. Landry
11. St. Mary
12. West Feliciana
0
50
100 Miles

Introduction

SHANNON FRYSTAK

In 2001 I was invited to be a fellow at Newcomb College Center for Research on Women, housed on the campus of Tulane University. Established in 1886, Newcomb College is one of the oldest women's colleges in the South and one of only seven southern schools that by 1916 "held a standard college designation within the Southern Association of College Women."[1] As was certainly the case for the thousands of women who entered its doors, my time at Newcomb was one of the best experiences of my life. For more than a year, like-minded fellow Louisiana historians, most of whom were researching and writing about Louisiana women and gender, surrounded me. We met regularly as a group to discuss our findings, or the lack thereof, and often found ourselves lamenting how little had been written on Louisiana women. As a result, we organized ourselves into a Friday-morning Louisiana women's reading group, where we scoured the library shelves, journals, and the Internet, searching for something—anything—new on the history of Louisiana women to discuss.

The Newcomb Friday group was fortunate to have access to a book on Myra Clark Gaines, a New Orleans socialite who legally fought for and ultimately won, after more than fifty years and seventeen Supreme Court appearances, the right to her father's New Orleans estate.[2] Barring the Gaines book however, in 2001, scholarship on Louisiana women was incredibly sparse. The first volume of *Louisiana Women*, edited by Janet Allured and Judith Gentry and published in 2009, rectified some of the lacunae in the literature. And in the past decade other works were published that show that women played integral roles in the history of this state from the colonial era to the present.

I am delighted to say that today the literature on Louisiana women is rich and continues to expand. Alecia Long's *The Great Southern Babylon: Sex, Race, and Respectability in New Orleans, 1865–1920* (Louisiana State University Press, 2005), Judith Kelleher Schafer's *Brothels, Depravity, and Abandoned Women: Illegal Sex in Antebellum New Orleans* (Louisiana State University Press, 2011), Carolyn Morrow Ware's *A New Orleans Voudou Priestess: The Legend and Reality of Marie Laveau* (University Press of Florida, 2007) and *Madame Lalaurie: Mistress of the Haunted House* (University Press of Florida, 2012), Kim Marie Vaz's *The "Baby Dolls": Breaking the Race and Gender Barriers of the New Orleans Mardi Gras Tradition* (Louisiana State University Press, 2013), Emily Clark's *The Strange History of the American Quadroon: Free Women of Color in the Revolutionary Atlantic World* (University of North Carolina Press, 2013), and Emily Epstein Landau's *Spectacular Wickedness: Sex, Race, and Memory in Storyville, New Orleans* (Louisiana State University Press, 2013) all address the more sensational past of Louisiana's women. Perhaps balancing them, Emily Clark's *Masterless Mistresses: The New Orleans Ursulines and the Development of a New World Society, 1727–1834* (University of North Carolina Press, 2007) and *Voices from an Early American Convent: Marie Madeleine Hachard and the New Orleans Ursulines, 1727–1760* (Louisiana State University Press, 2009) and Ellen Blue's *St. Mark's and the Social Gospel: Methodist Women and Civil Rights in New Orleans* (University of Tennessee Press, 2011) all look at the ways in which religion shaped and affected the activism of women in New Orleans. Lee Sartain's *Invisible Activists: Women of the Louisiana NAACP and the Struggle for Civil Rights, 1915–1945* (Louisiana State University Press, 2007), my own *Our Minds on Freedom: Women and the Struggle for Black Equality in Louisiana, 1924–1967* (Louisiana State University Press, 2009), Art Shiver and Tom Whitehead's *Clementine Hunter: Her Life and Art* (Louisiana State University Press, 2012), Peggy Frankland and Susan Tucker's *Women Pioneers of the Louisiana Environmental Movement* (University of Mississippi Press, 2013), and Janet Allured's much anticipated book on Louisiana women and second-wave feminism all look at how black and white women stepped out of the prescribed roles afforded them by their gender, race, and class to effect change in twentieth-century Louisiana. To be sure, as the ever-growing field of gender in Louisiana historical scholarship has shown, women were integral to the unusual history of this state.

After the publication of the first volume of *Louisiana Women*, and in talking with Louisiana scholars and historians at conferences and other scholarly events, we discovered that the amount of research being done on women all over the state had greatly expanded. Thus we approached the University of Georgia Press about the possibility of publishing a second volume. Having had such success with the first volume, the editors were more than happy when we presented them with a list of scholars doing work on Louisiana women—some famous, some not so famous—who embodied and continue to embody the spirit of Louisiana. The stories of women like Lulu White, infamous Storyville madam, stand alongside the stories of Lucinda Williams, Grammy-winning songwriter and folk musician. Lindy Claiborne Boggs, the wife of Senator Hale Boggs, who became a well-respected member of Congress in her own right, lived at the same time as Cora Allen, community activist and race leader. Their histories importantly further complicate the narrative of a state that is already complicated in myriad ways.

What this volume seeks to do, not unlike the first, is to rescue women's stories, many of which have been discounted or locked in archives or both. In their own ways, the authors all have addressed a reality that frequently has blurred with mythology. Whether in literature or film (see *Beasts of the Southern Wild*, *True Detective*, and the somewhat historically accurate *American Horror Story: Coven*, the latter based in part on the stories of Madame Lalaurie and Marie Laveau), the history of Louisiana is shrouded in myth and magic.[3] It is these myths that we are attempting to historicize in this collection with context and well-founded research. As the editors of the first volume wrote, we include these women in the history of the state "not as an addendum to the male version of events, but as an integral part of the state's sometimes checkered and colorful past."[4] And, like the first volume did, we hope to inspire other historians to delve deep and locate the hidden histories of the often-marginalized individuals who do not readily present themselves.

In many ways, the history of women in Louisiana is not unlike that of women in other southern states—or the nation writ large, for that matter. All were forced to conform to the social, economic, and political gendered mores and norms of their times. What the stories presented here suggest is that there were ways in which Louisiana's unique environment allowed these women to differentiate and shape themselves and their surroundings. With Spanish and French influences that affected language, architecture, dress, social conditions, and perhaps most importantly the non-Anglophone political and legal structure of the state (based on the Napoleonic Code) and varying regional religious influences—Catholicism in the southern part of the state and Protestantism in the north—Louisiana undeniably possesses a rich and anomalous history. Here, in some ways, women were able to operate under different strictures when it came to identity, work, and the arts and how they organized themselves politically.

This volume is organized slightly differently from the first. It is organized first topically and then chronologically under a theme. To be sure, the lives of the women written about are varied and complex and could easily be viewed as illustrating multiple themes, and this complicated placement. As editors we asked ourselves how each woman might view herself in the history of the state and we organized each part accordingly. The first, "Women and the Politics of Identity," highlights the lives of four groups of women who at times struggled with a sense of self, all the while creating lasting legacies for themselves, their families, and the state they chose to call home. Emily Clark's essay, "The Women across from Congo Square," looks at quadroon women—free women of color—

property-owning businesswomen who took advantage of their status, subverting the stereotype of *plaçage*, the system of "kept" light-skinned mistresses that many visitors to New Orleans had come to expect and that dominates much of the colonial New Orleans narrative. During the colonial era these women owned and managed properties notably, and ironically, across from the slave market in Congo Square, and they created successful businesses that survived well into the antebellum era. Giselle Roberts's essay about Sarah Morgan Dawson, author and chronicler of occupied Civil War Louisiana, documents the difficulties of straddling the fence between her family's Northern roots and the patriotism that was expected of a good Confederate lady. Janet Allured's essay on Janet Mary Riley explores the life of a woman who, as a lawyer and a religious devotee to the Society of Our Lady of the Way, fashioned a unique brand of feminism through her devotion to a life in service to Christ and her secular work of the law. Finally, Tania Tetlow presents the life of Marie Corinne Morrison "Lindy" Claiborne Boggs, wife of esteemed Congressman Hale Boggs, who in the wake of his tragic disappearance in 1972, re-created a life—political and consequential—all her own.

The second part, "Women and Work," explores the various ways in which Louisiana women not only economically sustained themselves and their families but also crossed fairly rigid gendered boundaries of acceptability to become enterprising women. Sara Brooks Sundberg looks at the life of Lucy Alston Pirrie, a Revolutionary War–era woman living on the Louisiana frontier who, taking advantage of liberal land policies of the time, acquired elite status and bequeathed a plantation and legacy to her children despite social prescriptions limiting women of the time. Michael Wade documents three generations of Patout women who successfully guided the evolution of a sugar plantation, through years of modernization and changing business and management practices, into one of the most successful sugar businesses in Louisiana. Emily Epstein Landau tells the legendary yet real-life story of Lulu White, a successful madam who ran a brothel in New Orleans's famous Storyville district in the early twentieth century, in turn altering our perceptions of the "tragic octoroon." And Carolyn Ware presents an important and little-known history of Croatian immigrant oyster-fishing families and the vital contributions Croatian women made to that industry and to Louisiana history and culture.

In its music, architecture, food, and visual and written arts, Louisiana possesses a history richly imbued with creativity. Part 3, "Women and the Arts," recognizes this tradition, addressing the often-marginalized histories of female artists and craftswomen. The five women presented in this section are writers, seamstresses, musicians, or, in the case of Cammie Henry, chatelaine and supporter of the arts. The essay on Carmelite "Miss Cammie" Henry was originally part of a dissertation begun by Lucy Gutman for a doctorate in American women's history at the University of Southern Mississippi. Sadly, Gutman passed away in 2010 before her dissertation could be completed. As one reviewer of the previous *Louisiana Women* volume noted, Henry's legacy is significant to the cultural and political history of the state, thus we thought it was important to include this work in Gutman's honor and because the story of Cammie Henry makes for an interesting study of a woman who promoted the complicated and controversial Lost Cause movement through her sponsorship of the numerous writers who graced her home, Melrose Plantation. While I contributed to the final research and writing on this piece, I did not have access to Gutman's original research, thus the soul of this essay is hers, as is the majority of writing and as are its conclusions. What Henry contributed to Louisiana culture is immense, not only because of the writers she sponsored and housed but also because Clementine Hunter, arguably Louisiana's most famous female folk artist, a laundress and cook at Melrose, began her artistic career upon being "discovered" there.

Part 3 also looks at the lives of four famous—and very different—female artists. Hellen S. Lee profiles Alice Dunbar-Nelson, a turn-of-the century "race woman" whose writings both reflected her political activism and influenced it. Dunbar-Nelson was the wife of the African American poet and novelist Paul Laurence Dunbar. Focusing nearly a century later, Mary Ann Wilson examines "chick lit" author Rebecca Wells, who found fame with *Divine Secrets of the Ya-Ya Sisterhood*, a best-selling book and then popular movie. Clearly affected by her life as a Louisianan and southern Catholic, Wells's work explores female identity, friendship, and what it means to be a writer. Susan Tucker looks at a different type of artist, Coralie Guarino Davis, a seamstress of Mardi Gras costumes who for sixty years documented her life straddling two worlds—the opulent, uptown world of the Mardi Gras participants for whom she created costumes and her working-class Italian immigrant community in New Orleans. Fully aware that her diaries would be read someday, Davis left behind a trove of information on the gender, ethnic, and class boundaries that existed in mid-twentieth-century New Orleans. Finally, Court Carney's essay on the Grammy-winning musician Lucinda Williams provides a window into the world of an artist who infuses her work with the soul of Louisiana and in doing so connects poetics of place to southern history writ large.

Part 4, "Organizing Women," documents the lives of women who in countless ways worked to alter the socially acceptable roles for women and, in doing so, created lasting change in communities across the state. Mark J. Duvall chronicles the life of Phoebe Hunter, cofounder of the Poydras Female Asylum, the first private Protestant refuge run by and for women in the antebellum South. Brittney Cooper's essay on Cora Allen's legacy as a "race woman" and African American female community leader in Shreveport during the racially volatile 1920s provides nuance to our understanding of black women's leadership strategies and their defiance of the racially and socially prescribed gender roles that black women were compelled to abide by in the Jim Crow South (often by threat of violence). Beth Willinger's essay on the New Orleans Christian Woman's Exchange looks at a group of women who through world wars, economic hardship, and natural disaster created a female community held together by similar interest and hardship, women who helped each other help themselves. Leslie Gale Parr writes on Sarah Towles Reed, a white teacher, union lobbyist, and educational advocate and reformer who fiercely defied regional convention and acceptable ideas of how women should operate in the twentieth-century Deep South. Reed's work as a labor, women's, and civil rights activist compelled her critics to charge her with being a "firebrand." Finally, Lee Sartain explores the life of another controversial female community leader, Georgia M. Johnson, who not only breached etiquette in her northern Louisiana community by speaking out against the racial status quo but also disregarded gendered conventions adhered to in the male-dominated National Association for the Advancement of Colored People. Assuming what was seen as a male position as the chair of the Alexandria NAACP's legal committee, Johnson ruffled many feathers with her head-on approach to racial justice—an approach that countered the NAACP's typically more moderate and measured ways—ultimately leading to her being ostracized within her local branch.

Of course, there are women whose stories have yet to be told. While the world watched, a young Ruby Bridges, along with the lesser-known Leona Tate, Tessie Provost, and Gaile Etienne, integrated two New Orleans public schools in 1960 in the city's Lower Ninth Ward, now famous only in the aftermath of Hurricane Katrina. More than sixty years later, Bridges, Tate, Provost, and Etienne continue to work for change in their communities. Dorothy Mae Taylor, with the help of her campaign manager, Oretha Castle Haley, whose life was chronicled in the first *Louisiana Women* volume, became the first African American woman in Louisiana history to be elected to the state house of representatives. Coca-Cola heiress Rosa Freeman Keller, her niece Betty Wisdom, and Felicia Kahn all challenged the elitist New Orleans power structure by inserting themselves in the harried civil rights movement in that city. Similarly, civil rights and women's rights advocate Sibol Holt continues in her eighties to address human rights issues in Baton Rouge, and feminist/activist author Ti-Grace Atkinson, also hailing from Baton Rouge, certainly deserves a chapter all her own. Famous restaurateur Leah Chase ought to be recognized for her activism and advocacy of civil rights in New Orleans. Similarly, Sybil Morial, wife of the late Ernest "Dutch" Morial, was a civil rights and women's rights activist in her own right as she supported her husband as first black mayor of New Orleans. Also worth recognition in her own right is the daughter of politician Maurice Edwin "Moon" Landrieu, Mary Landrieu, who served as U.S. senator for the state of Louisiana from 1997 to 2015. And of course there is novelist Anne Rice, who continues to inspire readers with her otherworldly works on the vampires and witches who are said to reside in Louisiana's backwoods. Finally we could include Brittney Spears, the pop artist, raised in Kentwood, Louisiana, and who has been inspiring young women with her music since the 1990s. It appears that the creativity and brazenness of Louisiana women knows no bounds, and thus the scholarship is sure to continue to be rich and varied. Perhaps a third volume is in order.

As is evident in this volume, the women written about here not only shaped but were shaped by Louisiana. As I write this, amid the revelry and tradition of Mardi Gras, the state stands alone in its culture, music, food, and, more importantly, its people. To be sure, these women embody what it means to be from and of Louisiana. Perhaps no one captures the essence of Louisiana quite like Lucinda Williams:

> Oh, my sweet Lafayette, how I'm going to miss you
> You feel so good, Lafayette, now I've come to greet you
> Tell all my friends I've come back again
> I couldn't stay away, I was gone only a day
> But I'm comin' back to my sweet Lafayette.[5]

NOTES

1. Georgen Coyle and Susan Tucker, "Newcomb: A Brief History of the College," Newcomb College Institute of Tulane University, revised 2011 by Susan Tucker, Mary Allen Johnson, and Beth Willinger, http://tulane.edu/newcomb/newcomb-college-history.cfm. See also Susan Tucker and Beth Willinger, eds., *Newcomb College, 1886–2006: Higher Education for Women in New Orleans* (Baton Rouge: Louisiana State University Press, 2012).

2. Elizabeth Urban Alexander, *Notorious Woman: The Celebrated Case of Myra Clark Gaines* (Baton Rouge: Louisiana State University Press, 2004).

3. See "Sorry, Louisiana Is Not Actually Made of Magic," Dave Thier, *Esquire.com*, March 11, 2014; and "In Defense of Louisiana's Magic," Lamar White Jr., *CenLamar*, CenLamar.com/, March 13, 2014.

4. Janet Allured and Judith F. Gentry, eds., *Louisiana Women: Their Lives and Times* (Athens: University of Georgia Press, 2009), 1.

5. Lucinda Williams, "Lafayette," *Happy Woman Blues*, Smithsonian Folkways, 1980.

PART ONE

Women and the Politics of Identity

The Women across from Congo Square
(1772–1840)

EMILY CLARK

April 27, 1804, was a good day for Marianne Brion. Her attorney, Charles Caune, brought gratifying news from the New Orleans Court of Pleas where he had represented her in a suit against her tenant Michel Meffre Rouzan. A bench of four judges, two of them French speakers and two of them speaking the English of the new U.S. territorial government, had found in favor of Brion's complaint against Meffre Rouzan for nonpayment of rent. The court ordered the deadbeat lodger evicted and satisfied Brion's demand for $329 in back rent.[1] The case is interesting not just for its satisfying revelation of a feisty female property owner who had her day in court and won against a man but also for the way it unsettles a well-entrenched myth about early New Orleans. Marianne Brion was a free woman of color who would have been generally known as a "quadroon," and Michel Meffre Rouzan was a French-born white man. According to what has been commonly believed about relations between two such people, it was Meffre Rouzan who should have had the power to give or deny Brion the roof over *her* head. Women like Brion supposedly lived in houses provided for them by men like Meffre Rouzan, who kept them as mistresses. Such an arrangement has come to be known as *plaçage*, a practice that has been an object of disapproving fascination since travelers to New Orleans began describing it at the beginning of the nineteenth century. Brion and two other free women of color who were her neighbors were not letting out rooms to make ends meet: among them they owned most of a city block in early New Orleans. The recovery of their life stories opens a window onto an alternate reality that makes it hard for the *plaçage* paradigm to retain pride of place among historic descriptions of New Orleans's free women of color.

During the final decade or so of Spanish colonial rule in Louisiana and the first years of American sovereignty, Marianne Brion, Marianne Coffy, and Marie Anstive owned, among them, nearly every square foot of the city block bounded by Rampart, Orleans, Burgundy, and St. Peter Streets on the northern boundary of the part of New Orleans now known as the French Quarter or Vieux Carré. Situated just opposite Congo Square and fronting Rampart Street, their property was located at the intersection of two mythic sites in the history of the city's people of African descent. The women who literally once owned this space are more qualified than anyone to play a part now in rewriting its history.

"The Quadroon girls of New Orleans are brought up by their mothers to be what they have been; the mistresses of white gentlemen," the British traveler and social commentator Harriet Martineau assured her readers in 1837. "Every young man early selects one, and establishes her in one of those pretty and peculiar houses, whole rows of which may be seen in the Remparts."[2] Twenty years before Martineau marked the quadroon cottages of Rampart Street indelibly on the map of the American imagination, Benjamin Henry Latrobe made a different Rampart Street destination famous. "Approaching the Common," on the edge of the city one Sunday morning in 1818, Latrobe reported that he "heard a most extraordinary noise, which I supposed to proceed from some horse-mill—the horses tramping on a wooden floor." When Latrobe got close enough to see what produced the racket, he found "that it proceeded from a crowd of five or six hundred persons, assembled in an open space or public square." The stomping and clapping that assailed Latrobe's ears that day came from hundreds of African men and women absorbed in the ritual of the ring dance, circling around one another to the beat of two drums and a primitive banjo for hours on this Sunday afternoon.[3] Latrobe had stumbled across Congo Square, the famous African dancing place of early New Orleans where the musical traditions that would eventually infuse jazz were sustained and celebrated. Between them, Latrobe and Martineau created two of the most popular itineraries for visitors to New Orleans in the two decades before the outbreak of the Civil War, travelers who often came in search of the exotic and the naughty, as some still do.

Nineteenth-century travelers who followed Latrobe's helpful instructions to walk "up St. Peter's Street" toward the commons that occupied the space where the city's ramparts had once stood would easily find the open space that came to be called Congo Square. If they hoped to get a glimpse of quadroon concubines slipping in and out of one of their "pretty and peculiar houses" when they reached Rampart Street, however, they would be disappointed. The block that Latrobe passed on his way to the spectacle, a block that occupied valuable real estate just across from the thrumming dance ground, was owned almost entirely by three free women of color: Brion, Coffy, and Anstive. Not one of them was a kept woman discreetly occupying a little cottage given her by a white lover. In fact, the lives of these three Rampart Street entrepreneurs diverge in nearly every particular from the stereotype presented by Harriet Martineau and dozens of others who described the free women of color of New Orleans in the nineteenth century.[4] The antebellum American reading public nursed an insatiable appetite for the sordid details of the quadroon's tragic immorality. The real stories of free women of color like Brion, Coffy, and Anstive would not have satisfied their salacious expectations, whether they visited New Orleans via armchair or steamboat. Without the retrieval of these women's histories, what we have amounts to a fanciful travelogue of the city's past.

The significance of Brion, Coffy, and Anstive lies in the ways they contradict and complicate the portrait of free women of color that has been reified in both the literary and the historical imagination. This is itself a densely woven fabric of fact and fiction that stretches back into the eighteenth century and across the Caribbean to colonial Saint-Domingue, which became the Republic of Haiti in 1804. Prior to the outbreak of the Haitian Revolution in 1791, marriage and other forms of sexual partnerships between white men and women of African descent were commonplace in the face of a skewed sex ratio among Europeans that created a shortage of potential wives of unmixed European descent. Some 7 percent of the marriages in the southern part of Saint-Domingue were between Afro-descended women and white men, for example.[5] The kinds of unions that European men formed with women of African ancestry ranged from transient liaisons to legitimate marriage. Other white men cohabited without benefit of marriage with women of color, or *femmes de couleur*, as they were known in Saint-Domingue. Often these relationships were life partnerships in which the men recognized their natural children and made them and their mothers legal heirs in their notarized wills. Many of these unions began when a free woman of color contracted to serve as the *ménagère* or manager of a European bachelor's plantation or urban household, an occupation for which she was remunerated at roughly the same rate as plantation overseers.[6]

Despite the wide range of types and quotidian circumstances reflected in Saint-Domingue's interracial partnerships, descriptions of Dominguan mixed-race women and their relations with white men developed into elaborate and sensationalized caricatures in the late eighteenth century. As European nations struggled to come to terms with the place of their colonies in their polities, differences in colonial practices were often exaggerated and held up as reasons to restrict colonial autonomy. The marriages and liaisons of French men with women of mixed African and European descent, known in the colony generally as *femmes de couleur*, became a particular focal point in the decade before and after the outbreak of slave rebellion in 1791. The figure of the *femme de couleur* was often referred to as *la mûlatresse*, a label used in Saint-Domingue not to indicate the precise phenotype of a woman born to an African mother and a white father, but to evoke a composite type that could actually be of any number of ancestral combinations. *La mûlatresse* comprised a constellation of stock elements. Her sexuality was naturalized and exaggerated. These women were said to be "naturally more lascivious than Europeans" and to "have reduced voluptuousness to a kind of mechanical art, which they have carried to the highest point of perfection." Another writer declared that "the whole being of a *Mûlatresse* is a book given to pleasure."[7]

The *mûlatresses* of these late-eighteenth-century descriptions had an insatiable appetite for luxury, one that most often took shape in the form of sartorial extravagance. They indulged themselves in "the most beautiful things that India produces," according to the French Caribbean writer Moreau Saint-Méry, and decorated these opulent fabrics with lace and masses of costume jewelry. There were, Moreau advised, "a fairly large number of mulattos in Saint-Domingue that could change their entire ensemble every day for a year."[8]

The trait of the *mûlatresse* that made her dangerous, rather than simply offensive to European notions of propriety, was her cold-hearted exploitation of white male lust to satisfy her taste for luxury. "Every night at bedtime," Moreau confided, "you can see the girls of color leaving their homes, often lit by a lantern carried by a slave, to go and spend the night at the home of the one they love most, or the one who pays best." Dominguan *mûlatresses* were said to eschew men of their own racial background to flirt with white men at balls to which they were admitted and men of color barred. There the women performed a seductive dance called the *Chica*, "a kind of lute where all the tricks of love and all its means of triumphing are put into motion." With the aid of her gorgeous clothes, the charms of the *Chica*, and her command of the arts of lovemaking, the *mûlatresse* was an irresistible temptress. She seduced men away from the wives and legitimate children who were the proper objects of their affection, and she diverted their allegiance from mother country to the colony and its unique diversions.[9]

At the very end of the eighteenth century and early in the nineteenth, the figure of the Dominguan *mûlatresse* was transported from her native territory to New Orleans. The relocation was physical—hundreds of Dominguan women of color sought refuge in New Orleans in the aftermath of the Haitian Revolution—but it was its figurative migration that was most powerful in fixing the extravagant, parasitic *mûlatresse* in New Orleans.[10] When travel writers described free women of color in New Orleans during the first decades of the nineteenth century, their accounts echoed those produced by earlier writers on the Dominguan *mûlatresse*. This is hardly surprising. Eighteenth- and nineteenth-century authors freely borrowed from one another in a practice that would be recognized today as clear plagiarism. Hearsay was considered an acceptable source. Harriet Martineau simply employed the conventions of her era when she confidently declared that, "the Quadroon connexions in New Orleans are all but universal, as I was assured on the spot by ladies who cannot be mistaken."[11] It would never have occurred to Martineau to consider her source and investigate the universality of the "Quadroon connexions" by knocking on the doors of some of those Rampart Street cottages. The actual doors are gone, but many of the women can still be found inhabiting the archives, Brion, Coffy, and Anstive among them.

Marianne Brion emerges vividly in the 1772 notarial act that freed her and four of her children from slavery. She was described in the manumission as a *mûlatresse* and was widely known to have been the daughter of French-born Claude Joseph Dubreuil, a wealthy planter and colonial official, and one of his enslaved domestics, an African-born woman named Nanette. It was often presumed by contemporaries, and subsequently by historians, that the origin of most free people of color was the phenomenon of white fathers freeing their mixed-race children.[12] In fact, this was not true in most cases, including Marianne's. She was not owned by her father when she was manumitted but by a man named René Brion and his wife, Marianne Piquery. The family was emancipated *graciosa*, or without payment or conditions. Marianne either chose or was given the surname of her last owner, but in her later life the surname of her biological father was often used interchangeably with it.[13]

Marianne Brion was not freed by her biological father, and other evidence suggests that she was not manumitted by her lover either. A bequest made to her ten years after she gained her liberty suggests otherwise. A free black man named Santiago LaFleur made Brion his universal heir, and in 1783 she inherited from his estate the first two of five contiguous lots she would eventually own on Rampart Street. The relationship between Dubreuil and LaFleur is otherwise undocumented, but people usually chose their husbands or wives to be their universal heirs. It seems quite likely that LaFleur was Brion's partner and probably the father of at least some of her children.[14]

The decade following Brion's manumission is almost impossible to reconstruct, but it cannot have been easy for her. She was thirty-eight years old in 1772, definitely middle-aged in eighteenth-century terms and a poor candidate for rescue by a besotted white lover. Typical occupations for free women of color in Spanish colonial New Orleans included petty marketing, laundering, and providing domestic services for a wage to households with no enslaved workers. These last two services could evolve into providing room and board for bachelors living in the city who could not maintain their own households, in a home the woman either rented or owned, in which she might or might not be present. Brion fits this profile. When she next emerges clearly in the historical record, it is as a successful—and somewhat infamous—landlady in the mid-1780s.

Andres Barba found himself in a tight spot as one of Brion's tenants at that time. He had leased two houses and a room from Marianne Brion at a rate of nineteen pesos per month. Barba understood the lease to be for a year, but Brion raised his rent to twenty-four pesos per month without warning before the year was up. Barba decided to stay put because he had sublet the houses to others and because it was too much trouble for him to move from the room that he was apparently occupying himself. At the end of the next year, Brion raised the rent to forty pesos, more than doubling what Barba had originally agreed to. This time Barba fought back and filed a complaint against Brion, claiming that her rent was exorbitant and seeking redress from the court. The outcome of the suit is not recorded, but given the success of Brion in her proceedings against Michel Meffre Rouzan two decades later, it seems unlikely that she was intimidated by the episode.[15]

The 1780s were good years for Brion, her unpleasantness with Andres Barba notwithstanding. After acquiring the two lots on Rampart Street through LaFleur's bequest, she bought a small piece of property behind them on St. Peter Street from another free woman of color to expand her presence in the neighborhood. Her children would all have been old enough to help out with her business in 1782: Marianne was eighteen, Adelaide was eleven, Annette fifteen, and Joseph fourteen. She was prosperous enough to buy at least two female slaves that decade who probably worked alongside Marianne and her children cleaning and maintaining the properties and collecting rent.[16] By the 1790s, Marianne Brion was comfortable by any standard. At middecade, she and her extended family lived in a house on Dauphine Street near Bourbon, where her household of eleven free people of color was served by seven enslaved men and women.[17]

At the beginning of the 1790s, Marianne may have owned even more bound workers, but in 1791 her servant ranks were reduced by one. An African woman of twenty-four had somehow managed to save the 650 pesos that Brion charged for her self-purchase. Under Spanish law, Brion could not refuse to free a slave who offered a fair price for herself, but she might have expected the African to remain in bondage a little longer. With no family in the colony when they arrived, newly enslaved Africans had a more difficult time accessing the networks that helped them earn their way to freedom. But this young woman was enterprising and had in her mistress a model of industry to emulate. On the threshold of freedom, Marie Anstive must already have known exactly what she wanted to do once she was free. Just nine years after she gained her liberty, she bought three large lots just around the corner from Marianne Brion's property on Rampart Street.[18]

It is impossible not to wonder about the relationship between these two women. Marianne Brion comes through in the historical record as a hard-nosed businesswoman, willing to stand up for herself in court against the white men upon whom women of her type were supposed to be dependent. Marie Anstive may have watched and learned as her owner strategized to maximize the opportunities that fell into her lap with Santiago LeFleur's bequest. Congo Square was just becoming a popular gathering place for enslaved Africans in the final decade of the eighteenth century.[19] Records for this period are spotty, but it seems likely that Brion exploited the properties fronting the dance ground, perhaps renting them to tavern owners or grocers who could provision the merrymakers and sightseers who flocked to the space on Sunday afternoons and after the workday was done. The bequest properties must have done well for Brion, because in 1794 she bought three more lots on Rampart, giving her ownership of all the lots opposite Congo Square on this block.[20] Perhaps Anstive watched as her mistress's properties prospered, overheard her talk about the desirability of buying more, and set her sights on following in her mistress's footsteps once she was free.

Anstive's former owner may have had a lock on the Rampart Street lots just across from Congo Square, but the properties around the corner on Orleans were close, and they were on the route that many would take from the cathedral to the dancing place after Mass on Sundays. In 1799 Marie Anstive bought property with a frontage of nearly 160 feet on the Orleans side of the block where Brion owned properties.[21] The former slave purchased two more properties on Orleans Street in 1820. She now possessed the entire block around the corner from her former mistress save one at the Rampart end of Orleans, which Marianne Dubreuil had already bought. Anstive was about sixty when she made this final move to consolidate her hold in the area.[22]

Marie Anstive met even fewer of the traditional criteria of the quadroon concubine than did Marianne Brion. Brion was described in various documents as a *mûlatresse rouge*, indicating that she was the kind of light-skinned free woman of color presumably favored by white men.[23] Anstive was African-born and is always described as a *negresse*. She did live near Rampart Street, but it was in the middle of an entire block of property that she owned, not in a little house supplied by a white lover. Her only child, Marie Joseph, is likewise described as a *negresse*, indicating that both parents were of unmixed African descent. If Marie Anstive got help in acquiring her real estate from the father of her child, it was from a black man. And Anstive did not follow Martineau's parenting model for free women of color and set up her daughter as some white man's mistress. Marie Joseph married Raphael Bernabé, identified as a *nègre libre*, at St. Louis Cathedral in 1813 before a large group of friends who celebrated with her and her mother the entry of another free black woman into the ranks of respectability.[24] Married though she was, Marie Joseph seems to have taken a page from her mother's independent outlook on life. She bore Bernabé two sons but separated from him at some point and presided over the swath of Orleans Street property her mother left to her until her own death in 1869.[25]

St. Peter Street was one block up from Orleans Street. The block around the corner from Marianne Brion's stronghold on Rampart Street and backing onto Marie Anstive's property on Orleans was never in the possession of a single entrepreneur, but it was mostly owned by free people of color. For example, free man of color Lindor Leduc received a lot near the corner of St. Peter and Burgundy as a bequest from Jacques Le Duc. Though their surnames are essentially identical, the relationship was not filial. Jacques Le Duc was a white man, while Lindor was identified in succession documents as a *nègre*.[26] Lindor's neighbor was Marie Coffy, who owed the St. Peter Street property nearest Rampart Street, a double lot with a frontage of fifty-four feet. There were no white lovers supplying free women of color on this part of the block either.[27]

Marianne Coffy is the most elusive of the trio of women in the historical record, but enough survives to confirm that her acquisition of the property did not involve a liaison with a white lover. Like Brion, she inherited the property, but in her case the bequest came from her mother, a free woman of color named Luison Almonester. Almonester, in turn, declared that she had inherited the property from a free man of color named Coffy, to whom she had borne five children. His name indicates that Coffy was probably African-born. Kofi was the Akan name for a boy born on Friday, and enslaved men born in Africa and named Cuffee appear in the historical record throughout the Atlantic world.[28]

A pattern involving free women of color does emerge around Rampart Street, but it is not the one that Martineau and others portray. A visitor walking across the city from the Mississippi River to Congo Square at the beginning of the nineteenth century would indeed have encountered property-owning women of African descent, but they presided over large tracts of urban real estate, not little cottages. And they came by those properties not through the patronage of white paramours but through their own hard work and that of partners and parents of their own racial background.

Rampart Street was on the edge of the old city, and when commentators like Martineau identified it as the provenance of free women of color, their marginality was underlined. The implication was that the upright citizenry of New Orleans sought to banish such an overt vice from the city limits. The concentration of property owners of color in general, and the three women across from Congo Square in particular, was not, however, the result of a plan to situate a shameful population on the city's margins. When men like Coffy acquired their property near Rampart Street in the eighteenth century, the neighborhood was on the undeveloped outskirts of the city. Land grants had been made to French settlers there in 1722, but almost none of the grantees built on these outlying sites, and many allowed their titles to lapse. Records of the transactions that transferred ownership of some of this property into the hands of free men of color like Coffy and LaFleur are lost. They may have been squatters whose ownership was recognized by the Spanish colonial government, or they may have purchased the land legitimately from heirs to the grantees or from the local government. Men like Coffy and LaFleur would have had little competition for these properties. Before the mid-1790s, the area near the city's defensive ramparts was virtually a no-man's land. A rudimentary fort had been built on or near the site of Congo Square in 1760, some two blocks north of what had previously been the city's north limit at Dauphine Street. When the fort was rebuilt in 1794 and officially named Fort Fernando, members of the free black militia served guard duty there.[29]

Perhaps it was the presence of black troops at Fort Fernando that provided the impetus for the area's development. Congo Square is not securely documented as a dancing ground until 1808. Before that time, accounts site the African dancing on the levee, at the riverfront. It is easy to imagine a scenario at the end of the eighteenth century in which a confluence of relatively sympathetic free black guards and a few intrepid free black business owners supplying refreshments helped turn the open space in front of Fort Fernando into the city's regular dancing ground for those of African descent.[30]

The city demolished Fort Fernando in 1804 and the dance ground no longer had the military for a neighbor. The site was now incontestably a destination for amusement. Marie Anstive and Marian Brion were not the only ones to recognize the commercial potential of this new entertainment zone. In 1808 Bernard Coquet bought into the neighborhood, putting together a parcel of land on the Burgundy Street end of the block dominated by Brion and Anstive. A small-time impresario who had managed two of the city's dance halls nearer the heart of town, he was known to cater to a clientele of all races. The white Coquet must have thought he could find his own niche in the vicinity of Congo Square. He did not stay long. In 1810 he sold all of this property.[31]

Marianne Brion's daughters did not sustain their mother's presence on Rampart Street beyond the mid-1820s. Annette died in 1814, and her property on Rampart Street was sold in 1815 to benefit her daughter. Her sister, Adelaide, sold her lot in 1817. Marianne Brion's namesake and eldest daughter, Marianne Piquery, sold her Rampart Street inheritance in 1825. Marie Anstive remained on her property on Orleans Street until her death in 1829, but some might make the case that Martineau could still have been right about the reign of quadroon mistresses on Rampart Street. After Brion's daughters abandoned the neighborhood, Anstive could have lived there a solitary anachronism, surrounded by light-skinned free women of color in "pretty and peculiar houses" who traded on their charms. But she didn't.[32]

Women like Anstive were indeed rare on Rampart Street in the 1830s, but it was hardly because the area had become the city's headquarters for love nests. It was a bustling strip where businesses occupied as much space as residences and men outnumbered women. Construction and building supplies featured prominently, servicing the city during this period of exponential growth. Eighteen sites were given over to building trades: carpenters, builders, and lumberyards up and down the street, and a bricklayer, joiner, slater, turner, and blacksmith at the ready to help realize the plans drawn up by the architect who had his office down the street. The block that had been owned by Marianne Brion and her daughters became home to a blacksmith shop and a lumberyard. A coachmaker, drayman, and two livery stables represented the transportation sector. Rampart was not just the haunt of laborers and tradesmen. More than twenty merchants, brokers, accountants, and clerks occupied space on the street, along with three attorneys and a notary public. A medical doctor, dentist, and druggist supplied health care. A trio of liquor stores anchored the block at Canal Street, and three taverns and a cigar maker provided other places for indulgence at the end of the workday.[33]

In 1832, Rampart Street was about equally divided between residences and businesses, with eighty-eight households and eighty-nine places of business. With about two-thirds of the households headed by men and half of the street occupied by men at work, the neighborhood was a distinctly male one.[34] Few, if any, of the women who did live on Rampart Street are good matches for Harriet Martineau's quadroon concubines. Eighteen were widows, including one who ran a boardinghouse. There were two married women living separately from their husbands—a more common phenomenon than might be expected. A mere seventeen single women headed households on all of Rampart Street.

There were only five free women of color heading households on Rampart, and only one of them, Arsene Latil, comes close to the portrait that Harriet Martineau paints of a kept woman. She was young, under thirty-five, and lived with her little boy on lower Rampart Street in the Faubourg Marigny. The others do not fit the stereotype nearly as well. Down the street lived middle-aged Marie Louise Labretonniere, a Haitian refugee who presided over a household that seems to have been knitted together by shared exigency rather than the indulgence of a white lover. She lived with another middle-aged free woman of color over the age of thirty-six, three free women of color in their late teens and early twenties, a little boy, and two enslaved female servants. New Orleans native Seraphine Christophe presided over a household of five adult free women of color, a scenario that suggests a pooling of resources among women who supported themselves. There were two other households of adult free women of color that suggest similar circumstances, the household shared by Zabeth Dutillet, a woman over the age of fifty-five, with an unnamed younger woman, and the apparent partnership of Justine Moreau and Adelaide Lambert, who shared a house on upper Rampart Street. It is worth noting that two white single mothers shared Rampart Street with these single free colored mothers. Unmarried mothers came in all colors in New Orleans.[35]

Harriet Martineau's geography of *plaçage* is only a piece of a much larger discourse that confined New Orleans free women of color to a single dimension. To be the unmarried partner of a white man was, to be sure, the real situation of some of the city's *femmes de couleur libre*, but the details of their lives have been left just as unexplored as those of Brion, Anstive, and Coffy. The history of Brion's own daughter, Marianne Piquery, is a case in point.

Piquery, who took the surname of the wife of the man who freed her and her mother, formed a life partnership with a white man born in France. Altogether she bore him seven children, Jacques in 1791, Maria Jacqueline in 1799, Charles in 1801, Louis in 1803, Marie Celeste in 1807, Anne Rose in 1811, and Michel in 1815.[36] At least two of Piquery's daughters wed free men of color. Marie Jacqueline married Louis Ferand, a native of Port-au-Prince who probably arrived in New Orleans with an influx of more than nine thousand other refugees of the Haitian Revolution in 1809. She was a successful dressmaker who declared a net worth of $1,500 in the marriage contract she executed with Ferand about two months before their wedding in 1818. When her younger sister Marie Celeste married Jean Fleming in 1826 at the age of twenty-one, Marie Celeste brought $2,500 in cash and $500 in goods to the new household. Neither of the grooms declared any worth. The daughters of Marianne Brion found in their mates love, a path to respectability, or both. They relied on themselves for material security.[37] One of Marianne Brion's sons, Jacques, also married. In 1825 he wed Catherine Andre Cavelier, a free woman of color who had already borne him two children who were legitimated by the marriage.[38]

The marriage of Marianne Piquery's children was not unusual in the 1820s among free people of color born into families with roots in colonial New Orleans. Some 165 free women of color married free men of color before the altar at St. Louis Cathedral between 1820 and 1830.[39] It is not really surprising that women like Jacqueline and Marie Celeste Piquery chose to marry. Both were women of means, and because Louisiana's civil law recognized and gave them absolute authority over the wealth that they brought into the marriage, it offered them protection from abusive or irresponsible mates that a nonmarital partnership did not. Marianne Piquery and her mother knew the disadvantages of such unions all too well from their own experience. After the birth of Louis in 1803, Marianne Piquery and her white lover had a falling out, and circumstances suggest that it was because he was not contributing sufficiently to family finances. It was not that he had failed to provide Marianne Piquery with the requisite house on Rampart Street to which quadroon mistresses were entitled. Quite the contrary. The white lover was in fact living in a house owned by his mistress's mother. When he failed to act as a responsible father should, Marianne Brion took him to court and had him thrown out of her house on April 27, 1804. The deadbeat lodger whose situation turned the rubric of *plaçage* on its head was Michel Meffre Rouzan.

NOTES

1. Judgment, *Marianne Brion v. Rouzan Junior*, Louisiana Court of Pleas (New Orleans), *Index to Minute Book, 1804*, April 27, 1804, Louisiana Division City Archives and Special Collections, New Orleans Public Library.

2. Harriet Martineau, *Society in America* (London: Saunders and Otley, 1837), 2:226.

3. Benjamin Henry Latrobe, *Journal of Latrobe: Being the Notes and Sketches of an Architect, Naturalist and Traveler in the United States from 1816 to 1820* (New York: D. Appleton, 1905), 179–80.

4. Other examples include Thomas Ashe, *Travels in America Performed in 1806 for the Purpose of Exploring the Rivers Alleghany, Monongahela, Ohio, and Mississippi, and Ascertaining the Produce and Condition of their Banks and Vicinity* (London: Richard Phillips, 1808), 3:269–74; John F. Watson, "Notitia of Incidents at New Orleans," *American Pioneer* 2, no. 5 (May 1843): 227–37; Frederick Law Olmsted, *The Cotton Kingdom: A Traveller's Observations on Cotton and Slavery in the American Slave States Based upon Three Former Volumes of Journeys and Investigations by the Same Author* (New York: 1984), 236.

5. Michel-René Hilliard d'Auberteuil, *Considérations sur l'état présent de la colonie française de Saint-Domingue. Ouvrage politique et législatif; présenté au ministre de la marine* (Paris: Grangé, 1776); Stewart R. King, *Blue Coat or Powdered Wig: Free People of Color in Pre-Revolutionary Saint Domingue* (Athens: University of Georgia Press, 2001), 187, 193–94; John D. Garrigus, *Before Haiti: Race and Citizenship in French Saint-Domingue* (New York: Palgrave Macmillan, 2006), 22–50, 56–57, 58, 73, 154, 191, 192, marriage statistic on 67.

6. King, *Blue Coat*, 187; Garrigus, *Before Haiti*, 56–57; Dominique Rogers, "Les libres de couleur dans les capitales de Saint-Domingue: fortune, mentalités et intégration à la fin de l'Ancien Régime (1776–1789) (PhD diss., Université Michel de Montaigne, Bordeaux III, 1999), 137–40.

7. Garrigus, *Before Haiti*, 111–14, 143–70; M. L. E. (Médéric Louis Élie) Moreau de Saint-Méry, *Description Topographique, Physique, Civile, Politique et Historique de la Partie Française de L'Isle Saint-Domingue* (Philadelphia: Chez l'Auteur, 1797; Paris: Dupont, 1797), 92–93; Francis Alexander Stanislaus, Baron de Wimpffen, *Voyage to Saint Domingo, in the Years 1788, 1789, and 1790*, trans. J. Wright (London: T. Cadell, Junior, and W. Davies, 1797), 111–13, published in French slightly later the same year as *Voyage à Saint-Domingue, pendant les années 1788, 1789 et 1790 par le Baron de Wimpffen* (Paris: Chez Cocheris, 1797), 1:147–48.

8. Moreau de Saint-Méry, *Description Topographique*, 93.

9. Ibid., 97; M. L. E. Moreau de St-Mery, *Danse Article: Extrait d'un Ouvrage de M. L. E. Moreau de St. Mery, ayant pour titre*: Répertoire des Notions Coloniales (Philadelphie: Imprimé par l'Auteur, 1796), 51–54.

10. Dunbar Rowland, ed., *Official Letter Books of W. C. C. Claiborne*, 1801–1816 (Jackson: Mississippi Department of Archives and History, 1917), 4:381–82; "Report of the Mayor of New Orleans to Governor Claiborne of January 18, 1810," *Moniteur de la Louisiane*, January 27, 1810.

11. Martineau, *Society in America*, 2:226.

12. I use the term "free people of color" throughout this essay in the same sense as contemporaries who used the French term *gens de couleur*—to refer to any person of any degree of African descent who was not enslaved. It had no connection to phenotype or *métissage*: a person born in Africa would be understood during the time period covered by this essay to be one of the *gens de couleur*. The term has subsequently been understood and used by commentators and historians to refer only to free mixed-race people, but this usage is anachronistic.

13. Acts of Jean Garic, September 23, 1772, Manumission of Marianne by René Brion, New Orleans Notarial Archives (hereafter NONA); Marianne Brion's sister, Cécile Dubreuil, was the great-grandmother of Henriette Delille, founder of the Sisters of the Holy Family. For more on this family see, Emily Clark and Virginia M. Gould, "The Feminine Face of Afro-Catholicism in New Orleans, 1727–1852," *William and Mary Quarterly*, 3rd ser., 59, no. 2 (April 2002): 414. On the origins of populations of free people of color in New Orleans and Saint-Dominguec, see Rogers, "Les libres de couleur," 67–72; Kimberly S. Hanger, *Bounded Lives, Bounded Places: Free Black Society in Colonial New Orleans, 1769–1803* (Durham, N.C.: Duke University Press, 1997), 17–54. Moreau de Saint-Méry, *Description Topographique*, 95, is typical of contemporary white Dominguan explanations for the growth of the free colored population.

14. Two of Marianne's children are identified as *mûlatre/esse* in the baptismal records that have survived, e.g., Baptism of Francois Adelaide, June 9, 1764, "St. Louis Cathedral Baptisms and Marriages, 1763–1766 (hereafter SLC B5), Archdiocesan Archives of New Orleans (hereafter AANO); Bap-

tism of [name not recorded], "petite mulatresse," September 9, 1768, "St. Louis Cathedral Baptisms, 1767–1771," (hereafter SLC B6), AANO. Had they been born to her of a white father, they would most likely have been designated *cuateron* (quadroon). The child of a *mûlatresse* and a *nègre* would have been identified as a *mûlatre/esse*. Marianne identified LaFleur as a *nègre*, a man of unmixed African descent, in Donation of property by Marianne Dubreuil called Brion to Adelaid Piquery, Acts of Michel de Armas, September 14, 1810, New Orleans Notarial Archives.

15. Barba's battle with Brion is detailed in Kimberly S. Hanger, "'Desiring Total Tranquility' and Not Getting It: Conflict Involving Free Black Women in Spanish New Orleans," *Americas*, 54, no. 4 (April 1998): 550–51.

16. Ages of Brion's children were calculated from the Manumission of Marianne by René Brion, September 23, 1772; Baptism of Joseph, September 16, 1769, SLC B6, and baptismal records noted in note 13 above.

17. "Recensement General de La Nouvelle Orleans, 1795," Archivo General de Indias, Papeles Procedentes de la Isla de Cuba, legajo 211, 63.

18. Manumission of Marie by Marianne Brion, Acts of Pedro Pedesclaux, September 15, 1791, NONA.

19. Freddi Williams Evans, *Congo Square: African Roots in New Orleans* (Lafayette: University of Louisiana at Lafayette Press, 2011), 135–63, provides a useful timeline for Congo Square. Although she accepts the authority of an undocumented secondary source that sites African dancing in 1786 at what became Congo Square, the earliest primary source for such activity is from an observation in 1808, Christian Schultz, *Travels on an Inland Voyage* (New York: Isaac Riley, 1810), 2:197.

20. Act of sale [by] Gilbert Guillemard to Marianne Dubreuil, September 15, 1794, referenced in Act of sale by Manette Devince to Marianne Piquery, Acts of Michel de Armas, April 2, 1814, NONA.

21. Act of sale by Ignace Balderas to Marie Anstive, Acts of Narcisse Broutin, December 10, 1799, NONA.

22. Act of sale, Succession of Catherine Molero to Marie Anstive, Acts of Christovel de Armas, June 30, 1820, NONA.

23. "*Mûlatresse rouge*" is a term that I have only encountered in this instance. It seems likely that it is primarily descriptive, indicating a complexion in which a rosy tint could be detected.

24. Manumission of Marianne by René Brion describes Marianne as a *mûlatresse rouge*; Anstive is identified as a *negresse* in Manumission of Marie by Marianne Brion and declares herself African-born in her will, Testament of Marie Anstive, Acts of Octave de Armas, April 7, 1829, NONA; Marie Joseph Pierre is described as a *negresse* in Testament of Marie Anstive, and in her marriage record, Marriage of Raphel Bernabé and Maire Joseph Pierre St. Martin, May 22, 1813, "Libro primero de Matrimonios de Negros y Mulatos en la Parroquia de Sn. Luis de la Nueva-orleans; en 137 folios da principio en 20 de enero de 1777 y acaba en . . .," AANO (hereafter "Libro primero").

25. In Testament of Marie Anstive, Marie Joseph Pierre is identified as the mother of two sons and the wife of Raphel Bernabé "separated in body and goods."

26. Burial of Santiago Phelipe Le Duc, August 23, 1807, SLC F6, 127; Declaration of Juan Bautista Leseur Fontaine, Testamentary Executor for Santiago Felipe Le Duc, Acts of Estevan Quinones, September 28, 1807, NONA.

27. Details regarding the chain of title of these lots and their measurements are found in Act of sale by Jean Baptiste Coffy to Pierre Isaac Bongue, Acts of Carlisle Pollock, September 13, 1820, NONA.

28. Ibid. The most famous African American bearing this name was probably mariner and abolitionist Paul Cuffee, who was named for his African father, Kofi, A. Mott, *Biographical Sketches and Interesting Anecdotes of Persons of Color* (York: W. Alexander & Son, 1826), 31–43; Lamont D. Thomas, *Paul Cuffee: Black Entrepreneur and Pan-Africanist* (Urbana: University of Illinois Press, 1988).

29. The apparent abandonment or neglect of land grants made in 1722 on the northern edge of

the city are clear in the chains of title documented in "The Vieux Carré Survey," Historic New Orleans Collection, New Orleans.

30. Manumission of Marie by Marianne Brion, Acts of Pedro Pedesclaux, September 15, 1791, NONA.

31. Ibid.; Act of sale, Succession of Leduc to Bernard Coquet, Acts of Steven de Quinones, April 26, 1808, NONA; Latrobe, *Journal of Latrobe*, 179–80.

32. Act of sale, William Parent, tutor of deceased minor, Annette Piquery, Acts of Michel de Armas, September 22, 1815, NONA; Act of sale, George Wertenbaker, agent for Adelaide Piquery to Francois Jahan, Philippe Pedesclaux, August 18, 1817, NONA; Act of sale, Marianne Piquery to Randal Curell, Acts of Felix de Armas, July 11, 1825. Testament of Marie Anstive in 1829 notes that she is living on her Orleans Street property. Last will and testament of Marie Joseph Pierre Barnabe, Acts of Octave de Armas, April 19, 1869, NONA, puts the death of Marie Anstive at 1829.

33. Based on *New Orleans Directory, 1832* (New Orleans: Perey, 1832).

34. Ibid.

35. Ibid.; 1830 U.S. Census provides household information for Latil, Labretonniere, Christophe, Dutillet, Moreau and Lambert. Christophe is identified as a native of New Orleans in the baptism of her daughter: Baptism of Celeste Ysavel Christophe, November 19, 1812, "St. Louis Cathedral Baptisms of—Slaves and Free Persons of Color, 1812–1814," AANO, 54. The refugee status of the Labretonnieres is documented in Baptism of Jean Honore LaBretonniere, June 2, 1818, "[St. Louis Cathedral] registro o libro 16 de bautismos de gente de color, 1818–1820," (hereafter SLC B30), AANO, 18, in which the child's mother is identified as a native of Jacmel, Saint-Domingue.

36. Baptism of Jacques Meffre Rousan, May 31, 1791, born February 26, 1791, "Libro de bautizados de negros y mulatos, [1786–1792], AANO; Baptism of Marie Jacqueline Rouzan, April 1, 1801, born November 12, 1799, "St. Louis Cathedral Baptisms of Slaves and Free Persons of Color, 1798–1801," (hereafter SLC B16), AANO; Baptism of Charles Meffre Rouzan, October 25, 1801, born June 24, 1801, SLC B16; Baptism of Louis Michel Meffre Rouzan, baptized as an adult September 29, 1819, born September 10, 1803, SLC B30; Baptism of Marie Celeste Meffre Rouzan, baptized as an adult September 29, 1819, born February 11, 1807, SLC B30; Baptism of Ana Rosa Meffre Rouzan, baptized September 29, 1819, born March 9, 1811, SLC B30; Baptism of Michel Meffre Rouzan, September 30, 1815, born November 3, 1814, "St. Louis Cathedral Baptisms of Slaves and Free Persons of Color, 1814–1816, AANO.

37. Marriage of Jacqueline Meffre Rouzan and Louis Ferand, September 28, 1818, "Libro primero"; Marriage of Catherine Andre Cavelier and Jacques Meffre Rouzan, September 7, 1825, ibid.; Marriage of Jean Fleming and Marie Meffre Rouzan, November 9, 1826, ibid.

38. Marriage of Jacqueline Meffre Rouzan and Louis Ferand, September 28, 1818, "Libro Primero"; Marriage of Catherine Andre Cavelier and Jacques Meffre Rouzan, September 7, 1825, ibid.; Marriage of Jean Fleming and Marie Meffre Rouzan, November 9, 1826, ibid.

39. Calculated on entries in "Libro primero."

Sarah Morgan

(1842–1905)

Family Politics and Confederate Patriotism in Civil War Louisiana

GISELLE ROBERTS

Sarah Morgan stood on the balcony of her Church Street home as cottony plumes of smoke wrapped Baton Rouge in a state of quiet despair. The town had been on alert for weeks now. Rumors, lies, and the inevitability of Union occupation had shaken the resolve of even the most self-possessed Confederates. "There is no word in the English language which can express the state in which we are all now, and have been for the last three days," Sarah wrote in her diary on April 26, 1862. "I feel such a craving for news . . . that I believe I am as crazy as the rest, and it is all humbug when they tell me I am cool." The federal assault on New Orleans had brought matters to a head. As Union ironclads effortlessly claimed muddy Mississippi and River Road riches, Baton Rouge sought to define its own terms of surrender. Politicians scurried out of the city, establishing a temporary state capital in Opelousas. Determined that invading troops would not reap slavery's bounty, the region's planters—including Sarah's brother-in-law John Charles LaNoue—piled whiskey-soaked cotton bales onto flatboats and set them alight on the river. "It had come from all directions," Sarah remarked, "but many men stood by who could claim an interest in the cotton that was burning, or was waiting to be burned, and either looked on, or helped with cheerfulness." "If the Yankees are fond of strong drink," she added, "I fear they will fare ill."[1]

The slashed and smoldering harvest may have departed Baton Rouge with all the patriotic aplomb of a full dress parade, but it took with it both military credit and domestic security. Sarah acknowledged that King Cotton's riverbed burial did not bode well for the fate of the city. "Nothing can be heard positively," she wrote anxiously. "We only know we had best be prepared for anything." If Baton Rouge acceded to the terms offered by the Union, there was a

SARAH MORGAN

Courtesy of Morgan Goldbarth.

possibility of staying put. But if the federal army shelled or burned the town, the Morgan family would have to reconsider their decision to "remain here, come what will." Sarah hoped for the best but prepared for the worst. Sifting through her personal papers and keepsakes, her clothing and jewelry, she filled a "treasure bag" with "a few necessary trifles and a few *un*necessary ones—I had not the heart to leave the prayer books father gave us—carving knife and pistol safe, I stood ready for instant flight." While Sarah toyed with the idea of lugging the piano out of town on a dray, her father's law library, the statue of Apollo and Diana, and her rosewood writing desk would all be left behind. "I never before knew how many articles were perfectly 'indispensable,'" she remarked. "This or that little token or keepsake, piles of letters I hate to burn, many dresses, etc. I cannot take conveniently, lay around me, and I hardly know which to choose among them, yet half must be sacrificed; I can only take one trunk." Sarah's personal papers sat "piled on the bed, ready to burn, with matches lying on them." Two "untouched" muslins—"the prettiest imaginable"—would share a similar fate. "It is useless to sew for fire," she concluded.[2]

The subdued arrival of the USS *Iroquois* on May 7, 1862, seemed almost anticlimactic to a town planning feverishly for booming cannons and flying shells. While the terms of immediate surrender were not met, the uncontested federal occupation of the arsenal and barracks signaled an end to southern governance in Baton Rouge. On May 13, 1862, fifteen hundred men under the command of Union general Thomas Williams made a brief stop—and an impressive show of force—in the city while en route to battle in Vicksburg. Most residents gawked uneasily at the men in blue, but Sarah obstinately vowed to "devote all my red, white, and blue silk to the manufacture of Confederate flags." "Henceforth, I wear one pinned to my bosom," she proclaimed. "The man who says take it off, will have to pull it off for himself; the man who dares attempt it—well! a pistol in my pocket will fill up the gap. I am capable, too." Constructing a five-inch flag—hand-pieced, slip-stitched, and embellished with a smattering of colonial knots for stars—Sarah tucked the stem into her belt, pinned the flag snugly to her shoulder, and promenaded the statehouse grounds with patriotic purpose. Sarah's neighbor Nettie Brunot joined her, sporting a "modest little [flag] of two inches hidden almost in the folds of her dress." The pair caused a sensation. "One old negro cried 'My young missus has got *her* flag a flying anyhow!'" "Now that *we* have set the example," Sarah remarked smugly, "I suppose the rest will follow."[3]

Sarah's pageantry flouted federal authority and ruffled old-school propriety. Her attempt at rebel rousing was a far cry from the halcyon days of winter 1861 when young ladies scrambled for sock patterns and Confederate hearts brimmed with southern pride. In the wake of secession, sacrificial patriotism had celebrated the southern feminine ideal writ large. Its flag-waving devotees had stood honorably in streets filled with the strains of "Dixie" and departing suits of gray. Like most women, Sarah had served her nation as a domestic patriot who extended submission and sacrifice to her Confederate family. She had sent her male kin off to war, cheered the troops, attended sewing societies and relief efforts, knitted socks, rolled bandages, and puffed with pride after trimming an officer's shirt with pearl buttons and ruffles. "Blessed is the Confederate soldier who has even [a] tooth ache, when there are women near!" she boasted. But the tables had turned with the arrival of bluecoats and the criminalization of all things Confederate. Robbed of domestic protection, some women in occupied cities turned to a politically charged patriotic ideal that celebrated, as historian Anya Jabour notes, "liberty and independence for themselves, as well as for their beloved country." In New Orleans, she-rebellion reached fever pitch as women discarded their knitting needles in favor of an unprecedented campaign of resistance. Some federal-cursing, flag-toting, bedpan-throwing women mocked Union funeral processions, sang Confederate songs, and hurled rowdy insults at their captors. Union general Benjamin Franklin Butler responded with Order No. 28, which threatened to prosecute every female agitator as a "woman of the town, plying her avocation."[4]

While some frustrated Confederates threw patriotic caution to the wind, well-to-do southern ladies often shied away from the darker undercurrents of rebel womanhood, clinging instead to the vestiges of feminine gentility that called for service and sacrifice. When a group of Union soldiers spied Sarah the following day with "flag again flying," Miss Morgan discovered that federal occupation had propelled her into uncharted territory. "I had not expected to meet them, and felt a painful conviction that I was unnecessarily attracting attention by an unladylike display of defiance, from the crowd gathered there," she cried. "I hope it will be a lesson to me always to remember a lady can gain nothing by such displays." Standing nose-to-nose with "fine, noble looking" soldiers "showing refinement and gentlemanly bearing in every motion" only heightened Sarah's feelings of regret. "They set us an example worthy of our imitation, & one we would be benefitted by following," she noted. "They prove themselves gentlemen, while many of our citizens have proved themselves boors, and I admire them for their conduct." Consigning her flag to the parlor mantel, Sarah pronounced herself "wonderfully changed" in sentiment. "To make a show, make me conspicuous and ill at ease, as I was yesterday—Never again!"[5]

Sarah's patriotism had heretofore ticked all the sacrificial boxes; she had rolled bandages, stitched uniforms, and waved flags in support of her Confederate family. But in occupied Baton Rouge, Sarah's decision to wear her love of country on her sleeve had turned her into a defender of the cause itself. The subtle shift was one of context and audience, but it marked the defining line between sacrificial patriotism and she-rebellion. One supported southern gender and class ideals, while the other subverted these ideals in assertive acts that risked censure from the enemy and the local community. Sarah's flag-flying had caused "great excitement" among the townsfolk and nothing more. Her impulsive display was hardly the stuff that landed women in prison at Ship Island. Her lingering discomfort, however, served as a sharp reminder that rebel womanhood was not a prudent alternative for ladies keen to protect their reputation under federal occupation. In Sarah's case, there were also family ties to consider: she was a devoted Confederate, but she was also a proud Morgan with a family heritage that spanned the sectional divide. Respect for the differing political beliefs of her immediate kin—a northern sympathizer and Union soldier among them—also shaped Sarah's views on the enemy, her interactions with federal troops, and her public pronouncements of southern loyalty.[6]

Born in New Orleans on February 28, 1842, Sarah Ida Fowler Morgan was the seventh child of Judge Thomas Gibbes Morgan and Sarah Hunt Fowler Morgan. Thomas, a native of Princeton, New Jersey, had moved in the 1820s to Baton Rouge, where he established a successful law practice and married Eliza Ann McKennan. After her death, he wed Sarah Hunt Fowler, a northern-born woman who had been raised by her guardian, George Mather, on his sugar plantation in St. James Parish, Louisiana. The couple spent the first years of married life in New Orleans, where Thomas worked as a collector of customs and Sarah raised their eight children: Lavinia, Eliza Ann, Thomas Gibbes Jr., Henry (Harry) Waller Fowler, George Mather, Miriam Antoinette, Sarah Ida Fowler, and James Morris Morgan. In 1850, the family relocated to Baton Rouge, where Thomas served as a district attorney and later a district judge.[7]

The growing sectional discord of the 1850s did not prevent Thomas and Sarah from creating a thoroughly southern life for themselves and their family. Indeed, the Morgans set the benchmark for well-to-do urban professionals in the city. Often described by locals as the "Aristocrats of Baton Rouge," the family occupied a handsome two-story home on Church Street with a well-tended garden and vegetable plot out back. They owned eight slaves who worked as domestic servants. The Morgan sons followed their father into the professional world: Philip Hicky (Thomas's son from his first marriage) and Thomas Gibbes Jr. chose law, while Harry studied medicine in Paris. Sarah and her sisters nurtured Morgan domesticity at home. After ten months of formal education, Sarah threw herself into a rigorous home-based program of intellectual improvement. On any given day she could be found "lost in the mysteries of Arithmetic, Geography, Blair's Lectures, Noël et Chapsal, Ollendorff, and reading aloud in french and english, besides writing occasionally in each, and sometimes a peep at Lavoisne." Everything was anchored in the pursuit of refinement and a rich tradition of family honor. "[If you] could only know something of the name you inherit," Sarah later informed her nephew, "I am sure you would strive to be worthy to be called by it." It was a reputation the family held dear and defended with their lives.

In April 1861, Sarah's brother Harry was mortally wounded on a New Orleans dueling ground after an acquaintance called him a liar. "Courage is what women admire above all things and that he possessed in the most eminent degree," wrote a grief-stricken Sarah. "Months after he died, passing a group of gentlemen in New Orleans, Jimmy heard them mention Harry's name, and one said 'I saw him when he stood up, and I saw him fall, and I never saw as brave a man.' 'That is the way with all the men of that family; they are as brave as can be, and those girls are not an inch behind them' returned another." Sarah could not take the bullet for her brother but stood tall as grief's tide washed unmercifully over the family circle. "Sarah has been the stay of the household," Judge Morgan told his son George. "I never saw such fortitude." The family was left to endure the tragedy without Thomas Gibbes Jr. and George, who had offered their services to the Confederate army. The day before Harry's death, twenty-three-year-old George had departed with the First Louisiana Volunteers for Norfolk, Virginia, where he joined Thomas Gibbes Jr., a second lieutenant with the Seventh Louisiana Infantry. James Morgan followed soon after, volunteering as a midshipman in the Confederate States Navy.[8]

Judge Morgan was proud of his sons but counseled his family against patriotic extremism. Sarah adopted her father's moderate views on politics. The Morgan's neighbors, the Brunots, may have been "bitter and uncompromising" Confederates, but Sarah preferred to stay "as quiet and hopeful as the most liberal of the Once conservatives." "It is a rope of sand, this Confederacy founded on the doctrine of Secession," she reasoned. "I want the South to conquer, dictate its own terms, and go back to the Union for I believe that apart, inevitable ruin awaits both." Judge Morgan also refused to view family honor through a political lens or cast out those kin who sat on the other side of the sectional divide. The family had relatives in the North, granted, but the Morgans also counted two prominent Union men in their immediate circle: New Orleans district court judge, and Sarah's half-brother, Philip Hicky Morgan, and Sarah's brother-in-law Major Richard C. Drum. Drum was a professional soldier who had married Sarah's sister Lavinia while stationed in Baton Rouge in the late 1840s. He served out the war in California. "There are few men I admire more than Major Drum," Sarah wrote, "and I honor him for his independence in doing what he believes Right." Philip Hicky Morgan also sided with the Union but refused to fight against his Confederate brothers. "Let him be President Lincoln if he will, and I would love him the same," declared Sarah. "Politics cannot come between me and my father's son. . . . If he is for the Union, it is because he believes it to be in the right, and I honor him for acting from conviction, rather than from dread of public opinion." Philip's presence at home was critical in the weeks following Judge Morgan's death in November 1861. "[He] said he would be our father," Sarah wrote, "and love us and care for us as the dear dead one did." The Morgan women chose to stay in Baton Rouge, but Sarah never forgot Philip's promise. "Are kind words recompensed in Heaven?" she pondered. "Then surely God will bless Brother for the words he spoke that evening."[9]

So while others proudly flung their flags in the air, Sarah Morgan made her way back through the crowd of blue coats and gray skirts, convinced that she had placed politics above family but would never do so again. Rebel patriotism flew in the face of Morgan honor and gentility, her half-brother and brother-in-law's standing, and her father's efforts to strike a balance between love of country and respect for kin. "Let me make home happy, and myself beloved in it, and a fig for the rest of creation!" she wrote. Unfortunately, it was not that simple. The politics of patriotism had become the wartime currency of social credit. Confederate men trod a familiar path: they volunteered for the army and affirmed ties to home and nation on the battlefield. But in occupied Baton Rouge, Sarah soon discovered that she could no longer satisfy public expectations while also safeguarding the reputation of her politically divided family. It was not Sarah's Confederate flag waving but her federal family ties and her conciliatory approach to the enemy that set tongues wagging. "I am begining to believe we are even of more importance in Baton Rouge than we thought we were," she wrote after hearing an "absurd" report that federal officers had been received at the Morgan home. "I suppose the story originated from the fact that we were unwilling to blackguard—yes, that is the word—the Federal officers here, and would not agree with many of our friends in saying they were liars, thieves, murderers, scoundrels, the scum of the earth, etc." "Such epithets are unworthy of ladies," she concluded. "I say it is unworthy of anything except low newspaper war, such abuse, and will not join in."[10]

In May 1862, however, the people of Baton Rouge faced more pressing concerns than a rumor or two about faltering Morgan loyalty. Since the arrival of the USS *Iroquois*, the town had sat in military purgatory—the U.S. flag flew from the barracks and arsenal, but it was a victory in name only. The federal troops that had met Sarah Morgan on the statehouse grounds had moved on to Vicksburg soon after, leaving Baton Rouge with a vow to destroy it if Confederates attempted to take back the city. Sarah and her family prepared their running bags and steeled themselves for an imminent attack. "We are hourly expecting two regiments of Yankees to occupy the Garrison," Sarah wrote on May 27, "and some fifteen hundred of our men are awaiting them a little way off, so the fight seems inevitable." Only forty Confederate guerrillas turned up the next day, firing on five Union soldiers as they rowed from the USS *Hartford* to the shore. Flag Officer David G. Farragut kept his promise and shelled the town. "As we stood in the door," Sarah wrote, "four or five shells sailed over our heads at the same time, seeming to make a perfect corkscrew of the air." In the streets outside, people were tangled together in a "heartrending scene. Women searching for their babies along the road, where they had been lost, others sitting in the dust crying and wringing their hands, for by this time, we had not an idea but what Baton Rouge was either in ashes, or being plundered, and we had saved nothing." The Morgans headed northeast for Greenwell, Sarah perched on a cart astride a "tremendous bundle" of family belongings, while her sister Miriam nestled "in a hollow between a flour barrel and a mattress." Later that day Sarah returned home with her brother-in-law Charles LaNoue. "It was a desperate enterprise for a young girl, to enter a town full of soldiers on such an expedition at night," she confessed, "but I knew Charlie could take care of me, and if he was killed I could take care of myself; so I went." The Morgan home was still standing but gunpowder and pandemonium had torn through every room. "The dirt and confusion was extraordinary," remarked Sarah. With the family's slaves now safely ensconced in Greenwell, she had no choice but to attend to the work herself. "I discovered I could empty a dirty hearth, dust, move heavy weights, make myself generally useful and dirty, and all this is thanks to the Yankees!"[11]

Sarah, Miriam, and their mother struggled with what to do next. "There is no refuge for us, no one to consult," Sarah wrote in tears. "Brother, whose judgment we rely on as implicitly as we did on father's, we hear has gone to New York; there is no one to advise or direct us, for if he is gone, there is no man in Louisiana whose decision I would blindly abide by." On her return to Baton Rouge a few days later, Miriam met with Union general Thomas Williams and "told him our condition," Sarah explained, "how our brothers were away, father dead, and mother afraid to remain, yet unwilling to lose her property by going away; how we three were alone and unprotected here, but would remain rather than have our home confiscated." The family's federal connections strengthened their case. Williams knew of Major Drum and assigned a sentinel to protect the Morgan home. Sarah conceded that while their property was now safe from lawless soldiers, the family's Confederate loyalty would again be up for debate. "If we win B.R. as I pray we will, they will say we asked protection from Yankees against our own men, are consequently traitors, and our property will be confiscated by our own government. To decline Gen. Williams kind offer, exposes the house to being plundered." "It was a singular situation," she wrote in her diary, "our brothers off fighting them, while these Federal soldiers leaned over our fence, and an officer standing on our steps offered to protect us." When Williams's aide, Lieutenant James C. Biddle, called on the Morgan women to discuss security arrangements, Sarah admitted that she liked the gentleman but "could not ask him to repeat his visit." "It wont do in the present state to act as we please," she remarked uneasily. "Mob governs."[12]

The Morgan family's decision to accept federal assistance came of necessity, not flagging Confederate loyalty, but their actions were interpreted as such by the southern "tribunal of patriotism"—who also knew about Philip Morgan and Richard Drum. "At Greenwell they are frantic about our returning to town, and call us traitors, Yankees, and vow vengeance," Sarah confessed. "Our friends forsake us, we are too proud to seek the protection of our enemies, and we stand between two fires of two 'public opinions,' besides the 'for true' fire of the gun boats and our own soldiers." Unwilling to blight her family name or dishonor her kin, Sarah's discreet allegiance to the Confederacy provided fertile ground for gossip, and the slander was compounded by the family's determination to treat occupying federal troops with respect. Mrs. Morgan and her daughters bowed to General Williams and his officers in church. They sent bandages and "nourishment" to a Union soldier and acquaintance after he was shot by Confederate guerrillas on the outskirts of Baton Rouge. A large barrel of flour had even been dispatched to the family with a note from General Williams begging Mrs. Morgan to accept it "in consideration of the present condition of the circulating currency." "These people have disarmed me by their kindness," marveled Sarah. "I expected to be in a crowd of ruffian soldiers who would think nothing of cutting your throat, or doing anything they felt like; and I find among all these thousands, not one who offers the slightest annoyance, or disrespect. The former is the thing as it is believed by the whole country, the latter the true state of affairs." When a federal soldier collapsed in Church Street, Sarah rushed outside with a pail of water to assist him while her friends and neighbors cried "Murder! and help!" from the patriotic safety of their balconies. "If he had been Satan himself lying helpless and bleeding in the street, I would have gone to him!" wrote Sarah defiantly. "May I never be discreet, or wise, if this is Christian conduct or a sample of either! I would rather be a rash, impulsive fool!" Miriam fretted about what the townsfolk would say—"in twenty four hours the whole country will be down on us"—and what the Confederate guerrillas would do if they reached Baton Rouge, but Sarah vowed to do "what Conscience alone dictates." She stopped short of nursing a group of sick Union soldiers that lay unattended in a nearby hospital, but she lamented the way war had corrupted the self-sacrificial tenets of women's "holy mission." "Where is the charity which should ignore nations and creeds, and administer help to the Indian or Heathen indifferently?" she asked. "Gone! all gone in Union versus Secession! . . . Die, poor men, without a woman's hand to close your eyes! We women are too *patriotic* to help you!"[13]

The more Sarah was backed into a corner by the public opinion of "long tongued slandering women," the more she used the political adventures of rebel patriots to redraw her own boundaries around genteel femininity and family honor. "What a consolation it is to remember there are no 'Politics' in heaven!" she scoffed. "The disgust I have experienced from listening to others, I hope will forever prevent me from becoming a 'Patriotic woman.'" "Do I consider the female who could spit in a gentleman's face merely because he wore United States buttons, as a fit associate for me?" she continued. "Lieut. Biddle assured me he did not pass a street in New Orleans without being most grossly insulted by *ladies*. . . . Such things are enough to disgust anyone. 'Loud' women, what a contempt I have for you! How I despise your vulgarity!" Brash patriotism and political resistance pulled at the fringes of Morgan family heritage. Sarah's half-brother, Philip, had probably endured similar taunts in New Orleans—he did not wear "United States buttons," but stories of his northern allegiance had run to far reaches of the Confederacy. Sarah regarded the acts by women "obliged to 'kick up their heels over the Bonny blue flag'" as an assault on the Morgan name, and she treated them as such. She wrote:

> O for a pen to paint the slaves
> Whose "Country" like a deadly blight
> Closes all hearts when Pity craves
> And turns God's spirit to darkest night!
> May life's patriotic cup for such
> Be filled with glory overmuch;
> And when at last their spirits go above in their pride,
> Spirit of Patriotism let these valiant abide
> Full in the sight of grand mass meeting—I don't want you to cuss them
> But put them where they can hear politics, and yet cant discuss them!

"I cant say worse than that!" she added. Rabble rousing and political grandstanding were the patriotic weapons of unrefined Confederate women, Sarah declared. Ladies kept their mouths shut and discreetly recorded their "indictment for high treason" in pen and ink. "All my violent feelings, which in moments of intense excitement were really violent, I have recorded in this book," Sarah wrote in her diary. "I am happy to say only the reasonable dislike to seeing my country subjugated has been confided to the public ear, when necessary." In any case, her brothers were fighting for the cause. "This excess of patriotism," she reasoned, "is unnecessary for me as my position is too well known to make any demonstrations requisite. I flatter myself that 'tells.'"[14]

By August 1862, the booming cannonade of war once again rolled into Baton Rouge. Having repelled a second federal attempt on Vicksburg, Confederate troops under General John C. Breckinridge headed southward to reclaim the state capital. Fighting began on August 5, 1862. Hoping to avoid another shell-induced stampede out of the city, the Morgan women departed Baton Rouge on the eve of battle, obtaining refuge at Dr. John T. Nolan's plantation seven miles east of the city. Out of immediate danger, they were still close enough "to watch what might be the downfall of our only home!" After the battle, Sarah gave up the estate as lost. "It was one scene of ruin," she wrote in disbelief. "Libraries emptied, china smashed, sideboards split open with axes, three cedar chests cut open, plundered, and set up on end." Miriam's piano had been dragged to the center of the parlor, evidently "too heavy to carry off." The Morgan family had paid dearly for putting family credit above outward displays of Confederate patriotism. "Ours was the most shockingly treated house in the whole town," Sarah cried. "We have the misfortune to be equally feared by both sides, because we will blackguard neither. So the Yankees selected the only house in town that sheltered three forlorn women, to wreak their vengeance on, just as our own people would have done . . . satisfied . . . that we were all Yankees." And while her heart had hardened a little after being "beggared"—"I would give my life to be able to take up arms against the vandall[s] who are laying waste our fair land!"—Sarah stoically refused to join the "wild fanatics" crying out against the northern marauders. This was not because she had abandoned the Confederate cause but because the "vandals" included Philip Morgan and Richard Drum. "Mrs Badger felt like beating me because I did not agree that there was no such thing as a gentleman in the Yankee army," Sarah wrote days after the attack. "I know Major Drum for one, and that Capt. Clark must be two, and Mr Biddle is three, and Gen Williams—God bless him where ever he is! for he certainly acted like a Christian."[15]

Unable to salvage much from the shattered remnants of their home, the Morgan women rented a "nutshell of a house" in Clinton, Louisiana, and settled down to the pinching economy of refugee life as "fugitives in a strange town." "The whole establishment consists of two rooms on each side of a passage as wide as the front door; and as it has a very low ceiling, with no opening, and no shade near, it is decidedly the warmest spot I ever inhabited," Sarah remarked indignantly. "We all sleep on the floor and keep our clothes in our trunks." Her "old wreck of [a] home" was at least a familiar sanctuary. "All its desolation," Sarah concluded, "could not be half so unendurable as Clinton." Morgan family honor had sat proudly on Church Street. Sarah now fell face first into scrimping modesty without the genteel trappings that had defined her life as a daughter-at-home. Little wonder she looked to the future "with a shudder." "If we are to be pennyless, as well as homeless, I'll work for my living," Sarah resolved. "How I wonder? I will teach! I know I am not capable, but I can do my best. I would rather die than be dependent, I would rather die than teach. There now, you know what I feel! Teaching, before dependence, death before teaching. My soul revolts from the drudgery." For the moment, $250 in savings and a good supply of dresses established the Morgan women "on the footing of ladies, if we chance to fall among vulgar people who never look beyond," but patriotic scrutiny followed them in hot pursuit. "We are as well known here as though we carried our cards on our faces," Sarah noted warily. "The whisper 'These are the Miss Morgans' being by no means unusual." "The dull round of this little place" turned on the "petty lies" that "we not only entertained Federal officers daily, but besides walking the streets daily with them, gave many a cozy dinner and supper party in their honor."[16]

Sarah vowed she would "grow mad" in Clinton. Fortunately for her, her sister-in-law, Lydia Carter Morgan, invited her to visit Linwood, the nearby Carter plantation. Mrs. Morgan remained in Clinton with her daughter Eliza, Eliza's children, and the family's slaves, while Sarah and Miriam rested their furrowed brows in plantation dreaming. Linwood became the tempest in Sarah's patriotic storm. Its quiet gentility, she confessed, would unfit her "for the rough old life that lies ahead." "From breakfast to dinner I remain on the balcony, and read aloud several Chapters of the Mémoire of Dumas, by way of practice," she wrote. "Then comes my french grammar, which I study while knitting or sewing, which takes very nearly until dinner time.... The evening, we always spend on the balcony." Sarah's brother Thomas Gibbes Jr. returned to Linwood in October 1862 with a shoulder wound from Antietam, and Sarah spent her evenings poring over a map of Virginia as he talked of war. An eager contingent of local troops populated General Albert Carter's parlor, slaves moved through the "big house" and the fields of sugarcane, and Sarah's greatest indiscretion was flapping her veil at a passing train of Confederate soldiers, who responded by throwing their caps skyward in a sea of "cheers and hurrahs." Linwood may have sat only twenty-five miles away from Port Hudson, and therefore "decidedly unsafe from Yankee vengeance," but for a moment it was a step away from war, an old southern flagship in a rare pocket of the Confederacy. "Our exile passes gaily here," Sarah wrote contentedly.[17]

Sarah's Linwood idyll came to an abrupt end when she fell from a horse in November 1862 and afterward spent months incapacitated by a back injury. "Ah me! how much more cheerfully I would have borne the breaking of an arm!" she wrote. "Spare me my feet! Merciful Father let me walk once more! Anything, save a helpless cripple!" Some doctors speculated that she might never walk again, but Sarah made a partial recovery at Linwood.

In January 1863, the Morgan women received confirmation that a Union colonel and his wife had taken up residence in their Baton Rouge home. "A stranger and a Yankee occupies our father's place at the table where he presided for thirty one years," she wrote indignantly. The federal confiscation of the Morgan family home was an act that left no room for respect, and Sarah branded the couple "Yankees" in the most derogative sense. "'What a fall was there, my country!' From Morgan hands down to—Yankees!... It will drive me mad to think of those people in our house, peering in the garret and reading all our letters and papers." Home had been Sarah's anchor, a training ground for womanhood, and in wartime a refuge from rebel patriotism's slings and arrows. Sarah had sung over her violets and roses in the garden, watched her mother pace the moonlit gallery, and sat by the old parlor lamp that shone brightly the day she was born. Now all had "passed in[to] the hands of strangers who neither know nor care for its history."[18]

By 1863, though, more tables and sideboards and old family treasures had slipped into northern hands. Countless numbers of slaves—including some owned by Sarah's family—had headed for Union lines. As federal forces closed in on Port Hudson and Linwood, the Morgan women regrouped, with plans to join Thomas Gibbes Jr. in Georgia. "No use of leaving my bones for the Yankees to pick," Sarah laughed anxiously. "Better sing Dixie in Georgia." But Thomas had no luck securing lodgings for his family in Augusta—it was already bursting with refugees. "The question has now resolved itself to whether we shall see mother die for want of food in Clinton, or, by sacrificing an outward show of patriotism, (the inward sentiment cannot be changed) go with her to New Orleans, as Brother [Philip] begs in the few letters he contrives to smuggle through," Sarah wrote. "It is a distressing dilemma to be placed in, as we are certain to be blamed which ever course we pursue." At Linwood, Sarah had found a welcome respite from the tumult of rebel politics. Life in New Orleans, she feared, would destroy the flimsy threads of patriotic propriety and family honor that she had worked so hard to protect. "To live surrounded by Yankees; to cease singing Dixie; to be obliged to keep your sentiments to yourself—for I would not wound Brother by any Ultra Secession speech," Sarah wrote. "If he is as friendly with the Federals as they say he is—to listen to the scurrilous abuse heaped on those fighting for our homes and liberties, among them my three brothers—could I endure it? I fear not." In the end, Sarah's and her mother's ill health tipped the scales in favor of New Orleans. In April 1863, the Confederate women traveled by schooner from Bayou Bonfouca to a Union home in an occupied city. "We sang Farewell dear land with a slight quaver in our voices," she related, "looked at the beautiful starlight shining on the last boundary of our glorious land, and fervently and silently praying, passed out of sight."[19]

Sarah's lofty Confederate farewell ended in a Yankee thud. Upon their arrival in New Orleans, the Morgan women were met by a group of federal soldiers who insisted that they pledge an oath of federal allegiance. "I prayed as hard as ever for the boys and our country, and felt no nasty or disagreeable feeling which would have announced the process of turning Yankee," remarked Sarah after raising her right hand. Her mother was not so accepting, Sarah noted, "launching into a speech in which Heaven knows *what* she did not say." "There was little she left out, from her despoiled house to her sore hand, both of which she attributed to the at first amiable man, who was rapidly losing all patience." Sarah felt humiliated by her mother's desperate cries of Confederate loyalty and the dishonorable fallout that landed in Philip Morgan's lap. Compelled to pull every federal string in his bow to prevent his stepmother's imprisonment, Philip supported Mrs. Morgan while she took the oath. "If she had done it at first," snipped Sarah in her diary, "she would have spared us a most painful scene, and saved me from fatigue that threatened to annihilate me for some time." Sarah, however, had underestimated the restorative powers of family life. Within days she happily declared, "I am getting well! Bless the Lord O my soul! Life, health, and happiness dawn on my trembling view again!" "Each of us have quietly taken possession of our different [domestic] departments already," she wrote. "Thinking we need company, Brother frequently invites what he calls 'a safe old secessionist' (an old bachelor of fifty three who was wounded at Shiloh) to dine with us; thinking it a fair compromise between the stay at home youth, and Yankees."[20]

While she grew stronger in New Orleans, Sarah conceded that their retreat to Philip's proud Union home had renewed "suspicion of belonging to a side we abhor with all our souls." "It seems base treason to remain under the protection of this hateful flag," she wrote helplessly. The arrival of southern prisoners from the Battle of Port Hudson in July 1863, however, unexpectedly revived Sarah's flagging Confederate credibility. Confined to the New Orleans Custom House while they awaited exchange, the prisoners were the same men who had bivouacked near Linwood. Within days of their arrival, Sarah and Miriam promenaded past the building in the hope of "seeing one of our poor dear half starved mule and rat fed defenders" or a soldier of Linwood past. Sarah was too embarrassed to catch a glimpse of those peering from the windows above, but her friend, Ada Peirce, provided a running commentary as the trio flew past a group of federal soldiers on patrol outside the building. As Sarah recorded in her diary, Ada said: "Look! he knows you, Sarah! he has called another to see you! They both recognise you! O look please and tell me who they are! they are watching you still!" Sarah added, "I would not do that again—!" "When we passed the last Yankee, with crimson cheeks we looked at each other and asked what would tempt us to try it over; and the answer was nothing—except the *certainty* of seeing a friend." News of their visit rushed through the Custom House and out into the world below. "Miriam and I are looked on with envy by other young ladies because some twenty or thirty of our acquaintance have already arrived," she wrote excitedly. "To know a Port Hudson defender is considered as the greatest distinction one need desire."[21]

Basking in her newfound Confederate favor, Sarah reacquainted herself with the simple pleasures of domestic patriotism. She worked up cravats, embroidered handkerchiefs, and prepared lunch baskets "of Chicken, soup, wine, preserves, sardines, and cakes" to send to the soldiers. "Ladies are naturally hero worshippers," Sarah remarked. "We are dying to show these unfortunates that we are as proud of their bravery as though it had led to victory instead of defeat." Sarah wrote to Confederate colonel Isaiah Steedman, a friend, with offers of assistance, and Miriam dispatched a bouquet to her beau (and future husband) Lieutenant Alcée Louis Dupré. Philip Morgan worried that his sisters had muddied the waters of propriety, and he cautioned them, saying, "[Send] any sum of money, purchase any quantity of clothing, send all the food you please, but for God's sake don't write to them!" Sacrificial patriotism, however, had already made its mark: the Miss Morgans were the "one topic of conversation" at the Custom House. Sarah remarked that the ladies "all call the third story Miss Sarah's department, and the second, Miss Miriam's, since [to them we] seem to reign over the occupants of each." And Sarah, who had once been wrongly accused of shouting "Hurrah for Lincoln" from the balcony of her Church Street home, now had the reputation of being engaged to Colonel Steedman, "a man," she boasted, "that every girl is crazy to win!" In the federally occupied streets of

New Orleans, under Philip Morgan's wing, Sarah's patriotic journey had come full circle. She had courted the wrath of rebel patriots in occupied Baton Rouge, quietly reaffirmed her southern sympathies at Linwood, and claimed Confederate repute in New Orleans. All Sarah's patriotic choices, her interactions with Union and Confederate soldiers, and her feelings about women and nationalism, were based upon her well-to-do upbringing and a familial code of honor that transcended the sectional divide. At Linwood and in New Orleans, Sarah's choices aligned with war's patriotic tapestry. In Baton Rouge and Clinton they did not. The Confederate context may have shifted and changed during the war, but Sarah's commitment to family remained steadfast, the core of her identity as a southern woman, a loyal patriot, and a proud Morgan.[22]

Sarah Morgan saw out the war in occupied New Orleans. In February 1864, the family was notified of the deaths of Thomas Gibbes Jr. and George Morgan. "Dead! dead! Both dead!" Sarah sobbed. "O my brothers! what have we lived for except you? We who would so gladly have laid down our lives for yours, are left desolate to mourn over all we loved and hoped for, weak and helpless; while you, so strong, noble, and brave, have gone before us without a murmur. God knows best. But it is hard—O so hard!" Sarah spent the late 1860s in Philip's household in New Orleans. After Miriam's marriage to Alcée Louis Dupré, Sarah and her mother relocated to South Carolina to make a home with Sarah's younger brother, James Morris Morgan. In 1873, Sarah accepted an editorial position at the *Charleston News and Courier*, marrying its charismatic editor, Francis Warrington Dawson, in 1874. The couple had three children: Ethel in 1874, Warrington in 1878, and Philip Hicky in 1881. Sarah continued to write articles and reviews for the newspaper until her husband's death in 1889. Thereafter she published short stories while waging a protracted and ultimately unsuccessful legal battle to secure her share of dividends from *News and Courier* stock. In 1899, Sarah moved to Paris to live with her son Warrington, and there she published a French version of the Brer Rabbit stories in 1903. She died in Paris on May 5, 1909.[23]

NOTES

1. Sarah Morgan Dawson, *Sarah Morgan: The Civil War Diary of a Southern Woman*, ed. Charles East (New York: Simon and Schuster, 1992), 47–49. On the Civil War in Baton Rouge, see John D. Winters, *The Civil War in Louisiana* (Baton Rouge: Louisiana State University Press, 1991), 113–24.

2. Dawson, *Sarah Morgan*, 48–49, 51, 86, 140.

3. Ibid., 64–65, 67. On women's patriotic dress, see Anya Jabour, *Scarlett's Sisters: Young Women in the Old South* (Chapel Hill: University of North Carolina Press, 2007), 250–51.

4. Dawson, *Sarah Morgan*, 229; Clara Solomon, *The Civil War Diary of Clara Solomon: Growing up in New Orleans*, ed. Elliott Ashkenazi (Baton Rouge: Louisiana State University Press, 1995), 369. On sacrificial patriotism, see Drew Gilpin Faust, *Mothers of Invention: Women of the Slaveholding South in the American Civil War* (Chapel Hill: University of North Carolina Press, 1996). On rebel patriotism, see Jabour, *Scarlett's Sisters*, 262, 239–280. On Confederate women, see George C. Rable,

Civil Wars: Women and the Crisis of Southern Nationalism (Urbana: University of Illinois Press, 1989); Laura F. Edwards, *Scarlett Doesn't Live Here Anymore: Southern Women in the Civil War Era* (Urbana: University of Illinois Press, 2000), 71–84; Giselle Roberts, *The Confederate Belle* (Columbia: University of Missouri Press, 2003).

5. Dawson, *Sarah Morgan*, 68–69.

6. Ibid., 67. See also Kimberly Harrison, *The Rhetoric of Rebel Women: Civil War Diaries and Confederate Persuasion* (Carbondale: Southern Illinois University Press, 2013), 62.

7. Dawson, *Sarah Morgan*, 67. For an account of Sarah's early life, see Charles East, introduction, in ibid., xv–xx.

8. Dawson, *Sarah Morgan*, 38–39, 70, 136; Sarah Morgan Dawson to Howell Morgan, May 23, 1880; Thomas Gibbes Morgan to George Mather Morgan, May 8, 1861, Francis Warrington Dawson I and II Papers, Rare Book, Manuscript and Special Collections Library, William R. Perkins Library, Duke University, Durham, North Carolina.

9. Dawson, *Sarah Morgan*, 22, 73–74, 259, 410. On political socialization within the family unit, see Anya Jabour, *Topsy-Turvy: How the Civil War Turned the World Upside Down for Southern Children* (Chicago: Ivan R. Dee, 2010), 22, 43.

10. Dawson, *Sarah Morgan*, 25, 69, 73.

11. Ibid., 85, 89, 90–91, 93, 103. Greenwell Springs is located in East Baton Rouge Parish.

12. Ibid., 104–8.

13. Ibid., 109, 112–14, 123–24, 129–30.

14. Ibid., 111, 115, 121–22, 130–31, 143.

15. Ibid., 200, 213, 233–36, 261.

16. Thomas Gibbes Morgan, Jr., to George Mather Morgan, October 7, 1862, Francis Warrington Dawson I and II Papers; Dawson, *Sarah Morgan*, 99, 153, 243–44, 250–51, 301.

17. Dawson, *Sarah Morgan*, 263, 271, 299, 329–30.

18. Ibid., 339, 384–85. See also Eliza Morgan LaNoue to James Morris Morgan, March 24, 1863, Francis Warrington Dawson I and II Papers.

19. Ibid., 430, 450, 483.

20. Ibid., 485–86, 488, 500, 502.

21. Ibid., 491, 518–19, 523.

22. Ibid., 520–21, 523–24, 540, 542.

23. Ibid., 597. On Sarah Morgan Dawson's later life, see Sarah Morgan and Francis Warrington Dawson, *The Correspondence of Sarah Morgan and Francis Warrington Dawson: With Selected Editorials Written by Sarah Morgan for the Charleston News and Courier*, ed. Giselle Roberts (Athens: University of Georgia Press, 2004); Giselle Roberts, "Sarah Morgan Dawson: A New Southern Woman in Postwar Charleston," *South Carolina Women: Their Lives and Times*, vol. 2, eds. Marjorie Julian Spruill, Valinda W. Littlefield, and Joan Marie Johnson (Athens: University of Georgia Press, 2010), 68–86; Katherine D. Cann, "A Most Awful and Insoluble Mystery: The Writing Career of Sarah Morgan Dawson," *Proceedings of the South Carolina Historical Association*, 1990, 75–86; E. Culpepper Clark, "Sarah Morgan and Francis Warrington Dawson: Raising the Woman Question in Reconstruction South Carolina," *South Carolina Historical Magazine* 81 (January 1980): 8–23.

Janet Mary Riley
(1915–2008)

An Angel with Teeth

JANET ALLURED

❁ ❁ ❁

In 1979, the Louisiana legislature revised Louisiana's matrimonial regimes law, also known as the community-property system, by doing away with the traditional "head and master" rule—which gave the husband control over the community property—and replacing it with "equal management" by both spouses. Providing the inspiration and legal guidance for this momentous reform of an ancient and archaic system was Janet Mary Riley, an attorney and the first female professor on the law faculty at Loyola University of the South in New Orleans. Hailed now as a feminist pioneer in Louisiana, at the start of this process Riley, a devout Catholic, did not consider herself a feminist and even opposed the Equal Rights Amendment (ERA) for a time. Riley's personal journey toward embracing women's equality illuminates a little-recognized source of feminist activism in the modern era, one that may have been especially important in the South: religion. Riley's dawning consciousness of the need for reform of state law was also the result of her research into the practice of community property, whereby she discovered case after case of husbands' abuse of "head and master" power; her years caring for female relatives (her mother and a divorced sister with dependent children); her training by the Ursuline sisters; and her exposure to the new rhetoric of women's equality and liberation. Hers was a long journey toward feminist consciousness but one in which religious devotion buttressed and dovetailed with her commitment to gender equality.

The reform of the matrimonial regimes system in Louisiana and simultaneously in the other seven community property states was part of a secular movement that historians typically refer to as the "second wave" of feminism, a term that describes the women's rights movement of the 1960s and 1970s. The second wave was multifaceted and vast in scope, for feminists critiqued not just the law

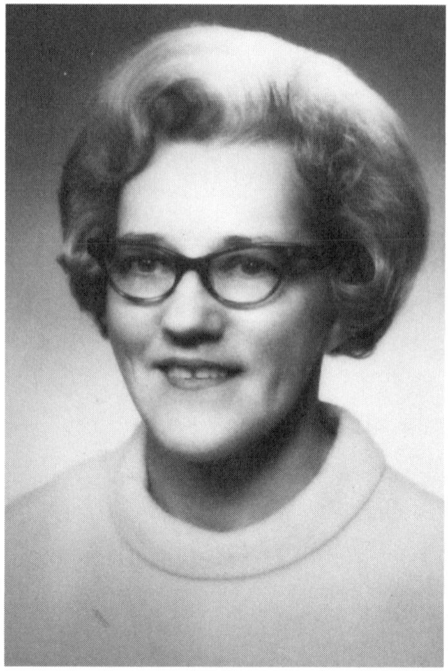

JANET MARY RILEY

Courtesy of Special Collections & Archives,
J. Edgar & Louise S. Monroe Library,
Loyola University (New Orleans, La.).

but virtually every aspect of society and of the patriarchal assumptions that underwrote the status quo. The victories were sometimes incremental and halting, but the inexorable push was in the direction of eliminating gender distinctions and discrimination in the public sphere (in education, hiring, pay, promotion), in public policy (for example, in pensions and public services), and in the law.

Scholars generally interpret the second wave as a secular movement, citing its organizational and intellectual wellsprings as the civil rights movement, the New Left, the antiwar movement, and even communism. The "gospel" texts that established the ideological framework of feminism include Simone de Beauvoir's *The Second Sex*, Betty Friedan's *The Feminine Mystique*, Kate Millet's *Sexual Politics*, Casey Hayden and Mary King's memo on women in the Student Nonviolent Coordinating Committee, and the report of President Kennedy's Commission on the Status of Women—secular all.[1]

Not only was the movement ideologically secular, it was also anticlerical, since feminists resented the patriarchal interpretations and practices of the denominations of their upbringings. Many, but not all, rejected their sacred traditions. The hostility that feminists so often expressed toward mainstream religion or the male control of existing denominations made it difficult for those who maintained a commitment to faith traditions to express themselves. In Louisiana as elsewhere, women organized independent feminist organizations seemingly devoid of religion. Most were led or founded by female faculty or students at universities, others by women active in the League of Women Voters. Yet many of these same activists attended religious services weekly. One of the first and most frequent places to provide space to feminist organizing in New Orleans, for example, was St. Mark's Community Center, a settlement house run by Methodist women.[2] Protestant, Catholic, and Jewish faith traditions in the United States nurtured subcultures that inspired feminist consciousness and produced leaders. Women found support for feminist ideas in liberal Christian churches like the Methodist, Episcopal, Lutheran, and Universalist Churches (the latter merging into the Unitarian Universalist Association in 1961), among Catholic clergy and "women religious," and in Reform Judaism.[3] For some women, then, religion was a fundamental motivation as they joined movements for social justice, just as theology had provided the grounding philosophy for Martin Luther King Jr. and members of the Southern Christian Leadership Conference, and for many peace activists.

Janet Mary Riley was one of many who embraced feminist values because of her religious devotion. While other Catholic feminists, like Rosemary Radford Ruether and Margaret Ellen Traxler, sought to end patriarchal practices in their church, Riley never (publicly at least) advocated such a position. Nor did she join an independent feminist organization, even though the National Organization of Women (NOW) had an active New Orleans chapter and worked in tandem with her to change the much-resented "head and master" rule. Rather,

Riley's commitment was to her faith, her church, and to the broader cause of social justice, which for her included women's equality in society at large.

This first generation of feminist legal reformers of which Riley was a part based their arguments against patriarchal privilege in the law on Western liberal traditions, in particular Enlightenment ideas that stressed equal citizenship, opportunity, individualism, and rationality. Riley articulated a liberal feminist legal theory (sometimes called "sameness feminism") that stressed that "the law should not treat a woman differently from a similarly situated man."[4] She was also of the mind that the law must evolve along with society. Because gender roles had clearly changed, Louisiana's law was no longer suited to modern society or to its constitutional principles.

Liberalism in any form faced an uphill battle in Louisiana. Riley's relatively modest goal of equal treatment for the sexes confronted an extremely conservative, male-dominated Louisiana State Law Institute (an advisory body to the Louisiana legislature) and an even more old-school, patriarchal, and alarmist Louisiana legislature dedicated to maintaining gender inequality for women as long as possible. (This same legislature did, however, acknowledge a changed role for women by ratifying the Nineteenth Amendment, which had granted women the right to vote in 1920.) As a result of male intransigence, the passage of reform legislation took years, much longer than in any of the other community property states, and almost fell apart several times along the way.[5]

Riley was up to the fight. Bright and talented, she combined determination with dignity and grace. Riley seldom backed down once she had decided upon the moral course of action. As a single woman, the reform to which she devoted many uncompensated hours and years of her life did not affect her personally. But she was concerned about the larger moral issue and the plight of some married women subjected to onerous "heads and masters" in the 1970s. While never publicly acknowledging that this was her guiding principle, she regarded the rewriting of the archaic provisions of the state's community property regime as her religious and moral responsibility, her duty to God.

Born in New Orleans in 1915, the third and last child of John and Mary Odile (Hymel) Riley, Janet Riley attended parochial schools and the public John McDonough High School before winning a scholarship to Ursuline College, the sister college to Loyola University of the South.[6] That scholarship was a life-changing event, she later said, without which she "would not have been able to go to college at all."[7] Upon her graduation in 1936, at age twenty, she taught elementary school in New Orleans "for two impossible years." Recognizing that teaching young children was not her calling, she went back to school to earn a degree in library science from Louisiana State University. She worked at the New Orleans Public Library first, and then for the army as a post librarian during World War II. In 1945, Loyola University of the South hired her to oversee its law library. A legal librarian during the day, she also took law classes at night. The only female in the class, Riley recalled the solitary and daunting environs: "In a sea of male voices, I was one lonely voice. It was awfully scary to open my mouth and speak."[8] Undoubtedly this experience helped her gain the coping skills necessary to face down the hostility she met in the reform years ahead. She graduated in 1952 and was admitted to the bar in 1953.

Riley attributed her highly unusual career choice to several influences. One was the Ursuline nuns, her spiritual mentors, teachers, and confidantes, who encouraged her to attempt a law degree and equipped her with the necessary skills. She also credited her older sisters, one a secretary and the other a teacher, who made a point of scaring Riley away from either of those professions.[9] Another life-long inspiration was the Society of Our Lady of the Way, a secular institute for unmarried women founded in Austria in the 1930s.[10] Approved by Pope Pius XII in 1947, secular institutes provided a missionary and spiritual outlet for laity who wished to devote themselves to Christ's work "in the world" as individuals.[11] Unlike women religious, who advertised their commitment by wearing habits, secular institutes encouraged "the law of discretion," whereby members kept their vows secret if making membership in the society known would hinder their apostolate. Their charge was to change society in quiet ways. "Consecrated seculars," the Society of Our Lady of the Way explained, "live their daily lives within the different strata of society. Exteriorly, they appear no different from others. Interiorly, they are consecrated to God and dedicated to the service of others." According to the society's literature, "each member tries to discern where God wants her to minister . . . [and] patterns her life after Mary: quiet, humble and aware."[12]

The commitment that Riley took was in every other way similar to joining an order of nuns. Secular institutes were one manifestation of increased lay activism in the 1930s, 1940s, and 1950s. The appeal of secular societies represents a transition in Catholicism before Vatican II that encouraged nuns to abandon habits and convents and come out into the world. Members took vows of poverty, chastity, and obedience but had no common apostolate and wore normal, undistinguishable "street" clothing.[13] Members of the Society of Our Lady of the Way were allowed to discern for themselves what their particular calling was, but their primary mission was to "reshape society" in the service of God. The organization's structure was democratic, its leadership elected by the general membership. Thus, women within the society exercised substantial control over their religious life and its expression, if not the Church, which had sanctified them.[14]

Riley took one-year vows beginning in 1966 and perpetual vows in 1973, but during her professional career she revealed to almost no one that she was a "bride of Christ." "Though I worked in a Catholic university," she recalled in an interview when she was in her eighties, "I never told my dean or colleagues. I thought that my work for the Louisiana State Law Institute, drafting and testifying for changes favoring women in Louisiana law, would be less effective if it were known that I had vows."[15] Yet her membership in this institute is key to understanding her life's work. Her decision to live singly and devote herself to an apostolic mission through her career as a law school professor gave her the inspiration as well as the time to study, to think, and to work for reform because she was not constantly being pulled into a domestic realm by the demands of a family.

The Society of Our Lady of the Way never had more than a few dozen adherents in the United States, and only a handful in New Orleans.[16] To strengthen the women's commitment and sense of community, the society sponsored an annual retreat, which Riley attended, and also appointed each woman a "ratio sister" to act as mentor and confidant. That was the extent of the community. Otherwise the society expected members to "dedicate themselves to the Lord" on their own. As the society's literature said, "We offer the road the disciples walked: hard work, self-discipline, no insurance of assurance other than the knowledge that you are fulfilling Christ's commandment: Love one another as I have loved YOU!" This task required "imagination, generosity, self-giving and patience to wait for results."[17] Patience was certainly something Riley would call upon frequently as she dealt with social injustice in the years to come.

Just as the society helped her live her faith through her career, Riley also credited her Ursuline education with equipping her with a social conscience.[18] Students at Ursuline College, she later remembered, were taught that:

> the state exists to serve the individual by using its God-given authority to create an environment in which he is assured those freedoms necessary to work out his salvation, for instance, freedom of speech and of religion, freedom from oppressive inequalities enforced by law, the freedom of fair trials, and freedom from unreasonable police searches. We were taught that, important as it is to support the form of government permitting freedom, it is personally more important to form a right conscience, including a social consciousness, an awareness of the problems of people outside our circles, and to aid in attaining a better society. Such an understanding of the function of government, and the development of a social consciousness, are necessary attributes of a lawyer.[19]

Riley put her social conscience to work almost immediately upon being hired at Loyola's law library. In the 1950s she served on the board of the Commission on Human Rights (CHR), an interracial group of students and faculty from black and white Catholic colleges in southern Louisiana who agitated for desegregation of archdiocesan events, organizations, and institutions. The founder of the CHR was Fr. Joseph Fichter, S.J., professor of sociology at Loyola, a contemporary of Riley's, an activist leftist Catholic, and likely an important role model. CHR members defied social norms by meeting together regularly as equals and by visiting area churches, sitting together as a group, to demonstrate their commitment to integration of Catholic spaces. The CHR lasted seven years before pro-segregationists within the church forced it to fold in 1956, a victim of the white supremacist backlash that came in the wake of the Supreme Court's *Brown v. Board of Education* decision.[20]

Riley's work on the CHR introduced her to civil rights attorneys in the state, including A. P. Tureaud and John P. "Jack" Nelson Jr. They asked her for assistance when several African American college students and Congress of Racial Equality (CORE) members, among them Oretha Castle and Rudy Lombard, were arrested for sitting at a lunch counter reserved for white customers in New Orleans in 1960. Charged by the state with "conspiracy to commit anarchy," the defendants were represented by Nelson, Lolis Elie, Robert Collins, and Nils Douglas. Nelson, Riley's friend, asked her to write the brief for this precedent-setting case, *Lombard v. Louisiana* (1963), in which the U.S. Supreme Court ruled that state action designed to enforce segregation violated the Fourteenth Amendment. This was one of the landmark rulings of the civil rights era, a triumphal moment for CORE, and Riley was justly proud of her authorship of the brief. Yet, while the male attorneys received considerable attention (not to mention career advancement) for arguing the case before the Supreme Court, Riley's role has received virtually no acknowledgement.[21]

While male attorneys such as her friend Jack Nelson may have respected her work, Riley nonetheless encountered gender discrimination that was typical for women lawyers of that generation. Upon passing the bar, she applied for jobs at law firms, only to be told over and over, "We don't interview women." Although she eventually received a job offer from a law firm, when Loyola offered her a teaching position in 1955, she took it, and thus became the first full-time female faculty member there and one of only a handful of female members of law faculties in the nation. The students were almost all male. When she walked into the room the first day, Riley remembered, the students' hostility was palpable: "I felt stiffened backs and an 'I dare you to teach me' attitude."[22] Even her home institution, Loyola, discriminated against her. As religious studies scholar Claire E. Wolfteich, the only academic who has written about Riley, explains: "Her single status led to lower salaries and difficulty gaining promotions. The school justified paying men [more] because they had to support families. Even single men were paid more, because some day they might get married and need to support families."[23] Riley found the assumption that she did not have dependents appalling, especially because she supported a niece and two grandnephews.[24] This inequality raised her consciousness about the unreasonable and entrenched discrimination women encountered.

Not long after joining the faculty, Riley took over a course in community property law. Finding a paucity of resources on the subject, she compiled a casebook on Louisiana community property law, which would be published by Claitor's in 1971.[25] *Louisiana Community Property—Cases and Materials on Lou-*

isiana Property and Marriage made her an expert in the field, and in 1973 the director of the Louisiana State Law Institute (LSLI), J. Denson Smith, asked her to chair a subcommittee that would study the matrimonial regimes section of the Louisiana Civil Code (Book III, Title VI). In 1938, the Louisiana legislature had created the LSLI to serve as an official advisory law revision commission and legal research agency of the state.[26] It consisted of twenty-eight members, three of whom were selected from the Loyola University School of Law. Riley had earlier served on the LSLI committee that successfully recommended a "no fault" divorce law in 1972.[27] Considering that the Catholic Church condemned divorce, this is perhaps surprising, yet it indicates that Riley recognized the need for changes in women's status.

The Louisiana legislature asked Riley's committee to recommend revisions to Louisiana's matrimonial regimes (also known as the community property system) because recent interpretations of Title VII of the Civil Rights Act of 1964, especially *Reed v. Reed* (1971), made it clear that sex discrimination in Louisiana's Civil Code would not withstand judicial scrutiny. In *Reed*, the U.S. Supreme Court ruled that women and men were equally qualified to administer estates, contending that the Fourteenth Amendment disallowed "unreasonable" gender bias.[28] (The term "unreasonable" proved problematic; opponents of gender neutrality would argue that the husband's control of community property did not match the definition of "unreasonable."[29]) Shortly after this ruling, the ERA passed Congress and seemed destined to become part of the U.S. Constitution in short order, at which point the institute asked Riley's committee to examine all statutes that treated the sexes differently and to propose revisions. Louisiana, like every state, had myriad "protective" laws that sought to shield girls and women from deleterious working conditions but did not offer the same safeguards to men. After some acrimonious debate, the committee came to an agreement that references to an employee's gender must be removed and replaced with gender-neutral terms such as "person," "employee," or "minor" (where applicable). In addition, the committee submitted recommendations on matters such as tutorship, custody, and parental power, most of which created little controversy. The legislature soon implemented the institute's recommendations.[30]

In 1974, the committee, which included two other women besides Riley and eight men, turned its attention exclusively to matrimonial regimes, and it devoted nearly all of its time for the next three years to working out changes in this system. In the midst of the committee's deliberations, Louisiana adopted a new constitution (1974) that included an equal rights clause, which dealt another blow to the old patriarchal system. Yet reform of the matrimonial regimes system was complicated because it regulated not only married persons' affairs but also inheritance rights, creditors' rights, testamentary rights, contractual rights, and judicial rights.[31] Reform would necessarily reach far and wide and would upset many interested parties beyond husbands who stood to relinquish their control.[32]

Riley understood that the court rulings, the new constitution, and the looming threat of the ERA all promised to bring reform to a matrimonial regimes system that had been largely unchanged since the colonial era. Louisiana was one of eight states having a system of community property that derived from continental European principles of civil law rather than from English common law.[33] Many praised the community property system as superior to the common law principle of *couverture* that applied in the former English colonies because not only was the wife half owner of all property acquired during the marriage (the "community of gains"), but she also retained separate ownership of all that she brought into the marriage or received from inheritance or donation during the marriage. Such a system recognized that the wife's contribution to the marriage was equal even when she did not contribute monetarily. As Riley put it, "neither spouse earns anything alone, but each is a better earner because of the cooperation of his or her spouse." Feminist reformers sought to preserve this principle in the new system.[34] Later in her life, Riley described the wife's role, and her own role in reform, this way: "[W]hichever path she chooses, working outside or inside, she is contributing to society's good and to the family in a monetary, economic way and should have equality. Her work in the home should be recognized. So when people tell me, 'Oh you're a feminist, you work to get women out of the home,' I say, 'No, I work for them to get equal protection whether in the home or out of the home.' But it was a hard thing to get across."[35]

Whatever the benefits of community property for women, Riley recognized that while the wife had an undivided half *ownership* of the community, she did not control the property during the marriage. Louisiana's Civil Code declared the husband the "head and master" of the community, meaning that he was responsible for managing the family's property, including real estate, both spouses' earnings, and the family business (if any).[36] The only way a wife could negate this control was if she had signed an agreement before the wedding ceremony refuting the community and specifying that she would administer her own property. She could also register intent to administer her separate property obtained by donation or inheritance. Almost no one did this, either because most did not know such an option was possible or, if they did, they were afraid that doing so would cast aspersions upon their husband's abilities and create conflict in the marriage. Furthermore, though frequently lauded as a "protection" for wives, renouncing the community was especially damaging to those who were not employed because they had no legal entitlement to any portion of their husband's salary.[37]

The matrimonial regimes code also contained other very limited protections for a wife. To prevent the husband from selling the family home out from under her, she could file a notarized Declaration of Family Homestead that would thereafter require the signature of both spouses before it could be mortgaged or sold, but this only applied to the family home and not any other community property. She could sue the "head and master" for mismanagement of community funds if she could prove his management was detrimental to the welfare of the community, but she bore the burden of proof. If successful, she could obtain a separation of property, but it only protected her from future mismanagement and offered no recompense for past damages. In practice, few did this. Furthermore, since she was not entitled to an inventory or an accounting of the community, mismanagement was difficult to detect until the damage was obvious, often too late.[38]

Besides the many practical problems that resulted from the husband's control, especially in the event of divorce or widowhood, most women, like Riley, found the gender inequality built into this antiquated system insulting and demeaning. As Riley recalled in a later interview, the law clearly had not kept abreast of the modern woman's changing life. Her husband's control of the community meant that the wife also was unable to establish credit in her own name while married (as was generally true elsewhere too), but the system presented problems even for single women. Because Louisiana law provided that when a woman got married, the "head and master" did not have to honor her past debts, a single woman was considered a poor credit risk since she could relieve herself of all her debts simply by getting married. Even if she continued to work, her earnings became community property that could not be attached if she failed to pay the debts she had incurred before she married.[39] Arguing from a doctrine of strict fairness and absolute equality, Riley was quick to point out that there were also provisions that discriminated against the husband: the husband's obligation to support his family and the wife's right to alimony regardless of fault. These and other provisions were clearly holdovers from the days when women could not be expected to find a respectable way to support themselves and their children. (In 1970, Louisiana women earned about half what male workers did.)[40] Riley maintained that these provisions did not provide equal protection to the husband and thus would not withstand a constitutional challenge.[41]

After researching the reforms underway in the other seven states that had community property systems, as well as those underway in Europe, Riley found Louisiana trailing behind. In 1965, France, the mother country whose *Code Napoleon* served as a foundational document for Louisiana's Civil Code, had eliminated the husband's status as head of the family and established joint management of family affairs by the two spouses. Drawing on the civil law reforms recently put in place elsewhere, Riley drafted a proposal technically known as "the joint and several management plan," informally referred to as "equal management." The proposal required action by both spouses to dispose of immovable property such as real estate, land, improvements, timber, and mineral rights. Joint action by husband and wife was also required for mortgaging property or leasing it, and both spouses had to agree to take action to sell movable property (such as furniture) used by the family.[42]

Robert Pascal represented the conservative opposition to Riley's plan. A law professor at Louisiana State University (LSU), family law specialist, and fellow member of the LSLI advisory committee, Pascal opposed Riley in committee deliberations, testified against her proposal (and against the ERA) before the legislature, and gave public speeches against her plan. In a 1974 letter to Riley expressing his outrage, Pascal referred to feminists as "mal-oriented 'women's liberation' zealots."[43] Pascal and others who sought to retain the old matrimonial regimes system based their arguments upon a traditional view, often religiously based, of the roles and rights of men and women. Pascal argued that the legal tradition that codified the position of the husband as the "head and master" was "consistent with societal practices that each has assigned roles." He explained publicly that he felt "strongly that marriage has broken down into sharp definitions of individuality" and there was a "loss of love in marriages." Coequal management of assets would not work, he asserted: "We cannot have dual control or joint control in marriage. We must have one head, not a two-headed monster."[44] Pascal thus believed that the new type of marriage based on partnership and mutual equality set up a competition between spouses, a competition that did not exist in the old system. Such an opinion failed to recognize that the vaunted "cooperation" of the traditional marriage rested on an inequality that seriously disadvantaged the wife and made it highly unlikely that she would ever refute or contest the husband's control. Riley countered that the equal management plan would "encourage couples to talk things over"; after all, less suspicion about what a husband did with the money would "make for a stronger family."[45]

While Pascal was arguably the most high-profile opponent of change, he certainly was not Riley's only challenger. Arguments against increasing women's power and participation in public life and in household financial management came from many quarters. Some Louisianans clung to the old notion of the family as a unit represented in the world by the head, the husband. David Conroy of the Louisiana Bar Institute, for instance, expressed the view of many when he declared that just as businesses were not run with copresidents, "the overall tendency is to feel that somebody ought to be in charge." Which somebody? Conroy answered, "Most couples prefer the husband to be the manager of the community."[46] Devan Dagget, executive director of the legislative council, believed the only problem with the current law was an "emotional" one, saying: "I think the concern is that the term head and master has become offensive." He suggested that the only necessary change would be to refer to the husband as the "administrator" instead of "head and master" of the community property.[47] The business community, particularly chambers of commerce, went even further, arguing that equal management would give the wife the power to stymie her husband's business dealings. Commerce in the state, businessmen insisted, would grind to a halt. Finally, defenders of the old system regularly cited the special "protections" or "privileges" women supposedly enjoyed and portrayed the new laws as a diminution in their status.[48]

Though Pascal did not typically quote the Bible, other opponents frequently cited scripture when defending gender inequality. As a devout Catholic who had professed vows, Riley paid attention to such arguments. Probably the most vocal and well-organized opponents of the ERA in Louisiana were Catholic laywomen. The Archdiocese Council of Catholic Women of New Orleans and the Catholic Daughters of America (CDA), an affiliate of the National Council of Catholic Women, spoke out against the ERA and showed up in Baton Rouge by the busload to testify against it. The CDA, with more than 180,000 members, deemed itself the largest organization of Catholic women in the world, and it was particularly strong in Louisiana. Not only did it have twelve thousand members statewide, the national regent (head) was Winifred Trabeaux of Plaquemine, Louisiana, and the chaplain of the national organization was Archbishop Philip M. Hannan of New Orleans.[49] Members could easily be mobilized to write letters to legislators and to newspapers and to travel to the capital, where they packed the galleries when the committee considering the ERA held hearings. In 1976, Phyllis Schlafly, a conservative Catholic and founder of STOP ERA, spoke in Baton Rouge at the biennial convention of the Catholic Daughters.[50] Assisted by Schlafly, the opponents' efforts succeeded, and, to Riley's frustration, Louisiana never ratified the ERA.[51]

But the conservative stance of the Catholic Daughters should not be taken as an indication of the mindset of all Catholics in Louisiana. The *Clarion Herald*, the New Orleans archdiocesan newspaper, contained a multiplicity of voices on the hotly contested women's issues of the day, with one exception: no Catholic whose words appeared in the *Clarion Herald* supported abortion rights. In 1974, the paper had a fairly left-leaning editor, Rev. Andrew C. Taormina, who lasted only eleven months before Archbishop Hannan asked him to step down following an editorial denouncing the pope's stance against artificial birth control. During Taormina's tenure as editor, however, the *Herald* endorsed the ERA in its May 16, 1974, edition.[52] Perhaps not surprisingly, the very next issue contained a sharp rejoinder from Archbishop Hannan, who assured readers that the endorsement was the opinion of the editor, not that of the archdiocese or the Catholic Church. Hannan made clear that "there is no official Catholic Church position on the ERA," further stating that he opposed discrimination against women and backed efforts to legally safeguard their rights.[53]

Hannan was right to stress that there was no official Catholic position on the ERA, for many Catholics, including Riley by this time, defended it. Catholic Women for the ERA, Christian Feminists, the National Assembly of Women Religious, the National Coalition of American Nuns Network, Priests for Equality, Sisters Formation Conference, and Catholics Act for ERA were all groups working for ratification.[54] Catholic feminists who supported the amendment used two basic arguments. The first was that ratifying the ERA was a "virtual mandate of the Second Vatican Council." An open "letter of conscience" that circulated widely in New Orleans, signed by the groups listed above, interpreted Vatican II to mean that "every type of discrimination, whether social or cultural, whether based on sex, race, color . . . is to be overcome and eradicated as contrary to God's intent." Second, they argued that support for the amendment did not equate to support for abortion; those who said differently were spreading "misinformation and confusion throughout the Catholic community about the meaning and impact of the ERA." Opposing the amendment, these Catholic feminists fumed, was "unfaithful to the American vision and authentic religious tradition and we ask that the promotion of inequality for women in the name of God and country cease."[55] In 1975, Riley's colleague, Fr. Joseph Fichter, S.J., a member of Loyola's Department of Sociology at the same time that Riley was on the law faculty, issued a press release in which he too endorsed the ERA. Fichter stated forcefully that there were many Catholic individuals such as him who strongly favored ERA and said that it was entirely consistent with Catholicism to support the ERA.[56]

Catholic feminism was well represented among the women religious in New Orleans as well, who likely provided role models for Janet Riley. The national conference to discuss the ordination of women to the priesthood, held in Detroit in 1975, included a delegation from New Orleans composed entirely of sisters. The fact that two of them were Ursulines is noteworthy because Riley credited the Ursuline sisters with being a tremendous inspiration to her. The New Orleans delegation also included Sr. Theresa Drago, a Carmelite and executive coordinator of the Sisters Council of the New Orleans Archdiocese, and Sr. Fara Impastato, associate professor of religious studies at Loyola—and Riley's colleague—and one of the first women in the United States to receive a doctorate in theology.[57] Women religious of New Orleans also went public in support of the ERA. In 1975, the Sisters Council of the Archdiocese voted unanimously to join ERA Central, and sent a "Declaration of Equality" to Governor Edwin Edwards and all state senators and representatives of districts within the archdiocese.[58] Clearly there was a conspicuous Catholic feminism in New Orleans in the 1970s in various quarters, many in close proximity to Riley.

Riley's legal education led her to oppose the ERA at first because, she said, the courts' recent interpretation of the Fourteenth Amendment in *Reed v. Reed* (1971) and its progeny gave the sexes equal protection. She worried that the ERA was "dangerously inflexible."[59] By 1976, however, she had reversed her position, citing changed circumstances. In a public statement in which she urged Louisiana legislators to back passage of the amendment, she said: "I now fear its . . . failure to pass could be used to rationalize a serious set-back in equality of rights when sex is the basis for difference in governmental treatment." Invoking her belief in God, she maintained that "it should not have become necessary for citizens under our Constitution to restate the obvious—that equality of rights shall not be denied by state or federal governments on account of sex—as this is a principle basic to God-given human dignity. But in the present climate, when the demand for that statement is so loud and clear, silence—or the failure to affirm the obvious—invites misinterpretation, a rejection of the principle itself." "[The] ERA, as a symbol of equality, is needed," she concluded.[60] Sr. Theresa Drago wrote to thank Riley for testifying in support of the ERA and praised her "objective analysis" and "honesty and integrity." Sr. Theresa wrote, "If the *Times-Picayune* quoted you accurately, your assessment of ERA echoes mine—a matter of basic equality. I am happy to be in such company."[61]

Though the issues were divisive and Louisiana Catholics expressed a variety of opinions, Riley found continual support for her positions on gender equality from many sources, including the Vatican. Catholics who supported the ERA frequently quoted Vatican II and Pope John XXIII's position on gender equality. A pamphlet entitled "Catholics and the Equal Rights Amendment" opened with the words of Pope John XXIII (pope from 1958 to 1963), who noted that "since women are becoming more conscious of their dignity, they will not tolerate being treated as mere material instruments, but demand rights befitting a human person both in domestic and in public life." Pope John XXIII began the process of reforming the church when he convened the council commonly referred to as Vatican II, but he died before it had finished its work. His successor, Pope Paul VI, who would lead the Catholic Church until 1978, continued the reform effort and concluded Vatican II in 1965. Paul VI tried to balance the demands of women for equality with respect for women's traditional roles. While he said that scripture recognized for women "the perfect equality of nature and dignity and therefore of rights," he was concerned that women maintain their femininity and not adopt a "masculine life-style." Paul VI incurred the wrath of feminists and of many Catholics by issuing the encyclical *Humanae Vitae* (July 25, 1968), reaffirming the Church's longstanding opposition to "artificial" contraception, and by upholding the ban on women's ordination.[62]

The difficulty with any scriptural analysis is always putting it into practice in the terrestrial world. Janet Riley later cited Pope John Paul II (pope from 1978 till 2005) to support her belief that women's ability to jointly control community property was entirely consistent with the Holy Scriptures. When her opponents argued that "the attempt to achieve equality between husband and wife in the management of family property was contrary to God's law," she called upon the authority of John Paul II, who, during his "year-long series of talks on the theology of marriage and the body," had said "that husbands and wives must treat one another as equals in a mutual, two-sided, sharing, personal relationship." The biblical references to man as "master" of his wife, she quoted the pontiff as saying, "was dictated by the social marginalization of woman in the conditions of those times."[63] Riley, then, found support for her belief that women's equality was just and right. That support came from the *Clarion Herald*, women religious (publicly and privately), her colleagues at Loyola, and the pope himself.

Endorsement of Riley's equal management plan came from the growing feminist movement in Louisiana as well as from the LSLI advisory committee that she chaired. Despite her committee's recommendation, the Council of the Law Institute rejected the proposal and instead presented Robert Pascal's alternative, a far more conservative "two fund" plan, to the legislature in 1977. Having her years of work dismissed by the very group that had appointed her to recommend reform, Riley resigned from the committee, joined forces with NOW, the League of Women Voters, and other women's groups around the state, and came out swinging against Pascal's proposal. The two-fund plan, she testified, was sleight. Because it would give each spouse control over his or her own earnings, it would seriously disadvantage homemakers. "The spouse who earns nothing or very little manages nothing or very little," Riley asserted.[64] While it would provide "equality of control of *categories* of property," it would not provide "equality of access to family income unless coincidentally the spouses each continuously have equal earnings."[65] When asked by legislators if equal management would not create the possibility of abuse of the community property by the wife—due either to revenge, extravagance, or poor judgment—she replied that husbands would "face exactly the same kinds of dangers that wives have faced since Louisiana was formed."[66] The League of Women Voters, easily the largest organization of reform-minded women in the state and capable of mobilizing women in every major Louisiana city, similarly issued a statement saying that "the two-fund plan does give some measure of relief to the employed wife. It does not, however, provide either relief or dignity for the wife who is not employed outside the home."[67] Their lobbying was effective, and Pascal's proposal died in committee.

In a 1980 interview with the monthly feminist newspaper *Distaff*, published in New Orleans, Riley recounted what happened next. According to her, some legislators, realizing the urgency of coming up with a suitable bill, approached her "about her original equal management plan and asked her about dusting it off and presenting it" again. Her bill passed the House Committee on Civil Law and Procedure in the summer of 1977 and was recommended to the house floor by Representatives A. J. McNamara and Diana Bajoie, the only woman representative in the Louisiana legislature. However, this bill stalled in the face of legislative discomfort over the magnitude of the changes.[68]

Riley said that it was due to her influence that the legislature ultimately decided to bypass the Law Institute and pass a joint resolution, which she authored, that created a joint legislative subcommittee and directed it to draft a bill that implemented equal management. The legislature also created a citizens' advisory committee consisting of six citizens, three of whom were required to be women, to assist the subcommittee.[69] The committees brought forth a version of Riley's equal management bill in the summer of 1978. "Women's groups from around the state mobilized to support it," Riley reported later. "It was very exciting." The Louisiana Bar Association and the Louisiana AFL-CIO also supported the bill.[70] When Governor Edwards's executive secretary, Ann Davenport, testified in support of the measure, it was clear that the governor would support reform. "As a wife and as a human being asking for equity," Davenport asserted, "Equal management is fair, it is constitutional, and it will work."[71] The legislature passed this equal management law but sent it to the Law Institute for further study.[72]

A modified version, watered down and not as strong as Riley wanted, passed in 1979 and took effect January 1, 1980.[73] In the new system, the words "husband" and "wife" disappeared and were replaced with "spouse." The new law applied to all married couples in the state that had not entered into marriage contracts stipulating otherwise and to all community property regardless of the date of acquisition.[74] Community real estate could not be sold, leased, or disposed of without consent of both spouses. Movable property, such as an automobile, which needed to be registered when purchased, could not be sold, leased, or mortgaged by only one spouse if registered in both names.[75] The law was imperfect and represented a compromise, but it would continue to be revised toward an equitable system reflecting modern principles of gender equality.[76]

The drive to end "head and master," according to Riley, "was the one issue that united all women in the state. I saw women with anti-ERA buttons sitting side by side with women wearing pro-ERA slogans. Both sides saw it as a victory for their cause when the bill passed; the anti-ERA women used it to show that states can handle women's rights locally and don't need a national ERA, and the pro-ERA women saw it as a natural step toward a national ERA. I don't know of one woman who opposed it." Indeed, the photo of Governor Edwards at the bill-signing ceremony includes black and white women activists representing a variety of professions as well as organized labor. "It brings Louisiana into the 20th century," Riley concluded. "But we have to understand that it wasn't handed to us by the legislature. We fought for it every inch of the way."[77]

Following the matrimonial regime reform and the death of the ERA in 1982, Riley's time and energy focused on caring for her ailing sister. After her sister died, she turned her attention to other "voiceless people" in need of legal advocacy. Children and elders in poverty as well as child and elder abuse became her new focus.[78] She retired from the full-time faculty at Loyola in 1986 but continued to teach seminars and courses as an adjunct professor until 1997. In 2002, Loyola established the Janet Mary Riley Distinguished Professorship when she and other law faculty members donated funds for its creation. Loyola also honored her with several other awards that recognized her service to humanity, her upstanding moral character, and her "unquestionable integrity."[79] She died in 2008 at age ninety-two, hailed as a "feminist hero."[80] Among the bequests in her will was one to the institute that had defined her life, the Society of Our Lady of the Way.

The experiences of Janet Mary Riley, who considered herself married to Christ, illustrate how feminism in Louisiana sprang from traditional organizations not typically considered wellsprings of the movement. Demonstrating her religious devotion through her work, Riley navigated the considerable opposition she faced with steadfast patience as she put her legal knowledge to work advancing human rights. Her faith taught her to interpret the opposition she encountered as a call from God and gave her the determination to persevere. She drew strength and inspiration from the vows she had pledged and from the women who made up her faith community as colleagues, spiritual advisors, and mentors. Her story indicates that, especially in the South, feminists might not come from expected places, and that we should not look for them just in the independent self-professed women's liberation organizations. Louisiana was a deeply conservative, Bible Belt state, where religion was a defining influence and the Catholic Church held enormous sway, especially in New Orleans and in the southern part of the state. Certainly, devotion to a faith tradition could cut both ways, as the actions of the Catholic Daughters and the words of the archbishop made clear. Yet Catholicism also encouraged its members to engage in social justice work. For Riley as for many other Catholic women, this meant embracing women's equality in the law, in the church, and in society.

NOTES

For their thoughtful critique of drafts of this paper, I am thankful to the scholars of the Delta Women Writers colloquium; the faculty members of the History Department at McNeese State University; law professors Dian Tooley-Knoblett and Herma Hill Kay; and historians Linda Kerber, Claire Wolfteich, and Mary J. Henold.

1. Beginning with Sara Evans's *Personal Politics: The Roots of Women's Liberation in the Civil Rights Movement and The New Left* (New York: Knopf, 1979), participants and scholars have located the origins of feminism in various New Left groups or movements. See Kate Weigand, *Red Feminism: American Communism and the Making of Women's Liberation* (Baltimore: Johns Hopkins, 2001); Dorothy Sue Cobble, *The Other Women's Movement: Workplace Justice and Social Rights in Modern America* (Princeton: Princeton University Press, 2004); Nancy F. Gabin, *Feminism in the Labor Movement: Women and the United Auto Workers, 1935–1975* (Ithaca: Cornell University Press, 1990); Gerda Lerner, *Fireweed: A Political Autobiograp*hy (Philadelphia: Temple University Press, 2002); Kimberly Springer, *Living for the Revolution: Black Feminist Organizations, 1968–1980* (Durham, N.C.: Duke University Press, 2005).

2. For a history of St. Mark's, see Ellen Blue, "True Methodist Women: Reflections on the Community of St. Mark's," in *Louisiana Women: Their Lives and Times*, ed. by Janet Allured and Judith Gentry (Athens: University of Georgia Press, 2009), 215–36, and *St. Mark's and the Social Gospel: Methodist Women and Civil Rights in New Orleans, 1895–1965* (Knoxville: University of Tennessee Press, 2011). St. Mark's was the location of many activities sponsored by New Orleans feminists in the 1970s.

3. The founding board of the National Organization for Women included two Roman Catholic sisters, and NOW welcomed women religious (a term for sisters who had active ministries and were not cloistered, as nuns were). Ann Braude, "Religions and Modern Feminism," in *Encyclopedia of Women and Religion in North America*, eds. Rosemary Skinner Keller, Rosemary Radford Ruether, Marie Cantlon (Bloomington, Indiana: Indiana University Press, 2006), 14–18. For the definition and switch in terminology from "nun" to "women religious," see Mary J. Henold, *Catholic and Feminist: The Surprising History of the American Catholic Feminist Movement* (Chapel Hill: University of North Carolina Press, 2008), 7. For information on Catholic feminism, see Henold, *Catholic and Feminist*, 17.

4. Nancy Levitt and Robert R. M. Verchick, *Feminist Legal Theory: A Primer* (New York: New York University Press, 2006), 16.

5. Louisiana ratified the Nineteenth Amendment on June 11, 1970, the forty-seventh state to do so. *Figaro* (New Orleans), March 17, 1973; Steve Mount, "Ratification of Constitutional Amendments," http://www.usconstitution.net/constamrat.html (accessed December, 30, 2012).

6. U.S. Census, manuscript schedules 1920 and 1930 for the Fifth Ward of New Orleans. Author interview with Shawn Holahan, great-niece of Janet Mary Riley (hereafter JMR), July 18, 2011.

7. JMR to Kathleen Lilly, Nov. 12, 1962, box 22, FF8, Janet Mary Riley Papers, Monroe Library Archives and Special Collections, Loyola University of the South, New Orleans, La. (hereafter JMR Papers).

8. Though she attended Ursuline College, her degree is actually from Loyola. *Times-Picayune*, November 30, 1993; *For the Record* (Loyola University Law Alumni) 3, no. 1 (Winter 1993): 11–12; *Times-Picayune* obituary, July 6, 2008.

9. Undated oral interview video with Janet Mary Riley available at the Louisiana Bar Foundation's website, www.raisingthebar.org/. Her sisters, Odile R. Holahan and Louise R. Melancon, told her: "Do not do this if you can possibly avoid it."

10. The Society of Our Lady of the Way was founded in 1936 in Steyer, Austria, by a Jesuit priest, Carl Dinkhauser, and Maria Elizabeth Strachotinsky. Avowed by Cardinal Innitzer in 1939, it was forced to meet in secret to escape persecution by the Nazis. Secular institutes were approved by Pope Pius XII on February 2, 1947, and this society was recognized by papal decree in 1948, the year when members were required for the first time to take the vows of chastity, obedience, and poverty. B. M. Ottinger and A. S. Fischer, eds., *Secular Institutes in the Code of Canon Law: A New Vocation in the Church*, rev ed. (1988; U.S. Conference of Secular Institutes, 2008).

11. "The apostolate in secular institutes includes the entire lifestyle of the member in their occupation (usually within public or private secular areas) or service to others within the context of a secular environment and in their relationships with family, friends and colleagues. This lifestyle includes prayer, spiritual reading, meditation and participation in the daily Eucharist. Secular institutes strive to be the 'light and leaven' for spreading Gospel values and social justice practices within secular society, in social activities and politics." United States Conference of Secular Institutes, http://www.secularinstitutes.org/index.htm (accessed July 6, 2011). See also Ottinger and Fischer, *Secular Institutes*.

12. Brochure published by the Society of Our Lady of The Way, in author's possession, acquired from one of the ten remaining members of the society (as of July 2009), Mary Ann Tady, of Cleveland, Ohio.

13. Society pamphlet, n.d., in author's possession; United States Conference of Secular Institutes, http://www.secularinstitutes.org/index.htm (accessed July 6, 2011).

14. Constitution of the Society of Our Lady of the Way, 1983, in author's possession. The constitution was written by the members, "accepted by the general assembly," and approved by the hierarchs in Rome.

15. Claire E. Wolfteich, *Navigating New Terrain: Work and Women's Spiritual Lives* (New York: Paulist Press, 2002), 37–39.

16. "From the Chronicle of the Society of Our Lady of the Way, 1936–1996," a self-published pamphlet on the history of the institute, lists no members in New Orleans in 1996, even though Riley was still alive at the time. The only other cities in the United States to have members as of that date were Los Angeles, with thirteen, and Cleveland, with seven.

17. Society pamphlet, n.d., in author's possession.

18. Riley left a bequest to the New Orleans Ursulines in her will, in addition to a bequest to the Society of Our Lady of the Way. Interview with Shawn Holahan.

19. JMR to Kathleen Lilly.

20. Joseph H. Fichter, *One-Man Research: Reminiscences of a Catholic Sociologist* (New York: John Wiley & Sons, 1973), chap. 3; see 101 for mention of Riley. See also R. Bentley Anderson, *Black, White and Catholic: New Orleans Interracialism, 1947–1966* (Nashville: Vanderbilt University Press, 2005), for an extended discussion of the Commission on Human Rights and other interracial efforts among Catholics in New Orleans. The black college students came from Xavier University in New Orleans, the only Catholic institution of higher education for blacks in the nation at the time. From Riley herself, see interview at www.raisingthebar.org; see also letter from JMR to Mrs. Eunice Toten, 9 October 1956, box 21, FF 15, JMR Papers.

21. Interview, www.raisingthebar.org; Wolfteich, *Navigating New Terrain*, 39; Shannon Frystak, *Our Minds on Freedom: Women and the Struggle for Black Equality in Louisiana, 1924–1967* (Baton Rouge: Louisiana State University Press, 2009), 128. Riley's brief for the case is in JMR Papers.

22. *Times-Picayune*, November 30, 1993; *For the Record* (Loyola University Law Alumni), 3, no. 1 (Winter 1993): 11–12; *Times-Picayune* obituary, July 6, 2008.

23. Wolfteich, *Navigating New Terrain*, 38.

24. Emily H. Wiesand and her sons, Craig and Brian. Emily had divorced and had cancer. Riley helped to support her niece, which helped her comprehend the difficulties women faced upon the dissolution of their marriages. Interview with Shawn Holahan.

25. Janet Mary Riley, ed., *Louisiana Community Property: Cases and Materials on Louisiana Property Law of Marriage*, 2nd ed. (Baton Rouge: Claitor's Publishing Division, 1981), v. She dedicated the book to her parents. Author interview with Shawn Holahan.

26. Louisiana Revised Statutes 24:201–4; Fred Zengel, "Civil Code Revision in Louisiana," *Tulane Law Review* 54 (1980): 943; "Handbook of the Louisiana State Law Institute," Baton Rouge, Louisiana (1963).

27. The no-fault divorce law was adopted in 1977. Louisiana Civil Code, article 138 (revised by Acts 1977, no. 735); "Handbook of the Louisiana State Law Institute," Baton Rouge, Louisiana, 1972; Janet Mary Riley, "A Revision of the Property Law of Marriage—Why Now?," *Louisiana Bar Journal* (1973): 29–41.

28. Serena Mayeri, *Reasoning From Race: Feminism, Law, and the Civil Rights Revolution* (Cambridge: Harvard University Press, 2011), 37, 61–62.

29. *Reed v. Reed*, 404 U.S. 71 (1971).

30. JMR to members of the Advisory Committee, February 22, 1974; JMR to J. J. Davidson, December 10, 1974, FF "Correspondence, 1974," JMR Papers. She indicated that in December 1973 "the council extended my assignment to recommend revision in all sexually discriminatory laws, not just Title VI." Louisiana House 1119, regular sess. (1976); Acts 1976, no. 624, section 5. The literature about protective legislation in the United States and debates about its effects on women's employment opportunities is too large to recount here, but a critical place to start is Alice Kessler-Harris, *Out to Work: A History of Wage-Earning Women in the United States* (New York: Oxford University Press, 1983).

31. *Morning Advocate* (Baton Rouge), June 15, 1974, reprint of an address to the Law Institute by Mack E. Barham, associate justice, Supreme Court of Louisiana.

32. In addition to Riley, who was technically known as the reporter, the committee consisted of Thomas A. Casey, Katherine Brash Jeter, Helen Kohlman, Thomas B. Lehmann, Max Nathan,

Robert A. Pascal, Eric O. Person, Robert Roberts, III, and Wayne S. Woody. Katherine S. Spaht, "Background of Matrimonial Regimes," *Louisiana Law Review* 39 (1979): 325; *Distaff* (New Orleans), September 1973.

33. The other states were Texas, New Mexico, Arizona, Idaho, Nevada, California, and Washington. Riley, *Louisiana Community Property*, 2nd ed., II A-2. The exact origin of Louisiana's Civil Code has been a subject of debate for decades, with some legal scholars emphasizing the Spanish roots and others pointing to the relatively high percentage of French sources. See, for example, Rodolfo Batiza, "Actual Sources of the Marriage Contract Provisions of the Louisiana Code of 1808: The Textual Evidence," *Tulane Law Review* 54 (1979): 77–116.

34. Janet Mary Riley, "Women's Rights in the Louisiana Matrimonial Regime," *Tulane Law Review* 50 (1976): 560; "Louisiana Community Property Law and How Its Effects Can Be Changed By Contract" ("A pamphlet for Louisiana citizens about to marry and for married persons from other states who come here to live"), January 1977, published by the Louisiana Department of Justice, pursuant to the authorization of Act 693 of 1975, with the cooperation of the Bureau on the Status of Women (June 1976). The pamphlet points out that "not all property owned by the husband or the wife is community property. Property owned by the man or the woman before their marriage, gifts made to the husband or to the wife alone, and property inherited by the husband or the wife alone are separate property. Income from separate property, however, is usually community property." E-mail correspondence with the pamphlet's coauthor, Louisiana lawyer Clay Latimer, March 3, 2010.

35. Wolfteich, *Navigating New Terrain*, 39.

36. The law established the husband as "head and master" in Louisiana Civil Code, 1870, article 2404, book III, title VI. The Matrimonial Regimes Law encompassed articles 2325–2437. "Head and master" first appeared in the Louisiana Civil Code in 1808 (article 66).

37. People who had married outside Louisiana and moved here had one year to file an agreement. See "Legal Rights of Louisiana Women," a 1972 NOW Legal Defense and Education Fund pamphlet (Karlene Tierney Collection, Newcomb Archives) that states: "Most immovable property is in the name of the husband alone. The property may be mortgaged or sold without the knowledge or consent of the wife. She is permitted to file a 'Declaration of Family Home,' a notarial act in the conveyance records, which prevents sale or mortgage without her participation. Unfortunately, she must wait six months after the property is acquired before she files such a declaration, during which time she is without protection. Our research reveals that few such declarations are on file, and that the availability of such protection is unknown to most women." The pamphlet was likely written jointly by Marguerite Rawalt, the legal counsel for the National Organization for Women, and Sylvia Roberts, a Baton Rouge attorney who worked for the NOW Legal Defense Fund.

38. "Louisiana Community Property Law and How Its Effects Can Be Changed By Contract."

39. *Morning Advocate* (Baton Rouge), June 12, 1975; *Louisiana Weekly*, August 9, 1975; "Women and Their Credit," Office of the Governor of Louisiana, Office of Consumer Protection, July 18, 1975.

40. Susan Holton, "Women Workers in Louisiana, 1970," pamphlet, Louisiana Commission on the Status of Women, State Department of Labor, Baton Rouge, July 1972.

41. Riley, "A Revision of the Property Law of Marriage," 33–35.

42. Ibid., 37–41; Janet Mary Riley, "Women's Rights in the Louisiana Matrimonial Regime," *Tulane Law Review* 50 (March 1976): 557.

43. Robert A. Pascal to Janet Mary Riley, chair of the LSLI Matrimonial Regimes Reform Project and cc'd to the entire committee, October 17, 1974, JMR Papers.

44. Cynthia Woody, "The Family as Legal Entity: Consideration of Changes," *State-Times* (Baton Rouge), February 2, 1974.

45. *Clarion Herald* (New Orleans), June 17, 1976.

46. Deidre Cruse, "Work Begins on Community Property Equal Management Plan," *Morning Advocate* (Baton Rouge), October 27, 1977.

47. Ibid.

48. Deidre Cruse, "Community Property Bill Said Equitable, Workable Plan; Bankers Fear Harm to Commerce," *State-Times* (Baton Rouge), June 7, 1978.

49. *Clarion Herald* (New Orleans), April 11, 1974 and March 27, 1975.

50. *Morning Advocate* (Baton Rouge), May 1, 1976 (Schlafly's appearance). The Catholic Daughters' opposition appears in newspaper reports on the ERA, in national statements issued by the organization, and in letters to legislators, e.g., *American Press* (Lake Charles, La.), March 10, 1975, and *Clarion Herald* (New Orleans), May 27, 1975, which reported that the national board of the 182,000-member Catholic Daughters of America took an official stand against the ERA. See also file folder "Opposition" in Ollie Tucker Osborne's papers, Collection 93, Edith Garland Dupré Library, University of Louisiana at Lafayette.

51. There are no secondary sources covering the battle for ratification of the Equal Rights Amendment in Louisiana. For other southern states, see, e.g., Donald G. Mathews and Jane Sherron De Hart, *Sex, Gender, and the Politics of ERA: A State and the Nation* (New York: Oxford University Press, 1990); Judith N. McArthur and Harold L. Smith, *Texas through Women's Eyes: The Twentieth-Century Experience* (Austin: University of Texas Press, 2010); Marjorie Julian Spruill, "Victoria Eslinger, Keller Bumgardner Barron, Mary Heriot, Tootsie Holland, and Pat Callair: Champions of Women's Rights in South Carolina," in *South Carolina Women: Their Lives and Times*, vol. 3 (Athens: University of Georgia Press, 2012), 373–408; Cynthia A. Kierner, Jennifer R. Loux, Megan T. Shockley, *Changing History: Virginia Women through Four Centuries* (Richmond: Library of Virginia, 2013).

52. *Clarion Herald* (New Orleans), May 16, 1974.

53. Ibid.; and May 23, 1974.

54. Henold, *Catholic and Feminist*, 223.

55. "Letter of Conscience" typescript, Karlene Tierney Collection, box 4, "ERA clippings, 1976," Newcomb College Institute Archives and Vorhoff Library Special Collections (hereafter Newcomb Archives).

56. "Point of View," radio station WGSU, New Orleans, by Fr. Joseph Fichter, May 7, 1975, in "Catholics Act—ERA" folder, Karlene Tierney Collection, Newcomb Archives.

57. *Clarion Herald*, March 4, 1976. Loyola faculty, including Sr. Fara Impastato, established one of the first women's centers in Louisiana in 1975. In the 1980s, Impastato cofounded the women's studies program at Loyola. "Women's Studies Honors Sister Fara," Loyola University of New Orleans, http://www.loyno.edu/newsandcalendars/loyolatoday/1998/09/srfara.html (accessed September 7, 2012).

58. *Clarion Herald*, June 3, 1976.

59. JMR to Prof. Warren D. Bracy, University of Toledo College of Law (n.d.), JMR Papers; JMR to Senator Fritz Windhorst, Baton Rouge, June 5, 1974, FF "Equal Rights Amendment," JMR Papers.

60. Typescript, Summer 1976, FF ERA, JMR Papers.

61. Sr. Theresa Drago to JMR, June 22, 1976, FF "ERA," JMR Papers.

62. Richard L. Camp, "From Passive Subordination to Complementary Partnership: The Papal Conception of a Woman's Place in Church and Society since 1878," *Catholic Historical Review* 76 (1990): 521–23.

63. Janet Mary Riley, "Analysis of the 1980 Revision of the Matrimonial Regimes Law of Louisiana," *Loyola Law Review* 26 (1980): 456–57.

64. Deidre Cruse, "Equal Management Would Mean Changes in Louisiana Marriage Laws," *State Times* (Baton Rouge), October 19, 1977.

65. Janet Mary Riley, "Community Property System Needs Revision," *The Code* (Loyola University School of Law), April 1976.

66. Deidre Cruse, "Work Begins on Community Property Equal Management Plan, " *Morning Advocate* (Baton Rouge), October 27, 1977.

67. Shirley Benton, "Will Community Property Laws Undergo Changes?," *Sunday Advocate* (Baton Rouge), May 29, 1977.

68. "Goodbye, Head and Master; Hello, Equal Management," *Distaff* 5, no. 1 (January 1980): 3–4; Bajoie's version was Louisiana House 1278, §§2352.1, 2353, regular sess. (1978); Spaht, "Background of Matrimonial Regimes," 334–37.

69. Spaht, "Background of Matrimonial Regimes," 335–36; Louisiana Congressional Resolution 54, regular sess. (1977). Subcommittee members: Senators Joseph Tiemann, Jesse Knowles, Claude Duval, Jackson Davis, Thomas Casey; Representatives Sam LeBlanc, Frank Simoneaux, A. J. McNamara, Clark Gaudin, Manuel Fernandez. On the advisory committee: Jack Caldwell, Katherine Brash Jeter, Raymond Simmons, Cynthia Samuels, George Bilbe, and Katherine Spaht. For Riley's authorship of the joint resolution, see her interview in *Distaff*, January 1980, and correspondence, 1980–83, box 23, FF 7, JMR Papers.

70. "Goodbye, Head and Master; Hello, Equal Management, " *Distaff*, January 1980, 3–4; "Community Property Bill Said Equitable, Workable Plan; Bankers Fear Harm to Commerce," *Morning Advocate* (Baton Rouge), June 7, 1978.

71. "Statement of Ann Davenport to House Civil Law and Procedure Committee, May 1978," typescript, Newcomb Archives; "Property Management Proposal Labeled Equitable, Workable," *Morning Advocate* (Baton Rouge), June 7, 1978. *The Louisiana Voter* (League of Women Voters), April/May 1978, noted that league members had gathered at the Governor's Mansion for sandwiches and "thanked Gov. Edwards for his support of equal management through the good offices of his executive secretary, Ann Davenport."

72. Louisiana House 1569, regular sess. (1978); Louisiana House Congressional Resolution 232, regular sess. (1978).

73. *Times-Picayune*, June 23, 1979.

74. Spaht, "Background of Matrimonial Regimes," 343; Richard W. Bartke, "The Reform of the Community Property System of Louisiana—a Response to Its Critics," *Tulane Law Review* 54 (1980): 305.

75. *Distaff*, December 1979; Louisiana Civil Code articles 2831–56 (1870) (repealed by Acts 1979, no. 709, §5, effective Jan. 1, 1980); Louisiana Civil Code articles 2326–28.

76. Cynthia Samuel, "Restoration of the Separate Estate from Community Property after the Equal Management Reform: Some Thoughts on Louisiana's Reimbursement Rules," *Law and Contemporary Problems* 56 (1993): 273–307; Kenneth Rigby, "Matrimonial regimes: Recent Developments," *Louisiana Law Review* 60 (2000): 405.

77. Pictured with Governor Edwards are Corinne Maybuce, Jean Reeves (League of Women Voters), June Rudd, Katherine Spaht, Pat Evans (director of the Bureau on the Status of Women), Susan Hymel, Mildred Clark, Roberta Madden (Women in Politics and Common Cause), Felicia Kahn (Louisiana Women's Political Caucus), and from the AFL-CIO, Fran Bussie and Sibal Taylor. Quotes are from "Goodbye, Head and Master; Hello, Equal Management, " *Distaff* 5, no. 1 (January 1980): 3–4.

78. *For the Record* (Loyola University Law Alumni) 3, no. 1 (Winter 1993): 11–12.

79. "Janet Mary Riley," *Loyola Lawyer*, Fall 2008, 8.

80. "Janet Mary Riley," obituary, *Times-Picayune*, July 6, 2008.

Lindy Claiborne Boggs

(1916–2013)

Wielding Great Power by Giving Away All the Credit

TANIA TETLOW

Lindy Boggs sat through a hearing of the House Banking and Currency Committee in 1973 as a brand new member of Congress. She listened patiently to her forty-six colleagues, all but two of them male, as they debated a provision in a bill designed to eliminate racial discrimination in lending. The Equal Credit Opportunity Act would create historic new protections to enable blacks to purchase a home and to finance a mortgage. Yet somehow, Congresswoman Boggs noted, her colleagues had entirely neglected the massive problem of gender discrimination. Recently widowed, Boggs had begun the complicated process of trying to establish credit for herself, individually, without a husband, so that she could function on the most basic financial level. In a far too real way she was coming to understand the full consequences of a system in which women could not get credit cards in their own name, much less mortgages or small business loans. Despite the outrageous omission, Boggs assumed, with her typical generosity, that her colleagues on the committee had simply failed to notice.[1] She would quietly persuade them to add gender and marital status to the bill and thus forever change the economic power of women. Born before women had the vote, Lindy Boggs pushed the country to realize its egalitarian ideals.

Lindy Boggs has always been described as "gracious." Indeed, her particular style was one too often required only of women, the willingness to give away all credit for their own accomplishments to others. But it was also an extraordinarily effective technique, one requiring enormous strength and sense of self. Lindy utterly conquered any trace of pride. She was unrelentingly optimistic about human nature and brilliant at inspiring others to live up to her high opinions of them. If she were a man, we would call these same traits extraordinary

LINDY CLAIBORNE BOGGS

Fourth from the left, with her family at the capitol.

Courtesy of Cokie B. Roberts.

political skill, a preternatural ability to connect with everyone. Instead, for her, it is labeled "southern charm."

In 1973, Lindy Boggs was perhaps the most unusual member of the freshman class in Congress because she already had been an important part of the institution for decades. She first came to Washington in 1941, at the age of twenty-four, when the city of New Orleans elected her husband to the U.S. House of Representatives. Hale Boggs would go on to serve fourteen terms and rise to the rank of majority leader of the House. For these thirty years, Lindy juggled raising three children with the full-time duties of a political spouse, doing a great deal of the work of politics and government behind the scenes. But she also was half of a renowned political partnership, not unlike Franklin and Eleanor Roosevelt.[2] She ran her husband's congressional office and managed his campaigns.[3] As Hale rose through the ranks, she also smoothed his rough edges. She made up for his infamous temper with her own infinite patience and doubled his significant charms.[4]

By 1972, Hale was majority leader, likely to become the next Speaker, and Lindy, at age fifty-six, had been near the center of Washington life for decades. On October 16 that year, Lindy woke to a phone call from Speaker of the House Carl Albert. Hale had been in Alaska campaigning for the reelection of Congressman Nick Begich, and his small plane had disappeared.[5] The military searched intensely for weeks, even using secret satellite technology, but the area was too vast a wilderness. The search found the remains of other long-lost planes, but it never found Hale Boggs's plane. Lindy spent months and then years imagining scenarios in which Hale might have survived a crash and was waiting for rescue. She listened patiently to psychics and less patiently to conspiracy theorists who blamed it all on Hale's service on the Warren Commission investigating the Kennedy assassination.[6] She never received closure, and for the rest of her life referred to Hale's "disappearance," not to his death.

Vacancies in the House of Representatives must be filled by election, not appointment as in the Senate. Lindy thus faced an agonizing choice. Running for Congress seemed a disloyal abandonment of hope, but she could not imagine letting anyone else take Hale's place. Lindy believed it necessary to carry on his work or, preferably, to hold his seat until he miraculously returned.[7] She also needed to feel drafted, to avoid displaying even a whiff of the arrogance that had been thoroughly trained out of her. Indeed, seemingly everyone in the political establishment, led by New Orleans mayor Moon Landrieu, wanted her to run.[8] Unlike many of the dozens of women elected to the House during the twentieth century to serve partial terms after the deaths of their husbands, Lindy would never be mistaken for a placeholder.[9] She was understood to be a political genius in her own right, the one who had already functioned as the local representative while her husband focused on serving as majority leader.[10] Lindy does not remember ever officially making a decision, but she did run using the name

"Mrs. Hale Boggs" and the campaign slogan "Let Her Continue." She transitioned from Hale's campaign manager to candidate with relative ease, and the outpouring of support ("We Love Lindy" became a slogan) seemed like a natural extension of the voters' loyalty to Hale and his accomplishments. She won the democratic primary with 75 percent of the vote against several opponents, and she won the general election by more.[11]

Representative Boggs may have been half of the Boggs partnership, enjoying overwhelming support from her district, but upon election she retained none of her husband's seniority. After the special election, Lindy entered Congress as the most junior of its 435 members and squeezed into a tiny freshman office, stuffing staff into cubicles. Her long-established relationships provided her with enormous informal clout, however. Senior leadership owed Lindy gratitude for her innumerable acts of service, but more than that, they adored her personally and apparently proved perfectly willing to bend the rules of seniority. When the Speaker offered her any of the four available committee vacancies, she asked instead to replace Hale on the Banking and Currency Committee. Rather than deny her request, the Speaker and minority leader jointly asked the House to expand membership of the Banking Committee by one.[12] It would be in this capacity that Lindy worked to spearhead new economic rights for women.

Lindy, named Marie Corinne Morrison Claiborne, was born on a Louisiana plantation in 1916, surrounded by the descendants of her family's slaves. She should have had the kind of life described in a Eudora Welty novel—a seemingly gentle, rural existence that revolved around hard work supporting the achievements of her husband and sons and benefiting from the racial hierarchy. Instead she ended up as one of the most powerful women in American political history, a liberal who supported civil rights.[13] She became a female heir to a family tradition that claimed an elected official in every generation since the 1630s in colonial Virginia and the first governor of Louisiana.[14] The Claiborne family tree includes at least eleven congressmen, three U.S. senators, two governors, a vice president, two ambassadors, and a secretary of war.[15]

In many ways, Lindy's childhood was idyllic, full of ponies and servants, a magical world where everyone who mattered was related to her. But there were also struggles. Her father died when she was two, a fire later destroyed the family home, and another fire destroyed her convent boarding school.[16] She was raised by strong women—her mother, grandmother, and the nuns of her school—whose primary role was service but in a way not inconsistent with wielding vast power. The nuns of St. Joseph's Academy taught her by example that women could run hospitals and universities. These convent women also instilled in her a strong sense of obligation to the world, which became the core of her identity, an ethic of service that supplanted any plantation attitudes about race. When Lindy struggled to explain her later liberalism on civil rights, she always did so with reference to her relationships with the black people who helped raise her and later helped to raise her own children. For her, the epiphany did not come from abstract political theory but from utter loyalty and an understanding that love is inseparable from treating people with dignity.[17] When asked how Lindy understood the truth of civil rights despite her background, her daughter answered, "It was very much born out of her faith. My mother took to heart the teachings that all humans are made in the image and likeness of God and so she felt that every human being deserved respect and kindness. She also genuinely loved pretty much everybody, especially the African Americans who helped raise her."[18]

From the time she was old enough to speak it appeared that Lindy had significant political skills. As a precocious only child she learned how to please the many adults who doted on her, exhibiting the charm that later came to define her.[19] When Lindy was fifteen, the convent school declared her ready for college and graduated her. She was not yet old enough for Newcomb College in New Orleans, the coordinate women's college at Tulane University, but even that did not deter her. She made an appointment with the dean, summoned her considerable charm, quoted Shakespeare, and talked her way in. She loved those four years. The common struggles of the Great Depression—from finding creative ways to pay for school to the consumption of fraternity-produced "wine" during Prohibition—fiercely bound her classmates together.[20]

The 1930s was an era when couples put off marriage because men struggled to find work, and it was an era in which women began to imagine having careers of their own. Lindy juggled dozens of beaus, sometimes getting in trouble for scheduling multiple dates on the same night in shifts. Yet she was far more entranced with the ambitions of Margaret Bourke White, the famous newspaper photographer of industrial life, than with the prospect of marriage. As a result, Lindy joined the school newspaper, hoping to start a career in journalism, and ultimately rose to the highest rank allowed for female students on the school newspaper—the Newcomb editor of the Tulane *Hullabaloo*.[21]

It was as the Newcomb editor that Lindy met the man who would later become her husband, the editor in chief of the *Hullabaloo*, Hale Boggs. Their meeting was as fateful for Hale as it would prove for Lindy. He was from a distinguished but cash-poor family on the Gulf Coast who had moved to the suburbs of New Orleans.[22] He paid his tuition at Tulane by doing odd jobs and writing some articles for the *New Orleans States* newspaper.[23] In contrast with the other men who courted her, Lindy got to know Hale's character by working with him.[24] As she put it, "I believed in him so much that I would have been working for him if I hadn't been married to him."[25] Hale started law school at Tulane before formally proposing, and Lindy enjoyed what she describes as one blissful year as a teacher in a rural elementary school, where she put together mock constitutional conventions with her young students. It was clear to her that Hale would choose a career in either journalism or politics, and given her own family's history, a life in politics perhaps seemed somewhat inevitable.[26] They married in New Roads, Louisiana, in 1938, with fifteen bridesmaids and groomsmen each because, according to Lindy, choosing among best friends and cousins proved far too difficult. They soon settled into an apartment in New Orleans and Lindy gave birth to their first child in 1939.[27]

Life did not stay simple for long. Louisiana was still recovering from the progressive yet luridly corrupt politics of Huey Long, who correctly predicted that the kind of power he had amassed would result in his successors going to jail. Hale was a young lawyer, a former part-time journalist, and a rising political star. He quickly became central to a reform effort called the People's League, which in 1940 fielded a slate of reform candidates for governor and the state legislature.[28] Members of the league decided that they should enlist their wives to help reform the elections process itself and to make a fair contest possible. A very young Lindy participated as part of this core group of blue-blood, "silk stocking" New Orleans women who went to the front lines to battle electoral corruption. There she quickly learned that "precinct captain" referred to more than just the police department. The group fought the outright theft of ballot boxes by physically guarding the polls. They brought flashlights in case the power was turned off and occasionally even got knocked over the head. Their courage worked: the People's League candidates won a majority of seats in the legislature and reformer Sam Jones beat incumbent governor Earl Long.[29] The reformers then asked twenty-six-year-old Hale to run for Congress against a long-time incumbent, Paul Maloney. In the fall of 1940, just after the release of the Jimmy Stewart movie *Mr. Smith Goes to Washington*, Hale ran ads with pictures of himself as an idealistic young man holding his baby daughter Barbara, whom he deemed his only political "boss." He defeated Maloney by about eight thousand votes.[30]

On the brink of World War II, Lindy and Hale moved to Washington. Lindy missed Hale's swearing in because of a serious eye problem that caused her temporary blindness, but she sent him a wire expressing her earnest admiration: "May you be the fine man you are today, each time you take an oath of public office."[31] The young couple arrived in the nation's capital just as Congress agonized over entering another world war. Lindy and Hale were members of the post–World War I generation of isolationists, young enough to vividly picture their peers fighting another apocalyptic European war. When Hale listened to committee hearings that made him worry he might have to change his mind and support the buildup, he insisted that Lindy come and hear for herself so that she would understand his decision.[32] Ultimately, in early 1941, despite his misgivings, he cast a deciding vote in the crucial resolution to continue the draft, only a few months before the Japanese attack at Pearl Harbor.[33] On December 7, Lindy saw smoke coming from the Japanese embassy as its diplomats quickly burned important papers.[34]

Hale's rise in politics was interrupted in 1942, when the New Orleans machine and Paul Maloney defeated his bid for reelection, with Maloney admitting his wish to teach the young upstart a lesson.[35] Hale then enlisted in the navy and at the same time served as a legal advisor and liaison to Congress for the duration of the war.[36] By 1946, Boggs's supporters convinced Maloney to step aside in return for a patronage job, and Hale returned to the House for the rest of his life with Lindy at his side.[37]

Meanwhile, Lindy juggled a growing family and the complicated Washington protocols of calling cards and white gloves.[38] She participated in the city's transformation from a place where politicians lived part-time, away from their families, to a community where they and their families lived year-round. Cheap postwar housing allowed more families to move to Washington, while maintaining a formal residence in their home districts. The invention of air conditioning also meant that members of Congress felt less compelled to flee the boggy city heat. And the advent of television made it easier to communicate with voters back home.[39] Now members of Congress came to know each other's spouses and children, even spending time together on weekends. It was a brief era that would only last until the advent of inexpensive air travel in the 1970s, which added pressure on legislators to go home every weekend after truncated four-day weeks in session.[40]

It was in this world that Hale and Lindy Boggs thrived, and the couple attracted powerful friends and mentors unusual for a junior congressman. As early as Hale's first term, Speaker of the House Sam Rayburn invited him into his inner circle, which included Lyndon Johnson and Harry Truman. A bachelor without children, Rayburn often invited himself over to the Boggs's for dinner.[41] A young Jack Kennedy, then also single, became a frequent guest as well. And the esteemed Washington columnist Walter Lippman included the Boggs in his "salons."[42]

Lindy supported Hale's work in Congress in every possible way. She organized the time-consuming labor of housework and child rearing, while juggling the enormous hosting duties essential to his eventual rise in congressional leadership.[43] Lindy managed all of this on Hale's nominal congressional salary, much of which went to Catholic school tuition for the children and hiring a full-time housekeeper to help. Lindy made the children's clothes and "catered" their annual garden party that included a thousand invited guests. For this event, she cooked for a month in advance, borrowing space in her neighbors' freezers. And on any given night, it was not uncommon for Hale to bring an extra four people home for dinner with no notice.[44] She thus learned to keep capers and caviar around to fancy up a meal in quick fashion. In one memorable case, Lindy recalls using canned cherries to throw together a flaming cherries jubilee. Everyone seemed quite impressed, but their expressions changed when they tasted it—she had accidentally used a can of black olives.[45]

Yet Lindy's partnership with Hale was not limited to cementing his political relationships over dinner. She also worked full-time running Hale's congressional office, with an official title and a small salary, a situation not uncommon then. When House Democrats elected Hale as majority whip in 1962, Lindy developed a system, using a loose-leaf notebook, to help him track every piece of legislation, sponsor, and vote. More than this, she got up at five o'clock in the morning to bake coffee cakes for Hale's weekly whip meetings.[46] Their son Tommy, now a powerful lobbyist, insists that his mother "did everything but vote."[47]

Beyond her substantial work supporting Hale's political career, Lindy herself played important public roles in government and politics. In 1954, she served as the president of the Democratic Congressional Wives Forum, and in 1958 she became the president of the Women's National Democratic Club.[48] Both of these groups helped train congressional wives for political work by educating them about public affairs. In 1960, Lindy cochaired John F. Kennedy's inaugural balls, raising money to pay for them and surviving the political quagmire of divvying out limited tickets to supporters.[49] After President Lyndon Johnson's support for the Civil Rights Act threatened his election in 1964, Lindy coordinated a whistle-stop train tour for herself and the first lady, Claudia "Lady Bird" Johnson, across the South. Hostile local crowds toned down their heckling in the presence of the women, which allowed Hale to give rousing speeches reminding them of their loyalty to their "grits-and-black-eyed-peas eating" southern president.[50] After Johnson won the election, he asked Lindy to chair his inaugural balls as well.

Lindy also enlisted other wives of male members of Congress and even of Supreme Court justices. These women provided the important but underappreciated work of governing behind the scenes—work that has long been marginalized in American political history. For example, when President Johnson asked for help establishing Head Start, his racially integrated program of early childhood education and a crucial part of his "War on Poverty" initiative, Lindy coordinated its efforts to focus on the poorest three hundred communities in the country, most of them located in the rural South. The political wives persuaded reluctant local officials to cooperate and found black churches willing to provide locations, food, and volunteers for the program.[51] Lindy's reputation and abilities were so clearly established that in 1965 President Johnson offered her a position in the economic division at the United Nations.[52] While she seriously considered the offer, even visiting the offices in New York, ultimately she decided, "I had enough on my plate" already.[53]

Splitting time between Washington and New Orleans made all the more obvious to Lindy the disconnect between lofty American ideals and racial realities. The family was forced to drive through the night between their two homes because there were no hotels that allowed their black housekeeper to stay with them. Lindy struggled to explain such absurdity to the children. One day on a segregated New Orleans streetcar, the children ran to sit in the back row, their favorite spot on the desegregated Washington buses. Lindy tried to call them back, but they refused. The older black women sitting behind the "colored only" sign looked up at her with eyebrows raised, waiting to hear her explanation. She told the children that the rear of the bus was reserved for people who had earned the privilege by working hard all day. They gave in, disappointed, and the women smiled at her effort to hide the ugly truth.[54]

Lindy and the children pushed Hale to do more on civil rights, at first to no avail. For Hale, however, walking the tightrope between his own progressive beliefs and the desires of his district proved to be his most difficult political and moral dilemma. In 1956, along with all but three members of Congress from the South, Hale made the decision to sign the "Southern Manifesto," a document that denounced the Supreme Court's decision in *Brown v. Board of Education* that found racial segregation of public schools unconstitutional.[55] Eight years later, in 1964, Hale also voted against the Civil Rights Act, which banned segregation in hotels, restaurants, and in employment. The only member of his counsel who advised him to vote for the bill regardless of the politics was Lindy.[56] The Boggs children also pushed him hard. They came of age in the era of the civil rights movement, brought home friends who were working in the movement, and referred to their own basement as the "underground railroad."[57] Hale's pragmatic choices in Congress may have saved his political career, but they did not come without consequence at home. The night of the Civil Rights Act vote, the children refused to let him back in the house, and Lindy did not stop them. Hale tearfully explained that it was important to the cause that he keep his seat lest he be replaced by someone far worse.[58]

The next year, Lindy and the children proudly watched Hale vote for civil rights and bravely face threats of violence as a result. The Voting Rights Act proved more politically palatable for a small but growing number of southern legislators, including Hale. It was easier for him to get away with the guarantee of voting as a fundamental civil right than it had been to regulate private businesses with the Civil Rights Act, and the final bill passed the House by an overwhelming margin, 333–85, with 22 southern votes in favor.[59] Hale agreed to vote for the bill but resisted his children's insistence that he also speak on its behalf. Yet when another member of his state delegation made the absurd claim that Louisiana blacks could vote without interference, Hale lost his temper and rose to correct him. As *Newsweek* reported, he gave an eloquent speech, arguing that the "fundamental right to vote must be a part of this great experiment in human progress under freedom which is America."[60] For his efforts, he received a standing ovation in the House and a burning cross on his lawn in New Orleans. The family also received death threats, and some friends refused to speak to them.[61] These reactions paled in comparison to the backlash Hale and Lindy suffered after his vote for the Fair Housing Act in 1968, which directly regulated private property rights in order to root out residential segregation.[62] This time, Hale faced a bitter reelection campaign and the very real possibility of defeat. Despite serving as the majority whip in Congress, with massive seniority and power, and despite an overwhelmingly democratic voting district, Hale barely held onto his seat against Republican Dave Treen, winning only 51 percent of the vote.[63] Still his national clout only increased and in 1970 Democrats elected Hale majority leader of the House.

It is hard to imagine that Hale Boggs would have risen so far without Lindy. She smoothed his rough edges, often apologizing to and appeasing those he had offended. While Hale possessed brilliant political skills and a certain brave bluntness, he could also be direct to the point of brusqueness.[64] In 1971, for instance, Hale took the House floor to attack the "gestapo tactics" of the all-too-powerful FBI, specifically accusing it of wiretapping members of Congress.[65] Moreover, when Hale drank, his temper became a real problem.[66] As Lindy delicately explained later: "He was full of contradictions, and he got more and more intense as his life became more and more complicated."[67] With her endless generosity and charm, Lindy played a crucial political role.

When Hale's plane disappeared in 1972, Lindy suddenly lost her center. Far too quickly, in the midst of her grief, she had to learn to become a member of Congress in her own right. Her greatest skill had been to demonstrate genuine respect for those with opposing views, and to make them feel listened to. Actually having to vote, however, required constantly taking sides, a role she hated. Her daughter Barbara reminded her that there was no "maybe" button in Congress.[68] And unlike Hale, she had no brilliant and adept wife to apologize for her hard votes.[69] Yet Lindy soon realized the tremendous power of actually being in the room where decisions were made, taking part directly rather than merely advising. One of the first steps in that transition was to realize the new role she would fill for women far outside of her district. As one of only sixteen women in the House and one in the Senate, she had begun receiving letters and visits from women all over the country and soon realized that she needed to represent all of them.[70] Only a year after she took office, she listened to Banking Committee members discussing racial discrimination in lending while ignoring the other similarly consequential discrimination suffered by their own mothers, wives, and daughters. They either did not see it or did not care, although Lindy always generously assumed the former. She took a copy of the bill and scribbled onto the categories of discrimination, "sex or marital status." She found a photocopy machine and passed out copies, explaining gently that she had a little amendment to make, noting, "I'm sure it was just an oversight" (that the drafters had left out gender).[71] Lindy felt and also believed pragmatically that she could accomplish more through polite persuasion than by the most justified self-righteousness. The other Banking Committee members bristled at first at her presumption. They insisted that wives and mothers did not require credit because women had men to support them. After spirited debate, they ultimately came around, and the amendment passed.[72] By opening up the possibility of personal and commercial credit, Lindy helped to change the lives of American women forever.

For Lindy, the revolution that she helped push forward for women was never an abstract movement for change. A few years after passage of the Equal Credit Opportunity Act, Lindy found herself in the precarious position of having to enforce the new law she had just helped create. Deciding to move out of her big house, where Hale's clothes still hung in the closet, Lindy sold it to her daughter Cokie Roberts, opting for smaller quarters. But when she tried to buy an apartment in Washington, the bank took its time deciding whether to approve a mortgage and demanded an unusual amount of financial documentation.[73] She was a member of Congress whose finances were both more than adequate and a matter of public record. She calmly warned the bank that they might be breaking the equal credit law that she, in fact, had authored. The bank quickly approved the mortgage.[74]

Lindy adapted to her newfound power and even came to terms with making hard political choices. Her extraordinary diplomatic skills ensured that no one ever stayed angry with her for long. According to historian Burt Solomon, Boggs's "sweetness of manner, her inoffensiveness, was more than charm; it was a political asset of consequence."[75] Speaker Tip O'Neill claimed that Boggs could smile at him, whisper in his ear, and get anything she needed for her district. Former civil rights activist and congressman John Lewis described the impact of her fundamental virtue and generosity: "Saying no to Lindy would be like saying no to Mother Theresa."[76] Colleagues found themselves unwilling to disappoint her, and she herself proved willing to continue asking for their help until they said yes.[77] She knew her own power, and she was unabashed about using it to help those who needed it most.

Over the years, Lindy amassed tremendous political power. In 1976, the still junior representative Boggs campaigned for a spot on the Appropriations Committee and was chosen by the House Democratic Caucus.[78] This enabled her to secure significant federal resources for her district, with a particular focus on flood control.[79] She also used the power of the purse to look after women. A number of agencies, including the military, had no choice but to address her concerns about gender. Departments quickly learned to hire and promote women to senior positions so they could participate in appropriations hearings and answer Representative Boggs's detailed questions on the subject.[80] Lindy pushed the military particularly hard about its progress, and, for example, was finally able to secure military status for members of the Women's Airforce Service Pilots ("WASPS") who flew noncombat missions during World War II, over the staunch opposition of some senior male colleagues who themselves had served in World War II.[81] She also used direct appropriations to address gender issues. She pushed for some of the earliest federal funding to tackle domestic violence at a time when few cared about endemic levels of brutality against women.[82]

Lindy Boggs helped spearhead the turn in second-wave feminism from the first legislative battles for basic formal equality (the rights to vote, contract, and own property) to the fight for economic and social equality.[83] The efforts of Boggs and her colleagues in the early 1970s constituted some of the first purposeful protection of women's rights by Congress. Until the 1970s, many of the advances in gender equality happened as an afterthought or even as a joke. Southern congressmen included gender in Title VII of the 1964 Civil Rights Act as a way to attempt to kill the bill. The amendment passed notwithstanding the strength of segregationist votes, and it managed to remain in the law, banning employment discrimination.[84] Until that point, and for too long thereafter, newspapers divided want ads into male and female, and women who might have discovered a cure for cancer found themselves working as secretaries. A decade later, the Supreme Court began applying the Equal Protection Clause of the Fourteenth Amendment, originally designed to protect formerly enslaved African Americans, to strike down laws that discriminated against women. In both cases, however, the lack of any legislative purpose to protect women watered down these protections.[85]

In the mid-1970s, Lindy Boggs worked at the forefront of efforts to end discrimination against women by the federal government and in the private sector. With the Economic Equity Act, she corrected the ways that tax policy devalued women's work and corrected government regulation of pensions to protect widows. She further sought equal rights for women in job opportunities and access to credit and higher education. The Equal Credit Opportunity Act made it possible for women to participate fully in the economy, to start businesses, buy their own homes, and function without financial oversight of fathers and husbands. And she supported the Equal Rights Amendment.[86]

Representative Boggs generally voted within the mainstream of the national Democratic Party, though often she proved quite liberal for a Deep South state like Louisiana.[87] At a time when it was still politically inexpedient to do so, Lindy did not hesitate to cross the usual political divides. She was southern yet represented a progressive urban district that would become majority black. She was a tireless proponent of civil rights and advocate for labor. And although a steadfast proponent of women's rights, she was a devout Catholic and culturally conservative.[88] There were two major challenges from her favorite constituencies that caused her pain. As her district became majority black (56 percent after a court-ordered redistricting in 1983), Representative Boggs faced serious African American political opposition, including a campaign by the respected civil rights leader Israel Augustine in 1984.[89] Although most of the local African

American political organizations opposed her, the strength of her reputation, as well as her bond with women voters of both races and decades of constituent work in the district, helped her win easily. She was never seriously challenged again.[90] The other issue with which she was forced to contend proved even more difficult. As a devout Catholic, Lindy firmly opposed abortion, and she thus faced opposition from a number of national women's organizations.[91] Given her accomplishments on women's issues, she clearly did not oppose abortion out of disrespect for women.[92] Unlike some more conservative "pro-life" members of Congress, whose concerns for children seemed to end at their birth, Lindy supported prenatal care, day care, and a full array of government services so that women would not feel that abortion was their only option.[93] But for many feminists during the height of the abortion debates, her anti-abortion stance made her untenable.[94] Walter Mondale publicly considered Congresswoman Boggs as a running mate in his 1984 bid for the presidency, but criticism of her views on abortion quickly took her out of the running.[95]

Despite these divisive issues, Lindy Boggs had two particularly gratifying crowning moments during her congressional career, times when she received well-deserved recognition. In 1976, the Democratic Party chose her as the first woman to chair a national party convention. She handled both the vast logistical duties and the public platform with her usual skill, and Jimmy Carter went on to win the election.[96] Ten years later, the Speaker of the House and majority leader of the Senate chose her to preside over the commemoration of the bicentennial of Congress. At a grand reenactment ceremony at Independence Hall in Philadelphia, Lindy Claiborne Boggs sat in George Washington's chair, although her feet did not reach the floor. She wondered with amusement what Washington himself would have thought of the image of a woman representing him. It was typical both of her generosity and of her feeling of personal kinship with American history that she assumed Washington would have enjoyed it.[97]

Lindy managed to suffer the grief and agonized uncertainty of losing Hale and eventually established her independence. For her New Orleans residence, she moved from the posh Garden District to an inherited family home on Bourbon Street, smack in the middle of blaring music clubs and adult entertainment. True to form, she happily walked every morning through the smell of stale alcohol to attend mass at St. Louis Cathedral.[98] Though remarriage was unimaginable to her, she did find companionship over the years, spending time with Tommy Corcoran, a respected lobbyist and former advisor to Franklin D. Roosevelt and Lyndon B. Johnson, until his death in 1981.[99] When she was in her seventies, Lindy was also very close to an old family friend in New Orleans, Herman Kohlmeyer, who dutifully escorted her to endless evening obligations.[100]

Lindy's three children have proven to be forces of nature in their own right, each using their inherited political skills in different ways. The youngest, Cokie

Roberts, is a prominent journalist who has worked for the likes of National Public Radio and ABC News. She brings historical understanding to her coverage unique to someone who grew up with Sam Rayburn and Lyndon Johnson at the dinner table. Tommy Boggs ran for Congress in Maryland in 1970 and lost narrowly. He subsequently became one of the most powerful lobbyists in the country and died in 2014 at the age of seventy-three. Oldest daughter Barbara Sigmund carried on the Claiborne tradition and served as the beloved mayor of Princeton, New Jersey. She also ran unsuccessfully for governor and the Democratic nomination for U.S. Senate in the 1980s, outperforming far more senior candidates. After Barbara lost an eye to cancer, she began wearing eye patches to match her outfits, including spangled ones for eveningwear.[101] By 1990, however, the cancer spread and it became clear that Barbara was dying. Lindy rode the train from D.C. to Princeton as often as she could to be with her daughter and ultimately decided not to run for reelection.[102] Twelve weeks after her announced retirement and four days after the Democratic primary, Barbara died.[103]

At age seventy-five, Lindy Boggs had certainly earned a rest, but she lacked any skill in that regard. Indeed, her only real vacation was an annual spring pilgrimage to Acapulco with Lady Bird Johnson (and Secret Service agents paddling after them in the ocean). In 1991 she accepted a position as counselor to the president of Tulane University in New Orleans, and her congressional staff of seventeen was drastically reduced to a single part-time student worker—me. I first met Lindy as a teenager after I wrote a letter explaining that I wanted to be her when I grew up. By some astounding good luck, I managed to spend the first years of her "retirement" with her. As I soon discovered, Lindy accepted every invitation and task that came her way and simply could not imagine disappointing people or slowing down. She would listen patiently for hours to constituent calls and personally try to solve their Social Security problems. In the evenings, I would go with her to accept yet another award, riding in Mr. Kohlmeyer's very large Cadillac, which he drove while peering over the steering wheel. The next day, we would put the "plaque du jour" in a teetering pile.[104]

In the spring of 1997, Lindy received a call from President Bill Clinton asking her to serve as ambassador to the Vatican. She spoke no Italian and could not quite imagine moving to another country to begin another career at the age of eighty-one. In an effort to be polite, she told him she would think about it. On one of her daily pilgrimages to the cathedral, however, she sat staring at the statue of Our Lady of Prompt Succor and thought, "Lindy Boggs, you are a big sissy. If the president asks you to do a job, you could at least give it a try."[105] But before she could communicate that rash decision to the White House, she turned on the news to hear herself being announced for the post. She was an absolutely perfect choice for a difficult position. As Louisiana senator John Breaux explained, she spoke "fluent Catholic," and could translate the Clinton administration to the Pope.[106] The Senate confirmation hearing was a lovefest, even featuring an adoring testimonial from longtime-conservative senator Jesse Helms, who did not believe in sending an ambassador to the Vatican.[107] That November, Vice President Al Gore swore her in, all the while laughing that Lindy had known him since birth, or really since before he was born.[108]

As ambassador, Lindy learned the complicated protocol of the State Department and struggled with the even more complicated rules of the ancient, secret world of the Vatican diplomatic corps. She found ways around the more challenging traditions, however, surprising and delighting the aging, celibate cardinals who ran the Vatican state by flirting with them.[109] The Vatican offered the possibility of unprecedented sources of information about the world because the Catholic Church often had access to more information on the ground than foreign leaders. It was and is a crucial listening post, and Lindy was a great listener.[110] She attended a merciless schedule of diplomatic events, driven around at break-neck speed by Italian police officers in a bulletproof Mercedes.[111] She adored Pope John Paul II, and he was often seen holding her hand in their photographs together.[112]

Finally, in her late nineties, Lindy Boggs slowed down. She looked back on a life in which she knew presidents from Herbert Hoover (who visited her family when she was a child) to Barack Obama. She survived both the great Mississippi flood of 1927 and Hurricane Katrina in 2005. And she kept the political family tradition alive, producing at least two more generations of public officials. After Katrina, she reluctantly left her beloved New Orleans to live in suburban Washington near all of her great-grandchildren, and on July 27, 2013, she died in her sleep at home.

The women of Congress now have a room of their own, just off of Statuary Hall, where they can rest and use what contained, until very recently, the only women's bathroom anywhere near the House floor.[113] There they can feel communion among the photographs of every woman to serve in Congress, beginning with a sepia-toned portrait of Jeannette Rankin in 1916. In 1991, the House of Representatives chose to name this room after the beloved Lindy Claiborne Boggs. It remains the only room in Congress named after a woman.[114]

NOTES

1. Lindy Boggs with Katherine Hatch, *Washington through a Purple Veil: Memoirs of a Southern Woman* (New York: Harcourt Brace, 1994), 276–77. The author interned for Lindy Boggs in 1989, worked for her after she retired from Congress in 1990–92, and remained close with her thereafter. This work is based on hundreds of conversations with her.

2. *Steel and Velvet*, directed by Bess Carrick and Dawn Logsdon (Louisiana Public Broadcasting, 2009), interview with historian Patrick Maney.

3. Burt Solomon, *The Washington Century: Three Families and the Shaping of the Nation's Capital* (New York: William Morrow 2004), 83.

4. Boggs, *Washington through a Purple Veil*, 210. Lindy compared her role to that of Bobby Ken-

nedy in his relations with his brother, the president; they were both behind-the-scenes organizers and the "buffer[s] from criticism."

5. Ibid., 245–46.

6. Ibid., 249–50, 254. See also "In Alaska Crash, Echoes of a Mystery," *Washington Post*, August 16, 2010, which describes conspiracy theories about Boggs's death and its relation to his Warren Commission service. On the Warren Commission generally, see "Warren Commission Born Out of Fear, Washington Wanted to Stop Speculation," *Washington Post*, November 14, 1993.

7. Solomon, *Washington Century*, 247.

8. Thomas Ferrell and Judith Haydel, "Hale and Lindy Boggs: Louisiana's National Democrats," *Louisiana History* 25, no. 4 (1994): 393. Governor Edwards and Mayor Moon Landrieu both urged her to run. Judith Haydel and Thomas Ferrell, "Lindy Boggs: A Democrat for All Seasons," *Southeastern Political Review* 28, no. 3 (2000): 433. Moon Landrieu described Lindy as the most viable candidate to keep the seat shortly after Hale almost lost it in 1970 following his Fair Housing Act vote, particularly in an election held on short notice. It was a decision "based on love of Lindy and her electability. She was the obvious candidate, universally respected and liked. Plus you had the sentimental aspect of taking her husband's place." Author interview with Moon Landrieu, January 23, 2014.

9. See generally Irwin Gertzog, *Congressional Women: Their Recruitment, Integration, and Behavior*, 2nd ed. (Westport, Conn.: Praeger, 1995).

10. Ibid.

11. Boggs, *Washington through a Purple Veil*, 261–66.

12. Solomon, *Washington Century*, 252–53; Boggs, *Washington through a Purple Veil*, 275. Lindy wanted the assignment to seek urban renewal funds that had been promised the district and then withdrawn after major construction projects had already begun. Author interview with Jan Schoonmaker, former legislative director for Lindy Boggs, January 27, 2014.

13. Haydel and Ferrell, "Lindy Boggs," 428.

14. Solomon, *Washington Century*, 39.

15. Haydel and Ferrell, "Lindy Boggs," 430.

16. Boggs, *Washington through a Purple Veil*, 4–42. When her father Roland Claiborne died, a nurse nicknamed the then-two-year-old Corinne "Rolinder" after her father, and that later was shortened to "Lindy."

17. Haydel and Ferrell, "Lindy Boggs," 428; Boggs, *Washington through a Purple Veil*, 29.

18. Author interview with Cokie Roberts, February 1, 2014.

19. In an interview conducted in 1976, she described her family as having made up for the loss of her father, saying it "had put an obligation on me to please them." "Lindy Boggs Makes History With a Gavel: The First Woman to Chair a National Convention," *People Magazine*, July 12, 1976.

20. Solomon, *Washington Century*, 23.

21. Boggs, *Washington through a Purple Veil*, 44–49.

22. Ferrell and Haydel, "Hale and Lindy Boggs," 393.

23. Solomon, *Washington Century*, 38.

24. Author interview with Lindy Boggs, October 11, 2011.

25. Gary Boulard, *The Big Lie: Hale Boggs, Lucille May Grade and Leander Perez in 1951* (Gretna, La.: Pelican, 2001), 22.

26. Ibid.

27. Boggs, *Washington through a Purple Veil*, 57–59.

28. Pam Tyler, *Silk Stockings and Ballot Boxes: Women and Politics in New Orleans, 1920–1963* (Athens: University of Georgia Press, 1996), 123.

29. Ibid., 129–31.

30. Boggs, *Washington through a Purple Veil*, 70–72.

31. Solomon, *Washington Century*, 36.
32. Boggs, *Washington through a Purple Veil*, 2–3.
33. Solomon, *Washington Century*, 48.
34. Boggs, *Washington through a Purple Veil*, 85–86.
35. Boulard, *The Big Lie*, 24.
36. Boggs, *Washington through a Purple Veil*, 96.
37. Paul Maloney got his seat back for four years. Hale served in the navy in D.C. with the War Department, and he did not run in 1944. In 1946 Maloney retired to a position as the New Orleans port tax collector, and Hale ran for his seat with the support of the mayor. Solomon, *Washington Century*, 59, 71.
38. Boggs, *Washington through a Purple Veil*, 80.
39. Ibid., 89; Solomon, *Washington Century*, 112.
40. Solomon, *Washington Century*, 112.
41. Ferrell and Haydel, "Hale and Lindy Boggs," 394.
42. Boulard, *The Big Lie*, 23; Boggs, *Washington through a Purple Veil*, 83.
43. Solomon, *Washington Century*, 112–13. Lindy's helper, Emma Cyprian, once famously refused to give the White House chef her recipe for President Johnson's favorite chicken dish, telling the White House that the president would have to come to her kitchen to get it. Boggs, *Washington through a Purple Veil*, 194.
44. Solomon, *Washington Century*, 80.
45. Author interview with Lindy Boggs, October 11, 2011.
46. Solomon, *Washington Century*, 126–27; Boggs, *Washington through a Purple Veil*, 174.
47. Haydel and Ferrell, "Lindy Boggs," 433.
48. Solomon, *Washington Century*, 111.
49. Boggs, *Washington through a Purple Veil*, 159, 161–64.
50. Ibid., 189–93.
51. Ibid., 196–98. Many southern Democrats opposed Head Start and other programs in the War on Poverty because these programs would be racially integrated. Taylor Branch, *Pillar of Fire: American in the King Years 1963–65* (New York: Simon and Schuster 1998), 444.
52. Haydel and Ferrell, "Lindy Boggs," 433.
53. Boggs, *Washington through a Purple Veil*, 199.
54. Author interview with Lindy Boggs, October 10, 2011. The District of Columbia ended segregation in 1954 after the U.S. Supreme Court held unconstitutional the segregation of the District's public schools in *Bolling v. Sharpe*, a companion case to *Brown v. Board of Education*. Solomon, *Washington Century*, 96.
55. The three dissenters—Albert Gore Sr., Estes Kefauver, and Lyndon Johnson—all had national political ambitions. Solomon, *Washington Century*, 101.
56. *Steel and Velvet*, interview with Patrick Maney.
57. Boggs, *Washington through a Purple Veil*, 156.
58. Solomon, *Washington Century*, 99–100.
59. Boggs, *Washington through a Purple Veil*, 204.
60. "Boggs for Civil Rights," *Newsweek*, May 17, 1965, 21. Cokie Roberts, daughter of Hale and Lindy Boggs, attributes her father's liberalism on race to his "innate sense that all men were created equal," and said that she and her siblings had been "instructed from birth about the dignity due all people and that racism was and is evil." Author interview with Cokie Roberts, February 1, 2014.
61. Solomon, *Washington Century*, 160; *Steel and Velvet*, interview with Cokie Roberts; Boggs, *Washington through a Purple Veil*, 203–5. Lindy described them as "socially ostracized." "Lindy Boggs Makes History with a Gavel: The First Woman to Chair a National Convention," *People Magazine*, July 12, 1976, 31–34.

62. Boggs, *Washington through a Purple Veil*, 212–13.

63. Ibid., 222.

64. Solomon, *Washington Century*, 224–46.

65. Lindy reports that she and Hale were informed by several sources that their home phone was in fact bugged. Boggs, *Washington through a Purple Veil*, 234. In a White House tape released more recently, Nixon discussed his dismay at the speech with Minority Leader Jerry Ford, saging, "He's on the sauce, isn't that right? . . . Or is he crazy?" "Nixon and Ford Discuss a Democrat's Attack on FBI Director Hoover," *Washington Post*, December 29, 2006.

66. Solomon, *Washington Century*, 111, 127, 213, 226; *Steel and Velvet*, interview with Congressman Thomas Foley; Haydel and Ferrell, "Lindy Boggs," 432.

67. Solomon, *Washington Century*, 226.

68. Boggs, *Washington through a Purple Veil*, 270.

69. Ibid., 272.

70. Ibid., 283. Boggs worked with the other women of Congress to create the Congressional Women's Caucus, which later accepted male members and became the Congressional Caucus on Women's Issues.

71. Ibid., 277. In her autobiography, and for decades leading up to it, Lindy Boggs remembered making the amendment to the broader Equal Credit Opportunity bill, a version of events that has been repeated in numerous sources. See, for example, "Boggs, Corinne Clairborne (Lindy)," History, Art & Archives, U.S. House of Representatives, http://history.house.gov/People/Detail/9543?ret=True (accessed February 26, 2015). However, the 1973 Equal Credit bill (H.R. 3210) was originally authored by Representative Bella Abzug to protect against only gender discrimination; it did not include race at all until it was amended two years later in 1976. Boggs's contribution must have been to the Housing and Urban Development Act (H.R. 246), which protected against racial discrimination in federally insured mortgages until the House Banking and Commerce Committee added gender and marital status.

72. Author interviews with Lindy Claiborne Boggs, October 11, 2011, and April 2, 2012. The reaction was "who do you think you are?"

73. *Steel and Velvet*, interview with Cokie Roberts.

74. Solomon, *Washington Century*, 254; Boggs, *Washington through a Purple Veil*, 314; author interview with Cokie Roberts, January 22, 2014.

75. Solomon, *Washington Century*, 271.

76. *Steel and Velvet*, interview with John Lewis.

77. Solomon, *Washington Century*, 286–87; Ferrell and Haydel, "Hale and Lindy Boggs," 402.

78. Solomon, *Washington Century*, 286. Solomon reports that Speaker Tip O'Neill gave Boggs a choice between the powerful Appropriations and Ways and Means Committees. Jan Schoonmaker, Boggs's former legislative director, remembers instead that Boggs affirmatively campaigned for the position with the House Democratic Caucus. Author interview with Schoonmaker, January 27, 2014.

79. Solomon, *Washington Century*, 351.

80. Ibid., 287. Not only did Boggs ask these questions during hearings of her own two subcommittees, she also submitted questions about gender and hiring to all of the other Appropriations subcommittees. Author interview with Jan Schoonmaker, January 27, 2014.

81. Boggs, *Washington through a Purple Veil*, 317–19; author interview with Jan Schoonmaker, January 27, 2014.

82. Author interview with Cokie Roberts, May 10, 2011; Haydel and Ferrell, "Lindy Boggs," 441.

83. Jean Gerhard, *Desiring Revolution: Second-Wave Feminism and the Rewriting of American Sexual Thought, 1920 to 1982* (New York: Columbia University Press, 2001).

84. Jo Freeman, "How 'Sex' Got into Title VII: Persistent Opportunism as a Maker of Public Pol-

icy," *Law and Inequality: A Journal of Theory and Practice* 9, no. 2 (March 1991): 163–84. As Freeman explains, the amendment was introduced by an opponent to the Civil Rights Act, Virginia congressman Howard K. Smith, and met with laughter, yet there remains controversy about whether that congressman actually acted on sincere motives.

85. As Justice William Rehnquist explained in *Meritor Savings Bank v. Vinson,* "The prohibition against discrimination based on sex was added to Title VII at the last minute on the floor of the House of Representatives . . . the bill quickly passed as amended, and we are left with little legislative history to guide us in interpreting the Act's prohibition against discrimination based on 'sex.'" 477 U.S. 57, 63–64 (1986). Three Supreme Court justices resisted application of the equal protection clause to women as going far beyond the purposes of the Fourteenth Amendment. *Frontiero v. Richardson*, 411 U.S. 677, 691–92 (1973).

86. Boggs, *Washington through a Purple Veil*, 331. For a detailed description of the unacknowledged impact of the varied provisions of the Economic Equity Act, see Patricia A. Seith, "Congressional Power to Effect Sex Equality," *Harvard Journal of Law & Gender* 36 (2013): 1–88 (noting Lindy Boggs' role as cosponsor at 21).

87. Haydel and Ferrell, "Lindy Boggs," 434–46. Boggs's voting record was much closer to northern Democratic colleagues than to her fellow southern Democrats.

88. Ibid., 439–43.

89. Frances Frank Marcus, "Rep. Boggs, 68, Faces Her Toughest Career Challenge in Louisiana Primary," *New York Times*, September 28, 1984; Solomon, *Washington Century*, 351. She received 60 percent of the vote. Haydel and Ferrell, "Lindy Boggs," 443.

90. Boggs, *Washington through a Purple Veil*, 332, 344.

91. Haydel and Ferrell, "Lindy Boggs," 440. Boggs voted for the Hyde Amendment banning the use of federal money for abortion.

92. Solomon, *Washington Century*, 287.

93. Ferrell and Haydel, "Hale and Lindy Boggs," 400.

94. *Steel and Velvet*, interview with Marcy Kaptur. "The issue of abortion 'marginalized her.'" "Feminism Critiqued in UCI Speech," *Los Angeles Times*, April 15, 1985. Congresswoman Shirley Chisholm reported taking heat for publicly supporting Lindy Boggs for vice president.

95. *Steel and Velvet*, interview with Patrick Maney.

96. Boggs, *Washington through a Purple Veil*, 307–11.

97. Solomon, *Washington Century*, 302; Boggs, *Washington through a Purple Veil*, 361; Lindy Claiborne Boggs, interview with author, April 2, 2012.

98. Michael Lewis, "Having Her Say at the See," *New York Times Magazine*, June 4, 2000.

99. Solomon, *Washington Century*, 301.

100. Boggs, *Washington through a Purple Veil*, 369; Iris Kelso, "Impressive Legacy of Lindy Boggs," *Times-Picayune*, October 7, 1990. Lindy and Herman were the same height, about five foot three, and loved to sing along to jazz bands.

101. Boggs, *Washington through a Purple Veil*, 338.

102. Ibid., 365; Solomon, *Washington Century*, 351–52; Frances Frank Marcus, "Lindy Boggs to Quit House, Ending a Louisiana Dynasty," *New York Times*, July 21, 1990.

103. Solomon, *Washington Century*, 353.

104. Haydel and Ferrell, "Lindy Boggs," 444 (listing her awards, a fraction of the total).

105. Lewis, "Having Her Say at the See."

106. Solomon, *Washington Century*, 375. After the Monica Lewinsky scandal, she joked about explaining Bill Clinton to the pope.

107. Solomon, *Washington Century*, 376.

108. John McQuaid, "Lindy Boggs Is Sworn in as Ambassador to Vatican, She'll Have Pope Saying 'Y'all' Soon, She Says," *Times-Picayune*, November 13, 1997. Lindy had held a toddler Al Gore on

her lap during the first congressional trip to China after Nixon's groundbreaking visit. She also later served with him in Congress, teasing him on a trip to Antarctica, when he huffed and puffed in the thin air, that she would be happy to carry him again. Author interviews with Lindy Boggs.

109. Author interview with Jennifer Dudley, special assistant to Ambassador Boggs, July 2005.

110. Solomon, *Washington Century*, 375.

111. Lewis, "Having Her Say at the See."

112. Interview with Jennifer Dudley.

113. This situation not rectified until 2011. "Women in the House Get a Restroom," *Washington Post*, July 28, 2011.

114. Donnie Radcliffe, "A Room with a Past for Lindy Boggs," *Washington Post*, July 30, 1991.

PART TWO

Women and Work

Lucy Alston Pirrie

(1772–1833)

A Woman's Life in Early Louisiana

SARA BROOKS SUNDBERG

The experiences of Lucy Alston Pirrie reveal much about a woman's life on the Louisiana frontier. Her life demonstrates how gender mixed with imperialism, law, and property in shaping this frontier. Lucy was born in 1772 on a plantation southeast of present-day Natchez, Mississippi, when Natchez was still part of British West Florida. This part of West Florida, known as the Natchez District, extended southward from Natchez into modern-day West Feliciana Parish and served as the backdrop for her life. When the American Revolution came to this region, Lucy experienced profound changes in her personal life. West Florida shifted from British to Spanish control, then to independence, before the United States annexed it, along with the rest of present-day Louisiana, in 1812. This "serial colonization" tested Anglo-American residents' loyalties and brought political instability to the region. Lucy's life story illuminates the private dimension of this contested frontier. She not only survived these tumultuous years, she and her family prospered and became wealthy, slave-owning landholders. Lucy's life demonstrates the critical role white women played in creating and maintaining family wealth and in transmitting Anglo-American culture to the Louisiana borderlands.[1]

Lucy's story unfolds chronologically in three parts during a period of serial colonization and early statehood between 1772 and 1833. The first finds her amid a political rebellion that arose in West Florida in response to the American Revolution. The second explores the cultural and legal implications of the American Revolution for Lucy and other women like her in West Florida, in terms of property ownership. The third examines how Lucy worked cooperatively with her family to build and retain their wealth in both land and slaves. While historians have largely depicted the West Florida borderlands as a male frontier, Lucy's experience reminds us that it was a family frontier.[2]

The portrait of middle-aged, matronly Lucy that gazes out over the ladies' parlor at Oakley Plantation today suggests nothing of the drama that accompanied her early life. Modern-day visitors to the plantation, a Creole-style house Lucy and her husband built in 1806, are more likely to be treated to a story about the romance and tragedy of Lucy's youngest daughter, Eliza Pirrie. In 1823, at the age of eighteen, Eliza eloped with a wealthy neighbor who died soon after from pneumonia, allegedly contracted while carrying Eliza across the swollen Homochitto River during their flight to Natchez. Alienated from her parents because of their elopement and pregnant with a son, Eliza is a sympathetic figure. More importantly, Eliza is remembered because her mother, Lucy, employed artist and naturalist John James Audubon as her tutor. Audubon completed work on several paintings that appeared in his influential *Birds of America* while living at Oakley. Oakley Plantation is now a state historic site commemorating his residence and work there.[3]

Lucy's life story, like her better-known daughter's, is filled with drama and tragedy and is historically even more compelling because it is rooted in the struggles over imperial frontiers in Revolutionary-era America. In 1772, the year Lucy was born, King Charles III of Catholic Spain met with advisors to discuss the growing number of British Americans settling along the Mississippi River in British West Florida. After the Treaty of Paris in 1763 formally ended the French and Indian War and officially designated West Florida as British, Anglo settlers like Lucy's father, John Alston, had taken advantage of British efforts to attract settlers to the fertile region through generous land grants. Although not listed among the earliest British land grantees in the region, Lucy's father, who migrated from North Carolina, in 1777 filed for a 450-acre grant from the British government, southeast of Natchez along Second Creek. Other Anglo settlements eventually extended all the way south to Baton Rouge, which worried the Spanish king who saw them as a threat to his hegemony west of the Mississippi. The king's advisors assured him that these settlements posed little threat to Spanish Louisiana, saying that settlers were motivated by economic prospects more than by any expansionist, political intent.[4] Regardless of the accuracy of their advice, Lucy was born and raised in volatile borderlands. In 1784, the region was sparsely settled, with 1,579 people spread out over the hundred miles of the Mississippi River and immediate hinterlands between Natchez and Bayou Sara, the main river landing in Feliciana.[5]

The political volatility of the region meant that the Alstons' considerable property remained secure only as long as their loyalties did not bring them into conflict with their Spanish neighbors to the south and west. By the early 1780s Lucy's family homestead, La Grange Plantation, contained roughly 800 acres and twenty-seven slaves, with some 185 acres cleared and ready to till and 35 acres planted in corn. The property included the family dwelling, fifteen slave cabins, a tobacco house, and other enclosures. Altogether it was appraised at nearly $7,000, a considerable sum for the times. Given the lack of a regular survey system and the dispersed pattern of settlement common to Anglo-Americans at the time, it is likely that the Alston homestead stood on the cultivated acreage, surrounded by cleared land and then by miles of forest or canebrake. In a memoir, Lucy's granddaughter recalled that her grandmother's family had amassed considerable wealth before emigrating from North Carolina and that Lucy had been reared in "luxury and refinement." Although the Alstons may have brought some of their finer household items with them, their home in Louisiana most likely was typical for British settlers on the southern frontier: a log or framed house with siding "one room deep and two or more rooms long, only 24 feet long and 6 feet wide." Modest, for a family with seven children, the building's structure allowed for additions.[6]

Lucy Alston was the fifth of seven children and one of two daughters of John and Elizabeth Hynes Alston and the first to be born in the new settlement. John and Elizabeth had come to West Florida with four young children in 1770 at the same time that a flood of Anglo-Americans sought refuge from growing Revolutionary War sentiment further north. Governor Peter Chester of West Florida officially declared the territory a refuge for Tories in 1775. Whether John Alston was "a true and loyal British subject," as his great-granddaughter claimed in her reminiscence, is a matter of dispute. What is certain, however, is that in May 1781 he played a significant role in the Natchez Rebellion, an attempt by Anglo-American rebels to retake Fort Panmure from the Spanish. Anglo-Americans, including Alston, seized the Natchez fort, only to relinquish it under Spanish pressure after the fall of Pensacola to the Spanish later that year. When Spanish authorities rounded up the rebels, Alston found refuge among friendly Chickasaw Indians living northeast of Natchez, but in autumn 1781 Spaniards captured and imprisoned him and then placed him on trial in New Orleans. Spanish authorities confiscated much of Alston's property and initially sentenced him to death, but he and others eventually were pardoned. Governor Bernardo de Gálvez released Alston and the other rebels from prison in 1783 "as a gesture of friendship and goodwill," in honor of the installation of the new British governor of Jamaica, Prince William, Duke of Lancaster. The duke dispatched a ship to transport Alston and the other rebels from their jail cell in New Orleans to Jamaica. Although temporarily exiled, Alston eventually returned to Louisiana and regained some of his property.[7]

Historians of West Florida have mostly analyzed the political and economic fallout from the Natchez Rebellion for rebels like John Alston. Refocusing on the consequences of the rebellion for Alston's family, this saga of political protest turns into a tragic family story. Backing up in time to 1781 again, we see that John and Elizabeth Alston and their seven children fled their home near Natchez immediately after the surrender of Fort Panmure to the Spanish. The family, with several of their slaves, had not journeyed far before forty-six-year-old Elizabeth's horse stumbled, tossing her to the ground. The accident left her seriously injured with several broken ribs, and the family was forced to return home, where she died some weeks later. Sometime afterward, John Alston and his eldest son escaped from Natchez. With the death of their mother and their father now declared a "fugitive rebel," Lucy and six of her seven siblings became legal orphans. In late July, Charles de Grandpré, the Spanish commandant of the post in Natchez, appointed Alexander McIntosh curator and guardian for the six children. It was McIntosh who had alerted the Spanish of their father's rebel attack on Fort Panmure.[8]

Court records document the plight of the children. McIntosh asked that the court appoint a manager for the Alston plantation and that it grant him permission to sell one of Alston's slaves because "his wards are destitute of necessities and cloathing [sic]." McIntosh explained that Lucy's youngest brother, five-year-old Henry, had died in August, just a few months after his mother. McIntosh complained that he could not protect the Alstons' slaves from thieves stealing them away to their father's hideout with the Indians, and he alleged that "the five children, his wards, are continually in company with evil disposed persons, receiving from them bad advice." McIntosh asked the court's permission to place the two girls in the Ursuline convent in New Orleans and to find trades for the two boys.[9]

The court seized and sold much of Alston's estate, leaving Lucy and the other children homeless. Before Alston fled Natchez, he had arranged for the children, accompanied by a favored slave, to live in a one-room cabin on a plantation in Point Coupee Parish. According to her granddaughter's reminiscence, Lucy vividly recalled the troublesome mosquitoes and frightening wolves that plagued them during their isolated, year-long stay in the woods. The displaced family subsisted on fish from False River, wild game, meat brought from the nearby plantation, and the proceeds from the sale of poultry raised by the slave, "Mammy Poll."[10]

The Alston girls had been two of the Natchez District's most economically and socially privileged female inhabitants. Now they and their brothers found themselves struggling for survival on a frequently lawless frontier and facing a highly uncertain future. Without the protection of their father or elder brother or husbands the girls confronted greater perils than wolves and mosquitoes. According to Lucy's granddaughter, Lucy's teenage sister Ann faced a particular dilemma: "Can you imagine a more distressing situation for a young and beautiful girl . . . in a few short weeks to be deprived by death of an affectionate mother, her beloved father a prisoner . . . without means, without friends, with a bare roof over her head . . . living in constant terror . . . without protection and at the mercy of any or all who might feel so disposed to molest her?"[11] Her sentiments illustrated attitudes concerning women's virtue and honor that were common among planters throughout the Lower South. Women found protection and security in marriage, if they retained their virtue. Of the sisters, Ann Alston met and married the manager from a nearby plantation in 1784, while Lucy, only ten years old, entered the Ursuline convent in New Orleans.[12]

No records tell us precisely when Lucy arrived at the convent, who deposited her there, or how long she stayed. Based upon her granddaughter's memoir and court records, it is likely she arrived in 1783 and stayed there for up to five years. We also do not know what Lucy thought about her time in the convent. The closest evidence comes from the documented experiences of Anglo-American girls, like herself, who boarded at the convent in the years following the American Revolution. For these girls, historian Emily Clark says, "the language, religion and customs were all alien and exotic" in New Orleans, and the convent "served the crucial role of acculturation." This seems to have been the case for Lucy, for by the time she left the convent she was fluent in French. Indeed, according to her granddaughter, "she had almost forgotten her mother tongue." Yet her classmates likely constituted a diverse group, including girls her own age who were daughters of Spanish and French-Creole families and daughters of free persons of color. Prior to her father's rebellion, Lucy had received tutoring at home on La Grange Plantation from "good and competent English teachers." Her time at the Ursuline convent surely challenged the rural isolation of this early education, acquainting her with cultural and economic groups outside the well-to-do, close-knit Anglo community of the Natchez District. Clark argues that the convent brought the daughters of the very wealthy, middle-class, and poorer inhabitants together under a common roof and a common curriculum.[13]

Lucy Alston's intellectual horizons likely expanded because of her educational training at the convent. Subject matter common to Revolutionary-era female education included basic literacy and domestic skills, but Lucy's abilities went far beyond that. Indeed, the plantation medical records attributed to her at Oakley Plantation suggest that she had attained advanced writing skills. Moreover, the Ursuline sisters complemented their female students' literacy with training in arithmetic, a subject commonly reserved for male students until after the American Revolution. Advocates for educational reform in the United States after the revolution linked female education to the health of the new nation. They campaigned for an expanded curriculum for young women they believed would eventually become mothers responsible for training children in the responsibilities of citizenship for the new republic. Young women like Lucy, who received an education at the Ursuline convent, had already benefited from an expanded curriculum that included both "literacy and numeracy." They had learned basic accounting procedures, knowledge that would prove essential to Lucy Alston in the future as she kept track of household and plantation accounts.[14]

When Lucy much later looked back over her life, she did not consider her experiences in West Florida during the American Revolution to be the most difficult years, but they were transformative years for her, as they were for West

Florida. In a single dramatic year, Spain reoccupied West Florida and Lucy's family almost came apart as a result of borderland politics. Exposing the precarious position of even well-to-do families, her life quickly shifted from one of material comfort to one of basic survival, and this took place at a highly impressionable age. Then her life at the Ursuline convent presented another challenge, and her studies and her classmates widened her experience. Given the tumult and diverse lifestyles she knew as a child, it is little wonder that Lucy Alston's granddaughter remembered her as a "woman of strong mind and great energy of character."[15]

It is likely that Spain resumed control of West Florida while Lucy was a student at the convent. Perhaps as many as one-third of the Anglo-American immigrants who migrated to British West Florida during the 1770s and early 1780s left after Spain assumed official control of the region in 1783. The Alstons remained in West Florida but moved southward into Feliciana. There they were again part of a distinct Anglo-American community that by 1802 one contemporary observer estimated comprised as much as "seven-eights of the population, some of whom came from Natchez" and others from Britain or the United States.[16]

After John Alston returned to Natchez from Jamaica, he must have retrieved Lucy from New Orleans, and Lucy kept house for her father until she married, probably in her early twenties. Her husband, Ruffin Gray, knew the Alston family through his sister, who had married Lucy's older brother Lewis. Gray and Lucy set up housekeeping on a plantation south of Natchez on a 220-acre Spanish land grant Gray had claimed along the Homochitto River. Lucy bore four children, two of whom died in infancy and one, Ruffin Jr., who would die in his early twenties. Only the Grays' daughter Mary Ann outlived both of her parents. The family remained in the Natchez District until Ruffin Gray's death in 1799.[17]

Five years prior to Gray's death, the United States and Spain negotiated an end to their dispute over the section of the northern boundary between U.S. territory and Spanish West Florida east of the Mississippi River. Pinckney's Treaty in 1795 established the thirty-first parallel as the new boundary, placing the Grays' plantation just over the line in U.S. territory rather than in West Florida. However, the transfer of authority from Spanish to American control did not take place until 1798. In 1796, Gray filed another Spanish land claim for seven hundred arpents, or about 673 acres, well below the thirty-first parallel, in Spanish territory near Bayou Sara in Feliciana, apparently intending to relocate his family there. Lucy's father and brothers owned plantations in Feliciana, and liberal land policies under the Spanish compared favorably with land opportunities in Mississippi. When Gray died in 1799, he left property, which Lucy would ultimately administer, in both the U.S. territory of Mississippi and in Spanish West Florida.[18]

Lucy's case as a newly widowed Anglo-American woman property holder provides a window into a unique legal world. Her lands lay on the periphery of multiple legal cultures: British (and later American) common law and Spanish civil law. Both common law and civil law granted single and widowed women substantial rights of ownership and management of property during the late eighteenth and early nineteenth centuries. Where the two legal systems differed was in the treatment of married women's property rights. Under Spanish civil law in Louisiana, and later under the Louisiana Civil Code, married women kept their legal identity, and they inherited half of the community property accrued during the life of the marriage. In comparison, under common law, married women lost their separate legal identity when they married. Moreover, common-law statutes generally guaranteed women only one-third of their husband's real and personal estate.[19]

Lucy's inheritance vividly reveals the impact of the law on women's ability to accumulate property in their own name. Lucy and Ruffin Gray had married and lived in the Natchez District while it was still a part of Spanish West Florida and under the jurisdiction of Spanish colonial law, and the couple resided under this jurisdiction during all but the last two years of their marriage. But when Gray drew up his will in 1798, it conformed to common-law principles and divided the couple's property equally between Lucy, their son, and their surviving daughter. Lucy's one-third share of the estate would represent $3,000 less than if the couple's community property had been divided in half according to Spanish civil law. In 1799, when Gray filed his will in the Natchez District and then died, the United States had acquired the region and finally and formally assumed jurisdiction. Gray's will legally conformed to American common law.[20] Even if the Natchez District had still been under Spanish control, it is not certain this would have made any difference in how Gray divided the couple's property or that Lucy would have protested his will. Anglo husbands frequently devised wills in Spanish West Florida that gave women less than Spanish law allowed. Anglo wives rarely protested, although at least some, including Lucy, understood their rights.[21]

Lucy would demonstrate her understanding of the particulars of civil law much later, in 1829, when she questioned her neighbor Rachel O'Connor about one of O'Connor's female relatives who had recently divorced her husband and claimed her separate property under Louisiana civil law, thereby protecting her property from her former husband's debts. Louisiana civil law drew upon Spanish legal precedent, among others, in matters of private law. Lucy not only understood the settlement involving the separate property under Louisiana civil law, she knew creditors who would personally bear responsibility for the couple's debts.[22]

Rachel Russ is another example of a West Florida woman who understood her property rights under civil law. Her case is particularly interesting because she not only understood the law but also, unlike Lucy, protested her husband's attempt to circumvent it. Abijah Russ, Rachel's husband, had devised a will that divided marital property equally between his wife and their five children. Rachel Russ filed a petition in 1805 that challenged his will, arguing that it did not conform to Spanish colonial law in force in the Baton Rouge District where they lived. The petition asserted

> that having contracted marriage while this province was under British rule, it is impossible to secure witnesses who could certify to the amount of property which the deceased husband brought in marriage, all the existing property being the product of thirty years of mutual duties and labors, during their married life, . . . the relatrix [Rachel Russ] makes use of her legal rights and claims as she has always claimed, half of the property of the said succession and her deceased husband all that property being community.[23]

The Spanish governor affirmed Russ's petition and granted her half of the couple's community property and her dowry, as she requested. Anglo-Americans like Lucy and her family and Rachel Russ constituted a distinct cultural community in West Florida and brought with them traditional beliefs about family property under British common law. Rachel Russ proved unusual in stepping outside that tradition in matters of inheritance to claim her marital portion under Spanish civil law. Russ was one of only two Anglo-American women in Spanish West Florida who protested their husbands' wills.[24]

This is not to say that women like Lucy did not venture into court at all to protect their property. Lucy made use of her knowledge of the law to insure that the family's property in land and slaves remained together as a working unit. She resisted the attempts of her own brother, acting as Ruffin Gray's testamentary executor, to immediately sell and divide the family's property, worth more than $21,000. She petitioned the court to allow her to administer the family estate intact until her children came of age, and the court agreed to her petition. Historian Cara Anzilotti uncovered Anglo-American widows of means in colonial South Carolina who behaved similarly to Lucy. She contends that they managed family property as "surrogates for their husbands" until their children were grown. Their actions proved critical to the continuance of family wealth and the advancement of the Anglo social order.[25]

Lucy lived in Spanish West Florida, a region "whose ruling residents' cultural background did not originate from their ruling country," and political loyalties there were fluid. While historians like Andrew McMichael have examined Spanish West Florida for its complex politics and fluid political loyalties, Lucy's experience as a widow in Spanish West Florida focuses attention on a different side of that story; that is, cultural adherence to law and its impact, within a context of conflicting legal systems in matters pertaining to women, family, and property. Despite the authority of Spanish colonial law, British common law and custom defined the legal boundaries for Anglo-American women like Lucy, and they continued to do so even as she moved southward, back into Spanish-controlled Feliciana.[26]

McMichael argues that along the Spanish West Florida frontier the availability of productive lands defined settlers' interests and loyalties as much as politics. James Pitot, a naturalized French businessman from New Orleans, toured Spanish Louisiana at almost the same time that Lucy moved to Feliciana. Pitot recorded the "excellent soil" he found in Feliciana and wrote that "Bayou Sara is navigable all the year, even as far as twelve to fifteen leagues during low water in small boats." Besides these qualities, Pitot found the air and water particularly healthful for this section of the lower Mississippi. Agricultural settlement began in earnest in this region in the 1780s. These promising lands offered opportunities for women as well as men. In 1796, Gray filed a land claim with the Spanish government for seven hundred arpents in the Felicianas. A year later, Lucy acquired two more parcels of land, both contiguous with Gray's claim. One comprised about 682 acres and the other 671 acres, making the total amount of land acquired in Feliciana by the Gray family about 2,000 acres. When Gray died in 1799, he left a twenty-seven-year-old widow, two children, thirty slaves, and two plantations, one in Mississippi and one in Feliciana, together totaling some 2,470 acres of land. Lucy qualified as a large landowner.[27]

After her husband's death, Lucy moved her family from Mississippi to Feliciana in order to manage and develop her more extensive properties in Louisiana. She oversaw the construction of the family's new home, Oakley Plantation, on Gray's land claim. According to her granddaughter's reminiscence, it was the early years at Oakley Plantation that Lucy remembered as the most trying times of her life, with the construction taking place as she was rearing children, complicated by an outbreak of smallpox. In 1802, she lost both her father, John Alston, and her sister, Mary Ann Stirling.[28]

In 1801, Lucy remarried, joining with Scotsman James Pirrie. Her decision, while not uncommon for young widows in the South, was not necessary or automatic. Research suggests that while rates of remarriage for women were high in the South prior to 1700, those rates declined significantly during the eighteenth century. Overall, younger widows under the age of fifty, like Lucy Alston Gray, were more likely to remarry than older widows, often because they owned less wealth than older widows or were single parents of small children (or both). That was not entirely true for Lucy. The Gray children were young, but Lucy had amassed considerable wealth and had already demonstrated that she understood how to manage it.[29]

Other wealthy widows in Lucy's neighborhood chose not to remarry. Lucy's neighbor Catherine Rucker Turnbull lost her husband the same year Ruffin Gray died. Only three years older than Lucy, she too qualified as a young widow. As with Lucy, the death of Turnbull's husband left her with several young children and a considerable inheritance. The fact that Catherine Turnbull remained a widow allowed her legal authority over her own inheritance. Her husband's will added incentive for Catherine to eschew remarriage. He appointed her executrix of his will, only as long as she did not remarry. Gray's will had made no such stipulation. In the end, the decision whether to remarry was not a simple one; both women likely made their decisions after carefully weighing their individual circumstances, personal need, and the wishes of their families.[30]

After her marriage to Pirrie, Lucy gave birth to three more children, one of whom died in infancy and another who died as a teenager. From this marriage, as from her first, only one child survived to adulthood, Eliza Pirrie. James and Lucy worked cooperatively to enlarge the homestead. The couple jointly purchased property on the north side of Oakley Plantation, contiguous with Gray's original claim. This claim added another 368 acres to Oakley Plantation, bringing the total acreage to about 2,335 acres. Probate records from the Gray and Pirrie families reveal the design behind the family's land claims and purchases. Ruffin Gray's original Spanish land claim provided the location for the plantation home, and Lucy's land purchases during her first marriage added to the size of the plantation as well as to the inheritance of their children. When the surviving children from Lucy's marriage to Gray came of age, she and the children divided the land equally into thirds, according to their father's wishes rather than according to civil law. After she remarried, Lucy retained the land from Gray's original Spanish claim along with their home. The two surviving children from her marriage to Gray each received one of the purchases Lucy had originally patented under the Spanish. After Lucy's son Ruffin Gray Jr. died in 1821, Lucy, as forced heir, repossessed the tract of land her deceased son had inherited, which she had originally purchased.[31]

For most women, widowhood complicated traditional ideas about the gender division of labor on a plantation. The West Florida economy, characterized by slave labor and cotton production, required plantation widows to engage in both the male world of commerce and the female work world of the household. Widows bought and sold slaves and land, negotiated with cotton factors, commissioned merchants in New Orleans, kept accounts, and sued in court to protect their assets and management prerogatives. Although Lucy's private papers are woefully scant, the documentary record demonstrates that she engaged in all of these activities during what would be two periods of widowhood. Considering Lucy's active management of the plantation, it is not surprising that a demographic profile of the slave population at Oakley at the time of her death reveals a population "artificially maintained" through slave purchases rather than natural increase, a pattern typical of productive plantations like Lucy's. Her livelihood, and that of her family, depended on slave labor, a fact that likely shaped her attitude toward them as a commodity to be bought and sold. Lucy's 1821 purchase, for seven hundred dollars, of an eighteen-year-old slave girl described as "sensible and sound with the exception of her right hand which has been burnt, and a slave for life" reflects the harsh reality of Lucy's immersion in commerce in early Louisiana.[32]

When John James Audubon met Lucy in 1821, he described her as an "extraordinary woman, raised to opulence by dint of industry." A member of the pioneer generation of settlers in West Florida, Lucy's "industry" included a vigorous work life on her plantation. She owned at least seventy-two slaves at her death, a large number for Feliciana at that time. Like many female slave owners, she undoubtedly dictated the work schedule of her slaves, especially in matters of food preparation and clothing. Lucy's accounts with merchants and the inventory of her property at her death included items for these responsibilities—two looms, fifteen spinning wheels, a carding machine, and bolts of cloth. She owned numerous vials of medicine, which she is reputed to have dispensed to her slaves and others in ill health. The documentary record does not reveal whether she also dispensed punishment to her slaves. Her widowed neighbor, Rachel O'Connor, reported, however, that Lucy fretted over slave discipline and feared slave insurrections. On one occasion, O'Connor reported that runaway slaves robbed Lucy while she lay sleeping in her bedroom. On another occasion, after Lucy became a widow a second time, O'Connor described Lucy "screaming and crying as loud as she could" at the neighbor's overseer, ordering him to check on her grandson's slaves, who had reportedly rebelled.[33]

As this incident implies, Lucy demonstrated strong will. Audubon complained that as a consequence of Lucy's "lack of understanding," she sometimes exhibited a "violent" temper. In an era when women were advised "to be always obliging, obedient, and cheerful, [and] never angry," it is possible that Lucy's assertiveness contradicted traditional expectations for female deference and cast her in an unfavorable light. Audubon noted that Lucy was "fond of quizzing her husband." She hired Audubon as a tutor for her daughter Eliza and later dismissed him after she questioned the bill he had submitted for his services. Behaviors such as these were better suited to settling a frontier or managing a plantation than satisfying cultural expectations for female submissiveness.[34]

Lucy was fifty-two years old when James Pirrie died in 1824. She owned Oakley Plantation until her death in 1833. During the latter years of her life, she spent significant time away from the plantation, in part because of poor health. Rachel O'Connor reported in July 1832 that "she [Lucy] stays so much at Dr. Ira Smith's [her son-in-law's home] that she knows very little about home or how it is managed." But, even before that, Lucy had been absent for months at a time, leaving the plantation under the care of an overseer. She also depended greatly on help from Dr. Smith. Her absences from home not only signaled that she was ill, they indicated a gradual generational change in the management of Oakley Plantation.[35]

Despite her absences, the inventory of Lucy's property at her death makes clear the continuity of her land ownership and the threefold increase in her overall wealth after she moved to Feliciana from Mississippi. At her death, Lucy still owned 1,529 acres in real estate, worth $14,200, about 21 percent of her estimated total worth of $66,734. Her probated wealth situated her within the top 5 percent of female property owners in West Feliciana Parish and would have placed her in the top 3 percent of male property owners. She clearly qualified as one of the elite planters in the parish, if not all of Louisiana, allowing her the means to travel and spend time away from the plantation. In 1826, O'Connor noted, rather wryly, that Lucy and her family had traveled to New York for the summer and that they "are the only people that don't appear to have some distress or other to sink their spirits."[36]

The acreage Lucy owned at her death included the land claim made by her first husband, Ruffin Gray, where the plantation house stood; another parcel that she and James Pirrie had purchased; and one of the parcels she purchased in her own name. Another parcel had already been deeded to her eldest daughter as her share of her father's estate. In her will Lucy expressed the desire that her property be equally divided between her two surviving daughters or sold if an agreement could not be reached between the two women. She also provided that her elder daughter, Mary Ann, be compensated for the fact that she had only received a third of her father's estate. After her son's death, Lucy received her son's property, increasing her share of her deceased husband's estate to two-thirds. In a spirit of fairness, Lucy sought to share the benefits she accrued from this legacy through her will with her daughter Mary Ann and her daughter's husband, Dr. Smith.[37] Rachel O'Connor, by then a close friend of Eliza Pirrie, believed there was more to Lucy's decision to provide additional property for Mary Ann, insisting: "The old lady only gave her youngest daughter about one-third of her Negroes . . . and very little of her land . . . which is all owing to the lies our honorable sheriff made and told her, which she found out before her death, but too late to make changes in her will."[38]

Whatever the precise motivation behind Lucy's bequest, her youngest daughter, Eliza, eventually owned Oakley Plantation and returned to live there in the 1840s. In her own way, Lucy sought to provide for the economic security of both of her daughters. Eliza Pirrie's inheritance allowed her to join the original Gray claim, which was contiguous with Lucy's claim, and then add one of her own purchases contiguous with these.[39]

Lucy Alston Pirrie's story reveals that the first generation of Anglo settlers in Spanish West Florida, both male and female, took advantage of liberal land policies—opportunities to purchase land to build plantation estates that would provide a legacy for their children. Lucy and her two husbands became successful planters in part because of lands they purchased or claimed through such land policies. Lucy, like many Anglo planters who came to Feliciana, began her new life there with considerable resources, including slave labor accrued from planting or trading in the Natchez District. That said, the family achieved the status of planter elite within the parish in large part because of the productivity of landholdings that Lucy helped to accumulate, and chose to keep, against the advice of her brother and the social expectations of women at that time. Lucy is exceptional for the amount of property she accumulated, but she is not unusual in the methods of accumulation. In West Feliciana Parish alone, forty-nine women were original landowners in the American period and accounted for the ownership of more than 10 percent of all the land.[40]

If Lucy had not hired John James Audubon as a tutor, Oakley Plantation would likely not be a state historic site and we would probably know very little about her. Aside from the portrait of her that hangs at Oakley and her granddaughter's reminiscences about her life, Lucy appears only briefly in notarial and probate records, a few merchant and plantation records, and the federal census. Rachel O'Connor recorded some observations about her in letters she wrote to her brother and his family about the affairs of the neighborhood around St. Francisville. The two women do not appear to have been close friends, but they did share a history as early female settlers in the region. It is notable that when Lucy became "dangerously ill," she sent for O'Connor. Perhaps it is in these expressions of neighborly kindness that we glimpse the connections among women in this generation of settlers in Louisiana. It is from O'Connor that we learn that Lucy suffered "monthly discharges" for four or five months at a time, suggesting that a probable cause for her death in 1833 may have been uterine cancer. It is also from O'Connor that we learn that, by the time of her death, the family no longer inhabited the Creole plantation home Lucy helped to build. It served, instead, as residence for the overseer.[41]

Lucy's grave in Beechwood Plantation's cemetery south of Wakefield, Louisiana, is simple yet substantial in size, appropriately reflecting her status as both pioneer settler and wealthy planter. As the child of one of West Florida's early British land grantees, Lucy represented a distinct Anglo-American community that developed in West Florida and then persisted into the late Spanish colonial and early American period. Pioneers like Lucy and her family, who adhered to the principles of British and later American common law, reinforced Anglo-American culture in this region. As suggested by historian Light Townsend Cummins, pioneer settlers like Lucy, who preceded the Louisiana Purchase in 1803 and persisted through the Spanish period, may have been "a decisive vanguard for the Anglo-Americanization of the lower Mississippi Valley." Indeed, she witnessed extraordinary political changes in the borderlands of colonial Mississippi and Louisiana and participated in the economic development of both regions as a pioneer settler.

Lucy's story is also a personal one. Her experiences reveal a back story to the political, cultural, and economic changes in West Florida. She weathered the family trauma caused by her father's political rebellion against the Spanish and emerged on the other side of these events a strong woman who helped to settle the Louisiana frontier. She faced the deaths of two husbands and five of her seven children, all the while managing to work cooperatively with her family to create and expand their wealth.[42]

Although they did not always occupy it, Oakley Plantation remained home to Lucy's descendants until 1947, when the lands that survived from the plantation were sold to the state of Louisiana. These lands now form the basis of the Audubon State Historic Site. It is fitting that among the final two generations of family members to own and occupy Oakley Plantation, it was the women in the family who played a predominate role in the plantation's management. After the Civil War, Lucy's granddaughter, Isabelle Bowman Matthews, owned the plantation along with her husband, although Isabelle appears to have been the most active in the plantation's management. When Isabelle died she bequeathed the plantation to her two unmarried daughters, Lucy Lyons Matthews and Ida Slocum Matthews. It is almost as if Lucy Alston Pirrie wanted us to remember the contributions she made to the settlement of early Louisiana and the creation of Oakley Plantation. The last family member to own and manage the plantation, and then finally sell it to the state, was Lucy's great-granddaughter and namesake, Lucy Matthews.[43]

NOTES

1. Lucy Alston Pirrie is known as Lucretia in some historical records. In this essay I refer to her as Lucy because that is the given name that appears on her grave monument in the private Beechwood Cemetery, near Wakefield, Louisiana. Because her last name changed over her lifetime (Alston, Gray, Pirrie), it is less confusing to refer to her in this paper by her first name. I am grateful to Ann Weller for making it possible for me to visit this cemetery. Stanly Arthur Clisby, *Old Families of Louisiana* (Baton Rouge: Claitor's Publishing Division, 2006), 189–95. I employ the geographic description for the Natchez District described in Light Townsend Cummins, "An Enduring Community: Anglo-American Settlers at Colonial Natchez and in the Felicianas, 1774–1810," *Journal of Mississippi History* 55 (May 1993): 136. Stuart Banner describes "serial colonization" in *Legal Systems in Conflict: Property and Sovereignty in Missouri, 1750–1860* (Norman: University of Oklahoma Press, 2000), 4.

2. An important exception to the male bias in the historiography of West Florida is Andrew McMichael, *Atlantic Loyalties: Americans in Spanish West Florida 1785–1810* (Athens: University of Georgia Press, 2008).

3. Herman de Bachell Seebold, *Old Louisiana Plantation Homes and Family Trees*, vol. 1 (Gretna: Pelican, 1971), 245.

4. Light Townsend Cummins relates the story of the Spanish king and his advisors, "An Enduring Community," 134–35; Alston's land grant is described in British Land Grants, Public Record Office, Kew Garden, co5/608, 285. I located Alston's land grant by comparing this description with a map drawn by Elias Durnford, Royal Surveyor for British West Florida in 1772, British Library, Map Room, K. Top.122.90.

5. Cummins, "An Enduring Community," 136; population numbers are derived from Winston De Ville, *The Natchez Ledgers, 1790–1791: A Finding Aid for Anglo-Americans in Pre Territorial Mississippi* (Ville Platt, Louisiana, 1994), vi.

6. May Wilson McBee, *The Natchez Court Records: Abstracts of Early Records, 1767–1805*, book A (Greenwood, Mississippi, 1954), 1; Fred B. Kniffen, *Louisiana: Its Land and People* (Baton Rouge: Louisiana State University Press, 1968), 132–33; Joseph Asbury Groves, *The Alstons and Allstons of North and South Carolina* (Atlanta: Franklin Printing and Publishing, 1901), 11.

7. Groves, *The Alstons and Allstons*; McMichael, *Atlantic Loyalties*, 15; Robert V. Haynes, *The Natchez District and the American Revolution* (Jackson: University of Mississippi, 1976), 135, 137, 142–51.

8. Groves, *The Alstons and Allstons*, 200; McBee, *The Natchez Court Records*; Haynes, *The Natchez District*, 135–36.

9. McBee, *The Natchez Court Records*, 2. Lucy's granddaughter remembered that Lucy was placed in the Ursuline convent in New Orleans. What became of the other children is not clear.

10. Groves, *The Alstons and Allstons*, 201–2 (see 198–207 for the full reminiscence). Sarah Pirrie Smith Stirling, Mary Ann Gray Smith's youngest daughter, likely wrote the reminiscence about her great-grandfather, John Alston, and other members of her family, including her grandmother Lucy Alston. See Groves, *The Alstons and Allstons*, 211, for a list of Lucy's grandchildren. The reminiscence identified Dr. Benjamin Farrar's plantation as a location where the children stayed. Farrar also owned property in Natchez. Court records corroborate the reminiscence except that when Alston's estate was auctioned by the court, Mammy Poll was not listed as a slave. See McBee, *The Natchez Court Records*, 1.

11. Ibid., 201.

12. Ibid., 203. See, for example, Cara Anzilotti, *In the Affairs of the World: Women, Patriarchy, and Power in Colonial South Carolina* (Westport, Conn.: Greenwood Press, 2002), 88–89. Student records for the convent during the years Lucy Alston would have been enrolled there are not extant. Her granddaughter's reminiscence combined with her guardian's request to deposit her there make it probable she was placed in the convent. See McBee, *The Natchez Court Records*, 2.

13. Emily Clark, *Masterless Mistresses: The New Orleans Ursulines and the Development of a New World Society, 1727–1834* (Chapel Hill: University of North Carolina Press, 2007), 146; Groves, *The Alstons and Allstons*.

14. Joan R. Gunderson, *To Be Useful to the World: Women in Revolutionary America, 1740–1790* (Chapel Hill: University of North Carolina Press, 2006), 92–93; Clark, *Masterless Mistresses*, 120; Kirsten E. Wood, *Masterful Women: Slaveholding Widows from the American Revolution through the Civil War* (Chapel Hill: University of North Carolina Press, 2004), 18. Lucy Alston Pirrie received accounts from factors and merchants in New Orleans. These accounts, addressed to her, required that she be knowledgeable about basic accounting procedures and arithmetic. See Oakley Plantation papers, Audubon State Historic Site, St. Francisville, Louisiana.

15. Groves, *The Alstons and Allstons*, 206.

16. McMichael, *Atlantic Loyalties*, 15; James Pitot, *Observations on the Colony of Louisiana from 1796 to 1802* (Baton Rouge: Louisiana University Press, 1979), 122.

17. Clisby, *Old Families of Louisiana*, 93; probate records, West Feliciana Parish Courthouse [hereafter cited as WF], St. Francisville, Louisiana, box 40, Partition of the Estate of Ruffin Gray, December 16, 1816.

18. Haynes, *The Natchez District*, 156; Craig A. Bauer, *A Leader among Peers: The Life and Times of Duncan Farrar Kenner* (Lafayette: Center for Louisiana Studies, 1993), 6; probate records, WF, box 40; notarial records, WF, book AA, 1824–1828, no. 108.

19. McMichael, *Atlantic Loyalties*, 6, employs the concept of peripheries of empire in writing about West Florida; the matrimonial regime under the Spanish is described in Nina Nichols Pugh, "The Spanish Community of Gains in 1803: *Socieded De Ganaciales*," *Louisiana Law Review* 12 (1971): 1–43. The common-law regime is described in Marylynn Salmon, *Women and the Law of Property in Early America* (Chapel Hill: University of North Carolina Press, 1986); under Spanish civil law and later under Louisiana civil law, husbands managed marital property during the life of the marriage, so wives experienced the most benefit from marital property at the end of the marriage when they inherited half of the community property instead of one-third under common law. For a comparison of women's property rights under Spanish civil and British common law, see Deborah Rosen, "Women and Property across Colonial America: A Comparison of Legal Systems in New Mexico and New York," *William and Mary Quarterly* 60, no. 2 (April 2003): 355–82. For a comparison of women's property rights under Louisiana civil law and American common law, see Sara Brooks Sundberg, "Women and Property in Early Louisiana, Legal Systems at Odds," *Journal of the Early Republic* 32 (Winter 2012): 633–65.

20. Survey of Federal Archives, *Archives of the Spanish Government of West Florida, Translations and Transcriptions, 1937–1940* [hereafter cited as ASWF], 4:193–99; Bauer, *A Leader among Peers*, 6.

21. Sundberg, "Women and Property in Early Louisiana," 660.

22. Allie Bayne Windham Webb, *Mistress of Evergreen Plantation: Rachel O'Connor's Legacy of Letters, 1823–1845* (Albany: State University of New York Press, 1983), 35–36.

23. ASWF, 10:283.

24. Ibid.

25. Ibid., 4:198; Anzilotti, *In the Affairs of the World*, 7.

26. McMichael, *Atlantic Loyalties*, 6.

27. Ibid., 4; Pitot, *Observations on the Colony of Louisiana*, 122; State Land Records, State Land Office, Baton Rouge, Louisiana, Greensburg Land District, tract book no. 4, Township 3S, Range 4W.

28. Groves, *The Alstons and Allstons*, 206.

29. Vivian Bruce Conger, *The Widows' Might: Widowhood and Gender in Early British America* (New York: New York University Press, 2009), 45–46.

30. Ann Alston Stirling Weller, *Alexander Stirling and Ann Alston in Spanish Feliciana: Ancestors, Descendants, and Allied Families* (A. Weller, 1999), 515–53; ASWF, 3:334–335; ASWF, 7:136.

31. State Land Office, Baton Rouge, Greensburg Land District, tract book no. 4; Succession of Ruffin Gray, probate box 40; Succession of Ruffin Gray Jr., probate record book C, 1832–1837 [WF].

32. Webb, *Mistress of Evergreen Plantation*, 197; Oakley Plantation papers; Minutes of the Third District Court Records, 130–1834, nos. 25, 31, and 37, [WF]. According to Laurie A. Wilkie, when the need for slaves rose faster than the natural rate of increase, slave populations were "artificially maintained" through purchases. This was typical of productive plantations like Oakley at that time. Laurie A. Wilkie, *Creating Freedom: Material Culture and African American Identity at Oakley Plantation, 1840–1950* (Baton Rouge: Louisiana State University Press, 2000), 57. See also notarial record AA 1824–1828, 107 [WF].

33. Alice Ford, ed., *Audubon, by Himself* (Garden City, N.Y.: American Museum of Natural History, 1969), 108; probate records, WF, probate record book C, 1832–1837, 308–14; Oakley Plantation papers. For a discussion of plantation mistresses' work and management of slaves, see Catherine Clinton, *The Plantation Mistress: Woman's World in the Old South* (New York: Pantheon Books, 1982), 16–25, 193; Wood, *Masterful Women*, 35–60. The Audubon State Historic Site in St. Francisville, Louisiana, which includes Oakley Plantation, suggests in its museum exhibit and historic house tour that Lucy Pirrie provided medicinal care to slaves and others on the plantation. See also Webb, *Mistress of Evergreen Plantation*, 37, 62.

34. Ford, ed., *Audubon, by Himself*, 108; Anzilotti, *In the Affairs of the World*, 117. Anzilotti makes a similar point about the contradiction between "social convention" and the reality of plantation women's lives on page 118.

35. Webb, *Mistress of Evergreen Plantation*, 71–72.

36. Probate records, WF, inventory record book B, 1830–1834, 34. See also Sara Brooks Sundberg, "Women and the Law of Property in Early Louisiana, 1782–1835" (PhD diss., Louisiana State University, 2001), 109; Webb, *Mistress of Evergreen Plantation*, 16.

37. Probate records, WF, inventory record book B, 1830–1834, 34; notarial records, WF, book E (1833–1836), Last Will and Testament Lucy Pirrie, 105–7.

38. Webb, *Mistress of Evergreen Plantation*, 108.

39. Wilkie, *Creating Freedom*, 52.

40. McMichael, *Atlantic Loyalties*, 20. Sara Brooks Sundberg and Adam Sundberg, "Female Landholders in West Feliciana Parish," unpublished paper presented at the Hemispheric Freedom Symposium, Baton Rouge, Louisiana, September 2012.

41. Webb, *Mistress of Evergreen Plantation*, 87, 94, 116.

42. Cummins, "An Enduring Community, 134.

43. Wilkie, *Creating Freedom*, 43–52.

Appoline Patout, Mary Ann Patout, and Ida Patout Burns

(1805–1879; 1836–1907; 1877–1956)

The Women of Enterprise

MICHAEL WADE

Two decades ago historian Glenn R. Conrad observed that the incidence of women actually running sugar plantations, and thereby controlling their destinies, was far greater than was generally known. He based this insight on his extensive knowledge of Louisiana's courthouse and business records.[1] The more widely focused work of historians Anne Firor Scott, Joanne Hawks and Sheila Skemp, and Catherine Clinton, among others, on plantation women has since supported Conrad's proposition that there were abundant research opportunities on the role of women in legal and industry records.[2] In Louisiana most such evidence concerns cotton and sugarcane production.[3] Cotton was the primary plantation crop of northern Louisiana. South Louisiana grew both crops, as well as rice, but sugarcane cultivation and milling historically predominated in the region south of Alexandria. After the War of 1812, sugarcane cultivation spread rapidly in Louisiana, first to the river parishes west of New Orleans and then to the south and west of the Atchafalaya Basin. Out on the southwestern Louisiana prairie, in St. Mary Parish, not one but three women played crucial roles in a relatively modest plantation's development into the raw sugar–manufacturing giant M. A. Patout & Son, Ltd.

Today M. A. Patout is Louisiana's largest raw sugar producer by a wide margin. Furthermore, it is the oldest sugar company in the United States still owned and operated by the original family. This company's history illustrates the important supporting roles that women played in the efficient operation of a complex business, which combined producing a crop with manufacturing a product for a national market. Even more significant, however, is that three of the Patout women were key forces in their company's growth from an eighty-one-acre cane farm in 1831 to a forty-thousand-plus-acre agricultural complex spanning

APPOLINE PATOUT

Courtesy of Mrs. George Broussard Sr.

several parishes. Without Appoline and Mary Ann Patout, in particular, and it would be tough to discount Ida Patout, it is likely that Enterprise Plantation would have been among the hundreds of sugar farms that failed to survive the century and a half following the Civil War. Their signal contributions to the company's success illustrate the need for wider research on women in the cane sugar industry, not least because their achievements overshadowed those of many of their male contemporaries and were surpassed by only a few in a time that largely assumed that women did not possess the ability to compete in a business especially notable for its failure rate.

Since 1996, M. A. Patout & Son, Ltd., has owned and operated three raw cane sugar factories: the flagship mill, Enterprise, in Patoutville (Iberia Parish); Sterling Sugars in Franklin (St. Mary Parish); and Raceland Raw Sugars Corporation in Lafourche Parish. Enterprise is the westernmost of the mills, located just under thirty miles south-southeast of Lafayette, the cultural capital of Louisiana's French Triangle.[4] Franklin, the parish seat of St. Mary Parish, is another twenty miles east of Patoutville. Fifty-four miles farther east is the Raceland factory, about thirty-five miles southwest of New Orleans. Even before M. A. Patout acquired Sterling and Raceland in 1994 and 1996, respectively, it was already the largest producer of raw sugar in Louisiana. The Enterprise factory features the latest in continuous, automatic vacuum pan technology and has the first and only cane diffuser in North America. The mill can process 22,000 tons of cane per day and 2.1 million tons over the course of the grinding season. Sterling and Raceland each have the capacity to process 12,500 tons of cane per day and 1.25 million tons for the season. All three mills produce sugar, molasses, and syrup on multiyear contracts. The company owns forty-three thousand acres of land and leases many thousands more.[5] M. A. Patout's remarkable rise to dominance in the past half-century owes much to female leadership in the family's first three generations.

French émigré Napoleone Geneviève "Appoline" Fournier Patout not only kept her family's plantation solvent following her husband's sudden death in 1847, but raised Enterprise Plantation squarely into the planter class even though, as a woman, she could not enjoy the full participation and respect that came with being a sugar planter in antebellum society. With the increasing assistance of her sons, she slowly rebuilt its fortunes after the Civil War. Like her mother-in-law, Mary Ann Schwing Patout found herself suddenly widowed in 1882. After completing her late husband's planting partnership with his brother, Mary Ann successfully executed an expensive, daring program of modernization in a period when most sugar mills were going out of business. Though her gender limited her access to the inner circles of male-dominated planter society, she clearly had the respect of her peers due to her formidable business skills. Ida Patout Burns, Mary Ann's daughter, made her contribution in a much different environment, as a company officer and a board of directors member after the business was incorporated following her mother's death in 1907. These three women, whose service to their family business collectively spanned more than a century, are heretofore largely unknown but noteworthy contributors to the growth of a Louisiana crop and industry with eighteenth-century roots.

When the Patouts arrived in New Orleans, sugarcane was a Louisiana crop with a long history but only quite recent success. Hoping that cane might be a cash crop for the fledgling Louisiana colony, Pierre Lemoine d'Iberville brought seed cane shortly after 1700, only to have it destroyed by flood. Jesuit missionaries planted cane in the 1740s and managed to produce a rough sugar by 1753. Finally, in 1795, after years of experimentation, the failure of commercial indigo cultivation, and the arrival in New Orleans of refugees from the 1791 Haitian Revolution, Antoine Morin successfully granulated sugar for Etienne de Bore. Thereafter, cane cultivation spread upriver and downriver from New Orleans, south and west into the Lafourche country, and eventually westward into the Attakapas District, which included St. Mary Parish.[6] It was there, on Louisiana's southwestern prairie, that French émigré Pierre Simeon Patout and his wife, Appoline, began Enterprise Plantation. In some respects, it is not much more imposing today than it was then. But outward appearances are not infrequently deceiving.

Enterprise sits on the South Louisiana prairie east of New Iberia, the parish seat. The milling complex can easily be seen from Louisiana Highway 90 to the north. Motorists are not likely to be impressed by its appearance. Other than the array of large, steel-sided buildings, not much else is apparent from that vantage point. Indeed, little to no traffic emerges from the exit where the secondary road to the mill bisects the highway. This sleepy picture holds true for about nine months of each year. While the Patout mill does not present itself as one of the country's most important agricultural corporations, drivers passing that way in late October will see steam billowing from the mill's smokestacks, a steady procession of heavily laden cane trucks leaving the highway for Patoutville, and an equally steady parade exiting back onto that thoroughfare for more loads of cane from all over southwestern Louisiana and as far north as Rapides Parish in the state's center. This activity continues well into December. Even then, signs of the place's history only begin to become apparent after one leaves the highway for the road to Patoutville.

The unincorporated hamlet of Patoutville, which has never had a very large population, is only a shadow of its former self. The general store, still standing, has been closed for decades. St. Nicholas Catholic Church, built at the behest of Appoline Patout, was moved to neighboring Lydia almost fifty years ago. The doctor's office and other small community establishments are long gone, though some of the structures remain. The cemetery, adjacent to the old church site, remains; it is filled with Patouts and their relatives and neighbors. Only Appoline Patout is buried outside the formal confines of the cemetery. The founding matriarch of the community, Madame Veuve (Widow) Patout was interred at the foot of the altar in the old St. Nicholas Chapel, which was destroyed by Hurricane Hilda in 1964. Her husband, Simeon, who predeceased her by thirty-two years, is also absent; he is buried a few miles away in St. Peter's Catholic cemetery in New Iberia.[7]

Simeon and Appoline emigrated from Ussy-sur-Marne, probably right after Christmas in 1828. Pierre Simeon Patout was a *vigneron*, a grower of wine grapes, in the old Champagne district east of Paris. The married couple boarded the *Crescent* with two infants from their 1826 union and three sons from Simeon's first marriage, to Marie Louise Morel. The family arrived in New Orleans in late January 1829. The 1830 census lists Simeon as a planter in St. Mary Parish who owned eight slaves. The family's arrival in St. Mary Parish fortuitously coincided with the continuing expansion of cane cultivation into the area's Isle Aux Cannes section south of Bayou Teche, although it is not clear that Simeon Patout immediately committed to cane cultivation. Family tradition holds that his initial plan was to start a vineyard. Simeon's business instincts were good. By 1840 he owned seventy-five slaves, a growing landholding (much of it unimproved), a successful general merchandise store, and a recently completed house, Enterprise, for his rapidly expanding family. During these same years, Appoline gave birth to six more children.[8]

It appears that Simeon spent part of the 1830s in an unsuccessful attempt to create a vineyard. Finding this difficult, he apparently turned to general farming and cattle raising while at the same time clearing and ditching land for sugarcane cultivation.[9] Given the considerable time required to develop a sugar plantation, the Patout store and the community that grew up around it must have provided a substantial part of the family income over the first decade and a half, because the first recorded sugar production at his budding plantation did not come until the 1845 season. The following year, in 1846, Simeon began developing another plot some miles away at Grand Lake. However, his tenure as a sugar planter was brief, and most of his thousand acres or so remained unimproved. Simeon Patout succumbed to yellow fever on September 21, 1847, leaving behind a crop in the fields, a widow, and nine children, one of them a newborn.[10]

Appoline, the Madame Veuve Patout, then forty-two years old, had to bury her husband, cope with the continuing yellow fever epidemic, and brace for the landfall of a strong hurricane, all while caring for children and attending to the transfer of Simeon's estate (held in two countries) to his heirs. To her also fell management of the *roulaison*, the arduous, expensive cane harvesting and sugar-making season on which their futures would depend. Agricultural historian Lewis Gray called it "a season of severe pressure when the manufacture of sugar was carried on night and day." For all practical purposes, Madame Veuve Patout spoke no English. Her eldest son, Armand Hippolyte, was only seventeen, but had been a store clerk for two years already. Additionally, she had the assistance of her stepsons, Isadore and Philippe, who remained at Enterprise as overseers for two years. Equally fortunate was that Madame Patout proved to be a shrewd businesswoman who did much more than simply mark time until her eldest natural sons might take over.[11]

In accordance with Louisiana's Napoleonic legal tradition, and apparently with the family's approval, the widow Patout became administrator of the estate. She purchased all community property at prices set by an impartial estate inventory conducted by male neighbors. She provided each heir with a mortgage representing their share of the inheritance, sold off the Grand Lake property, and authorized her Parisian sister, Zelie, to recoup ten thousand francs invested in Napoleon's treasury. Appoline may have subsequently returned to France to advance the claim, which Louis Napoleon's government finally recognized in 1854. At this juncture, she also appears to have sold the Patout property in Ussy-sur-Marne, probably to Simeon's sister.[12]

Following a good crop in 1848, milling problems led the widow Patout to have four cast iron friction rollers installed in her mill, so as to reduce by a third the horsepower required to operate the mill. They did not work well, and she was forced to restore the previous equipment. Despite this setback, the plantation had another successful season, and Appoline remained interested in technical improvements in the increasingly complex business of turning cane into sugar. In 1850, Isadore and Philippe purchased their own plantation just west of Appoline's, and operated as Patout & Patout. For a brief period thereafter, she relied solely on her son Hippolyte for assistance. Even then, however, it was clear that she was in charge, reporting Enterprise Plantation's production as that of A. Patout.[13]

Appoline Patout was a leader in the rapidly growing rural community out on Prairie Isle Piquant. A devout woman, she had long wanted to build a church for Isle Piquant Catholics. In 1849, she notified the archbishop of New Orleans, Antoine Blanc, that she had commissioned a design for a church. A year later, she prevailed upon neighbor Charles Olivier to donate ten acres adjacent to her house for a church, and construction began in 1851. In April 1852, the new pastor at St. Peter's Church in New Iberia, Father J. E. Blin, celebrated the first mass at St. Nicholas Chapel. In July, Blin reported a donation of eighteen acres to the church, ten from Olivier for the chapel grounds and eight from Patout for a cemetery. Biweekly masses by priests from St. Peter's were the rule for the first few years, but eventually, with Appoline providing monetary support, St. Nicholas received a priest of its own and "Madame Patout's Chapel" grew into St. Nicholas Parish.[14] Appoline's contributions to her small rural community later caused a person who knew her well to dub her the "Mother of Patoutville."

Meanwhile, Appoline continued to build on Simeon's legacy, purchasing more slaves and more land on her own. Apparently when it came to her labor force, Madame Patout could be a hard taskmaster. In 1851, she sued Darius

Legnon, a neighboring small farmer, in St. Mary Parish Court, demanding repayment because Richard, a slave she purchased from him, kept running away from her. Legnon responded that Richard ran away because of harsh treatment. This may well have been so. Duke University historian Thavolia Glymph has argued persuasively that the plantation household was a locus of power in which plantation mistresses wielded real, often violent, power.[15] A plantation mistress who also managed the plantation would thus have had ample prior experience with bending slaves to her will, whatever the method. In any event, the case was dismissed, with the costs borne by Patout. Presumably the court found Mr. Legnon's reasoning for Richard's derelict behavior more persuasive than that offered by Patout.[16]

Not easily deterred by the misfortunes attendant to raising cane and making sugar, Appoline began an expansion program in 1856, a year when the South Louisiana sugar crop was largely destroyed by the Last Island Hurricane. That year, Madame Veuve Patout's plantation produced only fourteen hogsheads, roughly sixteen thousand pounds, of sugar.[17] With much of the cane destroyed, she and other planters had to reserve much of what cane remained for the next year's seed. Even so, she was able to purchase almost one hundred arpents (an arpent equals .91 acres) of new land that year; she purchased three hundred arpents more on her northern boundary the following March. Appoline also bought and resold at a considerable profit several forty-arpent tracts in the late 1850s. Then, on April 12, 1860, a year to the day before Confederate cannons fired on Fort Sumter, she bought an additional nine hundred arpents from Charles Olivier, bringing her holdings north to the edge of the Grand Marais.[18]

By the start of the Civil War, Appoline Patout was a substantial planter. She owned twenty-one hundred acres of land, with some five hundred acres of it under cultivation or otherwise improved. Her plantation store was the retail and social hub for Isle Piquant. There were quite a few planters with larger holdings, especially with regard to improved acreage, in St. Mary Parish, but many, many more had smaller plantations and workforces. The Agricultural Census of 1860 valued Patout's plantation at $50,000. In addition, Patout listed livestock worth $8,000, machinery and implements valued at $12,000, and a personal estate estimated at $90,000. To work her land, she had 58 draft animals (horses, mules, oxen). Self-sufficient in meat production, she had 60 pigs, 50 sheep, and 104 head of cattle (four of them milk cows). To feed the animals, she raised her own hay and feed corn. Despite a dry spring and summer, and three severe storms in the late summer and early fall, she made 145 hogsheads of sugar. Certainly, the 107 slaves she owned did most of that work.[19]

The successful management of the plantation, however, was largely due to Appoline's own business acumen. While male planters might have questioned the propriety of a woman engaged in their much-admired profession, few could dispute her ability at it. Appoline Fournier Patout had been twenty-three when she arrived in Louisiana with two babies and three stepchildren. Married at twenty-one, she was a literate, politically aware, self-possessed, and intrepid person who had crossed an ocean to forge a new life in a strange land. While she undoubtedly deferred to her husband to some degree, she was also a contributing member of a plantation household who could read and calculate. She managed the household and perhaps even the store. She supervised a household staff of slaves, a job that required a firm hand, including corporal punishment to, as Elizabeth Fox-Genovese put it, "maintain order among people who were always supposed to be on call; among people who inevitably disappointed expectations."[20]

After Simeon Patout's death, Appoline had stepped up her involvement in the business. The phenomenon of widows managing their deceased husbands' plantations was not uncommon. Noting that in the South the odds of widowhood for a married white woman were virtually even, historian Kirsten Wood estimates that about 10 percent of antebellum plantation "masters" were women. These widows hired and fired overseers, foreclosed mortgages, secured the debts of others, negotiated contracts, and managed their relations with their enslaved workforces and other planters and farmers. In the process they developed their own versions of mastery. Add to this that they sometimes substantially expanded and improved their husbands' holdings, and Appoline Patout fits squarely into this mold.[21]

In 1857, Isadore Patout died at the age of thirty-six, leaving his brother Philippe to oversee the fortunes of Patout & Patout for his family and that of his late brother. Meanwhile, Appoline's eldest natural son, Hippolyte, was developing nine hundred acres of his own in Iberville Parish. Between 1849 and 1852, his younger brother Felix was at school, first at the College of St. Charles (Grand Coteau, Louisiana) and then at Georgetown University.[22] Though he was a capable planter, sugar production was never as compelling to Felix as was city life and other types of business. It was Appoline, then, who bought and sold land and slaves, employed overseers and storekeepers, and kept the mill running and in good repair. It was she who sued people over business disputes and determined contracts for Patout sugars and molasses. On the eve of the Civil War, this devout widow's public life clearly countered the prevailing concept of women as mere keepers of the household. She was an astute, hard-driving planter both able and willing to compete with her male counterparts in the sugar business.[23]

In November 1860, Louisiana Creole voters helped to carry the southernmost sugar parishes for presidential candidate John Bell, who advocated continued union under the U.S. Constitution. He lost, of course, to the Republican Abraham Lincoln, and the subsequent secession of eleven southern states led to war in April 1861. Even so, that fall Louisiana sugar planters brought in the best crop of the entire antebellum era. Still, the Civil War proved to be a devastating experience for Madame Patout and her family. With much less stake in his fledgling Iberville plantation, Hippolyte returned to Isle Piquant in 1863 to assist his mother. New Orleans had fallen to the Union in 1862 and its forces briefly occupied the Patout plantation in April 1863, confiscating wagons, livestock, food, and other supplies. Following Union departure, Appoline went to New Orleans, where she had a justice of the peace draft a petition swearing that she had taken the oath of neutrality required of foreign nationals and demanded payment for confiscations in the amount of $10,500.[24]

There was worse to come, however. Following General William Franklin's disastrous Great Texas Overland Expedition, retreating Union forces occupied and ransacked the Patout plantation for three days in November 1863. In Madame Patout's words, "Alone with her daughters, the petitioner was forced to let everything be done, to endure all outrage . . . since the soldiers were intent on seeing everything and appropriating all that they fancied." Following their departure, a band of blacks attached to Franklin's Nineteenth Army Corps carried off additional property. Elements of the Thirteenth and Nineteenth Army Corps made more visits in December and January, taking corn and dismantling barns and fences for military use. Determined to defend her property rights, Appoline went to General Franklin's New Iberia headquarters to seek compensation but was denied an interview. Years later, Emilien Landry, a neighbor of the Patouts, was asked to describe the Patout plantation at war's end. He testified simply that "immediately after the war the Patout Plantation was almost naked. The residence and a portion of the sugarhouse were standing and there was no fencing on it. There were a few cabins. It had during the war been very much devastated."[25]

Faced with the arduous task of rebuilding, Appoline entered a partnership with Hippolyte after the war. Confederate veteran Felix had moved to France, though in 1876, when his mother's health began to fail, he returned and joined the partnership the following year. Appoline died on March 1, 1879. Born in a small French village, she left behind a church, a community, and "one of the largest estates" of recently formed Iberia Parish. Following a protracted and disputed estate settlement, Hippolyte and Felix successfully purchased the plantation from the remaining heirs on April 4, 1881, and entered into a partnership to operate the plantation over the next five years.[26] Both Hippolyte and Felix were in their forties, and a return to male leadership of the family's fortunes seemed assured, as both men had male heirs nearing adulthood. However, the brothers only produced one crop together, a short harvest in 1881.

Hippolyte died unexpectedly at age fifty on April 8, 1882, leaving his wife, Mary Ann, in partnership with Felix. Both of Mary Ann Schwing's grandfathers were Germans from the Franco-German region of Alsace-Lorraine. Each immigrated to the United States and married there. Jacob Anselm's daughter, Christina, married John Godfried Schwing's sugar planter son, George, in Louisiana in 1833. Mary Ann was their second child. At age sixteen, in 1852, she married

Hippolyte Patout, nine years her senior, at her Iberville Parish home on Bayou Bouef. She brought to this union her own knowledge of the cultivation and culture of sugar learned from her parents. The couple had ten children, the last born in 1878. Mary Ann completed the partnership with Felix, purchased his interest in 1886, and made her eldest son, Hippolyte Jr., the plantation manager.[27]

Like Appoline, Mary Ann entered a male-dominated planting world. Perhaps emulating Appoline, who reported her crop returns and sugar production simply as A. Patout so as not to draw undue attention to her gender, Mary Ann used the term M. A. Patout in her business dealings. If anything, there were fewer female sugar planters after the Civil War than before, primarily because there were fewer plantations. Despite the enormous changes constituting what the historian Paul Johnson terms "the birth of the modern," relatively little had changed with regard to attitudes toward the place of women in industrializing societies. Women—southern, white planter women especially—were supposed to be domestic creatures. If they worked, women were expected to conform to gender-prescribed jobs such as teachers, secretaries, seamstresses, or perhaps nurses—all acceptable extensions of their domestic roles. On plantations, they ran the household, reared children, and managed the family garden. Though these were held to be their places in a hierarchical, male-run society, plantation mistresses inevitably learned important aspects of the business, sometimes from observation and conversation, but also because literate women were capable of providing clerical and managerial assistance in addition to fulfilling the social obligations expected of planter families. This was even more true after the Civil War, as the challenges of recovery gave way to rapid change in Louisiana's postwar sugar industry.[28]

The escalating transformation in sugar manufacturing technology following Reconstruction respected neither race, creed, nor gender. The advantage would go to those with financial and technological acumen, irrespective of sex. In this regard, the Patouts were enormously fortunate that one of their women broke the gender barrier and became a leader in the great shakeout in the Louisiana sugar industry, which dominated the last two decades of the nineteenth century. By 1880, southern Louisiana's sugar district had largely recovered from the war years, but plantations still using animal-powered mills and open-kettle sugar-making were rapidly being squeezed out by larger, capital-intensive, central mills employing steam engines to crush the cane and vacuum pans to reduce the resulting liquid to molasses and sugar.

In addition to achieving greater economies of scale, the new mills also reduced fuel costs and produced higher-grade sugars. Increasingly, open-kettle producers faced either modernizing their mills or selling their cane to central mills. The vast majority ceased to be planters in the traditional sense of that word and opted instead to become cane farmers. Enterprise was poised between past and present, using a modest steam engine to power a three-roller mill to crush cane and open kettles to make syrup and sugar. Sufficient for its cane crop and that of its immediate neighbors, the Patout mill needed new equipment. The Patout plantation had limped along in the years following the war, with attention to immediate needs, but nothing more.[29]

In 1887, M. A. Patout began an improvement program on the two hundred or so acres surrounding the home place. This initial effort centered on increasing transportation efficiencies. It included extensive ditching to improve drainage, and building or repairing 105 bridges. Given the rapidly eroding market for kettle sugars, to buy time until she could erect a central mill, she built a four-and-a-half-mile-long pipeline to ship syrup. This 23,000-foot line of two-and-a-half-inch pipe to a landing on Bayou Teche, laid after the 1888 season, ended the expensive, time-consuming practice of hauling sugar to that location on eight-mule team wagons, two hogsheads at a time. Previously, a roundtrip could take twenty hours if the roads were muddy. From Bayou Teche, the syrup went by barge to the Vaufrey Refinery in nearby Jeanerette. While the more common practice was to sell cane to central mills, shipping syrup enabled Mary Ann to keep her mill in operation until she could modernize it. For the 1891 and 1892 seasons, M. A. Patout shipped syrup equivalent to 1.45 million pounds of sugar each year.[30]

Having reduced costs associated with the processing of cane at the mill, Mary Ann and Hippolyte Jr. decided that a narrow-gauge railway would enable them to move cane from fields to mill more economically and in almost any kind of weather. Muddy roads could slow and even halt the timely delivery of cane to a mill, which optimally would have operated around the clock. Following the 1892 crop season, M. A. Patout concluded rights-of-way agreements with eighteen Isle Piquant landowners necessary for the development of an Enterprise rail system. The ensuing seventeen-miles of narrow-gauge railroad track comprised a circuit extending as far as ten miles from the Enterprise mill, enabling the mill to more efficiently gather cane from the dozens of small, white-owned farms whose development they had encouraged during the Reconstruction era transition from slavery to a free labor system.[31]

No record remains of the earliest locomotives, but in 1893, Enterprise processed cane equivalent to almost 3.4 million pounds of sugar despite a rain in late November that flooded cart roads for days. The rail system enabled deliveries to continue largely unabated. The large output in 1893 was augmented by a two-cents-a-pound federal sugar bounty that was to remain in place until 1905, another factor justifying the large capital investments. The company took delivery of a Porter locomotive with tender (fuel supply space) built especially for them in 1897 and a new Dickson full tender locomotive in 1901. Each pulled four-ton cars out to cane-loading sites, largely eliminating the need for dozens of mule-drawn carts, thus reducing labor and livestock costs.

In 1894, M. A. Patout returned to making its own sugar. Mary Ann spent

$24,523 for modern sugar-making equipment for a new refinery at Hubertville on Bayou Teche that began operating in 1895. Meanwhile, in the fall of 1894, she made slightly over 3.5 million pounds of vacuum pan sugars at the upgraded factory at Enterprise. The following year, Enterprise resumed piping molasses, this time to its own refinery. In the 1896 season, the Hubertville bayou-side refinery, equipped with a steam train, vacuum pans, and centrifugals (to mechanically separate molasses from raw sugars), granulated four million pounds of sugar.[32] For the 1898 crop, nearly new double-effect evaporators previously used in the syrup-making prairie mill at Enterprise were installed at Hubertville.[33] By the new century, M. A. Patout & Son had made the transition to central factory status without having to mortgage their property. Indeed, the industry journal *Louisiana Planter and Sugar Manufacturer* described the area surrounding the thriving hamlet of Patoutville as one of the richest parts of Iberia Parish, with Enterprise featuring a brand new sawmill and factory in addition to the modernized sugar mill.[34]

Adroit enough to keep the company's surplus capital working, Mary Ann Patout understood that the lumber milling operation would enable her to exploit the virgin cypress swamp that formed the southern part of Enterprise. It also put to good use the mules and wagons, which had been freed up by the installation of the railroad. Mary Ann was also active in local banking, buying stock in both the New Iberia National Bank and the People's National Bank of New Iberia. In 1887, her brother-in-law, Felix, became a founding director of the New Iberia National Bank, the region's first national bank. Mary Ann was later appointed to the board; she seems to have been the first woman in Louisiana to occupy that position in a bank of any magnitude. Her brother-in-law's likely influence notwithstanding, it represented a measure of the respect Patout's male peers had for her business sense.[35]

In 1901, under the direction of Mary Ann, M. A. Patout & Son was the leading sugar manufacturer in Iberia Parish, producing almost one million pounds of sugar more than its closest competitor. In 1904, the company installed new brickwork under the boilers, raised a new smokestack, and bought a Thornton derrick to improve the transfer of cane to the mill's carrier. Another departure was the change to the D74 cane variety developed at the Sugar Experiment Station, which had been established by the Louisiana Board of Agriculture on Louisiana State University property in Baton Rouge in 1886. The first sugarcane varieties grown in Louisiana were "Creole," from which Etienne De Bore first granulated sugar, and "Otaheite." These essentially Caribbean plants gradually gave way to "Louisiana Striped," "Louisiana Purple," and "D74." Styled "Noble" canes, these varieties featured larger stalk diameters, lower fiber content, and sucrose levels satisfactory for sugar production under Louisiana conditions.[36]

In 1906, the *Louisiana Planter* reported that a new, larger mill was en route to Patoutville. Capable of grinding one thousand tons of cane daily, the six-roller mill was powered by a Corliss Birmingham steam engine, with cane transmitted to the crushers by a new feeder. The resulting cane juice was processed by larger boilers and new evaporation equipment. In the 1906 season, Mary Ann's last, Enterprise produced 4.8 million pounds of sugar. Mary Ann Patout died suddenly on July 10, 1907, leaving an estate worth over $300,000, much of it invested in a company that had survived the great reduction in the number of sugar mills in the late nineteenth century and emerged modernized, ready for the challenges of a new century. The *Louisiana Planter* and the board of directors of New Iberia National Bank praised her "fine business qualities" and her "remarkable good judgment" respectively.[37]

Following Mary Ann's death, her children began planning for an arrangement that would permanently avoid another succession dispute such as had occurred following Appoline's death. The heirs created a family-owned, limited-liability corporation, with each family purchasing shares of stock according to its relative interest in M. A. Patout & Son. Each child had a one-eighth interest in Enterprise Plantation. Each also held an equal interest in Mary Ann's two-thirds holdings in the planting and manufacturing partnership with Hippolyte Jr. This partnership included the sugarhouse, the railroad and its rolling stock, the pipeline, and the refinery. As partner, Hippolyte held the remaining one-third interest. Each child, or inheriting grandchildren if their parent was deceased, sold his or her one-eighth interest to the new company, M. A. Patout & Son, Ltd., for $34,000, or 340 shares of capital stock. Hippolyte Jr. sold his heir's portion and his one-third of the partnership for $112,000, or 1,120 shares of stock. In addition, he became the company president, a position he held until his death in 1930.[38]

These changes were certainly in the best interests of the family and its business. However, they would substantially alter the possibilities for future leadership by women. Hippolyte's younger brother, William Schwing Patout, known as Willie, was also a member of the initial board of directors. Hippolyte Jr. was, of course, the logical successor to his mother's leadership, both through long experience and familiarity with the ever-more-complex operations of a growing company competing in a world market. Though the incorporation did indeed provide for stability across the generations, it also greatly diminished the possibility that another woman would lead the company by minimizing widowhood as a factor in determining a new director.

While community property laws with regard to inheritance continued to apply, stock ownership was now dispersed among the heirs of Mary Ann, and the board of directors would recommend to stockholders who should lead the company in cooperation with the board. At any given future time, the company president's widow would automatically receive half of her late husband's stock, but the days of a widow owning 50 percent of the entire operation were gone. It was not that there would be no role for women, however. Willie and Hippolyte's sister, Ida, became a director and the company's vice president, when the new corporation actually commenced business in 1911. Very few women in the country would have held such a position in this era, and once again it was a testament to ability rather than kinship or survivorship.[39]

Ida Patout Burns was no mere cipher. She undoubtedly learned much from her mother, both in terms of example and even particulars, about the business of sugar. She benefited from a very good private school education. Further, as the wife of New Orleans businessman James Henry Burns, she was well located for keeping up with the sugar business since the wholesaling of sugar was done in the Crescent City. Midway through World War I, she wrote Hippolyte that sugar prices were so high that people might soon be growing cane rather than vegetables in their backyards. She remained vice president through the prosperous war years and the depressed, crop-disease-challenged 1920s and 1930s. Upon Hippolyte's death, Willie became company president. With the support of Ida and his brother Rivers, the new board secretary, Willie continued modernization of the mill until his sudden death on the eve of the 1942 harvest. Two days later, the board named Ida president and William S. Patout Jr. plantation manager. Ida was empowered to employ a new sugar warehouseman to replace William Jr. A month later, under her direction, the company began a long-term program of modernizing M. A. Patout & Son's antiquated accounting systems.[40]

While this undertaking was timely, it could not prevent a short-term but serious crisis for the company. World War II exacerbated this condition with wartime regulations, excess-profits taxes, and the most rapid mechanization in industry history revealing glaring weaknesses in company recordkeeping and producing a serious cash flow crisis. In February 1943, the board authorized the hiring of an accounting firm whose audit not only regularized its piecemeal financial records but also found it $39,000 in refunds for extra taxes paid in 1942 and 1943. Additional refunds for fiscal 1943 and 1944 brought in almost $80,000 more to the company, considerably relieving the shortage of operating funds and any continuing threat to M. A. Patout & Son's solvency. Ida Patout Burns continued as company president until her death midway through the successful 1956 grinding season. She was succeeded as president by her son, J. Patout Burns, who moved from his position as the company's secretary-treasurer, a post then assumed by William Patout Jr., who continued as company manager until he turned the reins over to his son, Williams S. Patout III.[41]

Since then, M. A. Patout & Son, Ltd., has, by and large, been run by male family members. Though the family is justly proud of its history and is not reticent about the defining role of women in its company's success, few contemporaries are aware of it. Even fewer are aware of the now readily available documentary sources that might uncover important other female figures in what at first glance might appear to be a male-only business.

Under ordinary circumstances, plantation women did not direct the operations of these productive enterprises. They did, however, play important supporting roles that to varying extents mirrored those of their sisters in the middle and working classes. For example, they managed the plantation gardens, supervised food preservation, and oversaw meal preparations while their farm and housewife counterparts tended their gardens, did their own canning and curing, and personally saw to the cooking and cleaning. They saw to social obligations and the children, though often not as personally as did women of more modest means. When, as did Appoline and Mary Ann Patout, they successfully moved out of their supporting roles into management, they nonetheless maintained lower public profiles than had their deceased spouses, helping to obscure their historic roles.[42] All of these were vital, often undervalued contributions at a time when families were primarily units of production. With the growing importance of incorporation, and the parallel but more gradual transition of most families from production to consumption, women's functions changed accordingly. Rural southern Louisiana women might continue to garden, preserving a gendered connection to the earth rapidly being severed by the rise of the canning industry, refrigeration, and a national railroad network. Whether they did or not, they were increasingly drawn into a money economy, which diminished their traditional functions in favor of those that earned wages for, say, heading shrimp for so much a bucket at a local shrimp shed or doing some other basic processing work. With the growing use of processed foods, the plantation garden became less significant, as did the preservation of food. This meant a reduction of managerial functions ordinarily the province of plantation mistresses.[43]

At M. A. Patout & Son, Ltd., incorporation ensured that the business would endure but also added institutional layers of complexity to decision-making. Thus, Ida Patout Burns, a very capable businesswoman and leader, was important to her company's success. But, since she did not directly manage the company's operations, she did not play a role as central to its growth as did her female predecessors, Appoline and Mary Ann. Part of the reason is that, with incorporation, and the cessation of direction solely by a single planter, the business of the company for the first time was clearly separated from the household, its functions clearly vested in a management team selected by a board composed of stockholding family members. As of this writing, the six-member board of directors and the officers of the corporation are all male.[44] It has not always been so and may well change in the future. But it does seem unlikely that conditions exist for the emergence of another female chief executive at a company whose dominant position in Louisiana sugar owes so much to its women. Despite the many contributions of women to the industry, the sugar business culture remains very much a male preserve to this day.

What is more certain is that there are many more female sugar planters in Louisiana's past, some successful and some not, with careers worthy of scholarly attention. Historian Richard Follett has created a remarkable Louisiana sugar history website at the University of Sussex. Much of it is based on the annual crop reports of P. A. Champomier (1844–60, 1868–69), Louis S. Bouchereau (1868–77), and his son, Alcee (1878–1917). These three men, in effect early agricultural economists, produced their detailed reports by personally visiting the plantations whose activities they chronicled. The French-born Champomier noted that it required three months of travel, largely by horseback and boat, each year to produce his annual edition. Louis Bouchereau, who added valuable new detail to sugar reportage, perhaps died on the job; his final decline was attributed to exposure to extremely cold and wet weather during the 1877 harvest. Alcee Bouchereau's annual sugar pilgrimage required five months of his time, despite improved roads and transportation. There was more to report on a rapidly industrializing business, and he added increasingly sophisticated statistical tables to his work.[45]

This enormously useful scholarly site includes a Louisiana Sugar Harvest Database. Its General Statistics and Searches function enables searches of plantation records by categories, including one listing "Female Headed Plantations: Ordered by Year." Over the seven decades of reporting, there were 803 entries for Appoline's home parish of St. Mary. Interested scholars will find this a valuable springboard for deeper research into the largely neglected work of these planters, both large and small. A substantial number of these women were more than just caretakers of their farming and milling operations. One contemporary of Appoline's was Louisa Fuselier, who assumed management of the Fuselier family's horse-powered mill when her husband died. She continued with the traditional horse mill for three seasons and then invested in the relatively new steam technology pioneered by Norbert Rillieux in the 1840s. St. Mary planter Elizabeth Cochrane, like Appoline, continued to use horses from 1845 to 1862, in her final year producing a very respectable 240 hogsheads, or about a quarter-million pounds, of sugar.[46]

Admittedly, St. Mary Parish, in the heart of the Sugar Bowl, had a heavier planter population than most parishes. In southeastern Louisiana, Terrebonne Parish had 320 women planters; adjacent Lafourche Parish had 658. St. Bernard produced only 51 and Tangipahoa Parish on the north side of Lake Pontchartrain had none. On the Mississippi River, St. James Parish accounted for 826 entries and its eastern neighbor, St. John the Baptist, showed 450 females running plantations at various junctures. There were thus significant geographic variations in the sugar parishes. Furthermore, none of these figures signify that number of different women, given that many widows ran their businesses for many years and thus appeared as multiple entries. Nonetheless, there were twenty-eight parishes that produced sugar. In other words, Appoline, Mary Ann, and Ida were not alone.[47]

Though women scarcely register in histories of sugar planters other than as wives and mothers, in their time women who successfully managed and expanded their interests in an industry as fraught with risk as the sugar business were better known and appreciated at the time than they would be later when industry histories came to be written. Arguably, a greater percentage of late-nineteenth-century Louisianans living in their state's Sugar Bowl knew that the "M. A." in "M. A. Patout" stood for "Mary Ann." While certain social and political features of male planter culture remained more or less sacrosanct, the fact is that these successful female planters' business acumen, technical knowledge, and managerial ability could not be anything but respected by their contemporaries and their peers. These were women who, whatever their other qualities, exhibited business skills and competitiveness held to be largely if not exclusively the province of males in nineteenth and early-twentieth-century American culture.

NOTES

1. The late Glenn Conrad is one of the great figures in the development of Louisiana history. Conrad served as the secretary-treasurer of the Louisiana Historical Association, editor of *Louisiana History*, and founding director of the Center for Louisiana Studies at the University of Louisiana at Lafayette. He nurtured the careers of a number of Louisiana historians while maintaining an active research agenda of his own. Under his supervision the center published invaluable works like the two-volume *Dictionary of Louisiana Biography* (New Orleans: Louisiana Historical Association, 1988) and nineteen-volume *The Louisiana Purchase Bicentennial Series in Louisiana History* (Lafayette: Center for Louisiana Studies, 1995–2004).

2. Anne Firor Scott, *The Southern Lady: From Pedestal to Politics* (Chicago: University of Chicago Press, 1970); Joanne V. Hawks and Sheila L. Skemp, eds., *Sex, Race, and the Role of Women in the South* (Jackson: University Press of Mississippi, 1983); Catherine Clinton, *Plantation Mistress: Women's World in the Old South* (New York: Pantheon, 1984). See also Kirsten E. Wood, *Masterful Women: Slaveholding Widows from the American Revolution through the Civil War* (Chapel Hill: University of North Carolina Press, 2006). My friend and colleague Sheila Phipps provided invaluable assistance in getting me better acquainted with the issues and literature of nineteenth-century U.S. women's history.

3. Rice farming in southwestern Louisiana developed with the extension of rail lines west into that region in the 1880s.

4. Also known as Acadiana, the French Triangle is a subregion of Louisiana that historically has been heavily influenced by Acadian French and continental French culture. Its apex is either Pointe Coupee or Avoyelles Parish to the north (definitions vary). Its base is defined by Cameron Parish in western Louisiana and by Lafourche Parish to the east.

5. M. A. Patout & Son, Ltd., http://www.mapatout.com/ (accessed November 11, 2011).

6. J. Carlyle Sitterson, *Sugar Country: The Cane Sugar Industry in the South, 1753–1950* (Lexington: University of Kentucky Press, 1953), 3–6.

7. Michael G. Wade, *Sugar Dynasty: M. A. Patout and Son, Ltd., 1791–1993* (Lafayette: Center for Louisiana Studies, 1995).

8. U.S. Bureau of the Census, *Fifth Census of the United States (Louisiana, St. Mary Parish), Schedule of Free Inhabitants, of Slaves, and of Agriculture* (Washington, D.C., 1830); one of the slaves was seventeen-year-old Patsy. See Robert McCarty to Simeon Patout, June 15, 1829, St. Mary Mortgage Record no. 940, book 4, folio, 410, Clerk of Court's Office, St. Mary Parish Courthouse, Franklin, Louisiana; Simeon's youngest son, Felix, wrote that his father first worked as an overseer on a St. Mary Plantation, probably Martial Sorrel's, not too far from where Simeon eventually bought prop-

erty. Felix Patout to Ernest Burguieres, ca. 1917–18, copy in possession of Mrs. George Patout Broussard, New Iberia, Louisiana; U.S. Bureau of the Census, *Sixth Census of the United States (Louisiana, St. Mary Parish), Schedule of Free Inhabitants, of Slaves, and of Agriculture* (Washington, D.C., 1840).

9. There is a surviving, small brick building on the original property, which seems to have been for wine storage.

10. "Comparative Statement of Sugar Produced in the Parish of St. Mary in 1843, '44, '45, '46 and '47," *Franklin Planters' Banner*, February 10, 1848. Patout made ninety-nine hogsheads of sugar in 1845 at the home place on Prairie Isle Piquant. This report also shows another plantation near Grand Lake, with Jean Baptiste Meynard, with a cane crop scheduled for 1847; the assumption about the ability of the store to support the Patouts seems quite reasonable. At Patout's death, the store listed accounts receivable of $21,499.63 on store accounts and interest-bearing loans made by Patout. Succession of Simeon Patout, January 5, 1848, Original Estate Book A, no. 629, 52, Clerk of Court's Office, St. Mary Parish.

11. Lewis Cecil Gray, *History of Agriculture in the Southern United States to 1860*, 2 vols. (Washington, D.C.: Carnegie Institution of Washington, 1932), 2:749; Succession of Appoline Patout, March 2, 1879, Probate Book 5, no. 287, Clerk of Court's Office, Iberia Parish Courthouse, New Iberia, La., 322 (hereafter Succession of Appoline Patout).

12. Succession of Simeon Patout; Appoline Patout to W. P. Allen and R. B. Wynne, October 17, 1848, St. Mary Mortgage 7441, book 13, 398.

13. "Friction Rollers for Sugar Mills," *Planters' Banner*, May 17, 1849; Alanson B. Leavitt v. Appoline Patout, January 3, 1850, St. Mary Civil Suit 4107, St. Mary Parish Clerk of Court; Isidore [Isadore] Patout to Philippe Patout, December 24, 1849, St. Mary Recorded Mortgage 7732, Book 13, 595, St. Mary Parish Clerk of Court.

14. Appoline Patout to Bishop Anthony Blanc, November 2, 1849, Archives of the Archdiocese of New Orleans; Appoline Patout to Anthony Blanc, et al., May 7, 1852, Donation 176, Donation Book A, 204, St. Mary Parish Clerk of Court; Roger Baudier, *The Catholic Church in Louisiana* (New Orleans: Roger Baudier, 1939), 391. For a wealth of information on early priests in the area, see Glenn Conrad's annotation of William R. Burke, "A History of St. Peter's Parish: New Iberia, Louisiana, 1838–1888," in the *Attakapas Gazette* 26 (1991): 98–110.

15. Thavolia Glymph, *Out of the House of Bondage: The Transformation of the Plantation Household* (Cambridge University Press, 2008), 3–7. Glymph observed that, during the Civil War, domestic workers were often the first to flee the plantation, perhaps in reaction to the violence visited upon them by their mistresses.

16. *Appoline Patout v. Darius Legnon*, October 4, 1851, St. Mary Parish Civil Suit 4394.

17. A hogshead varied in weight, but 1,100 pounds was a fair approximation for a hogshead of sugar.

18. Wade, *Sugar Dynasty*, 61.

19. U.S. Bureau of the Census, *Eighth Census of the United States (Louisiana, St. Mary Parish), Schedules of Free Inhabitants, of Slaves, and of Agriculture* (Washington, D.C., 1860). P. A. Champomier, *Statement of the Sugar Crop, 1860–61*, vii, 30.

20. As her full name indicates, Appoline came from a family of Bonapartists; Elizabeth Fox-Genovese, *Within the Plantation Household: Black and White Women of the Old South* (Chapel Hill: University of North Carolina Press, 1988), 24. Noting that networks of households were the matrix of the plantation South, Fox-Genovese emphasized that this phenomenon enabled southerners to confine labor and gender relations to the private sphere, rather than to the public sphere of the market economy, as in the North (38).

21. Wood, *Masterful Women*, 3–10.

22. Wade, *Sugar Dynasty*, 58–59.

23. Ibid., 50–67.

24. *Hippolyte Patout v. the United States*, claim no. 239, French and American Claims Commis-

sion, record group 76, National Archives and Records Administration, Washington, D.C. Though the Patouts pursued the claim until 1918, they were unsuccessful in securing any payment for their losses. This was typical of the fate of most of the more than seven hundred claimants.

25. "Reclamation de Madame Veuve Patout contre les Etats-Unis, $56,234," George P. Broussard Family Papers, New Iberia, Louisiana; *Patout v. United States*; Richard Bache Irwin, *History of the Nineteenth Army Corps* (New York: G. P. Putnam's Sons, 1892), 132; Records of the Army Continental Commands, Department of the Gulf, record group 393, vol. 472, 16; David C. Edmonds, *Yankee Autumn in Acadiana: A Narrative of the Great Texas Overland Expedition through Southwestern Louisiana October–December 1863* (Lafayette, La.: Acadiana Press,1979), 29–49; George H. Hepworth, *Whip, Hoe and Sword, or The Gulf Department in '63* (Boston: Walker, Wise, 1864), 92; Michael G. Wade, "Justice Delayed: *Appoline Patout v. The United States*, 1864–1918," *Louisiana History* 31 (Spring 1990): 148. Emilien Landry was testifying to the condition of the plantation in regard to settling the estate of Appoline Patout.

26. Succession of Appoline Patout, 265–67, 270, 312–13, 323, 410–15; *Louisiana Sugar Bowl* (New Iberia, La.), March 13, 1879; Copartnership between H. and F. Patout, June 3, 1881, in Succession of Appoline Patout.

27. Schwing Genealogical Materials, J. Patout Burns Papers, New Iberia, Louisiana; "Genealogy of the Schwing Family," Schwing Family Papers, courtesy of Mrs. George P. Broussard, New Iberia, Louisiana; Wade, *Sugar Dynasty*, 161–65.

28. Paul Johnson, *The Birth of the Modern: World Society, 1815–1830* (New York: HarperCollins, 1992); Hawks and Skemp, *Sex, Race, and the Role of Women in the South*, xi; Scott, *The Southern Lady*, 17–18. Scott observed, "Like aristocrats, Communists, and bourgeois businessmen, southern men had no trouble finding theoretical support for a way of life that was decidedly to their advantage"; for the development of this view, see also Barbara Welter, "The Cult of True Womanhood: 1820–1860," *American Quarterly* 18, no. 2, pt. 1 (Summer 1966): 151–74.

29. Sitterson, *Sugar Country*, 261; *Louisiana Planter and Sugar Manufacturer* (hereafter *LPSM*), August 25, 1888, 91–92; *Louisiana Sugar Report, 1893–94*, 13 (see "Bouchereau, The Louisiana Sugar Report," in *Documenting Louisiana Sugar, 1845–1917*, University of Sussex, http://www.sussex.ac.uk/louisianasugar/sources/bouchereau, accessed May 5, 2015); Florence Blackburn, "Pumping Syrup by Pipe Line Unique Feature of Patout Mill," *Franklin (La.) Banner-Tribune*, August 21, 1952.

30. *LPSM*, April 13, 1889, 180; Florence Blackburn, "Pumping Syrup by Pipe Line; *LPSM*, August 17 and October 3, 1889; Alcee Bouchereau, *Statement of the Sugar Crop, 1890–92*, 19; Alcee Bouchereau, *Statement of the Sugar Crop, 1892–93*, 4 (see "Bouchereau, The Louisiana Sugar Report," in *Documenting Louisiana Sugar, 1845–1917*, University of Sussex, http://www.sussex.ac.uk/louisianasugar/sources/bouchereau, accessed May 5, 2015); Sitterson, *Sugar Country*, 261.

31. Iberia Corporate Conveyances, 1893, book 24, nos. 3992–4008, Iberia Parish Clerk of Court, New Iberia, Louisiana; William Edward Butler, *Down among the Sugar Cane: The Story of Louisiana's Sugar Plantations and Their Railroads* (Baton Rouge: William Edward Butler, 1980), 171–74; Alcee Bouchereau, *Statement of the Sugar Crop, 1893–94*, 4–5 (see "Bouchereau, The Louisiana Sugar Report," in *Documenting Louisiana Sugar, 1845–1917*, University of Sussex, http://www.sussex.ac.uk/louisianasugar/sources/bouchereau, accessed May 5, 2015).

32. Contract, March 13, 1894, Clerk of Court, Orleans Parish Courthouse, New Orleans; Alcee Bouchereau, *Statement of the Sugar Crop, 1894–95*, 5; Alcee Bouchereau, *Statement of the Sugar Crop, 1896–97*, 5; Alcee Bouchereau, *Statement of the Sugar Crop, 1898–99*, 7 (see "Bouchereau, The Louisiana Sugar Report," in *Documenting Louisiana Sugar, 1845–1917*, University of Sussex, http://www.sussex.ac.uk/louisianasugar/sources/bouchereau, accessed May 5, 2015); *M. A. Patout & Son vs. Iberia–St. Mary Drainage District*, Civil Suit 3520, December 17, 1900, Iberia Parish Clerk of Court; John Heitmann, *The Modernization of the Louisiana Sugar Industry, 1830–1910* (Baton Rouge: Louisiana State University Press, 1987), 216.

33. Multiple effect evaporation was the great achievement of the great Louisiana inventor Nor-

bert Rillieux, who successfully used the vapor given off by the first vacuum pan in the boiling of cane juice to provide the heat for boiling the more concentrated sugar juice in the second vacuum pan, repeating the process for the third and fourth pans. Double effect evaporators restricted the process to two pans. The great benefit of Rillieux's antebellum invention was that it provided approximately a 75 percent savings in fuel consumption. See Sitterson, *Sugar Country*, 147–49; Heitmann, *The Modernization of the Louisiana Sugar Industry*, 36–37.

34. U.S. Bureau of the Census, *Twelfth Census of the United States (Louisiana, Iberia Parish)* (Washington, D.C., 1900), 3b; *LPSM*, October 25, 1902; Michael Wade, interview with George Smith, December 22, 1984, Patoutville, Louisiana, M. A. Patout & Son, Ltd., Archives (hereafter M. A. Patout Archives), Patoutville, Louisiana.

35. *LPSM*, April 9, 1904; Minutes, Board of Directors, New Iberia National Bank, July 15, 1907; J. Patout Burns Papers; Glenn R. Conrad, ed., *New Iberia: Essays on the Town and Its People*, 2nd ed. (Lafayette: Center for Louisiana Studies, 1986), 51.

36. "History of Sugarcane in Louisiana," LSU AgCenter, http://text.lsuagcenter.com/ (accessed March 4, 2015).

37. *LPSM*, July 20, 1907,38; Minutes, Board of Directors, New Iberia National Bank, July 15, 1907; J. Patout Burns Papers.

38. Charter of M. A. Patout & Son, Ltd., December 12, 1910, Iberia Parish Corporation Charter No. 1973, Miscellaneous Book 6, 24; Hippolyte Patout to M. A. Patout & Son, Ltd., December 19, 1910–January 24, 1911, Iberia Parish Corporate Conveyances Nos. 23105–23112, book 70, 429–36; Ida Patout Burns to M. A. Patout & Son, Ltd., January 10, 1911, Iberia Corporate Conveyance No. 23083, book 73, 78.

39. Charter of M. A. Patout & Son, Ltd. There were, of course, female contemporaries of Ida Burns who were prominent in business circles. There just were not very many of them. The most remarkable example of female business success in the period may well have been Madame C. J. Walker (1867–1919). Born Sarah Breedlove in Delta, Louisiana, she was the child of former slaves. Orphaned at age seven, married at fourteen, and a widow at twenty, she survived the murder of her first husband, single motherhood, and some twenty years of laundry work at $1.50 a week to create a cosmetics industry for black women. A'Lelia Bundles, *On Her Own Ground: The Life and Times of Madame C. J. Walker* (New York: Scribner, 2001). The author is a great-great-granddaughter of Madame Walker; the biography was a *New York Times* Notable Book of the Year.

40. Ida Burns to Hippolyte Patout, April 16, 1917, Threadgill Family Papers, Dallas, Texas, courtesy of Eunice Threadgill; Arthur Keller, "Changes and Improvements in Louisiana Sugar Factories," *Gilmore's Louisiana Sugar Manual*, 1940–41, vi–vii; Board of Directors Minutes, September 30 and October 24, 1942, M. A. Patout Archives.

41. M. A. Patout Financial Report, November 23, 1943, J. Patout Burns Papers, New Iberia, Louisiana; Barton, Pilie, Sere & Wermuth to M. A. Patout Board of Directors, August 30, 1943, J. Patout Burns Papers; Mrs. Theo (J. Patout) Burns, Interview with Michael Wade, November 6, 1987, New Iberia, Louisiana, M. A. Patout Archives; President's Report to Stockholders, September 15, 1944, M. A. Patout Archives. William S. Patout III, continued his father's program of modernization, developing a reputation as a wunderkind of the Louisiana sugar industry. He served a term as president of the American Sugar Cane League and, following his retirement from active management, directed M. A. Patout's acquisition of Sterling Sugars and Raceland Raw Sugars Corporation.

42. Regarding the sometimes treacherous gap between the nineteenth-century understanding of the female nature and the often contradictory roles imposed on them by widowhood, see the range of three widows' responses (the first a Louisiana widow left with a large, debt-ridden plantation) to financial straits in Wood, *Masterful Women*, 146–49. On the often central and sometimes onerous household obligations of plantation mistresses, see Marli Weiner, *Mistresses and Slaves: Plantation Women in South Carolina, 1830–80* (Urbana: University of Illinois Press, 1998), 24–27, 43–47. By and large, those duties remained the same following the abolition of slavery; for postbellum women like

Mary Ann Patout there were enlarged possibilities for expanding the boundaries of femininity and domesticity. This point was convincingly made by Jane Turner Censer in her broadly conceived study of elite women in late-nineteenth-century North Carolina and Virginia, *The Reconstruction of White Southern Womanhood, 1865–1895* (Baton Rouge: Louisiana State University Press, 2003), especially the material on heroines in this period's novels, 42–48, and on the growth of public roles for women, 183–205.

43. Censer, *The Reconstruction of White Southern Womanhood*, 62–63, 77–78; see also Laura Edwards, *Gendered Strife and Confusion: The Political Culture of Reconstruction* (Urbana: University of Illinois Press, 1997).

44. M. A. Patout & Son, Ltd., http://www.mapatout.com/.

45. Documenting Louisiana Sugar, 1845–1917, University of Sussex, http://www.sussex.ac.uk/louisianasugar/ (accessed August 19, 2012). Follett, head of the Department of American Studies at the University of Sussex, is author of the award-winning *The Sugar Masters: Planters and Slaves in Louisiana's Cane World, 1820–1860* (Baton Rouge: Louisiana State University Press, 2005). As he correctly wrote in the project overview: "These remarkable records provide an unbroken time series of economic and production data with which scholars can examine an entire industry [it]. . . . permits users to rifle through the hundred thousand data entries that Champomier and Bouchereau filed a century ago and examine the social and economic history of the American South's most industrialized and capital intensive plantation regime. . . . No other public database detailing plantation life in this detail exists."

46. Documenting Louisiana Sugar, 1845–1917, University of Sussex, http://www.sussex.ac.uk/louisianasugar/.

47. Ibid.

Lulu White

(1868–1931)

Diamond Queen of the Demimonde

EMILY EPSTEIN LANDAU

In 1897 the New Orleans City Council passed an ordinance designating a bounded red-light district.[1] It became known as Storyville and soon earned a reputation as the nation's most spectacular and degraded vice district, securing New Orleans's reputation for immoral indulgence, sexual licentiousness, and political venality. Lulu White was Storyville's most notorious madam, the "Diamond Queen of the Demimonde," or as she was also known, the "Queen of the Octoroons." By "marketing miscegenation" in Storyville, White exploited New Orleans's longstanding association—part historical and part imaginary—with sex-slave auctions, quadroon balls, and interracial concubinage, as well as the literary trope of the tragic octoroon.[2]

Storyville was created as a reform measure, to consolidate and hide prostitution, to "segregate" it from respectable New Orleans and its legitimate business enterprises. Instead, Storyville highlighted the very aspects of New Orleans's culture that the authors of the ordinance hoped to obscure, namely prostitution, interracial sex, and government corruption. More than this, Storyville offered a liminal space in which to enact fantasies of white male supremacy while the South beyond its boundaries struggled to create, maintain, and enforce a strict color line, often resorting to terror and violence in doing so. Lulu White, though a singular character, came to represent the district in the eyes of respectable New Orleanians. In her keen exploitation of the desire to violate the miscegenation taboo during its strenuous and violent enforcement in the South, White reveals the complex dynamics between sex, race, and memory at play in the development and consolidation of Jim Crow.

Lulu White was born in Alabama in 1868, to Amanda Tipton, a "colored," eighteen-year-old "housekeeper," and Robert Hendley, a white man about whom little is known.[3] Lulu had one sister, Della, the mother of Spencer Williams, the jazz pianist and composer who wrote *Basin Street Blues* and *Mahogany Hall Stomp*, the latter named for his aunt's Storyville bordello. White left Alabama for New Orleans sometime in the 1880s, first appearing in the city directory in 1888, on a block devoted to "colored female boarding houses."[4] She may have married, hence "White," but no husband appears in existing records of her life. Sometime at the turn of the century she adopted a baby girl, but this daughter is absent from all public accounts of White's life in New Orleans until after Storyville's special status came to an end, and even her name is unknown. White left no diary, no cache of personal letters, no secret key to unlocking her motives and feelings. Her life was one of self-creation; she was a celebrity, and her movements through the public sphere became fodder for the press. It is through a careful reading of White's well-crafted persona, and the reaction it provoked, that we glean her significance in New Orleans.

Once in New Orleans, White quickly gained notoriety. By the early 1890s, she was a regular feature in the "Scarlet World" section of the *Mascot* and in other scandal sheets that focused on the city's underworld characters and goings-on. In 1894, she became the proprietress of her own brothel, and she had by then already posed in several series of extremely provocative pornographic photographs. White developed her identity as the Diamond Queen before Storyville's creation. The district became her stage for acting out the role.

The Storyville ordinance passed at the end of January 1897. White promptly secured a lot in a prime location in the district, in the middle of Basin Street.[5] Her partner in the endeavor was Assistant City Attorney George Washington Flynn, a member of the New Orleans Democratic machine, and its social organization, the Choctaw Club. Flynn, as a notary public, notarized the deal.[6] He then bought the property from White and arranged to sell it back to her over several years in a four-and-a-half-year mortgage. White therefore had the funds to construct and furnish what she would call Mahogany Hall.[7]

The bordello White built at 235 North Basin Street was spectacular inside and out. The building's domed roof could be seen from Canal Street to Esplanade.[8] Musicians who played there remember it as "plush" and luxurious.[9] Customers came in "dress clothes." According to legend, a maid might even check a man's shoes to ensure that the customers were, indeed, "well-heeled."[10] The women at Mahogany Hall were classified as "octoroons." This term, an outmoded and racist calculus meaning of one-eighth African descent or "blood," had purchase in New Orleans's infamous sex district at the turn of the twentieth century, and Lulu White drew customers in by advertising sex with light-skinned women of color to men of means in her "Octoroon Club," as Mahogany Hall was also known.[11] The customers at Mahogany Hall and other higher-end bordellos were white without exception.[12] Why did the district feature "octoroon" prostitutes, along with "colored," "white," and even "Jewish" and "French" women?[13] Why

LULU WHITE BORDELLO

From Emily Epstein Landau's collection.

did White fashion an identity for herself and her bordello based on such an atavistic racial category? A little context is in order.

Storyville's opening coincided with the landmark Supreme Court case, *Plessy v. Ferguson*. Homer Plessy himself was only fractionally of African descent. He was a Creole of color who had grown up in an activist community in New Orleans with a long history of fighting racial injustice in the name of equal rights for all.[14] His Supreme Court case grew out of a challenge to Louisiana's "Separate Car Law," passed in 1890. The men who challenged the law sought to obliterate the color line and eliminate "race" as the organizing binary of American society. According to these men, the 1890 Separate Car Law violated the first principle of American liberty, that "all men are created equal." "Citizenship is national and knows no color," they maintained, and they accurately recognized in the Separate Car Law the attempt by the Louisiana legislature to establish white supremacy through the false logic of "separate but equal." They set up the Citizens Committee to Test the Constitutionality of the Law and prepared to bring a case to do just that.

In bringing the case, Plessy's light skin tone—his own purported "octoroon" status—was central to the legal strategy of his attorney, Albion Tourgée. How better to demonstrate the arbitrariness of the law and the impossibility of its just enforcement than to have a person who *looked white* challenge a law based on *color*? Moreover, that Homer Plessy and his cohorts did not descend directly from slaves but from free people of color was again meant to highlight the arbitrary nature of segregation by "race." The law, one among many passed in the southern states in the years following Reconstruction, claimed to protect the racial sensibilities of both "races" and merely to codify the natural desire of each to maintain its distance from the other. This was not the case, however. Segregationist legislation portended a new racial dispensation, and *Plessy* was a watershed.[15] The promulgation of segregationist rhetoric was part and parcel of the strategies of white men to disenfranchise African Americans and retake the reins of power after the Civil War, emancipation, and Reconstruction disrupted white rule. As we well know, they were successful. Plessy lost his case, and the "separate but equal" doctrine allowed states to pass discriminatory legislation. In the years following the Supreme Court's decision, most African Americans lost the franchise through a combination of legal and extralegal measures, including intimidation, violence, and murder.

Meanwhile, a discourse of rape and retribution stoked the fires of race hatred. According to it, African American men were all potential rapists, their political and economic aspirations coded as desire for interracial sex and marriage across the color line. This discourse, ostensibly meant to protect white women from rapacious black men, was the justification for both legal segregation and extralegal violence. The 1890s were the most violent years of racial strife in terms of lynchings, some of which reached the level of grotesque spectacle, as well as the years in which racial legislation was passed by states and ultimately approved by the Supreme Court.[16] And even though the most severe and violent repercussions were reserved for black men accused of crossing the color line for sex, the developing rhetoric of white supremacy included all interracial liaisons in its disapproving language.[17]

Lulu White, with her "octoroon prostitutes," flourished in this period, set aside and confined within Storyville. The impulse to create such vice districts, to limit and bound them, was conjoined to the impulse to separate the races. The goal was to control and dominate public space, to establish a clear hierarchy in which whites were on top and where the middle-class notions of respectability, propriety, and legitimate profit took clear priority.[18] Yet, where *Plessy v. Ferguson* and the encompassing discourse of white supremacy mandated racial separation, Storyville promoted interracial intimacy. The district openly offered nonwhite women to its white customers. Where the ruling in *Plessy* obscured the ancestry and inheritance of Homer Plessy and other Creoles of color in New Orleans, Storyville highlighted the mixed-race population of the city by actively promoting the designation "octoroon." Lulu White even claimed to be from the West Indies, where Plessy's white grandfather had in fact come from. For nearly twenty years Storyville flouted the racial order that *Plessy* helped establish. Lulu White ruled the demimonde by claiming to inhabit the category the *Plessy* decision made moot. How can this be?

It presents a paradox that Storyville flourished precisely when the dominant public rhetoric of racial and sexual purity demanded that sex across the color line threatened the future of the white race and therefore the whole nation. To be sure, red-light districts are built upon the thrill of transgression and illicit sex, but the miscegenation taboo was at the height of its power as a bulwark of white supremacy and national/racial progress at this time. The taboo was the foundation of the lynching discourse and the continued oppression of white women as well as African Americans. Storyville violated these racial imperatives by offering sex with women of color to white men. Yet, in offering "octoroons" for the paid sexual pleasure of white men, Storyville violated the miscegenation taboo in a way that recapitulated the earlier order of the antebellum South, an order characterized by a racial patriarchy, undergirded by the institution of slavery. In the absence of slavery, in the wake of its destruction, white southerners created and embraced a mythological past and then aggressively "remembered" that past in shaping national policy.[19]

By featuring "octoroon" prostitutes and sex across the color line, Storyville thus called up memories of antebellum times. The district imaginatively recast the plantation household as a kind of sexual funhouse, open to all white men regardless of class. Though not all white men could afford the luxury of Mahogany Hall, Storyville offered a range of options for indulging transgressive fantasies. All any man needed for entry was sufficient cash and white skin.

Though White herself sought a better class of customers for Mahogany Hall, men who were on the ascendant in the New South world of commerce, the district as a whole effectively democratized an exclusive privilege of antebellum patriarchy, the sexual possession of women of color. When Lulu White promoted sex with octoroon women to her white customers, she certainly defied Jim Crow, but she also helped shape the developing culture of white supremacy. Thus Storyville prescribed a sexualized racial hierarchy even as it seemed to defy all social order.[20]

White embodied the "octoroon" fantasy and marketed it for her own profit. At the same time, she also embodied white southerners' fears about sexual and racial disorder. There are thus two sides to the octoroon fantasy: the sexual fantasy of racial and sexual dominance that recalled an older, bygone order in which white men were indisputably on top, and on the other side the fears and anxieties of a new, changed world order in which that dominance was over, where slavery no longer secured white privilege, where "invisible" or indecipherable "blackness" lurked and threatened, and where women sought new roles beyond the private sphere of home and family. This latter "fantasy" underlay the insistence on asserting and maintaining a strict separation of the races through the imposition of a legal color line, supported by political rhetoric and violent reprisal. We know that that line was based on a legal fiction, a product of sexualized racism and fear, and not based on any natural logic of difference. Yet American society organized itself around that legal fiction as if it were fact. Lulu White's life in defiance and support of the color line yields insight into the fluidity of desire and taboo, nostalgia and progress, and the spaces where they overlap. They overlapped in Storyville. Outside the district her life bore little resemblance to the identity she created for herself—"Diamond Queen"—and newspaper reporters were quick to deflate her puffed-up pretensions regarding both race and class.

Because Lulu White made the "octoroon" Storyville's sexual subspecialty, let us begin with a brief history of that figure in New Orleans history, myth, and lore. While present in literature dating back centuries, the iconic image of the light-skinned sexual slave girl coalesced into an American obsession in the antebellum period in part from a new focus in abolitionist writings after about 1831.[21] Through novels, plays, and poems themed around the "tragic octoroon," abolitionists denounced a slave system that corrupted the family, permitting and even encouraging interracial sex and adultery. The octoroon was always young and exceptionally beautiful, with perfect manners and an elegant demeanor. She had, writes literary scholar Anna Elfenbein, been "raised as a lady in the household of her father, who is, notwithstanding his sexual vagaries, descended from the best blood of the Old South."[22] The tragedy usually followed her father's death. He "has not seen to things. His concern with attending to pleasure rather than to duties . . . betrays his daughter, who possesses only the slightest evidence of Negro blood, to the auction block."[23] The octoroon's beauty, her light complexion, her virtue—all the things that made her resemble white women of the upper and upper-middle class—also made her especially attractive to the sex-slave trafficker, and especially valuable in the market.[24] The literature was sexually suggestive, even prurient, as authors took pains to describe the nubile octoroons as stunning innocents in imminent danger of ravishment (as well as products of previous ravishment).

The fictional "tragic octoroon" contributed to the image of New Orleans in America and abroad. It relied upon and reinforced previously existing knowledge of the city. New Orleans was already well known for its slave auctions featuring light-skinned women for sale as sexual slaves or concubines. Known as the "fancy trade" or simply "fancies," these women were, in Walter Johnson's words, "visions of sexual desire and the luxury of being able to pay for its fulfillment—enslaved versions of mastery itself."[25] Their possession indicated the power and prowess of their owners. Through the "tragic octoroon" literature, New Orleans was further associated with interracial sex, the moral decrepitude of slave traders, and planter lust. For those who opposed slavery, the traffic in "fancy girls" showed how a system of absolute power promoted sexual licentiousness, infidelity, and betrayal.[26] Where else could one find so clear an example of the corrupting influence of slavery? Furthermore, the lust provoked by slavery came dangerously close to violating propriety in the master's own home, so nearly white were its objects.[27] In the years around the turn of the twentieth century, when Lulu White ran a brothel of modern-day "fancy girls" for the pleasure of Storyville's wealthier customers, she reoriented the memory of the octoroon's tragic fate while maintaining her erotic appeal.

New Orleans publicized transgressions that the rest of the South repressed. Its flamboyant sex market in slave women magnified the sexual license that underlay plantation society and which was the special subject of tragic octoroon literature.[28] Many planters used slaves for sex. This was their prerogative, elaborating the privileges of patriarchy in an immediate and tangible way. The abolitionist discourse of the "tragic octoroon" at once highlighted the near-universality of sexual subordination under slavery and focused special attention on the light-skinned victims of planter lust. It also fixed New Orleans as the natural milieu for these degradations, associating the city in thousands of minds with the fancy trade, octoroons, and interracial sex. White's turn-of-the-century bordello full of beautiful octoroons celebrated what the abolitionists had deplored: absolute power and lust.

In addition to the markets in enslaved women, there were also markets for free women of color, known as quadroon balls. At these mythologized gatherings white men selected from an array of beautiful and cultivated light-skinned female Creoles of color. They entered into contracts for their care and promised to support them and any children resulting from the arrangement if the man sought to end the relationship and find a legitimate (white) wife. Much has been written about the facticity—or lack thereof—of these balls.[29] Yet enough visitors to New Orleans recorded their impressions of them to confirm that they did, in some form, take place, and that white, male visitors to the city felt in some sense compelled to witness at least one. Alexis de Tocqueville wrote of the one he attended in 1832: "Quadroon Ball. Strange sight: all the men white, all the women colored, or at least of African blood. Single tie created by immorality between the two races. A sort of bazaar."[30]

The relationships that formed at balls were known as *plaçage*, though it is not clear when that term came into use.[31] Most relationships between white men and women of color were not initiated at quadroon balls, and the relationships that fell within the definition of *plaçage* "ranged the gamut," in the historian Shirley Thompson's phrase, from temporary concubinage to life-long common-law marriage.[32] Here, however, we are concerned less with the accuracy of visitors' recollections and more with the circulation of their stories and their later resonance in Storyville.[33] One man remarked that the "quadroons . . . the light mulattoes of this country . . . pass their life in a prostitution."[34] Another wrote that he had "often heard of the beauty of the quadroons. I found them pretty. They are a very amiable looking people, and have the appearance of being virtuous; but they are generally prostitutes and kept *Mistresses*."[35] Another visitor, a woman, wrote that the Creole of color woman was "far more beautiful" than either the Anglo-American or the white Creole.

> The eloquent blood in her soft cheek speaks but too plainly of her despised descent. She seems to blush at the injustice of man, who visits upon her the sins of her fathers. The passer-by arrogantly bids her to stand aside, for he is holier than she; in bitter contempt, the women of the land shrink from her contact, and the large, sleepy eye, half hid by its curled fringes, is hardly raised, as gracefully and humbly she passes them by. Poor thing! what wonder, if, feeling that she is neglected and oppressed, she should turn in the desolation of her heart to other ties. Deprived too frequently of the many consolations of kindred affection; a solitary link in the chain of human sympathies—brotherless, friendless, alone! Let those who have never known what solitude of the heart is, speak harshly of the errors of the despised Quadroon. I can but pity her.[36]

In general, visitors commented on the women's beauty and fine manners, and they lamented their liminal, outcast status. That is to say, their observations did not take into account—in fact they erased—the large, endogamous population of the *gens de couleur libres*. Rather, they offered an image of a female population devoid of patriarchal protection and destined to support themselves through sexual liaisons with white men.[37]

The Civil War, emancipation, and Reconstruction brought immense change. Slavery, slave markets, and the slave trade ceased operations. Abolitionists folded up shop or switched their focus. White supremacy campaigns of varying degrees of violence proliferated as Reconstruction was overthrown and home rule reestablished in the former Confederacy. The retreat from Reconstruction included the elaboration of a racist discourse that provided the groundwork for legal segregation and racial oppression. The point is that Storyville's "octoroon" fantasy does not represent continuity from slavery days to the turn of the twentieth century. There was a decided rupture, during which social relations were thrown into chaos and power was briefly redistributed. The recapitulation of antebellum culture, in Storyville and elsewhere, was the attempt to recapture and reorder what had been lost and confused by the war and its aftermath—most generally, the racial patriarchy rooted in slavery.[38] Lulu White participated in this process by combining those elements of antebellum memory that recalled the special *sexual* privileges of planter patriarchy and serving them up in an atmosphere of luxurious debauch, redolent with nostalgia and taboo.

Lulu White was a saleswoman, but she was never selling mere commodities. Rather she commodified the complicated history of race in New Orleans in order to sell sex, using herself as her first "item." If you "bought" her story, or even if you did not, you might then visit her place of business. Throughout her career she strategically fashioned herself as part of her attempt to draw men to her bordello. In 1894, the *Mascot* reported that when Lulu was a small child, she had been "taken to New York by her father, who was a Wall Street broker, and after his death she fell heiress to No. 166 Customhouse Street." She was thus the fallen daughter of privilege; she came from money and the Customhouse property passed to her through the legitimate mechanism of patriarchy. White borrowed selectively from the old "tragic octoroon" narrative in her personal story, altering details here and there. For instance, in her story, her father was a northerner, his profession the apotheosis of capitalist success, quite the opposite of the impoverished, superannuated planter who usually filled the role in the literature. In White's narrative, her father's legacy may have condemned her to sexual slavery and prostitution, but it also gave her property.[39]

White understood the octoroon's prurient appeal. Yet, even as she drew on the mythic/historical resonance of the "tragic octoroon," she defied the essence of that figure. White claimed simultaneously to be an "octoroon" and white. In another instance, in 1894, she told the *Mascot* that though "some people take her to be colored," there was "not a drop of negro blood in her veins." Additionally, she claimed that she was a native "West Indian," as if that would clarify things.[40] Elsewhere White similarly referred to herself as a "famous West Indian octoroon."[41]

What did "West Indian" mean to Lulu White? What did White imagine it meant to her potential customers? There is no reason to assume that White was unfamiliar with the heritage of the *gens de couleur libres* and their place in the city's history, including the legendary quadroon balls and *plaçage*.[42] Moreover, writers like Lafcadio Hearn and others lavished praise on the beauty of the "*filles-de-couleur*" of the West Indies in terms comparable to the antebellum descriptions of the New Orleans Creole of color woman.

> Physically, the typical fille-de-couleur may certainly be classed, as white creole writers have not hesitated to class her, with the "most beautiful women of the human race." She has inherited not only the finer bodily characteristics of either parent race, but a something else belonging originally to neither, and created by special climatic and physical conditions,—a grace, a suppleness of form, a delicacy of extremities (so that all the lines described by the bending of the limbs or fingers are parts of clean curves), a satiny smoothness and fruit-tint of skin,—solely West Indian.[43]

Finally, the practices that titillated and shocked visitors to the city from antebellum times onward harkened back to the days of French colonialism and the history of sex across the color line in the French Caribbean as well as in New Orleans.[44]

White's repeated claim to be from the West Indies implicated her in the French colonial history of New Orleans—not as a former slave in Saint-Domingue but as part of the elite Creole population, hence her contradictory claim to be both "octoroon" and "white." This contradiction reflects either a lack of knowledge or, more likely, a disregard for fact. White had no obligation to "educate" her customers as to the cruelties of French colonial slavery, only to capitalize on the desire educated through the myriad discourses of sexual and racial proscription then at play. Her self-presentation as a "West Indian" and "octoroon," who had no "trace" of "negro blood," signified in multiple registers and captured the exotic, erotic identity she seems to have been going for. Yet White also embraced the identity of the octoroon as sex slave. White presented herself as proof of the successive elevations of generations of mixed offspring toward apparent whiteness, a racialized class ascent framed by desire. "In describing Miss Lulu, as she is most familiarly called, it would not be amiss to say that besides possessing an elegant form she has beautiful black hair and blue eyes, which have justly gained for her the title of the 'Queen of the Demi-Monde.'"[45] The strategy worked: Lulu White and her brothel full of women labeled "octoroons" gained great notoriety and her business boomed. For White and her customers at Mahogany Hall, "octoroon" resonated as a *sexual* category steeped in a history of colonialism, chattel slavery, and white domination, yet also removed from it. As the literary scholar Anne McKlintock reminds us, "The fetish is overdetermined."[46]

Mahogany Hall was faithful to the tradition of the antebellum hotels that had hosted New Orleans's spectacular slave auctions—venues where light-skinned female slaves were sold for sex.[47] Mahogany Hall even had a cupola, perhaps a conscious act of architectural homage to the St. Charles Hotel. Calling her brothel "unquestionably the most elaborately furnished house in the city of New Orleans," and "without a doubt one of the most elegant palaces in this or any other country," White drew on recognizable class markers to tout herself and her business.[48] Storyville generally sought to appeal to the rising, new-money, commercial classes in its offerings and its advertisements.[49] In the published guides to the district, known collectively as the Blue Books, one finds a kind of ironic, mocking tone, a simultaneous claim to class status and the mocking of that very claim in the context of bordellos and barrelhouses.

White's play on both race and class is evident earlier as well, in the pornographic photographs she posed in sometime in the 1880s or 1890s, before the opening of Storyville.[50] The pictures contain within them narratives that are useful in understanding White's later Storyville persona, especially insofar as they eroticize and burlesque middle-class morality while also playing with notions of racial dualism.[51] For instance, one group of photographs features White sexually positioned with a large dog.[52] The first two pictures in the series are not sexually explicit (in one she hugs the dog around the neck and in the next she sits on a chair with her skirt lifted, revealing her pubic hair). The photographs become progressively more graphic, with White holding the dog's penis, then preparing to fellate the dog, and finally being penetrated by him. Perhaps in this bestiality series there was a wink at the ritualized process of courtship, the complex social drama that had to precede intercourse for it to be considered legitimate, respectable.[53] In her photographic references to bourgeois aspiration and anxiety, White tapped the multivalent strains of sexual proscription and desire, taboo, and arousal that dominated sexual discourse at this time.[54]

Storyville, then, gave White a unique venue to live out the persona she had invented for herself and had developed over the decade or so she had lived in New Orleans. When Mahogany Hall opened for business in 1898, White published a small "souvenir" guide to publicize it. She began with a note of (false) modesty: "In presenting this souvenir to my multitude of friends," she began, "it is my earnest desire to, in the first place, avoid any and all egotism, and, secondly, to impress them with the fact that the cause of my successes must certainly be attributed to their hearty and generous support of my exertions in making their visits to my establishments a *moment of pleasure*." White continued, describing her bordello. Mahogany Hall was:

> erected specially for Miss Lulu White at a cost of $40,000. The house is built of marble and is four story; containing five parlors, all handsomely furnished, and fifteen bedrooms. Each room has a bath with hot and cold water and extension closets. The elevator, which was built for two, is of the latest style. The entire house is steam heated and is the handsomest house of its kind. It is the only one where you can get three shots for your money—the shot upstairs, the shot downstairs, and the shot in the room.[55]

White slides seamlessly from a description of her fine furnishings, which were indeed luxurious, to the underlying purpose of a visit: "the shot in the room."

She goes on, now juxtaposing the material accoutrements of her "palace" with the women inside, also objects of the finest quality:

> Her establishment, which is situated in the central part of the city, is unquestionably the most elaborately furnished house in the city of New Orleans, and without a doubt one of the most elegant palaces in this or any other country.
>
> She has made a feature of boarding none but the fairest of girls—those gifted with nature's best charms, and would under no circumstances have any but that class in her house.

She concludes with a few words about herself, highlighting the markers of bourgeois class status in a setting that simultaneously made them absurd: "As an entertainer Miss Lulu stands foremost, having made a life-long study of music and literature. She is well-read and one that can interest anybody and make a visit to her place a continued round of pleasure."[56] There are photographs of prostitutes in Mahogany Hall's booklet, and they all appear "white."[57] Only the text, often describing them as "octoroons," and their place at Mahogany Hall suggested a "drop of African blood." The actual genealogy of these women is unknown. Some of their names, Sadie Levy for example, suggest other ethnic heritages, though, of course, not definitively. The "real" identities of the women employed by White are not easily accessible. Women used pseudonyms and moved around a lot; they are difficult to trace. Moreover, who these women were outside of Storyville was less relevant than their ability to "pass" as "octoroons" within the rubric of the district. Lulu White's "souvenir" brochure and the Blue Books served as menus, in a sense, of the sexual offerings in Storyville. All these cases expose a world of commercial strategy and sexual fantasy, and not fixed and unchanging "race." Still, an affiliation with Lulu White and Mahogany Hall could be called upon to "prove" that a person was "colored" and *not white*. For instance, when a woman whom the police presumed to be white was arrested for violating the 1908 Louisiana law forbidding "interracial concubinage" she used her past affiliation with Lulu White and Mahogany Hall to "prove" that she was not white but rather "octoroon," and not, thereby, in violation of the law.[58]

Outside of Storyville, the country's "Handsomest Octoroon" became its most "Notorious Negress." White was a discomfiting figure in New Orleans when she ventured outside of Storyville; while within the district she certainly violated racialized gender expectations and the nascent Jim Crow order, the fantasy she served there instantiated white supremacy and the organizational logic of that order. Outside of the fantasy realm of Storyville, Lulu White did not fit into the picture of New Orleans that the city's boosters wanted to promote or inhabit. Lulu White *was* a "disorderly" woman: of the type of disorder that both racial segregation and the segregation of vice were supposed to eliminate or hide. The New Orleans newspapers treated her with disdain, focusing on her uncouth character, the nature of her business, and her associates. The latter group included pimps and gangsters, to be sure, but also policemen, lawyers, and politicians, because White was connected to some of the most powerful actors in the city and was perhaps one of them herself.

Lulu White's personal life most certainly included passion, heartbreak, and violence, providing fodder for the press. In 1904 White stormed into a men's club at 133 St. Charles Street and fired shots at the proprietor, George Lambert, White's former lover, a gangster and likely pimp, who had jilted her for another woman. "Lulu White seems to have no social club manners," wrote the *Daily Picayune*, "for the notorious negress broke up a poker game which was going on in George Lambert's place . . . Saturday afternoon." According to the *Picayune*, White showed up at the club with a pistol, began "abusing" Lambert, "and fired two shots at him." The other men in the room quickly got up, and one took the gun from White.[59] The poker players subdued White and spirited her out of the building before the police could arrive.[60] When they got there, the poker players turned them away.[61] The police nevertheless charged Lulu White with carrying a concealed weapon. The newspaper headline read: "Carrying Concealed Weapons—Lulu White. This accused is a notorious negress, proprietress of a den of infamy on Basin Street." The newspaper ridiculed the police's response, expressing mock bewilderment at the diminution of the charges: "Strange to say, no report was made of the affair until Sunday night. Yesterday, instead of making the proper charges against the negress, she was simply charged with carrying concealed weapons, a charge which will hardly be proven."[62] Indeed, they were right. With the aid of her lawyer, Edward Whitaker, White escaped penalty.[63] The following year, Whitaker was installed in the office of police inspector.[64]

White's connections in both legitimate and underworld New Orleans did not shield her in all cases. In 1905, for instance, she was charged with tax evasion and selling liquor without the proper licenses. White mounted an elaborate defense. First she claimed that Mahogany Hall did not "cater to beer much," having established her bordello as a "Wine Castle" in the Blue Books. The beer in question went to her prostitutes and so was not taxable, as it had not been sold at a profit. She had, she told the court, wished to keep her "girls" out of the saloons, which excluded them by law.[65] The prosecutor, in questioning the plausibility of this claim, confining his attention to one brewery, for one year, pointed out that she bought "over six thousand bottles of beer . . . from this one brewery alone. Do you mean to say that those girls drank nearly six thousand bottles of beer in the year 1904?" White's reply offers a privileged glimpse into daily life at Mahogany Hall. "Let me explain. In my house I don't allow the girls to go into any saloons . . . and I give them to understand that they can have all the bottled beer they want, just at the same price I get it from the brewery, to keep them from going." She claimed they drank "sometimes six dozen bottles a day, when I have twenty or twenty-five girls in the house . . . [they would] begin at nine in the morning and stopped around four in the afternoon, when they started 'getting ready for business.'"[66] White's explanation positioned her as the keeper, protector of, and provider for her "girls," while simultaneously maintaining her bordello's image as a "high-class" establishment. Even though White likely exaggerated the amount of beer the women drank, eventually conceding that a guest might buy a beer for fifty cents or a dollar, it is quite likely that the prostitutes also drank to excess.[67] She was convicted and ordered to pay her back taxes as well as a fine, together amounting to over a thousand dollars.[68]

A year later, White again found herself in court. This time she was there to testify on behalf of several police officers who stood accused of poisoning prostitutes at Willie Piazza's Basin Street bordello, another "octoroon" establishment. According to the *New Orleans Item*, two police officers had gone to Willie Piazza's place, ordered a round of beers for several of the prostitutes, and slipped a toxic powder into the beer glasses. The instigator of the "prank," wrote the *Item*, "sat in the 'Turkish Corner' of the 'mansion' and fairly split his sides with laughter while the doped victims writhed in agony. His alleged antics," the paper mocked, "were of the vaudeville order."[69] Piazza filed a complaint against the officers, and the badly played "joke" erupted into a major police scandal.[70] Worse than the poisoning, according to the *Item*, was that the police officers had been socializing with "colored" women.[71] At trial, Lulu White, whom the paper referred to as both "the lady herself" and "the notorious negro enchantress of Basin Street," sided with the police, and not her fellow "octoroon" madam, Piazza.[72] She denied having been a target herself in an earlier incident, and she revealed her strategic alliance with the law and specifically the chief of police, Edward Whitaker.[73]

Several years later, in November 1909, the *Daily Picayune* reported: "Lulu White, the negress of the Red-light District, who has had her swing for a long time" was "charged With Enticing Negress Below Legal Age." A fifteen-year-old girl named Marie Gaudette, whom the paper referred to as a "young negress," missing for three weeks, had been found by police at Mahogany Hall. Upon her "rescue," Marie accused her former boss, a white doctor, of seducing her.[74] Because there is no further substantive information about the incident in the newspaper or court records, it is impossible to know what happened. Perhaps teenage girls worked at Mahogany Hall. Perhaps White sheltered such girls from dangerous circumstances, offering them a place to stay, safe from lecherous doctors. White avoided prison but continued to skirt the edges of the emerging order.[75]

In 1911, White made the newspapers again for attempting to shoot a man. "Lulu White's Way" was the headline, and the story of how White "uses her pistol, but soon gets out of jail" was by then a familiar refrain. "This negress has a habit of taking a shot at a white man occasionally," wrote the *Daily Picayune*, "and yesterday morning she fired at George Killshaw, who is said to be a frequent visitor to the house." Killshaw may have been White's lover, but apparently Lambert, her earlier target, was not entirely out of the picture. "George

Lambert then came to the house, and he being persona non grata, was asked to leave." When he refused, White called the police. The officer "found Lambert under a bed. Lambert created a disturbance and was locked up."[76]

The newspapers made White's private life public, and used her behavior and her political connections to highlight the ongoing corruption in the city. In their excessive insistence on White's "blackness," they also reveal a defensive insecurity about the color line and the gendered social order. When White was safely bounded within the red-light district, "octoroon" could be construed as a sexual category signifying white male sex right and power. When she crossed the district's boundaries, her racial ambiguity and sexual and economic power threatened white supremacy. If miscegenation and prostitution functioned as metaphors for race despoliation and political corruption, Lulu White herself was a "master symbol" in the constellation of New South discourses.[77]

The problematic symbolism of Storyville's "octoroons," and its promotion of sex across the color line more generally, eventually led the city authorities to act. In 1917, the New Orleans City Council decided to make Storyville an all-white district. Interracial prostitution would be suppressed.[78] The body introduced an ordinance that read: "From and after the first day of March, 1917, it shall be unlawful for any prostitute or woman notoriously abandoned to lewdness, of the colored or black race, to occupy, inhabit, live or sleep in any house, room or closet situated outside of the following limits, viz.: From the upper side of Perdido Street to the lower side of Gravier Street, and from the river side of Franklin Street to the lower or wood side of Locust Street."[79] All "colored or negro" prostitutes and madams in Storyville would be compelled to move to the "uptown" red-light district, several blocks north of Canal Street. That area was not so much a vice district as a slum where vice flourished.[80]

The move was a long time coming, as reformers and others in New Orleans had decried the "notorious attraction" Storyville offered—sex across the color line—and sought to eliminate prostitution in the city.[81] On February 28, 1917, Lulu White received notice to vacate her premises at 235 North Basin Street and to leave Storyville, but she refused to move and filed a lawsuit in civil court to stop the city from evicting her.[82] The same day, Willie Piazza was served with an identical notice to vacate and also sued, along with at least twenty-five lesser-known "colored" prostitutes and madams.[83] Most of the women retained the same lawyer, M. D. Dimitry. The petitions were virtually identical, and George W. Flynn notarized most of them. Dimitry and Flynn had served as White's lawyers in the 1905 tax-evasion case. These two men's involvement in challenging the new law again point to the web of interests supporting Storyville's continued success, and to White's centrality in that web.

The petitions themselves are revealing. Each woman frankly stated that she ran a house of prostitution. Each, including White, stated she was of the "colored or negro race." The petitions claimed that the law forced them to give up their property without compensation or due process, and thus discriminated against them as "colored" women, in violation of the Fourteenth Amendment.[84] After a flurry of appeals, the women who had filed suit, including Lulu White, were allowed to remain in their houses and to operate their businesses pending the outcome of Piazza's case.[85] In the events that followed, Piazza won her case and the law was declared unconstitutional, the city applied for a rehearing of the case, and the City Council passed an amended version of the ordinance, closing the loopholes that had allowed Piazza her temporary victory.

The newly worded ordinance forced Lulu White to refine once again her self-presentation. In her new petition, she claimed that she was "*not* of the negro, colored, or black race," but that she "held herself out for the purpose of her business only as an Octoroon."[86] White said "her father and mother were both Spanish people of the Caucasian race; that her said parents were duly married in Havana, Cuba, where your petitioner was born of the issue of said marriage."[87] In this petition, White underlined both her own supposed racial self-fashioning as an octoroon and the superior salability of octoroon women in Storyville. Denying having even one "drop" of "negro blood," White claimed that she passed herself off as an octoroon for the purpose of attracting customers to her brothel. In fact White had been claiming for over twenty years that she possessed not one drop of "black blood" while hinting otherwise, blurring the color line from both sides.

Before the new law took effect, the city government ended the district's special dispensation and "closed" Storyville. Red-light districts all over the country were shut down as the nation prepared for war, with the aim of protecting young soldiers and sailors from the evil influence of vice.[88] The abolition of the quasi-legal space of Storyville had the unintended effect of permitting Lulu White to remain on Basin Street in contravention of the 1917 segregation-of-prostitutes ordinance. Prostitution did not cease, and White continued to live in Mahogany Hall and run her business there. Yet, after the district's special status came to an end, she suffered repeated raids by local police and federal agents. In 1918, for instance, agents of the U.S. Justice Department arrested White on eleven violations of different elements of the ordinance that abolished Storyville. White disputed the charges, claiming that she was running a legitimate business. She had put a hotel sign in front of Mahogany Hall and had opened a restaurant at her corner saloon. She took out this advertisement in a racing paper:

> ANNOUNCEMENT
> The proprietress of this restaurant has embarked in a legitimate business, and hereby respectfully solicits the patronage of all her former friends, as well as the public at large. Patrons will be served by waitresses who are REAL SOUTHERN BEAUTIES.
>
> Our specialty is Southern fried chicken and hot biscuits.

> LULU WHITE'S HOTEL
>
> 235 N. Basin Street.
>
> Adjoining this restaurant is Lulu White's Hotel, equipped with modern conveniences for making patrons comfortable.[89]

Her boarders were men, she insisted, not prostitutes, and White denied practicing prostitution herself over the previous "ten or fifteen years." She had, she testified, evicted all eighteen of the prostitutes living at Mahogany Hall, "sent a letter to that effect to the Superintendent of Police," and then "went to the City Hall and State office, and got a license to keep a restaurant and hotel."[90] She rented to the "transient trade," she insisted. Her only female residents were a maid who stayed with her through the night, because she was "afraid to stay alone," and her "legally adopted daughter," who had moved to New Orleans from her home in West Virginia after her husband had "gone to war." In spite of this the police harassed her four or five times a night, so that "I could not do anything wrong if I wanted to," she said.[91] She described the harassment:

> The police would come in and wake up the boarders and ask them their names and where they came from; Capt. Johnson gave his men instructions to go into my house every five minutes, and if the door was not opened right away, to break open the door. . . . [the boarders] would leave because they [the police] would wake them up every night five and six times and sometimes more often and when Capt. Johnson would come he would call me for everything he knew in the way of curse words. . . . Capt. Johnson even called me a Cock-sucker in front of the other officers, something which I have never done in my life.[92]

In contrast to White's earlier career, throughout which she received special consideration from the police force, she now faced not only constant harassment but also humiliation and denigration by the police. By this time Edward Whitaker had long since lost his position as police chief, and a new breed of "progressive reformers" reigned, with little sympathy for White and, perhaps more important, little desire to profit from prostitution.[93]

There is no doubt that White continued to run a brothel at Mahogany Hall after Storyville was supposed to cease operations, in spite of her claims otherwise. A federal agent who had been assigned to investigate prostitution in the former district testified in the spring of 1918 that he had entered Mahogany Hall with a partner. The maid had let them in and led them to White's famous mirror parlor, a "sitting room where there were two pianos, [and] the walls and ceiling were in looking glasses," and while the officers waited, three girls entered. "Some beer was ordered and paid for and some music by placing money in the music box, and dancing by one of the girls," who did the "Hoochy Macoochy" in the center of the room. The officer spoke to another one of the girls, "a thin slim girl [who] wanted me to go to bed with her and I put her off." The women were wearing loose "chemises" or "kimonos," one with "her bust hanging out."[94]

Two johns were busy upstairs, one of whom subsequently tried to hide himself behind an armoire.[95]

Found guilty of operating a bordello in violation of the ordinance "closing" Storyville, White was sentenced to pay a small fine but more terribly to "be imprisoned in the Parish Prison" for thirty days. Her lawyer filed an appeal. The appeal was rejected and the lower court's ruling affirmed. She applied for a rehearing on May 3, 1918, but before this case came up, White was arrested again—this time on federal charges for operating a brothel within ten miles of a military installation, Camp Nicholls.[96] On November 6, 1918, Lulu White and two of her boarders were again indicted for "unlawfully receiv[ing] and permit[ting] to be received for immoral purposes" two men into Mahogany Hall.[97] They were convicted, and "Lulu White, probably the most notorious operator of an immoral house in the old New Orleans district," was sentenced to serve a year and a day in the federal penitentiary.[98]

Most women convicted of the same crime spent only one or two months in the penitentiary. The judge had offered leniency to White on the condition that she sell her house and all her furnishings. As the *New Orleans States* put it: "'Lulu' must sell out or serve term in Pen."[99] White agreed to the arrangement but did not follow through in the time allowed and so earned the long sentence.[100] In March 1919, two federal marshals arrived in New Orleans to escort Lulu White to Oklahoma. "Heavy Men Take Lulu to Prison," read the headline.[101] According to her federal prison record, Lulu White, alias Lula White and Lula Hendley, who supposedly had no previous criminal record, was "Spanish" in her coloration and ethnicity.[102]

Prison was not kind to White. With the help of the prison doctor, she applied for a reduction in her sentence.[103] According to the physician, she had hemorrhoids, fistulas, and several tumors in her abdomen. He said that "according to her statements, she has been a heavy drinker, and drunk the greater portion of the time for 30 years. She is a nervous physical wreck, and has about all the ailments a human could possibly have."[104] Her lawyer, the same M. D. Dimitry who had represented prostitutes and madams in the 1917 segregation case, wrote to the U.S. attorney general in April 1919, pleading her case, but received no answer. Then on June 6, 1919, White wrote a letter in her own hand to the attorney general, A. Mitchell Palmer, requesting executive clemency and informing him:

> I am suffering dearly every day I am full of fistroyer [fistulas], rheumatism, and the doctor says I have two or three tumors in my abdomen—and can hardly walk and it is a matter of a short time I believe I will die, for God Sake do not let me die in this place! I am sixty years old and always tried to live within the law, I never served a jail term. This was a put up job on me by a man I thought was my friend.
>
> At the time I was running a restaurant and hotel, I am a tax payer and property owner for twenty five years in New Orleans, and, please be considerate and let me know my fate as I am suffering terrible pains.[105]

Lulu White's application included appeals from her lawyer, the prison doctor, and even from the original sentencing judge, Rufus Foster, who now believed that the example had been adequately supplied and that White should be released in the interest of mercy.[106] All of these appeals together convinced Attorney General Palmer to help White apply to the president of the United States for executive clemency.

In his letter to President Woodrow Wilson, Palmer wrote that he did "not at all agree with the view expressed by the judge that the sentence was severe," but he feared for White's health.[107] President Wilson commuted Lulu White's sentence by cable from Paris on June 16, 1919, and she was released from prison.[108] Twelve days later he signed the Treaty of Versailles.

White returned to New Orleans. In December, she leased out Mahogany Hall and moved into her corner saloon at 1200 Bienville Street, occupying the second-floor residence.[109] From there she ran what she called a soft drink company, but in fact she continued to operate a brothel.[110] To the U.S. Public Health Service, a division of the Treasury Department, White constituted a menace, and her "pardon" was astonishing. A Public Health Service official wrote to Palmer, requesting documentation that would confirm Wilson's role.[111] Palmer was quick to note that a commutation was not the same thing as a pardon, but he did forward the information.[112] Others were similarly incredulous about Wilson's intervention, with one reporter from the *Times-Picayune* implying a back-room connection.[113] Some observers suspected that White still maintained friends in high places with enough power to get the president's attention.

Lulu White's declining years are nearly invisible. She faced arrest several more times for running a brothel and for selling liquor in violation of the Volstead Act (Prohibition).[114] In 1929, she sold Mahogany Hall to Leon Heymann, the New Orleans department store mogul, for $10,000 cash. (He also bought the corner saloon business for $12,300.)[115] White was last arrested in February 1931, when she was living at 322 North Franklin Street.[116] She was charged with violating Act 199 of 1912—a state law that empowered authorities to define disorderly houses and to arrest their proprietors. Her health was very poor and she was apparently obese.[117] She died before her last case, several times delayed, came to trial.[118] The "notorious Basin Street enchantress" was said to have died in obscurity, poor and alone. In truth she had gone to be with relatives, but the notion of the tragic octoroon as always isolated and bereft of kin apparently persisted. In the 1930 federal census, her dwelling was listed as a rental property worth only $50, and she appears not to have left any estate.[119] Indeed, there was no recorded will for her and no accounting of her property at her death, despite the existence of her mysterious adopted daughter.

Lulu White is, and was, like Storyville itself, as much a myth as a reality. The "Diamond Queen of the Demimonde," the country's most famous octoroon, its most "notorious negress," was an image that Lulu White herself crafted, drawing on diverse social wellsprings with artistic virtuosity. Once the district lost its protected status and the publicity and advertising ceased, the image was impossible to perpetuate. With a federal law prohibiting prostitution, and another prohibiting the sale of alcohol, prostitution went underground, removed from the celebrity and commercial prestige it had enjoyed. The era of red-light districts passed, and the "spectacular wickedness" of Storyville went into hiding.[120] Furthermore, by the 1920s, the terms of white supremacy had largely been set. A democratic discourse embracing all whites as superior to all blacks helped remove African Americans from political participation while rhetorically elevating whites from different classes above them. Once disfranchisement was complete and racial segregation assured, the plantation imaginary ceased to resonate in the same way it once had. The liminal space of Storyville, and the liminal figure of the octoroon within it, faded away. There was no place for Lulu White. She died a relic of a different time, perhaps now truly a "tragic octoroon."

NOTES

1. New Orleans City Ordinance no. 13, 032 C.S. (1897). For the history of Storyville and Lulu White's place in it, see Emily Epstein Landau, *Spectacular Wickedness: Sex, Race, and Memory in Storyville, New Orleans* (Baton Rouge: Louisiana State University Press, 2013). This essay draws from the book.

2. By "marketing miscegenation," I mean the simultaneous promotion to white men of sex across the (perceived) color line, with women who themselves were labeled "octoroon" or otherwise designated "mixed." The naturalization of the notion of "mixed" race already betrays the essentialization of "race" as a biological category and hence is fraught with history, so let me emphasize that in this essay, and the book from which it comes, I am dealing with the world of advertising and desire within a straitening Jim Crow culture and not some permanent, biological entity.

3. U.S. Bureau of the Census, *Ninth Census of the United States* (Washington, D.C., 1870). Lulu White is not mentioned in this census, but she was probably about two years old by then. Nothing is known of her childhood or teenage years. Special thanks to Shelley Johnson Carey.

4. *Soards New Orleans City Directory* (New Orleans: L. Soards, 1888); Sanborn Fire Insurance Maps, City of New Orleans (Teaneck, N.J.: Chadwick-Healey, 1885–93). In 1894, the city renumbered all the houses in New Orleans to ease delivery of mail, and White's first New Orleans address translates into 110 South Basin Street in the present system, just uptown of the Canal Street dividing line, between Canal and what was then Gasquet Street and is now Tulane Avenue.

5. The transaction took place on July 3, 1897, but the record shows that White began negotiating to buy the property as early as June 14. Act no. 17 under notary George W. Flynn, July 3, 1897, Research Center, New Orleans Notarial Archives, New Orleans (cited hereafter as NONA).

6. Conveyance Office Book 166, folio 752 (August 2, 1897), and Conveyance Office Book 169, folio 193 (December 14, 1897), Conveyance Office, and Notarial Act no. 9280 under notary J. D. Taylor, July 26, 1897 and Notarial Act no. 9437, December 13, 1897, Research Center, NONA. I owe a debt of gratitude to Sally Reeves, the head of the notarial archives. Her knowledge of New Orleans architecture and her special attention to my project helped me immeasurably.

7. Conveyance Office Book 166, folio 752 (August 2, 1897), and Conveyance Office Book 169, folio 193 (December 14, 1897), Conveyance Office, and Notarial Act no. 9280 under notary J.D. Taylor, July 26, 1897 and Notarial Act no. 9437, December 13, 1897, Research Center, NONA; Martin Behrman, *Martin Behrman of New Orleans: Memoirs of a City Boss*, ed. John R. Kemp (Baton Rouge:

Louisiana State University Press, 1977); Edward F. Haas, *Political Leadership in a Southern City: New Orleans in the Progressive Era, 1896–1902* (Ruston, La.: McGinty Publications, 1988), 20. Years later, at the height of her fame, she would hire Flynn as her attorney.

8. *L'Hote vs. City of New Orleans et al.*, Division B Docket no. 54533 (1897), 47.

9. Interview with Manuel Manetta, Oral History Collection, William Ransom Hogan Jazz Archive, Tulane University, New Orleans.

10. Repeated to author by Shelley Johnson, a relative of one of the proprietors.

11. See Virginia Dominguez, *White by Definition: Social Classification in Creole Louisiana* (1986; New Brunswick, N.J.: Rutgers University Press, 1997). On legal definitions of race, see also Ariela Gross, "Litigating Whiteness: Trials of Racial Determination in the Nineteenth-Century South," *Yale Law Journal* 108, no. 1 (October 1998); *What Blood Won't Tell: A History of Race on Trial in America* (Cambridge: Harvard University Press, 2008). See also Emily Clark, *The Strange History of the American Quadroon: Free Women of Color in the Revolutionary Atlantic World* (Chapel Hill: University of North Carolina Press, 2013); Shirley Elizabeth Thompson, *Exiles at Home: The Struggle to Become American in Creole New Orleans* (Cambridge: Harvard University Press, 2009).

12. Interview with Manetta.

13. Storyville published yearly guides to the district, known collectively as "Blue Books." These guides featured advertisements for different bordellos as well as for liquor, pharmaceuticals, and local businesses. They also provided a directory of the houses and women working there, and this was organized by "race": "White," "Colored," "Octoroon," and, in some of the guides, "French 69" and "Jewish." See Landau, *Spectacular Wickedness*, esp. chapter 4.

14. For the history of the *Plessy* case and the Creoles of color in bringing it, see, for instance, Caryn Cossé Bell and Joseph Logsdon, "The Americanization of Creole New Orleans," in *Creole New Orleans: Race and Americanization*, ed. Arnold R. Hirsch and Joseph Logsdon (Baton Rouge: Louisiana State University Press, 1992), 201–61; Charles A. Lofgren, *The Plessy Case: A Legal-Historical Interpretation* (New York: Oxford University Press, 1987); Keith Weldon Medley, *We as Freemen: Plessy v. Ferguson* (Gretna, La: Pelican, 2003); Rebecca J. Scott, "The Atlantic World and the Road to *Plessy v. Ferguson*," *Journal of American History* 94, no. 3 (December 2007): 726–33; Scott and Jean Hébrard, *Freedom Papers: An Atlantic Odyssey in the Age of Emancipation* (Cambridge: Harvard University Press, 2012); Brook Thomas, *Plessy v. Ferguson: A Brief History with Documents* (Boston: Bedford Books, 1997); Barbara Young Welke, *Recasting American Liberty: Gender, Race, Law, and the Railroad Revolution, 1865–1920* (Cambridge University Press, 2001), esp. 338–51. On the crucial role gender played in the history of challenging segregation, see Barbara Young Welke, "When All the Women Were White, and All the Blacks Were Men: Gender, Class, Race, and the Road to *Plessy v. Ferguson*, 1885–1914," *Law and History Review* 13, no. 2 (Autumn 1995): 261–316.

15. See, for example, Glenda Elizabeth Gilmore, *Gender and Jim Crow: Women and the Politics of White Supremacy in North Carolina, 1896–1920* (Chapel Hill: University of North Carolina Press, 1995).

16. For a classic treatment, see Joel Williamson, *The Crucible of Race: Black-White Relations in the American South since Emancipation* (Oxford: Oxford University Press, 1984). More recent works include Crystal Nicole Feimster, *Southern Horrors: Women and the Politics of Rape and Lynching* (Cambridge: Harvard University Press, 2009); Amy Louise Wood, *Lynching and Spectacle: Witnessing Racial Violence in America, 1890–1940* (Chapel Hill: University of North Carolina Press, 2009).

17. For an especially good explanation of these processes, see Gilmore, *Gender and Jim Crow*, 61–89. See also Grace Elizabeth Hale, *Making Whiteness: The Culture of Segregation in the South, 1890–1940* (New York: Vintage Books, 1998).

18. See Landau, *Spectacular Wickedness*, chapter 3.

19. On Civil War memory and the Lost Cause, see David W. Blight, *Race and Reunion: The Civil War in American Memory* (Cambridge: Harvard University Press, 2002); Gaines Foster, *Ghosts of the Confederacy: Defeat, the Lost Cause, and the Emergence of the New South, 1865–1913* (Oxford: Ox-

ford University Press, 1988); Nina Silber, *Romance of Reunion: Northerners and the South* (Chapel Hill: University of North Carolina Press, 1989).

20. This is the central argument of my book. See Landau, *Spectacular Wickedness*, introduction and throughout.

21. See Ronald G. Walters, "The Erotic South: Civilization and Sexuality in American Abolitionism," *American Quarterly* 25, no. 2 (May 1973): 177–201; Jean Fagin Yellin, *Women and Sisters: The Antislavery Feminists in American Culture* (New Haven: Yale University Press, 1989).

22. Anna Elfenbein, *Women on the Color Line: Evolving Stereotypes and the Writings of George Washington Cable, Grace King, Kate Chopin* (Charlottesville: University Press of Virginia, 1989), 3.

23. Ibid. Other scholarly treatments of the tragic octoroon include Glenn Cannon Arbery, "Victims of Likeness: Quadroons and Octoroons in Southern Fiction," *Southern Review* 25, no. 1 (Winter 1989): 52–71; Judith Berzon, *Neither White nor Black: The Mulatto Character in American Fiction* (New York: New York University Press, 1978); Margaret Kellow, "The Fair Circassian: The Concubine in Feminist Antislavery Discourse," unpublished paper in author's possession; Margaret Kellow, "The Oriental Imaginary: Constructions of Female Bondage in Women's Antislavery Discourse," unpublished paper in author's possession; Susan Gillman, "The Mulatto, Tragic or Triumphant? The Nineteenth-Century American Race Melodrama," in *The Culture of Sentiment: Race, Gender and Sentimentality in Nineteenth-Century America*, ed. Shirley Samuels (New York: Oxford University Press, 1992), 221–43; James Kinney, *Amalgamation! Race, Sex, and Rhetoric in the Nineteenth-Century American Novel* (Westport, Conn.: Greenwood Press, 1985); Werner Sollors, *Neither Black nor White yet Both: Thematic Explorations in Interracial Literature* (Cambridge: Harvard University Press, 1997); Helen Taylor, *Gender, Race, and Region in the Writings of Grace King, Ruth McEnery Stuart, and Kate Chopin* (Baton Rouge: Louisiana State University Press, 1989); Jules Zanger, "The 'Tragic Octoroon' in Pre-Civil War Fiction," *American Quarterly* 18, no. 1 (Spring 1966): 63–70.

24. Walters, "The Erotic South." See Landau, *Spectacular Wickedness*, chapter 2. Two well-known examples of this literature are Harriet Beecher Stowe's *Uncle Tom's Cabin* and Dion Boucicault's play *The Octoroon*. Both works use New Orleans as a plot catalyst, for it was there, everybody knew, that light-skinned female slaves were auctioned off to white men of means. Harriet Beecher Stowe, *Uncle Tom's Cabin; or, Life among the Lowly*, in Stowe, *Three Novels* (New York: Library of America, 1982); Dion Boucicault, *The Octoroon; or, Life in Louisiana* (1859; Miami: Mnemosyne Publishing, 1969). See also Karen Sánchez-Eppler, *Touching Liberty: Abolition, Feminism, and the Politics of the Body* (1993; Berkeley: University of California Press, 1997), 41; George M. Fredrickson, *The Black Image in the White Mind: The Debate on Afro-American Character and Destiny, 1817–1914* (1971; Hanover, NH: University Press of New England, Wesleyan University Press, 1987), esp. 97–129; Mary Niall Mitchell, "'Rosebloom and Pure White,' or So It Seemed," *American Quarterly* 54, no. 3 (September 2002): 369–410.

25. Walter Johnson, "Masters and Slaves at the Market: Slavery and the New Orleans Trade, 1804–1864" (PhD diss., Princeton University, 1995), 130. See also Walter Johnson, "The Slave Trader, the White Slave, and the Politics of Racial Determination in the 1850s," *Journal of American History* 87, no. 1 (June 2000): 13–38; Walter Johnson, *Soul by Soul: Life inside the Antebellum Slave Market* (Cambridge: Harvard University Press, 1999); Mitchell, "Rosebloom and Pure White."

26. Walters, "The Erotic South."

27. Compare Drew Gilpin Faust, *James Henry Hammond and the Old South: A Design for Mastery* (Baton Rouge: Louisiana State University Press, 1982).

28. There is a large body of scholarship documenting the sexual abuses and excesses of the Southern slave system. Some examples include Peter W. Bardaglio, *Reconstructing the Household: Families, Sex, and the Law in the Nineteenth-Century South* (Chapel Hill: University of North Carolina Press, 1995); Peter W. Bardaglio, "'Shamefull Matches': The Regulation of Interracial Sex and Marriage in the South before 1900," in *Sex, Love, Race: Crossing Boundaries in American History*, ed.

Martha Hodes (New York: New York University Press, 1999), 112–38; Catherine Clinton, "'Southern Dishonor': Flesh, Blood, Race, and Bondage," in *In Joy and in Sorrow: Women, the Family, and Marriage in the Victorian South*, ed. Carol Bleser (New York: Oxford University Press, 1991), 52–68; Harriet A. Jacobs, *Incidents in the Life of a Slave Girl, Written by Herself*, enlarged ed., ed. Jean Fagan Yellin (Cambridge: Harvard University Press, 2000); Melton A. McLaurin, *Celia, a Slave: A True Story* (New York: Avon Books, 1991); Nell Irvin Painter, "Soul Murder and Slavery: Toward a Fully Loaded Cost Accounting," in *U.S. History as Women's History: New Feminist Essays*, ed. Linda K. Kerber, Alice Kessler Harris, and Kathryn Kish Sklar (Chapel Hill: University of North Carolina Press, 1995), 125–46; Deborah Gray White, *Ar'n't I a Woman: Female Slaves in the Plantation South*, revised ed. (New York: W. W. Norton, 1999). For the repression/elaboration complex, see Michel Foucault, *History of Sexuality*, vol. 1, *An Introduction*, trans. Robert Hurley (New York: Vintage Books, 1990); Michel Foucault, *Discipline and Punish: The Birth of the Prison*, trans. Alan Sheridan (New York: Vintage Books, 1979). See also Ann Laura Stoler, *Race and the Education of Desire: Foucault's* History of Sexuality *and the Colonial Order of Things* (Durham: Duke University Press, 1995).

29. See Kenneth Aslakson, "The Quadroon-*Plaçage* Myth: Anglo-American (Mis)interpretations of a French-Caribbean Phenomenon," *Journal of Social History* 45, no. 3 (Spring 2012): 709–34; Clark, *The Strange History of the American Quadroon.*

30. G. W. Pierson, "Alexis de Tocqueville in New Orleans, January 1–3, 1832," *Franco-American Review* 1, no. 1 (June 1936): 36.

31. Aslakson, "Quadroon-*Plaçage* Myth."

32. Shirley E. Thompson, "Ah, Toucoutou, Ye Conin Vous: History and Memory in Creole New Orleans," *American Quarterly* 53, no. 2 (June 2001): 232–66. See also Alecia P. Long, *The Great Southern Babylon: Sex, Race, and Respectability in New Orleans, 1880–1920* (Baton Rouge: Louisiana State University Press, 2004).

33. Landau, *Spectacular Wickedness*, chapter 2.

34. John H. B. Latrobe quoted in Joan M. Martin, "*Plaçage* and the Louisiana *Gens de Couleur Libre*: How Race and Sex Defined the Lifestyles of Free Women of Color," in *Creole: The History and Legacy of Louisiana's Free People of Color*, ed. Sybil Kein (Baton Rouge: Louisiana State University Press, 2000), 57–70.

35. Herbert A. Kellar, ed., "A Journey through the South in 1836: Diary of James D. Davidson," *Journal of Southern History* 1, no. 3 (August 1935): 358.

36. Matilda Charlotte (Jesse) Fraser Houston, *Texas and the Gulf of Mexico; or, Yachting in the New World* (1844; Austin, Tex.: W. Thomas Taylor, 1991), 55.

37. See Virginia Gould, "'In Full Enjoyment of Their Liberty': The Free Women of Color of the Gulf Ports of New Orleans, Mobile, and Pensacola, 1769–1860" (PhD diss., Emory University, 1991).

38. See Landau, *Spectacular Wickedness* and note 19 above on Civil War memory and the Lost Cause.

39. *Mascot* (New Orleans), January 20, 1894.

40. Ibid., December 15, 1894. White was not the only woman of ambiguous race to have claimed the West Indies as her native land. See Johnson, "The Slave Trader," 13–38. Alexina Morrison's lawyers suggested that she might be from the West Indies, as a way to indicate her "whiteness."

41. "The New Mahogany Hall," Williams Research Center, the Historic New Orleans Collection, acc. no. 56-15.

42. See Aslakson, "The Quadroon-*Plaçage* Myth." See also Landau, *Spectacular Wickedness*, esp. chapter 2, "The Quadroon Connexion." See also Emily Clark, "The Women across from Congo Square (1772–1840)," chapter one of this volume. On the iconicity of the "Mulatress" in colonial Cuba, see Vera M. Kutzinski, *Sugar's Secrets: Race and the Erotics of Cuban Nationalism* (Charlottesville: University Press of Virginia, 1993).

43. Lafcadio Hearn, *Two Years in the French West-Indies* (New York: Harper and Bros., 1890), 328. Thanks to Adam Rothman for pointing me to this book.

44. In The *Strange History of the American Quadroon*, Emily Clark argues that those practices did not simply originate in the French Caribbean but that women refugees from the Haitian Revolution and Cuban exile engaged in them exclusively. That is, she argues that native New Orleanians did not engage in quadroon balls or concubinage, only Caribbean women.

45. "The New Mahogany Hall."

46. Anne McClintock, *Imperial Leather: Race, Gender and Sexuality in the Colonial Contest* (London: Routledge, 1995), 149.

47. See Joseph Roach, *Cities of the Dead: Circum-Atlantic Performance* (New York: Columbia University Press, 1996); Joseph Roach, "Slave Spectacles and Tragic Octoroons: A Cultural Genealogy of Antebellum Performance," *Theatre Survey* 33, no. 2 (November 1992): 167–87.

48. "The New Mahogany Hall."

49. For an in-depth analysis of Storyville's advertising strategies, see Landau, *Spectacular Wickedness*, chapter 4.

50. Photographs of Lulu White, by anonymous photographer, 1892 (KI-DC: 2817, 70240, 70254, 70255, 70256, 70257, 70258, 70259, 70260, 70261, 70262, 70263), Kinsey Institute for Research in Sex, Gender, and Reproduction, Bloomington, Indiana. I am grateful to Catherine Johnson-Roehr at the Kinsey Institute for her help with these photographs.

51. The nature of White's voluntariness is, to be sure, open to interpretation. There are degrees of coercion and one could argue that her life as a colored prostitute, model, and madam was determined by the conditions of the Jim Crow South. However, such an interpretation would obviate White's profound individuality, her strategic self-fashioning, and her wealth and influence in New Orleans. It would render her a one-dimensional character, where I am seeking to show her as a fully formed, unique, and complex individual. I am not suggesting that the pictures were not exploitative; certainly they were. I do suggest that White exploited herself—down to her "one drop" of "African blood"—for profit. I elaborate this interpretation throughout the essay and in my book, *Spectacular Wickedness*. Alecia Long too writes that Lulu White both created and controlled the eroticized image of the octoroon and made the pictures herself to profit from that image. She writes that White "eagerly and creatively marketed herself and her girls as sexual objects" (Long, *The Great Southern Babylon*, 209).

52. According to Peter Gay, attending dog sex shows was itself a mode of bourgeois aspiration at the turn of the twentieth century. Peter Gay, *The Bourgeois Experience: Victoria to Freud*, 5 vols. (New York: Oxford University Press, 1984–1998), 2:353. See also Alain Corbin, *Women for Hire: Prostitution and Sexuality in France after 1850*, trans. Alan Sheridan (Cambridge: Harvard University Press, 1990), 124.

53. See, for instance, Beth Bailey, *From Front Porch to Back Seat: Courtship in Twentieth-Century America* (Baltimore: Johns Hopkins University Press, 1989); Elizabeth Alice Clement, *Love for Sale: Courting, Treating and Prostitution in New York City, 1900–1945* (Chapel Hill: University of North Carolina Press, 2006). There is another set of photographs in the Josie Arlington Collection, Manuscripts and Rare Books Division, Louisiana Collections, Earl K. Long Library, University of New Orleans. I am grateful to John Kelly and Florence Jumonville at the Earl K. Long Library for their help with these photographs.

54. For a fuller discussion, see Landau, *Spectacular Wickedness*, esp. chapters 4 and 5.

55. "The New Mahogany Hall."

56. Ibid.

57. Ibid.

58. *State v. Fred Miller and Felicia Carter*, Criminal District Court, Docket no. 36996 (May 19, 1909), City Archives, Louisiana Division, New Orleans Public Library.

59. *New Orleans Daily Picayune*, November 14, 1904; *State of Louisiana v. Lulu White*, First City Criminal Court, Parish of Orleans, Docket no. 40,733, City Archives, Louisiana Division, New Orleans Public Library; *City of New Orleans (appellee) v. Lulu White (appellant)*, Supreme Court of Louisiana, Docket no. 23,010, 18.

60. *New Orleans Daily Picayune*, November 14, 1904.

61. Ibid.

62. Ibid., November 15, 1904.

63. Russell Levy, "Of Bards and Bawds: New Orleans Sporting Life before and during the Storyville Era, 1897–1917" (master's thesis, Tulane University, 1967), 138–39.

64. *State of Louisiana ex rel. John Journee v. Board of Commissioners of the Police Department of the City of New Orleans*, Supreme Court of Louisiana, Docket no. 16,506, Supreme Court of Louisiana Collection, Mss. 106, Department of Special Collections, Earl K. Long Library, University of New Orleans. Former police inspector John Journée denied the charges brought against him for dereliction of duty and corruption, diagnosing the matter as a frame-up to put Whitaker in his job. He lost his case. See Levy, "Of Bards and Bawds," 121. Police inspector Whitaker was himself a spectacularly degraded character.

65. *State of Louisiana v. Lulu White*, Supreme Court of the State of Louisiana, Docket no. 15,896, 35.

66. Ibid., 29, 35.

67. Ibid. In contrast, Luc Santé writes that ten cents was steep for a bottle of beer at the same time in New York City's underworld. Luc Santé, *Low Life: Lures and Snares of Old New York* (1991; New York: Vintage Books, 1992). Elsewhere in the district a bottle or glass of beer cost a nickel.

68. *State of Louisiana v. Lulu White*, Supreme Court of the State of Louisiana, Docket no. 15,896.

69. *New Orleans Item*, December 7, 1906.

70. Ibid.

71. Ibid.

72. Ibid., December 22, 1906.

73. Ibid.

74. *New Orleans Daily Picayune*, November 4, 1909.

75. Ibid. Her listing in the city directory indicates that she lived in the district continuously, and then, in 1912, she increased her investment in Storyville by buying the property next to Mahogany Hall, on the corner of Bienville and Basin, where she opened up a saloon. Conveyance Office Book 249, folio 297, February 28, 1912, Conveyance Office. This saloon is the only extant Storyville structure. It is now a modest grocery store.

76. *New Orleans Daily Picayune*, September 10, 1911. According to Al Rose, White gave Killshaw $150,000 in 1907 to invest in Hollywood, thinking that she would like to try her hand at the movie business, and Killshaw disappeared with the money, double-crossing White and leaving her heart-broken. Rose's account is not to be believed—he provides neither evidence nor argument to support it. It is intriguing as part of the Lulu White myth in that it contains elements that are believable: White imagined herself a mogul of sorts and desired a much bigger stage on which to act out her own drama of life on the color line. There is some scant evidence that she may at one time have traveled to California.

77. Mark Thomas Connelly writes that "prostitution" was a master symbol at the turn of the century. *The Response to Prostitution in the Progressive Era* (Chapel Hill: University of North Carolina Press, 1980).

78. See Landau, *Spectacular Wickedness*, chapter 6; Long, *The Great Southern Babylon*, 191–224.

79. Ordinance No. 4118, C.C.S., February 7, 1917.

80. Louis Armstrong, *Satchmo: My Life in New Orleans* (1954; New York: Da Capo Press, 1968).

81. See Landau, *Spectacular Wickedness*, chapter 6 ("notorious attraction" quote on 171). See also Alecia Long, *Great Southern Babylon*, chapter 5.

82. *Lulu White v. City of New Orleans*, Civil District Court for the Parish of Orleans, Docket 5, no. 119,511, Division "E," City Archives, Louisiana Division, New Orleans Public Library. For Willie V. Piazza's response to the ordinance, see Long, *The Great Southern Babylon*, 217–24.

83. Civil Court Docket Books, City Archives, Louisiana Division, New Orleans Public Library.

84. *Agnes Morris* [Morrison?] *v. City of New Orleans*, Civil District Court, Parish of Orleans, Docket 5, no. 120,693, Division "A," City Archives, Louisiana Division, New Orleans Public Library. See also *Carrie Gross v. City of New Orleans*, Civil District Court, Parish of Orleans, Docket 5, no. 120,325, Division "D," Louisiana Division, New Orleans Public Library.

85. City Attorney Records (1917), City Archives, Louisiana Division, New Orleans Public Library.

86. *Lulu White v. City of New Orleans*, Civil District Court, Docket 5, no. 119,511. The wording is awkward and ungrammatical, but the message is clear.

87. Ibid.

88. See Landau, *Spectacular Wickedness*, chapter 6.

89. Newspaper ad for White's restaurant, December 1, 1917, clipping found in the Records of the War Department General and Special Staffs, War College Division and War Plans Division, Subordinate Offices—Education and Recreation Branch, Commission on Training Camp Activities, Entry 395, Reports Relating to Training Camp Activities, 1917 (National Archives Records Administration, College Park, Md.), record group 165, box 8, "Kentucky to Louisiana," emphasis in original (hereafter, War Department records, NARA College Park); testimony in *City of New Orleans (Appellee) vs. Lulu White (Appellant)*, Supreme Court of Louisiana, Docket no. 23,010, Supreme Court of Louisiana Collection, Acc. 106, Department of Archives and Manuscripts, Earl K. Long Library, University of New Orleans; *The State of Louisiana v. Lulu White and Clyde Robinson*, Docket no. 44,008, City Archives, Louisiana Division, New Orleans Public Library.

90. White's testimony, *City of New Orleans (Appellee) vs. Lulu White (Appellant)*, Supreme Court of Louisiana, Docket no. 23,010, Supreme Court of Louisiana Collection, Acc. 106, Department of Archives and Manuscripts, Earl K. Long Library, University of New Orleans, 18. In this trial White gave her age as "going on 53." In 1918 that would make her birth date 1866 or 1865, again confusing the record.

91. White's testimony, *City of New Orleans (Appellee) vs. Lulu White (Appellant)*, Supreme Court of Louisiana, Docket no. 23,010, Supreme Court of Louisiana Collection, Acc. 106, Department of Archives and Manuscripts, Earl K. Long Library, University of New Orleans, 18.

92. Ibid., 21.

93. See Long, *The Great Southern Babylon*, chapter 5.

94. Special agents' testimony from *City of New Orleans (Appellee) vs. Lulu White (Appellant)*, 7.

95. Ibid.

96. The charge was for a violation in May 1918.

97. *United States v. Lulu White, et al.*, U.S. District Court, Docket no. 4097, National Archives Records Administration, Fort Worth, Texas (hereafter NARA Ft. Worth).

98. She was found guilty of running an immoral house within five miles of a government military post. *New Orleans States*, March 1, 1919.

99. *New Orleans States*, December 2, 1918. Thanks to Tad Jones for bringing my attention to this article.

100. Her incorrigibility was underscored when she was arrested again for running a bordello during the period in which she was supposed to sell out. *United States v. Lulu White*, U.S. District Court, Docket no. 4015, Eastern District of Louisiana, NARA Ft. Worth [October 10, 1918].

101. *New Orleans States*, March 6, 1919. Thanks to Tad Jones for bringing my attention to this article.

102. Application for Executive Clemency, Justice Department Records, Rec. 33 p. 616–1185, record group 204, box 850, Series Title "Pardon", NARA College Park.

103. There was a rule that sentences of one year did not allow for parole.

104. Application for Executive Clemency, Justice Department Records, NARA College Park.

105. Ibid.

106. Ibid.

107. Ibid.

108. Ibid.; "Lulu White, Sentence Commutation 1919-08-23"; Case File Record 33-616, RG 204, box 850, "Pardon Case Files 1853–1946," microfilm at Law Division, Library of Congress, Washington, D.C.

109. Conveyance Office Book 315, folio 328, Conveyance Office Records.

110. *Soards New Orleans City Directory.*

111. Letter, William Edler, scientific assistant, United States Public Health Service, September 4, 1920, Application for Executive Clemency, Justice Department Records, NARA College Park.

112. Application for Executive Clemency, Justice Department Records, NARA College Park.

113. Ibid.

114. *State of Louisiana v. Lulu White and Clyde Robinson*, Criminal District Court, Docket no. 44,008, City Archives, Louisiana Division, New Orleans Public Library; *United States v. Lulu E. Hendley (Alias Lulu White) and Clyde Robinson*, U.S. District Court, Docket no. 6011, Eastern Division of Louisiana, New Orleans Division, Filed October 25, 1922, NARA, Fort Worth; *United States v. Lulu Hendley and Corrolanus Hopkins*, Docket no. 7633, U.S. District Court, Eastern Division of Louisiana, New Orleans Division, Filed December 12, 1923, NARA, Fort Worth; *United States v. Lulu E. Hendley and Corolanus* [*sic*] *Hopkins, and Clyde Robinson*, Docket no. 8465, Eastern Division of Louisiana, New Orleans Division, Filed June 11, 1924, NARA, Fort Worth; *United States v. Lulu Hendley, alias Lulu White*, United States District Court, Docket no. 13,432, NARA Ft. Worth.

115. Conveyance Office Book 447, folio 368, April 8, 1929, and Conveyance Office Book 451 folio 446, July 15, 1929, Conveyance Office Records.

116. This address for White also appears in the Conveyance Office records of White's sale on Mahogany Hall. Ibid.

117. Eleanor Early, *New Orleans Holiday* (New York: Rinehart, 1947), 242.

118. "8/21/31 Defendant dead," is the spare notation on the affidavit. There was a small notice in the *Times-Picayune* that a "Lula White" had passed away in the early morning of August 20. There is also a death certificate for a woman of that name from East Feliciana, a parish outside of the city, which matches the *Times-Picayune* notice. The East Feliciana woman was listed as married to a Dr. White with children, and her race was listed as "white." Though a stunning coincidence, our Lulu White's death certificate clearly indicates that she died out of state. *Times-Picayune*, August 21, 1931.

119. U.S. Bureau of the Census, *Fourteenth Census of the United States (Louisiana), Schedule 1—Population* (Washington, D.C., 1930), Enumeration District 36-62, 33.

120. On this process in larger contexts, see Timothy J. Gilfoyle, *City of Eros: New York, Prostitution, and the Commercialization of Sex, 1790–1920* (New York: W. W. Norton, 1994), 313–15.

Neda Jurisich, Eva Vujnovich, and Mary Jane Munsterman Tesvich

(1904–2002; 1929– ; 1955–)

Three Generations in a Croatian-American Oyster Family

CAROLYN E. WARE

Neda Taliancich Jurisich, born and raised on Croatia's impoverished Dalmatian Coast, arrived in southern Louisiana in 1928 to begin a new life as an oysterman's wife. At her family's urging, twenty-four-year-old Neda had married a Croatian emigrant she barely knew and then went back with him to America, hoping to build a better life there. She knew little about Louisiana apart from her New Orleans–based brothers' letters describing the city's "busy markets brimming with seafood, fruits and vegetables" and the "charming towns" along the lower Mississippi River.[1] Her brothers' depictions, and their settled lives in New Orleans, could not have prepared Neda for life along a remote Louisiana bayou on the brink of the Great Depression.

Croatian immigrants and their descendants have been an important ingredient in Louisiana's ethnic mix since the early nineteenth century, making significant contributions to the state's history, economy, and culture. Their transformation of the local oyster industry from small-scale, seasonal harvesting to a year-round farming enterprise shaped Louisiana's famous cuisine and tourism, as well as its fisheries. Croatian families founded a number of legendary restaurants in New Orleans and its environs, and Croatian-American oyster growers and processors still provide many of the oysters served in the city's restaurants and oyster bars.[2]

Relatively small, with five or six thousand members dispersed throughout the greater New Orleans area, Louisiana's Croatian community has attracted far less scholarly attention than more populous Louisiana ethnic groups, such as Cajuns, Creoles, African Americans, and Native Americans. In particular, Croatian-American women's impact on Louisiana history and culture has largely been overlooked. Yet the lives of female Croatian immigrants and their

NEDA JURISICH

Courtesy of Mary Jane Tesvich.

descendants offer a broader and more nuanced understanding of ethnic history and identity in coastal Louisiana, a reminder that the state is profoundly multicultural as well as multiracial. Croatian women's experiences add a critical ingredient to what is often called the multicultural gumbo of Louisiana.[3]

At the time of Neda Jurisich's arrival in the late 1920s, Croatian men had been living along the Gulf coast and employing their "ancient customs in all industries pertaining to the sea" for about a century.[4] The earliest Croatian settlers, well-traveled seamen, jumped ship in New Orleans, where they found employment on the city's riverfront or opened their own restaurants, oyster saloons, boardinghouses, and other businesses. By the 1850s, newly arrived fishermen from Croatia's Dalmatian Coast were settling downriver of the city in lower Plaquemines Parish, a soggy, mosquito-plagued frontier "hostile . . . in every way to humanity" but rich in oysters, shrimp, crabs, and fish.[5] Louisiana's coastal marshes offered an economic toehold for poverty-stricken Dalmatians who already "knew the ways of the water," were well acquainted with hardship, and were willing to work hard and live frugally in hopes of earning enough money to return home to Croatia.[6]

By the late nineteenth century, a steady stream of Croatian men and boys headed to Plaquemines Parish to fish oysters. Among the region's primarily French-speaking residents, they earned a reputation for being exceptionally industrious, honest, and so strong that a Croatian man could reputedly "take a barrel on his thick shoulders and lift it over the levee with the same ease that others would show in rolling it."[7] Their native-born Louisiana neighbors were said to be "amazed at the attraction that work held" for the newcomers, an attribute that still informs perceptions of local Croatians.[8]

Nineteenth-century Croatian immigrants reinvented Louisiana's oyster industry at a time when national demand for oysters was growing. In their hands, it became "probably the most efficient of the delta gathering enterprises," a systematic cycle of planting, cultivating, and harvesting oysters on privately leased water bottoms.[9] Their efforts, and those of later Croatians immigrants, helped to make Louisiana the nation's top oyster producer. Families of Croatian descent are among the industry's most prominent leaders, and in southern Louisiana, Croatian ethnic identity and oyster cultivation remain closely entwined.

It was Croatian women, however, who transformed these transient fishermen into a stable Croatian-American community. As they began joining their husbands in Louisiana in the early twentieth century, immigrant women became a significant force in their families' economic and cultural survival. Women in general, of course, have always been essential to managing the household economy, although their work has gone unrecognized until recently.[10] In coastal Louisiana, Croatian women raised children in small cabins perched above the marsh, planted vegetable gardens to feed their families, maintained households, and often assisted with family oyster businesses. Immigrant mothers offered their children access to mainstream American society through education and land ownership, but they also reinforced Croatian cultural ties by cooking traditional dishes, instructing their children in Roman Catholic practices, and teaching them the Croatian language and songs. Most crucially, generations of Croatian women instilled in their children the core values of hard work, perseverance, dedication to family, self-denial when necessary, and fortitude in the face of crisis. Musing about her mother, Neda Jurisich, and other immigrant women, Eva Vujnovich comments that for a very long time, "To me, the ladies have been working and holding up their men."[11]

In some respects, pioneering Croatian women in Louisiana had much in common with immigrant women elsewhere in the United States. By the beginning of the twentieth century, thousands of women from eastern and southern Europe were flocking to America's industrial regions, where they were "channeled into the bursting ghettos of expanding cities."[12] The majority worked long hours, lived in primitive conditions, and struggled to learn a new language and adapt to a new culture. In urban areas, married women often contributed to family income by taking in boarders or doing sewing at home. Unmarried women performed wage labor as factory laborers and domestic workers—typically work that no one else wanted. Like Croatian women in southern Louisiana, urban immigrants felt the stigma of being foreign, and they wanted better lives for their children.[13]

In other ways, however, Croatian immigrant women's experiences in coastal Louisiana were uniquely shaped by the region's geography, semitropical weather, natural resources, and cultural blend. In particular, the demands and rhythms of oyster farming created "not only a distinctive form of work with the Dalmatians" but an entire way of life "around which all their activities revolve."[14] Making a living from Louisiana's waterways offered Croatian families the independence and entrepreneurship they valued, but it also meant numerous risks and deprivations. Coastal life demanded adaptability and a strong will to succeed. For immigrant women raising their children in isolated oyster camps, with husbands gone for long periods and neighbors a boat trip away, it could be a lonely and uncomfortable life. The coastal marshes where oysters thrived were particularly vulnerable to floods and hurricanes that periodically destroyed homes and oyster boats and drowned entire families. Those who survived stoically rebuilt homes and businesses, sometimes several times during a lifetime.[15]

Today Louisiana has one of the oldest Croatian communities in the United States, and women play essential roles in many areas of local life. Southern Louisiana Croatians now work in a range of professions, but they remain most closely linked to the oyster industry. Oyster farming is an uncertain and risky occupation that demands as much of women as it does of men, and husbands and wives are both expected to work toward the family's betterment, without complaint or self-pity. When men spend days at a time on their boats, their wives assume additional responsibilities at home. Mary Jane Tesvich, whose grandfather, father, and husband all fished oysters, explains, "This is a rough business to be in. The husband's gone a lot. . . . We don't even question that. You raise your kids yourself."[16]

This essay traces the lives and influences of three generations of strong, resourceful women in one southern Louisiana family, whose collective experiences span more than a century. Matriarch Neda Jurisich, daughter Eva Vujnovich, and granddaughter Mary Jane Tesvich personify the challenges that Louisiana Croatian women have faced as first-generation immigrants and later as members of a small, close-knit ethnic community. All three women married Croatian-born oystermen, raised their children largely on their own, contributed significantly to their family's economic security, worked hard to offer their children advantages they lacked, and drew on inner strength to recover from setbacks and "turn trying circumstances . . . into opportunity."[17] Each succeeded in making her mark in her community, skillfully maneuvering within, and sometimes at the boundaries of, gender conventions.[18]

Each generation of women overcame particular challenges. Leaving her native Dalmatia in 1928, Neda Jurisich adapted to a new husband, a new country and language, and a new occupation. For forty years, she ignored traditional gendered divisions of labor and outperformed seasoned fishermen in the "men's work" of oyster farming. With her proceeds, she then bought land and built a home that rooted her family in America. Neda's daughter, Louisiana-born Eva Jurisich Vujnovich, straddled her parents' Croatian immigrant world and English-speaking American society, wrestling with the stigma of immigrant identity. After attending beauty college and managing her own hair salon for five years, she married a Croatian-American oysterman, raised six children, helped her husband build a successful New Orleans oyster processing business, and used her financial acumen to ensure the family's economic security. Mary Jane Vujnovich Munsterman Tesvich, a member of the third generation who spent a typical American childhood in suburban New Orleans, was the first in her immediate family to attend college. Widowed young, she found strength in her mother's and grandmother's stoicism and supported her children by working several jobs. Now remarried to an old-fashioned Croatian oysterman, she balances her career as a domestic violence victims' advocate with family responsibilities, and American feminism with Croatian ideals of wifely submission.[19]

Neda Taliancich Jurisich

Neda Taliancich was born on May 8, 1904, in Igrane, a Dalmatian Coast village where her family struggled to raise olives and grapes on tiny plots of rocky soil. Not long after Neda's birth, her older brothers emigrated to find work abroad, as did virtually all of Dalmatia's young men. The family's suffering was particularly intense during World War I, when blockades cut off food supplies and disease was rampant. Neda recalled drinking kerosene to stave off an epidemic that killed several family members, and eating grass because everything else had died.[20]

Neda began contributing to her family's livelihood at a very young age, as peasant girls and women typically did. As a child, she worked in the vegetable garden that fed the family, tended their few livestock, and made daylong journeys over a nearby mountain to collect firewood and foliage for the animals. Her formal education consisted of four years of schooling, during which she learned to read and write. After that, her parents needed her full-time labor. Neda hauled buckets of concrete and carted stones on her back for wealthier neighbors, who paid her wages to the family. For "anybody who needed help in the village," her daughter Eva Vujnovich explains, "she was hired out to do the job."[21] For the rest of her life, Neda remembered the shame of being poor and unschooled in a society that equated education with social status. She told her children that wealthier villagers such as schoolteachers had held their noses when she passed by, as if she stank. In response to these early challenges, she developed an exceptionally strong constitution, an even stronger will, and a determination that her own children would have access to education and other advantages.[22]

When Neda turned twenty-four in 1928, her family decided that she should marry. Her father's drinking binges were disrupting family life, draining their finances, and often ending in beatings for his wife and daughters. Marriage, one of very few options for changing Neda's situation, almost inevitably entailed emigration. World War I had killed many of Dalmatia's young men, and the remainder sought work in other countries. Neda was corresponding with a Croatian expatriate in Australia when her Louisiana-based brothers, Peter and Leopold Taliancich, wrote home about a new suitor. Their friend Frank Jurisich, fifteen years older than Neda, had admired her photograph and wanted to marry her. Neda's brothers encouraged her to accept Frank's long-distance proposal and come to America, where she would "no longer suffer starvation, wars, and lack of supplies."[23]

The couple exchanged photographs and letters, and Neda agreed to marry Frank before meeting him in person. Her decision may have been influenced by his good looks, but her American brothers were probably more compelling factors. Neda would have family in Louisiana, a tremendous social and cultural advantage. In 1928, during the traditionally slow summer months for oystermen, Frank traveled to Igrane to meet, marry (in June), and escort his bride back to America. These wedding trips were customary for bridegrooms able to afford the trip, but Frank had to borrow money from Neda's more prosperous and entrepreneurial brothers, who were apparently eager to facilitate the match.[24]

Neda's negotiation between familiar Croatian traditions and new American ways began immediately, when Frank insisted that Neda bob her long hair in the modern style. Her shocked parents threatened to disown her if she cut her hair, but Frank told his in-laws, "She's going to America. She needs to be American."[25] Within a month of meeting, the newlyweds were headed for Louisiana by way of New York, a shipboard honeymoon that Neda recalled as the happiest weeks of her life.[26]

Neda's brothers awaited them in New Orleans, where the couple briefly went their separate ways. Frank returned to Plaquemines Parish to prepare his Bayou La Chute oyster camp, while Neda remained in the city, home to a close-knit Croatian-American community of business owners. Staying with brother Peter's family in their comfortable New Orleans home, she helped her sister-in-law recover from childbirth. Neda's bonds with her brothers and their families, though sometimes strained, proved invaluable throughout her lifetime, especially as Frank Jurisich had no close relatives in Louisiana. Her relatives' homes offered a welcome change from the discomforts of bayou life, and Neda chose to give birth to both of her children, with the assistance of a midwife, at her brother Leopold Taliancich's New Orleans home.[27]

The next step of Neda's journey was a train voyage to Empire, a Plaquemines Parish fishing village sixty miles south of the city. Disembarking at a general store, she met several townswomen who voiced concern about her ability to survive life in the marshes. An undeterred Neda assured them that she would be all right with her husband, and the Jurisiches set out in Frank's small "putt-putt" boat for the hour-and-a-half trip to Bayou La Chute. Neda's first impression of the expansive prairie (as Louisiana's coastal marshes are known) was of "nothing but weeds and tall grass" and hordes of mosquitoes.[28] She was even more dismayed by her first sight of Frank's camp, an unpainted two-room cabin with a detached kitchen, sitting on piers above an island of oyster shells. On discovering that this was her new home, she realized that the "hard life she had tried to escape" would continue in this new setting.[29]

Despite her disappointment, Neda Jurisich tackled bayou life with characteristic vigor. One of her first tasks was learning to cook. Growing up, she had been too busy "working out" to cook anything beyond boiled cabbage and fish. Her family laughs about her early mistakes, but she soon became an excellent cook known for traditional Louisiana-Croatian dishes such as oyster spaghetti, oyster soup, and Croatian pastries. A proficient gardener, she grew a variety of vegetables and fruit trees in her garden, raised chickens, made her own bread, and harvested fresh crabs, fish, and oysters to feed her family. Although the Jurisich family had little money for many years, they never lacked good food, even when Frank was often gone for days at a time on his fishing boat.[30]

Neda also set about improving Frank's camp, now her home. She built coops for her chickens, constructed a bridge across a ditch on their homestead, made furniture for the family home, and painted "No Trespassing" signs to warn poachers off Frank's oyster beds. Her efforts continued throughout the years. According to family members, Neda was "always hammering nails everywhere."[31] Turning her carpentry and domestic skills to the family's oyster boat, she built benches that made culling (sorting) oysters much easier and sewed canvas gloves to protect workers' hands.

She soon discovered that her middle-aged husband was "not too much of a go-getter," and the family's oyster business was struggling.[32] During the Depression years, demand for oysters declined, prices fell to fifty cents a hundred-pound sack, and fishing families "had to shine [oysters] like gold to sell them."[33] Neda, young and ambitious, responded by becoming the family's primary planner, decision maker, and "pusher."[34] One of her first decisions was to join Frank Jurisich on the family boat, the *Bruseloff*. Dressed in men's trousers and work cap, she mastered the strenuous work of shoveling piles of seed oysters overboard for planting, harvesting them with long-handled tongs, and lugging hundred-pound oyster sacks. Her skills and strength earned the respect of seasoned fishermen, and Frank often had difficulty keeping up with her. Acknowledging the self-discipline that drove Neda to "be aggressive and get on the boat" for her family's benefit, her granddaughter commented, "I wouldn't say she loved it. She didn't. It was a hard life."[35] Through examples and stories of her triumphs over hardship, Neda Jurisich taught her children and grandchildren to value self-reliance, hard work, and loyalty.

Motherhood added a new, conflicting set of responsibilities. Neda gave birth to daughter Eva in New Orleans in 1929 and son Mitchell fifteen months later. The family's economic situation remained precarious for years. Frank Jurisich, kind and personable when sober, became paranoid and contentious when he drank, which was often. He would quarrel with hired deckhands, who would quit, leaving Neda to "run out there and help him with the oysters."[36] This pattern repeated itself for years, but Neda "learned how to work around" Frank's problems and remained a loyal (if outspoken) business partner and wife until his death in 1965.[37]

Fishing oysters with Frank meant long days on the boat, away from her children. Neda learned to be creative in juggling work and child care, but her solutions sometimes challenged local ideas of the maternal role. When her children were very small, Neda locked them in the camp's detached kitchen for several hours at a time, as she and her husband worked on nearby oyster beds. Shouting instructions over the water, she taught her young daughter to kill, clean, and cook chickens for the family dinner. Some years later, after moving to Empire for her children's schooling, Neda decided to rejoin Frank on their oyster boat. Again she left daughter Eva in charge of her younger brother for most of the day, with a neighbor checking on them periodically. Some non-Croatian townspeople were apparently "appalled and shocked to see this mother and wife leave with her husband each morning to plant, harvest, and bag oysters."[38] Daughter Eva Vujnovich jokes that today authorities "would have taken us away from her" for leaving them unsupervised, but independent-minded Neda "never worried about what other people said."[39] She focused on doing what was necessary to keep her family intact and financially viable, ignoring any criticism.

Neda's strong will and perseverance were equally evident in her relationship with her husband. During the early years of their marriage, Frank and Neda's very different personalities and priorities often clashed. They quarreled over their oyster business, their children's education, and Frank's drinking. Having endured her father's alcoholic bouts, she was not inclined to meekly tolerate her husband's drunkenness and periodically tossed Frank's bottles into the bayou. When their children were very young, the couple's battles boiled over when Frank, in a drunken rage, threw a basin of water in his wife's face. A furious Neda made the long boat trip to Empire and summoned the sheriff to their camp. Her unexpected response frightened Frank, and he apologized to her. Still angry, Neda took her two young children to New Orleans and stayed with her brother Peter for a while. In exchange, she helped tend his seven young children, who "tormented and teased" Neda about her imperfect English.[40]

This episode was a critical turning point in the Jurisich marriage. Neda seriously contemplated a permanent separation from her husband, a drastic step in a traditional culture that places a high value on family integrity. Divorce was rare in Croatian-American families in the early 1930s. When it did occur, the wife received most of the criticism because it was seen as her duty to hold her family together.[41] Ultimately Neda chose to reconcile with her husband in the best interest of her children—and for her own autonomy. Feeling like a servant in her brother's home, she decided, in daughter Eva's words, "'The heck with this, I'm going back to my husband . . . and be my own boss . . . and do what I can to help myself.'"[42] Her actions were a clear declaration of marital boundaries: she would not tolerate her husband's physical abuse. Frank never treated her roughly again, although he did still drink too much and "carry on" at times.[43]

One area of contention was their children's education, particularly their daughter's. Like most Dalmatian immigrants, Neda Jurisich believed that school offered the key to a better way of life. Typically, Croatian fishing families were determined to send their children to school and willing to tolerate long separations to do so. Croatian mothers and their children usually moved inland once the oldest child reached school age, rejoining the father at the fishing camp each summer—a custom that distinguished them from their often-illiterate French and Spanish neighbors in the marsh. Accordingly, as her daughter approached school age, Neda began planning a move to Empire, which had a one-room school. Frank Jurisich, however, resisted. Eva Vujnovich recalls, "He didn't want us to go to school, at all. He didn't believe that women should be educated."[44]

Neda put her foot down and eventually prevailed, as she usually did. By 1936,

Neda had scraped together enough money from oyster sales to buy a piece of land next to St. Ann Catholic Church in Empire. "She'd get this little piece of money," according to Eva Vujnovich, and tell her husband, "You're going to go into Empire and you're going to buy this lot . . . and you're going to get a house there. And these kids are going to school."[45] The Jurisiches paid $2,500 to have a house built to her specifications, and Neda moved her children in. This purchase had significance far beyond her children's education. For immigrant families, owning land represented "roots in, and identification with" their new country, and thus permanence and security.[46] Neda's beloved, sturdy house proved to be a good investment, surviving catastrophic hurricanes that sent other buildings adrift and sheltering three generations of family members long after the bayou oyster camp—and Bayou La Chute itself—was swallowed by Gulf of Mexico waters.[47]

With her children attending school in Empire, Neda sought ways to stay in town and earn money. Deciding to try a sideline business, she added a smaller building next to her home and opened a sandwich shop. Rising every morning at three o'clock to fry oysters, she made sandwiches to sell to workers at the local seafood cannery. After a few years, however, "she wasn't happy with that," her daughter Eva says, so she closed the shop and went back to work on the family's oyster boat.[48] However, she ensured that the shop building continued to produce income, first renting it out as an apartment and later converting it to a beauty salon for her daughter.

The Jurisich family's oyster business gained financial stability in the post–World War II years, as oyster prices rose and son Mitchell (a hard worker like his mother) began working full time with his parents. The business expanded to include two boats, and Neda and Frank Jurisich continued working together until they finally retired in the 1960s, handing over the business over to Mitchell. Their tenacity paid off, and now third and fourth generations of Jurisiches—Mitchell's sons and grandsons—run the business that Neda and Frank nurtured, using the same boats and farming many of the same oyster beds that have been in the family for almost a century.[49]

Neda faced a different kind of challenge in 1965, when Hurricane Betsy roared into lower Plaquemines Parish. Hurricanes are a regular feature of coastal life, and the Jurisiches usually evacuated for severe storms. This time, seventy-six-year-old Frank, ill and needing a wheelchair to get around, did not feel like leaving home, and Neda decided to ride out the storm with him and their son. When a nine-foot tidal surge flooded Empire and sent the Catholic church floating into Neda's yard, the family climbed into their attic to wait out the storm. They were stranded without electricity or running water for four days, and Frank became increasingly sick and then delirious. Finally, a National Guard truck managed to navigate the flooded streets and transported Frank to a regional hospital, where he died a month later. Neda remained by his side the entire time and grieved deeply for her husband of almost forty years. Her long-ago decision to remain in her marriage, on her own terms, had proved to be wise.[50]

To the end of her long life, Neda Jurisich remained an early riser, a hard worker who mowed her own grass and dug in her garden, an excellent and generous cook, and a faithful member of St. Ann Catholic Church. When she died in 2002 at the age of ninety-seven, she left a strong impression not only on her children, grandchildren, and great-grandchildren, but on the larger community as well. Mary Jane Tesvich commented that "Baba" (Grandmother) had taught her to "never give up, never look for handouts," and to "go to work and dig yourself out of whatever comes your way."[51]

Traditional immigrant stories may stress the intrepidness of the patriarch, but for this family, it is clear that matriarch Neda Taliancich Jurisich set a strong example and grew the family business for the next generation. Her life exemplified values that Louisiana Croatians consider central to their cultural identity: an emphasis on family relationships, hospitality, perseverance, self-sacrifice for the good of her family, and the ability to remain strong in a crisis. Her legacy includes the stories her children and grandchildren now retell about the obstacles she overcame.

Eva Jurisich Vujnovich

Eva Jurisich, Neda and Frank Jurisich's daughter, was born in New Orleans in 1929, the first native-born member of her immediate family. She spent her first seven years in the family's Bayou La Chute oyster camp, speaking only Croatian, entertaining herself with playthings she created, and performing domestic responsibilities such as cooking and caring for her younger brother while her parents worked. This isolated and somewhat lonely existence, she later told her children, inspired her desire for a large family of her own. These beginnings developed Eva's self-reliance and left no room for self-pity. The family lived at the camp "with nothing" yet "didn't think it was hard," she says. "You didn't cry" about difficulties.[52]

When her mother Neda moved her children to Empire in 1936, seven-year-old Eva was suddenly immersed in an English-speaking world that viewed her family's ways as foreign and strange. Attending a one-room school that spanned seven grades, she learned to understand and speak English almost without being aware of the process. One day, "I didn't know what they were telling me," and the next, "I knew what they were telling me."[53] As the first family member to become literate in English, she became her parents' translator: "I would have to read all their paperwork and everything and help them out with that English stuff."[54]

Eva Jurisich's youthful experiences with education, work, and recreation reveal her skill in crossing cultural boundaries. In many ways, hers was a typical small-town Louisiana experience: she competed on her high school girls' basketball team, jitterbugged to country-and-western music, played the organ in church, gave her girlfriends manicures, and sang along with them to Mario Lanza records. In 1947, she became the first in her immediate family to earn a high school degree. At the same time, she spoke Croatian at home with her parents and participated in various Croatian social events in the Empire area. She recalls feeling ambivalent about this immigrant identity: "When you grow up in a Croatian family, you feel like you're not equal to [other Americans]. . . . You're the immigrant. So you wanted to get away from that."[55]

Always a music lover, Eva would have liked to continue her education by studying music at Tulane University and becoming a music teacher. In reality, as the daughter of working-class immigrant parents, she had little say in choosing her career, although her options far outnumbered her mother's at the same age. Her family could not afford to send her to college, so they began considering potential occupations for her. Eva's uncles in New Orleans mentioned that she could graduate from a beauty academy there in nine months, and that was what she did. Staying with her cousin Lorraine Taliancich in the city (living alone would have given her a bad reputation, she says), Eva graduated from Moler Beauty College in 1948. Afterward she apprenticed as a "shampoo girl" for about a year at the Carriage Trade Salon on St. Charles Avenue, whose clientele included "all the debutantes in the city of New Orleans."[56] Although the apprenticeship offered valuable experience, her salary of thirty-five dollars a week was not enough to support her in the city, even living with family members.

Eva's mother, the family decision maker, devised a solution that allowed her daughter to return home to Empire and operate her own business. Neda converted the family's garage apartment into a salon, equipped it with seven hundred dollars of hairdryers and other equipment, and they opened Eva's Beauty Salon. Although the shop had no running water at first, and few people in lower Plaquemines Parish had money to spare, Eva did good business offering a shampoo, set, and dry-out for a dollar, as well as permanent waves, hot oil treatments, and manicures. For five and a half years she was a self-employed beautician, work that suited her in part because it allowed an active social life. Several nights a week she and her girlfriends visited local venues such as the Rex Club and the Delta Club, where she "danced my feet off" with various young men, she says.[57] When her former employer in New Orleans offered her a small raise to return to work for him, she turned him down.

As a teenager, Eva felt too young to think seriously about marriage. She was "waiting for the white knight," she comments.[58] Despite community and family pressure to marry a fellow Croatian, she wanted to marry an American man to escape the lingering mark of immigrant identity. Eva dated several Americans, but in 1954, at the age of twenty-five, she changed her mind and decided to marry a Croatian-born oyster farmer who had courted her for years. She had met Pete Vujnovich (better known as "Captain Pete") when she was sixteen and helping his sister make Croatian cookies. Captain Pete, seven years older than Eva, walked in the kitchen and was immediately smitten. Eva, on the other hand, was not interested at first. Aside from feeling too young for marriage, she worried that Pete wanted to marry her only because she was a Croatian girl. He waited for her for more than seven years until she finally realized that Pete "loved me unconditionally," she says. "Any way that I would come, he loved me." Their marriage, which would last fifty-four years until Captain Pete's death in 2008, appears to have been a very happy and collaborative partnership. Eva comments, "I'm glad I did marry [a Croatian]. It's better to marry somebody you understand."[59]

Pete and Eva's first important decision concerned where they would settle. They could live in New Orleans where he co-owned an oyster processing business with his brother or in Plaquemines Parish, where his oyster leases and boats were located. Eva Vujnovich recalls, "We didn't know where we wanted to live. We didn't know ourselves." They decided on New Orleans, moved into a house Captain Pete owned, and began building the large family that Eva Vujnovich describes as her "calling" in life. By 1957, she had three daughters—Mary Jane, Anna, and Lana—in diapers, followed soon afterward by sons Peter Jr., Frank, and Tony.[60]

When their children were young, the Vujnoviches made another significant and risky decision. Working-class Croatian Americans with "seventeen cents in the bank," in Eva's words, they decided to buy a house in the city's Lakeview neighborhood, a new housing development near Lake Pontchartrain that attracted upper-middle-class professionals.[61] The couple borrowed $32,000 from a friend in the finance business, a loan that was "big, big money" at the time. "We went and lived in a neighborhood where doctors and lawyers lived," Eva says. "We didn't belong there. But anyway, we took that chance and we made it."[62] Eva and Pete Vujnovich raised their six children on Chatham Drive, celebrated their fiftieth wedding anniversary there, and routinely hosted numerous relatives during hurricane evacuations. Perhaps more importantly, their children made lasting friends there.

Because her husband was frequently away from home, working on his oyster leases downriver, Eva Vujnovich handled most of the parenting as well as traditionally male chores such as cutting the grass. Daughter Mary Jane calls her mother the "backbone" of their family and explains, "For him to do his job, it was up to my mother to be mother [and] father."[63] True to Croatian tradition, Eva is modest about her behind-the-scenes contributions. A supportive and "stand-by-your-man" woman, in her daughter's words, she lets it appear publicly that her husband was the boss.[64] However, fellow community members recognize her strength, parenting and business skills, and contributions to the family's success, and they respect her for it.[65]

As a mother and wife, Eva continued to cross the boundary between American and Croatian culture. Marrying Pete brought Eva closer to the Croatian immigrant community she had once sought to distance herself from. Captain Pete was a long-time member and officer in several Croatian-American organizations, and in 1956 he was elected president of the United Slavonian Benevolent Association, then a hub of Louisiana Croatian life. Eva comments, "We were kind of famous, my husband and I, in the [Croatian] community, doing everything with the people." Eva also encouraged her Louisiana-born children to participate in their Croatian heritage, and much of the family's social life revolved around the dinner dances, picnics, and holiday celebrations hosted by Croatian clubs and oyster associations. Whatever was going on, Captain Pete and his family were there, dressed in their best clothes to make an impressive entrance. The Vujnoviches often brought their children's non-Croatian neighborhood friends along to social functions, becoming informal ambassadors for the Croatian community. However, Eva also taught her daughters and sons to enjoy the "American stuff" she loves, such as going to dances with American music and eating in non-Croatian restaurants. In their Lakeview living room, she coached her children and their cousins in the jitterbug and "danced up a storm," she remembers.[66]

In addition to her maternal responsibilities, Eva supported the family's oyster processing shop in various ways. Early in their marriage, when Pete wanted to leave a partnership with his brother to go out on his own, his wife told him, "Well, go ahead and do it. I'll help you if I can."[67] As a newlywed, Eva began helping out in the shop, especially when her husband was away. When they began a family, she brought a playpen to the office for her firstborn daughter and continued working. After going into labor at the shop before the birth of her second daughter, Eva spent the next decade at home, devoting most of her time to child rearing. She returned to the shop in 1968 when her youngest son was four. By then, she says, she was tired of the house and eager to get out. Shucking and washing oysters, waiting on customers, and delivering buckets of oysters all over the city, she did "pretty much anything . . . whatever nobody else wanted to do."[68] Thoughtful and observant, Eva "seldom spoke, but she saw everything" that went on in the shop, and she learned the business thoroughly.[69]

Initially it did not occur to Eva that she was in charge of the Rampart Street oyster shop in her husband's absence. When Captain Pete spent days at a time on the oyster boats, hired workers handled much of the sales and day-to-day business at the shop. These employees "realized who I was" and were "treating me like a boss," Eva says. "And me, I didn't feel like a boss."[70] When shop workers handed Eva money from their sales of shucked oysters, she was puzzled at first. "And I'd say, 'Why don't you keep it?'"[71] Once she "got the hang" of being in charge, however, she decided that she liked it. She also discovered that employees had been pocketing money from sales, and the business was about $100,000 in debt. Eva says, "So when I started coming there, it was a different story. I learned what the game was"—and the thefts ended.[72]

Through Eva's vigilance, the family's finances improved dramatically. She discovered a talent for investing and managing the business's profits, and with the money she made from selling oysters in the shop, she began paying down the couple's business debts. Within eight years, she paid off the entire debt and invested profits in CDs and other accounts.[73]

The money that Eva invested helped the family relocate following Hurricane Katrina in 2005. Forty years after Hurricane Betsy led to the death of Eva's father, Katrina upended the lives not only of Captain Pete and Eva, but several of their offspring. Because their Chatham Drive house had never flooded before, Pete and Eva initially decided not to evacuate in advance of the storm. At the last minute, though, they heeded warnings and left, taking little with them. Lakeview flooded when nearby levees broke, and the family—like all of their neighbors—lost their home and most of their possessions. Floodwaters also closed their Rampart Street oyster shop. To make things worse, son Peter Jr. and daughter Mary Jane also lost their homes in lower Plaquemines Parish. Neda Jurisich's old home in Empire, where Eva grew up, was torn off its foundation and washed off its lot. The loss of both her New Orleans home and her late mother's house was difficult for Eva. She and her husband were displaced for eight months, living with a daughter and her family. The worst part, Eva says, was that "I could never say 'I'm going home now.' That's a terrible feeling."[74]

Eva responded to the Katrina crisis with her usual strength and pragmatism. She and her husband decided to retire rather than reopen their oyster shop in flooded New Orleans, and they sold the building. Their Lakeview house was a total loss, so Eva found a house for sale in suburban Belle Chasse, next door to son Frank's family and near daughter Mary Jane's home. She bought it with money she had saved over years of investing, and the couple spent three peaceful years there before Captain Pete died in 2008. She comments that today her income derives from the investments she began making decades ago.[75]

In her mid-eighties, Eva remains at the center of family life, her Belle Chasse house usually full of her adult children and grandchildren. She has built a new social network in Belle Chasse, where she sings in the Our Lady of Perpetual Help Catholic Church choir, plays cards with other Croatian-Americans, and attends Croatian cultural events. Eva, who sent her children to Croatia as young adults so they could understand their roots, now appreciates belonging to a tightly knit ethnic community. Croatian-Americans, she says, are fortunate to have each other to lean on, and she concludes, "Without your heritage, you don't have much."[76]

Mary Jane Munsterman Tesvich

Eva Vujnovich's eldest daughter, Mary Jane, was born, educated, and raised in New Orleans but spent summers with her family at their oyster camp in Plaquemines Parish. Of growing up in a suburban New Orleans neighborhood in the 1960s, Mary Jane comments, "It was just a normal childhood." Many neighbors had large families of seven or eight children, so there were always neighborhood friends with whom to play football and basketball. At her Catholic school, however, she was aware of ethnic and class differences between her own family and her more affluent schoolmates, and sometimes she "kind of felt . . . the stigma of being Croatian" and working-class.[77] She was not alone in this. While many Louisiana Croatian oyster farmers are successful and highly respected leaders of their industry, white-collar professions are still considered more prestigious than making a living from the water.

In addition to her "normal" American childhood in Lakeview, Mary Jane participated in local Croatian-American life, attending ethnic dinner dances and other events with her family. Each summer, the Vujnoviches spent a month or so at their father's oyster camp near Port Sulphur, swimming and fishing, making crafts, and using their imaginations. Camp life, she recalls, was "a very basic and simple life" but a great deal of fun.[78] These summers kept the Vujnovich children in touch with their Croatian roots and taught them self-sufficiency. Mary Jane and her siblings learned to throw a pole or cast a net into the water to fish and to plant a garden to feed themselves. As a result, she says, "I'm not afraid to be without, if I had to [be]. I wouldn't panic and think the world was over. I'd get down there and dig up the ground and plant something. We learned that from [our parents] too."[79]

The sociable Vujnovich siblings often invited their New Orleans school friends to join them at the camp and were surprised to find that these children of wealthy professionals loved the simple oyster camp life. City friends' excitement over oyster camp summers helped Mary Jane realize the value of these traditional Croatian aspects of her life. Frequent visits with grandmother Neda in Empire were another important link to her rural Croatian ties, and stories of Baba's triumphs over hardship still inspire and guide Mary Jane.[80]

Like her mother and grandmother, Mary Jane considered education essential to financial independence. When she was in her teens in the 1970s, her father encouraged her to marry a traditional Croatian man she was dating, assuring Mary Jane that this man could take good care of her. Mary Jane, however, knew that "I never wanted to be stuck in a world of not being able to do for myself. So I wanted education. . . . I knew that was the secret to being where you could make a dollar if you had to."[81] After graduating from New Orleans's Cabrini Elementary School and then St. Joseph's Academy high school, she entered Southeastern Louisiana University.

Falling in love with and marrying Kenny Munsterman, a fellow SLU student who grew up in Plaquemines Parish, cut short her college career, and she left school when Kenny received his degree in business administration. The couple briefly lived in New Orleans East where Kenny managed a store, but both missed country life. They decided to move to lower Plaquemines Parish where Kenny would fish oysters with his brother-in-law, bringing Mary Jane Munsterman full circle back to her parents' and grandparents' roots.[82]

The young couple's finances were tight, and Mary Jane, like her mother and grandmother, worked to help her family get by. She found a position in a law firm, where she worked for three years before beginning her family of four children. A talented dancer like her mother, Mary Jane managed to turn her love of dancing into income when her youngest child was four. She applied to teach a dance class in Buras, although this was "really something I didn't think I could do. But I could teach, and I cared about people, and I cared about, from the Croatian work ethic, [doing] a good job. And that's what I promoted." Her classes grew from about a hundred students the first year to eight or nine hundred the next year, and she taught dance classes for the next eighteen years.[83]

When Kenny decided to establish his own oyster business, Mary Jane supported her husband's plan although they had small children and were "jack poor" at the time. They borrowed money to buy a fishing boat, worked hard and repaid the loan, and bought a larger boat. Through a series of mishaps, including their new boat sinking in a fierce windstorm, they lost much of their investment in the business. The practicality Mary Jane learned from her mother and grandmother supported her during this setback. Having grown up hearing the stories of her grandmother's life, she thought, "I guess I can make it too." She scrimped financially, and—like her mother—took care of many of the things a husband usually does around the house, because fishermen like Kenny "have that kind of job where they're not home every night."[84]

As previous generations of women in her family had done, Mary Jane responded to devastating loss with stoicism. Her greatest test came two days after Christmas in 1996, when her husband had a fatal heart attack on the family's oyster boat. Their teenaged son, training with his father, steered the vessel back to the dock, but Kenny was declared dead at a nearby hospital. Despite her acute grief, Mary Jane had to "buck up" for her family's sake, remaining strong so that her children could stay strong. "When disaster comes," she says, "you've got to hang tough. If I fell apart, then they would fall apart worse." Her mother and grandmother had taught her that "you've got to do what you've got to do" to carry on, and that lesson carried her through her shock. The Croatian community came out in large numbers for Kenny's funeral, providing an important source of support for her.[85]

As a cash-strapped young widow, Mary Jane took on additional jobs to support her four children. She was already teaching dance classes part-time, but she decided to approach the attorney whose law office she had worked in years before. By then her former employer was district attorney for the parish, and he agreed to hire her immediately. During the day she managed the D.A.'s office in Port Sulphur, and at night she taught dance. She comments, "We're taught like that. Do what you've got to do, and don't worry about yourself." That strength, she says, came from watching her grandmother and mother and hearing stories about their experiences.[86]

In 1998, she began dating Nedo Tesvich, a Croatian-born oysterman fourteen years her senior, whom she had known all her life. He had sold oysters to her father, and Mary Jane and Nedo had frequently danced together at Croatian social events through the years. Indeed, when she was about eighteen years old, her father had commented of Nedo, "Oh, that's the kind you need to marry. You're standing with a real nice guy." At the time, that only served to "push me further away" toward an American husband, she says.[87]

Now, decades later, Nedo Tesvich, a lifelong bachelor, was "looking for somebody to share his life with," Mary Jane says. "And I was too, I guess." One attraction for her, besides their mutual love of dancing, was the fact that they shared many of the same values. Nedo admired Mary Jane for making her children's welfare her first priority in the wake of Kenny's death. Croatians, she says, are "very strong people," and after a catastrophe "you're expected to carry on, to maintain your family. And it's all about family." She, in turn, wanted someone to help her guide her preteen and teenaged children. After a short courtship, Nedo and Mary Jane married in 2000. Marriage to Nedo brought Mary Jane back into the Croatian fold that she had wandered away from. She says, "When he entered my life, he still had the Croatian ways," and "all the traditions came back, which I was already aware and lived with."[88] He was and remains an active supporter of the Plaquemines Parish–based Croatian American Society, and he and Mary Jane participate in most of the association's cultural events. She has also recruited her mother and other family members into the society.[89]

Hurricane Katrina, which destroyed the Vujnoviches' New Orleans home in late August 2005, also devastated schools, churches, homes, fishing docks and marinas, stores, and other businesses in lower Plaquemines Parish. Nedo and Mary Jane lost their home in Port Sulphur, and Nedo's oyster boats sustained damage. Like many displaced commercial fishing families, Mary Jane and Nedo moved upriver to suburban Belle Chasse, in the northern tip of Plaquemines. The parish's largest and least-flood-prone community, Belle Chasse was largely untouched by the hurricane, and storm refugees who could afford it bought brick homes in the town's new subdivisions. For Mary Jane, the move to Belle Chasse meant a larger and nicer house, more amenities, and proximity to her mother, brothers, and their children, now settled in several Belle Chasse subdivisions.[90]

With the move to Belle Chasse, a new career opportunity "kind of fell into my lap," she says.[91] The district attorney offered her the lead position in forming a new domestic violence unit, warning her, "You've got to be self-motivated." She reminded him, "I'm Croatian. You don't have to worry about that."[92] Mary Jane's statement reflects Louisiana Croatians' sense of their ethnic identity being closely linked to the traits of reliability, honesty, and motivation—a perception that seems to be generally shared by local non-Croatians.[93]

As a victim assistance coordinator and trial assistant, Mary Jane now interviews domestic violence survivors, coordinates services for them, and acts as a trial assistant in domestic cases. Her new career gives her a fairly high profile in the community, and her salary helped tide her and her husband over until their oyster boats could be repaired. In Katrina, according to Mary Ann, "we lost everything," but a few years later, "We've got something." "We survived that tragedy," she says, just as previous generations of Croatian women have survived similar losses.[94]

Like many women, Mary Jane must maneuver around gendered expectations both at work and at home, but her responses may differ depending on realm. In her career, Mary Jane is willing to push when necessary. She says, "When I have a job and it requires me to be strong, I'm going to be strong." The domestic violence program, according to Mary Jane, "would have never worked if I wasn't brave enough to step on some toes along the way, and I had to do that to make it successful."[95]

However, in her marriage to an old-fashioned Croatian immigrant, she can choose to be "submissive when I have to be." During their courtship, Nedo held very traditional Croatian views on gender roles in marriage and told her that he expected to be the head of the household when they married. She, however, informed him that as spouses they would be equals. That does not mean, however, that their roles are identical. Through conversations with non-Croatian friends at work, Mary Jane recognizes that Croatian wives are willing to accommodate their husbands in ways that her non-Croatian office friends are not. According to Mary Jane, "They say, 'You're crazy! He's a man, he can do that himself.'" She jokingly calls herself a "mixed-up feminist" who manages to balance traditional ideas about gender roles with her own professional success and independence.[96]

For her, the issue is about "respect and the old-time values of how you treat your spouse in a marriage." Women's willingness to put up with certain things, she says, is tied to the oyster industry as well as to Croatian cultural ideals. Oyster farmer husbands, she comments, have "thrown dredges and lifted sacks" all day on the boats, "and their bodies are being torn up by their careers." Therefore, wives are reluctant to impose on them when they are home. "You can't depend on them too much . . . to be the babysitter, and to cook for you, and to share the duties," she says. "You're expected to do your own little duties and he'll do his own duties. And everything will be fine."[97]

Mary Jane has reconnected with the local Croatian community in recent years, as well as strengthened ties to the old country. She and Nedo recently built a home on the Dalmatian Coast and now spend a portion of their summers there, visiting relatives. Her now-adult offspring have more tenuous and ambivalent relationships to Croatian-American identity. Mary Jane comments that sometimes they seem to want nothing to do with their Croatian heritage, but then she discovers that one son proudly displayed a Croatian national emblem on his social networking site. She made a point of taking her children to Dalmatia and suggests, "If you can get [young people] over there and show them where they're from and what Croatia really means," then they appreciate it. "If you don't carry it through to your family," then you lose that culture.[98] Through visits to Croatia, extended family get-togethers, participation in Croatian American Society–sponsored events, and stories of her immigrant grandmother Neda's life, Mary Jane actively works to ensure that Louisiana Croatian culture is not lost to younger generations.

The lives of strong, determined Louisiana Croatian women like Neda Jurisich, Eva Vujnovich, and Mary Jane Tesvich illustrate significant aspects of Louisiana history and culture—especially of coastal life, which has been underrepresented in most scholarship. Their stories of adaptability, perseverance, and hard work reveal women's crucial place in the (publicly) male-dominated oyster industry, in family life, and in ethnic cultural maintenance. These women's experiences enhance our understanding of the remarkable ethnic diversity that makes Louisiana unique in the South, and they exemplify the Croatian community's transition from marginalized immigrants to a stable, successful, and influential ethnic group.

NOTES

1. Janice Buras, "Neda Jurisich—Hard Work Is Her Prescription for Life," *Down the Road* (Belle Chasse, La.), June 1994, 8.

2. Sources on Croatians' development of Louisiana's oyster industry include Milos M. Vujnovich, *Yugoslavs in Louisiana* (1974; Gretna, La.: Firebird 2000); Karen M. Wicker, "The Development of the Louisiana Oyster Industry in the 19th Century" (PhD diss., Louisiana State University, 1976). Anthropologist Tom McGuire addresses the reciprocal relationship between New Orleans tourism and coastal fisheries in "Louisiana's Oysters, America's Wetlands, and the Storms of 2005," *American Anthropologist* 108, no. 4 (2006): 692–705. Drago's Restaurant, Bozo's, and the Crescent City Steakhouse are only a few examples of beloved Croatian-owned restaurants, although some have closed in the wake of Hurricane Katrina and other events.

3. For an overview of southern Louisiana's ethnic diversity and history, see Nicholas R. Spitzer, "South Louisiana: Unity and Diversity in a Folk Region," in *Louisiana Folklife: A Guide to the State* (Baton Rouge: Louisiana Folklife Program), 75–82. In the same volume (Spitzer, *Louisiana Folklife*),

see also George F. Reinecke, "The National and Cultural Groups of New Orleans," 55–64; Rosan A. Jordan, "Folklore and Ethnicity: Some Theoretical Considerations," 49–55.

4. Gerald G. Govorchin, *Americans from Yugoslavia* (Gainesville: University of Florida Press, 1961), 93.

5. Ben Lucien Burman, *Big River to Cross: Mississippi Life Today* (New York: John Day, 1971), 278.

6. Ibid. For a history of Croatian immigration to Louisiana, see Vujnovich, *Yugoslavs in Louisiana*; Frank Lovrich, "The Dalmatian Yugoslavs in Louisiana," *Louisiana History* 8 (1967): 149–64; George J. Prpic, *The Croatian Immigrants in America* (New York: Philosophical Library, 1971); George J. Prpic, *South Slavic Immigration in America* (Boston: Twayne, 1978); Adam S. Eterovich, *Croatians from Dalmatia and Montenegrin Serbs in the West and South, 1800–1900* (San Francisco: R. and E. Research Associates, 1971).

7. Harnett T. Kane, *Deep Delta Country* (New York: Duell, Solan & Pearce, 1944), 93.

8. Ibid., 95. This reputation for honesty, a strong work ethic, and reliability still defines local Croatian-American identity. Members of Louisiana's Croatian American Society explicitly state that their core values include the importance of family and friends, hard work, perseverance, religious faith, and dependability. See, for example, Carolyn E. Ware, "Louisiana's Croatian American Society: A Case Study in Adaptation and Resilience," *Louisiana Folklore Miscellany* 23 (2013): 97–129.

9. Kane, *Deep Delta Country*, 101; Vujnovich, *Yugoslavs in Louisiana*; Donald W. Davis, *Washed Away? The Invisible Peoples of Louisiana's Wetlands* (Lafayette: Center for Louisiana Studies, 2010), 139, 325–55.

10. Although women's labor was crucial to rural life in pre–World War II Croatia, their status was considerably lower than men's. Govorchin writes that "women, especially peasant women, had been regarded as subservient and inferior to men physically, mentally, politically, socially, and in every other way," adding that in America, in contrast, "they have been recognized as equals" (Govorchin, *Americans from Yugoslavia*, 188). Old-country proverbs such as "One man is worth more than ten women" and "He who does not beat his wife is not a man" reflect this devaluation of women. Ibid. General scholarship on women and work includes Alice Kessler-Harris, *Women Have Always Worked: A Historical Overview* (Old Westbury, N.Y.: Feminist Press, 1981); Alice Kessler-Harris, *Out to Work: A History of Wage-Earning Women in the United States* (New York: Oxford University Press, 1982); Alice Kessler-Harris, *Gendering Labor History* (Urbana: University of Illinois Press, 2007); Deborah Gray White, *Ar'n't I a Woman: Female Slaves in the Plantation South*, 2nd edition (New York: W. W. Norton, 1999).

11. Eva Vujnovich, interview with author, August 2, 2011. According to E. Shapiro, immigration of Croatian women to America "accounted for a strengthening of Croatian family life." E. Shapiro, *The Croatian Americans* (New York: Chelsea House, 1989), 67.

12. Cecyle S. Neidle writes that in turn-of-the-century American industrial cities such as Pittsburgh, "Slavic women were employed at jobs that were considered inferior and unpleasant, such as tobacco stripping at stogie factories, laundries, canneries, and metal trades." Neidle, *America's Immigrant Women* (Boston: Twayne, 1975), 101. See also Doris Weatherford, *Foreign and Female: Immigrant Women in America 1840–1930* (New York: Schocken Books, 1986); Kessler-Harris, *Gendering Labor History*. On Croatian women's work in general, see also Govorchin, *Americans from Yugoslavia*, 188–89.

13. Susan C. Pearce, Elizabeth J. Clifford, and Reena Tandon, ed., *Immigration and Women: Understanding the American Experience* (New York: New York University Press, 2011). Croatian women's lives in rural Louisiana had close parallels to those of pioneer farm wives on the Great Plains, where immigrant women "lived under conditions more primitive than they had known at home, miles away from help" in cases of illness or emergency, and "worked unceasingly at hard physical labor" but still found this life preferable to working for others (Neidle, *America's Immigrant Women*, 88). In Louisiana, Coushatta women's economic and cultural contributions to their families' welfare offer interesting similarities to those of Croatian immigrants. Linda Langley, Claude Oubre, and

Jay Precht, "Louisiana Williams Robinson, Her Daughters, and Her Granddaughters," in *Louisiana Women: Their Lives and Times*, ed. Janet Allured and Judith F. Gentry (Athens: University of Georgia Press, 2009), 155–74.

14. Frank M. Lovrich, "Work among the Yugoslavs in the Mississippi Delta," *American Journal of Economics and Sociology* 27, no. 2 (April 1968): 135.

15. In 1893, one of the worst hurricanes on record killed more than two thousand people in Louisiana, including at least two hundred Slavic people living in and around Bayou Cook; this represented half of the Slavs then living in Plaquemines Parish (Vujnovich, *Yugoslavs in Louisiana*, 29). Some families were wiped out altogether, and hurricane damage dealt a crushing blow to the oyster industry in what has been described as the "greatest disaster that befell the Croatian immigration" (Vujnovich, *Yugoslavs in Louisiana*, 35). Fishermen experienced another devastating hurricane in 1917. More recent hurricanes such as Betsy (1965), Camille (1969), and Katrina (2005) caused extensive loss of property but not as much loss of life among oyster families. With better storm warning systems, most coastal residents evacuate in advance of severe hurricanes.

16. Mary Jane Tesvich, interview with author, August 2, 2011.

17. Allured, introduction to Allured and Gentry, *Louisiana Women*, 7.

18. Eva Vujnovich and Mary Jane Tesvich, interview with author, August 2, 2011; Janice Buras, "Neda Jurisich."

19. Mary Jane Tesvich interview, August 2, 2011.

20. Buras, "Neda Jurisich," 8; Neda Jurisich and Eva Vujnovich, interview with author, December 1994.

21. Eva Vujnovich interview, August 2, 2011.

22. Ibid.; Buras, "Neda Jurisich."

23. Buras, "Neda Jurisich," 9.

24. Eva Vujnovich, personal communication, May 28, 2012.

25. Eva Vujnovich interview, August 2, 2011.

26. Ibid.; Buras, "Neda Jurisich."

27. Eva Vujnovich, personal communication, May 28, 2012.

28. Buras, "Neda Jurisich," 10.

29. Ibid., 10.

30. Eva Vujnovich interview, August 2, 2011.

31. Eva Vujnovich, personal communication, May 28, 2012; Mary Jane Tesvich, "One of a Kind," *Down the Road* (Belle Chasse, La.), December 2002, 17.

32. Eva Vujnovich interview, August 2, 2011.

33. Jerrold Horst and Glenda Horst, *The Louisiana Seafood Bible: Oysters* (Gretna, La.: Pelican, 2011), 152.

34. Eva Vujnovich interview, August 2, 2011. Eva uses the term "pusher" as a compliment, to mean someone who works hard and pushes themselves—and others—to do what needs to be done.

35. Mary Jane Tesvich interview, August 2, 2011.

36. Eva Vujnovich interview, August 2, 2011.

37. Ibid.

38. Janice Buras, "A Look Back at Baba Neda's Life," *Down the Road* (Belle Chasse, La.), December 2002, 20. Other recent immigrants may have been more sympathetic to Neda's child-care solution. Peasant women and men in eastern Europe traditionally performed cooperative fieldwork and expected older children to care for younger ones (Weatherford, *Foreign and Female*, 156).

39. Eva Vujnovich, personal communication, May 28, 2013. Kessler-Harris suggests that this "constant tension between the two areas of women's lives: the home and the marketplace" provides "the crux of our understanding of women's working lives" (Kessler-Harris, *Women Have Always Worked*, 17).

40. Eva Vujnovich, personal communication, May 28, 2013.

41. Vujnovich, *Yugoslavs in Louisiana*, 68; Edward Kammer, "A Socio-Economic Survey of the Marshdwellers of Four Southeastern Louisiana Parishes" (PhD diss., Catholic University, 1941).

42. Eva Vujnovich interview, August 2, 2011.

43. Ibid.

44. Ibid.; Horst and Horst, *Seafood Bible*, 180; Vujnovich, *Yugoslavs in Louisiana*, 75; Kammer, "A Socio-Economic Survey."

45. Eva Vujnovich interview, August 2, 2011.

46. Vujnovich, *Yugoslavs in Louisiana*, 59.

47. Eva Vujnovich, personal communication, February 28, 2012.

48. Eva Vujnovich interview, August 2, 2011.

49. Eva Vujnovich personal communication, March 11, 2013; Horst and Horst, *Seafood Bible*, 151–52

50. Eva Vujnovich, personal communication, February 28, 2013.

51. Tesvich, "One of a Kind," 17.

52. Mary Jane Tesvich interview, August 2, 2011.

53. Eva Vujnovich interview, August 2, 2011.

54. Ibid.

55. Ibid.

56. Ibid.

57. Ibid.

58. Ibid.

59. Ibid.

60. Ibid.

61. Ibid.

62. Ibid.

63. Mary Jane Tesvich interview, August 2, 2011.

64. Ibid.

65. Ibid.; Horst and Horst, *Seafood Bible*, 180.

66. Eva Vujnovich interview, August 2, 2011.

67. Eva Vujnovich personal communication, March 11, 2013.

68. Eva Vujnovich interview, August 2, 2011.

69. Horst and Horst, *Seafood Bible*, 180.

70. Eva Vujnovich interview, August 2, 2011.

71. Ibid.

72. Ibid.

73. Ibid.

74. Eva Vujnovich personal communication, February 28, 2013.

75. Eva Vujnovich interview, August 2, 2011.

76. Ibid.

77. Mary Jane Tesvich interview, August 2, 2011.

78. Ibid.

79. Ibid.

80. Ibid.; Tesvich, "One of a Kind," 17.

81. Mary Jane Tesvich interview, August 2, 2011.

82. Ibid.

83. Ibid.

84. Ibid.

85. Ibid. See also Carolyn E. Ware, "Croatians in Southeast Louisiana: An Overview," *Louisiana Folklore Miscellany* 11 (1996): 67–85.

86. Mary Jane Tesvich interview, August 2, 2011.

87. Ibid. The traditional link of Croatian ethnicity to oyster fishing and working-class identity may also have played a part in both Eva Vujnovich's and Mary Jane Tesvich's ambivalence about marrying fellow Croatians.

88. Ibid.

89. Ware, "Louisiana's Croatian American Society."

90. Nine years after Katrina, many residents of the lower parish have chosen to remain in Belle Chasse because it is closer to New Orleans, more developed, and offers easier access to medical facilities, shopping, and other services. For commercial fishers, it is close enough to commute to their fishing boats downriver several times a week.

91. Mary Jane Tesvich interview, August 2, 2011.

92. Ibid. Of course, successful people in many other ethnic groups perceive themselves similarly. While Eva Vujnovich and Mary Jane Tesvich may identify these characteristics as distinctively Croatian, they are also associated with family example, opportunity, and other factors.

93. Many non-Croatians share this perception of Croatians as exceptionally industrious. In the 1970s, folklorist Nicholas R. Spitzer noted that when he asked a Cajun man in Plaquemines Parish about local Croatians, the man replied that "they're great people," but he added that "they work too hard." Robert R. Rathbone, "The Dalmatians of Louisiana," in *Report on Ethnic Groups in Louisiana* (New Orleans: Jean Lafitte National Park and Preserve, 1979), 320.

94. Mary Jane Tesvich interview, August 2, 2011.

95. Ibid.

96. Ibid.

97. Ibid.

98. Ibid.

PART THREE

Women and the Arts

Carmelite "Cammie" Garrett Henry
(1871–1948)

The Evolution of a Plantation Mistress and Chatelaine of the Arts

LUCY GUTMAN WITH SHANNON FRYSTAK

Carmelite Garrett Henry was the living embodiment of the Lost Cause movement and influenced the Southern Literary Renaissance through the writers and artists she selected to patronize her Louisiana plantation during the period between the two world wars. Henry used the leverage of a revered cultural movement that celebrated the Confederate tradition to emancipate herself from the restrictions of a gender-prescribed position, while simultaneously sustaining and expanding her status as a revered traditional southern lady. During the last fifty years of her life residing in the Cane River area of western Louisiana, "Miss Cammie," as she was called, revived the native crafts and hosted scores of white writers, artists, and photographers through the Natchitoches Art Colony (1921–37). These individuals shared her cultural beliefs and aided her in preserving the history and heritage of the Cane River and the Isle Brevelle Creoles of color—the Metoyer descendants of the eighteenth-century union of Marie Therese Coin-Coin, an enslaved woman, and Pierre Metoyer, a French planter and fur trader.[1] Henry's evolution was inspired, encouraged, and supported largely by the female friends she selected, all intellectually and artistically gifted women.

As Cammie Henry aged, she fulfilled her mission. To be sure, she made great cultural contributions to Louisiana history by virtue of the writers and artists who preserved and promoted ideas about Southern culture embraced by the Lost Cause movement through the work they produced in large part during their time spent at Henry's home. The ideology Henry advanced—the Lost Cause—was a conservative, indeed reactionary, cultural and political movement that was pervasive and highly influential during her formative years. A cultural phenomenon springing up after the Civil War and flourishing between

CARMELITE "CAMMIE" GARRETT HENRY

Courtesy of Northwestern State University of Louisiana, Watson Memorial Library, Cammie G. Henry Research Center.

1865 and 1913, the Lost Cause promoted a decidedly biased and racist white southern interpretation of the Civil War, its causes, battles, and aftermath, Reconstruction. It included publications, monuments, and activities all toward the perpetuation of the memory and legacy of the Confederacy and the antebellum South. Glorifying the idealized memory of the antebellum structure of society, as well as vindicating the Confederate cause and the soldiers in gray, the Lost Cause served as the basis for a white southern moral identity that included the idea of white racial superiority as well as an equally strong belief in states' rights, the perceived legal route to protecting the southern antebellum status quo.[2]

In the post-Reconstruction era, literature replaced the Civil War battlefields as the area of engagement to determine the superior culture as white and to vindicate the "ghosts of the Confederacy." As early as the 1880s, the Civil War was a favorite topic of American fiction, with literature becoming "not only Southern in type, but distinctly Confederate in sympathy."[3] Referring to the southern perception of the "godlessness of the truly damned Yankees," historian Rollin G. Osterweiss described the Lost Cause movement as a postbellum "legend," a nexus of myths that transformed the romanticism of the antebellum South into a fervent and distinctly regional mind and mood: a "phenomenon with power."[4] More recently, historian David Blight has discussed a "culture of reunion," the tenuous nature of southern memory, and restoring the role of African Americans to our national memory of a war wrought from slavery and sacrifice.[5] Novelist and attorney Albion Tourgee wrote about the white southern mentality in 1880, stating: "The South believed, honestly believed in its innate superiority over all other races and peoples. It did not doubt, has never doubted that, man for man, it was braver, stronger, better than the North."[6]

As the standard bearer for the ghosts of the Confederacy, through a formulaic literature and history during a time of massive transformation in every area of southern life, Cammie Henry did not want to relinquish the social and economic privileges that she, like many privileged white southern women, considered her due. Refusing to abandon the elitist and racial assumptions inherited from her ancestors, the mistress of Melrose Plantation, along with her mother, daughter (Carmelite "Cammie" Henry Wenk), and granddaughters, accomplished this through her membership in the United Daughters of the Confederacy (UDC). Founded in 1896, the UDC was arguably the most effective agent and catalyst for the promotion of the ideas, attitudes, and values of the Lost Cause. These "daughters"—aristocratic, southern white women—used the UDC to enter the public arena during the "club movement" era of the late nineteenth and early twentieth centuries. Through the organization, they formed the South's memory of the Civil War and shaped southern white culture through their influence and activities in educating the next generation about their "true" history.[7]

Henry's energetic drive to transmit antebellum southern culture and the values of the Lost Cause was akin to protecting a family legacy as well as a vindication of her ancestral heritage. Henry's Erwin forebears on her mother's side were central to her own identification with the southern aristocracy. Pruning the family tree in order to fit a more idyllic picture, Henry ignored the less attractive strains of her Erwin ancestry, such as alcoholism and depression. Still, Henry took pride in her ancestors, self-proclaimed aristocrats, who notably began with Joseph Erwin (1761–1829), her maternal great-grandfather and one of Louisiana's great sugar plantation barons of the first quarter of the nineteenth century.[8]

Henry's grandfather Isaac Erwin (1800–1872), the youngest son of Joseph Erwin, was a successful planter and shrewd land speculator who made Shady Grove, his Grosse Tete plantation, a prosperous venture prior to the Civil War. Isaac and his second wife, Carmelite Picou (1820–1917), Henry's namesake, were the parents of Henry's mother, Leudivine Erwin (1840–1935). The last social event at Shady Grove Plantation, hosted by the Erwins at the end of the Civil War, was the February 21, 1865, wedding of Leudivine to Stephen Garrett (1838–96), a captain in the Confederate army. At war's end, Garrett returned to his bride in Louisiana and, like numerous other white southerners, to a land in economic and physical ruin. The Garretts and later their three children lived on Scattery Plantation near Bayou Lafourche in Ascension Parish. Garrett was the overseer of the plantation, whose owner, Miles Taylor of New Orleans, held substantial acreage in Lafourche, Assumption, and Ascension Parishes.[9]

Although the Garretts never owned land or even their own house, Leudivine Garrett ensured that young Cammie fully recognized the Erwin family's wealth and social position before the war. As the middle child, Henry grew closer to her mother and to her younger brother, Stephen Neilson Garrett (1876–1955), after the death of her older sister, Ann Steele Garrett (1868–77). Mother Garrett influenced Henry with a love of books and romanticism for her aristocratic ancestry. On weekends and holidays, Garrett took her two surviving children for regular visits to the luxurious plantation homes of Erwin relatives who lived across southern Louisiana. Garrett advanced and encouraged the idea to young Henry that the Erwins were connected by kinship, marriage, and friendship to the network of wealthy white planter families whose homes stretched from the outskirts of New Orleans to the East Texas border. However, their most frequent visits were to the far more modest postwar home of Grandmother Erwin, where Henry heard firsthand accounts of the family's Civil War tribulations and abuse at the hands of the Yankees.[10]

Under the influence of her mother and maternal grandmother, young Henry came to feel that all of Louisiana was part of her extended heritage. By age ten she had begun a lifelong hobby of collecting newspaper and magazine articles about Louisiana, its people, and its history. Henry stored these articles in scrapbooks, which, by the end of her life, numbered in the hundreds. During her last fifty years, writers visiting Melrose Plantation used these scrapbooks in their research. As a young girl, Henry also read prodigiously, another habit that lasted until her final days. As she noted in one of her scrapbooks, "My fund of knowledge and love of good books comes from reading aloud to my mother until the day I was married. Now we often recall passages we read and enjoyed together."[11]

Henry's formal training provided the skills necessary to earn a living in contrast to her mother's elite, classical education. After attending local private female academies in Donaldsonville in southern Louisiana, in 1891 Henry completed her formal education at the Louisiana Normal College in Natchitoches, now Northwestern State University of Louisiana. Education for southern elite families had a conflicted legacy after the Civil War. The war had threatened the foundations of the South's paternalistic and patriarchal order. Reservations born of their wartime experience about the competence of men imbued many southern white females of the next generation with the motivation to educate themselves with marketable skills in order not to have to rely upon men for survival.[12] Indeed, after the war, many southern white women were expected to both help financially to support their families and conform to the chivalric images of southern womanhood. The unwritten curriculum at any southern white normal school dictated that female students learn to look and act like the ideal southern lady in order to effect change in their communities.[13]

Few of her generation of Louisiana belles learned as well as Cammie Henry to use the language of deference, compliance, and conformity in order to make her way within her culture to do as she pleased with her life and her resources. During her years at the Louisiana Normal College, Henry acquired the ability to earn a living in a socially acceptable way through teaching. It was here that she also met the younger generation of the Natchitoches white elite, including her future husband, John Hampton Henry. Immediately upon graduation she returned to her parents' home and worked as a teacher, ultimately becoming the principal at the Ginon Academy in Thibodaux, a job she only relinquished upon marriage in January 1894.[14]

John Hampton Henry brought to the marriage wealth, social position, the opportunity for his new bride to develop both her interest in the Lost Cause movement, and, in a serendipitous manner, a new and deep interest in the Cane River area where they lived. Yet even before Cammie Henry arrived at the altar, she was well trained to carry on southern aristocratic traditions including Old South conventions regarding the role and place of women. While her Erwin ancestry provided her a sense of identity as well as a belief in her upper-class position in the hierarchical setting of the late-nineteenth-century Deep South, her marriage into the Henry family formally secured her elite status. The Irish Catholic family of Joseph Henry had been well regarded in the Natchitoches area since the 1840s. A wealthy cotton planter who owned several plantations in northwestern Louisiana, Henry's social position was further secured by his service in the Confederate army as a second lieutenant. With marriage came access and acceptance in the upper reaches of a small, inbred, exclusive white society—an isolated and rural enclave in which social and cultural distinctions were carefully observed.[15]

In the early years of marriage, during Cammie Henry's visits with family in Natchitoches Parish in 1897 and 1898, she met Kate Chopin, the famous short story writer and local colorist who penned dialect tales about Creole life.[16] Henry learned about Chopin's important literary contributions to the Natchitoches area as well as the social and professional consequences that resulted from stepping out of the proscribed gender guidelines for proper matronly conduct. According to biographer and literary scholar Emily Toth, Chopin smoked cigarettes, wore her hair in a short, ear-length bob, and sometimes even wore a wig. She also showed her legs and allegedly had a romantic liaison with a married man in Natchitoches whose wife filed for, and achieved, a legal separation in 1891. To add to her already scandalous behavior, Chopin published *The Awakening* in 1899, in which she depicted a married woman's sexual awakening with a man other than her husband. Henry knew from Chopin's example that first-rate literature could be produced even in an isolated, rural backwater. She also witnessed the exorbitant social price Chopin paid for openly flaunting, at times flamboyantly, society's mores and norms.[17]

Henry's life was profoundly affected by the deaths of both her father and father-in-law in the late 1890s. Henry adored her father, naming her first son after him in 1894. The 1896 funeral and memorial service at St. John's Episcopal Church in Thibodaux for Captain Stephen Garrett became a Confederate social gathering for a fallen comrade, attended by members of the Braxton Bragg Camp No. 196, United Confederate Veterans. Following the services, Leudivine Garrett split the household furnishings between her son and daughter and began to divide her time living in their homes.[18]

Cammie Henry's husband inherited Melrose Plantation, then known as Yucca Plantation, upon the death of his father in 1899. Henry lived at Melrose for the next forty-nine years as the aristocrat she sincerely believed herself to be. Her ambition to own a plantation manor home had been a lifelong dream. As a child, Henry had collected many pages of images of antebellum homes in her scrapbooks, writing, "I'd love to live in such old-fashioned houses as these." Despite its rural location, she was grateful to be the mistress of a plantation. The early years as a new mistress of a plantation were stressful, however. Upon moving into the manor's big house in 1899, Henry promptly discovered that her dream of restoring the house and creating a home would be daunting. Melrose Plantation had fallen into a state of gross decay, having not been occupied by humans since before the Civil War. The plantation was isolated, located off dirt roads that were impassable during rains. And the long summer months brought tropical heat, humidity, and ubiquitous bugs and snakes, including a variety of poisonous ones like the cottonmouths native to the banks of the Cane River. Yet even in the face of pregnancy and motherhood, as well as a demanding and domineering spouse with a legendary violent temper, a man known to neglect her and the plantation business, Henry was successful. Indeed, all the while supervising renovations, Henry managed to carry to term eight pregnancies with no medical assistance other than from an old rural doctor who performed the deliveries. Between 1894 and 1915, Henry gave birth to seven sons and one daughter.[19]

With the restoration of the antebellum mansion at Melrose Plantation, Henry re-created a symbol of the Lost Cause. She sought and preserved bits and pieces of the Old South from surrounding decayed and sometimes deserted Cane River plantations. She salvaged an architectural record of the Old South by incorporating doors, fanlights, paneling, and chimneypieces from neighboring plantations. After restoring the house and outbuildings—Yucca House, the original plantation house; Ghana House, a small cabin once occupied by Marie Therese Coin-Coin, moved in from the fields; and Africa House, a barn—Henry began moving a number of former slave cabins from neglected Cane River plantations to her backyard. Two of these former slave cabins would later be used as a bookbindery and a weaving house. The others soon housed the writers and artists who came to visit. In 1903, Henry began enlarging the big house, adding first a kitchen wing and then twin hexagonal garçonnières (small, sometimes detached structures that housed teenaged male family members and single male guests) on either end of the house.[20]

Henry had learned well the social rules of her time, but she also knew how to do exactly as she pleased, within her given situation. As a wife and mother, Henry remained within the gender-prescribed roles expected of white, elite southern women. While her husband formally oversaw the running of the plantation, expanding his landholdings and supervising the field hands, Henry raised the children and supervised the servants. Despite her busy, often hectic schedule she continued her intellectual interests and activities, which included a large correspondence with book dealers, Louisiana historical associations, researchers, and authors, as well as the maintenance of her ever-growing scrapbook collection. Henry expanded her library of books about Louisiana and by Louisiana authors and continued her education through the mail with correspondence courses in the classics and the Bible.[21]

Eventually Henry also cultivated and planted the areas surrounding the big house in the style of the traditional estate gardens of the Old South. For half a century, cattle and hogs had grazed upon the grass and weeds surrounding the manor. Not only did she cultivate in her plantation gardens every flower and shrub native to Louisiana, Henry also planned the gardens so that there was always something blooming. Her passion for native flora brought her into contact with members of Louisiana garden clubs, including a fortuitous meeting with Caroline Coroneos Dorman, a horticulturist who helped her plan and plant the Melrose gardens.[22]

Caroline Dorman became Henry's closest friend and one of the most important influences on her life. An artist, author, teacher, horticulturist, and conservationist, Dorman lived with her older sister, Virginia, at an inherited family estate, Briarwood, about thirty miles north of Melrose. Henry and Dorman shared an interest in Louisiana native flora as well as a racial and class identity rooted in the Lost Cause. In contrast to Henry's deep and profound acquisitive nature, however, Dorman had little interest in, or access to, material wealth. A naturalist who preferred a simple, unadorned lifestyle, Dorman often accompanied Henry on her trips to southern Louisiana to gather native flora. While recognizing and encouraging her friend's many talents, Henry tried also to enlist Dorman in her salvage expeditions to abandoned properties. As she wrote to Dorman, "You've got to cultivate your talent—I intend to see to it—But you must get some of those valuable relics—send for me if you need any stealing—Sheriff ain't got me yet!!! Get them Carrie—they are going to be lost—no one else cares."[23]

As the years passed, the friendship between Henry and Dorman deepened. By the mid-1920s, Dorman often wrote to Henry of her love for and appreciation of her encouragement: "I lay up inspiration while I'm there [at Melrose]" and "Whatever is troubling you, always know that I love you." Henry also frequently wrote to Dorman with declarations of affection: "What would I do without you. You'll never know what you've meant to Melrose and to ME."[24]

Through Dorman, Henry met writer Ada Jack Carver (Snell), Dorman's former college roommate at Judson College and the daughter of an old and prominent Natchitoches family. Inspired by Chopin, Carver's writing talent became nationally known, beginning with the publication of her first short story in 1908. Although her personal life was a model of upper-middle-class conformity, Carver's writing broke through the barriers of her class and focused upon the people of the Cane River country, particularly the Creoles of color of the Isle Brevelle. A frequent guest at Melrose, Carver shared Henry's passion for the preservation of the southern past from a Lost Cause perspective.[25]

While developing relationships with the self-proclaimed upper-class elite of Natchitoches, Henry, a complex and often-contradictory character, also cultivated significant relationships with Creoles of color, particularly the Metoyers, descendants of the original owners of Melrose. Concentrated on the Isle Brevelle, an area south of Natchitoches located on a narrow strip of land surrounded by the Cane River, these descendants of interracial liaisons had achieved an elite status in a previously seigneurial society that long regarded them as "gens de coleur libre" (free people of color) prior to the Civil War. Ultimately they became a racial caste that took pride in French heritage and identified more with white than black society. These individuals were well-educated, cultivated, affluent, devout Catholics who held themselves apart from the poor whites and blacks who lived in the area.[26]

Henry was among the first to recognize the historical importance of the descendants of Claude Thomas Pierre Metoyer and Marie Therese Coin-Coin. Metoyer was a soldier-planter who arrived in Natchitoches in 1767 from La Rochelle, France. Coin-Coin was an enslaved woman owned by Marie des Nieges de St. Denis, the daughter of the French-Canadian, Louis Juchereau de St. Denis, who founded Natchitoches. Leasing Coin-Coin in 1767 and subsequently purchasing her, Metoyer and his concubine produced ten children. Prior to their parting in 1785—in order for the Frenchman to enter into a suitable, recognized marriage with a woman of his race and social background—Metoyer had manumitted his loyal and devoted slave and their children and as a parting token gave her a parcel of land on the Cane River, Melrose Plantation.[27] By the time of her death in 1816, Coin-Coin had managed both to buy her remaining children and grandchildren out of slavery and to acquire enough acreage to provide each one with a land grant.[28]

Henry was keenly aware that she was the mistress of antebellum buildings as well as curator of the plantation's unique history. Without Henry's intervention, much of the history, art, furnishings, and native crafts of the Cane River Creoles of color would have been lost. It was she who "rescued" their heirlooms, paintings, and furniture, acquiring pieces and displaying them in both the manor house and outbuildings. The writers, artists, and photographers whom she later patronized also captured on paper and canvas the Cane River history—images from a white perspective that was compatible with the Lost Cause movement that Henry cherished and promoted. Considering her love of the Lost Cause, it is ironic that during her first two decades at Melrose, Henry carefully cultivated and laid the basis for significant relationships and lifelong interracial friendships of mutual trust and respect with members of the Metoyer clan on the Isle Brevelle along the Cane River.

Henry's friendship with Madame Aubert Rocque, matriarch of the Metoyer clan and granddaughter of Grand-père Augustin Metoyer—the first son born to Metoyer and Coin-Coin—was particularly important in establishing the later Melrose group's credibility and acceptability among the Cane River Creoles of color. Every Sunday morning Henry sent her car and driver, Fuggerboo, a dark-skinned chauffer and house servant, to deliver Rocque to and from mass at St. Augustine Church. In the first half of the nineteenth-century Augustin Metoyer donated the land for the church and, with his brother, Louis, built St. Augustine's Catholic Church, still the center of communal life for the Metoyer descendants on the Isle Brevelle. Henry's cordial relationships with members of the Metoyer family lay the groundwork for the reciprocal Metoyer hospitality and openness extended years later to the white painters, writers, and photographers Henry invited to Melrose and who preserved the Metoyer history in their work.[29]

The Melrose group could not have come into being without the independence Henry acquired when she became a widow. Henry inherited Melrose

Plantation upon the death of her husband and was able to focus even more time and energy upon her cultural interests. John Henry Sr. died on March 2, 1918, from a sudden and unexpected massive cerebral hemorrhage. Cammie Henry no longer solely held the role of wife or the sense of security and belonging that went with it. Instead she possessed a new freedom as a widow no longer under the control of a domineering and sometimes violent husband. Whatever his behavior during the marriage, John Henry's succession document, based upon his handwritten last will and testament and promptly filed in Natchitoches Parish on March 7, 1918, left Cammie financially secure. In it John Henry referred to her as his "dear wife" and named Cammie and their eldest son, Stephen, executors of his estate. Few documents testify better to Cammie Henry's power of persuasion and influence than her husband's last wishes. Perhaps this difficult husband had come to feel respect and real affection for the woman he had made mistress of Melrose.[30]

Henry rarely discussed her feelings about her marriage or her husband, and she did not display sentimental mementoes around the house. While she seems not to have mourned her husband in an outwardly observable manner, Henry would grieve for the rest of her life over the loss of her son Isaac, who died on November 17, 1918, at the age of eighteen, a victim of the Spanish influenza epidemic. To help her daughter cope, Leudivine Garrett moved from her son's home in New Roads to Melrose and remained there for the rest of her life. Since Henry's eldest son, Stephen, was starting what would become an illustrious military career, her second son, John Hampton Henry, known as Jady, left college in his sophomore year to take over the business management of Melrose Plantation, which he did successfully until his death in 1969.[31]

In 1919, at the age of forty-eight, Cammie Henry took decisive action to remodel the big house once again. Despite having been left with a huge plantation, seven children (four of whom were under the age of twelve), and more than a hundred tenants and servants dependent upon management decisions, she had seemingly found her calling. With her newly acquired financial independence, Henry promptly added indoor plumbing to the manor, including indoor bathrooms, as well as a wing to the back of the house. She moved out of the marital bedroom as soon as the wing was complete. The back wing came from the local Markoe Plantation and included a sun porch, a new bedroom, which Henry occupied, and a quilting room that doubled as a sleeping room to accommodate still more of the steady and unending stream of guests.[32]

Several months after Henry's mother moved to Melrose, an old friend of hers and the late Stephen Garrett, Dr. Milton Dunn, became the first writer-in-residence at Melrose, arriving in August 1918 and staying until his death in 1924. Born in Jackson Parish, the widowed Dunn was a physician by profession but an amateur historian by avocation. As a teenager he had served with Henry's father in the regiment of Louisiana volunteers during the Civil War. Devoting himself to recording the histories of the soldiers in gray and maintaining a massive correspondence with Confederate veterans while at Melrose, Dunn wrote a history of Natchitoches, published in the 1920 *Louisiana Historical Quarterly*, in which he sought to preserve the "true" Confederate history. Dunn left to Henry his most prized possession, his library of Confederate books.[33]

Arguably the most significant possession Dunn left Henry, however, was the Colfax Cannon, which she acquired in 1921. The Colfax Massacre of 1873 has been described by one historian as "the bloodiest single instance of racial carnage in the Reconstruction era." Both Republican and Democratic contenders throughout Louisiana disputed the election of 1872. In Colfax, the parish seat of Grant Parish, freedmen, fearing the Democrats would seize the government, held the town hostage for three weeks. On Easter Sunday in 1873, rifle-bearing whites with this one cannon massacred some eighty blacks who had laid down their arms and were waving a flag of surrender.[34] A journalist noted in Dunn's obituary that he had volunteered for service in the "Colfax Riot" and at the time "was praised for his work in vindicating white supremacy in the South."[35]

Dunn had been the Grant Parish coroner prior to his move to Melrose, and it is evident that he exercised his considerable influence when Henry decided that she wanted the Colfax Cannon not only as a lawn decoration but also as a piece of Confederate memorabilia. As Henry gleefully wrote to Carrie Dorman, she sent her wagon to Colfax to collect "my cannon." Additionally, after she had the cannon mounted, she directed Dorman to create an "indestructible card marker" to put on the base. Unfortunately the cannon was an overt nonverbal statement to the hundreds of black house servants, field hands, and tenant farmers about the importance of knowing one's place. The Colfax Cannon remained the centerpiece of the front garden at Melrose Plantation until 1970, several decades after Henry's death.[36]

The widow Cammie Henry, now secure in her plantation home, rewrote her life. As a wife, Henry had been the personification of the southern lady. She embodied the Old South white feminine ideal of the plantation mistress: a cultivated, refined, genteel woman who usually exercised gender-prescribed methods of indirect persuasion and influence and upheld the class tradition of noblesse oblige. Yet after her husband died, Henry sought to alter her identity, and like other clubwomen of the Progressive era, for a time she was involved with a number of women's organizations in Natchitoches. In 1921 Henry joined the Natchitoches chapter of the United Daughters of the Confederacy, and through the 1920s she attended a few meetings of the Lesche Club, a literary circle founded in 1894 and the oldest women's club in the region. The middle-aged widow quickly concluded, however, that she was not one who would find satisfaction as a clubwoman. Rather than traveling out into the world, Henry's quest instead involved bringing those she selected from the world to be her guests at Melrose Plantation.[37]

In widowhood, Henry relied on her intellectual pursuits of the past to lead her to a new network of friendships and emotional support. Eventually she found a role that gave her life unique meaning. Without jeopardizing her status as an aristocratic southern lady, Henry not only reinvented herself, she also expanded her sphere. To be sure, her economic situation, interests, and intelligence allowed for the expanded gender, race, and class dynamics that she cultivated in these relationships. Emotional support from her informal group of female friends encouraged her transformation from wife to patron and chatelaine of a cultural center. Her choice of friends, and their encouragement, was critical to Henry's evolution—from one who clung to the traditional and conservative trappings of the southern woman to one who carved out her own destiny that gave power, control, and meaning to her life. The women who proved to be so influential in Henry's life were talented, ambitious, and shared her white, Protestant, elite background as well as the constellation of ideas and attitudes she held regarding the southern past. This Natchitoches-based circle included Caroline Dorman, who acted as her major emotional support and guide, the writer Ada Jack Carver, and Irma DeBlieux Sompayrac and Gladys Breazeale, both daughters of prominent Natchitoches families and cofounders of the Natchitoches Art Colony that existed from 1921 to 1937.[38]

Henry's friends Sompayrac and Breazeale hatched the plan for the first southern art colony, a plein air landscape painting school, during a March 1921 trip to New Orleans. The two former art students arranged a meeting with Newcomb College and Tulane University art professor Ellsworth Woodward to seek advice about their future vocations in art. The three discussed the need for a southern art colony, and having seen that Natchitoches and the surrounding area was a suitable setting, Woodward convinced his two former students to be codirectors and organizers of a colony where he and his fellow artists could teach. Initially visiting Natchitoches as an art instructor at the Louisiana Normal College in spring 1920, Woodward returned to Natchitoches that summer as the guest of Dr. and Mrs. William Thomas Williams, who had commissioned him to paint their home, Tauzin House, the oldest house in Natchitoches. During this summer trip Woodward met Cammie Henry and visited Melrose Plantation. Later Breazeale wrote to Henry, "Mr. Woodward was charmed with your home when he was here last summer." Soon after, Melrose became the home of the Natchitoches Art Colony.[39]

Born in 1921, the Natchitoches Art Colony was immediately successful and brought a growing awareness of the arts in the South and fostered patronage for them. The cultural preservation of the historic South and Confederate traditions intersected nicely with Henry's life when she began to open her home to the instructors and students of the colony. From the new art school's beginning, Henry fed the students and instructors who came to paint the Melrose landscape, and her plantation provided an atmospheric antebellum setting for socialization. Often partying and social events at Melrose and other Cane River plantations were the highlight of the art colony experience for both students and instructors. Will Henry Stevens, a colleague of Ellsworth Woodward at Newcomb College and founder of several art colonies in the southeastern United States, not only was a frequent guest at Melrose but also became the main instructor at the Natchitoches Art Colony. Among the students who became lifelong friends of Henry and part of the Melrose group were Edith (Eli) Mahier, an artist, former Newcomb student, and a native of Baton Rouge, and Alberta Kinsey, a New Orleans artist. In 1917, Mahier moved to Norman, Oklahoma, where she taught for decades at the University of Oklahoma. A student at the 1923 art colony's summer session, Mahier frequently visited Melrose, sustaining her relationship with Henry through a lifetime of letters and periodic visits. Kinsey was a member of the French Quarter's bohemian community of artists, writers, and stage performers, who stimulated each other's creativity, disregarded society's rules, and, perhaps most significantly, energized the effort to restore the historic Vieux Carré, notably the old French opera house, which had been destroyed by fire in 1919. Kinsey met Henry when she participated in the 1925 summer session, after which she made annual spring pilgrimages, painting the magnolias of Melrose to her heart's content. Embraced by the Melrose group, Kinsey was among the first to spread the word to her friends in the Vieux Carré group about the fledgling haven for talented artists.[40]

William Spratling, a Tulane University professor of architecture and part of the French Quarter's artistic and literary circle that eventually formed an important branch of the Southern Renaissance, learned about the Melrose Plantation group through his friend Kinsey. Spratling also associated with Woodward and Stevens and with others in the Vieux Carré artists' group. He made his initial visit to Melrose in the summer of 1925 with his friend Natalie Vivien Scott, a journalist, social worker, and award-winning playwright. Spratling and Scott were researching material for their book *Plantation Houses of Louisiana*, which would be published in 1926 and include a description of Melrose. In the autumn of 1925, Spratling displayed many of his drawings, including those of Melrose, at the New Orleans Arts and Crafts Club Exhibition, where the works of Will Stevens and Alberta Kinsey were also shown. Lyle Saxon, a feature writer for the *Times-Picayune* and member of the preservationist, literary, and artistic New Orleans circles frequented by Spratling and Kinsey, wrote that this particular art show included "Spratling's most ambitious work."[41]

Spratling returned to Melrose in 1926 to make sketches for his "Cane River Portraits" series, which *Scribner's Magazine* published in April 1928. His five portraits included Cane River blacks and Creoles of color, including Madame Aubert Rocque. He gained access to his subjects through the relationships Henry had cultivated for more than a quarter of a century. Irma Sompayrac also included Spratling's work with that produced at the Natchitoches Art Colony, which she marketed in some of the art galleries of New York City. Over the years, he maintained contact with the Melrose group and the Henry family. Spratling and his Vieux Carré roommate William Faulkner often stayed with the writer Lyle Saxon while in New York. Saxon, the director of the Louisiana Federal Writers' Project, student of New Orleans history, and coauthor of *Gumbo Ya-Ya*, a compilation of native Louisiana folk stories, eventually became a star of the Melrose Group.[42]

The success of the Natchitoches Art Colony brought an influx of reporters who spread the news of the colony—and coincidentally Melrose Plantation—to a nationwide audience. Mary Belle McKellar, daughter of a prominent Shreveport, Louisiana, family and herself a highly regarded journalist, was also a friend of Cammie Henry, Caroline Dorman, and Ada Carver, and remained part of the Melrose group throughout her life. McKellar was among the first to write feature articles about the art colony, beginning with her essay for the March 1923 issue of *Holland's*, a magazine of the South aimed at women in Texas and the Southwest. She later wrote "The First Art Colony of the South" for the feature section of the *Dallas Morning Star*, which appeared on Sunday, April 25, 1926. Apparently not unlike the other women who frequented the colony, McKellar was "high-spirited" and "fire-eating," according to one of her friends. The publicity that her writings, and those of others, brought to Melrose contributed to the influx of writers and artists who wanted to be part of the Natchitoches Art Colony.[43]

Attracted by the publicity surrounding Melrose, as well as the word-of-mouth praise for Henry and the art colony, author, musicologist, and folklorist Dorothy Scarborough visited the plantation in 1925, gathering material for *On the Trail of Negro Folk Songs*. Published in 1925, the same year she published *The Wind* (her most famous fictional work, later made into a movie by MGM starring Lillian Gish), Scarborough's book of folk songs fed into the Lost Cause ideal. She wrote that the songs she had collected revealed the "lighter, happier side of slavery, and re-create[d] for us the rustic merry-making of slaves on the many plantations of the South," and she asserted that "the colored mind is not essentially logical, and the folk-song shows considerable lack of coherence in thought." Scarborough's belief that slavery was beneficial to African Americans fit nicely with Henry's nostalgic, "moonlight and magnolias" view of the aristocratic antebellum South.[44]

Scarborough noted that during her stay at Melrose she had gained much of her information for her work from former slaves Israel and Jane Sudduth, whom Henry referred to as "Uncle Israel" and his wife, "Aunt Jane," then in their nineties. She witnessed the care rendered to them by Henry when they were no longer able to work. Seemingly in the tradition of noblesse oblige, a folkloric ideal demonstrated by the "good plantation mistress" from antebellum days, the mistress of Melrose cared for this couple daily, sending food at mealtimes to their cabin and guaranteeing for their lifetime the dwelling in which they resided.

Marie Therese Coin-Coin and her sons had constructed Yucca House, the original building for the plantation, in the late eighteenth century. When the Sudduths died in the mid-1920s, Henry had Yucca House renovated for Lyle Saxon. His decade-long stay at Yucca House would produce his fictional masterpiece, *Children of Strangers*, a 1937 novel centered on miscegenation and the Cane River Creoles of color of the Isle Brevelle. His time at Melrose became the golden era of the colony as his move inevitably brought his wide group of talented friends to Natchitoches. Having been at the center of the writers' group of the Southern Renaissance, which included renowned figures such as Faulkner, Tennessee Williams, Allen Tate, and Robert Penn Warren, Saxon invariably became integral to the success of the colony.[45]

Henry and Saxon met in 1923 and began their lifelong association and friendship. Saxon had learned about Henry and the Melrose Plantation through mutual friends connected to the Natchitoches Art Colony, the informal Vieux Carré literature group, and their mutual friend, Grace King, the elderly literary champion of the South and particularly New Orleans.[46] It was in March that Saxon met Henry at one of King's afternoon teas. At that meeting, Henry invited Saxon, Stevens, Breazeale, and several other artists to spend Easter at Melrose. Saxon wrote about this visit in a *Times-Picayune* feature article entitled "One is Closer to Heaven at Old Melrose Plantation," in which he insisted, "Aunt Cammie is one of the most charming persons you have ever seen." More significantly, however, he noted the existence of the infamous Colfax Cannon on the front lawn, writing, "You can imagine Aunt Cammie bringing home that cannon. It was the most characteristic thing she ever could have done."[47] Between 1923 and 1926, raconteur, bon vivant, journalist, writer, and legendary imbiber Saxon made numerous trips to Melrose before he finally decided to resign his position at the *Times-Picayune* to settle in at Yucca House. Henry had convinced Saxon to live at Melrose in order to concentrate on his writing. As she wrote to Caroline Dorman, "Lyle is magnificent and knit into my soul."[48]

Upon his arrival, guests to Melrose began to include Saxon's numerous gifted friends, including Edward Suydam, illustrator of three of Saxon's books; Edward Dreyer, a coauthor with Saxon of *Gumbo Ya-Ya*; Robert Tallant, a professor of English at Newcomb College, writer for the *New Orleans Item*, and another *Gumbo Ya-Ya* coauthor; Roark Bradford, novelist and night editor of the *Times-Picayune*; Sherwood Anderson, novelist and short story writer; Gwen Bristow, novelist and writer for the *Times-Picayune*; Rachel Field, popular author of children's and adult books; Harnett Kane, author, travel writer, and frequent contributor of book reviews to the *New York Times*; Joseph Titzell, writer, poet, and critic; Anne Parrish, novelist and author of children's literature; Julia Peterkin, novelist who specialized in the black experience and character; and photographer Doris Ulmann, who collaborated with Peterkin on *Roll, Jordan, Roll*, a photographic book of African American plantation life. Arguably, however, Melrose Plantation's most notable literary guest was William Faulkner. Other guests at Melrose included the famous surgeon Dr. Rudolf Matas; film star Margaret Sullivan; critic and *New Yorker* commentator Alexander Woollcott; author and playwright Rose Franken; novelist Ruth Cross Palmer and her husband, George William Palmer; journalist William Brown Meloney; authors Edith Wyatt Moore, Arthur Babb, Ross Phares, and James Pipes Register; journalist and literary writer Carolyn Ramsey; photographer Richard Avedon; and Francois Mignon, architect, writer, and designer of the Melrose gardens. Mignon first visited Melrose in 1938, and in 1939 Henry invited him to move there permanently. Henry convinced Mignon that she needed a literary aide and curator for the plantation library and its collections, as well as a tour guide for those visiting the buildings and grounds. Perhaps more so, she desperately needed an in-house friend after Saxon left to join the Federal Writers' Project. Mignon remained until 1970, when the Henry family sold the plantation, and he wrote about his experiences there in *Plantation Memo: Plantation Life in Louisiana, 1750–1970, and Other Matter*.[49]

Arguably it was Mignon who became the single most important person in the artistic scene at Melrose. Mignon single-handedly promoted the artistic career of Clementine Hunter (1886–1988), a field laborer, laundress, and cook at the plantation. While cleaning a bedroom, Hunter, then in her fifties, found some paints left behind by Alberta Kinsey that she asked Mignon if she could keep. History has it that Mignon found her a brush, tore an old shade from the window, and told her to paint a picture. Hunter would spend the rest of her life creating colorful "folk" paintings, reflecting her life at Melrose and capturing her families of origin, their marriages, and her friends, as she went about the chores and celebrations that otherwise constituted her world. Mignon became Hunter's unofficial agent, helping and guiding her until his death in 1980. Indeed, as a result of Mignon's tenacity, Clementine Hunter became one of Louisiana's most famous folk artists and the first African American to exhibit in the New Orleans Museum of Art, where her work remains to this day.[50]

Ironically, Melrose's most famous artist was thus the paradoxical exception to the writers and artists Henry sponsored in the Melrose group, who portrayed the southern past in the manner she most admired. Through her protégés, Henry reconstructed the cultural heritage of the antebellum South from an elite white perspective, one that Clementine Hunter viewed from the sidelines. The Melrose group also preserved a strand of Cane River culture that was in danger of being forgotten, that of the Isle Brevelle Creoles of color, the Metoyer descendants. The renovated big house, the grounds at Melrose Plantation, and Henry herself were living symbols of the Old South as created by the mistress of Melrose. While the upper-middle-class white guests of Melrose Plantation and the

Natchitoches Art Colony eulogized the lost Eden of the antebellum, agrarian South in their writings, paintings, and photographs, black servants like Hunter toiled and sweated, from their sunrise delivery of hot coffee and doughnuts on doily-covered trays to the slumbering white folks, to the laborious watering of the gardens under a scorching sun, to the cooking, cleaning, and laundering, all necessary to sustaining Henry's pastoral life.

Henry attempted to re-create the culture of the Old South at Melrose Plantation. It was there that she nurtured her carefully chosen, talented few, who transmitted the values and views of the Lost Cause to future generations. The writers Henry sponsored contributed to a cultural victory for the South. At Henry's dream factory, these individuals, with their pride and their prejudices, shared a common worldview that they preserved and transmitted. As Irma Sompayrac wrote to Henry, "I am still in a dream of Melrose and you." Ada Carver expressed similar feelings, once explaining: "I dreamed last night that Miss Cammie had created or developed a strange, lovely new flower at Melrose that the whole country was going wild over."[51]

Henry's most interesting creation, however, was the reinvention of herself as she expanded her sphere and stepped beyond her gender-prescribed role in the early-twentieth-century South. Her evolution from the mistress of Melrose to the chatelaine of a cultural center allowed her to nurture writers who embraced the ideas of the Lost Cause. The southern values and symbols that were promoted through their literature, in which a vanquished South wrote its way out of defeat and unconditionally won the day on the literary battlefield, were historically significant to a region attempting to recapture and sustain its lost heritage. Melrose was a haven for what was perceived to be an amoral and heartless modern world. As historian C. Vann Woodward, who drew a different meaning from the influence of the Old South myth and the Lost Cause movement, noted, "Juleps for the few and pellagra for the crew; it means a façade of Greek columns and a backyard full of slums." It appears, somewhat contradictorily, that Henry never had the dimmest awareness of the meaning behind what is generally perceived as a glorification of the antebellum South and slavery through the Lost Cause. "Miss Cammie" was never able to transcend the captivity of her culture.[52]

NOTES

1. For more information on Marie Therese Coin-Coin, see Elizabeth Shown Mills, "Marie Therese Coin-Coin: Cane River Slave, Slave Owner and Paradox," in *Louisiana Women: Their Lives and Times*, ed. Janet Allured and Judy Gentry (Athens: University of Georgia Press, 2009), 10–29.

2. Gaines M. Foster, *Ghosts of the Confederacy: Defeat, the Lost Cause, and the Emergence of the New South, 1865–1913* (New York: Oxford University Press, 1988), 4–6, 194; Charles Wilson Reagan, *Baptized in Blood: The Religion of the Lost Cause, 1865–1920* (Athens: University of Georgia Press, 1980), 7, 8, 15, 106. See also Charles Wilson Reagan, "The Lost Cause Myth in the New South Era," in *Myth America: A Historical Anthology*, ed. Patrick Gerster and Nicholas J. Cords (New York:

Wiley-Blackwell, 2006); David Goldfield, *Still Fighting the Civil War* (Baton Rouge: Louisiana State University Press, 2004).

3. Foster, *Ghosts of the Confederacy*, 4, 6, 194; Albion W. Tourgee, "The South as a Field for Fiction," *Forum* 6 (December 1888): 404–18; "Albion W. Tourgee," in *Contemporary Authors Online* (Gale, 2004), http://gdc.gale.com/gale-literature-collections/contemporary-authors.

4. Rollin G. Ostwerweis, *The Myth of the Lost Cause: 1865–1900* (Hamden, Conn.: Archon Books, 1973), 9.

5. David Blight, *Race and Reunion: The Civil War in National Memory* (Cambridge: Belknap Press of Harvard University Press, 2002).

6. Albion W. Tourgee, *Bricks without Straw* (New York: Fords, Howard, and Hulbert, 1880), 307.

7. Carmelite Garrett Henry's United Daughters of the Confederacy Certificate of Membership, folder 353, Melrose Collection, Cammie Garrett Henry Research Center, Watson Library, Northwestern State University, Natchitoches, Louisiana (hereafter cited as Melrose Collection); Cammie Henry Wenk's July 1946 Membership Application to the United Daughters of the Confederacy, in possession of the author; Karen Cox, *Dixie's Daughters: The United Daughters of the Confederacy and the Preservation of Confederate Culture* (Gainesville: University Press of Florida, 2003), 1–7, 160–63.

8. William Edward Clement with Stuart Omar Landry, *Plantation Life on the Mississippi* (New Orleans: Pelican, 1952), 196, "Joseph Erwin," in *Dictionary of Louisiana Biography*, ed. Glenn R. Conrad, et al. (New Orleans: Louisiana Historical Association, 1988), 287; Alice Pemble White, "The Plantation Experience of Joseph and Lavinia Erwin, 1807–1836," *Louisiana Historical Quarterly* 27 (1944): 288.

9. Leslie Sammons, "The Erwin Family" (undergraduate history research paper based on oral interviews with Erwin descendants, Louisiana State University, circa 1964–68), 1–25, copy in author's possession; Leslie Sammons telephone conversation with author, March 21, 2001; genealogy sheets, prepared by Eugene Lloyd Wenk, Jr., for the Genealogical Society of the Church of Jesus Christ of the Latter Day Saints, Salt Lake City, Utah, accession number 601, Lloyd Wenk Collection, box 1, Cammie Garrett Henry Research Center, Watson Library, Northwestern State University, Natchitoches, Louisiana (hereafter cited as Wenk Collection); Loree Oursler, "Portrait of Carmelite," *Natchitoches Times*, October 11, 1973, folder 604, roll 11, Francois Mignon Collection, Southern Historical Association, University of North Carolina at Chapel Hill (hereafter cited as Mignon Collection); Herman de Bachelle Seebold, *Old Louisiana Plantation Homes and Family Trees*, vol. 2 (Gretna, La.: Pelican, 1971), 319, 332, 336.

10. Wenk genealogical sheets; Seebold, *Old Louisiana Plantation Homes*, 319, 336; Clement and Landry, *Plantation Life on the Mississippi*, 47; Sammons, "The Erwin Family," 19.

11. Diane M. Moore, "Mistress of Melrose: Carmelite Henry," in *Their Adventurous Will: Profiles of Memorable Louisiana Women* (Lafayette, La.: Acadian Press, 1984), 6; Melrose Scrapbook, 205:124, Melrose Collection; Ora G. Williams, "Cammie G. Henry," in *Four Women of Cane River* (Natchitoches, La.: Natchitoches Public Library, n.d.), 19.

12. Moore, "Mistress of Melrose," 6; Drew Gilpin Faust, *Mothers of Invention: Women of the Slaveholding South in the Civil War* (New York: Vintage Books, 1996), 22–32, 256.

13. Amy Thompson McCandless, *The Past Is Present: Women's Higher Education in the Twentieth Century American South* (Tuscaloosa: University of Alabama Press, 1999), 18.

14. Williams, "Cammie G. Henry," 19–20; Moore, "Mistress of Melrose," 6.

15. Wenk genealogical sheets; Records of Louisiana Confederate Soldiers and Commands cited in Cammie Henry Wenk's July 1946 Membership Application to the Daughters of the American Revolution and the to the United Daughters of the Confederacy; Dana Henry Gibson, "Essay on Cammie Henry," Membership Application for the Daughters of the American Revolution, Melrose Collection.

16. For a time Chopin lived in Cloutierville, twelve miles from Melrose Plantation. She returned to her native St. Louis, Missouri, in 1884 as a widow.

17. See Emily Toth, *Kate Chopin* (New York: William Morrow, 1990), 132, 142–43, 161, 169, 317–18, 324–25, 411–12; Emily Toth, "Kate Chopin: Knowing What It Means to Miss New Orleans," in *Louisiana Women: Their Lives and Times*, ed. Janet Allured and Judy Gentry (Athens: University of Georgia Press, 2009), 114–36.

18. Invitation to Captain Stephen Garrett's 1896 Memorial Service, copy in possession of author; James Garrett, interview with author, March 12, 1998, New Roads, Louisiana; Wenk genealogical sheets.

19. Melrose Scrapbook 205:12, Melrose Collection; Wenk genealogical sheets; William Scruggs, interview with author, May 16, 1997, Baton Rouge.

20. Todd Cooper and Leslie Cooper, interview with author, November 20, 2000; Moore, "Mistress of Melrose," 15–16; D. D. Garber, "Mixed Architecture Adds Charm to Historic Melrose Plantation," *Dallas Morning News*, October 28, 1951, folder 582, roll 11, Melrose Collection.

21. Lloyd Wenk, interview with author, January 19, 1997, Shreveport, Louisiana; Pat Henry, interview with author, February 15, 1997, Natchitoches, Louisiana; Stephen Henry, Jr., interview with author, May 16, 1997.

22. Moore, "Mistress of Melrose," 15–16; Garber, "Mixed Architecture"; Fran Holman Johnson, *The Gift of the Wild Things: The Life of Caroline Dorman* (Lafayette: Center for Louisiana Studies, 1990), 22.

23. "Caroline Coroneos Dorman," in *Dictionary of Louisiana Biography*, ed. Glenn R. Conrad (New Orleans: Louisiana Historical Association, 1988), 1:251; Fran Holman Johnson, *The Gift of Wild Things: The Life of Caroline Dormon* (Lafayette: Center for Louisiana Studies, 1990), 22; Richard and Jesse Johnson, interview with author, March 29, 1999; Cammie Henry to Caroline Dorman, n.d., folder 626, Caroline Dorman Collection, Cammie Henry Research Center, Watson Library, Northwestern State University, Natchitoches, Louisiana (hereafter cited as Dorman Collection).

24. Caroline Dorman to Cammie Henry, March 15, 1924, Melrose Scrapbook 83:124, Melrose Collection; Cammie Henry to Caroline Dorman, March 1, 1925, folder 591, Dorman Collection.

25. Oliver Jackson Ford, III, "Ada Jack Carver: A Critical Biography" (PhD diss., University of Connecticut, 1975), 83, 111, 149, 151.

26. Gary B. Mills, *The Forgotten People: Cane River Creoles of Color* (Baton Rouge: Louisiana State University Press, 1977), xiv; Sybil Kein, "Who Are the Creoles?," in *Southern Historical Association Newsletter*, 2001, 7; Arnold R. Hirsch and Joseph Logsdon, *Creole New Orleans: Race and Americanization* (Baton Rouge: Louisiana State University Press, 1992).

27. For more on the complicated legal and intimate relationships between women of color and white men, concubinage, and plaçage, see Emily Clark, *The Strange History of the American Quadroon: Free Women of Color in the Revolutionary Atlantic World* (Chapel Hill: University of North Carolina Press, 2013).

28. Mills, *The Forgotten People*, xviii, 143; Daniel Graves, "The War for Southern Independence," *Profiles of Natchitoches History* (Natchitoches, La.: Museum of Historic Natchitoches, 1966), 15; Charles S. Gallien, "Melrose Plantation Served as a Cultural and Literary Center," *Natchitoches Times*, July 12, 1970, folder 583, roll 11, Mignon Collection; Gary B. Mills, "Patriotism Frustrated: The Native Guards of Historic Natchitoches," *Louisiana History* 18, no. 4 (1977): 438, 439, 449, 450; Cooper interview.

29. "Isle Brevelle Parish Observes the Centennial," *Catholic Action of the South*, November 11, 1954, folder 588, roll 11, Mignon Collection; Gary B. Mills and Elizabeth S. Mills, *Melrose* (Natchitoches, La.: Association for the Preservation of Historic Natchitoches, 1973), 49.

30. Death Certificate of John Henry, Sr., Registered #3976, Bureau of Vital Statistics, Louisiana Division of Archives, Baton Rouge, Louisiana; Succession Document of John Hampton Henry, Sr., folder 1101, Melrose Collection. John Henry's last will and testament is dated December 14, 1914.

31. Wenk genealogical sheets; James Garrett interview; Lloyd Wenk interview; Stephen Henry, Jr., interview; Pat Henry interview.

32. Scruggs interview; Lloyd Wenk interview.

33. "Dr. Dunn Lived a Useful Life, Friend Says," *Colfax Chronicle*, n.d., Melrose Scrapbook 70:25, Melrose Collection; Milton Dunn, "History of Natchitoches, Louisiana," *Louisiana Historical Quarterly* 3, no. 1 (January 1920): 53; inscription in book, Dunn Library, folder 1396, Melrose Collection.

34. Eric Foner, *Reconstruction: American's Unfinished Revolution, 1867–1877* (New York: Harper and Row, 1988), 437. See also Charles Lane, *The Day Freedom Died: The Colfax Massacre, the Supreme Court, and the Betrayal of Reconstruction* (New York: Henry Holt, 2008), especially the appendix, "How Many Died?," 265–66; LeeAnna Keith, *The Colfax Massacre: The Untold Story of Black Power, White Terror, and the Death of Reconstruction* (New York: Oxford University Press, 2009); Nicholas Lemann, *Redemption: The Last Battle of the Civil War* (New York: Farrar, Straus, and Giroux, 2007).

35. "Dr. Dunn Lived a Useful Life."

36. Cammie Henry to Caroline Dorman, September 1921, folder 626, Dorman Collection.

37. Cammie Garrett Henry's Membership Certificate to the United Daughters of the Confederacy; Mary Linn Wernet, interview with author, May 4, 2000; Mary Linn Wernet, "A Call to Order: Women's Organizational Records of the Cammie G. Henry Research Center, Northwestern State University," *North Louisiana History* 34, no. 23 (Spring/Summer 2003): 91. For more information on the women's club movement, see Noralee Frankel and Nancy S. Dye, *Gender, Class, Race, and Reform in the Progressive Era* (Lexington: University Press of Kentucky, 1994); Anne Firor Scott, *Natural Allies: Women's Associations in American History* (Urbana-Champaign: University of Illinois Press, 1992).

38. Sarah Bailey Luster, "The Natchitoches Art Colony: A Southern En Plein Air Art Colony (1921–1937)" (master's thesis, Tulane University, 1992), 42–44.

39. Ibid.; Gladys Breazeale to Cammie Henry, June 20, 1921, Melrose Scrapbook 68:118, Melrose Collection.

40. Luster, "The Natchitoches Art Colony," 65, 72–73, 84; Ted Olson, *Crossroads: A Southern Culture Annual* (Macon, Ga.: Mercer University Press, 2004), 101.

41. John W. Scott, "William Spratling and the New Orleans Renaissance," *Louisiana History* 45, no. 3 (2002): 287–88; Taylor D. Littleton, *The Color of Silver: William Spratling, His Life and Art* (Baton Rouge: Louisiana State University Press, 2000), 55; Lyle Saxon, "What's Doing?," *Times-Picayune*, October 25, 1925.

42. William Spratling, "Cane River Portraits," *Scribner's Magazine*, April 1928, 417–18; Luster, "Natchitoches Art Colony," 93; Littleton, *The Color of Silver*, 235; Thomas Bonner, Jr., "Lyle Saxon," in *Southern Writers: A Biographical Dictionary*, ed. Robert Bain, Louis D. Rubin, Jr., and Joseph M. Flora (Baton Rouge: Louisiana State University Press, 1979), 398–99. In 1930, William Spratling moved to Taxco, Mexico, where he resurrected the vanished folk art of silversmithing and in the process became rich and famous.

43. Robina Denham to Caroline Dorman, January 26, 1928, folder 528, Dorman Collection; Mary Belle McKellar, "The South Calls the Artists: Louisiana Has Opened a New Vista for Landscape Seeker Which Bids Fair to Found a New School of Louisiana Painting," *Holland's*, March 1923, 17; Mary Belle McKellar, "The First Art Colony of the South," *Dallas Morning News*, April 25, 1926, Melrose Scrapbook 78, Melrose Collection.

44. Roger Abrahams, foreword in Dorothy Scarborough, *On the Trail of the Negro Song* (Hatboro, Penn.: Folklore Associates, 1925), i, vi; Scarborough, *On the Trail*, 128, 272.

45. Francois Mignon, "Melrose Time Table," Old Plantation Scrapbook, 13, folder 599, Mignon Collection.

46. See Mary Ann Wilson, "Grace King: New Orleans Literary Historian," in *Louisiana Women: Their Lives and Times*, ed. Janet Allured and Judy Gentry (Athens: University of Georgia Press, 2009), 137–54.

47. Chance Harvey, *The Life and Selected Letters of Lyle Saxon* (Gretna, La.: Pelican, 2003), 79–80; Lyle Saxon, "Easter Sunday at Cammie Henry's: One Is Closer to Heaven at Old Melrose Planta-

tion," *Times-Picayune*, April 22, 1923, folder 638, Dorman Collection. See also Robert Bush, *Grace King: A Southern Destiny* (Baton Rouge: Louisiana State University Press, 1999); Wilson, "Grace King."

48. Cammie Henry to Caroline Dorman, July 5, 1925, folder 592, Dorman Collection.

49. *Plantation Memo: Plantation Life in Louisiana, 1750–1970 and Other Matter* (Baton Rouge: Claitor's, 1972); James W. Thomas, *Lyle Saxon: A Critical Biography* (Birmingham, Ala.: Summa Publications, 1991), 127; Wenk genealogical sheets. Francois Mignon lived with Ora Garland Williams, who wrote the foreword for Mignon's book on plantation life, and her husband, Judge Richard B. Williams, in their guesthouse on their Natchitoches estate during the final decade of his life.

50. Thomas, *Lyle Saxon*, 24; Art Shiver and Tom Whitehead, eds., *Clementine Hunter: The African House Murals* (Natchitoches, La.: Association for the Preservation of Historic Natchitoches, 2005), 20; Shelby R. Gilley, *Painting by Her Heart: The Life and Art of Clementine Hunter, Louisiana Folk Artist* (Baton Rouge: St. Emma Press, 2000), 44; Harvey, *The Life and Selected Letters of Lyle Saxon*, 106; Lee Kogan, "Clementine Hunter: Self Taught Artist," in *Louisiana Women: Their Lives and Times*, ed. Janet Allured and Judy Gentry (Athens: University of Georgia Press, 2009), 175–94; Ann Brittain, interview with author, May 28, 2000.

51. Irma Sompayrac to Cammie Henry, October 20, 1926, Melrose Scrapbook 81:8, Melrose Collection; Ada Jack Carver Snell to Cammie Henry, April 18, 1925, folder 519, Dorman Collection.

52. Osterweis, *The Myth of the Lost Cause*, 152; C. Vann Woodward, "The Old South Papered by the New South Fraud," *Washington Post*, July 9, 1961.

Alice Dunbar-Nelson

(1875–1935)

Looking at New Orleans

HELLEN S. LEE

When the twenty-year-old Alice Dunbar-Nelson, born Alice Ruth Moore, published her collection of stories and poems *Violets and Other Tales* (1895), she could hardly have imagined where it would lead her.[1] She often disparaged her own work as juvenile despite the positive reviews that it received from newspapers.[2] *Violets* would nonetheless catch the eye of future husband and poet Paul Laurence Dunbar and ultimately propel the career of the young New Orleanian as one of the most important African American writers, journalists, and activists of the early twentieth century.[3] Within fifty years, however, Dunbar-Nelson's celebrity and prominence would dwindle dramatically until Gloria Hull's efforts in the 1980s brought renewed attention to the once-famous author and activist. Dunbar-Nelson's success and subsequent obscurity attest to the vast possibilities and limitations that African American women writers encountered in the twentieth century.

Dunbar-Nelson is often remembered in a way that disconnects her from her upbringing in New Orleans largely because much of her personal, professional, and political life was spent outside of Louisiana as a "race woman" who worked tirelessly for the rights of African Americans across the country. Her early years in New Orleans, however, provided the context of the multiethnic, racially diverse, and regional divisions that contoured the trajectory of both her life and her work. The varied ethnic, racial, linguistic, and national genealogies of this international port city were foundational to what would come: her resistance and challenges to the stereotypical, monolithic, and static notions of African American women's identity and self-determination.[4] In each aspect of her life and work—her personal actions, her public political leadership and activism, and her writings in a wide array of literary genres, including poetry, short stories, essays, newspaper columns, letters, speeches, novels, and plays—she resisted the separation of the artistic from the political and the social from the personal.

Alice Ruth Moore was born on July 19, 1875 and grew up during what historians now refer to as the "Nadir," a particularly bleak time for African Americans, during which the relative political and social gains achieved during Reconstruction were struck down by Jim Crow.[5] She was the youngest daughter of Patricia Wright Moore, who had been born a slave in Opelousas Parish, Louisiana.[6] At the outbreak of the Civil War, Patricia's owner forcibly took her and his other slaves to Texas. When her owner finally released his slaves two years after the Emancipation Proclamation, Patricia moved to New Orleans, where she made her living working a variety of jobs—seamstress, laundress, and live-in domestic help—to support her two daughters, Alice Ruth and Mary Leila.[7] Because Dunbar-Nelson rarely spoke about her early life, there is some discrepancy in the record regarding her father. Many suggest that Patricia married Joseph Moore, assumed to be white, from whom Dunbar-Nelson inherited her fair skin and light hair. Based on birth certificates and city directories, however, historian Eleanor Alexander suggests a different story. Alexander posits that Dunbar-Nelson's parents never officially married and that her father may have been called John Moore or Monroe Moore. She also suggests that Leila and Alice may have had different fathers. Indeed, as Alexander and Hull have both pointed out, this would explain the mystery of Dunbar-Nelson's background, a secret that her husband Paul knew and would use to humiliate her over the course of their tumultuous marriage.[8] What is certain is that Dunbar-Nelson did not come from a background of privilege. During her earliest years she lived in a relatively impoverished neighborhood amid boardinghouses on Second Street in New Orleans.[9] Yet, by the time she reached adulthood, she and her sister had acquired college educations and the family had moved to Uptown, a desirable section of New Orleans.[10] Within a few years, the young mixed-race woman would become a leading political and literary figure, often mingling with the country's most influential African American elite.

Dunbar-Nelson married three times. Her first, famous, but short-lived marriage to Paul Dunbar lasted only six years, until his death in 1906. Ill-matched temperaments—exacerbated by his extended speaking tours, alcoholism, and heroin addiction—caused the couple to live apart for most of their marriage.[11] A few years after Paul's death, in 1910, Dunbar-Nelson secretly married Henry Arthur Callis, a fellow teacher at Howard High School in Wilmington, Delaware, where she had moved. The marriage lasted about a year. At thirty-four, she was twelve years Henry's senior, and speculation suggests that the marriage was kept private because of school district policies forbidding married women teachers, the difference in their social positions, or social stigmas regarding relationships between older women and younger men.[12] Several years after her divorce from

ALICE DUNBAR-NELSON

Photo by R. P. Bellsmith; courtesy of Special Collections, University of Delaware Library, Newark, Del., Alice Dunbar-Nelson Papers, MS 113.

Henry, she met Robert Nelson, a widower with two children, while working on her book *Masterpieces of Negro Eloquence* (1914). Two years later, when she was forty, the two married.[13] Alice and Robert worked together two more times: first at the Douglass Printing Company, with Robert as president and Alice as editor-in-chief, and then from 1920 to 1922 at the Wilmington *Advocate*, a newspaper focusing on local, regional, and national news and race politics.[14] This marriage lasted nearly twenty years, until her death on September 18, 1935, at the age of sixty. During this time she suffered from chronic ill health, including possible heart trouble.

Although often separated from each of her husbands during the course of her three marriages, Dunbar-Nelson was not alone while engaging in her literary, artistic, and political undertakings. Some have suggested that she sought companionship with other women and had close and passionate relationships with them. For example, historian Kevin Gaines explicitly refers to Dunbar-Nelson's sexuality and her struggle between "heterosexual, versus lesbian, sexuality" and discusses her "women lovers."[15] Taking a different tack, Hull concedes the difficulty of proving that Dunbar-Nelson was "anything other than conventionally heterosexual," yet she argues that Dunbar-Nelson "apparently needed multiple and varied channels for her erotic energy. During this period of her life [late 1920s to early 1930s], it becomes unequivocal that these included romantic relationships with women."[16] Based on evidence of fragments of poetry, numerous diary entries, and conversations with Dunbar-Nelson's niece, Pauline, Hull surmises that Dunbar-Nelson had a "tempestuous affair" in California with a younger married woman, the rising journalist and socialite Fay Jackson Robinson.[17] Further, Hull suggests that Dunbar-Nelson maintained a long-standing and especially close relationship with Edwina Kruse, the principal at Howard High.[18] In addition to mentoring the younger woman, Kruse "paid her expenses and gave her money, helped her family, was full of love and endearments and jealousy."[19] Dunbar-Nelson's diary entries are inconclusive but reflect depth of passion that she felt for these women in her life. Dunbar-Nelson was not unique in such affections, of course. Studies have long revealed same-sex relationships among white women during the nineteenth and early twentieth centuries, and similar relationships among African Americans also existed despite the heteronormative imperative and rigid patriarchal family structure among elite African Americans.[20]

It appears that it was the women in her family, however, who provided the most important support network in her life. When Dunbar-Nelson was a child growing up in New Orleans, her grandmother Mary Wright lived with the close-knit family and took care of the girls while her mother, Patricia, worked. Later, when her sister Leila moved with her husband James and their children to West Medford, Massachusetts, Alice and Patricia moved with them.[21] After

Leila and James ultimately separated, Alice, Patricia, Leila, and Leila's four children set up household in Wilmington. When Alice married Robert Nelson, he too joined the household.[22] The deep bonds among the women in the family were stable—preceding and sometimes outlasting the marriages and the deaths of three children—and they provided each other the social and economic support that would have been far more difficult had they lived apart.[23] In short, the shared household made it possible for these women to make it through financial difficulties, bouts of illness, and family deaths.[24]

For Dunbar-Nelson to make teaching her profession and achieve her goals and change social conditions for her fellow African Americans, education was crucial.[25] In this she was like many African American women during the Progressive era. As a girl she attended public school in New Orleans, and at the age of fourteen she moved to Baton Rouge to attend a high school run by Southern University.[26] After graduating in 1889 she returned to New Orleans to matriculate at Straight College (now Dillard University), from which she graduated in 1892 at the age of seventeen. Dunbar-Nelson would later pursue graduate studies at Cornell University, where she studied history, philosophy, literature, and education, and ultimately she wrote a master's thesis on William Wordsworth.[27] While continuing her education, teaching was her primary profession. During her lifetime she taught at elementary schools, high schools, vocational schools, and colleges in Louisiana, New York, North Carolina, and Delaware. Her most significant teaching work was from 1902 to 1920 at Howard High in Wilmington, where she taught English and drawing and eventually served as head of the English Department.[28] As it did for other aspiring young women of the early twentieth century, teaching was an avenue to obtain professional work, foster possibilities for advancement and promotion, and provide a reliable source of income.

Dunbar-Nelson's ability to overcome social and economic obstacles contributed greatly to her literary career. She effectively used her observations of the poor and working classes in the Crescent City to inform her writings. Having social and professional ambitions, but limited resources, Dunbar-Nelson found time to write amid a busy social schedule and full-time employment. While still at Straight College, she served as class poet, and she placed third in two short story contests in 1893.[29] A few years later, she published *Violets*, a collection of poetry, essays, short stories, and sketches that later caught the eye of her first husband. Dunbar-Nelson followed up that successful volume with *The Goodness of St. Rocque, and Other Stories* (1899), a more tightly edited short story collection that focused on New Orleans. She continued to write fiction, poetry, and screenplays, and she regularly submitted work to *Scribner's*, *Atlantic Monthly*, and other prominent literary magazines. Her work was published inconsistently, however, due to changing preferences of the publishers and readership of these literary venues.[30] With *Opportunity* and *Crisis* magazines, the principle publications for the National Urban League and the National Association for the Advancement of Colored People (NAACP), respectively, she found a more sympathetic and reliable outlet for her work. The *Crisis* published her dramatic one-act play *Mine Eyes Have Seen* (1918), the story of a young African American man being drafted in the final year of World War I, which highlighted the tensions between racial marginalization and national duty. She also wrote a few longer works, including *A Modern Undine*, a novella about a young southern woman who marries a northerner; *Uplift*, a satirical novel of an African American professional woman; and *This Lofty Oak*, a thinly veiled, fictionalized biography of Edwina Kruse, her principal at Howard High and life-long friend.[31] Because literary efforts did not pay regularly or well, she wrote her fiction and poetry quickly and without much revision when she could spare the time. Papers in her archives include scribbled notes on the margins of concert programs and reused notebooks.[32]

While the body of her fictional and poetic works comprises but a few volumes, her journalistic work reveals that Dunbar-Nelson was an incredibly prolific writer as well as an outspoken activist.[33] She was most productive as a columnist for periodicals, launching her career in 1894 by writing the "Woman's Column" for the *Journal of the Lodge*, an African American broadsheet based in New Orleans.[34] Later in life she would return to journalism to write for the *Pittsburgh Courier*, the most widely circulated African American periodical in the country, as a regular columnist ("Une Femme Dit" [A Woman Says]) from February to September 1926. Between 1926 and 1930, Dunbar-Nelson wrote the column "As in a Looking Glass" for the Washington *Eagle*, simultaneously penning "Little Excursions Week by Week," another column, syndicated by the Associated Negro Press in 1928. In January 1930, she returned to the *Pittsburgh Courier*, contributing the column "So It Seems—to Alice Dunbar-Nelson."[35] In all of these columns she wrote on a wide array of subjects, crossing genres as "literary critic, political analyst, social commentator, race theorist, humorist, stage and film critic."[36] In addition to this writing, she also managed periodicals, as she had with the Wilmington *Advocate*, acting as associate editor for the *A.M.E. Church Review* and the *Eagle*.[37]

For a woman living in the early twentieth century, professional positions were difficult to obtain due to sexism. For women of color, racism exacerbated the situation. To make a living, a woman of color required flexibility and ambition, both of which Dunbar-Nelson possessed to great extent. She took on a variety of jobs throughout her working life. Before moving to New York, she worked in New Orleans as a bookkeeper and typist for Paragon Printing Company, which was considered to be the largest black-owned business in the United States.[38] In all her roles, Dunbar-Nelson regularly championed women's rights, international peace, and "interracial cooperation as a strategy toward racial equality and social reform."[39] Aside from teaching and journalism, arguably her most lucrative work came in the form of speaking tours. As the widow of Paul Laurence Dunbar, Dunbar-Nelson was able to obtain moderate fees simply for reciting his "dialect" poetry.[40] Such paid speaking engagements, along with royalties from her first husband's work, provided a slight financial boost throughout her cash-strapped years.[41] In the last decade of her life, she tired of the piecemeal and poorly paid work as a journalist and public speaker and sought more steady employment. From 1928 to 1931 she served as the executive secretary of the Society of Friends' American Interracial Peace Committee.[42] Finally, in 1932, her third husband was appointed to the Pennsylvania State Athletic Commission. With this position, the couple finally achieved financial stability, which Dunbar-Nelson enjoyed until her death three years later.[43]

Dunbar-Nelson's literary endeavors were certainly a defining aspect of her life's work, but the writer also pursued other interests, including artistic and social activities as well as taking leadership roles in myriad political causes. She was an ardent aficionado of the arts and attended operas, plays, movies, and concerts whenever possible.[44] She studied art and music and played mandolin for a New Orleans orchestra.[45] As a young woman in New Orleans, she was a charter member of the Phyllis Wheatley Club, associating itself with the Women's Era Club, a national organization of African American women.[46] She also served as president of the Whittier Club, a social club based at her African Methodist Episcopalian church in New Orleans, and for which her sister Leila served as librarian. The two performed plays and dramatic "evenings" that Dunbar-Nelson wrote and produced.[47] After she had acquired celebrity and cultural influence, Dunbar-Nelson led the national organization and support of artistic and musical productions featuring African American artists and performers. In May 1929, for example, she organized a successful National Negro Music Festival called "We Shall Walk through the Valley in Peace" at the Philadelphia Academy of Music. The festival included performances by the Vaudeville entertainers Taylor Gordon and J. Rosamond Johnson, who cowrote "Lift Every Voice and Sing" with his brother James Weldon Johnson.[48] In 1932, she also led the Paul Laurence Dunbar Theater Guild in Philadelphia to encourage the dramatic arts in the local African American community.[49]

In addition to her many cultural activities, Dunbar-Nelson actively participated in a number of political organizations as part of the African American subset of the women's club movement of the late nineteenth and early twentieth centuries. As it did for many middle-class, elite, and aspiring African American women, this movement provided her the opportunity to combine her social, political, and intellectual interests in working on a variety of issues, ranging from antilynching and antisegregation (and antidiscrimination) to the women's suffrage campaign.[50] As Gaines has pointed out, Dunbar-Nelson was among the growing number of women becoming independent minded in politics, education, employment, and fashion.[51] Her diaries and newspaper clippings attest that she saw herself as firmly embedded within this realm of intelligent, social-activist women. She joined a variety of social clubs and political organizations, and often took prominent roles in them, writing for and speaking at such venues as the Delta Sigma Theta Sorority, the National Federation of Colored Women's Clubs, the Equal Franchise Association, the Circle for Negro War Relief, the Women's Committee of the Council of National Defense, the Women's International League of Peace and Freedom, the Welfare League, and the National Association for the Advancement of Colored People.[52] In addition to being a founding member of the National Association of Colored Women, Dunbar-Nelson had the distinction of being "the first African American woman to serve on Delaware's State Republican Committee."[53] She seemed to switch her political affiliation in 1922, when she served as "director of colored women" for the Democratic Party in New York.[54] In reality, she held no formal party affiliation and considered herself independent, allying with whomever she deemed was most consistent in the struggle to obtain justice and equality for African Americans.[55]

Her struggles for inclusion within the larger American society are clear in her earliest writings, specifically in *Violets* and *The Goodness of St. Rocque*. These collections, along with a few unpublished short stories, focused on New Orleans and are critical in understanding Dunbar-Nelson's attempt to be accepted artistically and politically. First, she wrote these pieces while living in Louisiana, situating herself as a southerner, a Louisianan, and a mixed-race writer, rather than as part of the broader category of "African American writer." This regionalism is evident among other southern writers and emerged in tandem with the rise of what is now known as the Harlem Renaissance and the New Negro movements, both of which sought to create a broader African American identity and literary tradition to gain political, social, and cultural inclusion and power.[56] That goal, however, had the consequence of fostering a narrower sense of African American writing that often privileged the modernist mode of the moment and eventually relegating into obscurity regional writers like Dunbar-Nelson and dialect writers like Paul Laurence Dunbar for ostensibly being too provincial or atavistic. Her New Orleans works also provide an important perspective of the city that complements the more widely read stories of better-known white female authors associated with the city, such as Kate Chopin, Grace King, and Ruth McEnery Stuart. Dunbar-Nelson's New Orleans stories add a crucial perspective to the literature of this period, one that provides ethnic and racial subtlety to representations of the city. Finally, in her later works, Dunbar-Nelson explicitly focused on social justice and addressed equal rights for women, social inclusion for African Americans, the antilynching campaign, and international peace. These issues were not ones Dunbar-Nelson had suddenly learned about as she moved in more cosmopolitan circles and gained celebrity status in places like Philadelphia, New York, or Washington, D.C.[57] Rather, they are presaged in Dunbar-Nelson's earliest writings, with their attention to local color, dialect, racial and ethnic conflicts, and class difference.

In both *Violets* and *The Goodness of St. Rocque*, her deeply nuanced descriptions of New Orleans reinterpreted the romantic and legendary aspects of the city. Read in their entirety as collections rather than as individual stories, they challenge binary stereotypes by insisting on complexity and nuance where racial and ethnic identities are concerned. Dunbar-Nelson transported readers into the romance of the Crescent City as a unique, exotic, dissipated, and anachronistic place by drawing upon specific details that she knew well. Tantalizing readers with an insider's view, she then disrupted that romantic vision with material reality and factual historical context. Rather than demonize the racialized and marginalized members of society, she brought attention to their humanity. This was not an uncomplicated endeavor, for Dunbar-Nelson, like many writers of the period, both black and white, fell prey to racialist discourse even as she represented African Americans in a positive light.[58] Rather than seeing her fraught and conflicted representations as a failure on her part as a writer, we might see them as evidence of how racialization and racist ideologies permeated the entire society.

Dunbar-Nelson had few real literary forebears. Certainly, the catalog of African American writers was already strong and continuing to develop, including such authors as William Wells Brown and Charles Chesnutt. Also widely circulating were the various slave narratives and memoirs such as those written by Olaudah Equiano, Frederick Douglass, Mary Prince, and Harriet Jacobs. African American women writers of fiction and poetry, however, were far fewer. Aside from the publication of poetry by Phillis Wheatley (1753[?]–1784) in the late eighteenth century, a collection of poems by Frances Ellen Watkins Harper (1825–1911), and the semi-autobiographical novel *Our Nig*, by Harriet Wilson (1825–1900), there were few predecessors for Dunbar-Nelson to learn from and emulate. As Hull reminds us, Dunbar-Nelson "is not writing out of an established black short-story tradition—especially not a black female tradition—but is in her own way helping to create one."[59] A black women's literary tradition thus was not something Dunbar-Nelson learned in school. There she likely was instructed in the canonical European and American literary traditions, and her literary allusions to Hester Prynne and Hercules along with her essay on Gustave Flaubert's *Salammbô* attest to this.[60] Nevertheless, she certainly was familiar with African American literature that circulated during her time. Knowledge of both types of literature placed Dunbar-Nelson in the midst of a conflict between her own multiracial position and the world of letters dominated by white writers. With this dichotomy of two very different literary histories, broadly speaking, and in the context of a more rigid Jim Crow environment that New Orleans became after the *Plessy v. Ferguson* Supreme Court decision affirming segregation, Dunbar-Nelson's own mixed-race identity became increasingly unsustainable, and her writings reflected her perseverance to maintain an indeterminate and liminal social position.[61] As Gaines suggests, "She existed between, never safely within, her society's repressive polarities of race, class, and heterosexual, versus lesbian, sexuality, a condition that disrupted the stable, privileged identity promised by black middle-class ideology."[62]

Through ostensibly sentimental, dialect-filled short stories that appealed to and fulfilled the desire of readers seeking to catch a glimpse of New Orleans life and focused on the minutiae of day-to-day existence—the lives of street-corner vendors and seamstresses engaged in the drudgery of piece work—Dunbar-Nelson addressed lofty themes such as tradition, virtue, and honor. In emphasizing seemingly mundane descriptions like the weather, Dunbar-Nelson symbolically drew attention to the romantic constructions of New Orleans in order to explore actual and complex social and cultural differences that demarcated the city from the rest of the country and even the rest of the Deep South. In "Little Miss Sophie," she wrote: "It was one of those, calm, blue-misted, balmy November days that New Orleans can have when all the rest of the country is fur-wrapped."[63] Here Dunbar-Nelson used reference to the balmy weather to set New Orleans apart as a special haven of warmth and beauty. Similarly, in "St. John's Eve," she described the weather as "hot and breezeless, and the men bent over their desks in their shirt-sleeves, and looked longingly at the moonlit streets, [all] the while they pushed their heads closer to the electric fans for a breath of air."[64]

If Dunbar-Nelson presented the weather of New Orleans as singular, different from the rest of the nation, then she also subtly contributed to the romantic and legendary notions of the city in contrast to actual turn-of-the-century modernization. She captivated readers by evoking familiar tropes of New Orleans as mysterious, dangerous, Old World, and chaotic. She further emphasized the city's difference by focusing on the famous French Quarter and the Third District, a largely Creole neighborhood. In her short story "Anarchy Alley," Dunbar-Nelson described one particular street, Exchange Alley in the French Quarter, as "the quaint, narrow, little alley that lies in the heart of the city" that embodied "all the phases of a Latinized portion of American, a bit of Europe, perhaps, the restless, chafing, anarchistic Europe of to-day, in the midst of the quieter democratic institution of our republic."[65] By referring to the street as quaint and small, she highlighted the contrast to the wide boulevards that were being built in other major cities during the late nineteenth century and early twentieth century. By describing New Orleans as delighting in this narrow alley, she highlighted a contrast between Old World and New World represented by the wide-open spaces that existed in other big cities. Her descriptions of the Third District made the contrast between "anarchistic Europe" and "our republic" further apparent. She not only described the area as full of "swamps and canals and commons and rail-road sections" and its "wondrous crooked, tortuous streets," she also stressed the atavistic nature of the neighborhood that the "city fathers seemed to have forgotten."[66] The contrast between the winding streets and the grand avenues of other major cities was augmented by the idea that the streets were forgotten, thus lost to the present and occupying their own reality. By focusing on this aura of timelessness, she appealed to a romantic and nostalgic vision of the city in direct contrast to modernization, industrial expansion, and technological innovation actually taking place at the time.

Perhaps the most significant way that Dunbar-Nelson enhanced the aura of New Orleans as unique and distinct from the rest of the country was in her portrayals of Carnival season. The New Orleans Mardi Gras and Carnival festivities were already infamous nationwide during the nineteenth century.[67] And Dunbar-Nelson surely knew that evoking Mardi Gras and Carnival would satisfy readers seeking to vicariously experience exotic thrills. In "Carnival," she wrote: "It is Carnival in New Orleans; a brilliant Tuesday in February, when the very air effervesces an ozone intensely exhilarating—of a nature half spring, half winter—to make one long to cut capers."[68] In "Odalie," she returned to this theme: "On Mardi Gras day, as you know, it is a town gone mad with folly."[69] In these passages she conjured up an image of an intoxicating atmosphere of celebration and festivity in sparkling contrast to the drab, late winter season. The excitement in this and other stories is so encompassing that not only did it permeate the very air of the city, it also infected an individual, caused one to be playful, pull pranks, and get into mischief.

Dunbar-Nelson thus relied on preconceived notions of Mardi Gras as creating an atmosphere that solicited the breaking of social rules and conventions. The invitation to break the rules was not limited to the residents of the city but also extended to visitors. In an unpublished story, "The Carnival in New Orleans," she wrote of the ease with which potential revelers could join in the merriment: "The charm of the Mardi Gras preparations to the out of town visitor, as well as to the at homes lies in the quaint little shops of Canal street in the French Quarter where suits for masking are for rent or sale, oftener the former."[70] This description integrated the visitor and placed him or her on Canal Street, inviting the visitor firmly within the matrix of the city. Moreover, she clearly stressed the rental of costumes for temporary indulgence and suggested that these social transgressions need not be considered permanent decadence. Instead, engaging in momentary mischief allowed visitors—and readers—to entertain fleeting participation in the reversal of social conventions before returning to daily life.

Even as she drew in readers by exploiting many familiar tropes and romantic visions of New Orleans, Dunbar-Nelson complicated the romanticized view of the city as decadent by disturbing much of the familiar imagery. For example, while she described the hedonistic festivities and disorder that Carnival encouraged, she also undercut this by contrasting order and careful forethought. In "The Carnival in New Orleans"—where she described the city as seeming "to lose its head and become a confused, incoherent mass of fun-seekers" and as a place for fleeting mischief—she also wrote: "New Orleans is peculiar in one respect: there is no store, large or small, that does not stretch out a roof above the side-walk, or banquette, as it is called, affording a real protection for passers by underneath and leaving a wide roomy gallery or balcony overhead. Thus, Canal Street, and other shopping districts, are long stretches of covered sidewalk where one may walk for several squares without encountering rain or sun."[71] In contrast to an image of a twisty, chaotic city that she described elsewhere, here she presented the city as planned, albeit on a small-scale, store-by-store basis, coordinated to protect customers from inclement weather. Moreover, the image of these covered sidewalks points to resourcefulness of the residents and shopkeepers of the city. Rather than simply accept the proclivities of the weather, the citizens effected ways to protect themselves against it. By presenting New Orleanians as inventive and attentive in this subtle detail, Dunbar-Nelson offered a different version of New Orleanians, one that countered the romantic view of dissipated carelessness.

Dunbar-Nelson further focused on this theme of order in her stories in contrasting the various neighborhoods of the city. While some of her descriptions may have encouraged viewing the city as a disorderly amalgam of peoples thrown together, in other places she carefully outlined how social and racial differences coexisted. She did not, however, present clear depictions of social and racial separation to reinforce them. She presented them to point out that notions of clear delineation and opposition were always misleading. For example, in "Tony's Wife" she highlighted the segregation of the city's different social and economic classes. She described Tony's corner store as being in "a semi-fashionable locality, far up-town, away from the old-time French quarter." By describing the location as "semi-fashionable," she implied that there were other areas that were either more or less fashionable—perhaps the Garden District as opposed to the French Quarter or the Third District—thus firmly placing this location as somewhere in between. Further, this "semi-fashionable" location was also linked with an earlier passage in which Dunbar-Nelson described the seasonal location of Mardi Gras as being "half spring, half winter." The recurrence of these images as not one or the other—not quite rich or poor, winter or spring—aptly described the city's liminality.[72]

As "Tony's Wife" indicates, Dunbar-Nelson's stories required a certain familiarity with the layout of the city in order to grasp fully the meanings that she implied. As literary scholar Pamela Glenn Menke notes, Dunbar-Nelson relied on the "substance of place," and her fiction depended upon "insider knowledge."[73] But for the reader who lacked that insider knowledge, she provided enough details of the city to both highlight the romantic vision and firmly embed it in a material reality. The street names and landmarks she featured are located in what are now the sections of the city known as the French Quarter, Marigny, Bywater, and Tremé. By including no less than twenty-three specific street names and landmarks in her two collections, she provided a double pleasure. For the nonlocal reader, the names of streets she identified carried with them the romantic traces of the Spanish and French past, while for the locals these names triggered the satisfaction of recognition and knowledge of place. Further, by including street names such as Bienville, Bourbon, Chartres, Galvez, Marigny, Orleans, Royal, and Toulouse, she alluded to the history of Spanish and French rule of the territory before the Louisiana Purchase made New Orleans part of the United States.

In a complex double move, Dunbar-Nelson depicted and reinforced romantic stereotypes of New Orleans and overturned and complicated them to present an open-ended view of New Orleans that refused to adhere to or reinforce notions of facile binary opposites. As literary scholar Thomas Strychacz has argued, her stories "foster an imaginative conception of race commensurate with the demographic gumbo of New Orleans without moving readers swiftly toward the interpretive closures exacted by a racist regime."[74] Thus, it is crucial to understand Dunbar-Nelson's reproduction of the stereotypes as a strategy to call attention to them as well as complicate and give nuance to them. This is most clear in the ways in that Dunbar-Nelson depicted Creole characters in her stories.

Illustrating Creoles with readily recognizable characteristics that signaled morality and industriousness was crucial, since northerners tended not to see their own binary views of racial formation as intolerant as much as they perceived New Orleanians as decadent. As her stories indicated, much of the negative perception of Creoles stemmed from the Spanish, French, British, and American legacies of different religious, linguistic, and social customs. Her stories indicate knowledge that for many northerners and easterners who had no real understanding of the tripartite racial and social system in New Orleans, and who understood whiteness strictly as Anglo, Creoles represented social and racial anxiety, being racially unintelligible. A long history in the region of racial intermixing brought about peoples with a wide array of phenotypical characteristics representing their Anglo, southern European, and African ancestors.[75] In her earliest writings, she depicts Creoles as encapsulating the competing and contradictory meanings of ethnic differences and similarities within the city as well as social inclusion and exclusion, including racial familiarity and fear that existed throughout the South. Even as Dunbar-Nelson relied on promoting an exotic view of New Orleanian Creoles, her attention to emphasizing their daily lives permitted her to make their differences seem less insurmountable for a northern readership by incorporating recognizable and ostensibly unique American values of hard work and morality. Ultimately, by presenting views that countered northern provincialism and prejudice, Dunbar-Nelson sought to recuperate New Orleans specifically, and perhaps Louisiana more broadly, through a morally redemptive view of Creoles.

By not simply indulging romantic stereotypes about Creoles, Dunbar-Nelson's depictions offered readers a clue as to the exaggerated and demonized understandings of how non-Louisianans saw Creoles as exotic, ethnically mixed European people. For example, in "La Juanita," she described the eponymous character as "the pride of Mandeville, the adored, the admired of all, with her petite, half-Spanish, half-French beauty."[76] She described another character, in "Odalie," as "ready for any new sensation, particularly if in the veins there bound the tempestuous Spanish-French blood."[77] In these examples, it was clear that the Creole represented a mixture of ethnicities, nationalities, and historical legacies that carried into the modern era. The strength of this cultural legacy was powerful. In an 1897 article, "A Creole Anomaly," for *Leslie's Weekly*, Dunbar-Nelson portrayed Creole men as clinging to "old customs, old ideas and localities. The French opera and the ancient absinthe café are his chief haunts, while the women, true to French customs, are seldom seen."[78] This representation of the stubborn refusal to adapt to modern, American customs served as a symbol of enduring cultural legacies. It was not only the men who were marked as different. Creole women were similarly described as belonging to the past. In "All Saints' Day," Dunbar-Nelson described them as "delightful, tignon-coiffed, black Creole women, flickering remnants of a beautiful people."[79] In both these cases, the emphasis on the old ("ancient" and "remnants") cultivated lingering and persistent images of the Old World.

Part of Dunbar-Nelson's depictions of Creoles as belonging to the Old World in contrast to the modernity of the United States satisfied the national inclination to define the turbulent political, social, and economic changes of the late nineteenth and early twentieth centuries as a move toward progress and modernity. When Dunbar-Nelson described Creole antipathy to Americans in "A Creole Anomaly," she was ostensibly describing Creoles' deep distrust and disdain for Americans: "The American is distasteful in every form. American ideas and infringements upon old traditions are resented with the usual Creole ardor."[80] But what is also apparent is that she echoed and reversed the misunderstanding and denigration that Americans had for New Orleanians. While in other moments she reiterated Americans' negative views of Creoles, here she also voiced the perspective of New Orleanians. In these moments, Americans were not described favorably. Instead they were lazy, colluding, and greedy. For example, in describing how Creoles and other Americans differ in their social practices, she wrote, "When the summer boarders and the Northern visitors undertake to give [a party], it is a comparatively staid affair, where due regard is had for one's wearing apparel, and where there are servants to do the hardest work. Then it is n't [*sic*] enjoyable at all. But when the natives, the boys and girls who live there, make up their minds to have fun, you may depend upon its being just the best kind."[81] In this passage, Dunbar-Nelson challenged the idea that Americans were serious, hard-working, and democratic by emphasizing the attention to the frivolity of appearance ("regard . . . for one's wearing apparel") and the relegation of the hard work to subordinates. As such, she cast Americans as vain, hierarchical, and lazy, employing the very terms by which New Orleanians and Creoles had long been criticized. Further, aiming at the heart of American ideals of fairness and due process, she charged Americans with corruption and collusion: "These English-speaking people could do nothing unless there was a trust, a syndicate, a company immense and dishonest."[82] Bringing attention to the burgeoning monopoly capitalism that would soon influence the entire nation's business endeavors, Dunbar-Nelson recuperated Creoles as recognizing corruption when they saw it, thus heralding their honor and morality. Creoles may have been of the Old World, but it was one of honor, decency, and honesty.

In referring to the Spanish and French heritages of Creoles and of New Orleans, Dunbar-Nelson subtly brought a history of cultural, ethnic, and sexual intermixing through descriptive details that carried much racial meaning. The effect of describing Creoles as atavistic fed the impulse of binary comparisons between old and new, ancient and modern, with "progress" as the privileged term representing the nation. In turn, this dual discourse paved the way for justifying any Yankee conceptions of binary racial categories. Dunbar-Nelson, however, complicated this bifurcated discourse by insisting on complexity and liminality. For example, she used the term "dusky" repeatedly throughout her stories. While the term may have been referring to the onset of darkness at twilight or even to a slightly dark color, "dusky" also was a euphemism for mixed-race peoples, especially when referencing skin or eye color. On occasions she described characters as a "dusky-eyed fiancée," "dark-eyed Creole damsels," or having a "dusky face."[83] Her emphasis on duskiness—describing something not completely black or white but incorporating both—insisted upon racial mixing rather than the ostensible racial purity upon which a binary racial system depends. In this way, her repeated attention to Creoles demanded that readers contend with a history of interracial sexual contact. She did not allow a view of the United States as a racially segregated nation but instead reminded readers that the nation had always been interracially linked, if not socially and culturally, then at least sexually. She rehearsed this idea in "Sister Josepha," in describing the protagonist, Camille: "She grew up with the rest of the waifs; scraps of French and American civilization thrown together to develop a seemingly inconsistent miniature world."[84] This "new world" embodied by the teenaged Camille was not one based on separation and exclusion but was an amalgamation, the combination of various aspects of the nation's past and formation. Further, even though that mixture may have appeared to be "inconsistent," her qualifier of "seemingly" suggested that it was only inconsistent at first glance but was intelligible after having considered a more encompassing definition of the American past and present. In this way, her references to Creoles served as more than romantic allusions to the past. They were reminders that American society at the turn of the century was partially integrated, thus suggesting a broader and more encompassing definition of America as having always been mixed.

Even as Dunbar-Nelson occasionally reiterated the racial and ethnic chauvinism of her era, she nevertheless offered an alternative vision of the relationship between the marginalized members of society and the nation at large. By contrasting the stereotypes and myths of New Orleans and Creoles with perceived notions of Americanness, she demonstrated the inability of stereotypes to represent honestly the diversity of the nation. Ultimately, the prevalence of deeply racist ideologies permeating the nation would demand that Dunbar-Nelson identify as an African American even as she resisted identifying solely as a black woman. Her social formation in the racially mixed South later influenced her refusal to embrace unambivalently the New Negro agenda of the early twentieth century, even as she undertook leadership roles in the African American women's club movement and through her political activism. At times, filled with despair and self-loathing, she turned to writing seemingly for the freedom to imagine a different kind of world, one where her unique liminal racial identity could find a voice and assertion. A complex woman living in a complicated era, Dunbar-Nelson exhibited the possibilities that an African American woman could achieve, all the while beset by the limitations presented by a country in the grip of racism and sexism. Perhaps the best way to describe Dunbar-Nelson is with her own words, as she described the title character in Flaubert's *Salammbô*, "She is an inexplicable mixture of the tropical exotic and the frigid snow-flower,—a rich and rare growth that attracts and repulses, that interests and absorbs, that we admire—without loving, detest—without hating."[85]

NOTES

I am grateful to Mary Farmer-Kaiser, Shannon Frystak, and Jake Mattox for their invaluable comments and suggestions on several drafts of this chapter. I'd also like to thank Shelley Streeby and Sara Johnson for their guidance and encouragement in earlier versions of this work. Special thanks to Rebecca Johnson Melvin and the staff of Special Collections, University of Delaware Library, for their gracious assistance.

1. Throughout this chapter, I refer to the writer as Alice Dunbar-Nelson, recognizing that her works were written or published under the names Alice Ruth Moore and Alice Dunbar, along with pseudonyms. See Gloria Hull, *Color, Sex, and Poetry: Three Women Writers of the Harlem Renaissance* (Bloomington: Indiana University Press, 1987), 101–2; Adele Morris [Alice Dunbar-Nelson], "Brass Ankle Speaks," in *The Works of Alice Dunbar-Nelson*, vol. 2, ed. Gloria Hull (New York: Oxford University Press, 1988), 311–21; "The Bicycle Race," box 17, folder 266, Alice Dunbar-Nelson Papers, mss. no. 113, Special Collections, University of Delaware Library, Newark, Delaware (hereafter ADN Papers).

2. Favorable reviews of *Violets* came from across the country, including from newspapers in New Orleans, Boston, Omaha, St. Louis, and New York. For newspaper clippings, see "Scrapbook No. 2," box 12, folder 233, ADN Papers. For Dunbar-Nelson's self-deprecating remarks, see Hull, *Color, Sex, and Poetry*, 37.

3. Her contemporaries were individuals such as W. E. B. Du Bois, Alain Locke, A. Phillip Randolph, and Mary Church Terrell. Hull, *Color, Sex, and Poetry*, 71.

4. One of these personal forms of resistance was to "pass" as white in public. In her refusal to accept second-class citizenship as a woman of color, Dunbar-Nelson frequently occupied the in-

between space of racial indeterminacy in her private life. Her diaries reflect these choices and her ambivalence toward collective identification solely based on race. See Hanna Wallinger, "Not Color but Character: Alice Dunbar-Nelson's Uncompleted Argument," in *Racial Thinking in the United States: Uncompleted Independence*, ed. Paul Spickard and G. Reginal Daniel (Notre Dame: University of Notre Dame Press, 2004), 83–102; Alice Dunbar-Nelson, *Give Us Each Day: The Diary of Alice Dunbar-Nelson*, ed. Gloria T. Hull (New York: Norton, 1984).

5. This period following Reconstruction is alternately referred to as either Home Rule or the Nadir, depending on perspective. For many white southerners, the withdrawal of the federal government in southern affairs meant that they were regaining self-determination. For African Americans, it meant a rapid decline of relative social and political gains, giving way to the rise of lynching and fierce re-establishment of Jim Crow laws. See Rayford Whittingham Logan, *The Negro in American Life and Thought: The Nadir, 1877–1901* (New York: Dial Press, 1954); Joseph Logsdon and Caryn Cossé Bell, "The Americanization of Black New Orleans, 1850–1900," in *Creole New Orleans: Race and Americanization*, ed. Arnold R. Hirsch and Joseph Logsdon (Baton Rouge: Louisiana State University Press, 1992), 201–61.

6. For biographical information, see Charmaine N. Ijeoma, "Alice Dunbar-Nelson: A Biography," *Collections* (University of Delaware Library Associates) 10 (2000): 25–54; Gloria Hull, "Shaping Contradictions: Alice Dunbar-Nelson and the Black Creole Experience," *New Orleans Review* 15, no. 1 (1988): 34–37; Eleanor Alexander, *Lyrics of Sunshine and Shadow: The Tragic Courtship and Marriage of Paul Laurence Dunbar and Alice Ruth Moore* (New York: New York University Press, 2001); Violet Harrington Bryan, "Race and Gender in the Early Works of Alice Dunbar-Nelson," in *Louisiana Women Writers: New Essays and a Comprehensive Bibliography*, ed. Dorothy Brown and Barbara C. Ewell (Baton Rouge: Louisiana State University Press, 1992), 122–38.

7. Alexander, *Lyrics of Sunshine and Shadow*, 54, 57.

8. Ibid., 50, 52–55; Hull, *Color, Sex, and Poetry*, 34; obituary, Patricia Moore, box 23, folder 442, ADN Papers.

9. Alexander, *Lyrics of Sunshine and Shadow*, 53.

10. Ibid., 46.

11. Hull, *Color, Sex, and Poetry*, 47. For an extensive study of the tumultuous relationship between Alice Dunbar-Nelson and Paul Laurence Dunbar, see Alexander, *Lyrics of Sunshine and Shadow*.

12. Ibid., 65; Kevin Gaines, *Uplifting the Race: Black Leadership, Politics, and Culture in the Twentieth Century* (Chapel Hill: University of North Carolina Press, 1996), 210.

13. Hull, *Color, Sex, and Poetry*, 66.

14. Ibid., 67.

15. Gaines, *Uplifting the Race*, 217, 226.

16. Hull, *Color, Sex, and Poetry*, 21, 95.

17. Ibid., 95. For remarks on Robinson, see entries dated March 19, 20, 29, 30, 31, 1930; April 15, 16, 1930; June 17, 1930; and March 18, 1931, in Dunbar-Nelson, *Give Us Each Day*.

18. Hull, *Color, Sex, and Poetry*, 63. For remarks on Kruse, see entries dated June 23, 1930, and September 6, 1930, in Dunbar-Nelson, *Give Us Each Day*.

19. Hull, *Color, Sex, and Poetry*, 62.

20. See Carroll Smith-Rosenberg, "The Female World of Love and Ritual: Relations between Women in Nineteenth-Century America," *Signs* 1, no. 1 (1975): 1–29. For a discussion of same-sex relationships among working-class African American women, see Karen Hansen, "'No Kisses Is Like Yours': An Erotic Friendship between Two African-American Women during the Mid-Nineteenth Century," in *Lesbian Subjects: A Feminist Studies Reader*, ed. Martha Vicinus (Bloomington: Indiana University Press, 1996), 178–207. For a collection of letters between two African American women across class lines, see Farah Jasmine Griffin, ed., *Beloved Sister and Loving Friend: Letters from Rebecca Primus of Royal Oak, Maryland, and Addie Brown of Hartford, Connecticut, 1854–1868* (New York: Knopf, 1999).

21. Hull, *Color, Sex, and Poetry*, 40–41.

22. The earliest entries in her diaries mention that they all shared the home in Wilmington. See entry dated August 7, 1921, in Dunbar-Nelson, *Give Us Each Day*.

23. Hull, *Color, Sex, and Poetry*, 60. The household suffered the loss of several children—niece, nephew, and stepchildren—over the years due to illnesses. See ibid., 66.

24. Dunbar-Nelson herself suffered from chronic high blood pressure, sciatica, vertigo, insomnia, bronchitis, and, in all likelihood, depression. See Gloria Hull, introductin to *Give Us Each Day: The Diary of Alice Dunbar-Nelson*, ed. Gloria Hull (New York: Norton, 1984), 27–28.

25. Education was one of the few ways that African American girls from working-class roots, as well as those from the middle class, could rise economically and in social class during the post-Reconstruction South with its strict racial binary system. See Jacqueline Jones, *Labor of Love, Labor of Sorrow* (New York: Basic Books, 1985), 143–46; Glenda Elizabeth Gilmore, *Gender and Jim Crow: Women and the Politics of White Supremacy in North Carolina, 1896–1920* (Chapel Hill: University of North Carolina Press, 1996), 31–43.

26. Alexander, *Lyrics of Sunshine and Shadow*, 59.

27. She drew upon her thesis and wrote a lengthy scholarly letter to the editor, later published in the correspondence section of *Modern Language Notes*. The letter is one of the few opportunities to read Dunbar-Nelson's writings published in a scholarly journal. Alice Dunbar, "Wordsworth's Use of Milton's Description of the Building of Pandemonium," *Modern Language Notes* 24, no. 4 (1909): 124–25. For her personal papers for her classes at Cornell University, see "Cornell Student Handbook," box 29, folder 478, ADN Papers. According to her own accounts, Dunbar-Nelson also took classes at the University of Pennsylvania, University of Chicago, Columbia University, and the School of Industrial Art, Philadelphia. See "Alice Ruth Moore Dunbar-Nelson [Biography 2]," box 23, folder 443, ADN Papers.

28. Hull, *Color, Sex, and Poetry*, 60.

29. Alexander, *Lyrics of Sunshine and Shadow*, 61.

30. Dunbar-Nelson, *Give Us Each Day*, 57.

31. She never completed and ultimately destroyed *Uplift*, and none of her other novels were ever published despite her and her niece Pauline Young's efforts to find willing publishing houses. See ibid., 29; Gloria Hull, "Alice Dunbar-Nelson: Delaware Writer and Woman of Affairs," *Delaware History* 17, no. 2 (1976): 89; Gloria Hull, introduction to *The Works of Alice Dunbar-Nelson*, ed. Gloria Hull (New York: Oxford University Press, 1988), xliii.

32. There are many instances throughout the archive of Dunbar-Nelson working on story ideas. For example, a short story manuscript, "The Bottle Man," was written on the back of a concert program. See box 17, folder 267, ADN Papers, among others.

33. Hull, *Color, Sex, and Poetry*, 90.

34. The *Journal of the Lodge* was a publication associated with the Grand Lodge of Masons in Louisiana. See I. Garland Penn, *The Afro-American Press and Its Editors* (Springfield, Mass.: Willey, 1891), 326; Hull, *Color, Sex, and Poetry*, 35.

35. Hull, *Color, Sex, and Poetry*, 83.

36. Ibid., 90.

37. "Alice Ruth Dunbar-Nelson [Biography 1]," box 23, folder 442, ADN Papers.

38. "A Brilliant Southern Writer/Editor of the Woman's Column," *Journal of the Lodge*, August 18, 1894, 1.

39. Gaines, *Uplifting the Race*, 227.

40. Gloria Hull, "'Two-Facing Life': The Duality of Alice Dunbar-Nelson," *Collections* (University of Delaware Library Associates) 4 (1989): 19. Dialect poetry was a complex form of writings by African American writers capturing dialect and local color, and which the largely white audience was all too eager to read as confirmations of their racist ideologies of African American inferiority.

41. According to Hull, Dunbar-Nelson arranged with her former mother-in-law to divide the

royalties from Paul's estate, with Matilda Dunbar receiving two-thirds and Dunbar-Nelson receiving the other third. See Hull, *Color, Sex, and Poetry*, 62.

42. Unlike her other volunteer and unpaid activities, she earned a small but stable annual salary of $2,000 for this position.

43. In an obituary, Dunbar-Nelson's death occasioned "both sides of the street bordered with long black carriages . . . as crowds increased outside the residence." See "Alice Dunbar Nelson, Noted Teacher, Author Crosses Bar," *Philadelphia Tribune*, September 26, 1935, box 28, folder 473, ADN Papers. Hull suggests that Dunbar-Nelson died of heart trouble. See Hull, "Two-Facing Life," 21. For Robert's professional successes, see Hull, *Color, Sex, and Poetry*, 103–4.

44. Hull, *Color, Sex, and Poetry*, 35, 73. See also Dunbar-Nelson, *Give Us Each Day*.

45. Alexander, *Lyrics of Sunshine and Shadow*, 47.

46. Ibid., 47–48.

47. Dunbar-Nelson, *Give Us Each Day*, 14; Alexander, *Lyrics of Sunshine and Shadow*, 47.

48. Dunbar-Nelson, *Give Us Each Day*, 319; Jennifer Wood, "John Rosamond Johnson," in *Harlem Renaissance Lives from the African American National Biography*, ed. Henry Louis Gates, Jr., and Evelyn Brooks Higginbotham (New York: Oxford University Press), 300.

49. Hull, *Color, Sex, and Poetry*, 73.

50. Hazel V. Carby, "'On the Threshold of Woman's Era': Lynching, Empire, and Sexuality in Black Feminist Theory," *Critical Inquiry* 12, no. 1 (1985): 264–65.

51. Gaines, *Uplifting the Race*, 225.

52. See "Miscellaneous Materials," box 27, folders 461–65, ADN Papers.

53. Lisa Materson, "African American Women, Prohibition, and the 1928 Presidential Election," *Journal of Women's History* 21, no. 1 (2009): 73.

54. Nikki Brown, "War Work, Social Work, Community Work: Alice Dunbar-Nelson, Federal War Work Agencies, and Southern African American Women," in *Post-Bellum, Pre-Harlem: African American Literature and Culture, 1877–1919*, eds. Barbara McCaskill and Caroline Gebhard (New York: New York University Press, 2006), 199.

55. "Alice Ruth Dunbar-Nelson [Biography 1]," box 23, folder 442, ADN Papers.

56. This is describing in very broad strokes what were intensely contentious and pluralistic cultural, social, and political movements. See Alain Locke, "The New Negro," in *Crossing the Danger Water: Three Hundred Years of African-American Writing*, ed. Dierdre Mullane (New York: Doubleday, 1993); W. E. B. Du Bois, Henry Louis Gates, Jr., and Terri Hume Oliver, *The Souls of Black Folk: Authoritative Text, Contexts, Criticism* (New York: Norton, 1999); Henry Louis Gates, Jr., and Gene Andrew Jarrett, eds., *The New Negro: Readings on Race, Representation, and African American Culture, 1892–1938* (Princeton: Princeton University Press, 2007); George Hutchinson, *The Harlem Renaissance in Black and White* (Cambridge: Belknap Press of Harvard University Press, 1997); Victor Kramer and Robert A. Russ, eds., *Harlem Renaissance Re-examined: A Revised and Expanded Edition* (Troy, N.Y.: Whitson, 1997).

57. Bryan, "Race and Gender in the Early Works of Alice Dunbar-Nelson," 124.

58. Gaines, *Uplifting the Race*, 3–4, 230–31; Kristina Brooks, "Between Love and Hate, Black and White: Narcissism and Double-Consciousness in the Diaries of Alice Dunbar-Nelson," A/B: *Auto/Biography Studies* 17, no. 1 (2002): 101–18.

59. Hull, *Color, Sex, and Poetry*, 53.

60. She makes reference to Hawthorne's protagonist in "The Maiden's Dream," in *The Works of Alice Dunbar Nelson*, vol. 1, ed. Gloria T. Hull (Oxford: Oxford University Press, 1988), 91. The Roman demigod is mentioned in "Tony's Wife," in *The Works of Alice Dunbar-Nelson*, vol. 1, 22; "Salammbo by Gustave Flaubert," in *The Works of Alice Dunbar-Nelson*, vol. 1, 65–71. Dunbar-Nelson's lesson plans include Booker T. Washington's *Up from Slavery*, amid a long list from American and British canonical authors, such as Wordsworth, Hawthorne, Coleridge, Irving, Chaucer, and Shakespeare, along with classics such as *The Odyssey*, Greek myths, and Arthurian tales. See lesson plans, box 29, folders 478–79, ADN Papers.

61. See Arnold Hirsch, "Simply a Matter of Black and White: The Transformation of Race and Politics in Twentieth-Century New Orleans," in *Creole New Orleans: Race and Americanization*, eds. Arnold R. Hirsh and Joseph Logsdon (Baton Rouge: Louisiana State University Press), 262–319.

62. Gaines, *Uplifting the Race*, 217.

63. "Sophie," in *The Works of Alice Dunbar-Nelson*, vol. 1, 144.

64. "St. John's Eve," box 19, folder 349, ADN Papers.

65. "Anarchy Alley," in *The Works of Alice Dunbar-Nelson*, vol. 1, 56.

66. "Titee," in *The Works of Alice Dunbar-Nelson*, vol. 1, 45; "Sophie," in *The Works of Alice Dunbar-Nelson*, vol. 1, 141.

67. Anthony J. Stanonis, "Through a Purple (Green and Gold) Haze: New Orleans Mardi Gras in the American Imagination," *Southern Cultures* 14, no. 2 (2008): 112.

68. "A Carnival Jangle," in *The Works of Alice Dunbar-Nelson*, vol. 1, 76.

69. "Odalie," in *The Works of Alice Dunbar-Nelson*, vol. 1, 184.

70. "The Carnival in New Orleans," box 21, folder 386, ADN Papers.

71. Ibid.

72. "Tony's Wife," 21.

73. Pamela Glenn Menke, "Behind the 'White Veil': Alice Dunbar-Nelson, Creole Color, and *The Goodness of St. Rocque*," in *Songs of the Reconstructing South: Building Literary Louisiana, 1865–1945*, eds. Suzanne Disheroon-Green and Lisa Abney (Westport, Conn.: Greenwood, 2002), 80.

74. See Thomas Strychacz, "'You Could Never Be Mistaken': Reading Alice Dunbar-Nelson's Rhetorical Diversions in *The Goodness of St. Rocque and Other Stories*," *Studies in American Fiction* 36 no. 1 (2008): 77–94.

75. For the imposition of northern values on the social and cultural formation of New Orleans, see, among others, Arnold R. Hirsch and Joseph Logsdon, *Creole New Orleans: Race and Americanization* (Baton Rouge: Louisiana State University Press, 1992), especially Joseph Logsdon and Caryn Cossé Bell, "The Americanization of Black New Orleans, 1850–1900."

76. "La Juanita," in *The Works of Alice Dunbar-Nelson*, vol. 2, 197.

77. "Odalie," 186.

78. Alice Ruth Moore [Dunbar-Nelson], "A Creole Anomaly," *Leslie's Weekly*, July 15, 1897, 43.

79. "All Saints' Day," box 21, folder 383, ADN Papers, mss. no. 113, Special Collections, University of Delaware Library, Newark, Delaware.

80. "A Creole Anomaly," *Leslie's Weekly*, July 15, 1897, 43.

81. "Fisherman of Pass Christian," in *The Works of Alice Dunbar-Nelson*, vol. 1, 42–43. I have made no changes to punctuation.

82. "M'sieu Fortier's Violin," in *The Works of Alice Dunbar Nelson*, vol. 1, 76.

83. "Little Miss Sophie," in *The Works of Alice Dunbar Nelson*, vol. 1, 145; "All Saints' Day"; "A Frenchtown Interlude," box 17, folder 296, ADN Papers; "By the Bayou St. John," in *The Works of Alice Dunbar-Nelson*, vol. 1, 90; "Sister Josepha," in *The Works of Alice Dunbar-Nelson*, vol. 1, 157.

84. "Sister Josepha," 157–58.

85. "Salammbo by Gustave Flaubert," 71.

Coralie Guarino Davis

(1926–2004)

Carnival Legacies

SUSAN TUCKER

New Orleans's Mardi Gras is often called "the biggest free party on earth." Yet much of the work that produces this celebration is not free and is, in fact, created within a multilayered system that is based on assignments by class, ethnicity, race, and gender. Some of the more visible layers have to do with the creation of costumes, ball gowns, other fancy dress, tableaux, and floats. Other layers revolve around those who wear the costumes and take part in these creations: those at the balls and on floats. There are also those watching, themselves almost performers on the streets, making their own little parties and masked on Mardi Gras Day.[1] Carnival, moreover, is not just one day. It involves months of preparation for public safety alone, as well as accumulations of fabrics and foods. It shapes traffic patterns as well as social calendars between Epiphany (January 6) and the beginning of Lent. Finally, social positioning through the Carnival "krewes" (those organizations that put on parades and balls) creates ties of commercial, government, and nonprofit work that last decades. Indeed, Carnival more often than not solidifies citywide allegiances to social class.[2]

Coralie Guarino Davis, like many others, moved between the spirals of beauty, exuberant fun, and sometimes parallel, often unequal strata of Carnival. Her life stands out because she left a record of "royal participation" and spectator status, work as a costume designer, and struggles with various class- and gender-prescribed roles. She did so in page after page that gives specific details—sometimes intimate ones, often hastily written and tired ones—of activities, interests, dress, food, and events for almost every day between 1939 and 2004. Her writings of nearly sixty-five years form the largest collection of one individual's diaries in the city of New Orleans.[3]

A starting point for exploring the complexity of Coralie's vision of her hometown and herself within it can be plucked from what she tells us about December 7, 1946. On this day, she—a dark-haired, attractive twenty-year-old of Sicilian, French, Spanish, and English descent—took the bus down Esplanade Avenue to the French Quarter. She first visited a seamstress to check on a ball dress made of "pink satin and net . . . sequins . . . silver rhinestones . . . silver dusts."[4] This was the dress Coralie would wear in February 1947 as queen of Elenians, a women's Carnival krewe. She would be costumed as Marie Antoinette and for the rest of her life would refer visitors to her home to a shadow box of the pink feathers that made up her headdress. She would also begin to collect books on Marie Antoinette.

Despite this focus on a French queen, the Elenians krewe was decidedly an Italian American women's organization, and such ethnic distinctions were important within Carnival. Elenians had been founded in 1934 as the Circola Elena di Savoia and named after the Italian Queen Elena (1873–1952), wife of King Vittorio Emanuele III.[5] "Elena," a name Coralie loved, reflected the European heritage of Italian American women in New Orleans, so often overlooked because of the concentration on French heritage in New Orleans. Queen Elena was actually Serbian and had been born a princess of Montenegro; her multiethnic background appealed to the New Orleans women. Elenians were one of the first women Carnival krewes in the city, and they were careful to show that they were worthy of a place in the city's annual celebration. Earlier women's groups had been founded in the 1890s, but none had lasted.[6] In their initial year, the Elenians invited Augusto Miceli, president of the New Orleans L'Unione Italiana, to speak. Miceli was one of the only Italian members of Rex and Comus, elite male krewes.[7] To the Elenian members, he represented inclusion, and he spoke of the need "not . . . to segregate ourselves, but rather to incorporate with the American life of the city." He was conscious of the Elenians' role in democratizing the events of Carnival.[8] One year later, in 1935, the Italian American men's krewe Virgilians was founded, eventually coming to be considered as hosts of one of the most elaborate balls in the city.[9]

Coralie was Italian on her father's side. Anthony Guarino (1901–84) was the son of Lena Gassissi and Joseph Guarino, both first-generation American children of late-nineteenth-century Catholic immigrants from Sicily. Anthony Guarino started as a truck driver and worked his way up to become a commission broker and real estate agent. Especially important to him were memberships in a number of mutual aid societies and neighborhood associations, including the Contessa Entellina Society, formed by New Orleanians who came from the same Sicilian village, the Italian American Cultural Society, and the Fun and Frolic Softball Club. Late in his life, Guarino also treasured his part in Endymion, a Carnival "superkrewe" organized in 1967 near the New Orleans Fair Grounds Race Course in a democratic response to older groups that excluded all but the elite, white, usually Protestant, Anglo-Saxon men.[10]

"THE SUNSET LIMITED" MAID

A Coralie Guarino Davis costume design.

Courtesy of Louisiana Research Collection, Tulane University.

CORALIE GUARINO DAVIS

As the queen of Elenians.

Courtesy of Vorhoff Library and Newcomb Archives, Newcomb College, Tulane University.

Anthony Guarino's daughter's participation in Elenians and later his in Endymion were important because they lived at a time when New Orleans Sicilians often were considered second-class citizens. Only a few years before his birth, nine Sicilian immigrants in the city had been given over to mobs chasing them, with nine shot while in prison and two lynched. While a number of Italian politicians, musicians, and business owners were making inroads into the middle class during his lifetime, neither Guarino nor later his daughter were allowed equal symbolic claim to the city's history as did so many other groups.[11]

Anthony Guarino's wife and Coralie's mother, Florence Ducros Guarino (1902–95), was more of an insider to elite New Orleans. She was an Episcopalian and, more critical to her identity, a descendant of the Catholic Pierre Denis de la Ronde, whose St. Bernard Parish plantation had long since disappeared but whose many descendants had much pride in their French and Spanish roots.[12] Perhaps for this reason, Florence agreed with her husband to have Coralie christened a Catholic.

The Creole family line was especially important to Florence's brother, Pierre [Duke] Ducros, and their father, Joseph Emile Ducros, who spent all their free time collecting family papers and undertaking genealogical research.[13] Florence sometimes took part in their pursuits, and she joined such groups as the Spirit of '76 Chapter, Daughters of the American Revolution (DAR); the Founders Chapter, Louisiana Colonials; the Descendants of the Founders of New Orleans; and the Dames of the Court of Honor. By far the lineage group that most interested Florence, and later her daughter, was the Daughters of the War of 1812, since Andrew Jackson had fought the battle of New Orleans partially on De La Ronde land. Along with other leaders, Florence and Coralie prepared over sixty celebrations of the annual January 8 commemoration of this battle.[14] Mother and daughter also contributed to dozens of other yearly teas, receptions, and public history reenactments held all over the city by members of numerous historical societies.

It was from this Creole side of the family that young Coralie also learned the benefit of diary writing, namely that a few details about one's life, suggesting the complexity of this life however poorly, sometimes continued in the hands of others after one died. In the 1930s, when Coralie was still in grade school, Uncle Duke showed her an unidentified woman's 1912 diary that he had purchased at a flea market. Coralie was so fascinated that he gave her a diary of her own at age eleven, and also ultimately the one from the unknown woman.[15] Coralie saved it with her own continuing diaries, inscribing opposite its title page, "I've read and re-read."[16]

An only child and thus often among adults, Coralie was also an early creative writer, sending poems to children's magazines and New Orleans newspapers and, as a teenager, trying her hand at short stories.[17] Her stories tell of young protagonists from families who have lost status, who watch as adults sell family heirlooms to keep up appearances in other ways.[18]

Coralie glimpsed such circumstances as she and her mother carried their contributions of sandwiches, cheese straws, pralines, and other food to homes and other venues where receptions were held. For example, on January 7, 1953, she wrote in her diary, "Daughters of 1812 reception. I made two flags for 1812 for their cakes. . . . Mom and I made 500 small sandwiches." From the next day's entry: "Invited to Military Ball of 1812 but we always go to the Banquet of LHS. All the Consuls were there as well as the leading society people like Mrs. Landry."[19] Throughout the diaries, Coralie tells of the neighborhoods of the city. Through membership functions of the Louisiana Historical Society (LHS), Coralie often visited Uptown homes where many of the elite lived, upriver from the central business district and the French Quarter. She lived in poorer downtown, when parts of the French Quarter and the Creole suburbs (such as the Faubourg Marigny) were considered slums. Coralie knew well the homes of relatives in the French Quarter, ones with grandiose high ceilings but little care taken for renovation or upkeep, and also those of aunts and uncles in more modest homes, downtown but not in the Quarter. Through third grade, Coralie attended a public school in Faubourg Marigny. She later remembered taking part in "soup parties" at the school when "[b]ig steaming pots of vegetable soup with French bread" were "more welcome than ice cream . . . [since] many of the other children rarely got a hot meal at home." One uncle, Vince, was a deliveryman for the Voorhies Company, a food purveyor, and young Coralie received an extra graham cracker or two from him during his stop at the school, a clue to the family's status straddling the line between the working and middle classes.[20] She later recalled that a cousin was married to a man "high up in the police force." He was considered "well-off."[21]

The family also provided other vantage points from which to see the varied cultures of New Orleans. As Anthony Guarino's membership in many Carnival groups suggests, the Sicilian family was a gregarious one. Besides his regular employment, he and his brothers worked nights in theaters around town. He and his brother Vince were "spear carriers in a play" and amazed young Coralie because they had been "on stage with Sarah Bernhardt." Vince later became assistant manager of the Saenger Theater. There, every week, members of the family attended plays and films. In addition, Florence Guarino saved for a yearly visit to the opera and sewed special dresses for Coralie for these events.[22] Also important to the family were trips to the Fair Grounds Race Track "early in the morning to see the jockeys and trainers school the horses." Many days the family also went to see the horses run, a pastime of both wealthy and average white New Orleanians.[23]

By the time Coralie was ready to enter fourth grade, both sides of the family had contributed enough money that she could move from the neighborhood public school to St. Joseph Academy, then on Ursuline Avenue. Always willing to place herself in terms of the city's social hierarchy, Coralie later noted in a short memoir that St. Joseph's was the parochial school for "the daughters of the better downtown families—French, Italian, etc." Before this time, she had not attended mass regularly, and the nuns made her acutely aware that her mother was an Episcopalian and that her father had lapsed in regular church attendance. The nuns were "delighted to educate a little heathen." Despite the obvious condescension, they made her first communion special: "So I wouldn't have to go to the altar alone, my three friends received with me and younger girls were my 'angels.' It was held in the . . . chapel, patterned off French chapels just as the school building was patterned off a chateau." The school grounds included a grotto "where we gathered to crown the Virgin each May," a ceremony that required special dresses and costumes.[24] The school then nurtured Coralie's love of pageantry and architecture.

St. Joseph's nuns also recognized and nurtured Coralie's talents, reinforcing her skills as an observer through art classes offered free only to a select few.[25] These after-school sessions continued through her high school years, providing the foundation for her acceptance as a first-year student in the fall of 1943 at H. Sophie Newcomb College, which was the coordinate college for women within Tulane University. Newcomb was a leader among southern women's colleges, a place where white women had been educated since 1887 to become influential in their professions and communities. However, Coralie's going to Newcomb meant crossing the line in a rigidly divided world. Noting that the college student body was made up primarily of Protestants and Jews, the nuns considered Coralie's choice an inappropriate one for a young Catholic girl.[26] She notes in her 1943 diary that they took her to visit Loyola University and Dominican College, hoping to change her mind.[27]

But Coralie and her family were fixed upon Newcomb. Two of her mother's distant De La Ronde cousins, sisters Marie de Hoa LeBlanc (1874–1954) and Emilie de Hoa LeBlanc (1870–1941), served as examples of what a Newcomb art education could do. Both were well known as art teachers and artists. Marie's career, in particular, was inspiring. She had enrolled at Newcomb in 1894, one year before the beginning of the College's pottery enterprise (1895–1940), and became one of its most respected designers. She won many awards, including those that allowed her to study at Harvard, the Art Institute of Chicago, and the Parisian Académie Colarossi.[28]

Coralie's mother had wanted to follow her older cousins to Newcomb, but she had been told by her father that she would not be able to "keep up with the other girls in clothes and parties."[29] This realization of economic handicap may well have been why Coralie would be Florence Guarino's only child. Certainly it was the reason that Florence shaped her life around heritage societies. These groups allowed her to conduct research and to tend to heritage by arranging public ceremonies and donating to libraries—in other words to announce herself as an educated woman even though she had not attended college. In these society functions, she often worked with cousin Emilie de Hoa LeBlanc.[30] All the same, she wanted more for her daughter: Florence wanted Coralie to attend Newcomb College.

Family members helped to ensure that this dream would come true. As Coralie later wrote, "I remember as a little girl going to D [Duke, the uncle who gave her the first diary] each week [with] $5 for college cost. During the depression that was plenty money. D said when the time came for college if he could afford it, he'd pay and the fund would be mine. Luckily, he could when 1943 came and I went to Newcomb."[31] She doesn't mention where the $5 comes from, but it is clear that it is her mother's side of the family saving, perhaps even hiding from her father the money they were saving for young Coralie.

Coralie then headed in a direction not available to many women of Sicilian descent. She was also conscious that a college education had not been possible for her mother. All her subsequent life, Coralie remained a devoted supporter of Newcomb College, seeing it as having given her a legacy of inclusion and achievement. As they had done for other art students, Newcomb's professors encouraged her drawing and painting, allowing her to join a community of artists. Here was a group of people, mostly women, united not by birth lines but by their interest in a particular form of work. Moreover, this community of artists practiced a love of the local that was quite different than one based upon family history. During the Newcomb Pottery period (1895–1940), instructors chose the local flora, fauna, and architectural details as inspiration for various crafts.[32] Three of the most well-known pottery designers (Sadie Irvine, Amelie Roman, and Henrietta Bailey) taught Coralie. Besides the fame of their past work, they also presented something of the iconoclastic role that artists could fill in New Orleans society. Like Emilie and Marie de Hoa LeBlanc, these three instructors had chosen careers over marriage, had chosen art as their life's work in much the same way that the first generation of nineteenth-century northeastern college women had chosen teaching.[33] The Newcomb pottery designers represented a model of independence. They were respected within and beyond the New Orleans community.[34]

Coralie's 1943–47 schooling at Newcomb meant also that she experienced the transformation of modernism within a serious art tradition. Slightly younger than many of those active in the Newcomb pottery enterprise, Caroline Wogan Durieux (class of 1916 and intermittently an instructor at the college) was one of the teachers at Newcomb during this time and certainly brought a different sensibility to the work and community life of a woman artist. Durieux had persuaded her parents to spend the money they would have used for her "coming out" debut after she graduated Newcomb toward her study at the Pennsylvania Academy of Art, thus pushing aside local tradition and seeking out new subjects and methods beyond New Orleans. Durieux would go on to marry, have a family, work with world-famous artists such as Diego Rivera, and be a significant player in all the WPA art projects in New Orleans.[35]

Similarly, the 1940s Newcomb art curriculum that Coralie undertook promoted experimentation.[36] Her design portfolios reflect recognizable aspects of the city's domestic architecture and interiors influenced by Frank Lloyd Wright's models of great expanses of long and wide windows and cantilevered roof-eaves.[37] Coralie gained confidence as a Newcomb artist because she was among a select group to finish the four-year program. Fifty-one students started as bachelor of fine arts students in 1943, but only eleven graduated in 1947. Many dropped out because the program was rigorous, others to marry or save money, often citing the imperatives of parents that college was not important for women's main roles as wives and mothers.

Two classmates (as the nuns had feared, one Jewish and one Protestant) stood out among her fellow graduates. One was May Hyman (Lesser), later well known for her depictions in vivid colors of medical workers. May's senior portfolio had been drawings of homeless people along the levee. The second among Coralie's most admired classmates, and her lifelong friend from Newcomb days on, was Lorys Sue Jones.[38] Lorys introduced Coralie to a more modest Uptown life than she had known in historical and lineage society teas. When they were seniors, Lorys also introduced Coralie to a McMain High School teacher, Olga Peters (Newcomb class of 1920).[39] Even more than Emilie and Marie de Hoa LeBlanc, Olga offered a role model of someone who moved independently beyond her economic and social background. Olga's mother was a milliner, but she was also a Carnival designer. Her daughter Olga had received a scholarship to study ballet at Newcomb and continued to study education at Tulane, traveling for her master's thesis to Milan and Paris to write about ballet and opera costume design. With this background, she was readied for teaching, ownership of a dance studio, and, like her mother, work as a Carnival designer.[40]

Coralie too left Newcomb prepared to use her art training for paid work. By October 1947 she had found a position as a draftswoman at Shell Oil Company. In itself, this job was unusual for women in the postwar years. Coralie was one among 72 women in the city employed in drafting, compared to 445 men.[41] Her Newcomb training also made her bold enough to consider another male-dominated field: during the fall of 1947 she took a course at Tulane in architecture. This ultimately proved a disappointment, especially when a male teacher tore up one of her drawings in front of the class.[42] Whether she was unsuited for architecture work is unknown, but she did not continue, and her disappointment was real. Years later, on May 10, 1984, she noted in her diary: "Left [work] a bit early to go to Edy's graduation from Architecture School. This is what I wanted years ago so I'm glad my godchild made it!"[43] Newcomb College had encouraged Coralie's interest in architecture by allowing her to write a special paper on the De La Ronde plantation ruins, and it had made her into a serious artist able to find work in her field. However, the criticism of the male world of the architecture school, for whatever reason, was more than she was prepared to stand and more, perhaps, than Newcomb College faculty and administrators were ready to help their female students meet.

In other ways too, her Newcomb experiences had hindered her from leaving the confines of her Sicilian and Creole communities. Like Coralie, most Newcomb College students at that time were local and stuck closely to groups formed around the neighborhoods and schools from which they came, never testing the boundaries of race and class in the city.[44] Coralie had wanted to be a member of Delta Zeta sorority, which had members from her neighborhood and had more members with French and German surnames than did any other sorority except the two Jewish ones. At that time, only Delta Zeta among all the Newcomb sororities had students with Italian surnames, six out of some thirty members over the four years Coralie was at Newcomb.[45] So even as she experienced Newcomb and its curriculum as a place to move beyond the prejudice toward Sicilians, she found that the boundaries sometimes held tight. Her diary entry from October 5, 1943, notes: "Didn't get sorority bid from Delta Zeta. Had my heart set on joining it."[46] Instead, besides her art friends, her social group at Newcomb and Tulane revolved around the Catholic Newman Club. As the nuns would have wanted, she continued through these college years, and indeed for the rest of her life, to attend Mass regularly.

During her entire academic and art education, Coralie was also being groomed by her mother and father to be a participant in Carnival. In 1941 Mother Florence Guarino had been a founding member of Venus, the first women's Carnival krewe to parade. Her daughter Coralie joined Elenians in 1942 and Venus in 1947.[47]

The immediate purpose of many of the Carnival balls lies within the families. In presenting their daughters to society, fathers and mothers optimize their chances to maintain and improve social connections and help their daughters find husbands who will be from the same social, racial, and ethnic group.[48] For women, the honor of being presented at a ball extends forever, and a queenship is a status that is celebrated not only in one year but also in subsequent years. Coralie remained loyal to her Italian heritage through her continued membership in Elenians. Witness her February 7, 1998, diary entry: "Elenian Queen luncheon. Only 18 of us. 3 queens died this year."[49] In certain anniversary years, a queen always "re-presents" among the group that selected her, receiving more attention than the annual luncheon and presenting gifts again for those attending. The queen is always an insider among insiders. Queenship or being part of the court as a maid, historian Reid Mitchell notes, is at once "a rite of passage, an act of submission, and a mark of honor." Queenship is the highest honor a female may desire in a particular Carnival realm.[50]

Within Elenians, during the 1940s, one could be presented more than once, as Coralie was, first as a maid in the winter of 1946, and then as queen in 1947. The choices of queen and members of the court are often based on who can pay for the costs, and whose fathers and mothers are to be honored, however obliquely. In February 1946, Coralie described in her diary all the ceremonial roles Elenians allowed their young women to play. One key element was gifts. On the day of the ball, Coralie's mother gave her "a lovely gold bracelet and earring set and a silver Owl charm" with topaz stones in honor of the event. Calling on her just before the grand march, her father gave her "the surprise of . . . [my] life . . . a two carat diamond ring." After the grand march, she then *gave* gifts: "I gave each of my callouts [those she asked to dance] . . . a key ring, money clip or silver belt buckle, and cuff links for the king."[51]

Young women being presented in "the courts" are called maids, indicating their young age, especially as daughters. Coralie explained in her diary something of the protocols of preparation, especially the physical process of being dressed by, and among, others. The morning of the ball, she visited the hairdresser, seamstress, and relatives. Her mother helped her bathe, and in the late afternoon they joined the queen and other maids and their mothers, as well as specially hired African American seamstresses and housekeepers at the auditorium where the ball was to be held. They were met by an Elenian officer who showed the young women "where we would come out from the stage and where we would stand. . . . Gloria, Pauline La Nasa (the acting captain)[among the Elenian maids] and I shared one dressing room. Our mothers and two maids [African American workers hired for the event] helped us to dress. I don't know what we could have done without those maids—they sewed us together and helped us with our headdresses. . . . By 8:45 . . . [we] were all gathered backstage, waiting for the curtain to go up. . . . At nine sharp, Pauline blew her whistle, and the past maids and queen came out in their white net dresses."[52]

The presence of the African American seamstresses and housekeepers is another telling part of the social hierarchy of the city. These women, the literal maids, were not always known to the white women dressing for the ball but given the assignment through contacts with wealthier women of the krewe or others outside the krewes in loftier social and economic realms. Some of these African American maids were not domestics at all in everyday life but themselves middle-class women, picking up extra money. Yet this job meant that they and the white women dressing for the balls met in an arena that reinforced the racial segregation of the city and highlighted the privileges given to whites of any class.[53]

The theme of the 1946 Elenian ball and its tableaux was Enchantment. Some of the young women being presented were dressed as witches. They appeared with a "young girl" who danced between them. As Coralie wrote, "The captain or chief witch came out and summoned the princesses who were captured . . . and enchanted into various animals. The narrator mentioned . . . wisdom . . . the

Owl! . . . Gloria and I came out, bowed and walked around . . . smiling. . . . I wasn't the least bit nervous as 5,000 people stared at me."[54]

After the ball there was a supper dance with another grand march and breakfast. After all this she wrote: "Came home with Mom and Dad about 4:30 a.m. after a glorious night—I got quite a kick out of parading around and having everyone look at me, and it was a big honor that I'll never forget."[55]

Her queenship of 1947 brought an even more privileged role, with more gifts, a more elaborate dress, and more honors, but she did not give as many details in her diary that year. The theme revolved around "visits of royalty" to some mythical country in Europe. The newspaper described queen Coralie, dressed as Marie Antoinette, "beautifully gowned in pompadour satin, fashioned with a tight bodice. The skirt, shirred with folds of blue satin, fell in long folds into a jeweled train. The dress was embroidered with rhinestones, sequined scrolls and jewels. Her mantel was of pink satin and the Marie Antoinette *fleur de lis* was encrusted with jewels."[56]

Six years after her reign as queen of Elenians, Coralie married a man who had attended this ball, George Davis, who had come to New Orleans as a young man from Mississippi.[57] It is significant that he was an outsider, neither a part of the group of Italian boys whose names appear on her dance cards or in her diaries, nor one of the Tulane University members of the Newman Club.[58] With Coralie so conscious of her dual heritage (Sicilian and Creole) and the ways she did and did not fit into any one particular, traditional New Orleans group, George Davis suited her better. They both liked volunteering for patriotic societies (he for those concerned with the Confederacy), reading local history, discussing conservative politics, and seeking personal improvement—for example, taking French classes together.[59]

Again in marriage she would straddle worlds, never finding an easy place, especially one with an adequate income. George Davis also worked for Shell, where Coralie was employed as a drafter, but he was laid off in the early 1950s shortly after she had resigned to stay home with their first (and only) child, in 1954. They lived near her parents in a small two-bedroom house that her father helped them purchase.[60] Her diaries are replete with renderings of the floor plan of the house, descriptions of painting rooms and cleaning, and considerations of the changes she wanted and could not make.[61] But she also had happy days where she moved toward crafting a life that combined traditional roles with her art education, her love of Carnival and New Orleans, and her work as a designer. Several entries from 1963 show this resilience, and her focus on costumes:

> January 13, 1963—Then, G [husband] & I took [son] to the auditorium for the Krewe of H_Ball—"Our Country's History." Very pretty ball with lovely costumes of American symbols and personages.

> January 15, 1963—I went with Dad and Mama for Ancient Scribes 5th Ball. I designed King, Dukes, and Krewe costumes which all came out well. It was a nice Ball and I got plenty of compliments.
>
> January 19, 1963—Heard from Edwin Ashby about [son] being in his Ball next Saturday so that means scurrying to find a Japanese costume!
>
> January 26, 1963—The Krewe of Andalusia's 7th Ball was "Japan—Land of the Rising Sun" and was beautiful—costumes very colorful. . . . But [son] was adorable—all made up like a Japanese and did his part very well.
>
> February 10, 1963—At 2pm, Mama, Dad, Geo [husband] & I escorted [son] to the Auditorium. Left him backstage while we got our seats. He was a Krewe Member in the Children's Carnival Club Ball & wore his "Uncle Sam" costume.
>
> June 12, 1963—Spent the day working on the Ball costumes—quiet, lovely day.
>
> June 20, 1963—Took the pencil sketches of costumes to Mrs. B . . . then came home for a quiet day with [son].
>
> July 5, 1963—I went to the grocery, ironed and worked on my costume sketches.
>
> July 18, 1963—I brought my sketches to Mrs. B . . . then went to the grocery.[62]

Coralie wanted always for her son to love Carnival as much as she did, and she wanted for him to have even more secure social contacts than she had had. When he participated in the Children's Carnival Club on January 22, 1967, she wrote, "Gabbed with lots of friends. All grandparents beaming, introducing kids to each other—making matches?"[63] Certainly then she knew well how these introductions, these functions of the balls, structured the contacts he could make that would benefit him later, that would connect him to the people she considered important.

She did not lose sight, however, of the ways an artists' community might transform any potential love of spectacle, might lessen the twin burdens of inclusion and exclusion. The entries above from 1963 show something of how, after leaving Shell, Coralie used her background in art, historical research, and knowledge of Carnival to become a seasonal designer. She also worked as an etiquette consultant to the courts of several smaller, newer krewes. She found this type of work through placing her own ads, through her Newcomb connections, the Italian community, the downtown neighborhood, her work at Shell, and friends in Lafayette and New Iberia.[64] She saw costume work as key to the success of any ball and at the same time as one part of the coordinated work of set and scenery designers, float designers, costume makers, and the usually secret members of the krewes.[65] Even though she did not work for the elite krewes, design work was attuned to what she had learned at Newcomb: art allowed passage into otherwise forbidden circles.[66] Not only did one learn details kept secret from the public and even from members of the krewes (what the themes would be and who would be queen, for example), but also as an artist one could see how such fluidity would work in other areas of life, outside the different strands of her Italian and Creole identities. Design work was a back door to directing part of Carnival. It made her feel very special, based as it was on talent, on merit, on the gifts and skill that her mother, the nuns, and her Newcomb artists' community had believed she possessed.

Coralie's costumes were elaborately imaginative. From 1954 to 1956, she designed for the Krewe of Maids of Troy. Their first theme, the Evolution of Transportation, showed in costumes "the world spinning dizzily on its axis with planes, streamliners and modern jet cars speeding about the horizon." She created a number of gowns around the names of trains and train routes through the city. There was the *Rebel* (with a Confederate flag in a frock of red and blue sequins spotted with silver stars), the *Super Chief* (a white satin "Indian princess" costume), the *City of New Orleans* (a yellow gown embroidered in black sequins making up a French Quarter railing alongside purple velvet masks), the *Sunset Limited* (more satin and sequins, here yellow and gold), the *Crescent City*, and finally the *Southern Belle*. "Her Majesty, who represented the Goddess of Transportation[,] wore a glittering frock of white brocade," with a "mantel of pale blue velvet, bearing an embroidered globe encircled by a silver sequined laurel wreath."[67] In later years, her costumes had to reflect "A Dream Fulfilled" (about a court marriage) and "A Fantasy in Silver."[68]

In 1957, Coralie designed for the Krewe of Andalusia in New Iberia, using their wish to portray "Discovery of America—a Visit with Isabella and Ferdinand." In 1960, she designed costumes that reflected "The Resources of Southwest Louisiana" for the Krewe of Faed Setum of Lafayette. For that ball, various colors and headdresses suggested (not an easy job) oil, sugar cane, sugar, tomatoes, yams, salt, oranges, sulfur, strawberries, rice, forests, corn, shrimp, and muskrat. In 1963 and 1964, for the Krewe of the Ancient Scribes in New Orleans, she designed around the themes of Happy Birthday and Good Will Tour. The former contained costumes of famous and literary children and presents at a party, with ponies and a carousel. The latter portrayed various countries through folk outfits and attire suitable for benevolent, traveling monarchs.[69]

Coralie considered the designs for floats and balls, their themes, and their costumes as "instructing" about cultural legacies. This was just one more reason to love Carnival: it was a form of public education, not unlike what she had learned from her mother's work, and her own, with historical society celebrations. As the themes above suggest, she drew widely in her research in order to portray ancient myths and European history, storytelling about the present and the past.[70] Again, Coralie had been prepared for work in libraries by her Creole family and their interest in genealogy, their searches for the context of historical events. She had also worked part-time as a researcher for novelist Frances Parkinson Keyes in the 1950s and 1960s.[71] Through the example of her father's love of life, theater, and his Sicilian family's gregarious adventures, she also looked forward to learning and exploring a varied city with many different types of people. Years later, she noted that Italian women in New Orleans had been less explored in general in all city histories than those of French, Spanish, and African descent.[72]

In her design work, research also taught her about things others might never have thought about. For example, zippers would not have been a part of the dress of people before the twentieth century, but the making of button holes was pricey. They were often sewed by rural Acadian women to whom this seasonal labor was allocated. In addition, synthetic fabrics such as polyester were out for people who wanted to be true to the period they represented, but they were necessary for keeping costs down. Coralie complained of various groups that "do not want to pay much, cannot pay much."[73]

Among her better-known competitors were "the Stouse Sisters"—Eveline, Claire, Yvonne, and Edith Stouse—daughters of a member of Rex, the most elite male krewe. The Stouse Sisters could afford both seasonal work and exacting standards because the Rex organization could pay more than the types of groups Coralie accommodated. Claire Stouse, who outlived her other sisters, passed most of their work along in the 1960s to Ilaine Hartman, whose grandmother ran a fabric store. Even though she came from "outside" the Rex community, Hartman, through her grandmother, had enough contacts to work all year, going on to achieve financial independence as a designer who employed her staff of costume markers.[74]

Coralie designed costumes for some four hundred people over time but is mostly unknown in the world of more prolific Carnival designers.[75] However, her career path itself, from attending Newcomb Art School and meeting Olga Peters (one of the best known of the early-twentieth-century designers) to immersion behind the scenes of Carnival, may match to some degree those of other seasonal Carnival workers who are subject to forces that are rarely apparent.

When George Davis died in 1967, Coralie was not established enough to continue work on Carnival. Instead, after trying teaching (which she found exhausting) and a return to Shell (which would not allow her holidays off with her child), she took a job as a library assistant at the University of New Orleans (UNO). She was interested in this work precisely because it allowed her to assist others in historical research. Again, though, her spheres of social and educational contacts were not aligned. There was, throughout the twentieth century, a strong prejudice in academia against genealogical and historical society endeavors, which she would not give up.[76] Though she would work at UNO more than thirty years and earned a master of library science degree from Louisiana State University, she was never promoted to librarian, a distinction that would have, at least in name, rewarded her for her specialty in research.[77]

Each time she was passed over for promotion, she became more active in historical and genealogical societies, thus drawing upon another gift her mother's side of the family and her mother had given her: a public role outside paid employment.[78] This public role remained the most steady of all her pursuits, besides diary writing, over her lifetime. For the Daughters of the War of 1812, she was national historian from 1967 to 1977, national vice president from 1977 to 1983, and president from 1983 to 1987. Her most substantive work was likely as a committee member in the 1980s and 1990s, advising the National Park Service, by then the owner of the Chalmette Battlefield, on the battlefield visitor center, the restoration of some of the rooms in the Beauregard House, and the planning for a cane field to show the work of the land.[79] These volunteer efforts gave her contacts who could encourage and sometimes even pay her to produce indexes to various local magazines, to compile and edit bibliographic essays on the city's history, and to publish several articles on Louisiana architects.[80]

For Coralie, the women in the Daughters of the War of 1812 and other groups served as peers with whom she could work on causes she considered linked to both history and citizenship. Here she received recognition. She also continued to use her contacts from Newcomb and Carnival. Women's patriotic societies have long been seen as groups more interested in social events than public history, more interested in myths of family than in actual research. Less recognized is the role they play in allowing women a part in preserving historic buildings and assisting others in safeguarding records and manuscripts, often uniting with women from different backgrounds in doing such work. Members have long seen themselves as tearing down some of the barriers of social and economic classes since descendants of all ranks may join.[81] While this more-or-less democratizing role has not always existed, Florence Ducros Guarino and especially her daughter Coralie came to focus their love for learning and much of their social aspirations in the Daughters of 1812.[82]

For Coralie, work for the Daughters of 1812 entailed her love for her city, for the nation, and for history in general. The organization gave her a voice that others had denied her, especially an ownership position in the Creole culture of New Orleans. Besides her key role in decades of commemorative events at the Cabildo and Chalmette Battlefield each January 8, Coralie was one of the central figures who maintained the Daughters of 1812 headquarters, the Jackson House. Tending this building endowed her with symbolic as well as literal placement within steps of the Louisiana State Museum. With the group, she also maintained monuments and graves in the city's oldest cemeteries. From the vantage points of the French Quarter and the graveyards, Coralie thought of herself as governing large portions of the colonial history presented to both natives and visitors of New Orleans.[83]

At the same time, she could never find a place within the hierarchy of Carnival decision makers. Even outside the confines of the Mardi Gras calendar (Epiphany to Lent), the elite krewes were those who oversaw all important events of the city. She revealed this stagnancy, as well as her place removed from these powerful men, in her uncritical way in her diary entry for October 17, 1953, on the 150th anniversary of the Louisiana Purchase:

> Quite a big day. Mom, Coco, Kathleen and I all went to Jackson Square dressed in our 1803 costumes for the big celebration. We had passes to admit us to the Square where the speakers' platform was. . . . Across from this platform was a huge grandstand, in the center of which was the Throne of Comus, where the Queens of Rex and Comus sat in their regal gowns. All the Ambassadors began arriving . . . just about every country was represented so NO [New Orleans] was the diplomatic capital of the country today. Then . . . finally President Dwight Eisenhower and Cecil B. DeMille . . . the long, well organized military parade started. . . . 17 floats of Rex and Comus, the 2 kings riding together. They descended the float to sit with their queens.

At this important celebration, it was Coralie, her mother, and her aunts who took traditionally gendered roles of caregiving, arranging food, making sure the scouts arrived on time, and seeing that they were part of the decorative backdrop. It was the men who sat as titular heads of the ceremony. Such could have happened anywhere in America, of course, but in New Orleans, the pageantry, and thus segregation by class, race, and gender, was repeated more often. In New Orleans, the city she loved, the men next to the national leaders would not necessarily be the leaders of industry or commerce or government but those whose families had secured their place in elite, exclusive krewes whose membership was based on birthrights.[84]

Coralie would not object even in her diary to this exclusion, to her place as a bystander. Other entries show rather that she enjoyed being as close as she could get to the elite krewes, always recording the themes of their parades, for example, and in later years careful to note invitations to (and attendance at) Rex balls. She remained unreflective about issues that would have caused her discomfort even if they ultimately brought change. She didn't want to miss seeing those people on the dais.

When, in 1991, African American city councilwoman Dorothy Mae Taylor introduced a city ordinance that prohibited granting parade permits to those krewes that discriminated on the basis of race, Coralie would be quiet. Taylor noted, in effect, that the same types of networks that let the elite white men trump others in sitting on the platforms of dignitaries in 1953 still existed. On December 19, 1991, the proposed ordinance was discussed in city council chambers, and a representative of one of the oldest Carnival krewes was asked, "Have you ever recommended for membership any Blacks, Jews, or Italians?" After a long pause, his first reply was quizzical: "I don't know if I have recommended any Italians or not."[85] Coralie was nearly silent on the topic in her diaries, noting only on January 25, 1992: "City Council report was that majority voters against Mardi Gras Ordinance . . . Comus and Momus cancelling. City in an uproar." On Tuesday, March 3, she noted, "Queen Eliz. Kelleher [of Rex] gown in gold was lovely. . . . Comus decided to keep it very private, cancelled the parade and didn't even put the Queen's and Maids photos in the paper."[86]

Coralie's virtual silence when it comes to Taylor's proposed ordinance is disappointing yet characteristic of that of the whole city. Taylor at first had included gender as one of the categories of discrimination in various Carnival organizations but gender parity at Carnival was unimaginable, and that part of the ordinance was nixed early. The women in Venus (the women's krewe to which Coralie and her mother both belonged) stated that they had worked hard to establish their own krewe, and they did not want men. Likely Coralie would not have written in her diary about the sign one of them carried even if she had seen it: "No penis in Venus," it read.[87] Coralie's diary does not mention the gender aspect of the proposed ordinance at all.[88]

As with the mention of Queen Kelleher in gold, Coralie in every diary for over sixty years put her design background to work and gave an account of the clothes of the Carnival season. Sometimes we learn of her own dresses, other times of the costumes of royalty. The entry for December 7, 1946, where we first met her in this essay—concerned with the pink frills, the outer, visible layers of life—would be indicative of the whole of her life.

Still, there was more than dressmaking: there was always the conscious work of recording what she had seen and done, leading to a cumulative body, her collection of diaries. That was a conscious part of her journey even as early as 1946. Then she was on her way not only to admire "the pink satin" but also to see the head of the Louisiana State Museum, to ask him to check on sources for local architecture.[89] She would continue research in her work for patriotic and historical societies and in the UNO Library, and she would reflect in her diaries, arguably a form of inner research. Through these dual practices, documenting and creating a legacy of her own, she negotiated a place in the metaphorical fabric of the city.

Drawing on her education and her experience in public endeavors, she knew the diaries would some day be read by outsiders, certain to pass beyond the city's caste system, to illuminate it. Her gift was a decidedly gendered one, based on what she learned struggling in a social milieu that held her firmly in place. Her own Carnival participation and its documentation are her legacy. Although her reactions on many changes are lacking—for example, her reactions to African American krewes or to the vast increase since the 1970s in the number of Carnival krewes—she leaves a record of her own movement through the twentieth century.

In several places in the diaries pages have been torn out that seem to have been at stages where she might have commented on changes regarding segregation and African Americans.[90] A glimpse at her preferred status as someone who believes in the difficulty of questioning lines of birthright, even in the literal segregation such lines can make, can be seen in 2004 (the year of her death), when the Daughters of 1812 had to face whether to admit a child conceived by an unknown donor by artificial insemination. Coralie was opposed to admitting this child just yet, and she noted in her diary that the decision needed a much bigger discussion.[91]

However, it was not just this trip or many others that she took to the various meetings of the Daughters of 1812, or her other trips, some as short as the one to the French Quarter in 1946, that were important to her. It is rather that the trips were opportunities for documentation. While she could not become the artist quite like the many people of her childhood and young adulthood believed her to be, she found a way to be more than simply an observer, both outside and especially inside the layers of social, ethnic, and gendered roles she had inherited. She became a creator of documents as well as fanciful costumes, leaving behind tangible evidence in one of the near constants of her life, her diaries. She also left instructions that these diaries should become the property of the Newcomb Archives, of the college her mother had wanted for her.

NOTES

1. While columns covering the "social scene" in the *Times-Picayune* routinely provide the names and themes of parades and balls, their authors almost never tell about the labor of producing Carnival. See, however, Lynn Jensen, "Life Is Sew-Sew for Rex Costumer," *Times-Picayune*, February 12, 1996; Mark Lorando, "Carnival in October," *Times-Picayune*, October 25, 2008; Errol Laborde, "Sow Me Something, Mister: Rex at 125: Some Theories of Evolution," *New Orleans Magazine* 31, no. 4 (1997); Brock N. Meeks, "Carter Church: The Mardi Gras Man," *Rising from Ruin*, MSNBC, December 26, 2005, http://risingfromruin.msnbc.com/meet_the_locals/index.rdf (accessed March 17, 2015). From time to time obituaries are published after the death of seamstresses and women designers. See, for example, "Grace Wood Blanchard, Designer and Draftsperson for Ball Gowns and Crescent City Connection," *Times-Picayune*, July 10, 2011; "Amy Marie Zeringue Roux," *Times-Picayune*, July 14, 2011. The obituaries of such women show that they generally worked in other fields as well as in design and sewing. For archival collections, see Louisiana State Museum; Louisiana Research Collection, Tulane University; and the Historic New Orleans Collection.

2. James J. McLain, *Local Government Revenues from Mardi Gras Parades in New Orleans* (New Orleans: University of New Orleans, 1987); Paul Spindt and Toni Weiss, *The Economic Impact of Mardi Gras Season on the New Orleans Economy and the Net Fiscal Benefit of Staging Mardi Gras for the City of New Orleans* (New Orleans: Carnival Krewe Civic Fund, 2009). Both studies show billions of dollars income for the city annually and millions of dollars spent annually by residents and visitors.

3. I found no comparably large collection of diaries in compiling *The New Orleans Guide to Collections on Women*, revised ed. (New Orleans: Newcomb College Center for Research on Women, 2002) or in a more recent informal survey of archivists in 2011 asking about New Orleans diary collections from men. Coralie Guarino Davis Collection (hereafter CGD Collection), boxes 4–6, Newcomb Archives, Newcomb College Institute, Tulane University, New Orleans (hereafter NA).

4. CGD Collection, Diary, December 7, 1946, NA.

5. Elenian Collection, box 1, folder 1, American Italian Research Library, Jefferson Parish East-bank Regional Library, Metairie, Louisiana.

6. Karen Trahan Leathem, "'A Carnival According to their Own Desires': Gender and Mardi Gras in New Orleans, 1870–1941" (PhD diss., University of North Carolina at Chapel Hill, 1994), 195.

7. Phyllis Hutton Raabe, "Status and Its Impact: New Orleans' Carnival, the Social Upper Class and Upper-Class Power" (PhD diss., Pennsylvania State University, 1973), 81–82.

8. Elenian Collection, box 1, folder 2, American Italian Research Library, Jefferson Parish East-bank Regional Library, Metairie, Louisiana.

9. Carolyn Kolb, "Virgilians, the Krewe with a Difference," *New Orleans Magazine*, February 2011, http://www.myneworleans.com/New-Orleans-Magazine/February-2011/VIRGILIANS (accessed March 17, 2015).

10. Coralie Guarino, application for admission to Tulane University, 1943, Student Records, NA; *New Orleans City Directory*, 1931, 1932, 1933, 1938, 1940; "Anthony Guarino," obituary, *Times-Picayune*, November 14, 1984. Some of the twenty families named Guarino listed in city directories in the years above worked selling produce, and the term "commission broker" may relate to selling produce. "Commission man," in *Division of Occupational Analysis, Dictionary of American Occupational Titles, Occupational Classification and Industry Index*, vol. 2, 2nd ed. (Washington, D.C., GPO, 1939), 54; Samuel Kinser, *Carnival American Style: Mardi Gras at New Orleans and Mobile* (Chicago: University of Chicago Press, 1990), 255.

11. Raymond Oscar Nussbaum, "Progressive Politics in New Orleans, 1896–1900" (PhD diss., Tulane University, 1974), 13–14.

12. Stanley Clisby Arthur and George Campbell Huchet de Kernion, *Old Families of Louisiana* (New Orleans: Harmanson, 1931), 394–400; Coralie Guarino Davis, collection 723, biographical files, Louisiana Research Collection, Howard-Tilton Memorial Library, Tulane University, New Orleans (hereafter LaRC); CGD Collection, box 2, folder 18, "Design," NA.

13. Joseph Emile Ducros, *Titre de noblesses des Denys De La Ronde* (New Orleans, 1928), English translation of Louis XIV granting of nobility to family, LaRC; Joseph Emile Ducros family papers, 1872–1965, collection 893, LaRC; CGD Collection, Diary, May 14 and August 28, 1947; March 1, 1993, NA.

14. U.S. Daughters of the War of 1812, Chalmette Chapter, scrapbooks 48–58, LaRC.

15. CGD Collection, Diary, April 13, 1953, NA.

16. CGD Collection, box 5, 1939 folder, NA. *The National Diary, 1912* (Cincinnati: Pounsford Stationery, 1911).

17. CGD Collection, box 3, autobiographical writing and notes for memoir, folder 7, NA.

18. CGD Collection, box 3, fictional writing, folders 5 and 6NA; see also stories in ibid., folders 2–4.

19. CGD Collection, Diary, January 7 and January 8, 1953, NA.

20. CGD Collection, box 3, autobiographical writing and notes for memoir, NA.

21. Ibid.

22. Movies and plays are documented in every diary, more than once weekly until the late 1960s and weekly or monthly after that. For opera attendance, see CGD Collection, Diary, April 26, 1940, NA.

23. CGD Collection, box 3, autobiographical writing and notes for memoir, NA; Sybil Boudreaux, head, Louisiana Collection, Earl K. Long Library, University of New Orleans, telephone conversation with author, October 14, 2011.

24. CGD Collection, box 3, autobiographical writing and notes for memoir, NA . See also CGD Collection, autograph book and scrapbook of St. Joseph, box 9, NA.

25. CGD Collection, box 3, autobiographical writing and notes for memoir, NA.

26. Similar sentiments can be found in Elsie Martinez and Margaret LeCorgne, *Uptown/Downtown: Growing Up in New Orleans* (Lafayette: Center for Louisiana Studies, University of South-

western Louisiana: 1986), 20. See also "Dagmar Adelaide Renshaw LeBreton," in *Newcomb College, 1886–2006: Higher Education for Women in New Orleans*, ed. Susan Tucker and Beth Willinger (Baton Rouge: Louisiana State University Press, 2012), 347–60.

27. CGD Collection, Diary, May 4 and May 5, 1943, NA.

28. For the careers on both sisters, see their respective student records and biographical files, NA; see also Jessie Poesch, *Newcomb Pottery: An Enterprise for Southern Women, 1895–1940* (Exton, Pa.: Schiffer, 1984), 101.

29. CGD Collection, box 3, autobiographical writing and notes for memoir, NA.

30. Daughters of the War of 1812, Chalmette Chapter, minute books, 1921–35, 1935–43, box 1, folder 15, LaRC; Daughters of the War of 1812, Chalmette Chapter, scrapbooks, 1925–27, 1931–37, box 1, folder 15, LaRC.

31. CGD Collection, box 3, autobiographical writing and notes for memoir, NA.

32. Richard Megraw, "'The Most Natural Expression of Locality': Ellsworth Woodward and the Newcomb Pottery," in *Bridging Southern Cultures: An Interdisciplinary Approach*, ed. by John Lowe (Baton Rouge: Louisiana State University Press, 2005), 144.

33. Barbara Miller Solomon, *In the Company of Educated Women: A History of Women and Higher Education in the United States* (New Haven: Yale University Press, 1985): 31, 119–23, 138.

34. Jessie Poesch and Sally Main, *Newcomb Pottery and Crafts: An Educational Enterprise for Women, 1895–1940* (Atglen, Pa.: Schiffer, 2003).

35. Earl Retif, "Caroline Wogan Durieux: A True Original," in *Newcomb College, 1886–2006: Higher Education for Women in New Orleans*, ed. Susan Tucker and Beth Willinger (Baton Rouge: Louisiana State University Press, 2012), 334–46.

36. Coralie Guarnino, student records, NA; CGD Collection, box 9, BFA scrapbook, NA.

37. CGD Collection, box 1, Newcomb College, Design Work, Interior Design Courses, NA; CGD Collection, box 11, artwork, NA.

38. Graduates Book, 1890–1952, NA; May Lesser interview with author, November 2, 1995; May Hyman, Student Records, NA; Lorys Jones, Student Records, NA.

39. CGD Collection, Diary, May 22, 1947, NA.

40. Olga Peters, interview with Adele Salzer, 1983, NA.

41. U.S. Bureau of the Census, *United States Census 1950, Detailed Characteristics: Louisiana* (Washington, D.C.: U.S. Census Bureau, 1950), table 73 ("Detailed Occupation of the Experienced Civilian Labor Force and of Employed Persons by Sex for the State and for Standard Metropolitan Areas").

42. CGD Collection, Diary, October 11, 14, 30, 1947, NA.

43. CGD Collection, Diary, May 10, 1984, NA.

44. Susan Tucker and Beth Willinger, "Part III: Lives," in *Newcomb College, 1886–2006: Higher Education for Women in New Orleans* (Baton Rouge: Louisiana State University Press, 2012), 263–86, especially 270.

45. See Tulane University yearbooks, *Jambalaya, 1944–47, Newcomb Archives.*

46. CGD Collection, Diary, October 5, 1943, NA.

47. CGD Collection, box 12, "Venus," NA.

48. For example, see "Reflections of the Past," *New Orleans Italian American Digest*, November 3, 2002 (see page 14 for a photo of Davis during her reign in 1944).

49. CGD Collection, Diary, February 7, 1998, NA.

50. Reid Mitchell, *All on a Mardi Gras Day: Episodes in the History of New Orleans Carnival* (Cambridge: Harvard University Press, 1995), 105.

51. CGD Collection, Diary, February 18, 1946, NA. For more information on these Carnival traditions, see Jennifer Atkins, "Dance and Gender in Old-Line New Orleans Carnival Balls, 1870–1920" (PhD diss., Florida State University, 2008); Carol Flake, *New Orleans: Behind the Masks of America's Most Exotic City* (New York: Grove Press, 1994).

52. CGD Collection, Diary, February 18, 1946, NA.

53. Employer 16 to Susan Tucker, August 10, 1982, notes, collection of the author. Related research was published in Susan Tucker, *Telling Memories among Southern Women* (Baton Rouge: Louisiana State University Press, 1988).

54. CGD Collection, Diary, February 18, 1946, NA.

55. Ibid.

56. "History of Dance Is Retold at Krewe of Elenians Ball: Miss Coralie Guarino Is Queen of Pageant," *Times-Picayune*, January 28, 1947.

57. "George W. Davis," obituary, *Times-Picayune*, August 18, 1966; CGD Collection, box 3, autobiographical writing and notes for memoir, NA.

58. See CGD Collection, diaries 1939–1947, especially April–May 1942 and 1943, and November 29, 1946, NA.

59. CGD Collection, Diary, December 1, 1952, January 31, 1953, January 12, 1954, January 8, 1956, January 30, 1960, NA.

60. CGD Collection, January 31, 1953, January 14, 1954, December 11, 1957, December 29, 1957, December 30, 1957, NA.

61. CGD Collection, Diary, March 15, 1953, October 12, 1954, December 22, 1960, April 16, 1963, July 14, 1965, May 10, 1979, November 24, 1992, NA.

62. CGD Collection, Diary, 1963.

63. CGD Collection, Diary, January 27, 1967.

64. "Costume Designer Seeks Carnival Ball Jobs, Up and Down the Street," *Times-Picayune*, March 8, 1954, want ads.

65. "New Orleans Carnival," *Shell News* 21, no. 1 (January 1953): 6–8.

66. Ibid.; Ilaine Hartman, conversation the author, October 17, 2011; Wayne Phillips, curator of textiles and costumes, Louisiana State Museum, New Orleans, interview with author, June 14, 2011.

67. Davis Collection, LaRC; "Growth of Transportation Depicted at Ball of Troy," *Times-Picayune*, February 6, 1954.

68. CGD Collection, LaRC. See also CGD Collection, Diary, January 9, 1953, January 26, 1953, February 4, 1953, February 8, 1954, February 17, 1954, NA.

69. Davis Collection, LaRC. See also "Faed Setum," *Lafayette Advertiser*, January 17, 1960.

70. CGD Collection, box 7, contains Coralie's portfolio of clippings on royal families. Books she used for Carnival include *Young Bess* by Margaret Irwin (1945) and Herbert Beerbohm Tree's *Henry VIII and His Court* (1911).

71. CGD Collection, box 1, "Frances Parkinson Keyes, 1961–1968," folder 2, NA.

72. She was always happy for her father for his role in Endymion and in Virgilians. See, for example, CGD Collection, Diary, January 13, 1964; Coralie Guarino Davis, conversations with the author, May 15, 1990, March 10, 2002, when I was compiling entries for the 1990 and 2002 editions of *The New Orleans Guide to Collections on Women*.

73. CGD Collection, Diary, February 5, 1954, NA.

74. Hartman conversation; Phillips interview.

75. Olga Peters and Leda Hincks Plauché have had the most recent attention. For the latter, see LaRC's Carnival Collection website, http://larc.tulane.edu/exhibits/carnival (accessed March 18, 2015).

76. Anne Billeter, "Why Don't Librarians Like Genealogists? Beginning Genealogy for Librarians," *Oregon Library Association* 7, no. 4 (Winter 2001): 2–6; Charles F. Bryan, "What Should We Do about the *Genies*?," *History News* 41, no. 1 (January 1986): 31–33; Richard J. Cox, "Genealogy and Public History: New Genealogical Guides and Their Implications for Public Historians," *Public Historian* 6, no. 2 (Spring 1984): 89–96; Elizabeth Shown Mills, "Genealogy in the 'Information Age': History's New Frontier?," *National Genealogical Society Quarterly* 91 (December 2003): 260–78.

77. Boudreaux conversation.

78. Lily Jackson, "Librarian Adept at Collecting the Collections," *Times-Picayune*, May 5, 1986; "Coralie Marie Guarino Davis," obituary, *Times-Picayune*, October 26, 2004. The public statements always identified her as a librarian, which she was, if not in job title then in educational attainments.

79. See U.S. Daughters of 1812, Chalmette Chapter, collection 656, box 2, folders 50–52, 66, scrapbooks 48–50, 58, LaRC.

80. Coralie Guarino Davis, *The Folk Architecture of Louisiana: A Selected Bibliography* (Monticello, Ill.: Vance Bibliographies, 1985); Coralie Guarino Davis, *Index to New Orleans Magazine, Volume 1, October 1966–volume 10, September 1976* (Baton Rouge: Louisiana Library Association, Subject Specialists Section, 1982); Coralie Guarino Davis, *A Selected Bibliography of the Architectural Works of James Harrison Dakin in Louisiana* (Monticello, Ill.: Vance Bibliographies, 1981).

81. Francesca Constance Morgan, "'Home and Country': Women, Nation, and the Daughters of the American Revolution, 1890–1939" (PhD diss., Columbia University, 1998), 154, 170–75.

82. For less sanguine looks at the way various patriotic societies re-created rather than changed class divisions, see Wallace Evan Davies, *Patriotism on Parade: The Story of Veterans' and Hereditary Organizations in America, 1783–1900* (Cambridge: Harvard University Press, 1955), 98; Karen L. Cox, *Dixie's Daughters: The United Daughters of the Confederacy and the Preservation of Confederate Culture* (Gainesville: University of Florida Press, 2003), 31, 34, 47, 83–84, 97; W. Fitzhugh Brundage, *The Southern Past: A Clash of Race and Memory* (Cambridge: Belknap Press of Harvard University Press, 2005).

83. The minute books and scrapbooks of the Daughters, Chalmette Chapter, LaRC, show these various tasks.

84. This was so for October 17, 1953, but also can be seen in almost all her entries for January 8 in any given year, the celebration of the Battle of New Orleans.

85. New Orleans City Council, Regular Meeting, December 19, 1991, proceedings, video tape 2, New Orleans Public Library, Louisiana Division, New Orleans.

86. CGD Collection, Diary, March 3, 1992.

87. David Winkler-Schmit, "Mardi Gras Sisterhood: All-Female Krewes Are Redefining Carnival—with a Woman's Touch," *Gambit*, February 13, 2007; Robin Roberts, "New Orleans Mardi Gras and Gender in Three Krewes: Rex, The Truck Parades, and Muses," *Western Folklore* 65, no. 3 (Summer 2006): 303–28.

88. New Orleans City Council Meeting, Proceedings, December 12, 1991, February 6, 1992. See also Report of the Blue Ribbon Committee on Carnival, which operated from January 30, 1992–April 14, 1992, New Orleans Public Library, Louisiana Division.

89. CGD Collection, Diary, December 7, 1946.

90. See, for example, CGD Collection, Diary, April 29, 1943, January 9, 1960, November 5, 1960, November 8, 1960, November 14, 1960.

91. CGD Collection, Diary, April 10, 2004.

Lucinda Williams

(1953–)

"Now Your Soul Is in Lake Charles": The Louisiana Motif and the Music of Lucinda Williams

COURT CARNEY

Born in Louisiana but claiming few long-term addresses, Lucinda Williams has crafted a career defined by critical acclaim, sustainable record sales, and a series of songs documenting the importance of place. In 1998, after two decades of working at the margins of fame, Williams centered her groundbreaking album *Car Wheels on a Gravel Road* on Louisiana. Using the state as an expanded metaphor for movement, family, and geography, Williams proved the potency of Louisiana as cultural signifier connecting the poetics of place to southern history writ large. The history of Louisiana—with its complicated racial matrix, international influences, and culture intimately defined by the significance of place—had a large influence on Williams, and her Louisiana is an elusive subject. In her lyrics Louisiana is a landscape of sojourn as well as a lodestar of memory and home, a place to leave and to which to return. The lyrics mention specific details about the state, but these appear through the blurry lens of childhood memories. Regardless, as a Louisiana woman, Lucinda Williams has consistently used the state as a vital touchstone and made it an emotional anchor to some of her most successful compositions.

For Williams, Louisiana is the location of a narrative about the search to find oneself within the tribulations of life. And in the middle of this motif sits the road, specifically Highway 61. Spanning six states and connecting New Orleans to Minnesota, U.S. Route 61 signifies the gnarled conduit of American myth, memory, and music. Running parallel to the Mississippi River, the road lays claim both to the ghost of Robert Johnson and the imagery of Bob Dylan and serves as a striking reminder of the mysterious entanglements of the past. In

LUCINDA WILLIAMS

Courtesy of Susan Wieand.

Clarksdale, Mississippi, the road crosses Highway 49, creating the imagined site of Johnson's deal with the devil and serving as the epicenter of American blues culture. In southern Louisiana the road often connects to prurient pursuits. In the 1930s, Huey Long pushed for an extension of the highway to facilitate travel between the governmental business of Baton Rouge and the nightlife of New Orleans. In the pre-interstate highway period, Highway 61 represented a fundamental aspect of the South Louisiana landscape. In the 1980s, this section of the highway—designated as Airline Highway for its generally rectilinear path—formed the infamous backdrop for Jimmy Swaggart's career-damaging liaison with a prostitute. Central to the geographic and cultural infrastructure of Louisiana, Highway 61 remains a powerful symbol of itinerancy and the transcendence of boundaries. The various names and histories of Highway 61 belie the basic point that the road *connects*: that New Orleans and Duluth share something, that a national relationship is constructed in tandem with regional cultures. As Highway 61 defines and redefines the concepts of place, time, and traveling in Louisiana, it also highlights the importance of these concepts to the state's musical legacy.

Throughout Williams's career, this road—both concretely and metaphorically—has connected her to the past as well as to a particularly defined sense of place. Living in Baton Rouge, a twelve-year-old Williams first heard Dylan's *Highway 61 Revisited*, a record that would have a profound impact on her.[1] Responding to the magnetism of Highway 61, Bob Dylan focused his 1965 masterpiece on the road as a way to situate his experiences growing up in the Midwest with the southern music over which he obsessed. Dylan took Highway 61 and populated it with both Abraham haggling with Jehovah as well as roving gamblers, the biblical rewritten as rural American parable. "From the time I was a small child," Williams recalls, "I had been influenced by southern poets and folk, blues, jazz, and country music. Here was a guy [Dylan] who was putting it all together, for the first time."[2] Lyrically, *Highway 61 Revisited* marked a culmination of his fusing of a more literate, if surreal, imagistic poetry with the blues form that served as the bedrock of his writing during this time. Dylan's eclectic tastes hit hard as he swerved from folk to garage rock to the blues, often in the same song. As a girl, Williams imbibed from this fantastically diverse source material—something that was mirrored by her upbringing. "I was almost thirteen and had just started guitar lessons," Lucinda remembers, when one of her father's students brought Dylan's record to her house. "My dad wasn't particularly interested," Williams points out, "but I was. . . . I got it."[3]

Born in Lake Charles in 1953, Williams grew up in a home filled with books, music, and moving boxes. The daughter of acclaimed poet Miller Williams and Lucille Day, a pianist, she was exposed to a wide array of musical and other cultural influences that would shape her career.[4] Much of Williams's childhood was spent traveling, as the family followed her father around to various teaching positions. This constant moving would have an influence on her sense of place and conception of home, two themes central to her songs. With Louisiana addresses in Lake Charles, Baton Rouge, and New Orleans as well as forays into Mississippi (Jackson and Vicksburg), there is an arc of wandering and mobility that looms large in Williams's biography. Lucy divorced Miller when Lucinda was fourteen—he would maintain custody of the children—and Lucinda's adolescence would be defined by the divisions within her family. She found a political voice at this time as well, and by the late 1960s Lucinda had become involved in various political causes. She was eventually expelled from high school after refusing to recite the Pledge of Allegiance, "as a protest against the Vietnam War."[5] By the time she was a teenager, with a dozen homes behind her, Lucinda had emerged as a well-read, rather worldly young woman without much regard for authority.

This sense of rooted rootlessness—a childhood defined so much by place, but also of no place—intensely affected Williams, especially as she began to write songs.[6] At the height of her mainstream success, in the late 1990s, Williams would confuse some of this early chronology: "I was born in Lake Charles, . . . and we lived there for about a year," she recalled to an interviewer. "Then I lived in Baton Rouge. Then when I was four we were in—wait a minute, wait a minute! We were in Vicksburg, Miss., when I was two, because my brother was born there. Then Jackson, Miss., when I was four."[7] Within this blur of movement, Williams experienced not only the geographic contours of Louisiana, but also the varying dynamics of the South. The sounds of the South would come to define her general perspective since so much of her life connects back both to the meaning of the blues and to the map of her youth. Southern life as defined by the blues is central to understanding Williams's life and career, and as an adult she would return to this landscape repeatedly in an attempt to document the cultural and emotional power of the region on her own life.[8]

With this backdrop of traveling and moving homes, Lucinda's father opened up a quasi-bohemian world of poets, writers, and artists for his daughter. The son of a Methodist preacher, Miller Williams had been born and raised in Arkansas in a household dedicated to various forms of activism related to civil rights. With degrees in biology and zoology, Miller taught science at Wesleyan College in Macon, Georgia, for several years, before radically shifting paths to pursue a life in poetry. As a university professor, Miller Williams threw parties for visiting poets, and as a young girl Lucinda met artists such as Flannery O'Connor, Allen Ginsburg, Charles Bukowski, and James Dickey.[9] These parties allowed Lucinda and her siblings, a brother and sister, to perform music for their guests and receive criticism by some of the most influential writers of the twentieth century.[10] Miller credited Flannery O'Connor with pushing him into a full-time focus on poetry on the university level. Without his knowledge, she pursued a professorship in English for him at Louisiana State University.

O'Connor also played an important role in Lucinda's creative education. "I ate [O'Connor's] stuff up. I was pretty young—fifteen, sixteen. Her stuff was so descriptive. . . . I loved that kind of writing, that very descriptive, realistic writing. I learned that instead of just saying 'I just left this last town,' why not say the name of the town? Describe the town. Don't just say 'I put my shoes on today,' say 'I put my cracked leather shoes on.'" Williams accompanied her father to visit O'Connor several times as a teenager, and she witnessed evidence of a writer's discipline—O'Connor would write every day, and if the shades were drawn they were to wait outside—as well as the less constructed side of a creative writer. "She raised peacocks," Lucinda recalled, "and they were running all over the yard. My dad says I was chasing the peacocks."[11] Although Williams would not live in Georgia long, she would find long-term inspiration in O'Connor as she began to develop her own creative pursuits. Her father's position at LSU would begin a long period of academic itinerancy, as he served as professor or poet-in-residence at a number of universities, including McNeese State College (in Lake Charles) and Loyola University (in New Orleans) as well as the University of Chile and the National University of Mexico.[12]

Williams's early musical background mirrored this creative milieu of artists, academics, and writers. Throughout her adolescence, her turntable featured blues, jazz, rock, country, and folk records, from Robert Johnson and Hank Williams to John Coltrane, the Doors, and Peter, Paul, and Mary. "I liked to stay inside," she once said. "I did my share of hopscotch and cartwheels and climbing trees and that kind of thing, but for the most part I liked to do indoor stuff like drawing and writing and reading." Williams turned to the guitar when she was twelve after brief forays with the piano, chord organ, and zither.[13] "I never learned how to play the piano because I wasn't patient enough," Williams recalls. "I sat and tinkered on it, but it was frustrating. I was desperate to figure out how to read sheet music so I could sing a song."[14] The guitar quickly emerged as her primary interest, and Williams began to pick out various folk and popular songs. As with her classroom education, Williams proved to be an idiosyncratic student, focusing more on what sounded right to her ears rather than practicing études, but through various lessons and listening to a large volume of music, Williams began to develop a fingerpicking style that she would continue to improve upon.[15] "I'd get all excited if I found a songbook with a song from a record I owned," Williams told an interviewer. "I spent hours learning new material. That became my whole life."[16] These songbooks provided young Williams with both instruction and a repertoire, and these melodies and chord changes learned at a young age shaped her own songs as she matured.

As she developed her guitar style, Lucinda also struggled to find a singing voice that reflected what she heard in her head as well as competed with her record collection filled with unique female singers such as Judy Collins and Linda Ronstadt. Aware of her vocal limitations—real or imagined—Lucinda decided early on, she later said, "that I was going to learn how to write songs really, really well, because I didn't want to have to compete as a singer. I didn't feel that it was my strong point."[17] The turning point for her in terms of discovering her personal strengths points to a constant theme of her entire career. In a 2012 interview with *The Believer*, Lucinda talked at some length of the two styles that came to define her voice as she discovered Bobbie Gentry, the country singer with a distinctive low voice, and Memphis Minnie, the blues singer. Gentry, born Roberta Lee Streeter in northern Mississippi, wrote and performed her own material in a series of well-received records in the late 1960s and early 1970s. These songs, especially her "Ode to Billie Joe," wedded stylized southern gothic lyrics to country-rock rhythms, but Williams was particularly intrigued by her strong and husky voice. Memphis Minnie, born Lizzie Douglas and raised in Algiers, Louisiana, taught herself the guitar and ran away to Memphis when barely a teenager. Her music, a combination of the rural blues of her childhood and urban culture, centered on her guitar playing and her "scratchy, different" voice, also provided a template for Williams. These two women, a white country singer from Mississippi and a black blues singer from Louisiana, would serve Lucinda well as she embarked on finding her own musical path.[18]

At the center of this musical education, whether Williams was conscious of this or not, swirled the sounds of Louisiana—jazz, blues, folk, country, swamp pop, Cajun, and zydeco—that helped define the culture of her birth state with its African, Caribbean, Creole, and Cajun influences. Various elements of Louisiana have colored each of her records in terms of rhythms, instrumentation, timbre, and lyrics. Of these forms, blues and traditional country serve as the most significant elements of Williams's early music. At times this is explicit, as in a cover of a Junior Wells or an A. P. Carter song, but often the blues and country exist as the emotional undercurrents of her music that characterize her phrasing and lyrical perspective. "The blues resonate in the way she finds and rides the central riff to her best songs," one journalist argues. "They echo in her vocal phrasing, they find succor and sustenance in the generous spaces she leaves for guitar solos."[19] As essential as the blues and country are to understanding Williams's musical approach, the blurry nature of her connection to these idioms has created problems for marketing her music. Williams, for example, has won three Grammy Awards in three different categories: "Best Country Song," "Best Contemporary Folk Album," and "Best Female Rock Performance." "Part of the difficulty Williams has had accessing a wider audience," one writer notes, "is the difficulty in pinning her music to any one tradition."[20] More than any genre, however, it is the music of a place—Louisiana—that has continued to shape much of Williams's recorded output.

In the early 1970s, Lucinda enrolled at the University of Arkansas, where she sporadically took classes over the course of a few semesters. Despite her interests in music and poetry firmly in place, Lucinda chose to pursue a degree in cultural anthropology. "At the time," Williams notes, "I wasn't interested in formal music training, I guess."[21] Her academic father certainly persuaded Lucinda to get a college degree, but she eventually left college behind. There was her father's continued traveling—Miller had relocated the family to Mexico City in 1970, where he was employed as the Fulbright professor in American studies at the National University of Mexico that year—and there was also the magnetic pull of music. The excursion to Mexico ignited Williams's desire to perform, and she became known for her folk performances at local schools. "We went to high schools, colleges. It was a little scary," she notes. "We were famous American folk singers as far as they were concerned."[22] As so often happened during this period, however, Lucinda's compass needle pointed toward southern Louisiana, and by 1971 or 1972 she was playing in various clubs in New Orleans. In particular, Williams found a recurring gig at Andy's Bar, a coffee shop/bar on Bourbon Street that featured folk musicians and was the first place in New Orleans to provide both Guinness stout on tap and the Sunday *New York Times*.[23] "Each person had a shift and you'd sit on a stool," Williams recalls, "but it was a big deal for me because it was a regular gig." This job proved to be important for the young singer also because it brought Williams a well-connected audience.[24] "I was just walking on the moon! This is what I wanted to do!" Williams says about her Bourbon Street experience as a performer. She called her father from New Orleans, explained her newfound desire to focus on music full time, and decided once and for all that she was finished with organized education. "That was probably one of the big early turning points," Williams says of her father's acquiescence to this new plan, "maybe *the* turning point."[25]

Within this diverse, mobile life, Lucinda Williams began to write her own material, and much of her adult life can be traced from the lyrics and sounds of her albums. Her discography, in other words, though only marginally biographical in a direct sense, offers an emotional map of her life, as her music reflects her choices, intents, and interests. During this period, most of Williams's repertoire consisted of covers of songs by Bob Dylan and Joni Mitchell and folk standards from the 1960s.[26] Positioned firmly within the folk tradition, Williams drew liberally from folk, country, and blues sources, which came to dominate her early songwriting. Between the late 1970s and early 2010s, Williams released twelve records that range from country blues to alternative country, heartfelt confessionals, and mature songs that oscillate between tender spirituality and raw sexuality. Overall, Williams's discography breaks down into several periods. The early one includes her first two records—*Ramblin'* (1979) and *Happy Woman Blues* (1980)—which showcase Williams at her sparsest and most connected to country and blues. After an eight-year hiatus, Williams returned with the second phase of her career with her eponymous record in 1988 and *Sweet Old World* in 1992. These records were centered more squarely on her songwriting and led to her breakthrough album *Car Wheels on a Gravel Road* (1998).

In many ways, *Car Wheels* bisects her discography, and her records after her late-1990s renascence explore a much different terrain. Her output in the 2000s picked up dramatically, and in the span of ten years Williams released five studio albums (*Essence*, *World without Tears*, *West*, *Little Honey*, and *Blessed*) as well as her first live record, *Live @ the Fillmore*. This productivity eclipsed the first half of her career (five records in twenty years) and introduced a lyrical focus far removed from her Louisiana-drenched early records.[27]

Williams's first experience in a recording studio developed out of her time in New Orleans and a friendship with Jeff Ampolsk, a folksinger who recorded a record for Smithsonian Folkways in 1977. Convinced that Mose Asch, the head of Folkways, would be impressed with her songs, Ampolsk urged Williams to send some of her material to the label. Eventually she complied, and Asch sent Williams a contract and $250 to make a record. "For some reason," Williams explained, "I thought this was a traditional archive stuff [*sic*], and they don't want to hear my own songs. So that's why I put [traditional] songs on there."[28] Situated between the Greenwich Village folk scene of the early 1960s and her blues record collection, Williams's first recording hints at a number of the themes she would develop through her career. Recorded over the course of a few hours in Jackson, Mississippi, *Ramblin' on My Mind* (later reissued as simply *Ramblin'*) featured traditional blues and country songs by Robert Johnson, Hank Williams, Memphis Minnie, and A. P. Carter. Accompanied by John Grimaudo on guitar, Lucinda Williams pursued a near-academic approach to the music, with her versions staying close to the parameters of the originals. With little production and with songs finished in just a handful of takes, *Ramblin'* achieves an unprocessed simplicity that makes it stand out considerably from Williams's later records.[29] This hurried foray into the studio, with the performances captured quickly as a way to preserve funds as much as a nod to early folk and blues sessions of the 1920s and 1930s, presaged her ultimate dissatisfaction with most things related to the sterile environment of modern recording.

Williams's versions of old songs afforded her the opportunity to record a second album for Folkways, which featured her own songs and was recorded in the late spring of 1980. Entitled *Happy Woman Blues*, Williams used this record to introduce a number of lyrical motifs that would delineate the central part of her career. Throughout this collection, Williams plays with the power and emotional strain of place, of region. From Little Rock and Houston ("Rolling Along") to New York City ("Happy Woman Blues," "Howlin' at Midnight," and "Maria"), and from Texas to New Mexico, Colorado, Canada, and Louisiana, Williams riddles these songs with place names in an attempt to locate her characters—and perhaps herself—within a definably real world. Firmly within the traditional idiom, though more fleshed out instrumentally than her debut album, Williams's *Happy Woman Blues* is rooted deeply in the South. Her Louisiana upbringing comes through in two songs that have an especially nostalgic pull. The opener, "Lafayette," reflects back on the culture of southern Louisiana when she sings, "I know where I belong," and this paean to the region of her birth connects to "Louisiana Man," a song that speaks of a "country man with a heart of gold." These two songs would be rerecorded and appear on later records, underscoring Williams's continual dissatisfaction with her studio output. According to Williams, the original recordings were recorded in three days without a drummer, but the "guy who was engineering it—he was kind of a combination producer and engineer—he decided to have a drummer come in while we were all out of the studio, and he put drums on the track!" "That was my initial step," Williams recalls, "into the manipulative, controlling arms of the music industry and recording." At that point, the release of *Happy Woman Blues* led to an eight-year hiatus, with Williams quietly drifting away from the public eye.[30] "I had a chance to move to L.A.," Williams recalls, "and moved in late 1984." "I did everything I could," she continues, "I opened up for everybody. I was beating the pavement, playing around—Raji's in Hollywood, the Palomino in the Valley, and all the folk clubs."[31]

During the 1980s, as she moved around the country—relocating to Los Angeles and then to Nashville—and kept writing songs, Williams eventually put together a demo tape for a new record. "I didn't know anything about the music business before then," she recalls, "I didn't have a manager, a lawyer, a booking agent, a band." Williams received a development deal with CBS Records to record an album, and she excitedly started writing and editing songs for it. Unfortunately, these songs failed to interest the artists and repertoire division of CBS, and executives there decided that Williams did not fit into their marketing strategy.[32] Turned down by CBS, Williams was picked up by a seemingly odd choice, Rough Trade Records, which signed her for $15,000. A British label that specialized in post-punk and experimental rock music, Rough Trade provided Williams with the opportunity to shift gears musically with her record *Lucinda Williams*.[33] Released in 1988, the record signified a fresh reintroduction to her songwriting as well as her first masterpiece. Featuring a clutch of solid songs, *Lucinda Williams* sold one hundred thousand copies and introduced the singer to a much wider audience than she had previously enjoyed. The Louisiana angle came through in "Crescent City," a reflective song about New Orleans, where "everything's still the same." Blending the general with the specific—"let's see how these blues'll do in the town where the good times stay" mixed with "Mama lives in Mandeville" and "the longest bridge I've ever crossed over Pontchartrain"—this song paints a nostalgic portrait of Louisiana as if through the images in a rearview mirror. Williams also affects the patois of Cajun Louisiana: "tu le ton son temps / that's what we'd say" and "I can hear my zydeco / and laissez le bon ton roulet [*sic*]."[34] Reflecting on this song years later, Williams noted, "I went through a lot of changes growing up in Baton Rouge and New Orleans with my brother, Robert, and my sister, Karyn, between 1965 and 1970. My music started there."[35]

The album featured high-quality songs, crisp production, and strong melodies, but its packaging shows that Rough Trade had difficulty figuring out how Williams should appear. The cover image eschewed obviously rural signifiers, such as in other promotional photographs at the time, in which Williams was pictured wearing a simple cotton dress. Instead Williams sports a leather jacket. According to the label, they opted to edit out a Confederate flag patch sewn to the jacket's sleeve. "To avoid this motif from becoming an unwanted point of discussion," Robin Hurley, Rough Trade's A&R representative, remarked in 2013, "Lucinda agreed that it should be airbrushed out."[36] Not quite rock, not quite folk, not quite southern, not quite urban, Lucinda Williams proved to be a difficult act to pin down.[37] Rooted in rock—Dylan's *Highway 61 Revisited* served as a clear influence on the mixing sessions for *Lucinda Williams*—but with country and folk overtones, the album served as her first bona fide success. With the album followed by several high-profile covers of her songs from it, most notably Mary Chapin Carpenter's version of "Passionate Kisses," Williams's profile rose considerably.

Williams followed the success of *Lucinda Williams* in 1992 with *Sweet Old World*. Compared to the spirited drive of her eponymous breakthrough, *Sweet Old World* sounds a bit more conservative, with moments that connect it to the traditional music of her early career. Part of the identity crisis of the record is due to the difficult time Williams had with the corporate machinations of the music business. "It sounded just like the radio," she told the *New York Times*, referring to the slick production of the early version of the record that RCA had contracted.[38] Despite this painful and drawn-out process, a practice that had now sadly become routine for Williams, *Sweet Old World* was finally released by the Chameleon label and included several high-caliber songs, including "Pineola," which became a fan favorite. Tightly composed, "Pineola" reflects on the suicide of Frank Stanford, a southern poet and family friend when Williams lived in Arkansas during the 1970s. "We recorded that album three times and it still didn't come out right!" Williams exclaimed. "That's the worst feeling in the world." This negative perspective on the process of recording *Sweet Old World* served as an ill omen as she began work on her fifth record in the mid-1990s.[39]

By 1995, Williams had begun to play a batch of new songs during live performances. These songs, filled with references to Louisiana and the South, connected immediately to her growing audience of fans of literate folk music, and Williams, feeling encouraged, set out to record the new material. The studio demons present during *Sweet Old World*, however, returned, and Williams soon embarked on a three-year quest to capture on tape the feeling and mood she felt these songs deserved. Moving from Gurf Morlix, who had coproduced *Sweet Old World*, to new producers Steve Earle and Ray Kennedy, Williams sought to enliven what she had decided was "flat, lifeless, not up to par."[40] Earle was entering his first creative peak since drugs had sidelined his career in the early 1990s, and his musical vision seemed to jibe completely with Lucinda's, at least on paper. In the studio, however, Earle and Williams—both famously headstrong—failed to finish an album together. Williams brought in Roy Bittan, keyboardist for Bruce Springsteen, to listen to the tapes and offer guidance on how to finish the record. Bittan was able to both maneuver Williams's longstanding trepidation with studio production and rescue supposedly less-effective earlier attempts at completing songs. "Kinda country," Williams described one of the finished songs, "but in that old-timey bluesy way."[41] With Williams finally pleased with the crucial mix of blues, country, and folk, the record, now entitled *Car Wheels on a Gravel Road*, came to epitomize not only Williams's evolution as a songwriter but the entirety of her career.

After decades of writing songs that touched on the concept and meaning of place, Williams crafted an entire record that used specific regional identifiers. Her lyrics were rooted in the quotidian South as well as the universal context of relationships. *Car Wheels on a Gravel Road* is centered on a series of Louisiana-related songs. In "Concrete and Barbed Wire," Williams focuses on the geographic and emotional distance between two separated lovers. "Somewhere in Louisiana," she sings, "my sugar's doing time." Both Algiers—in Orleans Parish—and Opelousas—in St. Landry—feature in the song and help situate the action within a knowable context. Even her ode to the Mississippi Delta, "2 Kool 2 Be 4-gotten," culminates with a hometown memory of "leaning against the railing of a Lake Charles bridge." At the emotional center of the record, however, "Lake Charles" and "Jackson" transcend any map, as Williams here places herself within the slippery framework of quasi-autobiographical songwriting. "Lake Charles" is about a man from Nacogdoches, Texas, who "had a reason to get back to Lake Charles"—Clyde Woodward, an ex-boyfriend with dreams of musical stardom and a debilitating and ultimately fatal alcohol habit. And in "Jackson," Williams leaves behind a partner, naming the towns through which she passes, including Lafayette and Baton Rouge. With direct, poignant lyrics addressing nostalgia, Louisiana, and roads as connectors and dividers, *Car Wheels* shows Williams's strength as a songwriter. Her songs follow not only tangible roads but also the intangible cultural paths wending through Louisiana and elsewhere in the South.[42]

In the years after *Car Wheels*, Williams's music continued to evolve stylistically even as she explored similar lyrical themes. Both *Essence* (2001) and *World without Tears* (2003) pushed against some of the expectations of *Car Wheels* with songs that were less defined by country music than by a desire to expand the borders of her music. Place still mattered to Williams on these records, but instead of the heavier Louisiana focus of her earlier songs, she began to write about California, Minnesota, and even Denmark. "Of course, I'm older now," she told an interviewer. "I'm in a different place in my life than when I wrote the songs for *Car Wheels* or *Essence* or whatever. Different things were going on."[43] Both of these records connect to the spirit of her earlier records (at least since *Lucinda Williams*), but her more diffused lyrical approach and broader musical palate hinted at the more diaphanous records she would come to make.

Her song “Bus to Baton Rouge,” on *Essence*, would be the last song as of 2014 that dealt directly with Louisiana. Significantly, this song’s narrator starts with “I had to go back” and ends with the reminder that “ghosts in the wind that blow through my life / follow me wherever I go.” From this point on, Williams began to deal more unequivocally with the ghosts of the past rather than simply evoke a more ambiguous sense of nostalgia. “I’ll never be free from these chains inside,” she concludes the song, “hidden deep down in my soul.”[44]

As Williams began to expand the lyrical focus of her songs in the early 2000s, she also began enlarging the tone of her music. “I’m looking for a crunchy, fucked-up sound that’s part electric and part acoustic,” Williams notes, as she continues to navigate the undercurrents of blues and folk that lay at the heart of her music.[45] This experimental approach to her sound and her songwriting came together in two albums released in 2007 and 2008. Both *West* and *Little Honey* offered stylistic developments that showed Williams moving away from her 1990s sound. Despite several upbeat songs, *West* is one of Williams’s darker records, inspired by the loss of a partner as well as the death of her mother. For much of her career, Williams had tended to avoid talking publicly about her relationship with her mother, and most biographies focused on her connection to her poet father. *West*, however, opened up this conversation, especially with songs such as “Mama You Sweet” and “Fancy Funeral.” Released within a year of *West*, *Little Honey* represented the less restrained side of Williams, then in her mid-fifties, as she brought together a sexually charged group of songs that echoed the music of *Car Wheels on a Gravel Road* but with a much more sensual lyrical focus. A duet with Elvis Costello and a cover of AC/DC insured that Williams had embarked on a different road than the one she was traveling in the 1990s.[46]

By the 2010s, Lucinda Williams had entered into the most prolific period of her career. In the two decades after *Ramblin’*, for example, Williams released only five albums, but between 2001 and 2011 she had released five studio records, her first live album, and a number of digital singles. This newfound fecundity culminated in *Blessed*, released in 2011 by Lost Highway Records, her label since the release of *Essence* in 2001. Replacing the overtly varied soundscapes of the two previous records, the songs on *Blessed* blended into a coherent, dynamic whole. On her tenth studio record, Williams distilled the grief and pain of other recent records while still gravitating toward the blues and folk motifs that had driven her best work. Lyrically, Williams had composed a series of blues haiku, and the quiet stillness of her rhyme and meter brought a knowing and stately quality to the proceedings. “A celebration,” she sings in “Sweet Love,” “my breath is yours to share / everything in me / and of me is yours forever.” Significantly, early copies of *Blessed* included raw demos of these songs, underscoring both her artistic distance traveled since the 1970s as well as the thematic constants that have underpinned her strongest work.

Thoughts of her family still weighed heavily on Williams's songwriting during this period, and she mentions songs, heretofore unrecorded or unreleased, that delve directly into the topic of mental illness as well as the concept of "survivor guilt," as Williams escaped the genetic threat of the disease. "I carry that stuff around me like an albatross around my neck," Williams says about her mother's illness. "This is the stuff," Williams argues. "That's what keeps me going. I have to write. I've written a couple of songs about my brother who's suffered from mental illness, which I am convinced is genetic because my sister has it, too." "Yeah, she had a rough time," she says about her mother. "Her mother [Williams's grandmother] had mental illness. Passed it down to her. It got passed to my sister and my brother. Somehow I managed to survive." No longer covering the blues, no longer name-checking Louisiana, instead by the 2010s Williams had developed a subtly new language. Informed by the blues in its sparseness, by folk music in its detail, and by Louisiana's nostalgic pull, her new songs were novel in their ability to evoke the emotional toll of the past and present in remarkable ways.[47]

Throughout her music and career, Lucinda Williams has conjured a landscape of myth and memory defined both by place and no place. Within this context, Louisiana serves a nostalgic role as well as a grounding one, regardless of whether a song is autobiographical or not. Ultimately, Louisiana is a convoluted, ambivalent motif in Williams's music and life, operating just on the margins of the remembered past but suggesting the breadth and complexity of Louisiana culture. "I have some relatives in Baton Rouge and Lake Charles," Williams related in 2007, "but it's actually strange for me to go back to Louisiana. There are just so many ghosts."[48] Running away from Louisiana perhaps as much as clinging to it, she repeatedly placed the state at the center of her most celebrated songs and yet the meaning of Louisiana, and by extension her connection to it, remained elusive. "Did you run about as far as you could go / down the Louisiana highway across Lake Pontchartrain," Williams sings. "Now your soul is in Lake Charles no matter what they say." In the end, her music signifies the fractured and ambiguous place that Louisiana, as a construct, represents within American music.

NOTES

1. "The first Bob Dylan album I heard," Williams notes, "was *Highway 61 Revisited.* It was 1965." Larry "Ratso" Sloman, "Happy Birthday, Bob! On His 70th Birthday, Famous Friends and Admirers Pen Tributes to Bob Dylan," *AARP Magazine*, http://www.aarp.org/entertainment/music/info-03-2011/bob-dylan-birthday-tribute.4.html (accessed January 20, 2014).

2. Ibid. Williams elsewhere said of Dylan, "He was the first artist who actually managed to incorporate both of the worlds I came out of, which was the more traditional folk music of America and the poetic, literary world. That's when I decided what I wanted to achieve." "Miller & Lucinda Williams: All in the Family," Poets.org (Academy of American Poets), http://www.poets.org/viewmedia.php/prmMID/5824 (accessed January 20, 2014).

3. Sloman, "Happy Birthday, Bob!"

4. See also David Baker, "To Advantage Dressed: Miller Williams among the Naked Poets," *Southern Review* 26 (Autumn 1990): 814–31.

5. Darcy Frey, "Lucinda Williams Is in Pain," *New York Times*, September 14, 1997.

6. "We'd get to a new town and we always had rental houses, so we'd run in and decide which room was gonna be ours. I was real shy as a kid, but I enjoyed the traveling and seeing different places." Roxane Orgill, *Shout, Sister Shout! Ten Girl Singers Who Shaped a Century* (New York: Margaret K. McElderry, 2001), 121–22.

7. Karen Schoemer, "Rambling Woman Blues," *Newsweek*, July 6, 1998, 68.

8. See also "Attitude is Everything: Ask Lucinda," *Middle Mojo*, http://middlemojo.com/2011/04/attitude-is-everything-ask-lucinda/4 (accessed January 20, 2014).

9. Orgill, *Shout, Sister Shout!*, 123. In an interview with Charlie Rose, Williams mentions her love of Flannery O'Connor's perspective on the South: "All of that dark southern gothic stuff. . . . I enjoy the eccentricity of it, I guess." Aired September 6, 2001, Charlierose.com, http://www.charlierose.com/view/interview/2962 (accessed May 31, 2012).

10. "We'd have writers over and sit around and have drinks. My dad would often read a new poem that he'd just written, and I would sing some songs. That was a fairly regular thing. I got feedback, which is of utmost importance when you're learning. I had this immediate, intelligent audience. Plus, I spent a lot of time sitting around just listening, observing, and absorbing things through a kind of osmosis." "Miller & Lucinda Williams."

11. Madeleine Schwartz, "Lucinda Williams," *Believer*, July/August 2012, http://www.believermag.com/issues/201207/?read=interview_lucindawilliams (accessed January 20, 2014).

12. "Miller Williams, 1930–2015," Poetry Foundation, http://www.poetryfoundation.org/bio/miller-williams (accessed March 18, 2015).

13. Schwartz, "Lucinda Williams."

14. Dan Ouellette, "Fruits of Her Labor," AcousticGuitar.com, http://www.acousticguitar.com/issues/ag128/feature128.html (accessed May 31, 2012).

15. "I learned rudimentary chord progressions and several different picking techniques. My right hand actually became more important than my left." Ibid.

16. Ibid.

17. Schwartz, "Lucinda Williams."

18. Ibid.

19. Grant Alden, "Lucinda Williams—World Without Tears," *No Depression*, February 28, 2003, http://nodepression.com/album-review/lucinda-williams-world-without-tears (accessed April 20, 2015). "And they're not blues, even though they are informed by something that might be described as a blues attitude." Bill Buford, "Delta Nights," *New Yorker*, June 5, 2000, 50.

20. "Miller & Lucinda Williams." "At one point CBS offered her enough money to record a demo tape, but when she submitted her work, the label's Los Angeles office found it 'too country' and sent it to Nashville; Nashville, in turn, found it too alternative and sent it to the trash. One by one all the major labels turned her down. One by one all the smaller ones did, too." Frey, "Lucinda Williams Is in Pain."

21. Schwartz, "Lucinda Williams."

22. Ibid.

23. "Max Clevenger (1926–2007)," reprinted from *Times-Picayune*, n.d., in Wrong Place Saloon, http://www.wrongplacesaloon.com/memMax.htm (accessed January 20, 2014).

24. See also Michael D. Ayers, "Interview," *Village Voice*, October 2, 2009.

25. Schwartz, "Lucinda Williams."

26. Elizabeth Bukowski, "Lucinda Williams," Salon.com, January 11, 2000, http://www.salon.com/2000/01/11/lucinda (accessed January 20, 2014).

27. See "Lucinda Willilams," Discogs, http://www.discogs.com/artist/Lucinda+Williams (accessed January 20, 2014).

28. Ayers, "Interview."

29. Ibid.

30. Schwartz, "Lucinda Williams."

31. Liner notes, *Lucinda Williams*, compact disc (reissue, Lucinda Williams Music, 2014).

32. Schwartz, "Lucinda Williams."

33. Frey, "Lucinda Williams Is in Pain." "It would be an unexpected home," Chris Morris notes, "for a drawling roots-based musician from Lake Charles." Liner notes, *Lucinda Williams* reissue.

34. Liner notes, *Lucinda Williams* reissue. Some confusion exists regarding these lyrics, as they clearly differ from accepted French spellings or their Cajun counterparts. The lyrics here are taken verbatim from the printed materials included with the CD.

35. Liner notes, *Lucinda Williams* reissue.

36. Ibid.

37. Ibid.

38. Frey, "Lucinda Williams Is in Pain."

39. Ibid.

40. Ibid.

41. Ibid.

42. Ibid.

43. Sam Adams, "Interview: Lucinda Williams," *A.V. Club*, March 10, 2011, http://www.avclub.com/article/lucinda-williams-52934 (accessed May 31, 2012).

44. Regarding *World without Tears*: "My dad told me this was a great body of work, that it's the closest to poetry of anything I've written." Ouellette, "Fruits of Her Labor."

45. Ibid.

46. "Lucinda Williams: Interview," ChicagoPride.com, March 4, 2007, http://chicago.gopride.com/news/interview.cfm/articleid/106384 (accessed January 20, 2014).

47. Schwartz, "Lucinda Williams."

48. "I don't really have any strong ties there to the South now that my mother's gone. She lived there for years and years, in New Orleans, right in the city. Then I moved her up to Arkansas because we had other family there." "Lucinda Williams: Interview."

Rebecca Wells

(1953–)

The Divine Saga Deep in the Heart of Louisiana

MARY ANN WILSON

The final chapter of Rebecca Wells's 2005 novel, *Ya-Yas in Bloom*, ends with a homegrown Christmas pageant bringing together three generations of children and grandchildren and all the elements that make up her own unique version of Louisiana: festivity, food (a table that "groaned with the fruits of the Louisiana earth"), family, music, and an irreverent take on religion, where the sacred and secular seamlessly blend.[1] The "wise women" in this family scenario are the Ya-Yas, Wells's fictional creations—hard-drinking, bourré-playing, outrageous women who dismantle the southern belle image as easily as one of them sideswipes the statue of the Infant of Prague in the school parking lot. Bicycle helmets and tiaras costume these actors along with Wise Men's robes and shepherds' crooks as the Walker clan witnesses the reenactment of what Christians celebrate as the Holy Family's story. But this family celebration is far from idyllic. Chief sassy matriarch Vivi has to be fortified with her trademark "bourbon and branch" to get in the right performative mood; one of the Ya-Ya grandchildren has only recently returned to the family after being kidnapped by a disturbed would-be mother; one of the grandfathers comes armed with a gun to protect his family against any future threats; and Siddalee, Vivi's daughter, is not here but away in another part of the country pursuing a career as an actress and playwright.

Like Siddalee, Rebecca Wells has ventured far beyond Louisiana's boundaries to explore her creative vision while still managing to remain tied to this landscape and culture that are the raw material of her art. In the process, she has explored issues of female identity—particularly the woman writer's identity—as affected by history and region, in her case, being Catholic in central Louisiana in the mid-twentieth century. She has also championed the healing power of writing at difficult times in her life. In two plays and four novels, she has captured a bittersweet and darkly humorous world of flawed mothers, wounded daughters, and female communities, giving her small Louisiana world a voice that resonates far beyond its cane fields and bayous. Beneath the sweet and sexy, beneath the flamboyant and outrageous, Rebecca Wells tells some hard truths about what it means to grow up female and southern and Catholic at various times in America's history; what it means to try to make sense of a deeply flawed human mother and an all too perfect spiritual one; what it means to have a safety net of friends who share your private dreams and nightmares; and finally what it means to be a writer and shape all that suffering into something solid.

Spanning the 1930s to the 1990s, Wells's stories foreground mother-daughter relationships, women's friendships, and marriage in the largely female world she creates. At the core of this fictional world is the theme of identity and how it emerges during particular historical periods, shaped by the forces of religion, race, and region, in this case pre–Vatican II Catholicism in the Jim Crow South of central Louisiana, "where the sin-loving Southern half of the state meets the atonement-hungry North," as one of her characters jokes.[2] Rebecca Wells anchors herself to a childhood world of memory and loss in a landscape rich, resonant, and distinctly Louisiana, a landscape familiar to her readers and fans around the world.

Born in 1953, Wells grew up in Alexandria, Louisiana, in a storytelling family on a working plantation and land her family had owned for centuries. There, this Catholic schoolgirl from Our Lady of Prompt Succor Parish reveled in the southern love of story, her own dramatic talents, and the perpetual drama that is life in Louisiana. "I grew up in a tiny kingdom of bayous and cotton fields," Wells says, in a "gumbo of stories, tales, histories. I saw friendships that last lifetimes." She goes on to ask, "How could I *not* be influenced by such rich characters, food, music, the beauty of the flat land stretching out forever, dotted like snow with cotton?"[3] She loved the seasonal world of rural Louisiana—harvesting cotton, crawfishing in the bayou—and the rhythms and rituals of black music and culture, such as Little Richard's music, which opens her first novel, *Little Altars Everywhere*. Wells absorbed it all and turned it into theater, acting in plays for and with her siblings. In high school she continued to act, and she expanded her repertoire at Louisiana State University (LSU), studying theater, English, and psychology. At LSU in the 1970s, during the second wave of feminism, Wells's interest in women's politics emerged. She was a member of LSU's first chapter of the National Organization for Women, lobbying on the steps of the state capitol in Baton Rouge for the Equal Rights Amendment. She also remembers feminist Bella Abzug coming to speak on campus. During this era in her life, the author was, in her words, "growing out of the southern belle-ness, the culture that formed [me]."[4]

REBECCA WELLS

Courtesy of Rebecca Wells.

Subsequent travels took her far beyond central Louisiana, to Colorado and the Naropa Institute where she studied language and consciousness with legendary poet Allen Ginsberg; to New York, where she studied the Stanislavski method of acting; and ultimately to Seattle where she settled into the theater community and wrote her first play, *Splittin' Hairs* (1982). Her early love for Louisiana's natural beauties and resources no doubt sensitized her to the forces threatening a larger world. Combining her developing artistic sensibility and her environmental concerns, she became active in Performing Artists for Nuclear Disarmament (PAND) while in New York, and she subsequently began a chapter in Seattle. Events closer to home like Hurricane Katrina and the 2010 Gulf of Mexico oil spill later elicited passionate responses from Wells. "The Louisiana brown pelicans and other wildlife have a soul that is no less radiant than our own," she wrote in a blog post, "but corporations have no soul." This Louisiana daughter continues to mourn the vanishing coastline and polluted waters of her native state.[5]

Clearly, like many writers whose emotional and psychological roots remain in the place of their birth—William Faulkner, Ernest Gaines, and Eudora Welty, for example—Rebecca Wells had to first venture far beyond her "landscape of the heart," as writer Elizabeth Spencer called it. From the vantage point of the expatriate, she began to create her fictional Louisiana worlds and offer her own cultural critique of what scholars of Louisiana literature Dorothy Brown and Barbara Ewell call "Louisiana's peculiar brand of southernness."[6]

With her two plays written and produced in the 1980s, *Splittin' Hairs* and *Gloria Duplex* (1987), Wells launched a theatrical career and staked out the terrain of her future fiction. *Splittin' Hairs*, a one-woman show written and acted by the author, is a multivoiced performance about its heroine, Loretta Endless, a character who later appears as the title character in the author's 2009 novel *The Crowning Glory of Calla Lily Ponder*. Readers follow Loretta from twelve-year-old girl to older woman hairdresser and antinuclear activist holding court in her South Louisiana hair salon. In the course of the play, Wells takes on the body language and dialect of characters as diverse as Bubba, a redneck sheriff; Erline, a liberated antiracist; and L. T., a shy black child who wants to skate in Erline's rink. At this early point in her career, the author was trying out different voices before she settled into novel writing and more fleshed-out scenarios. These southern stereotypes constitute a wholesale mythologizing—or in this case, demythologizing—of the South, reaching back to the plantation novels of the nineteenth century and continuing with Margaret Mitchell's 1935 novel *Gone With the Wind*, which plays a cameo role in Wells's *Divine Secrets of the Ya-Ya Sisterhood*. Several years after *Splittin' Hairs*, the popular novel *Fried Green Tomatoes*, by Fanny Flagg, and the play *Steel Magnolias*, by Louisiana native Robert Harling, added new voices to this chorus of southern characters, particularly women, appearing in popular and commercially viable genres.

Rebecca Wells is a performer who continues to give dramatic readings from her books and who firmly believes that acting and writing inform each other.[7] She often explains this embodied approach to writing, and the performative ethos that defines her fiction: "I . . . come to writing as a professional actress whose body has been trained to listen and smell and inhabit characters without judgment. When I write, I usually *see* the scenes in my head."[8] Rebecca Wells's plays were crucial building blocks for her fiction, her scenic imagination a match for the color and tragicomic opera of her Louisiana settings. Her 1987 play *Gloria Duplex: An Erotic Worship Service for Theater* debuted in Seattle and was performed in Louisiana at her alma mater, LSU, by Swine Palace in 1998. The play's New Orleans setting and stripper heroine, Gloria Tom Duplex, mine the urban rather than the rural ,ut contain Wells's trademark irreverence and the easy blending of sacred and secular that appears in all of her works. Gloria has a vision of God in the mirrored chandelier of the Kitten Paradise Temple and Lounge, and her journey to self-respect and acceptance, played out against the background music of gospel, New Orleans blues, and Cajun zydeco, lays the groundwork for Wells's future novels. Both of these early heroines—Loretta and Gloria—are performers in their respective arenas, artists if you will. Both, like their creator Wells, are prototypes of the larger-than-life Ya-Yas, whose local acts of rebellion mask deeper female yearnings and desires.

The *novelist* Rebecca Wells was born from a fortunate fall, which resulted in a broken foot, while she was dancing in one of her plays in Seattle. Forced to sit still, she faced her computer and began to write what would become her first novel, *Little Altars Everywhere* (1992), which won the Western States Book Award for the most promising new novel to come from a western writer. (The book was first published by a small Seattle press, Broken Moon, before being picked up by Harper-Collins.) Though it has been upstaged and obscured by its ostensibly more lighthearted and family-friendly successor, *Divine Secrets of the Ya-Ya Sisterhood*, Wells's first novel yields far more grist for the literary mill. Smart, heartbreaking, often funny, and more nuanced than the later book, *Little Altars* wrestles with Louisiana's geographic and psychic split and reveals the sources of the Walker family's troubled dynamic. It introduces readers to the Walkers; to Vivi and her three friends from childhood who constitute the Ya-Ya sisterhood; to the midcentury Catholic milieu of central Louisiana; and to the black characters who work for the Walkers and provide the counternarrative to the white family's dysfunction.

Because of the phenomenal meteoric success of *Divine Secrets* in 1996, most readers came to know the author through this later book. To judge from the postings on Amazon.com, when readers realized there was an earlier novel, they of course flocked to it. But they were shocked at what *Little Altars* revealed: Vivi's psychological and physical abuse of her children that explained their behavior and neuroses in the later books.[9] It is a story many women readers and

Ya-Ya fans have chosen to ignore, focusing instead on the sisterhood of these hard-drinking, card-playing refugees from the Girl Scouts who are only a small part of the story Rebecca Wells relates. In many ways, *Little Altars* serves as a template for its more popular sister, *Divine Secrets*, and astute readers see that it provides the essential subtext of the later, more popular book. It seemed to answer the questions many readers must have had: What were the roots of this family's pain and neuroses? Why did Sidda feel she had to leave home? And what in the earlier generation of women she belonged to produced the flamboyant and outrageous Vivi, whose performances hid so much past suffering?

Readers and interviewers inevitably ask Wells about the link between her fictional world and her life. So richly and fully imagined are the community of Thornton, Louisiana, and all its characters that readers and critics are tempted to draw autobiographical parallels. Wells is adamant, however, that this is fiction, not memoir. She insists that her work is the product of her own imagination "dancing a kind of psycho-spiritual tango with [her] own history."[10] But readers often resist such protests from authors, wanting the authenticity of lived experience and looking for it in the places where writers set their fiction. Fans of Ernest Gaines's *The Autobiography of Miss Jane Pittman*, for example, wanted to know who Miss Jane's ancestors were in the Louisiana parish of the book's setting. Editors at *Newsweek* asked for a picture of Miss Jane.[11] Perhaps Gaines unwittingly encourages this blurring of worlds through the intensely personal comments he makes about leaving Louisiana in fact but never in spirit. In one of his essays, "Bloodline in Ink," Gaines remembers the day he left Louisiana for California, headed west as Wells would do several decades later. He recalls seeing the faces of "my people, the past. . . what they would never be able to put into words."[12] His Faulknerian, writerly compulsion to "tell about the South" thus emerged from his desire to give voice to those who had none. Hence, it is not surprising that readers of a novel like *Miss Jane* would look for her real-life prototype in the southern Louisiana that Gaines sought to document. Gaines eventually came back to Louisiana, where he now lives on land near the plantation where he grew up, unlike Wells who has made her home in Seattle, in the Pacific Northwest—half a country away from her birthplace.

A similar controversy over the uses of history occurred in the critical reception of Kathryn Stockett's *The Help*. Now living in New York, worlds away from her native Jackson, Mississippi, the author protests that her work is fiction, but the nanny who works for Stockett's brother filed a lawsuit claiming that one of the novel's main characters is based on her. Though Stockett maintains the book is an homage to her family maid, Demetrie, she named her character Aibileen, echoing the name of Ablene Cooper, the litigant. The tenuous line between fact and fiction, how self-aware writers are about the fictional worlds they create—these issues provide a context for reading Rebecca Wells, who mines the landscape of her childhood and early adulthood in similarly provocative ways.

Shortly after *Divine Secrets* appeared, groups of Ya-Yas made pilgrimages to the crossroads town of Alexandria, Louisiana, to immerse themselves in the prototype of Wells's fictional Thornton, Louisiana. In one of the online postings discussing such a pilgrimage, the author cautions her fans about their upcoming trip in a gently worded cyber-drawl: "I know y'all all understand that my books are fiction, not autobiography. And while I certainly use the locale, food, music, scents, and dialect SHAMELESSLY in my work, Alexandria isn't Thornton, and my family isn't the Walker clan. I love my family and the community, which raised me, and I feel very tenderly toward them and also somewhat *protective* of them. But I also know that y'all are sisters of my heart and will respect their private lives."[13]

Wells remains fiercely protective of her central Louisiana world and continues to draw the boundaries between fact and fiction. But in her blogs, she moves easily between the fictional and the real, blurring the boundaries, often making statements like "Do you know what today is? It's Sidda's and Connor's wedding anniversary" or "I agree with my characters that October is the best month in Louisiana, bar none."[14] Perhaps these slippages testify to how this fictional world resonates with her, but they may also encourage her readers to cross the boundaries Wells has tried to maintain.

Little Altars Everywhere introduces the cast of characters who would become familiar to fans of Rebecca Wells's subsequent novels. Chief among them is Viviane Abbott Walker, Siddalee's mother, who deflates the idealized motherhood image over and over through her destructive drinking and her physical abuse of her children. Vivi also rails at having been born too early and thus being a woman "before you could do what you wanted."[15] And Vivi imposes the constraints she felt in her own life on her impressionable daughter Sidda, teaching her how to be popular and less bookish. Vivi is a good-looking, fashion-conscious woman who takes care of herself, plays tennis to stay fit, and slathers her face with cold cream at night to preserve it. Vivi fights time and gravity at every turn. Like another fictional Louisiana wife and mother, Edna Pontellier in Kate Chopin's *The Awakening*, Vivi is an erratic mother, in her own words "uneven," who often views her children as antagonists.[16] In this multivoiced narrative, we view Vivi Walker through her own eyes as well as the eyes of her adult children. Fun-loving, singing, dancing, outrageous, rule-breaking mother that she is, adored by her daughter Sidda, Vivi is also a bitter, angry woman whose narrative tells us she had four children in three and a half years and faced all family crises alone while her husband, Shep, fled to the duck camp. Ultimately Wells's novel evokes not just midcentury southern Louisiana but a whole era in which women's lives were scripted and controlled, and gender roles rigid. As argued recently by Trysh Travis in *American Literary History*, "The scenes of Vivi's married life explore the social causes behind the middle-class female malaise that Betty Friedan's *Feminine Mystique* called 'the problem that has no name.'"[17] Many women of Vivi's generation, Friedan argues, led lives of quiet desperation.

Frustrated, lacking creative outlets for their considerable talents, these women often turned inward and repressed a host of what were deemed improper feelings. While the women in Friedan's study had roots in New England or New York, Wells's character Vivi echoes their frustrations, exacerbated by her central Louisiana, Catholic milieu. Rebecca Wells was ten years old in 1963, the year *The Feminine Mystique* was published, a generation removed from the anxieties of her character Vivi. If she fails to show us the legacy of Friedan's book in Vivi's life, as Trysh Travis points out, Wells herself has obviously found the creative outlet Friedan's repressed suburban wives and mothers only yearned for.[18]

In a *Seattle Times* review of *Little Altars*, author Mary Ann Gwinn quotes Wells on the stratified southern society of her childhood. She recalls her high school years in the late 1960s and early 1970s, when "the hierarchy of high school was so ugly, especially for a woman growing up. In the South, you were initiated into the cult of popularity at a very young age. At the altar of popularity, it was not unheard of to sacrifice any part of yourself—your intelligence, your hair."[19] This cult mentality Wells identifies certainly is not specific to the region or time, but it does explain both her title for this first novel as well as the sacrifices she dramatizes in the lives of young girls. Paradoxically, Vivi Walker both subverts the southern belle image and reinforces it in the advice she gives her daughter: be popular, she says, but do not tell anyone you know how to cook. In an interesting regional twist, Wells has Vivi's husband, Shep, teach Vivi to cook, thus reinforcing the long-standing Louisiana tradition of men cooking, a skill they perfect in the all-male communities of fishing and hunting camps.

Besides these gender issues, religious pressures also surface in Wells's first novel. She complicates the preadolescent world of Siddalee Walker by having her parents be of different religions, with Vivi a Catholic and Shep a Baptist, thus making Sidda the child of what the nuns ominously call "a mixed marriage." This unholy yoking of husband and wife across the religious divide further stratifies Sidda's and Vivi's worlds and constitutes Rebecca Wells's pointed but often humorous critique of her own childhood religion. The religious difference between Sidda's parents mirrors Louisiana's own religious schism, with northern Louisiana primarily Protestant and abstemious and South Louisiana overwhelmingly Catholic and indulgent. Sidda, as the child of such disparate parents, inevitably feels conflicted in the town of Thornton, poised at the crossroads between north and south, Protestant and Catholic. Wells linked societal expectations for women with religious ones during this time, when she commented in a 2005 interview on the Ya-Yas' alcoholic tendencies: "The Ya-Yas do like their drink. They are women whose environment did all it could to trim back their spirits. They grew up when women were expected to get married, have kids, stay home and be a housewife, period. The Catholic Church expected them to be pure as the driven snow. Alcohol was the natural and, for the most part, socially acceptable way for these vital women to try to anesthetize their pain and frustration."[20] But Wells's attitude toward Catholicism is not so uncomplicated. In a 2006 interview she invokes one of her favorite writers, Flannery O'Connor, whose own blending of the fleshly and spiritual, the humorous and the deadly serious, she admires: "While I do not share her [O'Connor's] strict adherence to Catholicism, my life has been forever touched by the Catholicism of the first 18 years of my life, and I consider Catholicism to be not just a religion, but a culture."[21] *Little Altars Everywhere* evokes this Catholic school culture of midcentury America with its list of forbidden movies ("the Index"), money collected for pagan babies, saints' names chosen for the sacramental rituals of Holy Communion and Confirmation, and female saints' lives used as models of chastity and rectitude. The novel links the sacrificial, self-denying model for motherhood with the same sacrificial imperative imposed on the lives of Catholic schoolgirls. In the process, Wells paves the way for her later novels and their reimagining of the primary role model for Catholic womanhood, the Virgin Mary.

Beyond the social and religious stratification in this central Louisiana world lies the deep racial divide that marks black and white life in the South. Wells attempts in *Little Altars* a contrast between the Walker children's narratives and obsessive personal history, and the two voices of Willetta and Chaney, the black couple who work for the Walkers. They provide the validating narrative of the novel, with Willetta serving as surrogate mother to Vivi's children, shielding them from her anger, and Chaney acting as self-appointed family historian, documenting in stories and photographs, alongside those of his own family, the lives and histories of the Walkers.[22] These chapters in some ways reinforce Toni Morrison's argument in *Playing in the Dark: Whiteness and the Literary Imagination* that readers—and writers—must recognize the racial subtext, the parallel histories of black and white Americans, in white-authored texts.[23] But in other ways the reader recognizes that Chaney is really telling only the white story, appropriating their photographs, seeing his identity through theirs. His version of the Walker story corrects, revises, and ultimately deconstructs the white narrative as he sees Vivi's husband powerless at his father's death, in debt, with the only family wisdom passed on to him being "smoking and drinkin and how to sign a check."[24] Reinforcing this erasure of the black characters in Wells's text, Willetta relates Vivi's response to her when she tried to rescue the children from a beating: "She look at me all blankface like I be a stranger. Look at me like we hadn't been in that house together six days a week for ten—goin on eleven years . . . She look at me like I'm a nigger offa the street and she say: Willetta, you are a maid in this house. You are not a confessor, you are not a friend. You are a *maid*. Do not ever give me advice about how to handle my life again as long as you live. Do I make myself clear?"[25]

"It will take the rest of my life to even begin to unravel my complex relationship to black people," the author writes in a blog post shortly after Barack Obama's inauguration.[26] Certainly a whole body of works in the last few years—critical studies, memoirs, and oral histories—has testified to the truth of Wells's statement. Some works coming in the wake of Kathryn Stockett's *The Help*, such as *The Maid Narratives* and *Cooking in Other Women's Kitchens: Domestic Workers in the South, 1865–1960*, let the help speak for themselves.[27] I would argue that Rebecca Wells's novels, beginning with *Little Altars Everywhere*, attempt to untangle the web of race relations in the South and elucidate the power dynamic at work beneath the surface in segregated southern culture. But her novels also illustrate how difficult it is for the southern writer to tell these stories, to work outside the historical blinders of history, region, and internalized racism. She acknowledges these barriers: "I grew up in the apartheid of the Deep South. Where a black man could be beat[en] for meeting the eyes of a white man. I watched as my black 'father' [the man who worked the farm beside Well's biological father] averted his eyes as he talked to the 'boss man,' which is what he called my father. As a child, it was confusing. As an adolescent it was horrifying to realize, and as an adult it was unacceptable."[28]

Like many southern writers of her era, Wells reconstructs with some nostalgia and righteous anger what she witnessed as a child and shows a sensitivity to the racial conflicts at work in her own life and her novels. Wells identifies Ernest Gaines as an inspiration for her own fictive and real battles with race. Citing Gaines's *A Gathering of Old Men* as one of her favorite books, she identifies this novel as "one of the books that set me on the road to doing my best to confront the racism I grew up under."[29]

In unpublished notes titled "Growing Up Racist," which I was allowed to use for this essay, Wells reminisces about her early years in Alexandria in the 1960s at the height of civil rights and integration efforts across the South. In a telling metaphor of the lines being drawn during these years, she remembers the hedge planted between her house and those of the black workers. She remembers black children waiting across the road for their school bus, "openly defying [her] parents about racism" during her high school years, gradually becoming aware of the inequities around her. Moving away from Louisiana gave her some objectivity on these formative years, but the images she holds dear echo those appearing on the covers of books like *The Maid Narratives*: "grainy black and white photographs taken with my mother's Brownie camera of [the nurse Malinda] holding me in front of our first house."[30] These images could come from the album of any number of white children raised in a certain era of southern history, my own included. Admittedly, there is racial romanticizing at work here, a tapping in to a vast reservoir of internalized southern myths, perhaps a failure of this southern writer and others to imagine an equal relationship between black and white women, as critics like Tara McPherson notes. In *Reconstructing Dixie: Race, Gender, and Nostalgia in the Imagined South*, McPherson argues that "this desire [the desire for racial union] gets tripped up by the inability to imagine a connection that moves beyond the contours of white desire and emotion."[31] So instead of the parallel narratives Toni Morrison articulates, we have white narratives supported by black subtext. But there is also an attempt on Rebecca Wells's part—both in her personal reminiscences and her public fiction—to come to terms with the latent racism she compares to the "pesticides that I breathed in from the crop dusters that flew above my father's cotton fields."[32] And she would continue to revisit these decades and earlier ones in succeeding novels that represent central Louisiana's story within a larger cultural and historical narrative.

Four years after *Little Altars Everywhere*, Wells's blockbuster novel *Divine Secrets of the Ya-Ya Sisterhood* appeared, published by Harper-Collins. The novel enjoyed a respectable sales record in hardback, but its paperback edition a year later, in 1997, witnessed phenomenal sales, selling eighteen thousand copies in the first three months. What had happened in the year's interim? Malcolm Gladwell's book *The Tipping Point* points to the power of book club culture as a major factor.[33] Women's reading groups read, discussed, and passed the book on to sisters, mothers, daughters, and friends. Eventually communities of Ya-Yas emerged all over the country and even in England and Ireland. While earlier generations of women met to quilt or sew and in the process built strong female communities, modern women read and share books, often joining book clubs that sustain not only themselves but also the reputation and popularity of what they read. *Divine Secrets* quickly rose to the number one position on the *New York Times* best-seller list and stayed there for more than a year. It was made into a Hollywood film in 2002, which brought groups of women in tiaras and boas to theaters. The Ya-Ya frenzy inevitably made its way onto the Internet, creating a powerful cyber-sisterhood that replicated itself across the country.[34] The groundswell surprised and delighted the author and her publisher. Wells remembers coming to terms with the phenomenon: "I started noticing mothers and daughters coming. The daughters would be in their late thirties, early forties. The mothers were of the generation who went to high school during World War Two. Then I noticed that there started to be three generations coming, twentysomethings as well. And then to my total delight . . . there would be teenagers and fifth graders."[35]

The peculiar chemistry between book and audience that makes a best seller, coupled with today's powerful media outlets and the sheer force of Wells's personality as she gave readings on her book tours—all no doubt contributed to the book's success. But the author herself has identified the hunger for sisterhood and community as the driving force behind the book's rise to prominence. *Divine Secrets* capitalizes on and reinforces the somewhat muted sisterhood theme of the earlier *Little Altars Everywhere* with its focus on heroine Siddalee and her siblings. The author remembers wanting to write another book after *Little Altars*, going back to it, and reading the paragraph where Siddalee mentioned her mother's group of girlfriends called the Ya-Yas, who got arrested for something they did in high school. Wells's curiosity and her readers' meshed, and *Divine Secrets* was born.[36]

Again the question of autobiography surfaces. Readers encounter this group of women, childhood friends of differing personalities and family dynamics, who shared a common history of being born in the same era, being Catholic, and even being pregnant at the same time. If these characters are not modeled on actual women, the nostalgia for the kind of friendship they have is a familiar theme in Wells's interviews. She reflects on Sidda's generation and how different it was from her mother's: "Sidda (like most of her contemporaries) works outside the home. . . . But oh, how she longs for those long, lazy days her mother spent on the side porch with Caro and Teensy and Necie in that thick, humid Louisiana girl soup, sharing dreams and fears and hopes and fantasies. Those lazy days before air-conditioning locked the windows and closed up the porches."[37] When asked about the prototypes for the Ya-Yas, Wells admits to knowing people like them, but she insists they are not "factually real. They are an amalgam of memory, research, and imagination. Vivi is not my mother. Vivi is Sidda's mother. I am Rebecca; Sidda is Sidda." She admits that readers and fans often confuse these distinctions and fail to realize that her works, while they contain elements of her life, are "imagined" and thus contain only "emotional truth, not factual truth."[38]

Wells creates in this novel a heroine who, despite Wells's protests against autobiography in her fiction, mirrors the author's career path. She also voices through Sidda the mantra of forgiveness that has become one the author herself articulates as necessary given our fallible human nature. Sidda, now forty years old, is a successful director whose play about mothers and daughters, *Women on the Cusp*, has debuted to glowing reviews. She is estranged from Vivi because a *New York Times* interviewer calls her mother "a tap dancing child abuser."[39] Wells reaches back further here into Vivi's relationship with her fanatically Catholic mother, her absent father, the models for womanhood available in the 1930s, Vivi's flight from family and children, and her eventual incarceration for a period in a sanitarium. The ultimate theme is forgiveness, as expressed in the epigraph to the novel by Catholic theologian Henri Nouwen: "Forgiveness is the name of love practiced among people who love poorly. The hard truth is that all of us love poorly. We need to forgive and be forgiven every day, every hour—unceasingly. That is the great work of love among the fellowship of the weak that is the human family."[40] This redemptive and forgiving theme surfaces through the sisterhood of the Ya-Yas, who step in as surrogate mothers to Vivi's family when she beats her children in a drunken fit. In an episode that again channels Kate Chopin's heroine Edna Pontellier, Vivi confesses in her journal: "I walked for hours, and did not miss my children for a moment."[41]

Rebecca Wells dramatizes the religious forces that shaped women's identities during a particular historical moment, emphasizing the institutional lapses more than the maternal ones. She portrays a Catholic Church less than forgiving of Vivi's motherly weaknesses. The priest-confessor to whom Vivi runs admonishes her to repent of her sins and pray, to follow the lesson of the Blessed

Virgin Mary in bearing her cross silently and patiently. Vivi prays for a more humanized, fleshly Virgin Mary, one who shows the marks of her motherhood in an embodied way and connects to the very real demands of contemporary women. This subject is not unique to Rebecca Wells or her fiction. Feminist scholars such as Marina Warner in her book *Alone of All Her Sex: The Myth and the Cult of the Virgin Mary* articulate the same idea when they examine the Virgin as an index to western attitudes toward women.[42] Good Catholic daughter that she was, Wells identifies the dilemma for modern women and, in so doing, explains her own gradual shift to a female divinity more all-encompassing, tapping into the goddess discourse of the late twentieth century. Sacred and secular blend as Wells's sequence of novels progresses. The Virgin Mary becomes the Moon Lady of her 2009 novel, *The Crowning Glory of Calla Lily Ponder*, and in this book New Orleans rhythm and blues artist Aaron Neville sings "Ave Maria" as Sidda compares her own very earthly mother to the Virgin Mary: "My mother is not the Holy Lady, she thought. My mother's love is not perfect. My mother's love is good enough. . . . Maybe I am good enough."[43] Ultimately, the author expands and humanizes the sacred maternal images she and her characters find lacking.

Rebecca Wells finds the idea of sisterhood or women's communities a necessary antidote to our depersonalized, isolated postmodern condition. Certainly not new, the idea of women's communities reaches back into nineteenth-century culture and literature, as Kathryn Lee Seidel argues in *The History of Southern Women's Literature* (2002). Though Seidel's "Myths of Southern Womanhood in Contemporary Literature" does not include Rebecca Wells, Wells's literary and social communities, forged in bookstores, book clubs, and online groups, are clearly contemporary versions of the earlier sisterhoods Seidel identifies. She points out that during the nineteenth century "women begin to form friendships with other women, who are of great significance in their lives, and who in many ways provide the solace and nurturing that their husbands do not."[44] And the women's movement of the 1960s and thereafter emphasized the idea of female solidarity in the political sense as well as the personal, and thus fully connected women's power in the public arena to their enabling relationships in the private one. Wells herself continues the theme of female bonding when she talks about the writing of *Divine Secrets*: "I didn't write the book because I had a group of friends like the Ya-Yas. I think I wrote it because I wanted one."[45] But despite the rich network of readers her novels have spawned, and despite the idealized notions of female friendship Wells creates, there are those who find the novels a bit too real. A friend of mine recently revealed that she had been given copies of Wells's novels at various times in her life but that she could not bring herself to read them. She went on to say that she knew women like Sidda and Vivi, and she understood the painful lives they had led. So the books are still on her shelf, unread.

In *Divine Secrets,* Wells foregrounds two texts about women's lives that appeared in the 1930s when Vivi was a teenager: Clare Boothe Luce's play *The Women* (1936) and Margaret Mitchell's *Gone with the Wind* (1935). She skillfully embeds them in her larger narrative as she shows how a daughter of another era revisits the popular culture of her mother's generation. Luce's play satirizes the shallow, vapid lives of Manhattan society matrons married to wealth and fashion. Mitchell's novel, of course, dramatizes another moment in women's social and cultural history, the Civil War, when national and regional events forever shaped the future of their lives. Sidda is directing a revival of *The Women,* and the scrapbook of her mother's life with the early Ya-Yas serves as period research for her. But this scrapbook also transports the daughter back to the scene of Vivi's train trip to Atlanta at the age of thirteen to see the premiere of the movie *Gone with the Wind.* This iconic 1936 novel and the 1939 David Selznick film continued the mythologizing of the South for a whole generation of girls and women and established a kind of fantasy text for impressionable girls like the young Vivi. "I want to live in this movie, Necie," Vivi writes to one of her Ya-Ya sisters. "This is the kind of drama I was born for," she continues.[46] The romance of Margaret Mitchell's novel and the eventual film did, in fact, overshadow Scarlett's poverty and dispossession, and this selective memory of readers and viewers perpetuated a romanticized version of the South for generations to come, not unlike the selective memory of Wells's readers who displace the novel *Divine Secrets of the Ya-Ya Sisterhood* with its more sanitized Hollywood film version.

The novel *Divine Secrets* observes the dynamics of racism in a small southern town, and the author re-creates this convincing racial subtext in Vivi's trip to Atlanta. The subtext here, as in Mitchell's novel, serves as a moral and historical corrective to idealized narratives. The train Vivi travels on is segregated, but she is accompanied by Ginger, a young black maid and traveling companion old enough to have her own family, which she has left back home. Wells juxtaposes Vivi's decidedly white middle-class southern girlhood with Ginger's very different coming-of-age experience when Vivi makes her way back to the "colored" car and sees Ginger smoking, drinking, and playing cards:

> "Ginger," I said, "you know a lady doesn't smoke and drink and chew gum with strangers."
>
> And Ginger looked at the others, and they all started to laugh like they were old friends.
>
> "Miz Vivi," she told me, "Old Ginger ain't got to worry about being no lady. That yo' problem, baby. That yo' problem."[47]

Besides articulating the differences in what constituted proper behavior for white and black women of certain social classes in the decades preceding the women's movement of the twentieth century, this scene also enacts the racial inequities dramatized in *Little Altars*, as Lori Robison argues. "The implication here," Robison continues, "is that Ginger's body has escaped some of the cultural control that the white Ya-Ya's face."[48] But, unlike the photograph Wells remembers from her childhood, the scene also shows the author's awareness that Vivi's identity is necessarily constructed against Ginger's. The segregated train car reifies the boundaries between black and white, between privileged white girlhood and presumably and paradoxically its freer black counterpart. Again Wells links region and race as she explores the forces shaping female identity in formative periods of American, and in this case southern, history. Through intertextual references to the film version of *Gone With the Wind* as spectacle, juxtaposed with Vivi's impassioned, dramatic diary notations, Wells invites her readers to consider the performative nature of race and gender, as these intersect with class.

Almost ten years elapsed between *Divine Secrets of the Ya-Ya Sisterhood* and its 2005 successor, *Ya-Yas in Bloom*. In the interval, after a long period of illness and misdiagnoses, Rebecca Wells was correctly diagnosed with Lyme disease, an illness that had ravaged her body and spirit and permanently altered the course of her life. She calls this time her "horizontal decade."[49] After a period of silence and isolation and a reluctance to reach out and "confess" her weakness and vulnerability, Wells began to talk about her battle with the disease, and about the creative power of suffering, a subject inspiring the last years of her beloved Flannery O'Connor. She has revealed that two feminine images sustained her through it all: a picture of Our Lady of Guadalupe, the Mexican embodiment of the Virgin, and a picture of Flannery O'Connor after she was diagnosed with lupus, crutches in hand, standing on the steps of her Milledgeville, Georgia, home, "Andalusia."[50] Converting her own personal experience into social activism, Wells began to speak out about the horrors of Lyme disease and to call for research and a cure. She has been on the honorary board of the Lyme Disease Association and frequently posted updates and comments on a blog (lymeblog.com) to raise awareness of the disease and solicit personal stories of sufferers and survivors.[51]

The book Rebecca Wells was writing during this process of diagnosis and healing inevitably reflects a similar coming to terms with life in both Vivi, the mother, and Sidda, her now famous daughter. Using maternal metaphors to describe *Ya-Yas in Bloom*, Wells calls it a "miracle baby," a "victory of the imagination over my illness and fear."[52] The novel reaches back into the childhood of the four Ya-Yas and to the roots of their friendship. It also emphasizes more than the two previous books how Siddalee's career as a director emerged from her childhood experiences: her mother's theatricality, the Ya-Yas' singing, her own acting in family and amateur productions. More than any of her other novels, *Ya-Yas in Bloom* is Wells's portrait of the artist as a young woman. Celebrating life and family, forgiving and patient with human frailties, the novel, Wells says, was shaped by her bodily weakness and vulnerability in the face of a debilitating illness: "It's all a matter of what you train your eyes to see, and a willingness to embrace it all: the dark and the light. I try to write from this perspective."[53] The disease forced Rebecca Wells to temporarily withdraw from public life—book tours, readings, interviews—and concentrate on her physical health and well-being, a chapter in her life much like the earlier broken foot that launched her writing career.

Writing *Ya-Yas in Bloom* seems to have been both necessary and healing for its author, in keeping with the organic metaphor in its title. The novel is about growth and rootedness, from the family tree diagrams that grace the book's front pages to its sections: Sowing Sisterhood Seeds, Tending Young Buds, Bruised Plantings, A Bountiful Garden. But it is also about evolving spiritual vision—Wells's own and her character Vivi's—that includes a feminized deity capable of forgiving her imperfect human mothers and daughters. Vivi in particular learns to make peace with the warped Catholicism of her mother but not before she has wrestled the demons of her childhood and had a frank conversation with her friend Caro about religion and women's lives. Following an insulting conversation with a nun who accuses Vivi of being an unfit mother, she sideswipes the Infant Jesus of Prague statue in the parking lot (perhaps a Freudian swerve) and continues her musings about the image of divine maternity held up for all Catholic girls, the Virgin Mary. Vivi wants to reimagine and reinvent the Virgin and bring her down to the level of all-too-human, all-too-flawed motherhood. The real villain here seems to be Vivi's mother, Buggy, rather than the sacred mother, but the novel voices a reimagined Holy Lady—forgiving, strong, lighting the way for her daughters who are radiant, unstained, suffused with light. Wells explains Louisiana Catholics' worship of Mary and the material culture of this worship—statues in front yards, religious medals. She recognizes her own need, and other women's need, for what she calls "a female face of God," a "feminine deity."[54] This feminine deity in essence redeems and transforms her imperfect human daughters and mothers like Buggy, who, Caro says to Vivi, "fed you the Catholic Guilt Diet whole-hog. You were criticized for everything you did. There was no way you could accept that you were a lovely young girl, because your mother treated you like a *sinner*."[55] The novel revisits scenarios only hinted at in the earlier Yas-Yas books, correcting, revising, and filling in textual gaps. Wells evokes the country of childhood and the world of female identity as shaped by maternal forces both secular and spiritual, placing these in a Louisiana split between Catholic and Protestant, in a fictionalized town poised at the crossroads.

Rebecca Wells believes that creative expression can heal and save. Whether in the form of dancing, making music, acting, or writing, these acts throughout her novels transform and redirect her characters as they make their way through their troubled histories. The author witnessed this phenomenon in writing the latest installment of the Walker family saga and the secret history of the Ya-Yas. "Use everything in your life to create your art," says Wade, one of Sidda's theater friends from *Divine Secrets*.[56] This "everything" includes the pain and suffering as well as the love and support. At one point in her narrative, Sidda confesses her gratitude to Vivi for those moments of grace when she recognized her daughter's talents and publicly praised her: "That moment stays inside of all the other moments. . . . When I am up against the wall, when I am shaking with fear before a show opens . . . that memory of that moment stops me from hiding in the bathroom and throwing up. . . . It is one of the moments that is helping me stay (barely) glued together now that I'm working in increasingly high pressure settings. I wonder if Mama knows that. I wonder why I haven't told her."[57]

Wells departs from the Ya-Ya world in *The Crowning Glory of Calla Lily Ponder* (2009), but she creates the Ya-Yas' spiritual sister in the novel's title character. *Crowning Glory* tells the story of a hairdresser mother with healing hands and a dancing father with joy in his heart. The setting is split between the mythical, rural river town of La Luna, and New Orleans, a city with its own mythologies. Calla loses her mother early in the book but only after she learns from her the power to heal pain and suffering through the primary tools of the hairdresser's trade, her hands. Following the path her mother has inspired, Calla moves to New Orleans, becomes a hairdresser, falls in love with an oil rig worker who dies in an accident caused by negligence and corporate greed, moves back home to La Luna, and is eventually reunited with her first love after his wife dies. Presiding over all of these events is the Moon Lady, the female deity whose italicized monologues bookend the narrative. This brief summary fails to convey the rich sensory details, many of them about food, that bring both rural and urban Louisiana to life: the scent of red beans and rice; the raucous noise of Mardi Gras in New Orleans, the crowd moving "like one giant body of music"; and the pig roast, *cochon de lait*, that ends the book, celebrating the life and death of a town character, the smells of roasting pork almost enough to drown out the sorrow at his death. No doubt remembering these cultural signifiers was itself healing for Wells, as she wrote from her Pacific Northwest home and revisited the scenes that shaped her own destiny as a woman and a writer. In a 2010 interview, she discusses the healing power of food and music—both such communal aspects of her home state. She mentions her cousin's famous New Orleans restaurant, Upperline, and how it became a haven for post-Katrina refugees. She reveals that she loves to cook gumbo, red beans and rice, and crawfish étouffée.[58] Clearly, Wells blends all of these elements in her writing, filling her early novels with the sights and sounds of a Louisiana childhood and carrying us into a contemporary world of polluted water and corporate greed.

In the female space of a beauty parlor, fictional territory well trodden by writers as diverse as Eudora Welty and *Steel Magnolias* playwright Robert Harling, Wells takes us back to her early play *Splittin' Hairs*, the genesis of *Crown-*

ing Glory. She wrote *Crowning Glory* shortly before the tragedy of the Gulf of Mexico oil spill unraveled, and her environmental conscience and her anticorporate ethos infiltrate its narrative in appropriate places, beginning with the Moon Lady's opening words as she looks out over Louisiana and the Mississippi River: "That wide, robust river carries life and dreams of commerce and poisons out into the Gulf of Mexico. There I watch the Louisiana coast recede, losing a football-field piece of land every twenty minutes."[59] *The Crowning Glory of Calla Lily Ponder* thus moves beyond Wells's earlier vision to focus as much on the natural world as setting for, and victim of, human frailties, as it does on the web of family and regional ties that both nurture and inhibit. And there is a kind of redemption as, near the end of the book, Calla invests oil company "wrongful death" settlement money in the reincarnation of her mother's beauty salon. Ultimately the Mississippi, that mother of rivers, and that mythical female moon that waxes and wanes with the seasons and tides, emerge as characters in this narrative alongside the people of La Luna and New Orleans.

With such richly imagined and evocative books behind her, one can only speculate about Wells's future creative efforts. She is evasive about where her next book will take us. Maybe it will feature a whole new cast of characters, maybe a return to the Ya-Ya world that made her reputation and served as such a fertile source of characters and stories. Whatever comes next, readers and critics can look back on a strong body of work. Wells has done what many good writers do: begin with the regional and make it speak to and for a larger humanity.

Perhaps it is no accident that all of Rebecca Wells's novels end with a celebration—a baptism, a wedding, a family Christmas pageant. Ultimately, her books are about the power of personal and familial redemption, forgiveness, and love. In true South Louisiana fashion, she finds something to sing and dance about in life, in what the Moon Lady calls "the beating heart of Louisiana, in the lovely soul of the world."[60]

NOTES

1. Rebecca Wells, *Ya-Yas in Bloom* (New York: Harper-Collins, 2005), 247.

2. Ibid., 338.

3. "Rebecca Wells," *Author Interviews*, April 2005, http://writerinterviews.blogspot.com/2013/01/rebecca-wells.html (accessed August 29, 2012).

4. Rebecca Wells, interview by author, Lafayette, Louisiana, August 7, 2011.

5. Rebecca Wells, "Sheep, Oil and Outrage," *Goodreads*, http://www.goodreads.com/author/show/Rebecca_Wells/blog, (accessed June 21, 2010; page discontinued); see also Rebecca Wells interview.

6. Dorothy Brown and Barbara Ewell, eds., *Louisiana Women Writers: New Essays and a Comprehensive Bibliography* (Baton Rouge: Louisiana State University Press, 1992), 3.

7. See, for example, Rebecca Wells interview, May 5, 2010, http://www.blogtalkradio.com/book-club-girl/2010/05/05/rebecca-wells-discusses-the-crowning-glory-of-call (accessed November 18, 2012).

8. "Rebecca Wells," *Author Interviews*.

9. Some Amazon.com postings on *Little Altars Everywhere*: "I wish I had read this before its sequel" (July 17, 2000); "I read 'The Divine Secrets of the Ya-Ya Sisterhood' a couple of years ago and

fell in love with it. When I found out there was a book that came before . . . I had to read it" (June 3, 2002); "Luckily I read the DEVINE SECRETS OF THE YA-YA SISTERHOOD [*sic*] first and loved it so bought LITTLE ALTARS EVERYWHERE. . . . What a let down" (October 25, 2010).

10. "Rebecca Wells," KnowSouthernHistory.net, http://www.knowsouthernhistory.net/Culture/Literature/rebecca_wells.htm (accessed September 8, 2012).

11. Ernest Gaines, "Miss Jane and I," in *Mozart and Leadbelly: Stories and Essays*, ed. Marcia Gaudet and Reggie Young (New York: Knopf, 2005), 3–23.

12. Ernest Gaines, "Bloodline in Ink," in *Mozart and Leadbelly*, 41.

13. Quoted in "Rebecca Wells," *Twenty-First-Century American Novelists: Dictionary of Literary Biography*, vol. 292 (Farmington Hills, Mich.: Gale, 2004), 323.

14. "LymeBlog News: Rebecca's October Update," *LymeBlog News*, http://lymeblog.com/modules.php?name=News&file=article&sid=212, October 24, 2005 (accessed August 25, 2012).

15. Rebecca Wells, *Little Altars Everywhere* (New York: Harper Perennial, 1992), 198.

16. Kate Chopin, *The Awakening and Other Writings* (Peterborough, Ontario: Broadview Press, 2011), 164.

17. Trysh Travis, "Divine Secrets of the Cultural Studies Sisterhood: Women Reading Rebecca Wells," *American Literary History* 15, no. 1 (2003): 149.

18. Ibid., 150.

19. Mary Ann Gwinn, "One-Woman Show—Rebecca Wells Is Still in Control after All These Years," *Seattle Times*, January 17, 1993.

20. "Rebecca Wells," *Author Interviews*.

21. Rebecca Wells, "Meet the Writers: Rebecca Wells," interview with Mike Segretto, http://www.barnesand noble.com/writers/ writerdetails.asp?cid=968092 (accessed September 8, 2012).

22. Mary Ann Wilson, "Living on the Edge in Rebecca Wells' *Little Altars Everywhere*," in *Songs of the New South: Writing Contemporary Louisiana*, ed. Suzanna Disheroon Green and Lisa Abney (Westport, Conn.: Greenwood Press, 2001), 8.

23. Toni Morrison, *Playing in the Dark: Whiteness and the Literary Imagination* (New York: Vintage, 1993), 6, 16.

24. Wells, *Little Altars Everywhere*, 188.

25. Ibid., 138.

26. Rebecca Wells, "Inauguration 'Stars and Colors,'" Ya-Ya.com/news/news_items, January 20, 2008 (accessed May 15, 2014; site discontinued).

27. Katherine van Wormer, David W. Jackson III, and Charletta Sudduth, *The Maid Narratives: Black Domestics and White Families in the Jim Crow South* (Baton Rouge: Louisiana State University Press, 2012); Rebecca Sharpless, *Cooking in Other Women's Kitchens: Domestic Workers in the South, 1865–1960* (Chapel Hill: University of North Carolina Press, 2010).

28. Wells, "Inauguration 'Stars and Colors.'"

29. Wells, "Meet the Writers."

30. Rebecca Wells, "Growing Up Racist," unpublished notes, 2014, provided to the author by Wells, as noted in text.

31. Tara McPherson, *Reconstructing Dixie: Race, Gender, and Nostalgia in the Imagined South* (Durham: Duke University Press, 2003), 80.

32. Wells, "Growing Up Racist."

33. Malcolm Gladwell, *The Tipping Point: How Little Things Can Make a Big Difference* (New York: Back Bay Books, 2002).

34. Sarah Van Boven, "Getting Their Ya-Yas Out," *Newsweek*, July 6, 1998, 71.

35. Quoted in Gladwell, *The Tipping Point*, 171.

36. Bruce Barcott, "The Divine Ascension of Rebecca Wells," *Seattle Weekly*, July 29, 1998.

37. Wells, "Ga Ga for Ya Yas."

38. Wells, "Ya-Yas in Bloom."

39. Rebecca Wells, *Divine Secrets of the Ya-Ya Sisterhood* (New York: Harper Collins, 1996), 1.

40. Ibid., epigraph, n.p.

41. Ibid., 277.

42. Marina Warner, *Alone of All Her Sex: The Myth and the Cult of the Virgin Mary* (New York: Vintage/Random House, 1983), xxv.

43. Wells, *Divine Secrets*, 327.

44. Kathryn Lee Seidel, "Myths of Southern Womanhood in Contemporary Literature," in *The History of Southern Women's Literature*, ed. Carolyn Perry and Mary Louise Weaks (Baton Rouge: LSU Press, 2002), 431. Seidel's essay includes such southern women writers as Gail Godwin, Kaye Gibbons, and Dorothy Allison.

45. Van Boven, "Getting Their Ya-Yas Out," 71.

46. Wells, *Divine Secrets*, 112.

47. Ibid., 109.

48. Lori Robison, "Bodies, Southern Nostalgia, and the Construction of Whiteness in *Divine Secrets of the Ya Ya Sisterhood*," *Journal of Popular Culture* 42, no. 6 (2009): 1126.

49. Wells interview by author.

50. Ibid.

51. Rebecca Wells, "A Personal Letter about Lyme Disease," March 28, 2005 http://ya-ya.com/news/ (accessed November 18, 2012; site discontinued).

52. Ibid.

53. "Rebecca Wells," *Author Interviews*.

54. Rebecca Wells, "'Crowning Glory': A Story of Healing Beauty,'" interview, NPR, August 9, 2009, http://www.npr.org/ (accessed September 8, 2012).

55. Wells, *Ya-Yas in Bloom*, 117.

56. Wells, *Divine Secrets*, 182.

57. Wells, *Ya-Yas in Bloom*, 59.

58. Rebecca Wells, interview, May 5, 2010, http://www.blogtalkradio.com/book-club-girl/2010/05/05/rebecca-wells-discusses-the-crowning-glory-of-call (accessed November 18, 2012).

59. Rebecca Wells, *The Crowning Glory of Calla Lily Ponder* (New York: Harper-Collins, 2009), xii.

60. Ibid., 391.

PART FOUR

Organizing Women

Phoebe Bryant Hunter

(1760–1844)

Neither Northern nor Southern

MARK J. DUVALL

What a "strikingly ugly and wretched city to experience," exclaimed Mary Anne Hunter when she arrived with her respectable family in New Orleans from Philadelphia in 1815.[1] Like many northern families from New York, Boston, and Philadelphia, the Hunters moved to New Orleans following Louisiana's incorporation into the United States. Mary Anne's mother, Phoebe Bryant Hunter, was particularly appalled at the sight of the many destitute orphan girls roaming the streets in the family's newly adopted city. Within two years, however, Phoebe Hunter made contacts with other reform-minded women, as well as local philanthropist and legislator Julien Poydras, and established an orphanage to afford poor mothers and immigrant children direct aid in times of great distress. On February 22, 1817, the Louisiana legislature granted an article of incorporation to the Female Orphan Society (FOS). In short time, the FOS established the Poydras Female Asylum, making it the first private, Protestant refuge run by women and exclusively for women in the antebellum South.

Surely many citizens of Philadelphia and New Orleans were saddened after the *New Orleans Commercial Bulletin* announced Phoebe Hunter's death on January 8, 1844. From her work in Philadelphia during the yellow fever epidemics of 1793 and 1798 to her nearly thirty years of dedicated service to the FOS, Hunter spent the majority of her adult life serving the needs of poor people. Born in 1760 to a land-owning family in Chester County, Pennsylvania, she grew up in the Christian denomination called the Society of Friends, more commonly known as the Quakers. Hunter lived in Philadelphia following her marriage to Dr. George Hunter in 1786 and witnessed other young Quaker women founding and managing charitable organizations. In a northern city experiencing increasing immigrant populations and yellow fever outbreaks, Quaker men and women took a leading role in assisting those in need.[2]

As the writer of Hunter's obituary remarked, she had "studiously avoided" publicity, and thus the writer went so far as to note hesitancy about even announcing her death. But determining it "proper" and "an act of justice" to the city of New Orleans, Hunter's death was recorded, providing historians with one of the few pieces of evidence that sheds light on her life in Philadelphia.[3] It was not unique that a woman of her social, economic, and religious status avoided public recognition. It was also not unusual that Hunter, a Quaker before her marriage, participated in benevolent work in Philadelphia during the latter part of the eighteenth century. Hunter's life and her work stand out, though, because of the distinctive experiences she did have: she was a woman who was part of the Society of Friends, she witnessed the increase of benevolence provided by women in the North, and she worked directly with poor people during the yellow fever outbreaks in Philadelphia. These experiences certainly shaped Hunter's qualifications to provide aid and assistance to immigrant children facing hardship in New Orleans upon her family's arrival, as she worked tirelessly for many years. Hunter did not replicate the model of northern orphanages or the few Catholic benevolent institutions that helped indigent children in New Orleans. Instead, she and the FOS established political, economic, and social connections throughout the city that fostered the growth of the institution, helping it become a leading refuge for the city's immigrant children.

Phoebe Hunter spent forty-five years in Philadelphia before moving with her family to New Orleans in 1815. Born to parents Thomas Bryant and Mary Shaw in 1760, she grew up in a household whose members were steadfast in their Quaker religious beliefs. Thomas and Mary's marriage certificate states that they received the "consent of their parents and relatives" as they wed in Chester County in the summer of 1740.[4] Thomas Bryant was a taxpayer there from 1737 until his death in 1762. He and Mary had ten children, of whom Phoebe was their ninth. In 1771, Mary moved to nearby Philadelphia with Phoebe and three other daughters. Once there, the family of women registered with the Society of Friends Southern District's Monthly Meeting.[5] Hunter presumably lived with her mother until she married in 1786.

In late-eighteenth-century Philadelphia, the Society of Friends experienced some internal religious and intellectual challenges as Quakers debated their theology. For much of the eighteenth century, spiritual benevolence had been a pillar of Quaker identity. But following the Revolutionary War, ideological debate divided the Friends, eventually leading to the Hicksite schism in 1827.[6] Work within benevolent associations, and the Friends' presence among Philadelphia poor people in particular, emerged as a cause of division. People in northern seaboard cities like Philadelphia were then experiencing a market revolution firsthand. Commercialization and industrialization challenged previous social, economic, and religious relationships. Technological advancements provided new opportunities. Everyday life changed for thousands, and for a religious sect guided largely by simplicity, problems quickly emerged. Quakers who favored Protestantism and the ideas of the Second Great Awakening spawned by the market revolution welcomed outward, public benevolence. Those at odds with the growing commercialization and technological advancement resisted public benevolence.[7]

After Phoebe married George Hunter, for the duration of her life in Philadelphia she witnessed these competing forces shaping Quaker beliefs.[8] The March 1787 meeting of the Southern District reported that she had married "without the consent of her mother, after having been cautioned and advised against it."[9] The minutes further show that she also married "contrary to the advice of [her] friends" and was expelled from the Friends because a priest outside of the Society of Friends had performed the marriage. Though not a common practice for Quakers to marry outside their faith, publicly recognizing Hunter's marriage in the meeting minutes was more of a matter of business, to record her broken ties with the Friends, than an attempt to humiliate her. Three of Hunter's brothers and sisters were also "disowned" from the Quakers because of marriage outside the society. Nonetheless, Hunter's marriage in the Second Presbyterian Church of Philadelphia officially severed all ties between her and the Society of Friends and thus meant that she could no longer attend meetings, have her children baptized within the Friends, or participate in any other ceremonial activity.[10]

Very little is known about the Hunters' life in Philadelphia in the years immediately following her marriage.[11] George Hunter had moved from Scotland to Philadelphia with his brother, mother, and stepfather in 1774. Within two years, he had joined the Philadelphia militia as a volunteer. A year later he joined the American army in the hospital department as assistant apothecary; he had some experience as a young man in Scotland working as a druggist. In the early 1780s, George Hunter moved back to Philadelphia and began a "druggist business." The Philadelphia city directories list him as a druggist in 1794, 1797, 1798, as "chemist-druggist" from 1800 to 1809, and in 1813 and 1815 simply as "Dr. George Hunter."[12] Phoebe's 1844 obituary would note that she and George had been "intimately acquainted with Dr. [Benjamin] Franklin," who was their neighbor and a friend of George.[13] It would further note that the relationships and friendships Hunter fostered during her years in Philadelphia had provided the foundation for the family's "practical wisdom" and "proverbial good sense."[14]

Benevolent and charity organizations began to spring up in Philadelphia in the years after the American Revolution, founded by professionals and relatively affluent people (including Quakers), with the intent of aiding poor people and immigrants. When yellow fever outbreaks struck many poor immigrants in the city in 1793 and 1798, young Quaker women were among those getting involved.[15] This work provided a new role outside their traditional domain, the home, and through such volunteerism Quaker women helped change attitudes about poor people.[16] Between 1790 and 1810, over a hundred Quaker women participated in benevolent associations founded and operated by women.[17] Although Phoebe Hunter bore her seven children in Philadelphia between 1787 to 1803, which would have required her to spend a majority of her time in the household, the yellow fever epidemics were not simply part of her consciousness. Both Hunters worked with indigent people during the outbreaks, and Phoebe visited the homes of afflicted people, not only providing "relief and comfort for those suffering" but also "distributing from her own resources all needed aid."[18]

During this same period, a so-called revitalization movement took place within the Friends, the internal debate referred to above, which challenged the very foundations of Quaker faith. This revitalization coincided with the expansion of the evangelical movement and the Second Great Awakening. As benevolent and evangelical associations spread, Philadelphia Quakers had to choose what constituted appropriate religious and spiritual experience.[19] George and Phoebe Hunter's work with people afflicted with yellow fever seems a direct response to the growing benevolent ideals exhibited by concerned Christians and messages of the Second Great Awakening.[20] Many of those suffering in 1793 were recently arrived from Saint-Domingue, as the island of Haiti was then called. From May 1791 to April 1794 over three thousand French-speaking people moved to Philadelphia because of the revolution taking place on the island.[21] A little over twenty years later, Hunter would help establish the Female Orphan Society in New Orleans to aid immigrants afflicted by the yellow fever and cholera outbreaks there. In 1818, a year after its founding, the FOS reported that the many "unhappy sufferers" of the orphanage were "generally fugitives from the islands of Saint-Domingue and Cuba."[22] Although it is unknown what homes Hunter visited or exactly what groups of people she helped during the outbreaks in Philadelphia, it may not be happenstance that the FOS primarily served families from the Caribbean islands.

In Philadelphia, George Hunter directly treated people in his own household suffering yellow fever. In an October 1793 letter in the *Federal Gazette*, Dr. Hunter expressed his "gratitude" to Benjamin Rush, saying that he had found Dr. Rush's "method of treating [the] disorder to be successful."[23] He reported that the remedies prescribed by Rush worked in his own home, where his "family was taken ill" but now "almost all are restored to health."[24] The letter provided a hopeful assessment of the situation in the neighborhood around the Hunter family's home, as the doctor explained that a "great number of persons in our neighborhood [had become] well by the same means" suggested by Rush.[25] Three weeks later the Philadelphia *Independent Gazetteer* credited Hunter with having restored the health of people ranging from four to seventy years old.[26] Phoebe too, it would be said in her obituary decades later, "was constantly seen . . . visiting . . . the doors of the poor when the Yellow Fever prevailed."[27]

Within two years after the Hunters' arrival in New Orleans, nine women board members established the Female Orphan Society, and Hunter's benevolent activism would continue in her new home. The founders of the FOS consisted of wealthy, Anglo-American families recently arrived in New Orleans, who were attempting to take advantage of the opportunities the city presented. New economic markets and aspirations to create businesses inspired Americans to move to the city because of Louisiana's recent incorporation into the United States. The Hunter, Morse, Bryant, and Hennen families had moved to New Orleans from Baltimore, Philadelphia, and New York within the second decade of the nineteenth century. Quickly establishing themselves within the elite of New Orleans society, the women of these families founded the FOS and served as its first board members, while their husbands emerged as wealthy businessmen, doctors, lawyers, and politicians in the expanding American section of the city.[28]

After its February 1817 incorporation, the FOS placed six girls between five and ten years of age in temporary housing near the Hunter home upriver from the city. Phoebe Hunter was the driving force behind this early effort to accommodate orphans. Soon after, Julien Poydras, a wealthy and prominent New Orleans businessman, philanthropist, and legislator, donated his old plantation home on the corner of St. Charles Avenue and Julia Street, and on March 10, 1817, the home officially opened as the Poydras Asylum. Although a leader in establishing the FOS, Phoebe's name was not mentioned in the official minute books until her appointment as "superior directress" of the Poydras Home in January 1821.[29] Phoebe would go on to serve for twenty-three years in this role, overseeing expansion into a new building, assisting the board in purchasing rental property throughout the city to help defray the cost of running the orphanage, and witnessing a dramatic increase in the number of girls the FOS could house.[30]

The FOS adopted both a constitution and a system of rules that governed both the benevolent association and asylum and that give insight into the motives and goals behind their founding. An elected board of managers was responsible for "[providing] a house for the reception of indigent Female Orphans and Widows" and for appropriating "money and goods principally to the use of [the] establishment."[31] The board appointed a committee "to seek out and examine into the circumstances and claims of indigent Orphans and Widows" or "any female child, in want."[32] The full board, however, had the power to accept or reject candidates by a majority of votes. To "instruct the children in good morals and behavior; in all such knowledge as shall tend to make them useful members of society—in all useful Labor and the remnants of science," the board hired a governess to preside over the orphanage. It was the governess's duty "to ascertain as far as possible, the abilities and disposition of each individual under her charge, and to allot to her such employment and duties as best appertain."[33]

The FOS administrative structure resembled those of benevolent organizations from the North that had started in the late eighteenth century. As historian Anne Boylan shows, most of the societies in New York and Boston had a similar organizational framework.[34] Like the Society for the Relief of Poor Widows with Small Children, which was established in 1797 in New York, the FOS received an article of incorporation, lobbied for shares of public welfare funds, and had supporters who paid to be a part of the society but who were not involved in running the association or the orphanage. The FOS also resembled one of the first private women's associations in the South, the Ladies Benevolent Society of Charlestown established in 1813. Both benevolent societies had monthly visiting committees, were accepting of many Christian denominations, ran weekly and monthly meetings, and based all financial and administrative decisions on a vote by board members.[35]

As superior directress, it was Hunter's duty to manage FOS operations. She ran monthly meetings, put forth proposals, and hired teachers and caretakers for the children in the orphanage. Hunter also was required to continue the relationship established with the mayor and the New Orleans City Council upon founding of the FOS. Throughout the South, there were few public welfare systems that supported indigent children at the time. Conditions at the few public orphanages that existed, such as the Charlestown Orphan House, barely surpassed the living conditions of other poor white urban children.[36] Founded in 1790 as the nation's first public orphanage, the Charlestown Orphan House required guardians to surrender legal guardianship. And children entered into indentured contracts upon admittance. Private asylums in the South became virtually the only recourse for destitute families in the first half of the nineteenth century, especially in New Orleans, where the local and state government eventually came to depend on the FOS.[37]

A month prior to the FOS incorporation, a resolution had been passed: "Whereas the city council of New Orleans sees with the greatest pleasure the efforts of the women of this city, to establish an Association intended to help the needy orphan girls; resolved . . . to help them in this act of charity and to attain the realization of their ambitions in this respect."[38] Three months later, the council expressed "sincere pleasure and admiration . . . for the [FOS role in the] relief, maintenance, and education of female orphan children." It was also "deeply impressed with the necessity of encouraging and carrying into full effect the meritorious objects of said institution."[39] Through either direct monetary assistance or political backing, council members assured the FOS of their "willingness to relieve the distressed, as far as the means in their power will enable them."[40] Throughout the 1820s, the FOS "received orders from the Mayor for the adoption of orphaned children."[41] The early relationship between the city government and the FOS led to the city's growing dependence on the asylum. In October 1824, the FOS accepted twenty-four orphans from the mayor but required $1,400 per year for their inhabitance. The FOS also petitioned the mayor for an extra $200 to pay the salary of another governess to help oversee the increase of girls and also provide instruction in the Catholic faith, and the mayor agreed.[42]

As wives and daughters of prosperous merchants, lawyers, and politicians, Hunter and her fellow board managers were well aware of the advantages incorporation allowed them. Incorporation provided "concrete meaning to the influence" the society exhibited within the city.[43] Incorporation gave the FOS legal rights in New Orleans society, powers that women lacked in their own lives.[44] With these new collective privileges, the FOS gained access to political favor and economic advancement. The FOS also benefited from familial connections with the City Council. Nathan Morse and Thomas Bryant, for example, served on the council during Augustine Macarthy's term as mayor from 1815 to 1820. Their wives, Anne Bryant and M. C. Morse, were two of the first nine board members for the FOS.[45] The relationship with the mayor's office translated into direct access to public funds and political support. From 1817 to 1821, the mayor's office and State of Louisiana provided a substantial sum, nearly $5,000, to the FOS.[46] In October 1824, a visiting committee from the mayor's office reported on the "radiant health painted on the faces of the young girls."[47]

For a city challenged by death-dealing epidemics and inadequate public services for poor people, the FOS met a need in New Orleans. For Hunter, the FOS became an opportunity for her to enter the public sphere, even if only temporarily, and transcend her status as a home-bound wife. The FOS and its incorporation granted collective privileges to female board members like Hunter, who otherwise would not have been able to engage in politics or work so effectively at making and maintaining the social and economic relationships that fostered the institution.[48]

Sometimes her role took Hunter to unfamiliar places. The slave markets of New Orleans at the time sustained the city's economic relationships and businesses. In dealing with slaves, the women of the FOS entered a world largely unfamiliar to them. As the wives of slaveholding white men, women often directed slaves within the household but seldom participated actively in the slave market.[49] And as a northern white woman, Hunter had little experience buying or hiring out enslaved labor. Through the FOS incorporation, its managers exercised their right to buy and hire slaves outside of the control of their husbands. From March 1817 to July 1821, for example, the orphanage hired a slave for ten dollars a month.[50] Because white women could not enter the slave pens, they often chose to hire—rather than purchase—slaves because business could be achieved through correspondence and on their own terms. The practice of hiring slaves forced men, to some degree, to recognize the influence of such women. The market required exchanges of money, credit, and property, a world in which the FOS women necessarily engaged.

Despite their preference for hiring slaves and indentured servants, FOS women did also purchase them, and Hunter was involved in this. In October

1825, for example, the board directed her to determine a "fair price for James, the Negro hired in the garden being for sale at auction in a few days."[51] The women stated that they would go as high as $125 for the purchase but "he sold upwards of $200 [and] therefore he was not purchased by the Poydras Home."[52] In 1832, the asylum purchased its first slave, Rachel, for $200, and the board again directed Hunter to ask a man going to Norfolk, Virginia, "to inquire upon what terms a good male and female servant could be purchased for the Asylum."[53] It was the board members' responsibility to draw up contracts. Hunter also had complete autonomy when deciding which slaves to hire, for how long, and for what price. In a New Orleans economy that revolved around slave and indentured labor, problems often arose regarding availability of workers, skill, and fluctuations in prices, all of which the FOS experienced. "Because of the great difficulty of procuring labourers on advantageous terms," FOS minutes in 1823 noted that the market had forced them to "reduce the plan of [garden] cultivation to a sufficiency of vegetables," not the usual surplus sold in the local produce markets.[54] Regarding one laborer, the FOS found him "not qualified . . . and according to the agreement drawn up . . . [gave] him notice to quit the premises in one month."[55] The FOS began to be involved in affairs outside of the orphanage, such as buying and renting enslaved and indentured labor and renting properties to garner more income. And more and more children petitioned for acceptance, forcing the FOS to gather necessary support and money in order to keep the orphanage running smoothly.

As the population increased yearly in New Orleans, especially among immigrants, who represented the largest percentage of girls in the orphanage, Hunter had to balance poor people's needs with the capacity of the FOS to support them. At the first annual meeting of the FOS in January 1818, the secretary reported that nine girls lived in the orphanage. Seven years later, in January 1825, the secretary reported sixty-two resident girls. As the profile of the FOS rose, so did problems in finding room to house orphans and financial support to maintain their level of care.[56]

In a "special meeting" in May 1825, Hunter lay before the board estimates of several builders for the construction of new premises to house orphans. Hunter expressed concern that the building costs and expenses of the current year might exhaust the treasury, but "still felt justified in giving her vote . . . when she considered how very inadequate the present accommodations were to the healthful security of nearly one hundred children." Stating that "the greatest economy must be observed by the Managers," she said that she trusted in the "continued blessings of Providence."[57] After hearing Hunter speak, the board agreed to go ahead with the building in discussion, and construction soon began.[58] Hunter and the other board members faced a problem that institutions then and now experience: how to meet constituents' needs while keeping to a budget.[59]

Once the FOS moved its orphanage into the new building, the number of children it served increased dramatically. At the end of 1839, over 140 children lived in the orphanage.[60] The vastly increased number forced the FOS to search for new avenues of income to offset the costs. Through rental properties the FOS owned, the organization was able to gather thousands of dollars each year. Receiving legal assistance from Samuel Peters, the FOS chief counselor, Hunter and the board drew up legal contracts and leased their properties to tenants to the tune of $7,000 in 1837.[61]

That year, 1837, Hunter turned seventy-seven. By now her role in the FOS was diminishing, and she rarely attended board meetings in the years between then and her death in January 1844. Hunter's role in the early years of the FOS allowed it to thrive following her death. In 1844, the FOS was clearly in better shape than when it started twenty-seven years before: its treasury had expanded, the number of girls living within its walls had grown, and a new orphanage had been built. In 1857, the FOS and its orphanage moved into a new building, which the FOS built at the corner of Jefferson and Magazine Streets. The board reported that this facility could house approximately five hundred children and would be known as the Poydras Female Asylum in recognition of one of its earliest benefactors, Julien Poydras.[62] There the asylum would continue for another century. The building there still stands, though its role as orphanage ended in the late 1950s. It is now a retirement home.[63]

Phoebe Bryant Hunter lived in Philadelphia during an era when Christian women across the North began embodying the principles of the Second Great Awakening. Protestant evangelicalism then encouraged civic-minded women to serve poor people through benevolence and charitable works, and Quaker women in Philadelphia in particular heeded the call. Hunter, expelled from the Society of Friends, stayed true to her faith when she was involved in the city's yellow fever outbreaks of 1793 and 1798. During times that her own children suffered, she also chose to help others in need. Though not involved in a specific benevolent organization in Philadelphia, Hunter was aware of them, just as she was aware that it was largely other women of her own race and class who were involved in them.

Once in New Orleans, Hunter quickly identified the inadequacy of charitable assistance there, which fostered an environment that forced indigent families to beg. As a founder of the Female Orphan Society, Hunter went on to play many roles, serving as "directress," "superior directress," and head of many committees. Hunter led an institution that engaged the political, social, and economic forces of the city—and sometimes competed with them. As immigration to New Orleans rivaled that of the larger, urban cities of the North in the decades before the Civil War, the number of indigent families grew, and the city government relied on the institution to provide charitable assistance—and education—to needy girls.

Along with other board members, Phoebe Hunter ran a civic-minded institution in a bustling city that was emerging as a major economic hub in the South. With a focus on aiding poor immigrant children, she assiduously hired and purchased slaves, rented out properties, worked with contractors, and forged and maintained a supportive relationship with the mayor's office. In the South, especially, where women of similar social status were expected to focus on their own family and pursue few public relationships in the commercial and political forces that drove a city, Hunter challenged this status quo. She not only participated in benevolent work but also led an institution, engaging in political, social, and economic relationships to sustain the growth of the orphanage while continuing to provide charitable services to immigrant children in New Orleans.

NOTES

I am thankful for the many comments and suggestions by Shannon Frystak and Mary Farmer-Kaiser. Special thanks to the University of New Orleans Department of History, especially Mary Niall Mitchell, for all the assistance provided in graduate school.

1. Mary Ann Hunter to cousin Eliza, July 30, 1815, Vertical Files, Louisiana Research Collection, Special Collections, Howard-Tilton Memorial Library, Tulane University, New Orleans.

2. Sydney V. James, *A People among Peoples: Quaker Benevolence in Eighteenth-Century America* (Cambridge: Harvard University Press, 1963).

3. "The Late Mrs. Hunter," *New Orleans Commercial Bulletin*, January 8, 1844 (hereafter cited as Phoebe Hunter obituary).

4. Miriam L. Luke, *Some Descendants of Thomas Bryant, Chester County, Pennsylvania* (Madison: University of Wisconsin, 1977), 6–9.

5. Ibid., 9.

6. Bruce Dorsey, "Friends Becoming Enemies: Philadelphia Benevolence and the Neglected Era of American Quaker History," *Journal of the Early Republic* 18, no. 3 (Autumn 1998): 399. From the end of the eighteenth century to 1827, the Society of Friends experienced internal theological strife. One group of Quakers wanted to follow Protestant traditions, while the other wished to adhere to their "quietist roots" and continue to live simple, traditional lives. The latter (eventually labeled Hicksites because of their allegiance to the teaching of Elias Hicks) became hostile and disapproved of evangelical benevolence exhibited by Quakers in response to the growing number of urban poor people.

7. Ibid., 398–400.

8. William C. Kashatus, "The Inner Light and Popular Enlightenment: Philadelphia Quakers and Charity Schooling, 1790–1820," *Pennsylvania Magazine of History and Biography* 118, no. 1/2 (January/April 1994): 101.

9. Monthly Meeting of Women's Friends, Southern District of Philadelphia, March 28, 1787, 105, Quaker & Special Collections, Haverford College Library, Haverford, Pennsylvania.

10. Ibid.

11. George Hunter, "The Journals of Dr. George Hunter," edited by John Francis McDermott, *Transactions of the American Philosophical Society* 53, no. 4 (1963): 5–6.

12. Ibid., 6.

13. Phoebe Hunter obituary.

14. Ibid.

15. Margaret Morris Haviland, "Beyond Women's Sphere: Young Quaker Women and the Veil of Charity in Philadelphia, 1790–1810," *William and Mary Quarterly* 51, no. 3 (July 1994): 419. See

also J. Worth Estes and Billy G. Smith, ed., *The Public Response to the 1793 Philadelphia Yellow Fever Epidemic* (Canton, Mass.: Science History Publications, 1997).

16. Haviland, "Beyond Women's Sphere," 419.

17. Ibid., 422.

18. Ibid.

19. Dorsey, "Friends Becoming Enemies," 398.

20. Barbara Berg, *The Remembered Gate: Origins of American Feminism, the Women and the City 1800–1860* (Oxford: Oxford University Press, 1978); Lori D. Ginzberg, *Women and the Work of Benevolence: Morality, Politics, and Class in the 19th-Century United States* (New Haven: Yale University Press, 1990); Anne Firor Scot, *Natural Allies: Women's Associations in American History* (Urbana: University of Illinois Press, 1993); Nancy F. Cott, *The Bonds of Womanhood: "Woman's Sphere" in New England, 1780–1835* (New Haven: Yale University Press, 1977).

21. Gary B. Nash, "Reverberations of Haiti in the American North: Black Saint Dominguans in Philadelphia," *Pennsylvania History* 65 (1998): 49.

22. Female Orphan Society Board Meeting Minutes, *First Annual Report January 16, 1818*, Poydras Home Collection 67, no. 69, Louisiana Research Collection, Special Collections, Howard-Tilton Memorial Library, Tulane University, New Orleans (hereafter cited as Minutes, Poydras Home).

23. Letter, *Federal Gazette* (Philadelphia), October 1, 1793.

24. Ibid.

25. Ibid.

26. Miscellany, account of the yellow fever, *Independent Gazetteer* (Philadelphia), October 26, 1793.

27. Phoebe Hunter obituary.

28. George Hunter discovered salt in Louisiana while serving on President Thomas Jefferson's committee to explore the territory. Prior to Hunter's moving to New Orleans in 1815, he participated in four such trips (1796–1809) to explore Arkansas and Louisiana. Whether these missions provided the primary impetus for him to relocate his family to New Orleans in is unknown. But his experiences presumably played a role in the decision, for his family had long-established economic and social ties in Philadelphia. Dr. Hunter, along with his brother-in-law Thomas Bryant, established Hunter and Bryant's Steam Saw and Grist Mill in New Orleans in July 1815. Alfred Hennen was an attorney who served as president of the Louisiana Bible Society and the Bethel Union Society. Along with Dr. Hunter, Hennen served on the board of the First Presbyterian Church in New Orleans; Hunter served as president and Hennen as secretary. Thomas Bryant and Nathan Morse served on the New Orleans City Council during Augustin de Macarty's tenure from 1815 to 1820. Nathan Morse also served as head of the visiting committee to the FOS each year in the early 1820s. Hunter, "The Journals of Dr. George Hunter"; Louis Voss, *Presbyterianism in New Orleans and Adjacent Points* (New Orleans: Presbyterian Board of Publications of the Synod of Louisiana, 1931), 42.

29. I have not found any record in the Poydras Asylum files at Tulane University that specifically states that Phoebe Hunter was an official founding member of the Poydras Asylum. Only through unofficial sources, secondary works, and conversations with family members have I heard that Hunter was a founder of the home. I assume that she was a leading voice behind the scenes. Hunter's daughter, Mary Anne, was the first elected secretary, and her sister-in-law, Anne Bryant, served on the first board. Today a portrait of Hunter is displayed in the Poydras Home, now a retirement center, in remembrance of her dedication to the Poydras Asylum. February and March 1817, Minutes, Poydras Home.

30. January and May 1825, Minutes, Poydras Home.

31. Constitution of the FOS, Articles 1 and 3, approved and signed January 21, 1817, Minutes, Poydras Home.

32. Ibid., Article 4.

33. Rules and Regulations for the Government of the Poydras Asylum, Article 3, approved and adopted February 22, 1817, Minutes, Poydras Home.

34. Anne M. Boylan, "Women in Groups: An Analysis of Women's Benevolent Organizations in New York and Boston, 1797–1840," *Journal of American History* 71, no. 3 (Autumn 1984): 499.

35. Gail S. Murray, "Charity within the Bounds of Race and Class: Female Benevolence in the Old South," *South Carolina Historical Magazine* 96, no. 1 (January 1995): 59.

36. John E. Murray, "Fates of Orphans: Poor Children in Antebellum Charleston," *Journal of Interdisciplinary History* 33, no. 4 (Spring 2003): 526.

37. Ibid.

38. February 15, 1817, Minutes, Poydras Home.

39. Letter of City Council of New Orleans to FOS, May 17, 1817, Minutes, Poydras Home.

40. Ibid.

41. December 21, 1822, Minutes, Poydras Home.

42. October 27 and November 18, 1824, Minutes, Poydras Home.

43. Ginzberg, *Women and the Work of Benevolence*, 48.

44. Anne M. Boylan, "Women and Politics in the Era before Seneca Falls," *Journal of the Early Republic* 10, no. 3 (Autumn 1990): 365.

45. February 22, 1817, Minutes, Poydras Home.

46. Annual Report of the Treasury, 1821, Minutes, Poydras Home.

47. Visiting Report from the Mayor, October 1824, Minutes, Poydras Home.

48. Boylan, "Women and Politics in the Era before Seneca Falls," 365.

49. Walter Johnson argues that women in New Orleans indirectly participated in the slave market through three avenues. Before marriage, women could receive permission from her husband to have control over the property she possessed. A woman could also gain rights separate from her husband during marriage that enabled her to buy slaves. Because the FOS received legal recognition as a corporation within Louisiana, board members attainted the right to hire and buy slaves outside the control of their husbands. Women, however, were never allowed to go to the slave markets and purchase slaves directly. Walter Johnson, *Soul by Soul: Life inside the Antebellum Slave Market* (Cambridge: Harvard University Press, 1999), 89.

50. Financial papers, box 1, folders 1–5, Poydras Home Collection, Louisiana Research Collection, Special Collections, Howard-Tilton Memorial Library, Tulane University, New Orleans (hereafter Poydras Home Collection).

51. October 5, 1825, Minutes, Poydras Home.

52. October 12, 1825, Minutes, Poydras Home.

53. No date, sometime between May 1, 1832, and June 4, 1832, Minutes, Poydras Home.

54. January 16, 1823, Minutes, Poydras Home.

55. September 1821, Minutes, Poydras Home.

56. January 1818 and January 1825, Minutes, Poydras Home.

57. Special Meeting, May 17, 1825, Minutes, Poydras Home.

58. Ibid.

59. As migration increased to New Orleans, charitable orphanages like the FOS experienced a higher demand to place children. The FOS therefore decided to expand to a new building where it could accept more children. Natalie Dessens, *From Saint-Domingue to New Orleans: Migration and Influences* (Gainesville: University Press of Florida, 2007); Special Meeting, May 17, 1825, Minutes, Poydras Home.

60. Annual Report, 1839, Poydras Home.

61. Annual Report, 1837, Poydras Home.

62. Annual Report, 1857, Poydras Home.

63. In the summer of 1957, board members contemplated changing the Poydras Home to an institution that cared solely for aging women. By December that year, only two orphans remained in the boarding school, and they were allowed to stay until graduation. Annual Report, 1957, Minutes, Poydras Home.

Cora Allen

(1876–1935)

Louisiana Fraternal Orders and the Making of a Race Woman

BRITTNEY COOPER

On March 7, 1923, a Caddo Parish notary public certified that Cora M. Allen, along with four other women and one man, legally constituted the core officers of the Calanthe Temple Commission. Allen, "Grand Worthy Counselor of the Grand Court Order of Calanthe," headed the commission, which had been created to spearhead a large commercial real estate project, the Calanthean Temple, at 1007½ Texas Avenue in Shreveport, Louisiana. The Calantheans, the female auxiliary to the African American Knights of Pythias, was the first-known group of black women in the country to undertake such a large-scale commercial enterprise.[1] The Knights of Pythias were the third-largest male fraternal order among other long-standing fraternal groups such as the better known Prince Hall Masons. The Calanthean Temple opened in 1923, and it still stands today on Texas Avenue. When patrons entered the Calanthean in 1924, they encountered several businesses. Walker and Holland Cigar Company was located in the lobby. The dental office of Dr. W. M. Howard, the real estate offices of Green & Gross, J. V. Smith Lumber, Liberty Insurance Company, and the office of Dr. D. A. Smith, the lone male member of the Calanthean Temple Commission, were on the second floor. The medical offices of Drs. Sol E. Powell and G. M. Johnson and the office of Standard Life Insurance Company took up the third floor. Finally, the Order of Calanthe occupied the fourth floor, the top floor of the building, using it as its meeting space. Significantly, African Americans owned and operated each of these businesses.[2] The roof of the Calanthean had a tent-covered area known as the Rooftop Garden. Such notable musical figures as Duke Ellington and Louis Armstrong played there, and it hosted a variety of social functions.[3] The building was the centerpiece of Texas Avenue, the center of African American social life in early-twentieth-century Shreveport.

Known affectionately in the black community as "The Avenue," it was home to many African American businesses, fraternal temples, and churches.

As a commercial real estate venture, the Calanthean Temple was not remarkable, given a spate of similar ventures from white and black fraternal groups during the 1920s nationwide.[4] What made it unique was its African American female leadership. Moreover, the choice to build such an extravagant symbol of racial progress in a place as racially volatile as northern Louisiana in the 1920s took a great deal of courage. The local chapter of the Colored Knights of Pythias was organized in 1881, in the wake of a period of extreme racial violence that circumscribed and subjugated the political activities and organizing of Reconstruction era blacks in the city.[5] Shreveport was the capital of Confederate Louisiana after the fall of Baton Rouge, and the city itself had largely escaped Civil War violence. Within Caddo Parish in the postwar years too, the city witnessed markedly less racial violence than its surrounding rural areas. Between 1865 and 1884—and likewise before the war—because of extreme violence in its rural areas, Caddo Parish was considered "one of the worst places in Louisiana" for propagating racial violence.[6] By the 1920s, the Ku Klux Klan notoriously dominated local politics in northern Louisiana. In 1922, Klan bosses in Bastrop, a small city in the northeastern corner of the state, brutally killed three local white people who opposed their rural despotism. The Klan had so many political allies in Louisiana that, in order to alert federal authorities to the Klan's level of domination, Governor John W. Parker resorted to subterfuge, sneaking out a letter to federal authorities outlining the terrible conditions via one of his good friends. Because of violence against white dissenters, the state legislature targeted the Klan through several pieces of legislation designed to expose their membership and prevent them from wearing hoods in public. One act made any crime a felony if committed in a mask. Incensed at these efforts, the Klan made a series of costly political miscalculations in order to evade prosecution. Their efforts had the opposite effect and led to the swift suppression of their power.[7] Even so, by 1924, Shreveport was described as "the throne city of local Klandom," although most Klan activity seemed confined to Caddo Parish's rural areas.[8] Despite these volatile racial conditions, Cora Allen, as head of both the local and state chapters of the Calantheans, persisted in her plan to build a temple for their fraternal work.

Allen's life and leadership, especially her work in both local and national women's clubs and fraternal orders, significantly expands contemporary understandings of racial organizing and leadership in the Deep South in the early twentieth century. In particular, her local leadership highlights the connections between national initiatives and local implementation strategies that were a hallmark of racial leadership in her era. Moreover, Allen's fraternal work offers new information about a severely understudied area of African American racial leadership, namely the social service and institution building undertaken by women's fraternal groups. Allen and the four other women, F. E. Smith, L. B. Henderson, L. B. Horton, and Rosa L. James, who assisted in procuring funds and supervising the construction of the temple, complicate and enhance the national picture of race women's activism, since that picture rarely includes national recognition of local work undertaken by African American women in Louisiana, especially those outside of New Orleans.[9] Allen's wide-ranging organizational connections also indicate the high degree of cross-pollination among African American women's groups that enabled them to be effective as race leaders. Finally, Allen's National Association of Colored Women (NACW) correspondence and newspaper columns, along with her peers' perspectives on her leadership style, illuminate the ways that African American women in Louisiana negotiated conservative gender roles, both resisted and reinscribed the politics of respectability, and navigated class-based conflicts among black women in their quest for racial uplift.

Born Corinne Murdock in Delhi, Louisiana, in 1876, Allen relocated to Shreveport with her parents Oscar and Mattie and several siblings as a young child. Though young Cora attended school at the Thirteenth District Academy for a time, she did not complete a formal education. She married African American Baptist minister Luke Allen Jr., in 1893 at the age of seventeen. The couple would later adopt two orphaned teenagers, Ruby and Willie. In 1905, Reverend Allen assumed the pastorate of Avenue Baptist Church, which became the largest black church in the city in the 1920s. In the years that followed, Reverend Allen also served as president of the Louisiana Baptist Convention and became a well-respected and nationally noted preacher.[10]

As wife to a prominent black Baptist minister, Cora Allen inherited a conservative set of gender politics "drawn from biblical teachings, the philosophy of racial self-help, [and] Victorian ideology," all of which converged in a communal politics of respectability.[11] In churches, women served in traditionally feminine roles as nurses, church mothers, nursery workers, cooks, and the like. Like white women who subscribed to the cult of true womanhood, respectable black women believed in being pious, chaste, maternal, and submissive, but their racial subjugation lent a political dimension to their performance of these roles and demanded that they not limit their labor to the domestic sphere.[12] In service of their racial uplift efforts, then, many of these women assumed prominent public roles, in hopes that their effective performance of respectability would change the national view of African Americans collectively.[13]

Allen's tenure with the Louisiana Calantheans preceded her husband's ascension to the pastorate of Avenue Baptist. Consequently, despite conservative cultural expectations of preachers' wives, Allen eschewed a prominent church role in favor of continuing her work with the Calantheans and expanding into women's club work. In 1899, she became Grand Worthy Counselor of the Grand Court Order of Calanthe of Louisiana, the highest office in the state. She held this position until her death and was opposed for the position only once during her tenure. She also held the national position of "Supreme Worthy Inspectrix," the highest office a woman could hold in the order, for many years. In addition to being the head of the Calantheans, Allen was also a member of the Order of Eastern Star, the Household of Ruth, and the Woodmen of the World, all of which were fraternal groups.[14] In 1914, she started the Married Ladies Club, which was renamed the Mary Church Terrell Club in 1918. She revived the Louisiana branch of the NACW in 1926 and served as president from 1927 until her death in 1935.[15]

In 1900, Fannie Barrier Williams, a prominent public intellectual and member of the African American women's club movement, asserted that churches and secret societies had been the primary organizations in which black women received training for racial leadership. These organizations cultivated public speaking and debating skills, leadership ability, and racial pride in their members. Indeed, Williams insisted that "secret societies inculcated the types of values—'care for the sick, provisions for the decent burial of the indigent dead, the care for orphans, and the enlarging of the sense of sisterhood,'—that were central to the work of women's clubs. The inculcation of these values led to the 'development of the very conditions of heart that qualify women for the more inclusive work of those social reforms that are the aim of women's clubs.' Finally, both 'churches and secret societies' had 'helped to make colored women acquainted with the general social condition of the race and the possibilities of social improvement.'"[16] Notwithstanding the elitism of Williams's statement, her historical assessment of the important role of secret societies as a training ground for black female leadership demands consideration. Moreover, multiple generations of scholarship have focused on black women's club work. But very little has focused on the broad involvement of black women in fraternal orders and mutual aid societies.[17] Cora Allen's work as both a fraternal woman *and* a clubwoman provide a fuller picture of black women's leadership and activism in the early twentieth century. Though she had an active tenure as a club woman, it was her quarter-century of leadership in fraternal orders, particularly as a member of the Order of Calanthe, that shaped her relatively short tenure of club leadership in the last decade of her life.

Although scholars such as C. Eric Lincoln and Evelyn Brooks Higginbotham have considered the expansive role of the black Church in African American life and African American women's lives specifically, very little work has considered the role of early, non-Greek fraternal organizations in training black women for leadership.[18] Allen was a member of four fraternal groups. Though today "fraternal" tends to refer to male-only groups, in her time men and women were included under the banner of "fraternity." Among major groups like the Masons, the Elks, and the Pythians, women served in the respective female auxiliaries of the Order of Eastern Star, the Household of Ruth, and the Order of Calanthe.

Despite their service in an auxiliary capacity, these women referred to and understood themselves as "fraternal women." In fact, because fraternal membership was so prevalent among African American women, the NACW, the largest organization of African American women in the country, created its own Department of Fraternal Relations. Women's fraternal groups, consequently, are significant to the study of African American women's leadership. Though each fraternal group had differing gender ideologies and philosophies of women's leadership, these organizations provided women opportunities for significant oversight of racial initiatives in their communities.[19] For example, the black Pythians had a long history of financially supporting black women's independent institution building efforts on behalf of the Court of Calanthe, and Cora Allen maintained control of all matters related to the Calanthean Temple, without significant male oversight.[20] In fact, Charles Stump, a visiting correspondent for a Chicago-based newspaper, the *Broad Ax*, celebrated Allen's lead role in the administration of the Calantheans' affairs when he visited the temple in April 1924:

> I think I had the pleasure of going into the first building of its kind erected in the world, the Calanthean Temple. I know we have all over the country Pythian temples, Masonic temples, but I believe this is the first building in the world erected by a female fraternal order, and it is due to the wonderful training of Mrs. Cora Allen, the grand worthy counselor, which position she has held for about a quarter of a century, and she has well organized the women and you will get an idea when I tell you the beautiful four story building cost two hundred thousand dollars when finished and furnished. She will go down in history as one of the women of this race who believed in doing and she has erected a monument for herself.[21]

Stump's acknowledgment provided national exposure for the Calanthean Temple, while also affirming the important role black women played in racial leadership. In particular, the building of the temple suggested that black women were formidable institution builders within their communities. Although the Order of Calanthe was the female auxiliary to the Knights of Pythias, the successful construction of the temple challenged racial leadership ideologies that attempted to relegate black women to supporting, auxiliary roles and presaged a national push by fraternal women to have more leadership within their respective orders.[22] Thus, Allen and the Calanthean women were at the forefront of early-twentieth-century conversations and debates about the leadership roles race women could assume within local communities.

Black women also strategically capitalized on their membership in multiple organizations to buttress their broader racial uplift efforts. Allen's leadership role in the local, state, and national branches of the NACW constituted a significant spoke in a wheel of broad organizational connections. Her history and connection to myriad prominent race women of her day—including Mrs. S. Joe Brown, cofounder of the Iowa NAACP; Hallie Quinn Brown, famous elocutionist, writer, and professor; Nannie Helen Burroughs, founder of the National Training School for Girls and the Women's Auxiliary of the National Baptist Convention; and Mary McLeod Bethune, founder of the National Council of Negro Women—suggests that race women's work occurred at the nexus of several *overlapping* organizational networks that each provided opportunities for these women to reach and serve different parts of and interests in African American communities. Allen encountered many of these women as part of her work with the NACW, founded in 1896 after two smaller national bodies of black women decided to merge their efforts.[23] The goal of the new association was to provide national coordination for the social, political, cultural, and educational activities of women's clubs, which existed in and around the country. In many respects, though it was no simple replica, the NACW took its cues from the General Federation of Women's Clubs, which restricted its membership in most places to white women. At the same time, the NACW also had the aim of defending black womanhood from vicious and derogatory public attacks on black women's morality.[24] Exceptional kinds of racial achievement, like that signaled by the building of the Calanthean, played a critical role in combating myths about black women being lazy, lascivious, and childlike by demonstrating their intelligence, industriousness, and leadership capability.

In Shreveport, Allen served as founder and president of the Mary Church Terrell Club, one of the local clubs that fell under the purview of the NACW. Founded in 1914 as the Married Ladies Club, Allen renamed the club after Terrell in 1918 after hearing the prominent race woman and first president of the NACW speak. The club hosted a variety of programs—speakers, debates, "baby contests," and even a celebration of President's Day—and lent financial support to a range of civic endeavors.[25] It awarded an annual hundred-dollar scholarship to the highest graduate at the local "colored" high school. In 1928, its baby pageant raised over $1,000, which the club used to furnish the parlor at the Colored Pines, a convalescent home. In 1932, it financially contributed to the upkeep of the local segregated park reserved for African American recreation.[26]

The Terrell Club also engaged in debates and discussions over matters of political and social interest to local African Americans. A little-discussed area of black intellectual life in the 1920s and 1930s was the prominence of college debate clubs and teams. The *Shreveport Sun*, Louisiana's oldest weekly African American newspaper, routinely featured front-page stories about major debate tournaments at historically black colleges, including Howard, Fisk, and Wiley College. Wiley, whose debate team was the subject of the 2007 movie *The Great Debaters*, is located in Marshall, Texas, just thirty miles from Shreveport. Local churches also hosted debates about major public policy issues featuring students from local high schools. These events were always well attended. Allen, a well-respected orator, found these forensic activities intriguing. At the May 3, 1927, meeting, members of the Terrell Club staged a debate on the topic, "Resolved: That the South offers greater inducements and better advantages to our people than any other part of the country."[27] Mrs. Z. E. Baker and Mrs. R. E. Brown argued the affirmative; Allen and Mrs. Alice Davis argued the negative. The negative team won. The specific arguments of each team do not survive in the historical record. However, debates over what the South had to offer African Americans would have been especially prominent in the 1920s South, which was experiencing the effects of the first wave of the Great Migration northward. Well traveled via her work in the Order of Calanthe and the NACW, Allen had visited most major black urban areas and would have been exposed to the opportunities offered to black people in areas outside the South. However, the Terrell club debate is an example of the important intellectual and deliberative spaces that black women created for themselves through their work in women's clubs. Black women used these spaces to assess and adopt strategies responsive to the needs of their various constituencies.[28]

In 1926, after a schism over the leadership of the State Federation of Women's Clubs, Allen assumed the presidency of the Louisiana Association of Colored Women and used her considerable skills in diplomacy to unify the existing state clubs and make them an effective force in the national organization. In a full-page proclamation in the March 1926 issue of the NACW's newsletter, *National Notes*, Allen told Louisiana Association members, "I stand ready, supported by you to push our program to completion[;] how well I shall do this depends upon the support I shall receive from you."[29] Allen had received considerable support from the national association to assume leadership of the state federation. At the 1924 convention in Chicago, she was a featured panelist ("What the Women Have Accomplished in Business"), though records of her remarks do not survive. Several months after Allen assumed the presidency of the state federation, Mary McLeod Bethune recognized her during the 1926 biennial convention in Oakland "as a woman who put up a $150,000 building and asked a colored woman, Hallie Quinn Brown[,] to deliver a dedicatory address."[30] Though Bethune quoted the cost of the Calanthean Temple as $50,000 less in 1926 than Charles Stump had stated in 1924, the price tag remains significant, the equivalent of about $2 million today. Allen and Bethune, founder of Bethune-Cookman University, shared a history as local institution builders. Indeed, Allen was a vocal supporter of Bethune's 1926 campaign to raise funds for a national NACW headquarters in Washington, D.C. Allen donated one hundred dollars of her own money, matching the amount donated by the Louisiana association. Bethune also celebrated Allen's choice to have Hallie Q. Brown give the dedicatory address for the Calanthean Temple. At the time that the temple opened, Brown served as president of the NACW. Not merely a ceremonious selection, Allen's choice of Brown, a black female race leader and head of the largest organization of African American women that existed at the time, demonstrated Allen's women-centered gender politics and the importance of the temple not just as a racial achievement but also as an achievement for African American women.[31]

Using the model provided by the NACW, in early March 1928, Allen also launched the Shreveport City Federation of Women's Clubs. Composed of twelve local women's clubs, including the Mary Church Terrell Club, the federation held its first meeting at Avenue Baptist Church among "a packed house of the representative women of the city." In describing the event, the *Shreveport Sun* reported:

> It can be truthfully said that the Clubs made a wise selection that they can be proud of, a woman capable of leading any intelligent, national, and sound-thinking group. She [Allen] is a woman whose life shall ever be a living monument to the hearts and minds of citizens of Shreveport and even the nation because this heroic woman is beloved by leaders and their followers everywhere. One would never appreciate her intrinsic worth as a leader until he has witnessed her officiating over a body of critical pessimists and seen her satisfy all. Her poise and ease of carriage coupled with her ability to converse on almost any subject compel her to stand out as a leader among leaders.[32]

This description of Allen's leadership ability attests to the peculiar social agility that not only she but also many other race women cultivated as they negotiated between a range of competing political commitments, social values, and stereotypes to effectively do the work of racial uplift. Allen had a knack for diplomacy, which undoubtedly made her notable intelligence more palatable in a southern context in which many might have resisted one woman having such a prominent leadership role.

That Shreveport's African American citizens routinely invoked the language of "monuments" when referring to Allen is not accidental. In 1923, the United Daughters of the Confederacy were successful in a national campaign to get the U.S. Congress to agree to build a national monument in honor of "Mammy."[33] In fact, southern white women, fervent supporters of the Lost Cause, had been advocating such a "monument" since the end of Reconstruction. Brown railed against the building of the monument in an editorial in the *National Notes*. "Why," she asked, "erect a dumb statue to the black mammy, while thousands of living monuments attest the strength, the virility, they drew from the mammy's milk—the milk of human kindness?"[34] The reference to Cora Allen and the Calanthean Temple both as monuments dovetails with attempts by African American women and men to resist racist memorials to the lives of black women. Black women's fervency in building their own brick-and-mortar institutions created a powerful form of resistance, self-representation, and racial perpetuation that challenged the derogatory stereotypes inherent in white women's attempts to inscribe the public role of black women to that of involuntary nurturer.

In the summer of 1928, Allen brought her three decades of experience in the Order of Calanthe to bear in her new role as director of fraternal relations for the NACW. Allen believed that this national platform would allow her to "reach as many of our sisters as possible." Moreover, she viewed the appointment as fortuitous because a "new world of opportunities, influence, and power is unfolding itself before the American Negro women of today, as never before. An intelligent study and observance of the same enables us to observe and appreciate its spiritual, intellectual, and material significance."[35] She called for a new generation of "Paul Reveres," women who would spearhead racial uplift efforts.[36] Reminiscent of similar calls from earlier generations of race women like Frances Harper, Josephine St. Pierre Ruffin, Anna Julia Cooper, and Pauline Hopkins, who at critical moments reminded black women that their unique perspective qualified them for a special form of national duty, Allen's remarks also underscore the national significance with which she viewed the joint work of fraternal women and clubwomen.[37]

Though Allen was well respected for her work with the Order of Calanthe and her local and national club work, her activities took place largely within Shreveport's black middle-class milieu. The local paper routinely covered meetings of the Terrell Club, offering extensive descriptions of both the menu and party favors—"tiny pink baskets filled with mints"—and of the "the ladies" who were "very pretty in picturesque hats and gowns, the hostess [Allen] wearing beige crepe-georgette with contrasting corsage at the left shoulder and blending hosiery and slippers." The reporter took care to note that, "despite their beauty[,] . . . their allegiance to the club insures a beautiful harvest of . . . beneficial service to the community."[38] Although these descriptions might seem at different turns gratuitous, frivolous, and inconsequential, they demonstrate that Shreveport's clubwomen were a solidly middle-class group. Kevin Gaines, Deborah White, and other historians have written about the ways that clubwomen were often elitist in their approach to racial uplift.[39] On the one hand, African Americans during the post-Reconstruction era believed that attaining middle-class status was critically important for advancing the race, not just economically, but also ideologically. African Americans challenged prevailing racist ideas that black people were incapable of progress by attaining middle-class status. Furthermore, in the case of African American clubwomen, the attainment of middle-class status put them in the position to "lift as we climb," the NACW motto. A firm believer in this motto, Allen charged the Louisiana association to "work harder, stronger, longer and in a more systematic way on a more consistent program with better arranged plans, to plant the Banner of Lifting as we Climb many rounds higher up the ladder of progress."[40] Steeped in what Higginbotham has famously termed "a politics of respectability," Allen subscribed to middle-class notions of racial progress.

Consequently, among her many admirers, Allen had at least one critic. Just two weeks after the launch of the City Federation of Women's Clubs, Josepha Boyd created the Southern Women's Civic, Social, and Commercial Advancement Association. Though little information exists about Boyd's organization, she created the group to respond to perceived class exclusivity among existing women's organizations, most likely among those groups that constituted the City Federation of Women's Clubs. Boyd told a *Sun* reporter that, "of the many different organizations of our fair city[,] not one seems to be interested in the masses of our womanhood. The women who must rise at 5:30 of mornings to prepare their husbands and children to meet the day, then prepare themselves to make 7 o'clock time, get the Nordic men, women and children off on their journey for the day." Here Boyd painted a vivid picture of the lives of working-class black women in Shreveport, in stark contrast to Allen's middle-class interests. Boyd evinced a concern for "the washer-woman who must go to gather their bundles, [those who] must nurse petted children, and work in the offices, and cafes; these are the women that run the hubs of the organizations and so far, no consideration has been given to their welfare."[41]

Boyd offered an astute labor critique of the black club and fraternal movements to which Allen never publicly responded. After laboring all day in white organizations, businesses, and for white families, black working women still "rushed through the day always mindful of the duties awaiting them at home at the close of day." Boyd insisted that "the shoulders of the average Negro woman [carry] more duties than any other, and she gets less credit." In addition to making an explicit class critique of the differences between the experiences of working- and middle-class black women in Shreveport, Boyd also argued that the work of racial uplift was not just about changing political structures but also about creating an inviting social environment. Her association, she asserted, "hopes to make life a little brighter for the women and girls of this city by providing them with decent recreation, inspiration, and desires to work for their own uplift."[42]

Boyd's focus on the importance of recreation both converges and diverges with Allen's political philosophy. They agreed that an active social life was important for African American women, but Boyd explicitly advocated for increased recreational access among working-class black women. Moreover, both women accepted the self-help racial uplift philosophies of the time, but Boyd argued that working-class women needed to be invested in working "for their own uplift," while Allen touted the NACW philosophy of "lifting as we climb." Boyd further suggested that "if the women and girls of the city don't attend the show, church or visit, after their work is done, there is nothing left for them to do but 'WALK THE STREETS,' and this would start them down the path to 'SHAME and DEGRADATION.'"[43] Boyd's sexual policing of working-class black women betrays some investments in middle-class respectability, but her larger safety concerns were not unfounded. In the summer of 1927, the *Sun* published an editorial titled "A Warning to Race Girls," informing its readers that

> during the past three weeks, it is alleged, several unescorted colored girls and young women have been meddled, and others, insulted by young white men and boys at night in the streets, principally side streets. Young women and girls while on their way to church, show, entertainment or home have been stopped by these superior young white men, who do not believe in "social equality," and invited to accompany them on joy rides. Others have tried to force colored girls into their cars, parked less than half a block from Texas Avenue.

On one occasion, two girls who had refused such a request for a "joy ride" had been chased for half a block. The editorial went on to critique the obvious racism and sexual terrorism of the white men who perpetrated such acts against black women, but what it pointed to was a larger problem of sexual vulnerability among black women and girls that needed to be addressed.[44] Though Boyd's rhetoric of sexual policing fit within a long tradition of what Darlene Clark Hine has identified as the "culture of dissemblance," that quelled black women's public expressions of sexuality, the broader community narrative of protecting young girls suggests, in line with Danielle McGuire's findings, that black communities were forthright about the problem of sexual violence and fervent in their advocacy for protection of black women.[45]

The discussion about recreational opportunities for women and girls was part of a much larger conversation about the lack of available recreation facilities for all young blacks. A July 1927 *Sun* editorial railed against Shreveport's black leadership for not being more staunch advocates for the creation of parks and recreation centers for black children. Acknowledging racism in the allocation of public funds, the editor nevertheless argued that "the fight for equal rights and accommodations should never be given up until the battle is won. However, until that day comes, we have got to protect the interests of the youth of the group to the best of our ability—we have got to provide means for growth and development, or be satisfied with the knowledge that we are backward people." Thus the editor called on Shreveport's "43 Negro churches, twenty-three social clubs, and nearly a score of fraternal organizations" to donate the use of their property or to raise money to build playgrounds.[46] The conversation remained ongoing, and by 1931 Allen headed the Park Board for Colored Citizens. Local groups heeded the editor's call and contributed money to keep Lincoln Park open as recreational space for African Americans. The Mary Church Terrell Club contributed ten dollars, the second highest amount, to the effort.[47]

In one last thinly veiled critique of fraternal orders and mutual aid societies, Boyd declared that "we as a race are over dutiful in taking care of our DEAD, but very indifferent about the collective welfare of our living."[48] Fraternal orders were bastions of financial capital in black communities largely because of the lucrative burial insurance programs that they underwrote. Boyd herself was more concerned about providing black people a rich experience while they remained among the living. Although it is not clear what became of Boyd's group, her powerful intervention on behalf of Shreveport's working-class black women cannot be underestimated.[49] Her critique offered an early and important assessment of the ways that race, class, and gender worked to make black women vulnerable to sexual assault. Unlike Allen, who was never this explicitly political in print, Boyd explicitly confronted the challenges facing the "average Negro woman" in Shreveport. The presence of Boyd's southern civic group reveals a dynamic black women's community in Shreveport, one actively invested in improving conditions for African Americans, especially African American women and children. Even so, Allen's work, while differently focused, was no less political than that of Boyd's.

Though Allen's middle-class proclivities were short sighted, largely because her social tastes catered to a particular group, her woman-centered racial leadership model is an exemplar of early-twentieth-century racial organizing. Because she focused her social activism on business, women's leadership, and fraternal work, Allen demonstrated not in her rhetoric but rather through her activities that she believed an elevated, well-informed African American middle class would help to uplift the race. Allen should also be considered one of the pioneering figures in demonstrating the power of joint local and national organizational efforts in achieving racial uplift endeavors. The combination of fraternal efforts, the club movement, and the efforts of locally active women like Allen who were also nationally connected provided the organizational leadership paradigm that the National Association for the Advancement of Colored People would perfect and use to become a force in civil rights activism in the twentieth century.

Notwithstanding Boyd's local dissent, each of Allen's public roles gained her the respect of her colleagues, locally and nationally. Nannie Helen Burroughs, founder of the National Training School for Girls in Washington, D.C., and the National League of Republican Colored Women (NLRCW) had a great respect for Allen. Burroughs formed the NLRCW immediately following the 1924 NACW convention, attesting again to the ways in which race women creatively used their connections with one another to launch a range of ventures. The NLRCW had an explicitly political agenda in the face of the NACW's nonpartisan and increasingly domestic and insular commitments. In 1928, Burroughs spearheaded meetings with both President Calvin Coolidge and Secretary of Commerce Herbert Hoover in order to discuss the particular economic situation of African Americans. Allen was not present at the 1928 meetings of the NACW or the NLRCW, but Burroughs informed the club that before they met with Secretary

Hoover they needed "first hand information of the distress of our people in the South" and that they should get that information from Allen.[50]

By 1930, Allen had ascended to such prominence in the NACW that she became one of nine delegates to travel to the Quinquennial Meeting of the International Congress of Women (ICW) in Vienna, Austria, that summer. She shared the venerable company of such race women as NACW president Sallie Stewart, Mrs. S. Joe Brown, Hallie Quinn Brown, and Jane Edna Hunter, an attorney, social worker, and prominent clubwoman from Ohio. Most importantly, Allen's trip resulted in a significant evolution in her personal conception of her role as race woman. Allen referred to her experience as being part of "one of the greatest meetings of women the world has ever known."[51] She was particularly impressed at the accolades that Stewart received and the way in which "colored women" were consulted about and considered experts on the race problem. With her characteristic capacity for understatement, Allen also wrote about an ironic experience in which the NACW retinue found themselves surrounded by a group of Austrian musicians who began to play "My Old Kentucky Home" and "I Wish I Was in Dixie." "The Austrians wanted to do honor to us as Americans. We were happy to give our testimonials to the intelligent, honorable, and courageous manner in which our party received the courtesies extended to us."[52] That the women had to maintain their composure and a respectable demeanor in the face of such an outrageous courtesy demonstrates the necessity of their finely honed performance of respectability. At the same time, the trip inculcated in Allen a kind of global consciousness and the sense that she was not just a local or a national representative for her race but also an international one. Maintaining her dignity in light of that experience was a critical part of the training to be a racial leader and representative that she had received through her varied organizational work.

When Allen returned from the trip, she wrote a series of weekly articles recounting her experiences that ran in the *Sun* through the late summer and fall of 1930. This act of sharing each leg of her European tour in detail with her counterparts back home is part of a centuries-long tradition of black women's travel narratives about trips both in the United States and abroad.[53] It too was very much a part of race women's work for racial uplift. Rather than merely traveling for pleasure, particularly in the context of the swiftly approaching Great Depression, Allen's account of her journey allowed a certain amount of public scrutiny of her race work. Her readers participated as vicarious tourists to places that they might never have the opportunity to travel. The *Sun*'s celebration of Allen's trip revealed also a certain degree of "race pride" that one of Shreveport's own would be allowed to participate in such a magnificent trip. In addition to her weekly column, "My Trip Abroad," the *Sun* published at least five articles before, during, and after the trip, celebrating Allen. The *Sun* hoped that her published accounts of her travels would "prove both interesting and informing to those who have not, as well as to those who have, enjoyed the privilege of extensive travel."[54]

The black women who embarked on this trip saw themselves as racial ambassadors, called upon to represent the best of the African American community. The first opportunity that the nine NACW delegates had to be racial ambassadors occurred before they set sail from New York. Mrs. John D. Rockefeller hosted the ladies in her home for an interracial reception in New York City. Allen wrote in her column, "We shall never forget the heart-to-heart talk we had at this luncheon and the friendly relation that existed."[55] On several occasions while they were abroad, Allen noted that the entourage caused a stir, as many folks had presumably not encountered African Americans before, or simply found such dignified black women a novelty. Allen marveled that, during a tour of London, "two hundred or more school children observed us and surged to get near enough to shake our hands."[56]

Once they actually made it to the ICW conference, the delegation's duty to represent the race took on global dimensions. Allen told readers, "We created quite a bit of comment; and women of every foreign country wanted to meet us. Quite a few teas were given in our honor. . . . We were guests at a tea given by one of the Clubs of the city of Vienna. The affair was in our honor. The president, who is a very rich woman, was very anxious to have us tell them of our problems in America. And they in return told us of their own."[57] In another case, she explained, "We were the center of attraction wherever we went. Some thought we were from Africa, or some island possession, but our dropping a word here and there, they exclaimed, 'America! America!' It was amusing to see their efforts to classify us."[58] A conspicuously impressive group, the delegation handled their celebrity through a deft deployment of respectability that garnered them the respect of their peers.

When Allen returned to Shreveport, the City Federation of Women's Clubs hosted a celebratory program at the Avenue Baptist Church. A *Sun* reporter characterized Allen as "the embodiment of grace and dignity." After prefatory remarks and singing, Allen arose and "recounted the story of 'My Trip to the Orient,' in such a simple, intelligent and coherent manner as to demonstrate her ability as an expository and descriptive speaker of the highest type."[59] Here the reporter's characterizations of her speaking style are important: Shreveport residents respected Allen's leadership because of her grace and dignity, traits that had much currency under the regime of respectability; because of her great abilities as an orator, skills that were frequently celebrated by her peers both locally and nationally; and perhaps most importantly because of the accessibility of her content. Race women frequently discussed the importance of communicating ideas in a simple, clear, and nonconvoluted manner so that even people of lesser education and station could understand the ideas being brought to bear. Allen's willingness to do this while avoiding the air of condescension garnered her great respect among Shreveport's African American citizenry. The program ended with an attendee's recitation of a poetic stanza that one of Allen's fellow trip delegates had composed and distributed in honor of the women who traveled. Of Allen, the poet wrote: "Lady Cora M. Allen, so stately and fine; whose wisdom and counsel kept the party in line."[60]

Cora Allen's poise, courage, and ingenuity mark her as both distinctive and a representative figure of other race women who spearheaded racial leadership initiatives in the nineteenth and twentieth centuries. In particular, her endeavors at the intersections of fraternal and club work add new dimensions to existing studies of black female leaders. Her multiple roles as preacher's wife, clubwoman, and fraternal leader bespeak a multilayered gender politics, which she negotiated deftly and with the kind of poise that allowed her to disrupt prevailing negative stereotypes of black women as uncouth and undignified. Her skillful use of multiple overlapping networks of black women's organizations provides a larger critical model for investigating the ways that myriad other race women who were locally active had a national impact on African American uplift activities. A paragon of the respectable black woman, Allen used her skills as an orator and her knack for diplomacy to gain the respect of her peers, locally, nationally, and internationally, even as she tried, sometimes unsuccessfully as in the case of the women who joined Boyd's southern civic group, to make the privileges of her upper-middle-class lifestyle accessible to Shreveport's African American citizenry. As an institution builder, Allen's oversight of the Calanthean Temple project remains the signal accomplishment of her life. The temple was a rich point of convergence for African American business interests, cultural life, and social activism. That a group of black women managed to create such a culturally and socially significant space in the Deep South in the 1920s is a testament to black women's central role in African American racial uplift efforts. The Calanthe Temple Commission's work richly complicates the existing scholarship on women's activism in Louisiana, much of which focuses on women from New Orleans. Allen accomplished her feats of leadership not only in the Deep South, but in racially volatile, Klan-centered, 1920s Shreveport. For Allen to be successful in such a racially hostile environment attests not only to her ingenuity and skill as a negotiator but also to the pragmatic benefits of black women's intricately crafted politics of respectability. The rich tradition of fraternal activism coupled with club work among Allen and other women further underscores the breadth and depth of black women's leadership strategies, their communal and personal resistance to limiting gender roles, and their commitment to approaches that balanced broad national investments with deep forms of local and community engagement.

NOTES

1. The black Knights were organized in 1880 in Mississippi after being denied membership in the white Knights of Pythias, which organized in 1863 in Washington, D.C. The Shreveport chapter was founded in 1881. E. A. Williams and S. W. Green, *History and Manual of the Colored Knights of Pythias* (Nashville: National Baptist Publishing Board, 1917), 857.

2. *Shreveport, Louisiana, City Directory* (Shreveport, La.: Louis N. Brueggerhoff, 1924), 252.

3. Dan Garner, "The Legend of Old Blue Goose," in *Shreveport Sounds in Black and White*, ed. Kip Lornell and Tracey E. W. Laird (Jackson: University Press of Mississippi, 2008), 211.

4. See Elsa Barkley Brown, "Womanist Consciousness: Maggie Lena Walker and the Order of Saint Luke," *Signs* 14, no. 3 (Spring 1989): 610–33, for a longer discussion of black fraternal ventures in Richmond, Virginia, during this same time. Cora Allen was familiar with Walker's work because of their participation in the NACW and referenced Walker at least once in her correspondence with the NACW president. See letter to Sallie W. Stewart, November 17, 1930, in NACW Correspondence with the Louisiana State Federation of Colored Women, records of the National Association of Colored Women's Clubs, in which NACW business dealings with Walker and the Consolidated Bank & Trust of Richmond are noted. *Records of the National Association of Colored Women's Clubs, 1895–1992*, ed. Lillian Serece Williams (Bethesda: University Publications of America, 1994).

5. Williams and Green, *History and Manual of the Colored Knights of Pythias*, 857.

6. Giles Vandal, "The Policy of Violence in Caddo Parish, 1865–1884," in *The African American Experience in Louisiana: Part B—from the Civil War to Jim Crow*, Louisiana Purchase Bicentennial Series in Louisiana History, ed. Charles Vincent (Lafayette: Center for Louisiana Studies, 2000), 205–22.

7. David M. Chalmers. "Louisiana: Black Sheets among the Bayous," in *The African American Experience in Louisiana: Part C—from Jim Crow to Civil Rights*, Louisiana Purchase Bicentennial Series in Louisiana History, ed. Charles Vincent (Lafayette: Center for Louisiana Studies, 2000), 172–78.

8. Ibid., 172. The Klan tried to remove names from their local membership rolls and reregister the members on rolls in other states. But once their names were removed, many of those members refused to participate in Klan activity for fear of prosecution.

9. Many of the women mentioned in this essay used their initials rather than first names in order to make it more difficult for local white people to call them by their first names, a tacit act of disrespect that failed to recognize African American women as adults. "Race man" and "race woman" were terms used to denote male and female racial leaders who had a high degree of visibility and were known publicly for their advocacy of racial uplift.

10. Williams and Green, *History and Manual of the Colored Knights of Pythias*, 924; William Hicks, *A History of Louisiana Negro Baptists* (Nashville: National Baptist Publishing Board, 1914). See also *Annuals and Journals of the Black Baptist Conventions in America* (Nashville: Historical Commission, Southern Baptist Convention, 1977). In 1939, Leland College, a now-defunct theology school in southern Louisiana also named a building after Luke Allen Jr. See "Sessions to Be Held in Luke Allen Memorial Auditorium on Leland College Campus," *Shreveport Sun*, October 14, 1939, 3. See also photo with caption: "[The Avenue Church] now boasts the largest membership of any church in Shreveport," *Shreveport Sun*, November 12, 1927, 8. For adoption info, see Caddo Parish Clerks Book, no. 118, 663–65. Many thanks to April Dahm for sharing the adoption information with me.

11. Evelyn Brooks Higginbotham, *Righteous Discontent: The Women's Movement in the Black Baptist Church, 1880–1920* (Cambridge: Harvard University Press, 1993), 186. See also all of chapter 7.

12. Barbara Welter, "The Cult of True Womanhood," *American Quarterly* 18, no. 2 (1966): 151–74.

13. For additional discussion of the ways that African American women blended their views of domesticity with their commitment to public transformation of racial discourses, see Claudia Tate,

Domestic Allegories of Political Desire: The Black Heroine's Text at the Turn of the Century (New York: Oxford University Press, 1992); Carla Peterson, *Doers of the Word: Black Women Speakers and Writers in the North, 1830–1880* (New York: Oxford University Press, 1995).

14. A. E. Perkins, ed., *Who's Who in Colored Louisiana* (Baton Rouge: Douglas Loan, 1930). See also Thomas Yenser, ed., *Who's Who in Colored America: A Biographical Dictionary of Notable Living Persons of African Descent in America*, 3rd ed. (Brooklyn: Thomas Yenser, 1932), 23; Yenser, *Who's Who in Colored America*, 4th ed. (Brooklyn: Thomas Yenser, 1937), 9.

15. *National Notes* (NACW) 28, no. 6 (March 1926): 13–14. See also Records of the City Federated Clubs of Shreveport, 1980, author's personal collection.

16. Fannie Barrier Williams, "The Club Movement among Colored Women of America," in *Can I Get a Witness? Prophetic Religious Voices of African American Women: An Anthology*, ed. Marcia Y. Riggs (Maryknoll, N.Y.: Orbis Books, 1997), 118. For additional information on the black women's club movement, see Darlene Clark Hine, *Hine Sight: Black Women and the Re-construction of American History* (Brooklyn: Carlson Publishing, 1994); Deborah Gray White, *Too Heavy a Load: Black Women in Defense of Themselves, 1894–1994* (New York: W. W. Norton, 1999); Stephanie Shaw, *What a Woman Ought to Be and to Do: Black Professional Women Workers during the Jim Crow Era* (Chicago: University of Chicago Press, 1996); Paula Giddings, *When and Where I Enter: The Impact of Black Women on Race and Sex in America* (New York: Quill/William Morrow, 1984); Cynthia Neverdon-Morton, *Afro-American Women of the South and the Advancement of the Race, 1895–1925* (Knoxville: University of Tennessee Press, 1991). Scholarly studies by these historians have sought to recapture and make visible Black women's participation in the first wave of the feminist movement via the clubwomen's movement (Giddings, White) and various forms of community socialization that made Black women's race work almost compulsory in many respects (Shaw and Hine).

17. See Brittney Cooper, "'They Are Nevertheless Our Brethren': The Order of Eastern Star and the Battle for Women's Leadership, 1874–1925," in *"All Men Free and Brethren": Prince Hall Fraternalism and the Rise of a People*, ed. Peter P. Hinks and Stephen Kantrowitz (Ithaca: Cornell University Press, 2013), 114–30.

18. For a discussion of black women and the church, see Higginbotham, *Righteous Discontent*; C. Eric Lincoln and Lawrence Mamiya, *The Black Church in the African American Experience* (Durham: Duke University Press, 1990).

19. In their important article on different models of leadership in women's fraternal groups, historian Orit Kent and sociologist Bayliss Camp argue that there are three general models that characterize the leadership styles of women's groups: proprietorship, helpmates, and pilgrims. The proprietorship model, considered the most masculine of the three, revolves heavily around hierarchy and merit based ascendancy through the recognized ranks and degrees of the order. The "helpmateship" model acted in an auxiliary capacity to its male leadership and "did not attempt to inculcate strong bonds between female members." Based upon Kent and Camp's evaluation, the Calantheans and the members of the Household of Ruth used a helpmateship model. The Eastern Stars, who jockeyed heavily for independent control of their organization, were considered the most proprietary of the three. As a tool of social analysis, Camp and Kent's model has much to offer, particularly when analyzing the work of a woman who was a member of a singular organization. But the models meet severe limitations when we apply them to black women's *actual* patterns of participation within these varying groups. Many women, like Cora Allen, were members of multiple groups. See Bayliss Camp and Orit Kent, "Proprietors, Helpmates, and Pilgrims in Black and White Fraternal Rituals," in *What a Mighty Power We Can Be: African American Fraternal Groups and the Struggle for Racial Equality*, ed. Theda Skocpol, Ariane Liazos, and Marshall Ganz (Princeton: Princeton University Press, 2006), 102.

20. See Williams and Green, *History and Manual of the Colored Knights of Pythias*. By way of example, the Alabama Pythians in the early 1900s financially supported the Tuggle Institute, founded

by Calanthean Carrie Tuggle. The school was later run by Calanthean Fannie Blevins, an acquaintance of Cora Allen. The Tuggle Institute went on to become Tuggle Elementary, the school that Angela Davis attended as a child in Birmingham, Alabama.

21. Charles Stump, *Broad Ax* (Chicago), April 5, 1924.

22. From 1920 to 1925, the Order of Eastern Star engaged in several court battles with their respective local Prince Hall Masonic orders, over who would retain the most power to lead the order. See Cooper, "They Are Nevertheless Our Brethren."

23. Those two organizations were the National Federation of Afro-American Women based in Boston and the Colored Women's League based in Washington, D.C.

24. For a discussion of the clubwomen's movement, see White, *Too Heavy a Load* and other works cited in note 16.

25. Women's clubs all over the country hosted "baby contests" as part of the NACW's campaign to champion reproductive health and "proper family structure" in black communities. Though the details of the Shreveport clubwomen's participation are not known, these contests often provided a pretext for examining women for sexually transmitted diseases and for imposing conservative ideas of nuclear family structure on local black families. For more on this practice, see Michele Mitchell, *Righteous Propagation: African Americans and the Politics of Racial Destiny after Reconstruction* (Chapel Hill: University of North Carolina Press, 2004), 96–101.

26. See "Louisiana Federation Report," *National Notes* (NACW)30 (July 1928): 6; *Shreveport Sun*, May 21, 1927. See also "Local Clubs Contribute Liberally to Upkeep of Lincoln Park," *Shreveport Sun*, August 6, 1932.

27. "Negative Win in Debate, 'Resolved That the South Offers Better Advantages to the Negro Than Other Sections of the U.S.," *Shreveport Sun*, May 21, 1927.

28. For more information on black women's debating societies and their use as a tool of political deliberation, see Carla Peterson, *Black Gotham: A Family History of African Americans in Nineteenth Century New York City* (New Haven: Yale University Press, 2011). See also Elizabeth McHenry, *Forgotten Readers: Recovering the Lost History of African American Literary Societies* (Durham: Duke University Press, 2002).

29. *National Notes* (NACW) 28, no. 6 (March 1926): 13–14.

30. "Minutes of the Fifteenth Biennial Session, August 1926," in *Records of the National Association of Colored Women's Clubs, 1895–1992*, ed. Lillian Serece Williams (Bethesda: University Publications of America, 1994), 29.

31. Ibid., 12, 29.

32. "City Federated Clubs in Annual Meet," *Shreveport Sun*, March 17, 1928, 7.

33. For further discussion, see Kimberly Wallace-Sanders, *Mammy: A Century of Race, Gender, and Southern Memory* (Ann Arbor: University of Michigan Press, 2008); Micki McElya, *Clinging to Mammy: The Faithful Slave in Twentieth Century America* (Cambridge: Harvard University Press, 2007).

34. Hallie Q. Brown, "The Black Mammy Statue," *National Notes* (NACW) 25 (1923): 3.

35. Cora M. Allen to Sallie Stewart (NACW president), February 25, 1929, NACW Records, *Records of the National Association of Colored Women's Clubs, 1895–1992*, ed. Lillian Serece Williams (Bethesda: University Publications of America, 1994).

36. Ibid.

37. See White, *Too Heavy a Load*, chapters 1–3.

38. "Dr. Sol. E. Powell Addresses Mary Church Terrell on Sociological Causes of Disease," *Shreveport Sun*, May 28, 1927.

39. See Kevin K. Gaines, *Uplifting the Race: Black Leadership, Politics and Culture in the Twentieth Century* (Chapel Hill: University of North Carolina Press, 1996), introduction and chapter 3. See also White, *Too Heavy a Load*.

40. *National Notes* (NACW) 28 no. 6 (March 1926): 13–14.

41. "Southern Women's Civic Social & Advance Assn. Organized by Local Woman," *Shreveport Sun*, April 7, 1928.

42. Ibid.

43. Ibid.

44. "A Warning to Race Girls," *Shreveport Sun*, June 18, 1927.

45. For more on the culture of dissemblance, see Hine, *Hine Sight*. See also Danielle McGuire, *At the Dark End of the Street: Black Women, Rape, and Resistance—a New History of the Civil Rights Movement* (New York: Vintage, 2010).

46. "Shreveport Negroes Either Don't Know or Don't Care," *Shreveport Sun*, July 2, 1927.

47. "Local Clubs Contribute to the Upkeep of Lincoln Park," *Shreveport Sun*, August 6, 1932.

48. "Southern Women's Civic Social & Advance Assn. Organized by Local Woman," *Shreveport Sun*, April 7, 1928.

49. There was no more coverage of the organization in any extant issues of the 1928 *Sun*.

50. "Meeting Minutes," Nannie Helen Burroughs Papers, box 309, Minutes of the National League of Republican Colored Women, Library of Congress, Washington, D.C.

51. Cora M. Allen, "My Trip Abroad, Series D," *Shreveport Sun*, September 20, 1930.

52. Cora M. Allen, "My Trip Abroad, Series H," *Shreveport Sun*, October 18, 1930.

53. For more on African American travel narratives, see Farah Jasmine Griffin, *Who Set You Flowin?: The African American Migration Narrative* (New York: Oxford University Press, 1996); Carole Boyce Davies, *Black Women, Writing, and Identity: Migrations of the Subject* (New York: Routledge, 1994); Cheryl J. Fish, *Black and White Women's Travel Narratives: Antebellum Experiences* (Gainesville: University Press of Florida, 2004).

54. *Shreveport Sun*, August 30, 1930.

55. Cora M. Allen, "My Trip Abroad, Series A," *Shreveport Sun*, August 30, 1930.

56. Cora M. Allen, "My Trip Abroad, Series B," *Shreveport Sun*, September 6, 1930.

57. Cora M. Allen, "My Trip Abroad, Series H," *Shreveport Sun*, October 18, 1930.

58. Cora M. Allen, "My Trip Abroad, Series I," *Shreveport Sun*, October 25, 1930.

59. *Shreveport Sun*, July 19, 1930.

60. Ibid.

The Women of the New Orleans Christian Woman's Exchange

(1881–)

From "Helping Women Who Help Themselves" to a Mission of Historic Preservation

BETH WILLINGER

Margaret W. Bartlett, a socially prominent and wealthy widow, believed there to be "a great desire among many of our 'best people' to have an efficient organization of ladies, ready and willing to do whatsoever their hearts and hands may find to do for the encouragement, improvement and reclamation of their own sex."[1] Her invitation, "The Ladies Call," was printed in the March 27, 1881, *New Orleans Daily Picayune*. Some forty "prominent ladies" of New Orleans accepted her invitation and met at the St. Charles Hotel on April 1 for the first gathering of what would be called the Christian Woman's Exchange—"the first association organized and chartered in New Orleans by women, for women."[2] More than 130 years later, The Woman's Exchange, as it is now called, is "one of the oldest continuously run non-profit organizations owned and operated by women" in the United States.[3]

The long history of the Christian Woman's Exchange (CWE) provides a background for exploring how an organization of women, by working together, improved the social and economic conditions of thousands of other women and ultimately the condition of the city itself. This essay foregoes a formal institutional history of the CWE to focus on several of the women whose leadership, though largely unseen and unknown to those outside the organization, enhanced or altered the course of the CWE. It also attempts to make visible the women who most often are ignored and nameless in studies of philanthropic organizations, the "needy" women whose lives were somehow bettered by the voluntary work of the organization's members.

Margaret Bartlett's plan to found an organization of women dedicated to improving the lives of needy women was part of a national reform movement. The CWE's original mission to "help women who help themselves" in securing a livelihood was transformed over time in response to world wars, economic recession and depression, natural disasters, and, importantly, changing attitudes about women's work and family roles. Such unanticipated societal changes would ultimately bring about the CWE's decision to join another movement in the late twentieth century, this one to preserve the houses and history of the Vieux Carré.

Bartlett could not have foreseen that her desire to help needy women would expand to include a rooming house for businesswomen or lead to CWE's ownership and preservation of historic homes. Still, in 1881, she showed remarkable foresight in her intention to help women achieve economic security by providing a retail outlet for the sale of items handmade by women in their own homes.[4] Bartlett had observed that "avenues for self support open to ladies in reduced circumstances" were so few that there was "great suffering . . . among a large class . . . anxious for employment [but with] no opportunity to dispose of their handiwork."[5] She was knowledgeable about the work begun by the Philadelphia [Pennsylvania] Ladies' Depository in 1832 to ameliorate "the condition of needy women" and had visited the New York Woman's Exchange with the thought of replicating the organization in New Orleans. Thus in 1881, the New Orleans Christian Woman's Exchange became the first such organization in the Deep South and the twelfth of some seventy-two to be organized in the country by 1891.[6] The woman's exchange movement drew upon the interplay between the Arts and Crafts Movement begun in Great Britain and the European philosophy of self-help and self-improvement through the acquisition of vocational skills. These dual influences are evident in the objectives put forth by Bartlett and adopted by the CWE. Their first objective was "to provide the ways and means for the encouragement and relief of our impoverished women who cannot be crushed into beggary and sin, but who earnestly seek to help themselves." Their second objective aimed "to provide some means of improvement in the education of our young women, by which they may become artistic workers in all the great and grand affairs of human life, both practical and ornamental."[7]

Characteristically, woman's exchanges nationally provided a venue for the sale of women's traditional work in the decorative and domestic arts, and many also offered an "edible department" or lunchroom where food prepared by women was sold. While the objectives of the New Orleans Christian Woman's Exchange paralleled those adopted by exchanges elsewhere, it was the only one to include the word "Christian" in its name. The insertion drew criticism from "A Church Member" whose letter in the *Daily Picayune* questioned "the policy of making our Women's Exchange a religious work instead of one of noble philanthropy" and urged the inclusion of non-Christian women, particularly Jewish women, in its membership.[8] These arguments apparently held some sway. Although "Christian" remained in the organization's name, apparently at the insistence of the founder, the by-laws maintained, "All white women, without regard to religious belief, may become members."[9]

At the April 1, 1881, organizational meeting of the Christian Woman's Exchange, twenty-four women of the city's most visible and respected families were elected to the board of managers.[10] Bartlett was elected president, and among the four vice presidents elected were Mrs. R. M. (Caroline Gratia Williams) Walmsley, whose husband was president of the Louisiana National Bank, and Mrs. T. G. (Ida Ann Slocomb) Richardson, whose husband, Dr. Tobias Richardson, was dean of the Tulane University School of Medicine.[11] Mrs. Theodor (Mary Emma) Auzé, whose husband was a prominent cotton broker, was elected secretary.[12]

The organizers were women accustomed to the idea of doing good deeds for those less fortunate. They had been born of privilege and married well. Bartlett, daughter of the well-to-do McComb family, had been a founder of the Seventh Street Orphan Home and provided the funding for the construction of the Presbyterian church and parsonage on Thalia Street.[13] Ida Richardson was a daughter of the affluent Slocomb family and reputed to be the wealthiest woman in New Orleans. She served on the CWE board of managers and was president for many years of St. Anna's Asylum for the Relief of Destitute Females and Their Helpless Children. She later gave funds for the construction of the Richardson Building to house Tulane's School of Medicine, and in 1908 she was awarded the *Picayune*'s Loving Cup for public service.[14]

Yet while members of the CWE were likely to have engaged in benevolent work as their Christian duty or joined with others in religious, patriotic, or hereditary auxiliaries and associations, few had specifically organized around the needs of women. Moreover, even amid the women's club movement of the turn of the century, it was unusual to have a board composed of women only. Some questioned whether this organization of strong-minded women could work together to accomplish anything of substance.[15]

The answer soon was evident. Less than two weeks after their initial meeting in 1881, the CWE board of managers rented four rooms at 41–43 Bourbon Street for use as their headquarters and salesroom.[16] By mid-May they had opened the first Exchange Shop for the sale of high-quality articles made by local women and "confidently expected that great relief will be afforded to a class of needy persons who have hitherto been debarred the means of supporting themselves by their own efforts."[17] For June, the CWE's first full month of operation, the women reported paying $234 to sixty-one consignors (the purchasing power of approximately $5,150 in 2010 dollars).[18] Several months later, they leased the entire building at 41–43 Bourbon Street and opened a lunchroom that was "supplied almost entirely from the entries in the salesroom," including salads, gumbos, breads, "jellies, cakes, rolls, ice cream and other dainties."[19] By the end of the year, after seven months in operation, salesroom receipts totaled $908.55 (estimated at $20,000 in 2010) and lunchroom receipts added another $754.20 (approximately $16,600 in 2010).[20]

The immediate success of the CWE's Exchange Shop and lunchroom may be attributed in part to the weekly marketing campaign sponsored by one of the city's most prominent feminists, Eliza Jane Nicholson, editor and publisher of the *Daily Picayune*. Nicholson, who had written under the pen name Pearl Rivers, was the first woman publisher of a daily metropolitan newspaper in the country.[21] She made available free to the CWE each Sunday, for one year, one-and-a-half columns for articles promoting the organization. She also offered the CWE the "engagement of a correspondent to furnish the notes."[22] The correspondent to whom Nicholson referred, quite likely, was Martha Field, a young widow who was hired that year as the first woman to hold a staff position on the *Picayune*. Field, whose pen name was Catharine Cole, was present at the first meeting of the CWE and "kindly consented to write articles relative to the Exchange."[23]

The column, titled "Exchange Notes" and signed "XChange," typically began with a virtuous message urging "active exertion for the good of others" or deploring the condition of women.[24] For example, in a July 1881 column, the author takes aim at those who would criticize women for their lack of thoroughness and self-reliance, insisting: "The fault is certainly not their own. Girls are educated so superficially that when any emergency arises they are unequal to it."[25] The author would then segue into the CWE's efforts to alleviate this condition (e.g., providing training) and conclude with a review of the handmade items for sale in the Exchange Shop and the foods available in the lunchroom. Whether written by Cole or by Mrs. Auzé, CWE secretary, as a marginal note in the minutes suggests, the articles rendered a close reporting of the meeting minutes, and though a bit doctrinaire, they also expressed a gender ideology consistent with that of Cole.[26] Like other women of her social standing, Cole held a strong sense of noblesse oblige, feeling women had an obligation to care for those less fortunate and to uphold a high standard of moral conduct. She celebrated what she considered to be woman's essential nature and moral superiority and accepted the South's belief in separate spheres for women and men, even as she recognized the need for women to work outside the home. Perhaps for this reason, and as a workingwoman herself, Cole was critical of the low wages and labor conditions under which women worked.[27]

Cole wrote numerous articles about the work of the CWE and mentioned it often in her other unsigned weekly column, "Woman's World and Work." At the annual meeting of the CWE in 1884, Field was made an honorary member.[28] Perhaps in a somewhat exaggerated attribution, her brother-in-law, Bernard Shields, once contended: "New Orleans owes [Catharine Cole] its Training

School for Nurses, its *Woman's Exchange*, and its kindergartens."[29] The truth is that Cole's writing, signed or unsigned, was instrumental in broadening views of women's work and worth, in New Orleans and throughout the South.

Cole's articles and "Exchange Notes" were directed, by-and-large, to a readership with funds to patronize the CWE's shop and lunchroom. Few articles spoke to those who would be consignors. A sentence in an early "Exchange Notes" column stated simply: "To all needy gentlewomen who desire to help themselves this Exchange has opened a door."[30] Advertisements directed to consignors were placed in the want ads section of the paper. One of the first read: "Christian Woman's Exchange is now open for the reception of articles for sale and orders for work at 41 and 43 Bourbon Street. Orders taken for cakes on WEDNESDAYS and SATURDAYS. Articles for sale received every week day at 11:00 A.M. Contributions of any kind gratefully received."[31] The procedures for women to place their items for sale at the Exchange Shop changed somewhat over time. Initially women who joined the CWE at an annual subscription fee of five dollars were given three tickets to be "distributed to a worthy person, who thus became entitled to bring their work to the rooms." A committee would then determine if the items "were up to a certain standard of excellence" before being placed in the salesroom.[32] Consignors were required to pay a fee of two dollars annually. They set their own price for their goods to be sold and were charged a 10 percent commission on the sales.[33] The financial participation of both members and consignors was thought to establish a cooperative spirit in which both parties were "stock-holders."[34]

More than two hundred of the city's most prominent women joined the CWE within the first year, each given "the privilege of affording three fellow creatures the means of gaining a livelihood."[35] In setting out to "help those who help themselves," however, CWE members drew a distinction between the "worthy" and "unworthy" poor. Historian Anne Firor Scott notes that white women's societies nearly always made such a distinction, viewing with special sympathy once-prosperous widows who had fallen on hard times or were too old to work ("ladies in reduced circumstances").[36] This philosophy is similarly revealed in the CWE's acceptance of not only handcrafted items but also "family heirlooms" that "owners were willing to sell in order to pay their debts during hard times."[37]

CWE members also made assumptions of worthiness based on race. After a lengthy "discussion in regard to applicants for tickets," a motion that "any member shall be permitted to assist anyone in distress without regard to color" was "finally withdrawn."[38] In many ways, the motion was a bold one, particularly given the beliefs and customs then prevalent in the South. However, Kathleen Sander concludes in her study of the woman's exchange movement, *The Business of Charity*, that such attitudes were not specific to the South, as managers nationally rarely "reached beyond 'educated,' white, middle- and working-class women to embrace those of the immigrant or lower classes."[39] One can imagine that the CWE member's proposed motion considered a domestic worker's chocolate cake or handmade baby blankets as appropriate and salable items that could bring additional income to the worker. Yet, for other CWE members, it would appear that having the motion withdrawn was preferable to assisting women of color or having a vote on the issue recorded in the minutes.

Little is known of the consignors locally or nationally. This is in part a consequence of the exchange movement's national policy of maintaining the anonymity of consignors so as not to reveal the names of women who were in financial distress.[40] Items bore the number assigned to the consignor, never her name. In the CWE's "Consignor's Books" and "Inventory" can be found each consignor's number, name, address, list of articles consigned, and amount paid, but nothing about the consignor herself. The CWE minutes hold an occasional mention of a woman expressing her gratitude for the opportunity afforded her. A daughter wrote as an adult to tell of her mother supporting their family by selling her work through the exchange. One woman who regularly sold bread for the lunchroom was reported to have bought a stove with her earnings.[41] Many of the CWE consigners lived outside the city and state, and it is thought that some consigners sent their wares to more than one exchange.[42]

In addition to newspaper coverage of the CWE—its merchandise, successful consignors, and fashionable managers—the CWE also gained patronage from the Woman's Department of the 1884–85 World's Industrial and Cotton Centennial Exposition held in New Orleans in present-day Audubon Park. Julia Ward Howe, author of "The Battle Hymn of the Republic" and president of the New England Woman's Suffrage Association, was chosen to head the Woman's Department. Howe secured the participation of nineteen states, each having a woman commissioner in charge of organizing her state's exhibit. The selection of the Louisiana commissioner fell to the president of the Christian Woman's Exchange, Caroline Walmsley, who had been elected president at the first annual meeting of the CWE, a year after its founding, and was reelected each of the next twenty-five years. Walmsley appointed Jenny Caldwell Nixon chief commissioner of the Louisiana women's exhibit. Mary Emma Auzé, CWE secretary, was chosen local secretary of the Woman's Department.[43]

The Woman's Department, alternately called the Department of Woman's Work, exhibited women's decorative arts, handicrafts, literary accomplishments, and scientific studies and also regularly sponsored classes and demonstrations to foster art appreciation and the development of practical skills.[44] Notable among these classes were those offered by the brothers William and Ellsworth Woodward. Their classes created a group of women trained in the design skills needed to produce the crafts, notably hand-painted ceramics, and an appreciation of the decorative arts by women patrons. An immediate outcome of the classes was the formation of the Ladies' Decorative Art League and the New Orleans Art Pottery (later the Art League Pottery Club), which allowed the women to continue the design of clay work learned at the Cotton Centennial. These wares were then placed for display in the CWE's Exchange Shop.[45] The symbiotic relationship between the CWE and the Woman's Department likely stemmed in part from the dual influences shaping both, namely the Arts and Crafts Movement and the ideology of self-help and self-improvement as a means to women's economic security.

Under Walmsley's leadership, the CWE thrived. In 1887, its board of managers reported payment to consignors of $87,069.54 (approximately $2,080,000 in 2010) over a five-year period and expressed "an earnest desire" for permanent headquarters to accommodate their growing success.[46] That same year, two prominent New Orleanians and board members, Mrs. Charles L. (Florestile) Howard and Mrs. Charles A. (Marie Louise) Whitney, both of whom were widows, donated funds for the $28,000 purchase of a twenty-six-room, three-story building at the corner of Camp and South Streets on Lafayette Square.[47] The gifts were considered to be two of the largest in the United States given to charitable organizations by women in their own names in the late nineteenth century.[48] In addition to appreciating greater space for the Exchange Shop and lunchroom, CWE members remarked that "the possession of a home" enables us "to greatly enlarge the scope of our work, and increase the number of women benefited."[49]

Enlarge they did. While the raison d'être of the CWE remained the business of running the Exchange Shop "for the sale of woman's work," the organizational structure of the CWE also bore similarities to women's benevolent associations and settlement houses forming throughout the country.[50] For example, in their new headquarters on Lafayette Square, CWE members created community services such as New Orleans's first free circulating library and first day nursery for working mothers with young children. They provided the first office of the Travelers Aid Society and shelter for homeless women, founded a sewing school and held various vocational and literary classes for the education of young women, offered an employment bureau, and managed a full-service lunchroom favored by businessmen.[51] In offering this wide variety of services to women and the community, the CWE's operation was more analogous to the Young Women's Christian Association than to other woman's exchanges.[52] As there was a dearth of social service agencies in New Orleans at the time—it was not until 1896 that Kingsley House, the "oldest Settlement House in the South," was founded in the city, and not until 1911 that the New Orleans YWCA was formed—it may well be that CWE members felt compelled to take on these various services to address the needs of women, particularly those new to the city.[53] It was here in 1887 that the CWE began renting furnished rooms to single workingwomen at affordable rents, an unusual though not unique offering among woman's exchanges.[54]

As with the consignors, little is known about the residents of the CWE rooming house during this early period. The board referred to residents as either "permanent" or "transient," though no precise definition has been found. Presumably transients were women who stayed less than a month, with some staying just a few nights. The permanents, on the other hand, often stayed for years. While meals could be purchased in the lunchroom of the CWE, and meals were provided to women in need, the CWE residence appears always to have been intended as a rooming house, not a boardinghouse that included two or three meals a day in the rental fee. Nor was it intended as a settlement house where CWE members served as volunteer social reformers or settlement workers to immigrant communities. Residents with surnames such as Boyd, Dupry, Lutrell, Sims, Thornhill, and McWhan suggest that there was no particular ethnic or migrant group of women served.[55] Moreover, despite the organizational name, there is little to suggest that members considered themselves Christian missionaries.[56] Jews as well as gentiles appear to have been admitted as roomers. There was no mandatory Sunday worship or even a chapel or prayer room on the premises as was often found in rooming houses or boardinghouses for young migrant women.[57] Rather, members of the board of managers managed: their primary concern was hiring and supervising employees, balancing the budget, and maintaining their property and investments. Only occasionally did they involve themselves in the hands-on daily operation of either the residence or the retail shop.

The only existing records of the women who lived at the CWE residence on Lafayette Square are contained in three rent receipt books covering the years 1913 to 1919. These list tenants as "Miss" or "Mrs." with their surname—seldom a first name—and the payment received from each. Rents averaged about $6.25 per month.[58] In 1918, there were fifty-seven roomers, the majority of whom were long-term or "permanent." The year began with thirty-three residents, and one year later twenty of those women were still in residence. Of these, nearly half had been renting a room since 1913. Nine of the 1918 residents were listed as "Mrs." Quite likely these women were widows, not divorcees, as divorce was considered socially and morally unacceptable at the time and legally difficult to obtain, even for women in abusive or adulterous marriages. Fewer than 10 percent of women in the United States at the time never married. For the "permanents," then, it would appear that the CWE was not a home away from home—it was home. Although it was somewhat unusual for a woman to live in a rooming house or boardinghouse, it was especially rare for a person to live alone. Regardless of age, most single adults lived with family members.[59]

In keeping with their primary mission, CWE board members measured their success by sales completed and monies paid to consignors and only rarely by the number of consignors paid or roomers housed. In 1913, Mrs. George Halbert, recording secretary, reported that during CWE's thirty-two-year existence the exchange had paid nearly $500,000 (estimated at $11.4 million in 2010) to women for work they had accomplished at home.[60]

The CWE's payment to consignors and success in managing its various departments positioned it as one of the most financially successful exchanges nationally.[61] While the philanthropic intent of the CWE was to promote economic security among needy women through self-help, the exchange movement also fostered the development of managerial and administrative skills among well-to-do women members. CWE members engaged in a kind of "domestic feminism" that positioned their benevolence and volunteerism on behalf of women and "women's work" as ideological support for women's traditional family roles and the right for women not to have to engage in work outside the home.[62] At the same time, their philanthropic work permitted them the freedom to work outside their homes in nontraditional roles and allowed them to expand their sphere of influence into areas otherwise denied them in the late nineteenth and early twentieth centuries. This apparent dichotomy was acknowledged early on in "XChange Notes," whose author insisted: "There is little doubt that the Woman's Exchange is an object of interest. . . . Representing, as it does, individual capacity in the extension of every variety of work that is especially womanly, it exhibits also, as an organization, the result of a practical business capacity, the possession of which is rarely credited to women."[63]

The CWE's carefully crafted by-laws, beautifully handwritten and meticulous minutes, detailed recording of debits and credits, and ease with handling money suggest that board members were privy to an education, likely through private tutors and schools, that was unavailable to the majority of women or men in New Orleans. In 1922, the CWE's reputation for making sound financial decisions was cemented. Faced with ever-mounting maintenance costs and repairs to their headquarters, and with many of the services and resources they had earlier provided no longer needed—or assumed by other agencies and organizations—board members voted to sell their building on Lafayette Square. They leased the building to the New Orleans *Daily States* for $4,000 a year, with a five-year, $80,000 purchase option, and then moved the Exchange Shop to a rental property at 524 Royal Street in a fashionable row of antique shops.[64]

Two years later, the CWE board purchased the "Grima House" at 820 St. Louis Street for their headquarters, paying $17,500. They then spent about $16,000 in repairs and renovations, including conversion of the third-floor ballroom into five rooms for rent to single workingwomen. Having disposed of the furnishings of their former home, they committed $845 to furnish twelve single rooms: five rooms on the third floor and seven rooms on the second and third floors of an annex. Their purchases included "dressers, chairs, pillows, bedsprings, mattresses, wash stands, bowls, pitchers, and slop jars."[65]

Several CWE members responded generously to an appeal by the board for the donation of furnishings for the new headquarters.[66] Mrs. George (Elise) Whitney and her brother furnished a large bedroom on the second floor as a memorial room for their mother, Mrs. Nelson McStea, donating their mother's tester bedroom set and other furnishings attributed to local cabinetmaker and importer of fine furniture Prudent Mallard. Other "memorial rooms" were furnished by Mrs. Robert (Leila Hardie) Moore Sr. in memory of her mother, and by Mrs. E. E. Soulé for her mother, Mrs. Esty. Additional donations included furnishings for the sitting room, central hall, and loggia, a rosewood bookcase, and several antique beds.[67]

In 1924, the serious illness of the CWE president, Mrs. Eugene Roberts, had prompted the board to invite one of the vice presidents, Leila Moore, to assume the presidency and oversee the Grima House purchase. Moore, who had furnished the "Hardie Room" in memory of her mother, was about forty-eight years old when she began her nine-year tenure as CWE president, the second longest term in the organization's history. Earlier that year Moore had hosted several prenuptial social events for her son, Robert Jr.; traveled to Europe with her husband and younger son, Francis; and reigned as queen of the Mystic Club Ball, one of the city's most exclusive Mardi Gras balls.[68] The Mystic Club Ball was begun in 1923, and Moore was only the second woman to be honored as royalty. Unlike other balls that debut young unmarried daughters of elite male members, the Mystic Club is alone among the established mystic societies in honoring the wives of its members. For many years, it was also alone in having the costumed queen of the ball printed on the front page of the newspaper the following day.[69] In 1924, the *Times-Picayune* gave detailed coverage of the ball's "Mandarin's Joy Ride" tableau, noting, "Mrs. Robert Moore was selected to be queen over the island court." With her appeared six "ladies in waiting," three of whom shared an involvement in CWE management, including her daughter, Mrs. L. Kemper Williams.[70] However, none of Moore's many civic activities was mentioned. Rather it was her husband's business career—as vice president of Moore, Hyams & Company, Inc., Investment Securities—and membership in the Boston Club, an exclusive men's club, that received the unstated recognition of the Mystic Club organization.[71]

Robert Moore served as a member of CWE's Men's Advisory Committee and, along with several other men, had advised the organization regarding the purchase of the Grima House. In 1927, when the *Daily States* exercised its option to purchase the CWE's Lafayette Square property for $80,000, Mr. Moore advised the organization regarding the payoff of its $18,000 loan on 820 St. Louis Street and the investment of some $60,000 in profit (approximately $733,000 in 2010).[72]

The two years between vacating their headquarters on Lafayette Square and purchasing the Grima House permitted board members the time to reflect on who might best be served by their rooming department. The St. Louis Street location raised concerns about the wisdom of providing a home for women in the French Quarter given "the questionable character of the surrounding neighborhood."[73] At that time, Norma Wallace, the French Quarter madam, maintained a bordello at 328 Burgundy, and then at 410 Dauphine, both just a few blocks away. Storyville, the district identified as a sixteen-block area in which a "public prostitute or woman notoriously abandoned to lewdness" was legally required to live, was just adjacent to the French Quarter on Basin Street. Although officially shut down in 1917, its activities spilled across Basin Street as the Quarter became the place for late-night music and other "immoral" activities such as tango dancing.[74] CWE members proposed that if no women under thirty years of age were accepted as residents, the objection could be waived. After all, they reasoned, the neighborhood was "better than that surrounding the YWCA" on Gravier Street in the Central Business District.[75]

Other considerations figured into the CWE's focus on the needs of the "older business woman." In a letter sent by board members to CWE associate members, they ardently explained:

> It has been forcibly brought home to the members of the board of the Christian Woman's Exchange that there is no place in the city provided for the older woman who is thrown upon her own resources for support. The younger woman is provided for by more than one splendid organization, but the older woman, whose earning powers are not so great as that of her younger sister, is forced to seek her lodging in out of the way rooming-houses, or with reluctant relatives and her lot is far from enviable. She is a tragic figure.[76]

The CWE managers were keen observers. In 1920, nearly 53 percent of the single, widowed, or divorced women in New Orleans were in the paid labor force. Among women workers, approximately 34 percent were twenty-five to forty-four years old, and 24 percent were forty-five and over.[77] Not only was it considered inappropriate for women to live alone, the lower wages paid to women made doing so nearly impossible. The housing market was tight, Louisiana had a higher rate of renter-occupied housing units than most other states, and most units averaged more than five residents. Few householders lived alone and even fewer owned their own homes.[78] Therefore it is not surprising to find that nearly 30 percent of workingwomen in New Orleans lived with a (reluctant) relative other than their mother, father, or husband (15.2 percent), or in a boardinghouse or lodging house (13.5 percent).[79]

The first of several hundred women to rent a room at the "Residence of the Christian Woman's Exchange" over the next fifty years was a woman identified as Miss Wishaar, the historic event recorded into the minutes as a seventeen-night stay beginning November 1, 1924, for Room No. 1 on the third floor of the main house for $10.20.[80] By 1930, fourteen permanent "lodgers" were renting rooms at the residence, five of whom were widows and nine unmarried. All of the residents were white, and just two were born in Louisiana. The women averaged forty-four years of age, and a higher percentage were employed in occupations typically identified as middle-class than women nationally. Six of the residents were in professional or managerial positions as shop owner, manager, teacher, or solicitor. Three did clerical work, two were in sales, one worked in tourism, and one was not employed.[81] Nationally, most women workers were clerical workers, manual operators such as seamstresses, or private household service workers.[82]

Thus, even though the French Quarter was considered déclassé at this time, there were several favorable conditions to recommend life at the Residence of the Christian Woman's Exchange. Rent for a room included utilities and housekeeping services: beds made and floors dust-mopped daily except Sunday, bed linens changed weekly, and fresh towels delivered twice a week.[83] In addition to these services, the residence provided single women the comforts of a well-managed home, a historic address, and the companionship of other middle-class women. Each resident could enjoy the privacy of her own room and entertain her guests in a communal sitting room furnished with a piano, overstuffed chairs, and, in the 1950s, a television. There was a shared bathroom on each floor and a refrigerator available to all residents on the loggia. Though no meals were offered, the location in the French Quarter—near restaurants, laundries, and other services and within easy walking distance of workplaces on Canal Street and in the Central Business District—made living at 820 St. Louis Street an attractive and affordable option.

There were other events taking place in the 1920s French Quarter that made living there interesting, even if not socially proper. Writers and artists such as Sherwood Anderson, Caroline Durieux, William Faulkner, Lyle Saxon, Natalie Scott, and William Spratling were making the Quarter their gathering place and creative center. Helping to foster this artistic milieu was the founding in 1924 of another women's organization, Le Petit Salon. With the novelist and historian Grace King as president and the nationally recognized advice columnist and journalist Elizabeth M. Gilmer (Dorothy Dix) as vice president, the salon was founded "to keep alive the love of the old traditions of New Orleans and where possible to keep and preserve old historic buildings." True to its charter, the salon purchased and restored the home at 620 St. Peter Street, built in 1838, for its headquarters. Although not viewed favorably at the time by those who wished the Quarter to maintain its bohemian character, the restoration and preservation of the building was later considered "one of the most significant acts to save the architectural heritage of New Orleans," a purpose the CWE would later adopt.[84]

While the society columns of New Orleans newspapers often reported the activities of Le Petit Salon side-by-side with those of the CWE, only a few women participated in the leadership of both.[85] But together the members of these two socially prominent organizations promoted "a rare atmosphere of tradition and culture" by their influx into the French Quarter for meetings, concerts, teas, and receptions.[86]

Across Royal Street from the Exchange Shop, at 531 Royal, was the Clark & Washburn antique store, opened in 1928, with Mary Washburne and Gay T. Clark proprietors.[87] Mary Annie Moore Washburne had moved to New Orleans from Kentucky in 1923 to live with her daughter, son-in-law, and their two young children, shortly after the death of her husband. In Kentucky, Mrs. Washburne was credited with organizing and serving as chair of the country's first American Red Cross World War I canteen.[88] Precisely how Washburne moved from her civic work in Louisville to a career buying and selling antiques is unknown. However, in 1928 she traveled to Europe for the first of what would be at least seven buying trips to France or England in the next ten years. In 1929, she and Mrs. Clark opened Little Antique Shop, Inc., at 527 Royal Street, specializing in French and British antiques. For the next several years, she served as president of the business, with Clark serving as vice president and treasurer. In 1930 and 1931 they traveled abroad together, but by 1935 Washburne appears to have been running the shop alone, and she continued to do so until she retired in 1943.[89]

Sometime around 1937, Washburne became a roomer at the Residence of the Christian Woman's Exchange. The CWE minutes report that "Mrs. Washburne's room" had just been painted, so it is quite likely she had been a resident well before this time. The room she occupied, a spacious 430 square feet with thirteen-foot ceilings, was known also as "the Whitney Room," as it was furnished with Mrs. Whitney's mother's fine antique tester bed and armoire mentioned previously. When Washburne moved into this furnished room, at approximately sixty-five years of age, the monthly rent was $26 (about $400 in 2010). When she "departed" in 1955, at over eighty, her rent had increased to $50 (still about $400 in 2010).[90]

Washburne moved her shop several times, but it was always across the street from the Exchange Shop on the first floor of what is known as Casa Merieult, or the Merieult House. In 1938, the Merieult House, 527–533 Royal Street, was purchased and restored by Robert Moore's daughter, Leila Hardie Moore Williams, and her husband, L. Kemper Williams, as their residence.[91] For at least five years, then, Washburne would have leased her store from Colonel and Mrs. Williams. The Williamses were considered part of the "smart set" whose activities frequently were recorded in newspapers' society pages. Like her mother, Leila Williams would be recognized as queen of the Mystic Ball, in 1936. Like her mother, she too served on the CWE board of managers.[92]

In their home at Royal and Toulouse streets, the Williamses entertained guests associated with his work as president of a lumber manufacturing business and his civic work as chairman of the New Orleans Housing Authority and president of the Community Chest. His civic work would earn him the *Times-Picayune* Loving Cup in 1938, an award his father had received in 1924 for his donation establishing Kingsley House and the New Orleans Day Nursery.[93]

Though Kemper Williams was nearly fifteen years older than his wife, she preceded him in death and in her will donated their French Quarter property for the establishment of the Historic New Orleans Collection.[94] Today the Historic New Orleans Collection's retail shop and welcome hall occupy the spaces that once were home to Washburne's antique shop.

As a French Quarter proprietor, Washburne would have known about the rooms available for rent at the Residence of the Christian Woman's Exchange. However, it is unclear how other prospective residents, whether staying for a few nights or for years, knew of the housing opportunities offered by the CWE. A long-time resident of the Quarter reported that the women "had to know someone" to be approved for residency. Information appears to have been largely by word of mouth, as suggested by the 1929 annual report: "All transient [*sic*] seemed delighted to find so well looked after abode + ask for cards to circulate as they go." This was apparently quite successful, as the 1932 report stated that "practically every one who comes here from out of the state has been sent by someone who has stayed in the house and recommended it."[95] Occasionally an ad announcing the availability of furnished rooms would appear in the newspapers such as this one posted under "Rooms for Rent" in the October 1, 1927, *Times-Picayune*: "Christian Women's [*sic*] Exchange. 820 St. Louis. Rooms. Rates reasonable for permanent or transient." Or this one from 1950: "Comfortable rooms for employed ladies. References required. Christian Woman's Exchange, 820 St. Louis St. 60 years of faithful service to worthy women."[96] While an occasional ad might appear, no listings ever appeared in the New Orleans City Directory under headings such as Apartments, Apartment Houses, Boarding Houses, Furnished Rooms, Hotels, Housing Rentals, Clubs, or Societies.

Another long-term resident, Mrs. (Bertha Frances) Oliver was about sixty-seven in 1942 when she moved in. She would stay until 1962. Oliver, who was born in Ireland, was a widow with a British war pension and was retired from her position as a governess. Her daughter Mave rented a room in the annex of the residence for a few years in the late 1940s.[97] Her surrogate daughter, Lin Emery, the internationally acclaimed kinetic sculptor, also lived at the residence for several years and certainly was the most illustrious tenant known to have lived there. Oliver had been Emery's governess in New York and Florida, beginning when Lin was about five years old, and then moved to New Orleans because of her preference for a damp climate. Shortly after she arrived, she enticed her former charge to visit her at the CWE residence. Emery, then only fifteen years of age and enrolled at Syracuse University, recalls that when she first came to New Orleans to visit with Oliver, the house manager set her up in a room on the ground floor of the annex that was half the size of Oliver's. Dominated by the open hearth of the former kitchen and furnished with a cot, it was quite a contrast to Oliver's spacious room that held her large collection of scientific books and novels.[98] Before permanently moving to New Orleans, Emery would return to the CWE residence much as she would to a family home, renting a room during several personal and professional transitions.

Oliver not only filled in the early gaps in Emery's education brought about by her young widowed mother's frequent moves between homes in New York and Florida, she also carefully selected Emery's schools, arranged for tutors in French and Latin, and enrolled her in painting classes.[99] An extremely well read, highly intelligent, and socially conscious woman, Oliver had been a member of the socialist Fabian Society in England and was said to have corresponded with Albert Einstein about several of her ideas.[100] Although theoretically responsible only for Emery's intellectual development, Oliver was far more, and the two formed a lasting emotional and intellectual relationship. Emery once remarked that Oliver was "a very mystical woman" and described her as being highly resourceful and an excellent researcher, skills illustrated by Oliver's finding the CWE residence and locating educational opportunities for Emery even after her official duties had ended.[101] For example, in the summer of 1943, Oliver arranged for Emery to live with a Mexican family in Mexico City while participating in a summer program at Universidad de Mexico to learn Spanish. The two also spent the summer of 1948 together in Taos, New Mexico, where Emery's paintings were on exhibit at the Harwood Museum.[102] Emery seems to have shared with Oliver a driving curiosity that led Emery to her use of various media such as clay, plaster, and metal and the study of welding, architecture, and engineering. It is quite possible that Oliver's scientific interests also influenced Emery's work as a kinetic sculptor and the development of her highly complex massive sculptural masterworks.

While the residence attracted an array of women, the members of the CWE did not intend for their benevolence to challenge boundaries of race and class. Potential residents were required to provide references and were interviewed by a few members of the board (later just the house manager). All residents were white, as were CWE members and the majority of CWE employees.[103] Rarely was a reference to race recorded in the minutes and then only to identify the "colored" maid.[104] Some of the residents, like Washburne and Oliver, though possibly in "reduced circumstances," had independent means and held some social standing. For example, Washburne's family was among the first families of Virginia and Kentucky. Her genealogical research tracing her maternal line back 3,250 years was featured in a *Times-Picayune* article and was accepted by the National Society of Magna Charta Dames, of which Washburne was a member.[105] Oliver's ancestral home in Ireland was said to have been a castle.[106]

Even women living in the more modest furnished rooms were independent and self-supporting. Martha Foster occupied Room 11 on the third floor from 1951 to 1962. She worked in the linen room and as a room inspector at the Hotel New Orleans on Canal Street and faithfully paid half her monthly rent of $22.50

every two weeks. In her mid-fifties, she too was a widow and had moved to New Orleans from Texas when her daughter came to the city for nursing school.[107]

There were few house rules, no curfews, and residents had their own keys, so they could come and go as they pleased. Although the residence was often considered "chaperoned" or "sheltered" housing by board members, residents were in little need of supervision, and little supervision was given. The house manager lived on the first floor and by and large served as the liaison between the two groups of women, collecting rents, dealing with requests for needed repairs, and supervising housekeeping and maintenance. Still, the board often expressed concern for the welfare of the roomers, cautiously raising rents and sometimes reducing them. For example, during the Great Depression, the board reduced monthly room rents by five dollars "as a temporary measure to meet the present economic situation" and reported that "the residence is perhaps more than ever filling the purpose for which intended," as six of the permanent residents had either lost their jobs or had their salaries cut.[108]

There was little social interaction between residents and members of the board or among the roomers. Residents kept pretty much to their own rooms and to themselves.[109] In contrast to the boardinghouses of the late nineteenth and early twentieth centuries, there was no expectation for organized activities designed to socialize young rural women, promote middle-class ideals of family, or structure leisure time for moral purity.[110] Moreover, as there were no common meals and no kitchen available for cooking (only hot plates for warming beverages were allowed in the rooms), residents had no scheduled opportunity to come together over meals. Some residents had a main meal at their place of employment and then bought sandwiches and snacks at the corner grocery. Washburne was reported to have had her meals sent to her room each day from Antoine's Restaurant, the venerable New Orleans establishment just a block away. Oliver and Emery regularly went in the late afternoon to Morrison's Cafeteria on Canal Street. To the entertainment of many French Quarter residents, Emery would pick Oliver up in her oversized 1936 Buick and pull out a wooden crate for the petite Oliver—always wearing her white gloves—to step onto so that she could more easily get into the car.[111]

The well-appointed boardroom served also as the sitting room and was a place for residents to meet with guests, both male and female, though rarely with one another. A 1953 letter from the board to residents cautioned: "Sitting rooms are to be kept strictly as sitting rooms. This does not mean that a Guest [resident] may not sit down and do some embroidery work. We just want to limit activities in the sitting rooms to those one would carry on in her own living room."[112] The donation of a piano to the boardroom was viewed unfavorably by several residents, particularly Washburne, who requested of the board that the "piano be removed" as she was "annoyed by persons playing it."[113] Her request was denied but made clear that the sitting room was not a place where residents gathered to join in song or socialize, just a "sitting room." Life at the residence, however, did not necessarily mean a lonely existence. When Emery bought property in the French Quarter and renovated one of the two buildings on the lot for Oliver, Oliver chose instead to stay at the residence, telling a disappointed Emery that she preferred not to live alone.[114]

But change at the residence was underway. The April 1955 annual report of the House Committee noted cheerily: "Of course Mrs. Oliver's TV set is a major change at the Exchange. All indications are that it is a valuable addition, and the atmosphere of the Board Room is now one of a cheerful living, sitting and gathering place rather than one of an occasional happening-to-meet place among the ladies of the House."[115] Emery, who at the time was making sets for WDSU television programs, inserts an amusing correction to the minutes: the TV had actually been given to her by a man she was then dating who worked at WDSU and wanted to watch television when he came to visit with her in the sitting room. She doubts that Oliver ever watched it.[116]

In the 1950s, with residents averaging forty-eight years of age, the board expressed growing concerns about the number of aging residents, anxious perhaps that the failing health of their permanent residents required services for which they were ill-prepared to offer. This assumption is somewhat validated by the illness of Washburne in 1953, which prompted the board to notify her daughters of her illness and apprise them that they would assume no responsibility for their mother in the event of a future illness.[117] It was not uncommon for rooming houses to have several elderly long-term residents like Washburne and Oliver. The mature women set a tone of stability and gentility and removed any suspicion that the rooming house was anything other than a highly respectable residence. In the French Quarter, this may have been particularly important to other women wishing to rent a room there. However, the balance seems to have shifted away from the middle-aged working woman, and in an effort to right the ship, the House Committee sent a letter to residents about a number of housekeeping items. One pertained to the retirement of residents: "Since the Exchange is designated for employed women, Guests coming to reside at Exchange after September 1, 1953 will be permitted to remain at Exchange six (6) months after retirement, thereby, keeping Exchange to original use for which it was intended, that is, for employed women."[118] Then four years later, an announcement went out to residents regarding "the retention of guests of the Exchange after they cease to be employed," stating that "as of the above date of December 6, 1957, no lady approaching retirement age and/or ceasing to be employed may continue as a tenant of the Christian Woman's Exchange. We suggest, therefore, that any person now employed and anticipating a change in her status should make some other arrangement for her future, since it will be impossible for her to remain with us."[119]

The policy brought about a number of changes at the residence, beginning with a significant drop in the average age of those living there—from an average age of forty-eight in the 1950s, to thirty-seven in 1960, and thirty-five in 1965. In the 1960s, many of the new residents were young women from New Orleans who were making their first move to independence. It was deemed inappropriate for young single women to live alone, and the "chaperoned" Residence of the Christian Woman's Exchange likely served as a favorable alternative for daughters and parents alike. Nevertheless, on a residence card from the 1960s, Jessie Robinson, the house manager, wrote of a young New Orleanian: "Her mother decided she did not approve of her living away from home so she forfeited her deposit."[120]

The tenor of the residence also changed with the introduction of younger workingwomen. Unlike the residents of the 1940s and 1950s whose futures had all but passed, the residents in the 1960s would occasionally go out to dinner together and congregated for the twice-weekly airing of *Batman*, the camp comedy television show. Judy Voiron Sentis, a New Orleanian and resident in 1966, describes herself and her housemates as a new breed of women: independent working girls in their twenties who wanted a safe, convenient, and respectable place to live. In Sentis's mind, "we girls were the future!" Sentis worked for a dental laboratory on Dauphine Street and remembers the French Quarter as a neighborhood community, comprising primarily Italians, who looked after and respected the CWE residents as girls trying to make a living. "We were well watched," she said. "The Quarter had eyes."[121] Another of the residents—a high school classmate of Sentis, Iris Guerro—introduced Sentis to her future husband.[122] Toula Rush, a Greek citizen who came to New Orleans in search of her estranged husband, the father of her son, found the residence a supportive and welcoming place to live. Alone, sending her parents and baby in Greece nearly every penny she earned from her job as a waitress at Terry's Restaurant, she vividly recalls the kindness and generosity of other residents. A special memory is Christmas—the tree that filled the central hall and the pink angora sweater all the "girls" pitched in to buy her.[123]

The changing characteristics of the roomers coincided with social changes taking place nationally in the late 1960s and early 1970s regarding both the greater number of women joining the labor force and the liberalization of sexual attitudes and practices. In this respect, the board seems to have exchanged one set of tribulations for another. The young roomers presented problems largely associated with their moral conduct and high rate of turnover. They were careless about leaving doors unlocked, which led to at least one break-in and attempted rape, and often were judged "not desirable" in the words of Robinson, the house manager. On the residence card of one resident, Robinson wrote: "Evicted because of morals (lack of)." About another, she wrote: "We do not want further dealings with her." Several roomers were asked to leave because they were "upsetting the harmonious living conditions at the residence," others for failure to pay their rent, and others because they complained too much about the condition of the residence.[124]

The greater employment opportunities and freedoms gained by women in the 1960s also made having one's own apartment more affordable and desirable. Consequently, there was less demand for the furnished rooms at the residence. In addition, the increasing number and types of jobs available to women reduced the need for women to make a living through consignments. The Exchange Shop had been moved from Royal Street to the CWE property in 1946 and had become largely an antique store for the consignment of silver and decorative pieces. For example, a 1948 "Report on shop activities" provides a long list of items sold, most of which were glass pieces (including Baccarat), hand-painted china, and furniture such as a drop leaf table, five chairs, and two fiddleback chairs. Handmade items were few, consisting mainly of five rag rugs, four chair mats, and baby clothes.[125] In the 1950s, the Exchange Shop had a listing in the classified section of the City Directory under "Antiques." By the late 1960s, both the shop and the residence were operating at a substantial financial loss.[126]

The board of managers was stuck in time. Over the years, it had become self-perpetuating. Members remained on the board until they died and then were replaced by a friend or relative of another board member. It was an honor to be selected for membership, but few brought practical expertise to the board, either from volunteering at the exchange shop or residence or from managing a business. The passion and need for social reform that was the hallmark of the early board members had been co-opted and institutionalized in governmental agencies. Most members maintained an interest in some small feature of the residence or shop. As a result, few board members were ardently involved in the organization or understood its total operating costs. Money was tight, membership was down—in part because the board did not want to pay the postage to send out dues notices—and no fund-raising activities had ever been undertaken.[127] Major repairs to the residence were delayed, and small repairs were made possible thanks only to personal donations from board members.[128]

While the architectural and historical importance of the Residence of the Christian Woman's Exchange had garnered tourist attention at least from the 1940s, in April 1960 the Orleans Parish Landmarks Commission designated the Grima House a city landmark.[129] This recognition fostered serious discussion among board members as to the usefulness of their current work against their responsibility as owners of an historic property. Members arguing to maintain the Exchange Shop and residence looked to the CWE constitution and by-laws. Their resistance to a changing mission was strong. Members arguing in favor of a new focus on historic preservation pointed to the reduced demand for furnished rooms as well as the increased difficulty of managing the residence as a rooming house. They argued that women no longer wanted "sheltered housing."[130]

Shingo Manard (later Woodward) was said to have been the catalyst behind the idea that the Grima House "was of such historic importance as to be worthy of becoming the primary focus of the Exchange."[131] Manard's mother-in-law, Mrs. Bryant Manard, had been on the board for years and was responsible for bringing her daughter-in-law onto the board in 1952. The younger Manard's membership in another women's organization, the Junior League of New Orleans, had trained her in the leadership skills needed to accomplish organizational goals. She brought this training to her CWE presidency in 1963 when she appointed committees to evaluate why the Exchange Shop was losing money. She also initiated the preservation process by locating records and documents on 820 St. Louis Street dating to the earliest known property transfer (1792) and building records (1818).[132] During Shingo Manard's last year as president, in 1965, Hurricane Betsy caused extensive damage to the residence, forcing the board to decide the purpose of the repairs—renovation or restoration. Both were decided upon. The rental rooms on the second and third floors of the annex were to be renovated to bring in higher rents, and the kitchen on the first floor of the annex was to be restored.[133]

Joining the movement to preserve the buildings of the Vieux Carré, the board began the arduous task of restoring the residence to its original splendor.[134] New members invited to the board were selected because of their interest or knowledge of historic homes and preservation.[135] Shingo Manard herself lived in the historic Garden District at Sixth and Coliseum Streets.[136] The first project to be undertaken by the board was the restoration of the 1831 open-hearth kitchen. Avery Bassich (Mrs. Beauregard) assumed the lead and became the "undisputed authority on early 19th century kitchens."[137] The fervor of the CWE founders and early board members returned as board members undertook extensive study of the architecture, social customs, and household furnishings of the home's early period, 1830–60. The New Orleans Town Gardeners volunteered their time, expertise, and finances in restoring the courtyard to the early period garden design. The first floor was closed to renters, and the Louisiana chapter of the National Society of the Colonial Dames of America volunteered their efforts in furnishing the hall and front parlor. In 1971, the principal rooms of the main house, the 1831 open-hearth kitchen, and the courtyard parterre were opened to the public for tours. In August 1971, the Hermann-Grima House and Complex—formally renamed in honor of both Samuel Hermann, who built the house in 1831, and Judge Felix Grima, who purchased the house in 1844 and whose descendants lived there until 1921—was listed in the National Register of Historic Places by the U.S. Department of the Interior.[138]

By the end of 1972, the board had closed the second floor to renters. Robinson was replaced by a professional museum director, William C. McKemie, and for the first time, responsibility for house operations and maintenance was given to a man.[139] In 1974, the director recommended that the board reach a decision as to whether to continue the rental program. Rental income was below budget projections, and tenants in the "mansion house" brought problems "ranging from the projection of an unsuitable image, to outright damage to the museum and the collection." The board voted to discontinue room rentals on the third floor, leaving only five rooms in the annex and the apartment over the Exchange Shop as rentable spaces.[140]

The CWE board officially terminated the rental program in December 1975. The last recorded payment of $85 (approximately $344 in 2010) was from Imogene Fuller for the month beginning November 7 and ending December 7, 1975.[141] The Exchange Shop was closed for several years but reopened in 2011 for the sale of juried work by women artists and artisans. In 1996, the CWE purchased the Gallier House from Tulane University, and both museum houses now are accredited as one institution by the American Association of Museums.[142]

Over time, the work of the Christian Woman's Exchange, like the work of so many philanthropic associations nationally, was rendered either obsolete or unnecessary as governmental agencies and large bureaucratic organizations assumed much of the responsibility for those in need. Yet for many decades, the CWE offered hundreds of women a venue for the sale of their handmade products and family heirlooms, provided temporary and long-term housing to thousands of women, and allowed members of the board the opportunities for leadership largely unavailable to them in business or industry. The by-laws of the Christian Woman's Exchange were revised and no longer state as its purpose "the amelioration of the condition of needy and worthy women by enabling . . . them to earn a livelihood." The mission of The Woman's Exchange is now directed to "historic preservation by restoring and maintaining the Hermann-Grima/Gallier Historic Houses and interpreting their contribution and place in New Orleans."[143] That preservation now includes the history of the women of the Christian Woman's Exchange as well as the domestic history of another era.

NOTES

1. "The Ladies Call," *New Orleans Daily Picayune*, March 27, 1881.

2. "Christian Woman's Exchange," *New Orleans Daily Picayune*, April 3, 1881; Charles L. "Pie" Dufour, *Women Who Cared: The 100 Years of the Christian Woman's Exchange* (New Orleans: Christian Woman's Exchange, 1980, 12.

3. The name Christian Woman's Exchange was changed to The Woman's Exchange (TWE) effective January 26, 1999. For information on the current mission of the organization, see "About Us: The Woman's Exchange," Hermann-Grima and Gallier Historic Houses, http://www.hgghh.com/aboutus.

4. Kathleen Waters Sander, *The Business of Charity: The Woman's Exchange Movement, 1832–1900* (Urbana: University of Illinois Press, 1998), 21–22, 64.

5. "Christian Woman's Exchange," *New Orleans Times*, April 17, 1881; Dufour, *Women Who Cared*, 7.

6. Sander, *The Business of Charity*, 121–23. The New Orleans Woman's Exchange was the only woman's exchange with a religious reference in its name. Other woman's exchanges founded in the South include the Exchange for Woman's Work, Charleston, S.C. (1885); the Woman's Exchange, Little Rock, Ark. (1887); the Exchange for Woman's Work, Memphis, Tenn. (1887); the Woman's Exchange, Houston, Tex. (1887); the Woman's Exchange, Augusta, Ga. (1888); and the Woman's Work Exchange, San Antonio, Tex. (1890).

7. Dufour, *Women Who Cared*, 7; "Christian Woman's Exchange: An Interesting Meeting in Furtherance of an Important Movement," *Daily Picayune*, April 3, 1881. The third objective adopted read: "We mean an earnest effort to reclaim the Lord's own from the pernicious amusements and allurements of the world, and to cultivate in our hearts the high Christian grace of compassion, as shown by our Lord's example when He kindly said to the guilty woman, 'Go and sin no more.'"

8. Reported in Dufour, *Women Who Cared*, 9, 11; Sander, *The Business of Charity*, 64.

9. Christian Woman's Exchange Collection, Manuscripts Collection 257, Louisiana Research Collection, Tulane University, New Orleans, Louisiana (hereafter cited as CWE). All minutes of the board of managers are located in CWE unless otherwise noted. In reality, the majority of CWE members were Episcopalian, Methodist, or Presbyterian, and it was not until the late twentieth century that a Catholic board member was appointed (personal correspondence with Mamie Sterkx Gasperecz). Board meetings began with the Lord's Prayer, but only rarely was any reference to religion or beliefs included in the minutes.

10. "Christian Woman's Exchange," *Daily Picayune*, April 9, 1881.

11. Dufour, *Women Who Cared*, 9; John P. Dyer, *Tulane: The Biography of a University, 1834–1965* (New York: Harper & Row, 1966), 323; New Orleans City Directory, 1890 (Walmsley); "Semi-annual Statement of the Louisiana National Bank," *Times Picayune*, January 3, 1905.

12. New Orleans City Directory, 1886.

13. "Death of Mrs. Margaret W. Bartlett," *Daily Picayune*, December 30, 1890. The church was listed in the 1890 New Orleans City Directory as the Franklin Street Memorial Church at Franklin, corner of Euterpe, and in the 1900 directory as the Bartlett Memorial Presbyterian Church.

14. Dyer, *Tulane*, 75; "Mrs. Ida B. Richardson Dead: Was City's Great Benefactor," *Daily Picayune*, April 10, 1920.

15. "Christian Woman's Exchange," *Daily Picayune*, April 9, 1881; "Exchange Notes," *Daily Picayune*, September 24, 1881.

16. Minutes of April 18, 1881, CWE. The street numbers in the French Quarter were changed in 1894, whereupon the address became 227 Bourbon Street (Collins C. Diboll Vieux Carré Digital Survey, Historic New Orleans Collection, http://www.hnoc.org/vcs/).

17. "Christian Woman's Exchange," *New Orleans Times*, April 17, 1881.

18. "Exchange Notes," *Daily Picayune*, July 10, 1881. All 2010 monetary conversions are estimates provided by Lawrence H. Officer and Samuel H. Williamson, "Purchasing Power of Money in the United States from 1774 to 2010," MeasuringWorth, 2011, based on the Consumer Price Index, http://www.measuringworth.com (hereafter cited as MeasuringWorth).

19. "Exchange Notes," *Daily Picayune*, September 10, 1881; July 3, 1881.

20. "Exchange Notes," *Daily Picayune*, January 15, 1882; MeasuringWorth.

21. Patricia Brady, "Eliza Jane Nicholson (1843–1896): New Orleans Publisher," in *Louisiana Women: Their Lives and Times*, ed. Janet Allured and Judith F. Gentry (Athens: University of Georgia Press, 2009), 94.

22. Minutes of the board, June 3, 1881.

23. Minutes of the board, April 1, 1881.

24. "Exchange Notes," *Daily Picayune*, August 11, 1881.

25. "Exchange Notes" *Daily Picayune*, July 24, 1881.

26. Minutes of the board, June 3, 1881. Written in margin: "Exchange Notes written weekly by Mrs. Theo. Auzé."

27. Joan B. McLaughlin and Jack McLaughlin, eds., *Louisiana Voyages: The Travel Writings of Catharine Cole, Martha R. Field* (Jackson: University Press of Mississippi, 2006), xii.

28. "Christian Woman's Exchange: Its Prosperity and Usefulness, as Shown in the Third Annual Meeting," *Daily Picayune*, April 9, 1884.

29. Quoted in McLaughlin and McLaughlin, *Louisiana Voyages*, xii. Emphasis added.

30. "Exchange Notes," *Daily Picayune*, April 8, 1881.

31. Undated newspaper clipping pasted on page 4 of "Christian Woman's Exchange for Woman's Work, Book No. 1, Christian Woman's Exchange, April 1881, Record of Correspondence," CWE, hereafter cited as "Record of Correspondence."

32. "Christian Women's [*sic*] Exchange: The Depot on Bourbon Street, and the Popularity It Has Already Achieved," *Daily Picayune*, June 10, 1881.

33. "By-laws of the Christian Woman's Exchange," n.d., ca. 1881, box 1, Hermann-Grima House Archives (hereafter cited as HGH). The archives holds the early official documents and most of the documents and materials from the 1950s forward, including the "Record Card for Residence" from the mid-1950 to 1975; "Record of Correspondence." At the board meeting of May 16, 1927, the 10 percent commission fee was reaffirmed for items made by hand, and the commission was raised to 15 percent on furniture, glass, silver, etc. In 1950, the commission on all items was made 15 percent [minutes of the board, April 14, 1950].

34. "Rules and Regulations for Consignors" n.d., ca. late 1950s, HGH; Sander, *The Business of Charity*, 24.

35. Dufour, *Women Who Cared*, 12.

36. Anne Firor Scott, *Natural Allies: Women's Associations in American History* (Urbana: University of Illinois Press, 1991), 14.

37. "History of the Christian Woman's Exchange," n.d., box 1, 3 pages, HGH.

38. Minutes of the board, April 18, 1881.

39. Sander, *The Business of Charity*, 108.

40. Ibid., 107, 109.

41. Vol. D, CWE. The exact number of consignors is unknown, though it is assumed that the number was somewhat greater than a thousand. A September 30, 1934, "Accounts Payable (Consignors) Trial Balance" sheet lists payment to fifty-six consignors, whose numbers ranged from 4 to 991. Payments ranged from a low of $.01 to a high of $346.80, with most payments under $3.

42. Vol. D, CWE; Sander, *The Business of Charity*, 106.

43. Herbert S. Fairall, "Woman's Department," in *The World's Industrial and Cotton Centennial Exposition, 1884–1885* (Iowa City: n.p., 1885), 353–78, see especially 367, 422; see also Suzanne Ormond and Mary E. Irvine, *Louisiana's Art Nouveau: The Crafts of the Newcomb Style* (Gretna, La.: Pelican, 1976), 7–11. In 1887, Jenny Nixon became the first faculty member appointed to the H. Sophie Newcomb Memorial College of Tulane University, New Orleans.

44. Fairall, "Woman's Department"; Mrs. E. M. Ordway, who Walmsley appointed superintendent of the Science Department, was among the first seven faculty members of Newcomb College.

45. Ormond and Irvine, *Louisiana's Art Nouveau*, 11–14; "Personal and General Notes," *Daily Picayune*, January 5, 1890. It is unknown if the pottery pieces were for display only or were also placed for sale in the Exchange Shop. A somewhat longer link from the classes offered by Ellsworth and William Woodward at the Cotton Centennial led to the Ladies Decorative Art League and New Orleans Art Pottery, and from there to Newcomb College and the beginnings of Newcomb Pottery in 1895.

46. "Christian Woman's Exchange. The Grand Results of Six Years' Labor—but Much More to Be," *Daily Picayune*, September 9, 1887.

47. The amount of $28,500 in 1887 has the "purchase power" of $674,000 in 2010 (MeasuringWorth).

48. Sander, *The Business of Charity*, 67. Larger gifts were made by Sophia Smith, who left $400,000 in her 1870 will to create Smith College, and by Josephine Louise LeMonnier Newcomb, whose initial gift of $100,000 to the administrators of the Tulane Educational Fund in 1886 established the H. Sophie Newcomb Memorial College. Both gifts established women's colleges and were not technically given to a "charitable" organization.

49. Sander, *The Business of Charity*, 72.

50. Ibid., 63; Scott, *Natural Allies*, 12–14.

51. "Grima Mansion Bought as Home," *Times-Picayune*, November 25, 1923.

52. Sander, *The Business of Charity*, 72.

53. New Orleans YWCA Manuscripts Collection 637, Louisiana Research Collection, Tulane University, New Orleans, Louisiana (hereafter cited as YWCA); Kingsley House, http://www.kingsley-house.org/about.

54. Sander, *The Business of Charity*, 71–72. The other woman's exchanges offering rooms were the Exchange for Woman's Work of Richmond, Virginia, the New York Exchange for Woman's Work, and the Woman's Industrial Exchange of Baltimore.

55. Rent receipt books for 1913, 1916, and 1918, Volume B—Rentals, CWE.

56. Dufour, *Women Who Cared*, 9–11; "Christian Woman's Exchange," *Daily Picayune*, April 9, 1881.

57. Record card for residents, HGH; Lynn Weiner, "'Our Sister's Keepers': The Minneapolis Woman's Christian Association and Housing for Working Women," *Minnesota History* 46, no. 5 (Spring 1979): 189–200; Lisa M. Fine, "Between Two Worlds: Business Women in a Chicago Boarding House 1900–1930," *Journal of Social History* 19, no. 3 (Spring 1986): 511–19.

58. Rent receipt books, Volume B—Rentals, CWE. Thirty-six rooms were rented in 1918: seven on the second floor, sixteen on the third floor, and thirteen on the fourth. As the building was reported to have been a three-story building, rooms on the fourth floor must have been converted attic space. The amount $6.25 in 1918 has the same purchase power as $90.50 in 2010 (MeasuringWorth).

59. Data on families prior to World War II is sparse. See James R. Wetzel, "American Families: 75 Years of Change," *Monthly Labor Review* (U.S Bureau of Labor Statistics), March 1990, 5–6. A household is a house, an apartment, a mobile home, a group of rooms, or a single room that is occupied as separate living quarters. Separate living quarters are those in which the occupants live and eat separately from any other persons in the building and that have direct access from outside the building or through a common hall.

60. Christian Woman's Exchange annual report, 1913, box 1, folder 11, CWE; MeasuringWorth.

61. Sander, *The Business of Charity*, 123.

62. The first use of the term "domestic feminism" appears to be in Daniel Scott Smith, "Family Limitations, Sexual Control, and Domestic Feminism in Victorian America," *Feminist Studies* 1 (Winter–Spring 1973): 40–57. Smith's definition focuses on women gaining greater freedom and control within their families, particularly over reproduction. The definition used here focuses on women organizing on behalf of women by promoting the production of products made by women in the home.

63. "Exchange Notes," *Daily Picayune*, February 19, 1882.

64. "History of the Christian Woman's Exchange: Part III," box 1, HGH. It is not known if the *Daily States* continued any portion of the rental program.

65. Minutes of the board, October 3, 1924. The relative value and purchasing power of $17,500 and $60,000 in 2010 is $223,000 and $765,000 respectively (MeasuringWorth). The building at the back of the main house was always referred to as the "annex" by CWE members, though this type of structure is more commonly referred to in New Orleans as the "slave quarter."

66. Letter, "Christian Woman's Exchange, 524 Royal Street, New Orleans, 1924," box 1—Correspondence, CWE.

67. Minutes of the board, November 7, 1924; annual report, April 14, 1925, box 1—Adminstrative, CWE.

68. "Annual Review of the Recording Secretary," sheet 6, box 1, HGH; "Pre-nuptial Compliments Feature Many of Week's Parties," *Times-Picayune*, April 27, 1924; *Register of New Orleans Society*, 1936, 17.

69. Karen Leathem and Wayne Phillips, Louisiana State Museum, e-mail correspondence with author, October 30, 2012.

70. "Mandarin's Junk Lands on Island of Many Jewels," *Times-Picayune*, March 3, 1924; Dufour, *Women Who Cared*, 96–97.

71. "New Investment Banking Concern Arises from Old," *Times-Picayune*, June 15, 1923; "Board Chairman of Hotel Is Dead," *Times-Picayune*, February 16, 1948.

72. Minutes of the board, March 4, 1927; letter from Moore Hyams & Co., Inc., to Mrs. Robert Moore, president, April 2, 1927, box 1, CWE; minutes of the board, November 7, 1924.

73. Minutes of the board, August 3, 1923.

74. Christine Wiltz, *The Last Madam: A Life in the New Orleans Underworld* (New York: Faber and Faber, 2000), 10, 17–18.

75. Minutes of the board, August 3, 1923. The YWCA constructed a three-story building for its headquarters and twenty-room residence hall at 923 Gravier Street in 1922 (YWCA).

76. Letter from Moore Hyams & Co., Inc., to Mrs. Robert Moore, president, April 2, 1927, box 1, CWE.

77. Joseph A. Hill, *Women in Gainful Occupations 1870 to 1920*, Census Monographs 9, Bureau of the Census Library (Washington: U.S. Government Printing Office, 1929), tables 161 and 168.

78. Frank Hobbs and Nicole Stoops, "Demographic Trends in the 20th Century," U.S. Census Bureau, Census 2000 Special Reports, Series CEN SR-4 (Washington, D.C.: Government Printing Office, 2002), chapter 4. Data is provided for 1910 and 1940 but is missing for 1920 and 1930. Available online at http://www.census.gov/prod/2002pubs/censr-4.pdf.

79. Hill, *Women in Gainful Occupations*, table 92.

80. Minutes of the board, November 7, 1924. The relative worth of $10 in 1924 would be approximately $128 in 2010. (MeasuringWorth).

81. Department of Commerce-Bureau of the Census, *Fifteenth Census of the United States 1930, Population Schedule*, Enumeration District No. 36–63, 10-A. This is the earliest record available on the women who lived at the residence.

82. U.S. Census Bureau, *Historical Statistics of the United States: Colonial Times to 1970*, Part I, Series D, 182–232.

83. "Sept. 15, 1954, Maid's Duties," box 67, HGH.

84. Genevieve Munson Trimble, *Le Petite Salon: A History of Its Fifty Years, 1924–1974* (New Orleans, 1974), 11, 17.

85. "Society," *Times-Picayune*, October 16, 1924; Trimble, *Le Petite Salon*, 43–44; Dufour, *Women Who Cared*, 95–97.

86. Trimble, *Le Petite Salon*, 6.

87. The correct spelling of Washburne is with an "e," though the "e" was frequently omitted. It is unknown if Mary A. Moore Washburne was related to the Robert Moores (e-mail correspondence with Sallie Williams [Mrs. Bill Washburne Williams], July–August, 2012).

88. John S. Wurts, "Mary Annie Moore, 1518–1519," in *Magna Charta: Families of Royal Descent, Part VI* (Philadelphia: Brookfield, 1950), 1518–19.

89. *New York Passenger Lists, 1820–1957 and Border Crossings: From Canada to U.S., 1895–1956*, records for Mary M. Washburne, Ancestry.com; New Orleans City Directory, 1927–35, 1938, 1940; *Kentucky Death Index, 1911–2000*, Ancestry.com; Wurts, "Mary Annie Moore, 1518–1519."

90. Minutes of the board, October 8, 1937; annual report, House Administration, April 5, 1955, box 1, HGH. Washburne was apparently moved to Kentucky at that time. She died in Jefferson, Kentucky, in 1959 at the age of eighty-seven. *Kentucky Death Index, 1911–2000*, Ancestry.com; rent receipt books, vol. B—Rentals, CWE.

91. Collins C. Diboll Vieux Carré Digital Survey, Historic New Orleans Collection, http://www.hnoc.org/vcs/.

92. *A Small Portrait of Leila Moore Williams, Co-founder with Lewis Kemper Williams of the Historic New Orleans Collection* (New Orleans: Historic New Orleans Collection, 1976), 6; "Splendor of Old Guatemala Depicted in Annual Ball of Mystic Club at Auditorium," *Times-Picayune*, February 23, 1936.

93. *A Small Portrait*; "Award Loving Cup for 1937," *Times-Picayune*, June 25, 1939.

94. "Mrs. Williams Taken by Death," *Times-Picayune*, December 14, 1966; "Estate Provides for Museum," *Times-Picayune* October 5, 1967; "Important Bequest," *Times-Picayune* October 6, 1967.

95. Annual report, April 1929; House Report Annual Meeting, April 1, 1932, box 1, CWE.

96. "Rooms for Rent," *Times-Picayune*, September 17, 1950.

97. Rent receipts for 1948, vol. B, CWE; list of rooms & tenants, September 15, 1950, box 67, HGH.

98. Lin Emery interview with the author, June 1, 2011. Emery is known particularly for her large kinetic works that are inspired by the forms of nature and made of polished aluminum. Her most visible New Orleans sculpture is located in Sculpture Garden of the New Orleans Museum of Art.

99. Ibid.; Philip F. Palmedo, *Lin Emery* (Manchester, Vt.: Hudson Hills Press, 2012), 15.

100. Palmedo, *Lin Emery*, 14; Emery interview.

101. Quote from Edward Lucie-Smith, *Lin Emery: Borrowing the Forces of Nature* (New Orleans: New Orleans Museum of Art, 1996), 7.

102. Emery interview; Palmedo, *Lin Emery*, 137–38.

103. The by-laws of the Christian Woman's Exchange 1881, stated: "All white women, without regard to religious belief, may become members of the Christian Woman's Exchange." The by-laws were revised in 1972, deleting "white," box 1, HGH. It was apparently an unstated policy that roomers at the residence would be white, as no written records documenting such a requirement were found among the CWE papers.

104. Minutes of the board, November 10, 1950; November 14, 1952.

105. "Traces Family Tree Back 3250 Years!," *Times-Picayune*, July 29, 1951.

106. Emery interview.

107. Diane Robin, interview and correspondence with the author, June 2011; record receipt book, vol. B, CWE; record card for residence for Martha Foster, box 67, HGH.

108. House Report Annual Meeting, April 12, 1932, box 1-A, CWE.

109. Emery interview; Robin interview.

110. Weiner, "Our Sister's Keepers"; Elizabeth Kirkland, "A Home Away from Home: Defining, Regulating, and Challenging Femininity at the Julia Drummond Residence in Montreal, 1920–1971," *Urban History Review* 34, no. 2 (Spring 2006): 3–16.

111. Emery interview.

112. Letter, "Dear ——," from House Management Committee, September 30, 1953, box 1-A, CWE.

113. Minutes of the board, November 14, 1952.

114. Emery interview.

115. Annual report, House Committee, April 5, 1955, box 1-A, CWE.

116. Emery interview; Palmedo, *Lin Emery*, 138.

117. Minutes of the board, April 1953.

118. "Dear ——," September 30, 1953.

119. "To the Ladies Residing on the Premises at 820 St. Louis Street," December 6, 1957, box 67, HGH.

120. Record card for residence, 1960s, box 67, HGH.

121. Judith Voiron Sentis interview with author, April 2, 2012.

122. Ibid.

123. Toula Rush Hatzioannidis interview with author, November 17, 2011.

124. Letter, "Miss ——," from Mrs. Jessie M. Robinson, January 14, 1968; letter, "Dear Mrs. ——,"

from Mary McLellan, July 14, 1969; letter, "Dear Mrs. ——," from Mary N. McLellan, January 2, 1970; letter, "Miss ——," from Mrs. Morgan L. Shaw, September 1, 1971; record of residence card, 1965–71, box 67, HGH. The transgressions remained unspecified.

125. "Report on Shop Activities, October 1948," box 1, CWE.

126. Mrs. M. Truman Woodward Jr. (Shingo [Mrs. John P.] Manard) interview, December 12, 1980, HGH files; Dufour, *Women Who Cared*, 51, 54.

127. Woodward interview.

128. Helen Shaw interview, June 14, 1994, HGH.

129. Minutes of the board, March 8, 1940; "History of the Christian Woman's Exchange," n.d., box 1, 3 pages, HGH.

130. Woodward interview.

131. Quoted in Dufour, *Women Who Cared*, 51.

132. Woodward interview; Dufour, *Women Who Cared*, 51.

133. Mrs. James M. Batchelor, Mrs. Philip R. Farnsworth, Mrs. Morgan L. Shaw, "Introduction, Chapter I, Betsy's Destruction Brings on Construction," box 1, HGH.

134. Ann Haddow interview with the author, May 10, 2011.

135. Haddow interview.

136. Manard interview.

137. Quoted in Dufour, *Women Who Cared*, 54.

138. "818–820 St. Louis Street," Collin C. Diboll Vieux Carré Digital Survey, Historic New Orleans Collection, http://hnoc.org/vcs/; Dufour, *Women Who Cared*, 85, 89.

139. Letter, "Mrs. Jessie M. Robinson," from Mrs. Morgan L. Shaw, December 5, 1972, box 91, HGH.

140. "Director's Report," January 4, 1974, box 91, HGH.

141. Rent receipt books, box 67, HGH; MeasuringWorth.

142. Personal correspondence, Mamie Sterkx Gaspercz, executive director of the Hermann-Grima/Gallier Historic Houses; Hermann-Grima/Gallier Historic Houses, http://www.hgghh.org/.

143. "By-laws Revision 1972"; "By-laws Revision 1978"; "By-laws Revision 2008," box 1, HGH.

Sarah Towles Reed
(1882–1978)

Southern Firebrand

LESLIE GALE PARR

A single ambition shaped Sarah Towles Reed's life: to advance public school education in New Orleans. The teacher, labor union lobbyist, and educational reformer fought for more than fifty years to bring democracy into the classroom, safeguard intellectual independence, and secure economic justice for the teachers of New Orleans. Reed courageously defied southern convention and powerful opposition by publicly defending her support for such controversial causes as labor rights, racial justice, and sexual equality. As her obituary stated, "She earned a reputation as a firebrand early in her career and never lost it."[1]

Time after time, Reed led her forces in the overwhelmingly female teaching corps into frays with the predominantly male educational establishment. As early as the 1920s, she demanded equal pay for equal work, working with other teachers to bring women's salaries into line with men's. She was instrumental in overturning the prohibition of marriage for women teachers during the Great Depression, when many states were first adopting or reinforcing marriage bans for single female teachers. In the same decade, Reed overcame many of her colleagues' prejudices against unionization and convinced them to join an American Federation of Labor (AFL) affiliate that proved to be a powerful and influential weapon in the fight for educational reform. The New Deal also inspired Reed to overcome her segregated upbringing and work closely with black teachers. During the early Cold War years of the 1940s, she challenged educational authorities at a time when many teachers fearfully shunned controversy and secured an important victory for academic freedom.

Reed spent her early years in West Feliciana, one of the most conservative parishes in southern Louisiana, where her father, Daniel Towles, had inherited Weyanoke, his family's plantation near St. Francisville, in 1878. Towles did not

SARAH TOWLES REED

Courtesy of Leslie Parr/UGA Press.

succeed as a planter. When cotton prices plummeted, he lost the property and took his family to live with his wife's cousin at nearby Ouida Plantation and managed the modest 320-acre farm. His daughter Sarah was born there in 1882. After the panic of 1893, he realized that Ouida could no longer support his family, which eventually grew to include seven children (not including three who died before the age of three). Towles moved his family to New Orleans after he secured a position at the New Orleans Custom House, thanks to the influence of his brother-in-law, Governor Murphy S. Foster.[2]

Reed's parents always emphasized the importance of education to their children and were thrilled when, in 1900, Reed won a scholarship to H. Sophie Newcomb College, which had opened four years earlier as the women's coordinate college of Tulane University. Reed flourished at Newcomb and showed an early interest in progressive reform and women's rights. In one class essay, Reed speculated about the women who eventually would be elected to public office once suffrage was won. A woman in office, she wrote, "will treat the position as no sinecure. Less obtuse than man, she will not prove so docile as men fondly hope." The woman officeholder, Reed predicted, could "be trusted to register an absolute veto against squalor and disease. . . . She will write a requiem for heinous injustice."[3] No doubt her Newcomb professors, some of whom participated in suffrage groups and progressive organizations, influenced Reed. Possibly too she learned from the examples of women reformers active in New Orleans at the time including Sophie Bell Wright, who ran a day school for girls and opened a free night school for working boys; Laura McMain, director of the Kingsley settlement house; and Kate and Jean Gordon, energetic sisters who were active in nearly every reform effort in town. After graduating from Newcomb in 1904, Reed continued her education, receiving a master's degree at Tulane in 1906, a bachelor of arts in education from Newcomb in 1914, and, in 1924, one of the earliest law degrees earned by a woman at Loyola University.

Sometime before August 1921, Sarah Towles secretly married Elkanah Reed, known as Eck, who worked in a general store in St. Francisville. The need for secrecy was vital for the young teacher, whose income was important to her family and who was subject to the Orleans Parish School Board (OPSB) regulation prohibiting women from marrying while employed as a teacher. No one outside the family knew of the marriage until Eck was killed in an automobile accident. When school officials read his obituary in August 1921, they learned for the first time that Reed had been married. Never minding that she was now a widow, they promptly fired her from her teaching position at Sophie B. Wright High School on the grounds that she had automatically forfeited her position when she married. Principal Alice Lusher appealed to the school board to reinstate Reed, and in September the board allowed her to return to her classroom.[4] Reed never remarried and never revealed any information about her marriage. She lived the rest of her life with her sister Roberta Towles, also a teacher in New

Orleans public schools. Both sisters took active roles in teacher organizations and spent many evenings together telephoning other educators, organizing, and attending meetings.

Reed gradually became the leading voice of New Orleans teachers and their organizations. Recognizing that women teachers were the most vulnerable members of the public school teaching force, she championed women's causes and the goal of sexual equality. In one of her first public appearances, she took up the feminist standard, demanding equal pay for equal work in a school system that routinely paid women teachers less than their male counterparts. Representatives from the Newcomb Alumnae Association, the Louisiana League of Women Voters, the New Orleans Woman's Club, the National Woman's Party, and the Louisiana Equal Rights Party, as well as teachers and other interested women, including the Gordon sisters, joined Reed at the Orleans Parish School Board meeting in 1921 to endorse the women teachers' petition. As one newspaper reported, women "jammed the room, hung over the windows from the hall and crowded into the open door of the School Board office."[5]

In her speech, Reed pointed out that men and women teachers had to meet the same qualifications, cover the same amount of material, and work the same hours. A salary scale based on gender alone, she argued, discriminated against both women teachers and girl students since it obviously placed a higher value on the education of boys, whose teachers, more likely to be men in New Orleans's sexually segregated schools, were paid more.[6] When Reed and the women teachers lost their fight in 1921, they responded by organizing the High School Teachers Association. Its representatives kept the issue alive by repeatedly going before the school board with petitions for equal pay. The board just as often put them off. It was more than a decade before they could claim victory.[7]

In 1925, Reed led the drive to organize another teachers' organization, the New Orleans Public School Teachers Association (NOPSTA). The new group hoped to strengthen the power of public school teachers by extending membership to include all white New Orleans teachers and principals (maintaining the strict racial segregation that characterized the New Orleans school system). Reed represented the association before the school board and at the state legislature, where she lobbied on behalf of bills benefiting the state's teachers. In an attempt to unify the teaching corps, which had been badly fractured along gender lines during the salary equalization struggle, NOPSTA put aside salary equalization for a time and urged all teachers to work together to increase their steadily deteriorating salaries.[8]

Although NOPSTA met with some success in protecting teachers' pay, the arrival of the Great Depression placed their economic circumstances in even greater jeopardy. Teachers' paychecks were often delayed, and their salaries, already low, shrank by 14 percent to 26 percent during the first two years of the 1930s.[9] The city's already dismal financial situation grew desperate when Senator Huey P. Long, angered by the refusal of the city's politicians to back his candidates and bills in the state legislature, forced the city into bankruptcy. In 1932, New Orleans banks demanded that the school board repay its overdue loans and redeem its bonded debt.[10] As it had done many times, the board raised money by cutting teacher salaries.[11]

Facing the continual threat of salary reductions and alarmed by an announcement in 1931 that dismissed teachers did not have the right to a public hearing, Reed realized that teachers needed more political clout than they could muster among themselves.[12] She had always understood that organization was essential to achieving teachers' goals, and when the Depression stimulated a resurgence of interest in labor organizations, Reed began to consider the advantages of affiliation with a national union. Always closely attuned to the political currents of the day, she could hardly have failed to notice the surge of union activity during the early New Deal years. After the 1933 passage of the National Industrial Recovery Act, specifically Section 7(a) protecting workers' rights to bargain collectively, laborers joined unions in the greatest numbers since World War I.[13]

The economic crisis and the union movement swirling around her led Reed to broaden the context in which she viewed herself and other teachers, as she began to understand that their concerns were very much like those of workers everywhere: job security, fair wages, and decent working conditions. It was at this juncture that the American Federation of Teachers (AFT) contacted Reed to request her help in organizing a local affiliate of the American Federation of Labor (AFL) in New Orleans.[14] Immediately sympathetic to the union's invitation, she eagerly began recruiting teachers to create an AFT local. Reed worked hard to convince her colleagues that the problems they faced in the economic crisis were beyond the means of existing teachers' associations to solve. Allies in the local labor council and the national union, she understood, might mean the difference between success and failure for teachers when pressing their claims before the school board and the state legislature.[15] In 1934, Reed, her sister and fellow teacher Roberta Towles, and eight other teachers applied for a charter to create the New Orleans Classroom Teachers' Federation, Local 353, of the American Federation of Teachers, AFL. In accordance with the AFT's practice of conforming to local racial norms, the union included only white teachers. All administrators were excluded from membership.[16]

It was not an easy task to persuade teachers to join a union. Many teachers saw themselves as professionals and were reluctant to enter a working-class organization, particularly one that some considered politically radical.[17] Consequently, like many AFT locals, the New Orleans Classroom Teachers' Federation (CTF) represented only a minority of the city's teachers. Despite its small membership, the union scored significant victories during the 1930s, including passage of a new, stronger tenure law for New Orleans teachers in 1936. Under Reed's leadership, teachers crafted the text of the bill, lobbied legislators, and secured the support of the governor, lieutenant governor, and state superintendent of education to get it passed. Vividly remembering that teachers had been fired for purely political reasons during the Huey P. Long regime, teachers ardently supported passage of the law. The final language guaranteed all New Orleans teachers, black and white, a public trial before dismissal, clarified tenure requirements, and gave them tenure for life after a three-year probationary period.[18] Shortly afterward, the state legislature passed a similar bill that gave teachers throughout the state lifetime tenure based on the same requirements established for New Orleans teachers. Like the New Orleans law, the state tenure act stipulated that after the probationary period a teacher could be fired only if found guilty of willful neglect of duty, incompetence, or dishonesty, after a hearing before the parish school board. A charged teacher could choose to have a private or a public hearing. The same bill also established a teacher retirement system.[19]

Reed and the Classroom Teachers' Federation secured another triumph for teachers in 1936 when they succeeded in eliminating the marriage ban for women. This was a remarkable achievement considering that the widespread practice of denying teaching jobs to married women (and firing women teachers who married during the school year) had grown even more prevalent during the Depression. By the time World War II began, 87 percent of school systems in the United States denied employment to married women and 70 percent automatically fired women who married while under contract. Although the legality of dismissing women teachers who married had been debated in New Orleans since the early 1920s, it was not until Reed forced the issue that the Orleans Parish School Board rescinded its restrictions, long before most school systems did. Reed used her legal knowledge to test the school board's rule that "the marriage of a female teacher ipso facto vacates her position and is considered equivalent to a resignation." After convincing four women teachers who had married over the summer to report back to school in the fall, Reed argued before the state attorney general that the teachers' status as tenured faculty members protected their jobs. He agreed with Reed that there were no grounds to dismiss them since they were not guilty of any of the conditions that made it legal to fire a tenured teacher.[20] The school board had no choice but to drop its longstanding regulation. The triumph was a particularly sweet one for Reed, who had herself experienced the ignominy of dismissal because of marriage.

Reed and the union continued to score victories for teachers during the 1930s, including, in 1936, a partial restoration of salaries that had been cut earlier in the Depression.[21] The next year, the union secured significant salary increases for white teachers and, finally, a single-salary plan based exclusively on experience and qualifications, not gender. In 1938, the state Board of Education ordered all parishes in Louisiana to adopt a similar single-salary schedule. The resolution specifically prohibited discrimination between men and women teachers.[22]

Salary inequities still existed, however, between white and black teachers. African American teachers received significantly lower salaries than their white counterparts and received no raises at all in 1937.[23] This glaring injustice, coupled with a frightening incident of racial violence on property she owned in West Feliciana Parish, propelled Reed into her first public interracial protest. Years earlier, Reed and her sister Kate had managed to buy at auction the Weyanoke house and one hundred acres of the land that had once belonged to their father. Reed and Towles struggled to rehabilitate the dilapidated dwelling, doing much of the work themselves. Reed even learned how to install plumbing, and the two sisters frequently traveled from New Orleans to spend the weekend at their rural house. With only their teacher salaries to support them, Reed and Towles rented out part of their land to help with expenses. They were aware that two black tenants on their property, Willie and Irene Scott, had organized a local of the Louisiana Farmers' Union, and, while approving of the cause, they warned them to be careful, knowing that the surrounding white landowners would be hostile to any such activity. When some of the neighbors learned that a white organizer had violated racial norms by spending the night in the couple's cabin, they broke into the house, found Irene Scott, and proceeded to beat her.[24] Reed and Towles, outraged by the attack and already sympathetic to the labor movement, immediately understood the connection between unionism and civil rights and resolved to do more to assist their African American colleagues in New Orleans.

Two weeks after the announcement of the 1937 salary schedule, an interracial delegation of fourteen teachers, headed by Reed, Towles, and Veronica Hill, an activist and leader in the African American teacher corps, marched into the school administration building armed with a petition demanding raises and a "fairer deal" for black teachers. When the elevator operator refused to take them to the third floor where a school board meeting was underway, the women went outside, climbed a fire escape, entered an open window on the fifth floor, and took the stairs down to the third floor. There they either threw the petition through an open transom window, slid it under the locked door, or handed it to the president of the board when he opened the door, depending on which version of the now-legendary story one believes.[25] The next morning's newspaper announced the board's decision to grant raises to African American teachers.[26]

Shortly after the fire escape episode, Reed and Towles met with Hill and other African American teachers in Orleans Parish to advise them about establishing a black AFT local. It was a propitious time to organize. African American teachers remained upset about discriminatory salaries and frustrated by the dilapidated condition of their school buildings, large class sizes, inadequate supplies, and inferior textbooks. Both white and black schools had been hit hard by the

Depression, but, not surprisingly, black schools suffered more. While African American schoolchildren in Louisiana had traditionally received only a fraction of funds spent on white students, during the 1930s that figure fell from 22 to 17 percent.[27] The teachers responded warmly to Reed's union pitch and decided to take the bold action of organizing the League of Classroom Teachers, Local 527, of the American Federation of Teachers, AFL.[28]

Energized by its new national affiliation and the recent salary victory, the new union petitioned the OPSB for equal salaries in 1938. In New Orleans, the League of Classroom Teachers pointed out, the average white teacher, with a pupil load of thirty-five, received $47.77 per pupil in annual salary, while the average black teacher, with a pupil load of fifty-five, received only $21.78 per pupil per year.[29] It took another five years and a court case led by New Orleans civil rights attorney A. P. Tureaud, but finally, in September 1943, African American teachers in New Orleans received paychecks equal to those of their white counterparts.[30]

Reed's efforts to assist black teachers alarmed those in the white New Orleans community who opposed any tampering with segregated norms. Her participation in the Southern Conference for Human Welfare (SCHW), a group that excited a great deal of hostility among southern traditionalists, further tarnished her reputation. Members of the SCHW, a New Deal–inspired interracial reform group organized in 1938, contended that racism prevented the South from achieving its true potential and determined to advance the region by encouraging political, social, and economic reform.[31] Somehow Reed persuaded the OPSB to pay for her trip to Birmingham to attend the inaugural meeting of the group.[32] Reaching out to liberals across the South, the organization sought to mobilize support for voter registration reform, antilynching laws, federal aid to education, abolition of poll taxes, and full citizenship for all Americans regardless of race. The SCHW also condemned the new House Un-American Activities Committee (then headed by Marin Dies).[33]

Opponents of the New Deal and any kind of racial "mixing" attacked the SCHW and liberals in general for their "radical" ideas. Some found in anticommunism a convenient weapon with which to fight a variety of initiatives, both race related and labor related. As a prominent union member and a supporter of black unionizing efforts, Reed repeatedly clashed with the Crescent City's white conservative community, whose attitude toward liberalism and radicalism of any kind had hardened by the late 1930s, partly in reaction to the interracial organizing drives in the city by the Congress of Industrial Organizations (CIO). The campaign to organize both white and black dockworkers into the CIO's International Longshoremen's and Warehousemen's Union in New Orleans had encountered violent attacks on workers and picketers and police raids of CIO headquarters.[34]

After the Soviet-Nazi nonaggression pact in 1939 and the end of the Popular Front era, the political climate in the entire United States became increasingly less tolerant of radical or unconventional ideas. Teachers faced closer scrutiny than ever before, and investigations and policies aimed at rooting out communists from the educational world gained momentum. The National Education Association, the largest teachers' organization in the United States, recommended in 1941 purging teachers whose conduct was deemed "inimical to the best interests of our country."[35] Even the AFT felt compelled to take action, expelling communist-dominated locals in New York and Philadelphia.[36] In New Orleans, groups such as the Louisiana Coalition of Patriotic Societies, the Young Men's Business Club, and the Association of Commerce's National Defense Committee sought to weed out "un-American" activities on the part of teachers and led their own crusades against "subversion."[37]

Reed's perceived lack of patriotism came under attack in 1941 when the Orleans Parish School Board charged her with violating its new Americanism rule prohibiting teachers from joining any group that aimed to overthrow the government, eliminate private property, hinder conscription or national defense, or promote class or religious hatred.[38] The charges against Reed resulted from an investigation by her principal, John Conniff at Alcee Fortier High School for boys, who had called students into his office and asked them if any of their teachers "were going against the democratic way of life." If so, they were to give statements to the Association of Commerce's National Defense Committee.[39] After seven of Reed's students questioned their teacher's patriotism, the Association of Commerce advised school authorities to transfer her to another school to teach a presumably less dangerous subject than civics.[40] Conniff had repeatedly clashed with Reed and eagerly endorsed the plan, which he had earlier suggested to the school board himself. After the board confronted Reed with the charges and listened to her objections to the students' affidavits, it decided not to act on the allegations that Reed characterized as "so obviously false and malicious that they do not merit consideration."[41] For the time being, the board put the matter aside.

Two years later, the school board again tried to rid itself of the troublesome teacher and to discredit the union with which she was so closely identified. Reed and the CTF were obvious targets for those who wanted the schools to remain free from all taint of radicalism. The union was always suspect in this regard, and, as Jacqueline Leonhard, school board president from 1950 to 1952, noted, "to many people Reed *was* the union."[42] This time, the OPSB suspended her for failing to fill out a school board questionnaire concerning teachers' after-school activities. Reed, declining to participate in an investigation clearly aimed at identifying teachers who moonlighted in war industries, simply signed the questionnaire without filling it in and returned it to the principal. When Conniff told Reed to complete the form, she refused. "It was none of the school board's business," she retorted.[43] Reed responded to her suspension by immediately demanding a public hearing as guaranteed by the teacher tenure law. At the end of the hearing, the board found her guilty of neglect of duty, reinstated her anyway, but withheld her pay for the period of her suspension.[44] Reed, who saw her suspension as an attack on teacher tenure, sued for restitution of her lost pay, hopeful that the court would uphold the tenure law in its decision. She also wanted the school board to reverse its verdict.[45]

New Orleans teachers came out in large numbers to support their colleague at civil district court in May 1944. When Reed's lawyers introduced a report that her civics classes scored higher in tests than students in other schools, the teachers applauded and cheered so loudly the judge halted the proceedings. The teachers stopped only when the judge threatened them with contempt of court.[46] The school board attorney then presented reports of Reed's uncooperative behavior and her frequent criticism of school authorities and offered into evidence the affidavits collected by the Association of Commerce in 1941. For the first time the allegations against Reed were made public. It is clear that many of the statements were simply false and most of them harmless, unless interpreted as part of a larger, subversive agenda. One student had claimed that Reed belittled a Baptist church on St. Charles Avenue for spending money on a neon sign and reported that she had advised a Catholic boy not to confess to a priest "as it is none of his business."[47] Three boys had alleged that Reed seemed to approve of communism, although one of them also said he overheard her admit to being a fascist.[48] Two other boys, in identical affidavits, had quoted Reed as saying that "the South was not a fit place to live" and that she was indifferent to religion.[49] Finally the judge ruled in favor of the school board. Reed did not fill out the questionnaire as she had been directed to do, he said, and her attitude in court indicated that she did not think the board had any right to inquire about her after-school activities. The judge concluded that the school board did have that right.[50]

If school authorities hoped that the trial would tame Reed, they were disappointed. She never lost her willingness to challenge authority when she thought it necessary, and never curtailed her dedication to progressive teaching techniques. Her Fortier High School students had always engaged in lively debates about current events, politics, and government, and she filled the shelves of her classroom with newspapers and magazines, including the *New Republic* and the *Nation*. She unbolted desks from the floor and rearranged them to encourage participation. Her civics class resembled a legislative assembly room in which one student held the position of chairman, called the assembly to order, and asked class members for reports on world events, national and local politics, and other topics.[51] Indeed, minutes of the class meetings kept by the day's secretary reveal animated discussions and debates on topics many would consider too controversial or too complex for high school students to understand: the CIO, immigration laws, the fairness of the sales tax, economic conditions in the South, housing problems in New Orleans, sit-down strikes, Louisiana's low literacy rate, and the Spanish Civil War. One student's contribution to the news report concerned freedom of speech, which triggered a lengthy debate. In another class, "A big slum discussion immediately started but had to be put down to get on with regular business." New Deal policies and Roosevelt's speeches were common topics in Reed's civics classes throughout the 1930s and early 1940s, and several of her classes analyzed the democratic and undemocratic features of New Orleans government.[52]

Reed's classes extended far beyond the confines of the Fortier High School building. She took her students to the polls, the courthouse, the parish prison, and to city council and school board meetings. At a meeting of the school board, one of Reed's civics classes presented two petitions: one calling for the construction of an auditorium at Fortier, which the board agreed was a good idea, and another to lengthen the Christmas vacation, which the board rejected.[53] Her classes collected food for the Alexander Milne Home School for Destitute Orphan Girls and made scrapbooks about current events and problems in the United States.[54] Her aim, she said, was to make civics come "alive" to her pupils and "to bring out everything in the child that we can so that each child has some avenue of expression. The consequence is, I think, the children do develop a great deal, and I try as much as humanly possible, to stand aside and let them discuss, and they like it."[55]

In her classroom, as in her public life, Reed subscribed to the sentiments expressed in the CTF charter: "We believe in democracy and in the schools as the chief agency of democracy. We believe that servility breeds servility," it stated, affirming the teachers' intention "to democratize the schools by encouraging and promoting teacher and pupil participation."[56] Reed saw a direct connection between political democracy in the classroom and political democracy in the world outside of it, and she tried to make the connection clear to her students. To many of her critics, this was pedagogy verging on subversion.

The reemergence of anticommunism in an even more virulent form after World War II created philosophical and political problems for Reed and other liberals. The dissolution of the Soviet-American alliance, the invasion of eastern Europe by the Soviet Union, and the reports of Stalin's purges worried Americans. Members of the House Un-American Activities Committee, charged with investigating un-American propaganda and subversion, announced its intention to "expose and ferret out the Communists and Communist sympathizers in the federal government." President Truman responded to the success of red-baiting by giving it federal legitimacy in 1947, when he issued an executive order calling for a new loyalty-security program in the U.S. government, the first ever initiated in peacetime.[57]

In this Cold War environment, at a time when liberals such as Reed became increasingly vulnerable to charges of disloyalty, the Orleans Parish School Board used the growing anticommunist sentiment to finally silence her. In 1948, in a transparent attempt to force the sixty-six-year-old teacher to resign, as well as to show the community that it was diligently guarding the schools against communist influence, the board charged Reed with "not stressing the American way of life as superior in every respect to Communism or other 'isms,'" and informed her that she would no longer teach civics. In her new class, the school superintendent warned, anytime "the American way of life is brought up in your class it will be your bounden duty to extol the American system."[58]

Reed's past conflicts with the school board and her principal, her work for the teachers' unions, her close identification with organized labor, her support of African American teachers, her ties to the political left, and her unconventional pedagogy—any one of these might have been enough to antagonize school authorities. Taken together they would have been more than enough to crush another teacher. Neither Reed nor her union, however, was intimidated by the proceedings against her. Even as they fought the charges, Reed and the union engaged successfully in another battle with the board over teacher sabbatical leaves.

Again Reed demanded a public hearing and rallied her supporters behind her. Calls and letters soon poured into the school superintendent's office from the Central Trades and Labor Council (CTLC), representatives from a committee of Tulane and Loyola professors who had organized to support Reed, and other concerned citizens. It took courage to openly deny charges of disloyalty in 1948. A more cautious person would have acquiesced to the board's transfer in the hope that the matter would remain private. Reed, however, was rarely cautious. Instead, she and the union bolstered her defense by organizing another committee of thirty teachers, while gathering supportive statements from parents and faculty. The CTLC agreed to pay all expenses necessary to fight the accusations against Reed.[59]

During the hearing, the board used as evidence statements it had collected from five of Reed's current students who reported that their teacher "advocated equal distribution of nation's wealth," supported repeal of the Taft-Hartley Act, voiced her preference for Henry Wallace for president, and "pointed out certain phases of superiorities of Communism over the Democratic way."[60] The board also brought out again the 1941 affidavits that questioned her patriotism and recounted many of its numerous clashes with Reed.[61] The board's case, however, paled in comparison to the large number of students and teachers who testified on her behalf, the several dozen more who were prepared to speak for her, the nearly two hundred students who had volunteered to do whatever they could to help her, and a CTF survey of 250 students who all denied that Reed had made statements denigrating democracy.[62] In the end, faced with an outpouring of support for Reed from her students, colleagues, women's groups, and the general public, the board dropped its plan to transfer Reed and let the matter go, not without some embarrassment.[63] Reed celebrated the board's decision, calling it "a great victory for academic freedom in the classroom. The case was a very special illustration of democracy at work in the New Orleans public school system. It has been wonderfully educational for my boys." She noted that controversies were bound to erupt in her classes where students often took the lead, but she had no intention of changing her teaching methods: "I am proud that I got across to my students the fact that America, even in its greatness, is no finished product wrapped up in cellophane, just to be looked at. It's a living, growing thing and so, while we have privileges, we also have duties and responsibilities. These I have always emphasized."[64]

In the days following Reed's public hearing with the school board, the New Orleans press carried letters from citizens who described the charges against Reed as ludicrous. As Ethel Hutson, former suffrage leader and women's rights activist, wrote to the *Times-Picayune*:

> If there is one teacher in the public schools of New Orleans—or in any school anywhere—who is known for independence, courage in fighting injustice and oppression, and unwillingness to allow anyone to impose on her or on anyone else, it is, and has been for close on to 40 years, Mrs. Sarah Towles Reed. She has worked and written and spoken and fought for the rights of teachers against arbitrary and unfair action, rulings, decisions of Boards and Superintendents for more than a generation.[65]

Another writer rejoiced that Reed had once again won a battle for all teachers, not just for herself. "Teachers may no longer cower and shrink from the intimidation of Communism as a means of whipping them into line," she said.[66] A fellow teacher wrote to Reed personally and thanked her for protecting teachers' rights: "Instead of being accused of not stressing Democracy, to the contrary, I think you should be given the Congressional Medal of Honor for being one of those courageous individuals whose high democratic ideals make it possible for this great Democracy of ours to survive and progress. May there always be Sarah Reeds and more power to them!"[67]

As the overwhelming support for Reed shows, liberalism in the South was strong enough to defeat its foes, at least on issues of academic freedom and free speech, despite the conservatism of the national mood. On issues of race, however, southern liberals were soon to show themselves to be too cautious and essentially ineffective. Reed's approach to integration is a case in point. Although she had supported African American teachers in their efforts to organize a union and fight for better schools and equal pay, she was hesitant when the issue of union integration arose.

Reed had worked closely with the black teachers' union from its earliest days and regularly attended its meetings. In 1946, she helped organize an interracial liaison group that met every month, and more often during emergency situations. The two locals merged their committees on kindergarten classes and began sharing an office and legislative fund.[68] Integrated groups of teachers appeared before the Orleans Parish School Board to address their mutual concerns. In 1950 an interracial delegation convinced the board to overturn its policy of not hiring married women.[69] The next year, the presidents of Locals 353 and 527 spoke to the board about improving the condition of black schools, and Veronica Hill, president of 527, asked Reed to serve on a committee to explore the conversion of some white schools to black ones, a move opposed by whites who wanted keep the schools in their neighborhoods all-white. The two unions sponsored an integrated forum to discuss this "very touchy subject," as Hill described it.[70]

In 1954, after the *Brown v. Board of Education* Supreme Court ruling, the AFT ended its official tolerance of segregation and directed all segregated locals to submit reports explaining why they were not integrated. Two years later, after repeated warnings to New Orleans's white local that it was jeopardizing its standing with the national by insisting on segregation, the AFT suspended the local until it integrated. The black local would remain in the national since it had no problem with integrating. The AFT required all locals to be fully integrated by the first day of 1958 or lose their charters.[71]

Reed had already left teaching when the crisis over union integration erupted. After teaching for more than forty years, she retired in 1951 at the age of sixty-nine. She did not retire from union work, however, and labored tirelessly to save her precious union from expulsion. While Reed herself favored integration, she feared the consequences of trying to force it on other members of the white union who did not share her racial views and who would quit the union before accepting a merger with the black local. She pleaded in vain with the national union to extend the integration deadline. In September 1957, Local 353 brought the issue of integration to a vote. It voted to remain segregated and consequently lost its affiliation with the national.[72] Local 527 agreed to accept any member regardless of race and became the only official AFT local in New Orleans. The old Local 353 continued in existence without national affiliation and merged with NOPSTA in 1968. Finally, in 1973, Local 527 merged with the local unit of the National Education Association to form the integrated United Teachers of New Orleans.[73]

At first glance, Reed's diffident stand on union integration seems out of character for an outspoken liberal who had never hesitated to stand up for her beliefs, however controversial, even when her job was in jeopardy. Her reluctance to mount an aggressive campaign to put an end to segregated locals can be understood only in light of the prevailing hostility against integration by the dominant Louisiana white population. Reed's lobbying efforts with state legislators were crucial to the success of teachers' bills. An integrated teachers' union could not expect to win allies in the Louisiana legislature.

Reed's social and political background may also have influenced her ambivalent approach to the issue. As a southerner with roots in plantation country she may not have been able to muster the passion necessary to ardently advance the cause of integration. It could also be argued that her inability to move beyond a New Deal framework limited her ability in subsequent years to understand the social forces that pushed against that era's patient approach to racial integration. Reed had reached her political maturity during the New Deal, which worked to ameliorate conditions for blacks but largely ignored segregation. But segregation was the only issue that mattered in the mid-1950s South. Reed was forced to choose between a firm stand in favor of integration, while watching her union die, and a compromise that would prolong segregation but keep the union alive, albeit without its national affiliation, until the "old diehards," as she called them, could be persuaded to integrate. Like many southern liberals, Reed chose the moderate, gradualist course of action and, as a result, separated herself from the revolution exploding around her.

Reed continued to work with Local 527 while remaining a member of the former 353 and the New Orleans Public School Teachers Association. Her lobbying efforts with the Louisiana legislature finally ended in 1972, when illness prevented her from catching the early-morning bus to Baton Rouge. On May 8, 1978, Reed died at the age of ninety-six. In 1988, the Sarah Towles Reed High School opened in eastern New Orleans.[74]

Throughout her life, Reed embodied the ideals of her Progressive era roots and her New Deal outlook. She was part of the generation of women that included Francis Perkins, Molly Dewson, Lucy Randolph Mason, and Eleanor Roosevelt—women who brought Progressivism into the New Deal, fought for social reform all of their lives, and advanced the role of women in public life. Like these contemporaries, Reed dedicated her life to public service and social justice. While some in the New Orleans community considered her a radical and a dangerous influence on her students and other teachers, other New Orleanians rushed to her support when school authorities attempted to quiet her. Her champions—teachers, professors, and members of women's clubs and labor unions—protected her as she rallied them to her cause. Reed and her allies belie the stereotypes of southerners as reactionary and parochial and southern women as deferential and docile. Reed's outspoken views and her intrepid campaigns on behalf of equal rights for women and blacks, and for academic freedom, economic justice, and unionization, earned her the animosity of some in the community. Just as important, however, they also attracted the support of others—liberals who, like Reed, understood the value of democracy in southern public education.

NOTES

1. *New Orleans States-Item*, May 10, 1978.

2. Sonora Towles Marsh, *The Story of a Good Citizen: Sarah Towles Reed* (privately published, n.d.), 3, Sarah Towles Reed Collection, Archives and Manuscripts Division, Earl K. Long Library, University of New Orleans (hereafter STR Coll.).

3. Pamela Tyler, *Silk Stockings and Ballot Boxes: Women and Politics in New Orleans, 1920–1965*

(Athens: University of Georgia Press, 1996), 15, 18; Kathryn W. Kemp, "Jean and Kate Gordon: New Orleans Social Reformers, 1898–1933," *Louisiana History* 24 (Fall 1983): 390; Sarah Towles, untitled manuscript, Newcomb notes and papers, n.d., STR Coll.

4. Orleans Parish School Board Collection, minutes of Sept. 9, 1921, Archives and Manuscripts Division, Earl K. Long Library, University of New Orleans (hereafter referred to as OPSB min.)

5. *New Orleans Item*, October 15, 1921.

6. OPSB min., October 14, 1921; Sarah Reed manuscript drafts, STR Coll.

7. *Times-Picayune*, October 23, 1921; OPSB min., August 12, 1932.

8. Papers of the executive board of New Orleans Public School Teachers Association (NOPSTA), 1925–26, STR Coll; OPSB min., February 12, 1924.

9. Roman Heleniak, "Local Reaction to the Great Depression in New Orleans, 1929–1933," *Louisiana History* 10 (Fall 1969): 303.

10. Douglas L. Smith, *The New Deal in the Urban South* (Baton Rouge: Louisiana State University Press, 1988), 22, 25.

11. OPSB min., August 12, 1932.

12. Michael Provosty, city attorney, to A. J. Tete, secretary, OPSB, June 27, 1931, OPSB general files.

13. George B. Tindall, *The Emergence of the New South, 1913–1945* (Baton Rouge: Louisiana State University Press, 1967), 505.

14. Allie Mann, vice president, American Federation of Teachers, to STR ("My dear Mrs. Reed"), May 5, 1934, STR Coll.

15. Marjorie Murphy, *Blackboard Unions: The AFT and the NEA, 1900–1980* (Ithaca: Cornell University Press, 1990), 67–68.

16. Constitution and By-laws of the New Orleans Classroom Teachers' Federation, Local 353, American Federation of Teachers, effective August 1, 1938, STR Coll.

17. New Orleans Classroom Teachers' Federation, Local 353, American Federation of Teachers, 1937–38 Yearbook, STR Coll.

18. Guy Clifford Mitchell, "Growth of State Control of Public Education in Louisiana" (PhD diss., University of Michigan, 1942), 410; *Times-Picayune*, June 9, 1936; *Faculty*, June 1936, STR Coll.

19. Mitchell, "Growth of State Control of Public Education," 405, 411; *Times-Picayune*, June 19, 1936; *Faculty*, June 1936, STR Coll.

20. Claudia Goldin, *Understanding the Gender Gap: An Economic History of American Women* (New York: Oxford University Press, 1990), 161; Lessley P. Gardinor, second attorney general, to Hon. A. J. Tete, secretary, OPSB, October 7, 1936, OPSB general files.

21. Myrtle H. Rey, President's Annual Report, New Orleans Public School Teachers Association, 1936, STR Coll.

22. New Orleans Classroom Teachers' Federation, Local 353, *1937–38 Yearbook*, STR Coll; Mitchell, "Growth of State Control of Public Education," 467; *Times-Picayune*, March 1, 1938.

23. *Times-Picayune*, August 18, 1937.

24. West Feliciana Parish notarial records, book 29, 579; Nora Marsh, interview with author, November 30, 1993; statements by Irene Scott, Reuben Cole, and Willie D. Scott, notarized by Herman Midlo, notary public, July 2, 1937, Harold N. Lee Papers, Howard-Tilton Library, Tulane University, New Orleans.

25. *New Orleans Item*, September 1, 1937; Veronica Hill, interview with author, April 1, 1996, Gretna, La.; OPSB min., August 31, 1937. A slightly different version of this story appeared in *Times-Picayune*, September 1, 1937.

26. *Times-Picayune*, September 1, 1937.

27. Adam Fairclough, *Race and Democracy: The Civil Rights Struggle in Louisiana, 1915–1972* (Athens: University of Georgia Press, 1995), 23.

28. "September 23, 1937," Record Book and Minutes of the New Orleans Federation of Classroom

Teachers, AFT Local 527, William H. Davis Sr. Collection, Archives and Manuscripts Division, Earl K. Long Library, University of New Orleans.

29. *The Voice of the New Orleans League of Classroom Teachers, Local 527*, Alexander Pierre Tureaud papers, Amistad Research Center, Tulane University, New Orleans; Veronica Hill, interview with author, April 1, 1996.

30. *New Orleans Item*, August 24, 1943.

31. Linda Reed, *Simple Decency and Common Sense: The Southern Conference Movement, 1938–1963* (Bloomington: Indiana University Press, 1991), xx.

32. OPSB Report to the President and Members, December 9, 1938, STR Coll.

33. Pamela Jean Turner, "Civil Rights and Anti-communism in New Orleans, 1946–1965" (master's thesis, University of New Orleans, 1981), 5; *Times-Picayune*, November 24, 1938. Also attending the first SCHW meeting was Virginia Foster Durr, a founding member of the group, who, like Reed, came out of the Old South slave-owning tradition and did not question her racial views until she became a New Dealer. Like Reed too, Durr was attacked for her political views. In 1954, the Internal Security Committee, headed by Senator James Eastland, called Durr to testify about her allegedly "subversive" activities. For a full account of this episode, see Hollinger F. Barnard, ed., *Outside the Magic Circle: The Autobiography of Virginia Foster Durr* (Tuscaloosa: University of Alabama Press, 1985), chapter 18.

34. David Lee Wells, "The ILWU in New Orleans: CIO Radicalism in the Crescent City, 1937–1957" (master's thesis, University of New Orleans, 1979), 7.

35. *New Orleans Item*, July 4, 1941.

36. Murphy, *Blackboard Unions*, 170; David Caute, *The Great Fear: The Anti-communist Purge under Truman and Eisenhower* (New York: Simon and Schuster, 1978), 432.

37. William V. Moore, "Civil Liberties in Louisiana: The Louisiana League for the Preservation of Constitutional Rights," *Louisiana History* 31 (Winter 1990): 60–63; *New Orleans Item*, January 10, 1941; *Times-Picayune*, August 10, 1940; OPSB min., January 10, 1941.

38. OPSB min., January 10, 1941.

39. OPSB, Hearing in the Matter of the Alleged Failure of Mrs. Sarah Towles Reed, Teacher at Fortier High School, to Adequately Stress Americanism in Her Civics Classes, 1948 transcript, 57 (hereafter referred to as OPSB hearing on alleged un-Americanism), STR Coll.

40. OPSB min., March 11, 1941.

41. STR to president and members of OPSB, April 21, 1941, STR Coll.

42. Jacqueline T. Leonhard, interview with author, May 30, 1996.

43. OPSB min., Feb 9, 1943.

44. *New Orleans Item*, March 18, 1943.

45. *New Orleans States*, April 8, 1943.

46. *New Orleans States*, May 5, 1944.

47. Martin Kombar, Affidavit, December 30, 1940, Civil District Court, Parish of Orleans, State of Louisiana, no. 249–672, Division "E," docket 3, *Mrs. Sarah Towles Reed v. OPSB*, Answer (hereafter referred to as Civil District Court, *Reed v. OPSB*), STR Coll.

48. Robert E. Brown, Affidavit, December 30, 1940, Edmund Brown, Affidavit, December 30, 1940, Civil District Court, *Reed v. OPSB*, STR Coll.; William von Phul Trufant, Affidavit, January 18, 1941, Civil District Court, *Reed v. OPSB*, STR Coll.

49. John Parran and Kenneth Muller, Affidavits, January 25, 1941, Civil District Court, *Reed v. OPSB*, STR coll.

50. *Times-Picayune*, July 12, 1944; *New Orleans Item*, July 12, 1944.

51. Marsh, *The Story of a Good Citizen*, 6; STR notes, n.d., STR Coll.

52. STR notes, n.d., STR Coll.

53. OPSB min., December 13, 1935.

54. Ida B. Little, superintendent, Alexander Milne Home School for Destitute Orphan Girls, to STR, Fortier High School, November 24, 1944, STR Coll.; STR scrapbooks, n.d., STR Coll.

55. OPSB hearing on alleged un-Americanism, 159, 156.

56. *Constitution and By-laws of the New Orleans Classroom Teachers' Federation*, Local 353, AFT, effective August 1, 1938, STR Coll.

57. Richard H. Pells, *The Liberal Mind in a Conservative Age: American Intellectuals in the 1940s and 1950s* (New York: Harper and Row, 1985), 267; Caute, *The Great Fear*, 27–28.

58. Lionel J. Bourgeois, assistant superintendent, Instruction, OPSB, to STR, Alcee Fortier High School, May 24, 1948, STR Coll.

59. "Reed Case Victory for Academic Freedom, "*Federation Review* (Teachers' Federation, A.F.L., New Orleans), September 1951, 4.

60. *Times-Picayune*, August 28, 1948.

61. Ibid.; OPSB hearing on alleged un-Americanism, STR Coll.

62. *Times-Picayune*, August 28, 1948; *New Orleans Item*, August 27, 1948.

63. OPSB min., August 27, 1948; Lionel J. Bourgeois to President and Members of OPSB, August 27, 1948.

64. *New Orleans Item*, August 28, 1948.

65. *Times-Picayune*, September 5, 1948.

66. Ibid.

67. Nancy DiMartino to STR, August 31, 1948, STR Coll.

68. Edith Rosepha Ambrose, "Sarah Towles Reed: Teacher and Activist," *Louisiana History* 37 (Winter 1996): 57–58.

69. Jonie Griffin, "'We Believe that Servility Breeds Servility': The Classroom Teachers' Federation and Human Rights in New Orleans, 1925–1958," paper presented at the Southern Historical Association meeting, Atlanta, November 1991; Samson P. Bordelon, "The New Orleans Public Schools under the Superintendency of Lionel John Bourgeois" (PhD diss., University of Southern Mississippi, 1996), 49.

70. Griffin, "We Believe that Servility Breeds Servility"; OPSB min., February 1951; Veronica Hill, president, Local 527, to STR, January 22, 1952, STR Coll.

71. William Edward Eaton, *The American Federation of Teachers, 1916–1961: A History of the Movement* (Carbondale: Southern Illinois University Press, 1975), 59–160; Murphy, *Blackboard Unions*, 198–99; meeting of the Executive Board, Local 353, June 19, 1957, STR Coll.

72. CTF ballot, September 26, 1956, STR Coll.; Griffin, "We Believe that Servility Breeds Servility"; Ruby Dowling to Carl Megel, president, AFT, September 20, 1957, AFT Archives, Archives of Labor and Urban Affairs, Walter Reuther Library, Wayne State University, Detroit.

73. Murphy, *Blackboard Unions*, 198–99; Donald E. DeVore and Joseph Logsdon, *Crescent City Schools: Public Education in New Orleans, 1841–1991* (Lafayette: Center for Louisiana Studies, University of Southwestern Louisiana, 1991), 278.

74. *Times-Picayune*, May 10, 1978; *Times-Picayune*, August 5, 1988.

Georgia M. Johnson

(1894–1969)

"We Are but Americans": Civil Rights Activism in Alexandria, Louisiana

LEE SARTAIN

African American women in the twentieth-century civil rights struggle in the United States have been generally recorded as a collective body of activists who contributed their social networks to fund-raising, membership drives, and campaigning.[1] This has tended to obscure the talents of minor characters who were leaders, though not always presidents, of local branches of the National Association for the Advancement of Colored People (NAACP) and who fought for civil rights for African Americans within their communities. Georgia M. Johnson of Alexandria, Louisiana, exemplifies such a person, a forceful individual in a racially conservative city in the Deep South who was extremely active in the civil rights movement during midcentury. She helps to define the role women often undertook in the early struggle not because of her conformity to social and gender expectations but because of many of the organizational taboos she breached. Certainly, Johnson was self-conscious of the dual nature of discrimination, sexism and racism, within the community in which she worked and the white society she encountered during the 1940s.

Georgia Johnson articulated a coherent ideological stance for her activism through a blend of religious belief and class consciousness. Her prolific and long letters to the New Orleans NAACP branch and to the association's national office in New York give a great deal of insight into the motivation of an individual who found it restrictive to work within a highly centralized organization that did not always accept women other than in a traditional gendered role. While women were accepted as secretaries and chairs of committees on entertainment or fund-raising, since this fitted the concept of women as collectivist organizers working in the background, it was often harder for them to gain acceptance as organizational leaders in the public eye. Johnson, however, was unique in Louisiana in this period by undertaking the position of chair of the legal redress and legislation committee in an NAACP branch, where such a post, like president and treasurer, was a decidedly male preserve.[2] The NAACP branch constitution stated that the committee existed to "examine local ordinances for possibilities of discrimination, work for better equal enforcement of the laws . . . and work for the repeal of discriminatory laws." Its more significant and prominent role, however, was the investigation of "all cases reported to it for legal redress" and to "watch over all litigation in which the Branch is interested."[3] Such a high-profile position led to intense personal politicking within the branch between the militant Johnson and the gradualist male leadership in the city, as well as direct threats from the white establishment attempting to suppress her investigations into racism in the city.

Alexandria, located in Rapides Parish in central Louisiana, had short-lived NAACP branches in 1921, 1927, and 1930. Isolated and remote branches were inspired usually by single issues that directly affected the city's black community and reflected the difficult social and political conditions under which the segregated black population lived. For example, Alexandria had a small and reasonably secure black middle class, comprising clergymen, teachers, and businesspeople whose organizing proclivities contributed to sporadic civil rights activities. In 1921, the city's black elite organized a branch under the leadership of Reverend H. R. Norris in response to a constitutional convention being held in the state in which voting rights were of prime interest, particularly as the issue of black female enfranchisement was at stake after the states ratified the Nineteenth Amendment. The 1927 branch was organized in response to the devastating Mississippi floods that year, while at a national level the NAACP campaigned against labor peonage in levee camps in Mississippi and Louisiana and publicized discrimination in federal aid to blacks who had been displaced from their homes and workplaces.[4] By April 1930, Alexandria was "proud of the fact" that it had chartered a branch with 102 members, although it soon disbanded, probably due to the difficulties of sustaining interest in a civil rights group during the devastation of the Depression.[5]

In May 1941, an Alexandria NAACP branch established itself again, this time to organize statewide campaigns to equalize black teachers' salaries with those of whites and to undertake vigorous voter registration drives.[6] This time a rapidly expanding war economy gave clear focus to the campaigns. There were five military bases within a twenty-five-mile radius of Alexandria that acted as the center for all basic training of U.S. armed forces, and population growth in the period was considerable. Before 1941, the total population of the town stood at twenty-six thousand, of whom eleven thousand were black. By the end of that year, the population had grown to forty-one thousand whites and twenty-six thousand blacks.[7] This substantial African American population included soldiers as well as civilians employed in wartime industries.

Outside of the major metropolitan areas of New Orleans and Baton Rouge, most of Louisiana was seen by George W. Lucas, president of the New Orleans NAACP branch (1921–30), as a remote and dangerous hinterland.[8] While New Orleans, in the southeastern part of the state, was seen as being more French- and Spanish-influenced and Catholic due to its colonial past, northern Louisiana was thought to be more "Americanized," having more in common with other southern states, with Protestantism predominant among blacks and with its more Anglo-American culture.[9] Alexandria, therefore, reflected the social conditions of other cities across the nation, while its exaggerated military composition led to general wartime stresses and a subsequent rise in civil rights militancy. Madison S. Jones, a national NAACP field officer, deemed Alexandria as "the roughest place, as far as race relations are concerned" in Louisiana in the early 1940s.[10]

It was in this daunting social atmosphere that the Alexandria NAACP branch was kept alive almost single-handedly by Georgia Johnson, chair of the branch's legal redress and legislation committee. She had been a member-at-large of the NAACP since 1920, motivated to join by her staunch belief in exercising her citizenship via the ballot. As soon as the Nineteenth Amendment was ratified in 1920 she attempted to register to vote. Johnson eventually was the first black woman to do so in Rapides Parish, although she much later admitted that it was a constant struggle to reregister over the next forty years.[11] Her personal example was an unequivocal message to the broader African American community and perhaps also an intentional act of defiance to the white authorities. Johnson's high-profile and long-term dedication to civil rights won her personal support in the African American community in Alexandria and led to her prominent role in the NAACP branch in 1941.

Madison Jones's report on his visit to Alexandria in December 1942 demonstrates the virtual invisibility of individual women and the general expectation of their backroom status within NAACP branch offices. The national officer noted that the Alexandria branch "is rather small at the present time, and plodding, but doesn't know just what to do. However, there are some younger men on the Executive Committee who should be able to take over."[12] Such a statement is blatant, yet predictable, in its failure to note Georgia Johnson's central contribution to the branch. Of an official NAACP visit to the mayor of Alexandria, Jones reported, "I went . . . in the company of the Branch president and [was] joined later by a Miss Johnson, secretary of the Branch."[13] Jones mistakenly assumed that Johnson occupied the secretarial post, a typical role for women in local branches. In fact, Georgia Johnson had acted as secretary during the early 1940s, typing all the annual reports and keeping in regular contact with the New York office, a constitutional requirement of an elected branch secretary.[14]

It appears that Johnson was acutely aware of her multifarious branch roles and claimed a leadership position, as she saw it, almost by default, rather than one she had actively sought. She stepped up, she wrote to NAACP director of branches Ella Baker in 1945, "not because I wanted to [or] had the time but some one had to act or others would have suffered."[15] Moreover, she assumed a large part of the moral responsibility in fighting the civil rights cause believing that those who should also have accepted the call, particularly the city's black elite, were shirking their duty. Indeed Johnson's legal redress committee was often the only fully operational aspect of the branch, but in 1945 a faction in the branch caused Johnson to be removed from her post. A pro-Johnson faction in the branch complained to the national office that hers had been "the only committee working . . . through appalling handicaps. Oftimes going over the wishes . . . of some of the members of the branch [in] defending the rights of soldiers [in Alexandria's segregated army camps]."[16]

Although very little can be ascertained about Johnson's childhood or education, she was born around 1894. Her professional career, which lasted from the 1920s through the 1960s, indicates an extremely busy entrepreneurial spirit and a reasonably educated woman. To Ella Baker she described her career both as a livelihood and a way by which to advance her community, seeing herself as a "business and a general civic worker for a number of years for my group."[17] Like so many women who joined the NAACP, Johnson had been a public school teacher and a principal. In the 1930s she was the first black social worker in the parish and at one point also sold insurance. During her time working for the city's NAACP in the 1940s, Johnson was editor and manager of the *Alexandria Observer*, a black newspaper, and at the same time she owned a café, the Royal Garden. In the 1950s and 1960s she became an independent booking agent for southern artists, "booking bands, orchestras, spirituals and shows, [and] all types of theatrical musical presentations," and by the late 1960s she was the owner of the Holly Oak Cemetery. Her business acumen gave Johnson economic independence from the white community and insulated her from political pressures from the black social establishment. Economic independence underscored her political autonomy and she was able to protest against segregation and racial injustice without significant financial ramifications.[18]

Johnson remained unmarried throughout her life, although family was important to her, as can be seen by her employment of her two nieces (as managers) and her nephew in the Royal Garden. Religion too was central to Johnson, a committed Methodist who had a powerful understanding of the message of Christ's suffering, martyrdom, and redemption, which she related directly to herself and her role in the civil rights struggle. This view of Christianity was widespread among African Americans, who had suffered under slavery and then segregation, and it can be attributed to many local leaders fighting for civil rights locally on a day-to-day basis. Indeed Johnson took great solace in viewing Christ as "crushed and misrepresented," which connected with her personal difficulties being associated with the NAACP and to the black population as a whole, suffering oppression.[19]

Johnson's perception of the fight for constitutional rights was essentially elitist. She believed that it was the job of a self-selected social elite (in her own words, "well thinking educated members of the branch") to work for the liberation of the entire black population.[20] Well-informed, middle-class leaders from within the community were needed both to lead the fight for equality and to guide by personal example so that the lower classes could emulate them. In 1941 Johnson stated, "Action is paramount. Thinking is in order. Classes should think for the masses, but help by pulling them along and helping them find themselves in this great civilization."[21] However, Johnson's was not just a middle-class moral example to all African Americans. Her activism, based on individual fortitude, aimed at achieving equality in American society. Not only did Johnson regularly register to vote, she expected others to be inspired by her actions to follow suit and to be brave enough to join the NAACP, even if it meant enduring repercussions from the white community. This is very much in keeping with what research has shown of other black female leaders, such as Lillie M. Jackson and Juanita J. Mitchell of Baltimore, Lula B. White of Houston, Daisy Bates of Little Rock, and Rosa Parks of Montgomery, Alabama. The growing literature on African American female leadership and the civil rights movement suggests that across the United States individual women developed leadership roles by associating with national organizations like the NAACP while utilizing their local social and professional networks.[22]

This concept of leadership differed from that of Ella Baker (director of branches from 1943 to 1946), who had a "radical democratic" vision of the civil rights struggle. Baker, a better-known activist who helped to found the student-led and student-dominated, nonhierarchical Student Non-Violent Coordinating Committee (SNCC), objected to the undemocratic structures in the NAACP and disapproved of a movement based solely on middle-class attitudes. Johnson had some sympathy with the idea of leaders emerging from within a community rather than being imposed, and her extensive correspondence with Baker in the mid-1940s suggests she had significant empathy with Baker as a national NAACP female figure. Yet Johnson differed from Baker with her belief in an elite-based movement, akin to the views held by the noted black intellectual and NAACP founder, W. E. B. Du Bois (editor of the NAACP journal, *Crisis*, from 1910 to 1934), in his early years with the association. In particular Johnson would have sympathized with Du Bois's ideas of an African American "talented tenth," an elite who could lead the black masses to attain their full political rights by their erudition and understanding of the race situation.[23]

Such an understanding of an elite directing the NAACP in Alexandria led to occasional frustrations with the apparent inertia of "the masses," although it was the black middle classes Johnson blamed for the failure of civil rights progress in Louisiana.[24] When lawyer A. P. Tureaud of the New Orleans NAACP branch and Thurgood Marshall, NAACP special counsel, both failed to respond to Johnson's request for legal help during a 1944 voter registration campaign organized by the branch, she wrote to Tureaud, "I do not understand colored people. No matter how great or how important their position is[,] they are poor business people."[25] Her impatience led her to privately attack various officials in the NAACP, both at the local and national levels, for the slow pace of change in race relations. She felt that not every black person had her passion and strength for the fight. A "protest committee" organized in January 1945 and consisting of sixty Alexandria NAACP members sent a petition to the New York office. The dissidents argued that some branch officers suffered from a "lack of vision as to the great work of the N.A.A.C.P."[26] Johnson, cochair of the committee, accused branch leaders of not having acting upon atrocities perpetrated on black soldiers in the city. She confided to Ella Baker that year: "[Seeing] incident after incident . . . happening among citizens and soldiers coming from other sections of this country [to Alexandria] and . . . [sentiments] . . . growing more and more intense. . . . [N]o one [in the branch was] acting. . . . [S]ome have resorted to mud-slinging and have forgotten the real principle upon which the [NAACP] is built[,] that is to Advance and not to degrade."[27] Part of the problem, as Johnson saw it, was that the other branch leaders continually tried to "appease the white people."[28] Johnson had little patience with a gradualist approach to civil rights matters, whereby black elites compromised on segregation as they negotiated with white power structures for meager gains. Johnson was uncompromising in her expectations of NAACP leaders and her stance that they should confront racism or they would otherwise be an ineffectual elitist clique that accommodated bigotry. In 1946, she reflected upon such inadequacies of the Alexandria branch officers, whom she saw as merely being interested in maintaining their own status. She wrote to Baker, "I know Negroes and their organizations, they want only a little group of their friends to sop while the others stand and look on."[29] As an example of her own commitment to standing up to white power, Johnson declared that she had resigned from being a school principal at the Rosenwald School in the area and as a social worker in the parish, telling Baker, "I could not be an uncle tom."[30]

Johnson clearly understood gender expectations within the organization and wider society. Women had a role in black middle-class society as morally virtuous people who needed protecting from male indecorousness and sometimes shielded from their own sensitivities. For instance, of his meeting with the mayor of Alexandria, Madison Jones expressed shock at the foul language the mayor had used "in front of my two colleagues, including a lady, and also his own secretary."[31] A. P. Tureaud of the New Orleans NAACP branch wrote to Johnson that she was "too sensitive about things," which made her "too hasty" in her opinions, particularly when she condemned the leadership of a statewide NAACP voter registration drive for failing to be more effective.[32] Furthermore, Johnson related to Baker, a black minister in Alexandria, Reverend E. Charles Curtis, "bluntly warned me to be careful because I was a woman."[33] Within the

NAACP, men believed that women should be shielded from vulgarity and protected from harassment and violence.[34]

In any case, Johnson's prominent civil rights profile did lead to physical threats to her well-being. In early 1939 her house was burned down under mysterious circumstances, which may have been related to her activism.[35] Such recrimination may have negatively affected Johnson's business enterprises. She wrote to Baker in 1945: "When a member of our race group displays his or her militancy they are denied many things from a financial point of view. . . . When I think of the time I spent when I could . . . have been doing [other business] and I am not . . . rewarded . . . [I am] very much discouraged and see no hope for the race as a whole. When you are militant you are simply placing a rope around your own neck."[36] Despite such a view, Johnson continued to believe that "the day will come that all men and women regardless of color will have their rightful place in this nation and that we will no longer be the FOOT MATS of this American Country and will not be Semi-slaves as we are but Americans." "Of one Blood God made all Nations to Dwell upon the face of the Earth," she wrote to Baker.[37] Her religious and political ideals informed and reinforced her civil rights work, despite all threats to her welfare.

Equality and integration in Johnson's civil rights philosophy meant a fair share of civic and economic opportunities for African Americans, but not necessarily actual social mixing with whites. She believed in fair chances for blacks to achieve a decent education at all levels, fair employment opportunities throughout a lifetime, and the ability to participate and represent one's community in the national body politic. It was, in fact, belief grounded in the U.S. Constitution: equality before the law (and thus opportunity) but an implicit acceptance of social distinctions. Some people would be successful in their life pursuits, others would not, but it was unfair to impede an individual's progress simply because of racial stereotyping and discrimination. This unfairness was made ever more apparent during America's involvement in World War II, which was supposedly based on ideals of democracy and freedom.[38]

As a center for military training, Alexandria was a perfect place to observe the paradoxes of white American leaders' rhetoric and to witness the work of grassroots civil rights leaders on the ground. Johnson's daily work as chair of the legal redress committee was grueling. This was a significant assignment aimed at mitigating racial discrimination and prejudice against Alexandria's black population, civilian and military. The complexity of this task was amplified by the substantial rise in the city's population due to the training centers and expanding war industries, but this was an opportunity for the NAACP to showcase employment discrimination as well as campaign for job opportunities for black people. It was a daunting mandate for the small group that made up the city's NAACP branch, which received little to no help from the New York office.

In 1941, Johnson declared that the Alexandria NAACP branch was examining the defense industries, civil service, and other job opportunities in the city. After a mass meeting of one hundred "outstanding citizens" at the Shiloh Baptist Church on September 29, Johnson, acting as the meeting's chair, stated that "Alexandria [is] in the midst of one of the greatest National Defense Programs in the nation [and the NAACP has] . . . lots to do in the city."[39] However, the branch committee on labor and industry, responsible for "improving the status of colored people in labor, industry and agriculture," was generally inactive over the following years and by 1944 was defunct.[40] The failure to have an active labor committee was partly due to the intense factionalism between the older race leaders, who controlled the committee, and a more militant group, with Johnson as its standard bearer. Meanwhile, the chair of the legal redress committee spent her time investigating and defending cases involving the civilian and military black populations, observing that there was "much police brutality in this section," with "persons of color being beaten by officers nearly everyday."[41]

While Johnson was sometimes merely recording such abuses and lodging complaints to city officials, her committee work also led to major legal cases undertaken by the branch to save black people's lives. A case in point occurred during 1944 when Johnson investigated the case of Herbert Anderson, who was accused of murdering the chief of police, W. H. Bishop, after Bishop had beaten Anderson's fiancée. Within the Alexandria branch it was only Johnson who wanted to pursue the case, and she found the branch obstructing her committee's work. After a bank rejected a branch check for $134.27 due to apparent lack of funds, Johnson accused branch leaders of misappropriating $184.50 that had been raised for Anderson's legal fees, noting, "Branch should have had several times this much."[42] Johnson also fought to get black men appointed to the jury in order to secure a fair trial for Anderson. Despite such efforts and prolonged legal entanglements, the state executed Anderson in June 1945. Johnson accused the NAACP branch of not being active enough in the case yet also put the blame on "White Southern Lawyers," who had access to the local court system that excluded blacks, for "keeping our group financially . . . depressed while they grow fat."[43]

Much of the work that Johnson undertook through her committee concerned black soldiers at the training camps around Alexandria, particularly "soldier slaying" cases.[44] World War II saw a growth of African American militancy, including the NAACP's "Double V" campaign to fight fascism abroad and at home, which saw national membership grow tenfold from 1940 to 1946, and white racists reacted to this by attempting to reassert control over blacks in military uniform.[45] In line with her committee guidelines, Johnson had to enter areas that posed personal dangers to an NAACP investigator, male or female, even more so due to the military context. No case was more dangerous than researching the Alexandria Riot of January 10, 1942, the largest domestic unrest in the country during the war. The riot erupted after the arrest and treatment of a drunken black soldier on Lee Street in Little Harlem, and it expressed the general resentment black soldiers felt about their experiences in the segregated army camps and city facilities. During the riot, police made over three thousand arrests, and at least twenty-eight African Americans were shot.[46] Madison Jones later in the year reported that it was a constant source of fear among whites that a larger rebellion would take place, and he observed that "a great deal of ammunition is missing from many of the army camps. . . . [O]ne unit had been stood up in the sun last August, at attention for an hour, in order to make them break down and confess. . . . At Camp Claibourne there are several Negro tank divisions and the boys are very vocal in saying that they expect to drive their tanks down the streets of Alexandria before they drive to the front."[47] White authorities were so anxious that they situated a machine gun on top of the city hall for some time after the riot in case of further unrest. Johnson's determination to investigate the causes of the riot came up against hostility from the white population and authorities, as she explained in 1945 when she received threatening telephone calls and was "stopped in the streets by . . . many of the members of the 'White Group.'"[48] In this atmosphere of fear and heightened racial tension, Johnson was taken to the city courts twice for formal interviews concerning her research into the riot and also became a frequent visitor to the police station.[49]

The Japanese attack on Pearl Harbor, coming just a month before the Alexandria riot, had fueled a spirit of wartime unity and patriotism, which resulted in the federal government censoring the full story. So successfully was the riot suppressed in the media that most historical works mentioning the event include only a line or paragraph of detail despite it being the largest race riot in the United States during World War II. Johnson's work to reveal the circumstances surrounding the riot had little impact, even on the NAACP in New York, suggesting that the organization was complicit in pursuing civil rights through accord rather than displaying disunity by issuing militant calls in the aftermath of Pearl Harbor.[50]

This failure did not prevent Johnson from continuing her investigations in Alexandria. For a while, what was known as "the three soldiers case" became the focus of a national campaign. The case involved three black soldiers, Richard F. Adams, John Bordenave, and Lawrence Mitchell, who were accused of raping a white woman at Camp Claiborne about twenty miles south of Alexandria.[51] There was confusion over jurisdiction of the case, as the alleged crime had taken place on military grounds. The three men were convicted of rape on August 10, 1942, by the federal district court in New Orleans, but they also faced a court-martial. The trial took place at Camp Maxey, Texas, and the soldiers were again convicted and sentenced to die, despite Johnson's attempts at raising money to get proper legal representation. The national office in New York took up the case, and in 1944 President Franklin D. Roosevelt commuted the soldiers' sentence to life imprisonment; they were paroled in 1947.[52] Similarly, in 1944 at Camp Livingston, just across the Red River from Alexandria, a black private named Eddie Anthoney was accused of attempting to rape a white woman. Johnson employed local white attorney, John R. Hunter, who managed to get the soldier acquitted of the charge during a court-martial hearing.[53]

An assertive black woman investigating cases of black men accused of attacking white women must have caused a considerable stir among the white community and authorities of Alexandria. Indeed, historian Danielle McGuire suggests that such social and political resistance by black women was going on across the South at this time, countering countless fallacious accusations against black men of raping white women. One of these black women was Rosa Parks of the Montgomery chapter of the NAACP in 1944.[54] These events were an extension of the NAACP antilynching campaigns of the 1920s and 1930s against the killing of black men by white mobs, albeit during the 1940s it was the state and military authorities who were primarily imprisoning or executing African Americans for breaches in racial and social codes. The justifications put forward by white segregationists for lynching was almost always based upon the alleged sexual savagery of black men and the concomitant protection of white feminine purity. However, the NAACP antilynching campaign reversed this concept by focusing on protecting black men, their wives, and their families from white savagery. The idea that black men were lynched simply for sexual transgression was a falsehood debunked early on by the national office and by activists such as Ida B. Wells, who saw this purely as a method of social and economic control over the black community.[55]

Johnson's defense of black soldiers struck at the very heart of white social power. Here was an uncompromising African American woman defending the rights of black men to have fair trials in both civilian and military courts, as well as their right to associate with women of any race and to serve in the U.S. military without repression so that they could fight for *true* American values. At one point, the state district attorney singled Johnson out with a direct warning after one of her periodic arrests, saying, as Johnson related to Ella Baker, "We are going to do all we can to teach you a lesson. You dictated the policies . . . to get negro [*sic*] soldiers free accused of raping white women. . . . [Y]ou had better leave that . . . Nigger Organization [NAACP] alone and that nigger paper [*Alexandria Observer*]." Johnson told Baker that a state judge had concurred with this, saying, "Well[,] you are an agitator and we know you are a good educated nigger woman but you have these white people against you fooling with that Nigger organization."[56]

As a result of her having such a public profile in Alexandria's civil rights struggle, in 1945 systematic official persecution took place against Johnson. On July 29 that year, two police officers visited Johnson and alleged that her nephew had stolen some sugar from "Cotton Brothers Baking Company." The police forced their way into Johnson's café, the Royal Garden, and after they "found no sugar," they instead claimed that "two cans of lard" worth ten dollars had been stolen. As Johnson reported to Baker, the officers "carried me to Jail [and] kept me there a day." One of Johnson's nieces, a café manager, was also arrested. Johnson told Baker, "Monday they came with a warrant [which they] would not allow me to read. . . . [I]nstead [they] called me a smart Negro agitator fooling with that Negro Organisation N.A.[A.]C.P. and said lots of things. They were glad they had me [as] they were going to make an example out of me. . . . Having references from various outstanding white[s] and Negroes I . . . [got] out on a Bond of $750." The charge was receiving stolen property. At a personal cost of $100, Johnson employed a white lawyer who informed her that it was well known that "you were never at the place . . . [Royal Garden] [b]ut you spent your time with that nigger organization." It is clear that the harassment over the alleged theft was due to her public affiliation with the NAACP. However, when Johnson made it clear that she was prepared to sue the city authorities over police procedural irregularities, the case was dropped.[57]

As if persecution from reactionary whites were not enough, Johnson also suffered defamation from within the Alexandria NAACP branch due to her civil rights militancy and her breach of gender propriety. The central charge, as stated by the branch president, Spencer Bradley, was that Johnson was "not good with finance."[58] As a result, she lost her position as a committee chair in the chapter's election held on November 13, 1944. Johnson did not accept that the election had been legitimate, and a long, abusive campaign began between the two branch factions. The situation was inflamed further when Johnson refused to turn over the financial books for her committee.[59]

A. P. Tureaud reported to Ella Baker that what became known as the "Alexandria problem" was partly due to a "clash of personalities," but he acknowledged that the real issue had erupted over "election irregularities."[60] A small cadre of officials had unconstitutionally rescheduled the November 1944 branch elections from eight o'clock to a half-hour earlier, and no one had been "elected by ballot."[61] This was essentially a coup in order to reappoint the current leadership, minus Johnson. In response, the "protest committee" mentioned earlier was formed on Johnson's behalf, its sixty signatories indicating substantial support from within the branch and also throughout the city's network of black churches. The protesters, in turn, accused the branch leaders of being financially incompetent and lacking commitment to the equality cause. The committee further defended Johnson by insisting that she was "paying [her] own expenses, for example, postage, trips to prison[,] making interviews at Army Camps . . . and other duties too numerous to mention."[62]

One of the central accusations leveled at Johnson was that she had no head for the complex financial issues involved in running an important committee and for branch fund-raising—a treasurer's role that was generally a male preserve in other branches in Louisiana and elsewhere in the South.[63] This seems curious considering Johnson's involvement in her various businesses. A case in point, used by the branch hierarchy, was Johnson's omission from branch accounts of twenty dollars that she had raised. The Methodist minister Reverend J. M. Murphy, protest committee chair, explained that he had personally raised the twenty dollars from his congregation, specifically in Johnson's name and for her committee work, not for the NAACP. Johnson's methods of circumventing the bureaucracy of the local branch to use money she raised for her own committee work was simply to not "even mention the Alexandria Branch to get money." She told Ella Baker, "I can go to any of these churches in the city any Sunday [to] speak and get a collection. . . . I do not have to . . . mention the N.A.[A.]C.P. to get a little money."[64] This was possible since she had been a longtime activist working with the Alexandria network of black churches, and she was comfortable sidestepping the NAACP bureaucracy to achieve her committee's remit.

In retaliation, during an attempted branch meeting in April 1945, Johnson had the city's NAACP leaders arrested and indicted for civil libel. This included the arrest of the president, Spencer Bradley, its vice president, Freddie Spears, and Earl Smith, the new chair of the legal redress committee. They were subsequently released on $100 bonds. Johnson was persuaded to drop the charges due to pressure from the New York office, which did not want the bad publicity in Alexandria and foresaw factionalism leading to the collapse of the branch.[65] This was not a personal vendetta. The goal all along for Johnson was to get NAACP national authorities interested in the irregularities of the election and to attempt to reinvigorate the branch, to make it a more vibrant and effective body. Still, she failed to arouse national office action, notwithstanding its potential to highlight racism in the armed forces training camps. Despite much correspondence between Johnson, Tureaud, and Ella Baker, very little was done to investigate the claims of the protest committee. While the personal wrangling continued into 1946, Baker declared to Johnson that as the election problems of 1944 had gone on for over a year and new elections had taken place in November 1945, the issue was now moot.[66]

The issue was by no means irrelevant, however, and it continued to provoke resentments in the civil rights struggle in Alexandria. By mid-June 1945, Johnson and the protest committee had set up a rival NAACP branch in the city, which collected membership dues under the guise of being the official organization. With the factionalism and the reluctance of the state and national organizations to investigate, the Alexandria NAACP branch went dormant for most of 1946 only to resurface again in 1947 with Johnson's dissident group firmly in control. Johnson was back as chair of the legal redress committee, with her primary defender, Reverend Murphy, serving as president. The usual battles commenced on the civil rights front, including a protest against a local registrar who had refused to let blacks register to vote. "As a result the books are now open to all citizens of the parish," declared Johnson.[67] The branch also continued lobbying the mayor of Alexandria, J. A. Blackman, to improve black education, fight racial injustice, secure the vote for all American citizens, and put a stop to lynching.[68] The old guard of the NAACP had been ousted by the protesters of 1945, and the branch seemed to work better as a cohesive unit. Rather than Johnson's legal committee existing as an independent wing of the branch, which is how it seemed in the first half of the 1940s, it became a significant part of the branch's operating structure.

Georgia Johnson's individualistic methods continued to mark her NAACP career. By the end of 1947 she was suing a local black lawyer, Louis Berry, for "criminal libel," after he had accused her of "embezzlement without having receipts and affidavits to prove [from whom and] when you collected the funds." Johnson dropped the case due to national NAACP insistence that it would ruin the organization's citywide reputation and again prevent the chapter from being effective. While she worked untiringly for NAACP goals of racial equality, Johnson did not adhere to rules she considered inconvenient to the advancement of her own work. Her participation in the Alexandria branch lapsed during the late 1940s and 1950s, mainly due to unremitting personality clashes. She reemerged in the mid-1960s, by then in her seventies but with renewed vigor, as the chair of the labor committee of a revived NAACP branch. Yet her approach to activism got her into trouble again with the new branch hierarchy. In 1968, Johnson accused the branch president, "Old Houston Jackson" ("Old Ignorant Jackson," Johnson called him), of kowtowing to white politicians in the city. Johnson once refused to attend a mass meeting of the branch, as she was aware that white politicians were going to be there, "and I know I will get angry," she wrote to NAACP field director for Louisiana, Harvey Britton.[69]

Johnson's idiosyncratic methods of operating continued, and she bypassed the branch hierarchy by sending money she had raised locally to the central office in New York. For example, having personally solicited a twenty-five-dollar check in 1968 from J. Hall LeBlance, a "liberal white man of Alexandria," Johnson sent the donation directly to New York, thus depriving the local branch of its share. This was due to her perception that the branch was not being run as effectively or radically as she would have liked and, therefore, ought not to be trusted to appropriately spend the funds that she had raised. Johnson had a fierce regard for her own independence and a strong self-belief in her approach to confronting racism in her home city. Unfortunately, because her actions often breached expected gender protocols this often led to frequent conflicts within the branch, as in 1944 with her unceremonious expulsion.[70]

Johnson was an indisputable leader of the Alexandria NAACP branch despite her profession that it was an "unwanted position" and only hers by default. Her power base was located throughout the broader African American social and religious community rather than in a narrow and strictly political or organizational arena, and the African American population in the city recognized that she was a dedicated and courageous advocate on their behalf. Johnson represented an important black constituency, namely her church and social networks, frustrated by racial repression and imperceptible change. Yet, curiously, she never declared herself a leader, only stating that she was working for "my race," even though as a self-styled member of Du Bois's "talented tenth" she saw this as a measure of her class and Christian duty.[71]

Johnson became a prominent leader in her community despite many social obstacles and organizational conventions that prevented many other women from leadership positions. Her activism emerged from a broad base that included middle-class expectations of social involvement and professional employment as well as deeply held religious values, all of which motivated her to work for the advancement of the entire African American community in Alexandria. As an unmarried woman she worked to support herself but also employed members of her extended family in her various businesses. For Johnson this was not just about survival but a way to flourish. In turn, this fed into her appreciation of civil rights and what U.S. citizenship meant to her as an African American and as a woman. Johnson's economic independence gave her some liberty in pursuing racial justice and shielded her from the worst of white financial and political pressures, which helped maintain her integrity in her civil rights work.

Georgia Johnson was rarely constrained by officialdom, and her frustration at the slowness of change led her to circumvent many conventions. This subsequently led to Johnson's disaffection with the Alexandria NAACP branch and also the hierarchy's growing aversion to her distinctive manner. Her uncompromising leadership went against many gender expectations of female participation in the civil rights struggle, and it ultimately led to her isolation within the branch (particularly from its male leadership) and her unconstitutional removal as chair of the legal committee. She was not a strict organization person and could not remain quietly in the background while male leaders of the branch did not pursue, unflinchingly, her progressive agenda. Johnson's approach pushed beyond organizational boundaries and challenged male leadership in Alexandria, illustrating the constraints upon all women in the NAACP and the sexism, as well as the racism, they were forced to confront.

NOTES

1. For a critique of historical analysis about black women in the early civil rights struggle, see Bernice McNair Barnett, "Invisible Southern Black Women Leaders in the Civil Rights Movement: The Triple Constraints of Gender, Race, and Class," *Gender and Society* 7, no. 2 (June 1993): 162–82; Gerda Lerner, ed., *Black Women in White America: A Documentary History* (New York: Pantheon Books, 1972), xvii; Paula Giddings, *When and Where I Enter: The Impact of Black Women on Race and Sex in America* (New York: William Morrow, 1984); Peter J. Ling and Sharon Monteith, *Gender in the Civil Rights Movement* (London: Routledge, 1999).

2. Lee Sartain, *Invisible Activists: Women of the Louisiana NAACP and the Struggle for Civil Rights, 1915–1945* (Baton Rouge: Louisiana State University Press, 2007), 99–108.

3. Constitution and By-laws for the Branches of the NAACP, 1937, Article III, Section 1 (d), 9.

4. Roy Wilkins with Tom Mathews, *Standing Fast: The Autobiography of Roy Wilkins* (New York: Da Capo Press, 1994), 119–25.

5. *Louisiana Weekly*, May 3, 1930.

6. Annual Report of Branch Activities, Alexandria, 1941, part 25, reel 17, frame 765–69, microfilm, NAACP Papers, Cambridge University Library (hereafter NAACP Papers).

7. "Alexandria, La.," memorandum to Walter White from Madison Jones, June 21, 1942, part 1, reel 8, frame 798, NAACP Papers.

8. From comment made by George W. Lucas, New Orleans branch president, cited in Mary White Ovington, *The Walls Come Tumbling Down* (New York: Arno Press, 1969), 227.

9. Jerry Pervis Sanson, *Louisiana during World War II: Politics and Society, 1939–1945* (Baton Rouge: Louisiana State University Press, 1999), 5–6, 221–26; Adam Fairclough, *Race and Democracy: The Civil Rights Struggle in Louisiana, 1915–1972* (Athens: University of Georgia Press, 1995), 2–5, 15–17.

10. "Alexandria, La.," memorandum to Walter White from Madison Jones.

11. Georgia Johnson to Ella Baker, March 25, 1946, reel 7, A. P. Tureaud Papers, Amistad Research Center, Tulane University, New Orleans (hereafter Tureaud Papers).

12. "Alexandria, La.," memorandum to Walter White from Madison Jones.

13. Ibid.

14. Constitution and By-laws for the Branches of the NAACP, 1937, Article II, Section 4 (d, g), 5.

15. Georgia Johnson to Ella Baker, April 30, 1945, reel 7, Tureaud Papers.

16. "Protest," Alexandria NAACP Branch to the National Executive Committee of the NAACP, January 3, 1945, reel 10, Tureaud Papers.

17. Georgia Johnson to Ella Baker, March 25, 1946, reel 7, Tureaud Papers.

18. Georgia Johnson to Ella Baker, April 30, 1945; Johnson to Baker, March 25, 1946; quote from Johnson to Mary Jamieson, January 8, 1966, NAACP Field Director Reports, reel 1, Amistad Research Center; Johnson to Harvey Britton, November 22, 1968, Amistad Research Center.

19. Quote from Georgia Johnson to Ella Baker, March 25, 1946; Stephanie J. Shaw, "Black Club Women and the Creation of the National Association of Colored Women," *Journal of Women's History* 3, no.2 (Fall 1991): 12; Peter Ling, "Social Capital, Resource Mobilization and Origins of the Civil Rights Movement," *Journal of Historical Sociology* 19, no.2 (June 2006): 204–9.

20. "Alexandria Branch N.A.A.C.P.," undated letter circa 1941 by Georgia Johnson to addressee unknown, part 25, reel 17, frame 771, NAACP Papers.

21. Ibid.

22. For other female leaders in the NAACP, see Daisy Bates, *The Long Shadow of Little Rock: A Memoir* (New York: David Company, 1962); Belinda Robnett, *How Long? How Long? African American Women in the Struggle for Civil Rights* (Oxford: Oxford University Press, 1997); Merline Pitre, *In Struggle against Jim Crow: Lula B. White and the NAACP, 1900–1957* (College Station: Texas A&M University Press, 1999); Charles Payne, *I've Got the Light of Freedom: The Organizing Tradition and the Mississippi Freedom Struggle* (Berkeley: University of California Press, 1995); John A. Kirk, *Redefining the Color Line: Black Activism in Little Rock, Arkansas, 1940–1970* (Gainesville: University Press of Florida, 2002); Dayo F. Gore, Jeanne Theoharis, and Komozi Woodard, eds., *Want to Start a Revolution? Radical Women in the Black Freedom Struggle* (New York: New York University Press, 2010); Danielle L. McGuire, *At the Dark End of the Street: Black Women, Rape, and Resistance—a New History of the Civil Rights Movement from Rosa Parks to the Rise of Black Power* (New York: Vintage Books, 2010); Lee Sartain, *Borders of Equality: The NAACP and the Baltimore Civil Rights Struggle, 1914–1970* (Jackson: University Press of Mississippi, 2013).

23. Barbara Ransby, *Ella Baker and the Black Freedom Movement: A Radical Democratic Vision* (Chapel Hill: University of North Carolina Press, 2003), 9, 106, 135–36. For more on Du Bois and the "talented tenth," see David Levering Lewis, *W. E. B. Du Bois: Biography of a Race, 1868–1919* (New York: Henry Holt, 1993); Shawn Leigh Alexander, *An Army of Lions: The Civil Rights Struggle before the NAACP* (Philadelphia: University of Pennsylvania Press, 2012).

24. "Alexandria Branch N.A.A.C.P.," undated letter circa 1941 by Georgia Johnson to addressee unknown.

25. Georgia Johnson to A. P. Tureaud, October 9, 1944, part 4, reel 8, frame 564, NAACP Papers.

26. "Protest," Alexandria NAACP Branch to the National Executive Committee of the NAACP, January 1945.

27. Georgia Johnson to Ella Baker, April 30, 1945.

28. Ibid.

29. Georgia Johnson to Ella Baker, March 25, 1946.

30. Georgia Johnson, to Ella Baker, April 30, 1945.

31. "Alexandria, La.," Memorandum to Walter White from Madison Jones, December 21, 1942.

32. A. P. Tureaud to Georgia Johnson, October 5, 1944, reel 7, Tureaud Papers.

33. Georgia Johnson to Ella Baker, March 25, 1946.

34. Glenda E. Gilmore, *Gender and Jim Crow: Women and the Politics of White Supremacy in North Carolina, 1896–1920* (Chapel Hill: University of North Carolina Press, 1996), 63, 75, 101; Stephanie J. Shaw, *What a Woman Ought to Be and to Do: Black Professional Women Workers during the Jim Crow Era* (Chicago: University of Chicago Press, 1996), 81; Lynne Olsen, *Freedom's Daughters: The Unsung Heroines of the Civil Rights Movement from 1830 to 1970* (New York: Scribner, 2001), 16; Marisa Chappell, Jenny Hutchinson, and Brian Ward, "Dress Modestly, Neatly . . . as If You Were Going to Church: Respectability, Class and Gender in the Montgomery Bus Boycott and the Early Civil Rights Movement," in Ling and Monteith, *Gender in the Civil Rights Movement*, 69–100.

35. *Louisiana Weekly*, January 7, 1939.

36. Georgia Johnson to Ella Baker, March 25, 1946.

37. Georgia Johnson to Ella Baker, April 30, 1945.

38. On blacks and World War II, see Richard M. Dalfumie, *Desegregation of the U.S. Armed Forces: Fighting on two Fronts, 1939–1953* (Columbia: University of Missouri Press, 1969); Neil A. Wynn, *The Afro-American and the Second World War* (London: Paul Elek, 1976); Patricia Sullivan, *Lift Every Voice: The NAACP and the Making of the Civil Rights Movement* (New York: New Press, 2009).

39. "Alexandria Branch of the NAACP Holds Mass Meeting," unknown newspaper clipping (probably *Alexandria Observer*), September/October 1941, part 25, reel 17, frame 771, NAACP Papers.

40. Constitution and By-laws for Branches of the NAACP, 1937, Article III, Committees, Section 1(e), 9.

41. Georgia Johnson to A. P. Tureaud, August 1, 1943, reel 7, Tureaud Papers.

42. Georgia Johnson to Ella Baker, March 25, 1946.

43. Georgia Johnson to Ella Baker, April 30, 1945; Tomiko Brown-Nagin, *Courage to Dissent: Atlanta and the Long History of the Civil Rights Movement* (Oxford: Oxford University Press, 2011), 24–25.

44. Annual Report of Branch Activities, Alexandria, 1941.

45. On violence against black soldiers, see Harvard Sitkoff, "Racial Militancy and Interracial Violence in the Second World War," *Journal of American History* 58, no. 3 (December 1971): 661–81; Dalfumie, *Desegregation of the U.S. Armed Forces*; Sullivan, *Lift Every Voice*; Neil A. Wynn, *The African American Experience during World War II* (New York: Rowman and Littlefield, 2011).

46. Fairclough, *Race and Democracy*, 74–75; Sitkoff, "Racial Militancy and Interracial Violence," 667–69.

47. "Alexandria, La.," Memorandum to Walter White from Madison Jones, December 21, 1942.

48. Georgia Johnson to Ella Baker, April 30, 1945.

49. Georgia Johnson to Ella Baker, March 25, 1946.

50. Fairclough, *Race and Democracy*, 78; Sitkoff, "Racial Militancy and Interracial Violence," 667–69; William M. Simpson, "A Tale Untold? The Alexandria, Louisiana, Lee Street Riot (January 10, 1942)," in *The African American Experience in Louisiana, Part C: From Jim Crow to Civil Rights*, Louisiana Purchase Bicentennial Series in Louisiana History 11, ed. Charles Vincent (Lafayette,: Center for Louisiana Studies, 2002), 191–203.

51. For a history of how African Americans were socially and legally controlled by accusation of rape and threats to black women's bodies, see McGuire, *At the Dark End of the Street.*

52. Georgia Johnson to Ella Baker, April 30, 1945; Johnson to A. P. Tureaud, January 5, 1943, reel 7, Tureaud Papers; Fairclough, *Race and Democracy*, 78.

53. *The Crisis* (NAACP), September 1943; FBI Report on the New Orleans Branch of the NAACP, November 11, 1944, FBI File on the NAACP, New Orleans Public Library; 34th Annual Report of the NAACP for the Year 1943, 43, Spingarn Collection, Howard-Tilton Memorial Library, Tulane University, 3, 10–11; Annual Report of Branch Activities, Alexandria, 1944, part 25, reel 17, frames 774–77, NAACP Papers.

54. McGuire, *At the Dark End of the Street*, 15–47.

55. Robert L. Zangrando, *The NAACP Crusade against Lynching, 1909–1950* (Philadelphia: Temple University Press, 1980), 4; Gilmore, *Gender and Jim Crow*, 63, 75.

56. Georgia Johnson to Ella Baker, March 25, 1946.

57. Ibid.

58. Spencer Bradley to Roy Wilkins, January 17, 1945, reel 7, Tureaud Papers.

59. Earl Smith to Ella Baker, May 22, 1945, reel 7, Tureaud Papers.

60. A. P. Tureaud to Ella Baker, February 4, 1946, reel 7, Tureaud Papers.

61. "Protest," Alexandria NAACP Branch to the National Executive Committee of the NAACP, January 3, 1945.

62. Ibid.

63. Sartain, *Invisible Activists*, 68.

64. Georgia Johnson to Ella Baker, March 25, 1946.

65. Freddie Spears to A. P. Tureaud, April 18, 1945, reel 10, Tureaud Papers; Earl Smith to Ella Baker, May 22, 1945, reel 10, Tureaud Papers.

66. Ella Baker to Georgia Johnson, March 20, 1946, reel 7, Tureaud Papers.

67. Annual Report of Branch Activities, Alexandria, 1948, part 25, reel 17, frames 779–83, NAACP Papers; Shannon Frystak, *Our Minds on Freedom: Women and the Struggle for Black Equality in Louisiana, 1924–1967* (Baton Rouge: Louisiana State University Press, 2009), 21–23.

68. J. M. Murphy, Georgia Johnson, and Elizabeth Williams to J. A. Blackman, March 4, 1947, part 15, reel 2, frame 5, NAACP Papers.

69. Daniel Byrd to Georgia Johnson, October 12, 1947, part 15, reel 2, frame 70, NAACP Papers; Donald Jones to J. M. Murphy, December 1, 1947, part 15, reel 2, frame 72, NAACP Papers; Georgia Johnson to Harvey Britton, March 9, 1968, NAACP Field Director Reports, reel 3, Amistad Research Center; Britton to Johnson, March 19, 1968, NAACP Field Director Reports, reel 3, Amistad Research Center; Johnson to Britton, November 22, 1968, NAACP Field Director Reports, reel 4, Amistad Research Center; Johnson to Britton, May 31, 1968, NAACP Field Director Reports, reel 4, Amistad Research Center.

70. Georgia Johnson to Harvey Britton, May 31, 1968; Johnson to Britton, June 21, 1968, NAACP Field Director Reports, reel 4, Amistad Research Center.

71. Georgia Johnson to Ella Baker, March 25, 1946.

Contributors

JANET ALLURED is professor of history and director of women's studies at McNeese State University. Allured is coeditor with Judith Gentry of the first volume of *Louisiana Women: Their Lives and Times* (University of Georgia Press, 2009) and with Michael Martin of *Louisiana Legacies: Readings in the History of the Pelican State* (Wiley-Blackwell, 2013). She is currently completing work on a manuscript on second-wave feminism in Louisiana, 1950–85, to be published by the University of Georgia Press.

COURT CARNEY is associate professor of history at Stephen F. Austin State University, where he teaches courses on African American history. He is the author of *Cuttin' Up: How Jazz Got America's Ear* (University Press of Kansas, 2009) as well as articles on race, memory, and American music.

EMILY CLARK is Clement Chambers Benenson Professor in American Colonial History at Tulane University. Her most recent book is *Strange History of the American Quadroon: Free Women of Color in the Revolutionary Atlantic World* (University of North Carolina Press, 2013).

BRITTNEY COOPER is assistant professor of women's and gender studies and Africana studies at Rutgers University. Her first book project, *Race Women: Gender and the Making of a Black Public Intellectual Tradition*, is forthcoming from University of Illinois Press. Cooper is also cofounder of the Crunk Feminist Collective and a weekly columnist on race and politics at Salon.com.

MARK J. DUVALL has taught history at Mary Institute and Saint Louis Country Day School in Missouri since 2009. Much of the research for his essay was completed while in graduate school at the University of New Orleans from 2007 to 2009. The author wishes to thank the entire graduate faculty at UNO.

MARY FARMER-KAISER is the James D. Wilson/BORSF Memorial Professor of southern studies and is a professor of history and dean of the Graduate School at the University of

Louisiana at Lafayette. She is the author of *Freedwomen and the Freedmen's Bureau: Race, Gender, and Public Policy in the Age of Emancipation* (Fordham University Press, 2010).

SHANNON FRYSTAK is an associate professor of African American and women's history at East Stroudsburg University of Pennsylvania. Her book *Our Minds on Freedom: Women and the Struggle for Black Equality in Louisiana, 1924–1967* was published by Louisiana State University Press in 2009. Her current research focuses on the women who managed Cross Keys Plantation.

LUCY GUTMAN earned a bachelor's degree in American history from Wellesley College in 1958 and master's degrees from Bryn Mawr College (social work), University of Arizona (American history), and Northwestern State University of Louisiana (counseling and guidance; and American and British literature). When she passed away in 2010, she had completed all her coursework and much of her dissertation for a PhD in American women's history from the University of Southern Mississippi.

EMILY EPSTEIN LANDAU teaches U.S. history at the University of Maryland, College Park, and lives in Washington, D.C., with her husband and two daughters. Her book *Spectacular Wickedness: Sex, Race, and Memory in Storyville, New Orleans* (Louisiana State University Press, 2013) is a scholarly history of the notorious red-light district. Her next book will be about murder ballads and their meanings in twentieth-century Appalachia.

HELLEN S. LEE is an associate professor in the Department of English at California State University, Sacramento, where she teaches nineteenth-century U.S. literature, twentieth-century U.S. multi-ethnic literatures, and cultural studies. Her research focuses on late-nineteenth-century and early-twentieth-century representations of working-class, racialized, and immigrant women in the United States and the circum-Caribbean region.

LESLIE GALE PARR teaches photography and the history of journalism and photography at Loyola University New Orleans where she is the A. Louis Read Distinguished Professor of Communication. Parr also directs Loyola's Center for the Study of New Orleans. She is the author of *A Will of Her Own: Sarah Towles Reed and the Pursuit of Democracy in Southern Public Education* (University of Georgia Press, 2010).

GISELLE ROBERTS is an honorary research associate in the Department of History at La Trobe University in Melbourne, Australia, and coeditor (with Melissa Walker) of the Women's Diaries and Letters of the South series published by the University of South Carolina Press. She is the author of *The Confederate Belle* (University of Missouri Press, 2003), and editor of *The Correspondence of Sarah Morgan and Francis Warrington Dawson* (University of Georgia Press, 2004) and *A New Southern Woman: The Correspondence of Eliza Lucy Irion Neilson, 1871–1883* (University of South Carolina Press, 2012).

LEE SARTAIN is course leader in American studies at the University of Portsmouth, England. His books include *Borders of Equality: The NAACP and the Baltimore Civil Rights Struggle, 1914–1970* (University Press of Mississippi, 2013) and *Invisible Activists: Women in the Louisiana NAACP and the Struggle for Civil Rights, 1915–1945* (Louisiana State University Press, 2007), which won the Jules and Frances Landry Award for best book on a southern topic. He also coedited *Long Is the Way and Hard: One Hundred Years of the National Association for the Advancement of Colored People* (University of Arkansas Press, 2009).

SARA BROOKS SUNDBERG received a doctorate from Louisiana State University and is professor of history at the University of Central Missouri. She has published several articles on women in the early South and trans-Mississippi frontier and she is coauthor, with Carol Fairbanks, of *Farm Women on the Prairie Frontier: A Sourcebook for Canada and the United States.*

TANIA TETLOW is the Felder-Fayard Professor of Law and Associate Provost for International Affairs at Tulane University. Her research focuses on violence against women and discrimination by juries. Professor Tetlow worked for former congresswoman Lindy Boggs from 1990 to 1992.

SUSAN TUCKER is curator of books and records and oversees the Newcomb Archives and Special Collections within the Vorhoff Library of the Newcomb College Institute, Tulane University. Her most recent work is as coeditor, with Beth Willinger, of *Newcomb College, 1886–2006* (Louisiana State University Press, 2012) and coauthor, with Peggy Frankland, of *Women Pioneers of the Louisiana Environmental Movement* (University Press of Mississippi, 2013). She is also the author of *Telling Memories among Southern Women: Domestic Workers and Their Employers in the Segregated South* (2002), which served as the basis for the novel and movie *The Help.*

MICHAEL WADE is professor of history at Appalachian State University, where he was founding director of the Public History Program and department chair. His publications include *Sugar Dynasty* (Center for Louisiana Studies, 1995), a history of Louisiana's largest raw sugar producer; *A Frontier Boyhood* (Hubbard Center at Appalachian State University, 1987) about early settlers in the Texas Panhandle; and numerous articles and book chapters. His current project is researching the desegregation of the Louisiana state colleges, 1954–75. He is a fellow and past president of the Louisiana Historical Association.

CAROLYN E. WARE received her doctorate from the Program of Folklore and Folklife at the University of Pennsylvania and is an associate professor of English and folklore at Louisiana State University. Her publications include *Cajun Mardi Gras Masks* (University Press of Mississippi, 2011), with Carl Lindahl; *Cajun Women and Mardi Gras: Reading the Rules Backward* (University of Illinois Press, 2006); and numerous scholarly articles and presentations on Croatian folklife in Louisiana, tourism and Cajun Mardi Gras celebrations, veterinary medicine and human-animal connections, and the civil rights movement in Plaquemines Parish, Louisiana. She served as editor of the *Louisiana Folklore Miscellany* from 2008 to 2012.

BETH WILLINGER is retired from Tulane University where she served for twenty-five years as the executive director of the Newcomb College Center for Research on Women, founding director of Tulane's women's studies program, and a term as interim dean of Newcomb College. Her research focuses on the current socio-economic status of women in Louisiana and the history of Louisiana women. Among her publications are the highly regarded report "Katrina and the Women of New Orleans" (2008), and *Newcomb College, 1886–2006* (Louisiana State University Press, 2012), edited with Susan Tucker. In 2003, the Louisiana Endowment for the Humanities named her "Humanist of the Year" for her contributions developing the academic field of women's studies and her research aimed at bettering the lives of women in Louisiana.

MARY ANN WILSON is professor of English at the University of Louisiana at Lafayette where she teaches American literature, southern literature, humanities, and women's studies, and is a fellow of the Center for Louisiana Studies. She has published widely on American women writers such as Joyce Carol Oates, Grace King, and Rebecca Wells. Her Catholic girlhood in Birmingham, Alabama, mirrors Rebecca Wells's own experiences. She is at work on an essay linking Wells, Flannery O'Connor, and the concept of suffering, and her current book project is tentatively titled *Every Good Impulse: New Orleans Women's Book Clubs, 1880–1925*.

Index